DANIEL HERAUD

CARNET DE ROUTE / ROAD REPORT INC.

Legal deposit: 4 th quarter 1998
Bibliothèque nationale du Québec
Bibliothèque nationale du Canada

Print and bounded in Canada

ISBN: 1-895100-40-2

SUMMARY

The mediocrity race..?

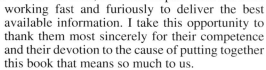

You've no doubt noticed that over the last few years, this book, along with its closest rival, is available at your bookstore at an earlier and yet earlier date. For decades, automobile guides were out for the Montreal Book Show that takes place in early November. But since then, it's a race to see who'll get the book out first. At the end of October, in mid-October, at the end of September, in mid-September... And why not in mid-July? Then everyone could read it during their holidays. This race is a bit mad, for in the long run, it jeopardizes the quality of the content. American carmakers give out their information on upcoming models between June and July, Asian car producers do so between September and October and Europeans, namely German automakers, wait until Christmas...

This simply means that books printed at the end of September are deprived of 25% of their authentic content. Worse still, in the attempt to always arrive first at the finish line, 80% of the some of the competition's photos aren't from the year stated on the cover of the book, but rather from the year before. It's quicker and less nerve-wracking than waiting for the carmaker's photos. But this is false representation. The funniest thing is that this approach doesn't do anyone a favor, since for years now, sales figures from year to year are absolutely identical, within a one or two per cent margin. Nobody really robs anybody else's readers. But rather, everyone is deprived of something essential, namely, quality information.

In spite of the difficulties encountered in preparing the material that's vital to writing our «Bible» on time, the Road Report team has been working fast and furiously to deliver the best available information. I take this opportunity to thank them most sincerely for their competence and their devotion to the cause of putting together this book that means so much to us.

You'll see that Road Report is even better this year, that is, the longer and more detailed texts appear on the page on the left, while technical charts appear on the right, as some of you had suggested. We also tried to include more detailed photos for each model, something others wanted to see in the book, so there are a total of more than a thousand photos in all. The minimum-maximum price listings, that serve as a buyer's guide when it comes to bargaining with the dealer, are included in the equipment charts, including brands and types of tires that come as standard equipment on the various models. The next time we meet, we'll be at the dawn of the third millennium and for the occasion, Road Report will outdo itself to offer you the best car info out there. Happy trails and we'll see you next year.

Daniel Héraud

CREDITS

Cover Page: Renault Zo
Author's picture : Jacques Grenier
Credits for photos in these pages: Lise Champagne, Michel Condominas, Gérard Héraud, Daniel Héraud, Jean D'Hugues, Benoit Charette and from the manufacturer's press services.

Chief Editor:	Daniel Heraud
Collaborators:	Luc Gagné
	Benoit Charette
Cover Design:	Imagidée, Gilles Leduc
Proofreading-Translation:	Rachelle Renaud
Translation:	Allan McVicar
Techninal advisor:	Jacques Gervais
Technical consultant:	François Viau
Color:	Imagidée, Jean-Denis Lalande
Printing:	Québécor Inc.

INTERNATIONAL COLLABORATORS

Germany:	Helmut Herke
Canada:	Sammy Chang
France:	Michel Condominas
	Gérard Héraud
United-States:	Alan McVicar
Great-Britain:	Nick Bennett
Italy:	Andréa Andali

SPECIAL THANKS

To produce this edition of *Road Report*, we had to count on numerous individuals working in the automotive and publishing fields. To all of those whether close by or far away, who have participated in the creation of this book, a sincere and grateful thank you.

Factual information pertaining to the automobiles listed herein, specifically information under the headings "ENGINE," "TRANSMISSION," "PERFORMANCE," and "SPECIFICATIONS," has been supplied by the manufacturers of such automobiles and the author, publisher, and distributor of this book can accept no responsibility for the accuracy or completeness of such factual information. The commentary and recommendations contained herein are made to the best of the author's knowledge. Author, publisher and distributor accept no responsibility for any loss or damage caused by the use of any of the materials contained in this book, and they explicitly disclaim any and all guarantees.

INDEX

Manufacturer's Identification .

Model Identification .

Flag of builder's country of origin.

Text of evaluation in twenty points, classified by decreasing order of qualities and defects with the conclusion and the average value which allows vehicles to be classified and compared.

In "Data", the indices are explained as follows:

The **insurance rate** multiplied by the suggested retail price of a specific model gives the approximate total premium. It has been established for a person 35 years of age, married, living in a metropolitan area, without an accident in the last six years and no driver's license suspension. The base premium for $1 million of property and personal liability, $250,000 collision and $50 for multiple risks.

The **depreciation** risk is calculated based on our "Used car guide" for three years. If the vehicle exists for less than three years, the number of years follows in parenthesis.

The **cost per mile** is calculated by category. It is based on the use of the vehicle during a three-year period at the rate of 12,000 miles per year and includes the insurance rate, registration costs, interest rate, fuel cost, tire wear, maintenance and repairs, depreciation and parking costs.

OLDSMOBILE — **Intrigue**

The Intrigue is a brisk seller, as is the case for the Oldsmobile brand itself. So much so that the carmaker now exhibits its name on the Intrigue's exterior! This car's mission is to blot out all memories of the Cutlass Supreme and its unimaginative design, for it's more like the popular Japanese midsize models. Of course, it does share the Buick Century-Regal and Pontiac Grand Prix platform, but it offers a more refined silhouette generally inspired by the Aurora.

A Nice Formula...

MODEL RANGE

The Oldsmobile Intrigue is a 4-door sedan that's available in three trim levels: GX, the base model, equipped with disc brakes, ABS, climate control and alloy rims; the GL, the mid-range model that has added driver's bucket seat that's power-adjustable, 60/40 split-folding rear seatbench, fog lamps and heated exterior mirrors; and finally, the GLS, that has leather seat coverings, a passenger's bucket seat that's power-adjustable, faux-bois trim, sound system including tape deck and CD player and an electrochromic interior rearview mirror. This year, all three versions can be equipped with the «Autobahn» options package that includes H-rated tires and higher performance brakes (12-inch discs up front and a different power braking system).

TECHNICAL FEATURES

Two different engines will be available for part of the year. The GX and GL will be equipped with the 3.8L 3800 Series V6, whereas the GLX will be animated by the new 3.5L DOHC V6. But the latter will replace the 3800 Series V6 during the course of the year. The Intrigue has a steel body mounted on a monocoque chassis. All panels are galvanized on both sides, except the roof. With a drag coefficient of 0.32, aerodynamics are in the average range. The four-wheel independent suspension consists of MacPherson struts up front and a three-link setup at the rear. There are coil springs and an anti-roll bar at each extremity. Disc brakes, an antilock braking system and traction control are standard features, as is the latest Magnasteer II that's a progressive, variable assist system.

PROS

+ STYLE. Inspired as well by the Aurora, the Intrigue is elegant and its distinctive looks attract passersby, especially when clad in dark shades that really add class. This simple design will look lovely for many a moon.

+ EQUIPMENT. Compared to the Cutlass Supreme, the Intrigue offers a lush interior and scads of luxury items. Not at all like traditional American cars sold at tempting prices, but really low on the totem pole when it came to equipment, unless, of course you added on lots of options... which had a way of becoming awfully expensive!

+ PERFORMANCES. The new 3.5L DOHC V6 bestows on the Intrigue a trait that was really lacking: an engine worthy of its chassis and sophisticated suspensions. With 215 hp, accelerations and pickup are akin to those of the Regal supercharged model. The newcomer lets you really let loose at the wheel, without adversely affecting fuel economy, since fuel consumption sat at around 19 mpg during our road test.

+ RIDE COMFORT. On the highway the Intrigue behaves like an import. The suspension is perfectly adjusted and disguises road faults like magic. And the thickly upholstered seats provide lots of support, which adds to travel pleasure.

+ HANDLING. The Intrigue takes curves with superb assurance, thanks to the effective suspension and tires that have excellent grip on wet or dry surfaces.

+ QUALITY. With this vehicle, Oldsmobile is exhibiting a very high level of craftsmanship. Assembly and fit and finish are superb. Everything is uniform and fits perfectly together, with not the slightest gap or such. The same goes for the equipment on this car that's above average when it comes to caliber (tires, headlamps, wipers, etc.).

+ NICE FEATURES: We really liked the two neat levers on the steering column that control headlamps, turn signal lights and wipers, as well as the great visibility all-round, due partly to the generous-size exterior mirrors.

CONS

- TRANSMISSION. The shifter has gears set too far apart; and you have to know how to adjust the accelerator pedal pressure in just the «right» way to shift into overdrive or to downshift at the right moment. And there isn't much braking effect in 3rd gear.

- PERFORMANCES. The 3800 Series V6 achieves average accelerations and pickup, when compared to the Intrigue's rivals, but they're quite acceptable. You often get the impression you're driving faster than you really are. The new DOHC V6 should add a bit of pizzazz!

- STEERING. It's precise and very direct, with only 2.5 turns lock-to-lock. Yet the Magnasteer system is crippled by over-assistance, so it gets light and sensitive in strong winds or when driving over poor pavement.

- MATERIALS. Some of the plastic used inside the cabin affects the look of other items (especially the leather trim) , because of its lackluster shade (gray) and shiny texture.

- COCKPIT SETUP. The center console is too low, more so than on the Buick Century-Regal and Pontiac Grand Prix. And the shifter is smack in front of the climate control dials.

- NOISE. It's strange that such a sleek bod generates so much wind noise, unless its stay in the wind tunnel was a bit too short for its own good...

CONCLUSION

The Oldsmobile Intrigue demonstrates, as did the Buick Regal and Chevrolet Malibu, that General Motors is once again able to build current-standard vehicles able to compete with Japanese products.

Final verdict:

 Over 65%,

between 55% and 65%,

 below 55%.

Manufacturer's Logo.

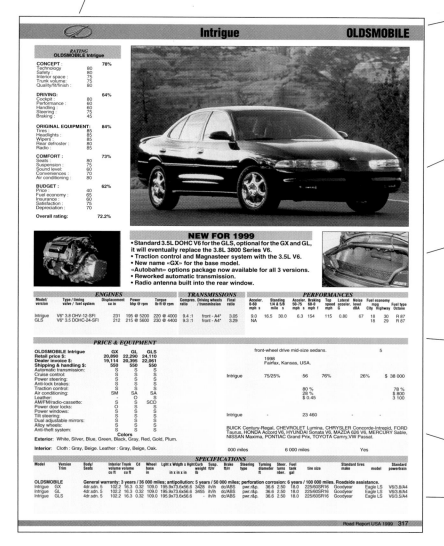

Basis of evaluation for rating all the vehicles according to the scale presented on page 8 and according to manufacturer's data plus all the results of our team road-test. Each analysis is divided in specific sections for a better understanding.

NEW FOR 1999
An update for every new characteristics of every models.

Minimum and maximum prices plus all the major equipments for all models. Also, the available colors for exterior and interior.

Main available power train, engines and transmissions as well as their performance.

Historical facts, sales statistics, competitors, main improvements and equipment.

Technical data.

IMPORTANT WARNING

This book is put together with preliminary information given by the manufacturer's during the summer season preceding the arrival on the vehicles on the market. The difference between our data and those of the official catalog's of the company published in the fall season does not constitute a mistake but simply a change they often make witout warning. All the information is accurate at the time of printing.

Road Report is written simultaneously for Quebec, Canada and the United States. It is therefore possible that some models shown will not exactly conform to those sold locally.

TYPES OF ENGINES

H	Horizontal cylinders
L	In-line cylinders
V	V cylinders

FUEL SUPPLY

EFI	Electronic fuel injection
MPEI	Multiple point electronic injection
MI	Mechanical injection
SFI	Sequential injection (multiple point)
TBI	Throttle body injection
EMI	Electronically controlled mechanical injection
RI	Rotary diesel injection
TR or TBO	Turbocharger
Ti	Turbocharger plus intercooler
S	Supercharger

TRANSMISSIONS

M4;M5;M6	Manual 4-speed; 5-speed; 6 speed
A3;A4 A5	Automatic 3-speed; 4-speed; 5-speed
2WD	2-wheel drive
4WD	4-wheel drive

MODELS

cpe	coupe
sdn	sedan
wgn	station wagon
van	van
p-up	pickup
a-t	all terrain
2dr	2-door
3dr	3-door
4dr	4-door

SIZES

cyl	cylinder
cu.ft	cubic feet
hp	horsepower (SAE)
in	inches
ft	feet
lbs/ft	torque: feet-pounds
L	volume in liter
db	sound level in decibels
mph	miles per hour
mpg	miles per gallon

OTHERS

*	original equipment or standard
#	not available at print time
NA	not available
NR	not recommended (towing)
HD	heavy duty
Cd	air drag coefficient
dc	disc
dr	drum
ABS	anti-locking brake system
TCS	traction control system

SUSPENSIONS

si	semi-independent
r	rigid rear axle
r&p	rack and pinion
pwr	power assisted
ball	recirculating ball steering
	sector and roller

1999 EVALUATION SCALE

Notes in %	**0**	10	20	30	40	**50**	60	70	80	90	**100**

CONCEPT

Technology:	drag coefficient		platform		powertrain			propellant		materials	
Safety:	NHTSA	structures		doors	environment		seat-belts	air bags			
Interior space: EPA cu.ft	57	64	70	78	85	88	92	99	106	113 120	
Trunk: EPA cu.ft	3.5	5.5	7	9	10.5	12.5	14	16	17.5	19	21
Quality/fit/finish		appearence			assembly			materials			finish

DRIVING

Cockpit:		seat		visibility			commands		controls		
Performances: 0/62 in s.	16	15	14	13	12	11	10	9	8	7	5
Handling: lat. G force	0.66	0.68	0.70	0.72	0.74	0.76	0.78	0.80	0.85	0.90	0.95
Steering:	ratio		precision		calibration			assist	return		
Braking: 62 to 0 in ft.	215	200	180	165	150	130	125	120	110	105	100

ORIGINAL EQUIPMENT

Tires: grip:		dry		wet	winter		comfort			noise	
Headlights:		range		brightness	efficiency		antifog				
Wipers: coverage			speed		intermittent			Kind of blade			
Rear-defroster:			area covered			speed					
Radio:	MA/MF		cassette		CD		sound quality	power		richness	

COMFORT

Seats:		seat		lateral support		back support			padding		trim
Suspension:		damping		amplitude		roll			pitch		frequency
Sound level: dBA	73	72	71	70	69	68	67	66	65	64	63
Conveniences:											
Air conditioning:		quicknest		distribution		hot		cold	power		commands

BUDGET

Price $ US	30,000	27,000	24,000	21,000	18,000	15,000	12,000	10,500	9,000	7,000	6,000
Fuel economy: l./100	20	18	16	15	14	13	12	11	10	8	6
Insurance:% of retail price	16	14	12	10	9	8	7	6	5	4	3
Satisfaction: %	5	10	20	30	40	50	60	70	80	90	100
Depreciation: %	100	90	80	70	60	50	40	30	20	10	5

ABS : Initials for anti-locking brake system. This system detects and prevents wheel lockup during hard braking. Sensors at each disc or drum brake detect a sudden speed decrease indicating the beginning of lockup. Fluid pressure to that brake is reduced and reapplied at the rate of several pulsations per second till the wheel regains rotation speed. The sophistication of these systems varies between makes. Some are mechanical, others detect deceleration and lateral G-forces (centrifugal force in a turn) to prevent spinouts or large shifts in direction: always possible with more simplistic devices.

ADJUSTABLE STEERING COLUMN: Changes the angle of the steering wheel or its length, to accommodate the driver.

AIR DAM: A device to deflect air, usually under the front bumper or other locations. It can be fixed or movable.

ALL-WHEEL DRIVE and 4-WD: All wheels, front and rear, provide traction. A differential splits the torque between the front and rear axles.

ALTERNATOR: The belt-driven alternator supplies current for ignition, battery charge, AC and other accessories.

AUTOMATIC TRANSMISSION: Automatic shift change: offering 3, 4 or 5 ratios is also set up for holding the transmission in lower gears for torque or grade retard.

BAGGAGE COVER: Cloth or cover to conceal baggage in coupes, sedans or station wagons.

BODY BELT LINE: Artificial line dividing the sheet metal lower body from the glazed upper body.

BORE/STROKE: Dimensions that allow figuring the cylinder displacement. The bore is the diameter of the piston and the stroke is the distance it travels. Displacement formula is B/2 squared X Pi X S X number of cylinders = volume. Keep consistent measurements, inches or centimeters, to get cubic inches or cc volume. of the engine displacement

CAMBER: Lateral wheel angle, relative to a vertical plane, to compensate for tire roll in the turn.

CAMSHAFT: A steel part with lobes to operate intake and exhaust valves either directly or through rocker arms. It is gear, chain or belt-driven.

CARBURETOR: Meters fuel in proportion to the air needed by the engine and controls the air through one or more throttle blades.

CASTER: Forward or rearward inclination of the steering axis.

Cd: Coefficient of drag of the automobile body, usually measured in a wind tunnel. Multiply the Cd by the frontal area to get a comparison index from car to car. The lower the number, such as .029 , the higher the efficiency.

CLUTCH: Couples or disengages the engine and the transmission.Has one or more discs engaging by friction. Many clutches are used in automatic transmission. The clutch action can be timed for progressive engagement.

COMPRESSION RATIO: When the piston is at the bottom of its stroke, the cylinder and combustion chamber are filled with air. The ratio between that and the combustion chamber volume is the compression ratio. Higher compression ratio improves combustion efficiency. Supercharged or Turbocharged engines may need a lower nominal compression ratio, while a Diesel needs 22:1 compression to initiate ignition.

COMPRESSION STROKE: After intake, the piston moves up to compress the airfuel mixture. More compression improves efficiency: the fuel octane limits the maximum compression that can be used.

CONNECTING ROD: The part which connects the piston to the crank. The rod conveys the alternating piston motion to rotary crank motion and vice versa.

CONTROLLED SHOCKS: The shock settings can be externally changed by an electronic control.

COUPE: 2-volume body with 2 main seats and 2 mini-seats, and a sports look.

CRANKSHAFT: The crankshaft turns on main bearings and has offset journals, just like a bicycle crank, to transform the alternating piston motion to a rotary motion.

CYLINDER HEAD: The part over the block which contains the combustion chambers and intake valves, as well as intake and exhaust ports. It carries the valves and valve train parts.

CYLINDERS: The barrel-shaped part of the block in which the piston forms a moving wall and which is closed off at the top by the combustion chamber. Cylinders can be laid out IN-LINE, in V6 or V8 or horizontally opposed (BOXER) as in VW Beetle or Subaru.

DIESEL: A denser fuel than gasoline. It requires much higher compression ratios to spontaneously ignite. *Cetanes*, not octanes, rate Diesel fuel and is a measure of ignitability under compression, while octanes measure the resistance to ignition due to compression. A direct injection sprays into the cylinder. Glow plugs may be used but not a conventional ignition or fuel injection into the manifold.

DIFFERENTIAL: The gear train which allows the drive wheels to turn at different speeds up when going around a corner. You will find differentials in the front and rear drive trains in the 4WD, while transmitting torque to both wheels, as well as in the transfer case.

DISC BRAKE: The disc turns with the wheel and the caliper with pads applies friction for efficient stopping power. *Ventilated disc:* Fins between the 2 sides of the disc circulate air and cool the disc. Disc brakes work at very high temperatures and cooling is important.

DOHC: One cam operates the intakes, the other the exhausts, which allows timing refinements.

DRIVE RATIO: Determines the final drive ratio between the transmission output and the drive wheel rpm. Numerically higher ratios make the engine turn faster. More wear, but also more power.

DRUM BRAKE: A drum turns with the wheel. Shoes with friction-lining material rub against the drum and retard it during brake application.

ELECTRONIC IGNITION: Electronic ignition replaces points and may also control timing in conjunction with the computer.

ENGINE TORQUE: The turning effort delivered by the engine at any given rpm. Torque is pull on a moment (lever) arm, given in lbs/ft. or in m/kg. 1.0 lb/ft = 0.1382549 m/kg. Pulling on a wrench applies torque to the bolt.

FLOOR PAN: Bottom of the car, which also includes reinforcing and suspension mount members.

FUEL INJECTION: Atomizing the fuel under pressure, as it exits from a nozzle, so it can mix with air.

FULL-TIME 4WD: All 4 wheels always driving.

GAS SHOCK: May use gas pressure to prevent foaming up of the fluid or to produce additional lift. On some shocks, electronic controls adjust damping. In a suspension a spring temporarily stores, then releases energy and the shock absorber dissipates: damps out - energy and converts it to heat.

GRILL: Decorative air inlet to the radiator and engine.

HEAT EXCHANGER: A heat exchanger is used to transfer heat from engine oil or transmission oil or a power steering to the engine coolant or to ambiant air.

HYDRAULIC SHOCK: Uses internal oil forced through orifices by the motion of a piston in a cylinder to generate daming forces.

HYDROPNEUMATIC SUSPENSION: Uses gas pressure to maintain and adjust height, and fluid to control damping.

INDEPENDENT SUSPENSION: Each wheel moves independently of the other.

INDIRECT INJECTION: Used on Diesel engines with a pre-chamber to improve ignitability. *Jets* are calibrated orifices to meter fuel.

KNOCK SENSOR: Detects combustion noise and is used in conjunction with the computer to alter spark or fuel supply. See: *Octane.*

LEAF SPRING SUSPENSION: A stack of flat leaf springs of decreasing lengths connects to the axle at a spring pad and pivots on the frame or body. Since the leaf gets longer when it deflects, a swing shackle compensates for the length change.

LIMITED SLIP DIFFERENTIAL: A device which limits the rpm difference between 2 wheels by engaging a clutch or other coupling.

LOCKING DIFFERENTIAL: It can lock the 2 output shafts to each other. *Viscous coupling*: A clutch filled with high viscosity silicon to increase the lockup as the difference in rotation speed increases.

MACPHERSON: Independent suspension with a single lower control arm, connected to a housing with a shock absorber and a coil spring. The upper portion of the shock pivots on the unit body. There are modified MacPhersons with upper and lower control arms, as on the Honda, which maintain better camber control when the car leans in a turn.

MANIFOLDS, INTAKE AND EXHAUST: Castings or tubular assemblies with the passages that connect each cylinder to the intake or exhaust side of the engine. Their shape can have a large affect on performance.

MANOMETER: One way to measure air or fluid pressure.

MANUAL TRANSMISSION: Provides a choice of gear ratios to match car speed with engine speed. The driver selects the gear ratio through cable or rod controls and couples the pair of gears needed to the input and output shafts, while disengaging the clutch to interrupt power flow.

MASTER CYLINDER: Part of the brake system, when the driver applies pedal pressure it provides the pumping action to deliver fluid to the individual wheel cylinders, drum or disc.

MECHANICAL INJECTION: A pump controls the fuel delivery. *EFI*: Electronic fuel injection. *MPI* or *EMPI*: Electronic multiple injection. SFI: sequential fuel injection, each cylinder fed in turn according to firing order.

MODULATION: How well the driver can control the brake or steering, so that the input force results in a proportioned output.

MULTIFUEL ENGINE: Engine capable of utilizing several types of fuel.

MULTIVALVE ENGINE: Engine with 3, 4 or more valves per cylinder.

OCTANE: The fuel's ability to resist detonation (knock) or preignition.

OIL PAN: The section under the engine which holds the oil supply and the oil pump.

OVERDRIVE: In the manual or automatic transmission, a final drive ratio that is higher than 1 to 1. The engine is turning slower than the transmission output shaft. Great economy but no acceleration.

OVERHANG: What extends behind the rear wheels or ahead of the front wheels.

OVERSTEER: The vehicle has a tendency to turn at a tighter radius than steering wheel input and at the limit the rear is kicking out. During oversteer, the driver applies reverse lock to the steering to keep from spinning out.

PANHARD ROD: It provides lateral control by connecting the body to the opposite side of the axle housing. Now the back of the car can't swing out on a turn.

PART-TIME 4WD: A differential or a slip coupling divides the power between the front and rear. Usualy includes a lockup feature.

PUSH ROD ENGINE V6/V8: A cam which runs inside the block operates the valves through lifters, pushrods and rocker arms, in succession.

QUARTER PANELS: Side body panels at the backlight, trunk and rear wheels.

RAILS: Lengthwise sections in the chassis or unit body, U, C or box-shaped. They are generally tied in by cross members.

RIGID SUSPENSION: The 2 wheels are connected by a rigid axle. On a rear-wheel drive car, the rigid axle includes the differential.

RACK-AND-PINION: Two hypoid gears at right angles to each other that transfer power from a drive shaft sitting lengthwise to the differential and the axle shafts of the rear wheels. It also provides a final drive gear ratio. The pinion is powered by the driveshaft and the ring gear drives the differential.

ROTARY ENGINES (WANKEL - MAZDA): A rotor controls intake and exhaust and moves eccentrically within the housing to complete intake compression and exhaust in one turn.

SEDAN: Body with 2 or 3 volumes and 2, 3, 4- or 5 doors offering 4 to 6 seats.

SERVO: Another word for assistance. The driver's input is multiplied by allowing it to control an outside power source.

SHOCK ABSORBER: Controls the amplitude (travel) and speed of suspension and wheel travel due to road undulations and also partially controls body movements such as roll, pitch, loading and unloading. Shock absorbers cannot substitute for larger springs or stabilizer bars.

SHOULDER BELT: Upper part of safety belt harness.

SIDE VALVE ENGINE: Used on antique, in-line and V8 engines with side valves (valves next to the cylinder as in an old Ford).

SKIRT: Air deflector along the side of the car.

SOHC: Single overhead cam located in the cylinder head. It may operate the valves through cup followers or through rocker arms and controls both intakes and exhausts.

STABILIZER BAR: Long torsional bar connecting a pair of wheels and the body to limit roll during the turn. It does not support the car vertically, but stabilizes it by opposing roll.

SUPERCHARGER: A crank-powered belt or chain drives an external pump (supercharger), which feeds air to the engine to increase output, compared to a naturally-aspirated engine (the piston pumps its own air). There are Roots blowers (Ford Thunderbird SC) or spiral blowers (VW Corrado).

SYNCHRONIZATION: During the shift in a manual transmission, a small internal cone clutch equalizes gear and synchro sleeve speeds so engagement can be completed without grinding.

TIMING BELT DRIVE: A toothed timing belt that powers one or more cam shafts: flexible, quiet, doesn't require outside lubrication. When one breaks, you require a new engine.

TIMING CHAIN: A chain of either roller or toothed type that drives one or more cam shafts.

TIRE ASPECT RATIO: Speaks of the ratio of the height to the width of the tire cross section. Example: 185/60 R 14: the 60 says that 60 percent of 185 mm width is the height. Less than 60 percent (low profile) helps handling; larger than 65 percent gains comfort.

TOE-IN: A steering geometry designed to have the wheels tip toward each other.

TOE-OUT: The same, but with the wheels toeing away from each other. It is equally important at the front and as the rear.

TORQUE CONVERTER: A hydraulic coupling used with automatic transmissions to provide slip, as with a manual shift clutch, and to multiply torque.

TORQUE TUBE DRIVE: A tube or an arm extends forward from the drive wheel axle housing to near the center of the body to handle axle windup torque. An antique last seen on Opels, Vegas and early Fords, but very effective.

TORSION BAR SUSPENSION: A torsion bar is a straight coil spring. The bar works in twists: one side fixed in the frame and the other connected to the suspension arm. Most torsion bar suspensions offer initial ride height adjustment.

TRACTION CONTROL: Often combined with ABS to apply braking to the wheel that shows traction loss, which restores torque transfer to the opposite wheel.

TRANSFER CASE: Used on 4WD vehicles to shift into 2WD, N or 4WD in High or Low range.

TRANSMISSION HOUSING: The outer case of the transmission which contains the shafts, gears, clutches (automatic) and the transmission fluid.

TUNNEL: A long, tunnel-shaped section of the floor pan, in the middle of the car, makes room for the drive shaft and sometimes the exhaust.

TURBOCHARGER OR SUPERCHARGER HEAT EXCHANGER: Same concept. Either of the two devices adds heat. By cooling, the temperature of the air delivered to the engine is reduced and efficiency improves.

TURBOCHARGER: A form of supercharger which is driven by the engine's exhaust instead of by a crank-driven belt. It adds power, can add efficiency and is used not only in sports car performance but in big, Diesel trucks.

UNDERSTEER: At the limit, the vehicle is understeering when it tries to go out nose first; during understeering you need to increase the steering wheel angle.

UNIT BODY: The body, floor pan and various reinforcing sections combine into a single, structural shell as opposed to a separate frame and body connected by mounts.

VALVE: Works like a sink stopper, this mushroom-shaped part with a long stem is closed by a spring and opened by a cam shaft. Intake valves admit air, exhaust valves let out burned gases.

VENTURI: Senses air flow. The carburetor is designed to atomize the fuel, mix it with the air so the engine can burn it to make power. The number of throttle plates in the carburetor decides the number of barrels. A 2-barrel has 2 venturis, 2 throttles.

WASTE GATE: A valve controlled by intake manifold pressure which bypasses some of the exhaust to stay within pressure limits tolerated by the engine.

WHEEL RIM: Retains the tire.

TECHNICAL

HONDA

This Japanese carmaker started doing research on electric cars in 1980. In 1996, it developed the EV, a car that runs on nickel metal hydride batteries. This builder, famous for its high-efficiency and low pollutant emission engines, wanted to design a highly efficient electric engine. The powertrain is lodged in a single housing, that includes the engine itself, regulator and transmission. The engine, loaded with powerful magnets, achieved a 96% maximum efficiency, providing enough juice for the wide range of engine speeds and electrical current. The small EV weights 3,500 lb., has a road automomy of 130-215 miles and can attain an 80 mph maximum speed.

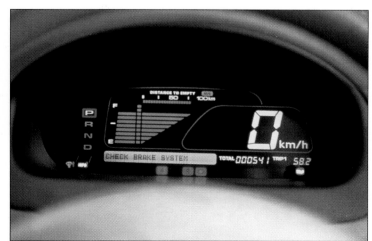

Technical

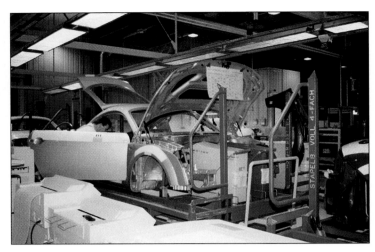

AUDI

It's in Hungary, 100 miles from the capitol city of Budapest, that Audi decided to build its new TT coupe. The ultramodern plant, strictly managed and run in the «German style», is located in the charming town of Györ. This plant, built after the fall of the Wall of Berlin, produces all the various engines in the Audi lineup. The plant was extended so as to include the TT model assembly line. The convertible version of this TT coupe will be unveiled soon. Clockwise, you can see various elements involved in assembling this car. The car body is assembled elsewhere and arrives on the platform, along with a few accessories. Pre-assembled mechanical components arrive on the assembly line on remote-controlled dolleys. Once in place, the engine and suspension components are mounted by employees who work in a squeaky-clean environment. Once cars are assembled, they're checked over and tested before being stocked on the lawn surrounding the plant.

Technical

DODGE

The ESX2 was exhibited at the last Detroit Auto Show. It's the second-generation model of a hybrid vehicle developed by Chrysler. It's equipped with a 1.5L direct fuel injected Diesel engine that's super efficient (70 mpg) It charges the high-performance lead battery that feeds the electric engine controlling vehicle power. To cut down drastically on weight, the body is made of an aluminum structure covered with six elements of thermoplastic polyester that reduces usual production costs by 20%. The ESX2 is the size of a Dodge Intrepid and weighs 1,200 lb less, yet it provides more generous cabin space. It accelerates from 0-60 mph en 12 seconds and road autonomy is 420 miles.

Technical

TOYOTA

At the latest Tokyo Auto Show, Toyota gave an update on its fuel cell research. To illustrate the application of this process aimed at creating pollution-free energy, the Japanese firm equipped a RAV4 with an alloy storage module that stores the hydrogen that feeds the fuel cell, so as to produce the 20 kW needed to cover 155 miles, which is equivalent to an 80 mpg consumption. Of course, under pressure, some metal alloys can absorb and release hydrogen. So a 220-lb. module of metal hydride can «absorb» 700,000 cu. ft. of hydrogen gas, without any risk of exploding.

Technical

CADILLAC

During the Golf war, infra-red imaging technology allowed the American military to accomplish its mission at night. Cadillac is the first carmaker to have adapted this process to the automobile. Its DeVille 2000 could be equipped with this device that lets you see via a display on the windshield what's lurking beyond the headlights' span, so as to provide safer travel.

Technical

During the 22nd «Toyota Idea Olympics», a competition that gives awards for the most original ideas related to vehicle design, the winner was this «360 Degree Free-Moving Mode Car» (on the left) with directional all-wheel drive and rotating cabin, so the pilot feels like he or she's flying above the traffic.

The Prize for Excellence was awarded for the «Mechanigator» (above) that's controlled by the driver's hip movements. As shown above, this wheelchair can also climb thanks to caterpillar strips, so it can climb up sidewalks, stairs and get around on all kinds of surfaces, such as sand and ice.

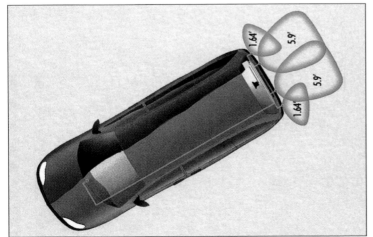

The reverse radar system developed by Ford is a very unusual option that can equip the latest model Windstar minivan. Four sensors installed on the bumper set off an alarm if something or

someone is behind the vehicle. The alarm signal rhythm accelerates as you approach towards the point of impact.

TOKYO AUTO SHOW

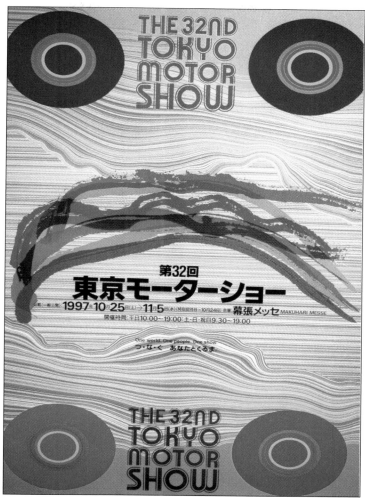

• TOKYO

The last Tokyo Car Show was held in the Makuhari complex in the suburbs of the Japanese metropolis. As is often the case, there was a wide diversity of vehicles shown and of course, it's tough taking photos without flocks of young and beautiful people also getting into the picture. Japanese beauties to show off car beauties. A tricky endeavor, not encountered anywhere else...

Tokyo Auto Show

• BMW

Only German carmakers were really able to present something that caught your attention in this sea of Nipponese products. BMW exhibited a new-design coupe-convertible called Z07 whose classic looks are inspired by those of the limited edition 507 sold in the fifties of which only 252 models were built, powered by a V8 engine.

The Z07 design consists of an aluminum structure supporting body panels made of the same metal, whereas bumpers are made of a carbon fiber composite. To be true to its ancestry, the engine is the 4.4L V8 that equips the M5, assisted by a six-speed sequential transmission. Wheels sport magnesium rims for the occasion.

Tokyo Auto Show

• DAIHATSU

The FR-X (upper left) is a small, plump 2+2 sports coupe equipped with a 850 cc engine, while the Naked (upper right) is a all-out utility vehicle that's very solid and compact that's powered by a 660 cc engine!

• DAEWOO

The d'Arts is a city slicker, shown here in the Style version that was designed for the Tokyo Auto Show. It looks a bit «kitsch» with its two-tone paint job, spoked wheels and chrome accents, but the Japanese are just wild about it. It's less than 13 ft long and is a Korean creation, but it's also built in Rumania, Poland and India and is equipped with an 800 cc engine developing 52 hp.

Tokyo Auto Show

• HONDA

Clockwise, the J-WJ represents the stylistic study of an AWD very compact vehicle equipped with a variable speed transmission linked to a 1.5L VTEC engine. The J-MW is equipped with the same engine and transmission but it's a small station wagon with a minivan design providing a high-perched cockpit. The J-VX is a mini sports coupe based on the «Small is Smart» concept. It's animated by a direct fuel injection 1.0L 3-cylinder VTEC linked to a continuously variable transmission (CVT). A very compact electric generator, affixed to a heat engine, increases engine power to accelerate and recycle kinetic energy when slowing down in order to reduce fuel consumption.

Tokyo Auto Show

• ISUZU

The VX-2 (shown above) is a futuristic vision of Isuzu's concept of an all-purpose vehicle. The Zaccar (on the left) has a different open rear end design and is equipped with a direct fuel injection diesel engine. The V-Cross (opposite) that sports a very sci-fi silhouette is already sold in Japan and is the cause for quite a stir.

• KIA

Besides the two-door semi-convertible version of the Sportage SUV, this Korean automaker exhibited its concept sports coupe that will soon be put on the market, a coupe called KMS-4 motivated by a 2.0L 4-cylinder engine developing 151 hp. This coupe will be fitted with solar energy panels and emergency braking system.

Tokyo Auto Show

• MAZDA

The unveiling of the latest Miata roadster model was a focus of interest at the Tokyo Auto Show. It's more rocket-like and muscular than the former model, and is no longer equipped with pop-up head-lamps, it has more lively en-gine, revamped instrument panel, bigger trunk and roof top now fitted with a glass win-dow and electric defroster. We could also admire the latest Sentia (lower right), the creami-est vehicle in the Mazda lineup, that was formerly imported in North America under the name 929 Serenia.

The Demio (lower left), half-station wagon, half-minivan, is really popular in Japan due to its compact and multi-purpose attributes and is available in an electrically powered version.

Tokyo Auto Show

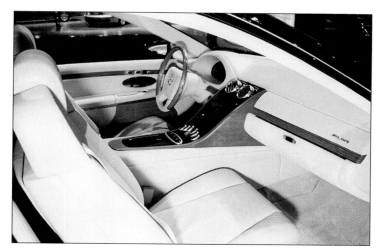

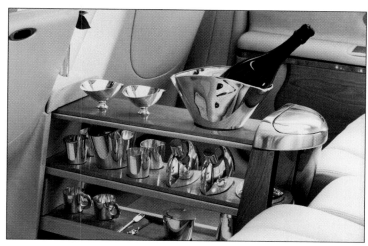

• MERCEDES-BENZ

The Maybach, bearing the German designer Wilhelm Maybach's name, will soon be the top-of-the-line model produced by the German carmaker. It will come in a limited one thousand unit edition and will share the upcoming S-Series' platform and mechanical components, but it will be furbished with even more refined, posh equipment items. This chauffered sedan has rear reclining seats, elaborate bar and a complete multimedia communications system including three telephones, computer, television set and tape recorder. The body is made of composite materials, aluminum and magnesium and is fitted with a powerful lighting system controlled by a microprocessor.

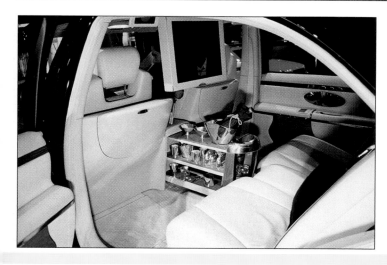

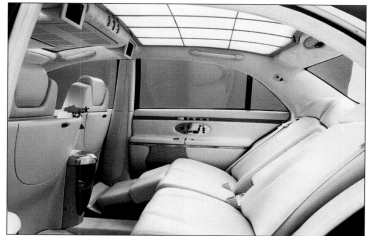

Tokyo Auto Show

• MITSUBISHI

Clockwise, you can take a look at the Maia prototype, an SUV with a modular cabin design and hatch door that opens in three different ways. The more rounded out Tetra is a good example of new all-terrain body design. Access is much easier due to lower ground clearance, wider doors and hinged rear hatch. Opposite, the HSR study is a forerunner of the sports coupe for the next century, that's equipped with unique-design high-tech hinged doors. And the cabin can be raised or lowered depending on driving mode to provide good visibility and higher-yield aerodynamics. The controls and instrument panels are really imaginative.

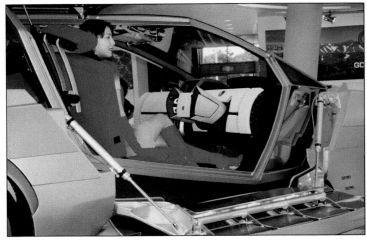

Tokyo Auto Show

• NISSAN

Clockwise, behold the R'nessa, the key vehicle in the Nissan exhibit. It's a big station wagon with modular seats, offered in regular and high-performance versions. Opposite, the Altra EV is the first electrically powered vehicle geared to the North American market, equipped with lithium-ion batteries, hidden under the floor, providing a road autonomy of 120 miles. The AL-X (below) is a hybrid urban vehicle built of aluminum and equipped with a heat engine that recharges the batteries, while the Cube (left) offers maximum cabin volume for a minimal format, that allows you to go from the front to rear seats without having to get out of the vehicle.

Tokyo Auto Show

• SUBARU

A new, revised and improved Exiga (above) enjoyed center stage at the Subaru stand. It's a big all-wheel drive station wagon van driven by a new compact version of the 2.5L flat-4 engine. A dynamic control (VDC) system stabilizes handling and an optical safety detector (ADA) keeps an eye on driver maneuvers.

The Elten (opposite), reminiscent of the famous 360, is an engineering concept of a hybrid urban vehicle that's equipped with a continously variable transmission (CVT) and solar panel roof.

The Casa Blanca (below right) is a retro version of the Impreza and a spanking new sports sedan version was exhibited (left).

Tokyo Auto Show

• SUZUKI

Clockwise the CT-1 is an electric SUV concept vehicle built to transport light loads in an urban setting. It's equipped with neat, power sliding side doors.

The UW-1 represents a compact mini-station wagon concept. It's powered by a 1.0L 4-cylinder engine and the cabin can accomodate five passengers without affecting trunk volume that's quite reasonably sized.

The C2 is a charming little roadster whose single-panel hard top can be removed by rotating it, leaving the trunk volume intact and unscathed. It's animated by a remarkable 1.6L V8 that develops 250 hp paired up with a 6-speed manual or 5-speed automatic transmission.

Tokyo Auto Show

• TOYOTA

The Prius (above) is the first hybrid automobile in the world to be actually and successfully sold. It was first sold in Japan at the same price as a regular compact car, thanks to Japanese government subsidies. Depending on driving style, the on-board computer activates either the 1.5L gas engine or the electric engine, or both simultaneously, without the driver's intervention. The driver can view on a cathode screen the type of power feed chosen, aimed at reducing consumption and pollutant emissions.

The MR-S roadster (opposite) is animated by a 1.8L engine set in the middle at the rear. It's linked to a sequential transmission exactly like the one used in Formula 1 racecars.

Tokyo Auto Show

• TOYOTA

The e-com (below) is a small electric car that's no different from its counterparts, but it does have more of an ovoid design. Its NiMH batteries provide a road autonomy of 60 miles without having to recharge and last three times longer than lead batteries.

The Funcoupe, exhibited last year in Frankfurt, has original looks and is akin to that of a leisure-loving car.

The New (opposite) is a four-wheel drive SUV with very modern design and stripped down to basics interior. Technical touches can still be things of beauty and Toyota states that the dashboard is a «village» design, which is a bit confusing, or maybe the country isn't what it used to be...

Tokyo Auto Show

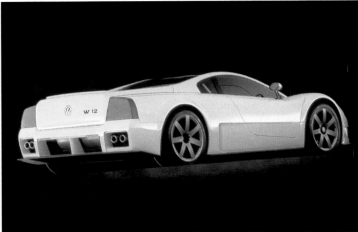

• VOLKSWAGEN

BMW and Mercedes-Benz each introduced a new model at the Tokyo Auto Show, so VW followed suit and exhibited an innovative design car. The W12 coupe was created by Ital Design, yet it's blessed with ultra-conservative classic looks. But the W12 engine is more original, since the popular German builder has just acquired Rolls Royce and Lamborghini. It is in fact made up of two VR6 engines, joined together and set at a 72° angle, that develop 420 hp at 5,800 r.p.m. thanks to its 4 valve per cylinder distribution activated by a total of 4 OHC's. This extremely compact unit is built of aluminum, but the rocker arm covers and timing chain are made of magnesium.

Tokyo Auto Show Curiosities

The Jimmy Wide is the latest version of this vehicle to be sold by Samurai. Wider wheel tracks provide better stability, a sorely lacking trait that had explained its removal from the roster.

The Hyundai model coined the Atos or Andro is in fact a tiny 4-door, 5-passenger minivan powered by a 55-hp 1.0L engine sold exclusively on Asian markets.

It's hard to imagine that this Swiss chalet style cabin interior is that of a Japanese bus aimed at servicing ski resorts...

You can take a look at the very sleek rear end design of the latest Accord station wagon that's no longer sold in North America.

The Lincoln Town Car sold in Japan is quite lovely with its lens-shaped headlamps that give it a more high-tech apprearance than is the case for the domestic model.

The Toyota Spacio is the minivan in the Corolla family. Following Japanese fashion trends, the front end is what you could call retro, or in other words, it's bygone bizarre.

Tokyo Auto Show Curiosities

This Honda motorcycle, equipped with a car-like comfy seat and trunk, is an interesting specimen in the two-wheeler vehicle segment.

No doubt inspired by the Plymouth Prowler, this rather interesting product graced the stand of a merchant who makes very stylish wheel rims.

Araco sells hinged seats that offer maximum comfort, aimed at replacing the rear seatbench now found on most all-terrain SUV's.

Two very famous Canadian actors did a comedy routine at the Mazda stand. From left to right, you can see Jim Robinson and Mike Benchimol...

How can you not bring home a dozen doughnuts after meeting these charming sales persons? In Japan, sexual harassment isn't an issue yet...

Can you see the car model? No? Well, we can't either, which is the common plight of photographers covering the Tokyo Show, but no one really complains...

DETROIT AUTO SHOW

• AUDI

From an all-wheel drive vehicle to a 4X4, there's only a hop, skip and a jump, a move that the German carmaker didn't hesitate to make so as to jump aboard the lucrative SUV bandwagon. Its SUV (below), based on the A6 Avant, benefits from an air suspension that automatically adjusts ground clearance according to speed. When you get right down to it, it's a question of terminology...

• ACURA

In keeping with what has become something of a tradition for this brand, the TL-X is the concept car that was behind the next generation Acura TL model that will be sold in the fall of 1998. It was designed in California and will be built in Ohio and will double Acura sales. It'll be offered with a V6 engine and a sequential shifter automatic transmission.

Detroit Auto show

• ASTON MARTIN

Jack Nasser, the power behind the Ford throne who's the owner of the British company, proudly presented this design study of a Super Aston called Project Vantage whose silhouette is an Ian Callum creation. The body design is modern, yet reflects traditional brand stylistics, whereas the cabin design has a new look with tawny leather and shiny aluminum accents. The body, built of aluminum honeycomb and composite material, has trimmed its weight down by half, while still providing maximum structural rigidity. The 6.0L V12 (two V6's joined together), associated with a 6-speed «manumatic» transmission featuring fingertip shifting, should hit 200 mph and go from 0 to 60 mph in 4 seconds.

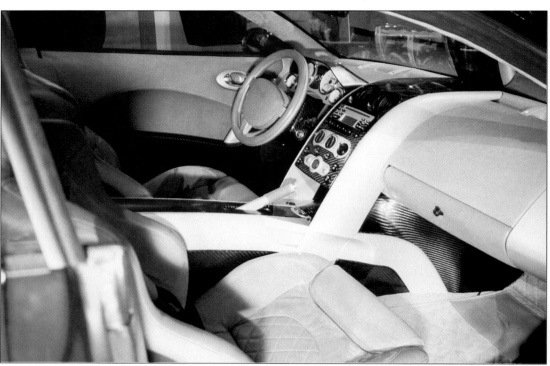

Detroit Auto show

• BUICK

The Signia project reflects perfectly the current SUV family car trend. Its heavy silhouette won't go down in automobile history, but the sliding rear hatch door is neat for it allows for easy access to the modular cargo hold. An offshoot of the Park Avenue Ultra's architecture, the Signia is equipped with a 240-hp 3.8L supercharged V6. The vehicle is equipped with an automatic all-wheel drive transmission, but it isn't geared for off-road rambles. A hybrid power source is being experimented with so as to dramatically reduce fuel consumption and pollution emissions. The screen located in the middle of the instrument panel lets you control main vehicle functions that can be adapted to each driver.

Detroit Auto show

• CHRYSLER

Right off, the Chronos strikes you due to its unusual size, since it's more than 16 ft long and almost 7 ft wide. Its 20 and 21-in diameter wheels are in keeping with vehicle format, as are mechanical components borrowed from the Viper, namely a 6.0L V10 engine that now develops 350 hp (!) associated with a 4-speed automatic transmission. This 5,180 lb. luxury car looks a lot like the Chrysler d'Elegance designed by Virgil Exner in 1953. The Chrysler LHS (below) has had a makeover and is still the cream of the crop model built by the # 3 American carmaker, while its offspring cousin the 300M borrows elements from the former 300 versions that are remembered as sports cars dressed up in their Sunday best...

Detroit Auto show

• FORD

Ford wants to check out the small pickup Courier F1's popularity (above left) on the North American market. This vehicle is a light delivery truck by vocation. Built in Brazil, it's equipped with 1.3 and 1.4L engines that keep fuel bills nice and low. On the right is the Alpe, a design that's a meld of an all terrain vehicle and a four-door station wagon. This trim vehicle is based on the Escort platform and is driven by a 2.0L engine. Opposite is the new Super Duty truck in the F-Series that comes in 250-350-450 and 550 versions.

Below, Ford didn't waste any time imitating Dodge and now equips its F-150 and Ranger pickups with a fourth rear door for easier access.

Detroit Auto show

• HONDA

When the MV99 for Mini Van 99 was unveiled, it still didn't have a definitive name. It was only later that we found out that the replacement for the Odyssey would bear the same family name. The cabin design was wild and maybe not wonderful, but vehicle size was a clear indication that Honda had decided to get into the fray, competing with the biggest rivals out there.

• GMC

General Motors gave a foretaste of what its new pickup trucks would look like when they'll be reworked for 1999, by showing this GMC Sierra Ace. The rear end of the cabin is noticeably longer, so there'll be more leg room for seatbench occupants.

Detroit Auto show

• JEEP

The shining star of Chrysler's opening show, the Jeepster, explores traits characteristic of an all terrain vehicle and a sports coupe, in the Suzuki X-90 style, but it's a lot more original. This vehicle can leave the highway and head for field and vale thanks to its variable ground clearance and its Quadra-Trac all-wheel drive. The powerplant is the new 275-hp 4.7L V8 that will soon equip other vehicles built by Jeep, beginning with the latest Grand Cherokee. The Jeepster design is neat with the trim front and rear overhang and the safe tubular structure that serves as a frame for the top. This approach will maybe restitute the sports car's popularity, something it lost to the 4X4's.

Detroit Auto show

2-40-A

• LEXUS

It's the very first time that the SUV RX300 (below), derived from the ES300-Camry, was shown in North America. It's a direct rival to the Mercedes-Benz ML320 and is blessed with a very mod bod. On the right, the LX 470 replaces the LX 450, still inspired by the Toyota Land Cruiser.

• MERCURY

This Ford division set out to broaden its traditional mature clientele and appeal to younger age groups, so it resurrected the Cougar for the name and the Probe for the technical philosophy. But it should be noted that the car's lower body and mechanical features no longer hail from Mazda, but from the Ford Contour, such as the 2.0L Zetec 4-cylinder and 2.5L Duratec V6.

Detroit Auto show

• MITSUBISHI

The SST got its stylistics from the California team. It's a geo-mechanical concept of the sports car of the 21st century that expresses its temperament via muscular aspects akin to those of the human body. It's impressive with its 20-in diameter wheels and very clean, lean look interior.

• OLDSMOBILE

The Alero replaces the Achieva with real flair. In fact, the basic recipe is still the same, but the body and cabin design, inspired by the Aurora and Intrigue, have a lot more pizzazz. It's still available as a coupe or sedan, powered by a 2.4L 4-cylinder or 3.4L V6 engine with automatic gearbox only.

Detroit Auto show

• PLYMOUTH

The Pronto roadster is an example of what a small, affordable sports vehicle built by Chrysler and with the younger set in mind, could look like. The body is an injected polyethylene skin (the same material used for soft drink bottles) which cuts production costs by 80%. It's equipped with the 225-hp 2.4L supercharged engine that powers Neon racecars. The engine is set in the main rear section of the steel unibody. The car interior has attributes typical of this type of vehicle, that is a compact instrument panel and leather-clad bucket seats.

Detroit Auto show

• PONTIAC

The Montana Thunder is the end result of the down-and-out nightmare that afflicted Pontiac designers when they realized they'd never outstrip their homologues at Chrysler... But even if the overall effect is a bit strange, some details are quite noteworthy, such as the power hatch door, built-in computer and turn signal indicator lights in the side mirrors. Below, the latest version of the Grand Am that still sports the unique style that appeals to so many buyers. What you don't see in the photo: it's furbished with a dashboard reminiscent of the country music singer Dolly Parton's attributes...

Detroit Auto show

• SUBARU

Paul Hogan of «Crocodile Dundee» fame had made the trip to Australia to unveil this Outback sedan and he was not a happy camper...

• SUZUKI

This vehicle looks more like a home-made specimen than a serious concept vehicle, since it has the 4-door Sidekick's front end design with a pickup truck box at the rear.

• VOLKSWAGEN

The New Beetle was the hottest item at the 1998 Detroit Auto Show, upstaging the star introduced by Chrysler, who wasn't prepared for such a turn of events.

• VOLVO

Volvo will be importing the 40-Series animated by a 1.9L engine, that it builds in association with Mitsubishi in Europe.

NEW-YORK AUTO SHOW

• CHEVROLET

An identical twin to the Suzuki Vitara, the Chevrolet Tracker has had a complete overhaul. Since it first appeared in 1994, it had hardly changed at all and the onslaught of the new rivals like the Honda CR-V's and RAV4's gave it a back shelf, antique status... It's still offered in a short 2-door convertible model with a 90-hp 1.6L engine and in a long 4-door station wagon model, animated by a 2.0L engine developing 127 hp. The newcomer has a new beefier chassis, reinforced front axle (2.0L), roomier cabin and cargo hold, handier instrumentation and all-wheel drive that can be activated at any speed under 60 mph.

New-York Auto Show

• HONDA

The only and sadly relative success of the first Odyssey, more of a station wagon than a van, forced Honda to take another look at its strategy. To be on a par with the competition, the new Odyssey is just as spacious as the Nissan Quest and Toyota Sienna. It's motivated by a new 3.5L V6 borrowed from the Accord and will be built in Alliston, Ontario in Canada.

• HYUNDAI

The ill-named Avatar that replaces the Sonata is still equipped with a transverse V6 engine and four-speed automatic transmission.

New-York Auto Show

• INFINITI

Peekaboo, it's back. The G20 was taken off the Infiniti roster in 1997 but it's back.. It has a fresh, new look, but it's equipped with almost the same mechanical features as the former model. Stay tuned...

• LINCOLN

To everyone's surprise, Lincoln unveiled the LS6 and LS8 models that will be the lower end cars in the luxury Ford division as of year 2000. This RWD car shares the same structural makeup as the impatiently awaited «small» Jaguar and could be powered either by a 3.0L V6 or a 3.9L V8, linked to a manual (LS6), automatic or sequential SelectShift transmission. Infiniti, Lexus, Catera and company, get ready...

New-York Auto Show

•MERCEDES-BENZ

The Stuttgart firm introduced 4 models that will be equipped with a 4.3L V8 powerplant: the C43, CLK430, E430 and the all terrain ML430, vehicles to be part of the 1999 lineup.

• TOYOTA

The Solara coupe, a Camry offshoot that shares its ancestor's mechanical attributes, will be built in Cambridge, Ontario in Canada.

• VOLVO

The Swedish builder is broadening out its lower end model range. It announced that it'll be importing a compact model built conjointly in Europe with Mitsubishi. The S and V40's will be animated by 1.9L 4-cylinder engines.

GENEVA AUTO SHOW

• GENEVA

The Geneva Auto Show is undoubtedly the automobile show-case that best deserves the term international, since Switzerland and especially Geneva, are international business and political centers. You run into people from all around the world looking for the most unique, one-of-a-kind and prestigious products.

Geneva Auto Show

• AUDI

The A6 Avant station wagon caught up with the sedan in a hurry and is now sold in a front-wheel or all-wheel Quattro version, driven by a 193-hp V6.

• BERTONE

The Pickster is a high-performance pickup truck that will be more at home in chic neighborhoods than down on the farm or on a construction site. But on the other hand, on a German fast-track highway, it will show off its 320-hp BMW engine to make emergency deliveries. Its 21-in wheels are equipped with puncture proof Michelin tires and in a pinch, two passengers can be accomodated on the pop-up seats built into the frame floor.

Geneva Auto Show

• BMW

The 3-Series has had an ultra-conservative facelift, since it integrates most stylistic touches inaugurated on the most recent models. It's longer, wider and higher, so it benefits from better handling and offers more generous cabin and cargo space. It will be imported in North America with two 6-cylinder engines: a 2.5 and 2.8L.

• DAEWOO

The Korean automaker has reworked two of its models distributed in Europe. On the right, the Lanos is a reasonably priced compact vehicle equipped with 1.5L and 1.6L engines. The Leganza is similar to the Hyundai Elantra. It comes as a sedan or station wagon powered by a 133-hp 2.0L engine with manual or automatic transmission.

Geneva Auto Show

• FERRARI

Pininfarina has put some subtle new touches on the 456's front hood and bumper cover design, while Ferrari has refined the suspension and installed unusual instrument gauges and a traction control device.

• JAGUAR

The Coventry company marks the fiftieth anniversary of its XK model by unveiling the R version of its latest coupe that's motivated by a supercharged V8 that develops 370 hp.

• FORD

Ford revolutionized its traditional way of doing things by offering a daring design and new name for the successor of the Escort, that's been its star seller at century's end.

Geneva Auto Show

• HYUNDAI

The Korean carmaker sure got some attention with its latest prototype, Euro-I inspired by roadsters from the fifties, beefed up with a bold body design that's typical of the Hyundai lineup. The cockpit layout and wire electronic controls are borrowed from racecars. If the general public likes it, Hyundai will build it at some future date...

• KIA

Carnival is the name of this minivan that hails from Korea. It has conservative, traditional looks and is driven by 2.5 and 2.9L V6 engines, but it has clever shelves mounted on the front seat backs, a feature worth mentioning.

Geneva Auto Show

• MERCEDES-BENZ

Above is shown the new CLK convertible and the Designo version of the SLK (on the right) that's outstanding because of its understated interior design...The Maybach, already exhibited in Tokyo, had a living room-office layout to show off in Geneva, aimed to attract business executives and company. A noteworthy item: the rather unusual ceiling design at the rear end.

• MITSUBISHI

The Spacestar (below) is a new model that will replace a vehicle that's well-known in North America under the name Colt Wagon or Expo LRV. It's a vehicle that sits somewhere between the station wagon and minivan and it no longer has a sliding side door. Hard to say if the engineering concept L200 (on the right) is an all terrain SUV with a platform or a 4-door pickup truck!

Geneva Auto Show

• OPEL

The Zaphira is a new SUV that now joins the lineup, between the Omega Caravan wagon and the Sintra minivan (identical to the Venture-Trans Sport's) in the European GM model range. Designed along the lines of the Astra platform, it sports a neat third seatbench that can be folded down into the floor, as is the case on the Honda Odyssey.

• PEUGEOT

The anagram concoted by Peugeot to name this concept vehicle, forerunner of the next generation 207, can't be translated into a language other than French. It should have read Vingt-Coeur for conqueror and not Two-O-Heart as some foreign magazines translated it. It's a convertible coupe with a brilliant design, a real gem.

Geneva Auto Show

• RINSPEED

The E-Go Rocket is another flight of fancy created by the Swiss builder Rinspeed. It's another single-seater similar to record-breaking speedsters. Under the hood, there's a 410-hp V8 that can make this car hit 162 mph.

• ROLLS ROYCE

Launching a new model isn't terribly typical of the British automaker that's just come into the Volkswagen fold. The Silver Seraph is a big luxury sedan boasting a classic and distinguished style that incorporates traditional company traits such as the vertical grille, chrome accents and leather and wood trim. Strange enough, there's a BMW 322-hp V12 under the hood!

OUR COVER PHOTO

• RENAULT

This intriguing Zo has all it takes to end up on the cover of Road Report. It's a fascinating creature with its name inspired by zoomorphic, a shape akin to that of a beetle and a shiny frame that's maybe a bit overdone. It's a roadster reminiscent of the single seater due to its trim size and also a dune buggy with its bathtub form. Zo is an all terrain vehicle equipped with an air suspension that varies ground clearance depending on driving mode selected: low on the highway or perched high on rough turf.

The Clio (above) is the most popular Renault model. It's been redesigned in a unique «pontoon» style that the French automaker is trying to resurrect.

Geneva Auto Show

• SBARRO

Our friend Franco celebrated forty years of love and passion for cars, surrounded by his wife Françoise and students from the most recent cohort at his design school Espace Sbarro. This year he presented (clockwise) an Ocean version of the Citroën Berlingo, similar to dune buggies in the sixties, the Be-Twin, a roadster with shiny wheels, equipped with a dual driver cockpit, no doubt destined to be used in driving schools. Below, the Crisalys is a coupe with a folding hardtop that transforms into a convertible. Its body is mounted on the frame via rubber elements to reduce noise and vibration and it's equipped with a V6 Peugeot engine.

Geneva Auto Show

• SEAT

The Bolero (opposite) demonstrates the idea of a sports sedan with a bulky style like that of the Audi A6 and the upcoming TT coupe. It was elaborated by researchers from the Spanish firm Seat that belongs to the Volkswagen group.

• TATA

This Indian firm is trying to make it on the European market by introducing (above) a small economy sedan as well as an all-terrain vehicle called Safari.

• VALMET

This Swedish company has created a four-door convertible (landaulet) version of the Honda CR-V that's quite interesting with its electrically powered top and glass rear window fitted with both wiper and window washer.

We've been talking about alternatives to gas and clean emission electric or hybrid cars for ages but we never got beyond simply exhibiting prototype models at Auto Shows, so we had ended up thinking the whole idea was a pie in the sky dream. GM made a pitiful attempt to market an electric car whose road autonomy didn't extend beyond the length of the battery recharger cable, so it seemed that no hope of ever succeeding such a feat was possible before the end of the century. But then there was Toyota, the dynamic Japanese giant full of awesome energy and resourcefulness and of course this carmaker had been wisely putting money aside, the result of ultra-conservative management.

At the most recent Tokyo Auto Show in October 1997, Toyota exhibited several vehicles that meet no or low pollution emission standards, such as the Prius that's been sold on the Japanese market since December of the same year and that's been a smashing success.

Its design principle is quite simple. Up front, the power train consists of including in the same housing a

1.5L 4-cylinder gas engine linked to a continuously variable transmission (CVT). A motor and electric alternator are set between the two. There isn't a direct link between the heat engine and the axles. The heat engine is standard and turns at a maximum of 4,000 r.p.m. and only activates the alternator that recharges the batteries when needed. These serial nickel-metal hydride batteries are the size of a C battery with 40 modules linked

to yield a rated current of 240 volts. They're set flat between the seatbench and the trunk and are never charged beyond 66% of their capacity so as to last as long as the car itself, namely 155,000 miles. They feed power into the electric engine that develops 40 hp at an r.p.m. range of 960 to 2,000 tr/mn. The electronic fairy orchestrates these components so that each plays its piece at the right moment. The sophisticated electronic control unit lets you use the system as needed, for example, the electric engine is activated for starting, but if more power is needed and there isn't enough energy on reserve in the batteries, the heat engine kicks in to provide the proper juice. While going downhill or when braking, kinetic energy is converted into electrical current and directed towards the batteries. Electric energy is constantly being replenished as long as there's gas in the tank, so you don't have to hook up the battery to recharge it. When starting up in cold weather, a conventional battery located in the trunk sends impulses to stimulate the pertinent battery electrons before each startup. The block heater cable also maintains electric power during cold nights. The neat thing about this system is that the electric car is 100% autonomous, since it generates its own electrical energy from an engine that's two times less of a pollution source than a conventional engine. This solution may not be perfect, but at least it exists, is affordable and reduces pollutant gas emissions by 50%.

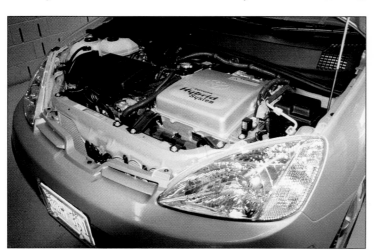

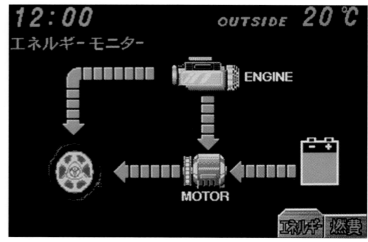

TOYOTA Prius
Take a Ride in
Tomorrow's Car...

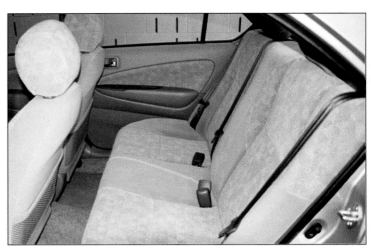

Developing and marketing the hybrid Prius represents a remarkable technological first for the Japanese carmaker Toyota. Even if a lot of automakers say they're ready to follow suit, Toyota will still take the credit for being the first to have sold such a car on the Japanese market, then in 1999, on American and Canadian markets.

MODEL RANGE

For now, the Prius is a 4-door sedan that's about as long as the Corolla, but we know that a coupe based on the same technology will soon be available. Standard equipment includes an automatic continuously variable transmission, power steering, air conditioning and an antilock braking device. When it hits the North American market, it will be equipped with side-impact airbags as well as the two front-impact airbags that are already included.

TECHNICAL FEATURES

The Prius has a steel monocoque body. Its clean silhouette is really efficient, since even with the wide exposed surface due to its unusual height, it yields a drag coefficient of 0.30. The body is both rigid and lightweight since it's made of high-resistance steel. Lexus soundproofing techniques have been applied so as to keep the cabin nice and quiet. The independent front suspension consists of MacPherson struts and at the rear, there's a torsion axle. Disc and drum brakes benefit from an ABS device and the car is equipped with power rack-and-pinion steering. The power train includes the heat engine, generator, electric engine and continuously variable transmission all enclosed in the same housing set transversely between the front wheels.

PROS

+ POLLUTION CONTROL. Thanks to this hybrid system, gas pollutant emissions are cut in half on the current model and there's talk of improving this even more by the time it's sold here.

+ EFFICIENCY. The hybrid power source lets you economize on gas since current consumption is less than 40 mpg, yielding an average road autonomy of 775 miles.

+ DRIVING PLEASURE. This car is amazingly easy to drive, for the computer takes care of everything. After turning on the engine, all you have to do is choose forward or reverse and accelerate.

+ VEHICLE SIZE. The Prius is quite a trim little car, but it offers more cabin space than a Corolla because seats are perched high. The trunk isn't convertible since it lodges the batteries, but it can hold a fair amount and loading access is nice and handy.

+ RIDE COMFORT. The relatively flexible suspension and nicely upholstered seats provide good passenger comfort and the engine is very quiet, except for the whistling turbine noise emitted by the variable transmission.

+ SCREEN. It's set in the middle of the instrument panel and it can serve as a navigation system when such is available and it shows a graphic image of the energy source and management.

+ CONVENIENCE FEATURES. The Prius has all sorts of hidden storage spots, so it's really a neat and handy car.

CONS

- VEHICLE WEIGHT. The Prius weighs about 440 lb. more than a conventional automobile of its size, so you feel like you're at the wheel of a big American beauty with such a cushy suspension and such. Vehicle weight also affects performances, according to test figures, but you feel like you're travelling faster than you really are.

- WHEELS. They're small to cut down on rolling resistance, so they don't cope too well with heavy loads and weight shift on curves, since the inner wheel is overloaded on such maneuvers.

CONCLUSION

One may think Toyota is taking a shining light lead role in the fight against pollution and wasted resources so as to improve its image for purely commercial reasons, nonetheless the Prius is the first mass-produced hybrid car on the planet, it's finally here and will be sold at North American Toyota dealers as of next year...

RATING TOYOTA Prius		
CONCEPT :		**73%**
Technology	90	
Safety :	80	
Interior space :	65	
Trunk volume:	50	
Quality/fit/finish :	80	
DRIVING:		**60%**
Cockpit :	75	
Performance :	20	
Handling :	70	
Steering :	75	
Braking :	60	
ORIGINAL EQUIPMENT:		**72%**
Tires :	70	
Headlights :	75	
Wipers :	75	
Rear defroster :	70	
Radio :	75	
COMFORT :		**77%**
Seats :	80	
Suspension :	80	
Sound level :	70	
Conveniences :	80	
Air conditioning :	75	
BUDGET :		**66%**
Price :	60	
Fuel economy :	100	
Insurance :	70	
Satisfaction :	50	
Depreciation :	50	
Overall rating:		**82.8%**

NEW FOR 1999

- According to information received just before printing, this hybrid car should be sold by the end of 1999 as the year 2000 model.

	ENGINES				TRANSMISSIONS			PERFORMANCES									
Model/ version	Type / timing valve / fuel system	Displacement cu in	Power bhp @ rpm	Torque lb-ft @ rpm	Compres. ratio	Driving wheels / transmission	Final ratio	Acceler. 0-60 mph s	Standing 1/4 & 5/8 mile s	Acceler. 50-75 mph s	Braking 60-0 mph f	Top speed mph	Lateral acceler. G	Noise level dBA	Fuel economy mpg City Highway		Fuel type Octane
Prius	L4 1.5 DOHC-16-EFI electric engine	91.3	58 @ 4000 40 @ 2600	75 @ 4000 225 @ 940	13.5 :1	front - AVC	3.927	13.8	22.0	36.5	11.0	144	100	NA	66	56	R 87

PRICE & EQUIPMENT

TOYOTA Prius	4dr.sdn.
Retail price $:	**20,000**
Dealer invoice $:	-
Shipping & handling $:	-
Automatic transmission:	S
Cruise control:	-
Power steering:	S
Anti-lock brakes:	S
Traction control:	-
Air conditioning:	S
Leather:	-
AM/FM/radio-cassette:	S
Power door locks:	S
Power windows:	S
Tilt steering:	S
Dual adjustable mirrors:	S
Alloy wheels:	-
Anti-theft system:	-

Colors

Exterior: White, Silver, Blue, Bordeaux.

Interior: Medium grey

AT A GLANCE...

Category: front-wheel drive hybrid compact sedans.   **Class :** 3

HISTORIC

Introduced in:	1997
Made in:	Japan.

DEMOGRAPHICS

Model	Men./Wom.	Age	Married	College	Income
Prius	50/50 %	42	72%	50 %	$ 40 000

INDEX

Safety:	80 %	Satisfaction:	NA
Depreciation:	NA	Insurance:	$950
Cost per mile:	$ 0.22	Number of dealers:	1 233

SALES

Model	1996	1997	Result
Prius	Not on the market yet		

MAIN COMPETITORS

CHEVROLET Cavalier, DODGE-PLYMOUTH Neon, FORD Escort, HONDA Civic 4 dr., HYUNDAI Elantra, MAZDA Protegé, PONTIAC Sunfire, SATURN SL, SUBARU Impreza, VOLKSWAGEN Jetta.

MAINTENANCE REQUIRED BY WARRANTY

First revision:	Frequency:	Diagnostic plug:
3000 miles	6 000 miles	Yes

		SPECIFICATIONS														
Model	Version Trim	Body/ Seats	Interior volume cu ft	Trunk volume cu ft	Cd	Wheel base in	Lght x Wdgth x Hght in x in x in	Curb weight lb	Susp. ft/rr	Brake ft/rr	Steering type	Turning diameter ft	Steer. turns nber.	Fuel tank gal	tire size	Standard tires make model	Standard powertrain
Prius	base	4dr.sdn. 5	95.3	12.4	0.32	100.4	168.3x66.7x58.7	2734	ih/sih	dc/dr/ABS	pwr.r&p.	30.8	3.6	13.2	165/65SR15	- -	L4/1.5/AVC

This just in ...

• MERCEDES-BENZ

In March 1999, The German automaker will officially unveil its new S-Class luxury sedan. Mercedes has learned its lesson, as can be seen in these photos, for the newcomer's body design is much more appealing and vehicle size is less pretentious. It will still be animated by 6, 8 and 12-cylinder engines and a two-door CL coupe will be introduced at the Frankfurt Auto Show in September 1999.

• JAGUAR

At the lower right, you can see the Jaguar X200 prototype that'll share most of its mechanical features with the upcoming Lincoln LS.

• VOLKSWAGEN

At the lower left, the European VW Bora will be the next North American Jetta.

TOYOTA Solara

HONDA Odyssey

ROAD TESTS
AND
ANALYSIS

PLYMOUTH Prowler

JEEP Grand Cherokee

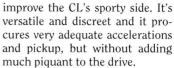

It never pays to be too ahead of one's time. Few car experts really understood Acura's approach when it started selling the CL coupe. Today, the arrival of the Toyota Solara derived from the Camry, throws new light on the future of the coupe market. The «baby boomers» have become «empty nesters», so one day they'll be deserting the minivans that were once crammed with their offspring, or the arrogant 4X4's that finally never did get them everywhere they had a yen to go, and they'll be beginning their retirement years in the cushy and refined comfort of a two-door coupe.

MODEL RANGE

The Acura CL is offered in a single two-door 2+2 coupe in base or De Luxe 2.3 equipped with either a 2.3L 4-cylinder engine paired up with a standard 5-speed manual transmission or an optional 4-speed automatic, or a 3.0 version powered by a 3.0L V6 linked to an automatic gearbox. Both these models are very richly equipped. The only difference between them is that the automatic transmission is standard on the 3.0 version and optional on the 2.3 model. We notice that there still isn't any traction control system listed in the catalogue.

TECHNICAL FEATURES

The CL coupe, built on the Honda Accord platform, shares the same wheelbase, and is equipped with the same main mechanical components as the car from which it's derived. The steel monocoque body is fitted with some galvanized panels and doesn't seem to benefit from wonderful aerodynamics, since the carmaker hasn't published its coefficient. The four-wheel independent suspension consists of a double wishbone arrangement and coil springs, coaxial shocks and anti-roll bar both front and rear. The 2.2L engine has had its displacement increased to 2.3L a year ago and now its power by 5 hp. The SOHC 4-valves per cylinder engine benefits from variable valve timing and lift that's electronically controlled, a system known as VTEC. The all-aluminum V6 engine, the same as on the Accord, is built at the Anna plant in Ohio. It also benefits from electronic fuel injection and the VTEC system.

PROS

+ STYLE. It's quite original, very sleek and has a futuristic touch, especially at the rear where the taillight design resembles that of

Cushy Cocoon...

the prototype unveiled in Detroit in 1995. The over-all look is elegant and fine finish details and equipment items are a cut above what most of the rivals have to offer.

+ RIDE COMFORT. It's pretty cushy, for the cabin truly accomodates four passengers, although the ceiling clearance is a bit low in the rear seats. The suspension handles the worst road faults, in spite of only average travel. And the noise level is nice and low at cruising speed, since most noise interference is blotted out by the effective sound dampening, be they road, engine or wind nonsense.

+ CONVENIENCE FEATURES. This aspect is a pleasant surprise on a model of this type, for the trunk holds enough luggage and storage spots inside the cabin include a

glove compartment, door side-pockets, console compartment and a shelf built into the dashboard.

+ PERFORMANCES. They're particularly brisk with the 4-cylinder engine, that's got lots of pep and the competent suspension helps the car stay on the straight and narrow and the front-wheel drive really does its stuff. Steering is an important factor, for it's nicely powered, just a tad firm, but it's accurate and benefits from a good reduction ratio.

+ CABIN DESIGN. Inside the car, there's a touch of class with the wood appliqués, leather trim seats, meticulous finish job and plastic components that for once look great.

+ PERFORMANCES. The V6 engine outclasses the 4-cylinder in this regard, but it doesn't really

improve the CL's sporty side. It's versatile and discreet and it procures very adequate accelerations and pickup, but without adding much piquant to the drive.

+ BRAKES. They're effective, since even without ABS, sudden stopping distances are quite short and they're easy to apply as needed with such a sensitive and progressive pedal. Their endurance is surprising for a Japanese model, for they never flagged during our intensive braking tests.

CONS

- BUDGET. These coupes don't come cheap, but they are richly equipped and they do provide a smooth, silky ride. But they aren't too well-known, so depreciation is pretty dramatic.

-TEMPERAMENT. The CL coupe is fun to drive, but it isn't a true blue fast car, not even with the V6 engine that doesn't make much difference at all.

-MANEUVERABILITY. It could be more effective, for you have to take a second shot at every little move, by giving the steering wheel a few whirls.

- STRUCTURAL RIGIDITY. There's room for improvement, for the body on our two test cars emitted lots of rattles and squeaks and some finish details are unworthy of such classy cars.

- TRUNK. It isn't convertible and can't handle big, bulky objects since it only connects with the cabin via a ski-size pass-through and the trunk opening itself isn't too wide.

- ANTILOCK BRAKING. It isn't wonderfully reassuring since it sometimes only kicks in a few fractions of a second later, so there's wheel lock over a short distance.

- INCONCEIVABLE. The front seatbelts aren't height-adjustable and the original radio is a poor excuse for same.

CONCLUSION

The Acura CL was the first luxury coupe designed to try to convince a particular clientele of the virtues of the comfort offered by a refined and high-performance car, without it being an out-and-out sports car. It's a new trend that other serious-minded carmakers are adopting, which leads one to believe that something will end up happening in this market segment. ☺

RATING ACURA CL

CONCEPT : 68%
Technology	80
Safety :	80
Interior space :	40
Trunk volume:	60
Quality/fit/finish :	80

DRIVING: 66%
Cockpit :	80
Performance :	60
Handling :	50
Steering :	80
Braking :	60

ORIGINAL EQUIPMENT: 82%
Tires :	85
Headlights :	80
Wipers :	90
Rear defroster :	75
Radio :	80

COMFORT : 71%
Seats :	75
Suspension :	75
Sound level:	50
Conveniences :	75
Air conditioning :	80

BUDGET : 62%
Price :	40
Fuel economy :	75
Insurance :	55
Satisfaction :	85
Depreciation :	55

Overall rating: 69.8%

NEW FOR 1999

- Different design alloy rims on the 3.0 CL.
- Rear holding net.
- Horn sound simlar to that of the TL.

ENGINES

Model/version	Type / timing valve / fuel system	Displacement cu in	Power bhp @ rpm	Torque lb-ft @ rpm
2.3CL	L4 2.3 SOHC-16-MPFI	137	150 @ 5700	152 @ 4900
3.0CL	V6 3.0 SOHC-24-MPFI	183	200 @ 5600	195 @ 4800

TRANSMISSIONS

Compres. ratio	Driving wheels / transmission	Final ratio
9.3 :1	front - M5*	4.27
	front - A4	4.29
9.4 :1	front - A4	4.20

PERFORMANCES

Acceler. 0-60 mph s	Standing 1/4 & 5/8 mile s		Acceler. 50-75 mph s	Braking 60-0 mph f	Top speed mph	Lateral acceler. G	Noise level dBA	Fuel economy mpg City Highway		Fuel type Octane
9.0	16.7	30.5	6.5	128	118	0.74	67	25	31	R 87
10.0	17.3	31.0	7.0	131	112	0.74	67	23	29	R 87
8.5	16.3	29.6	6.2	131	124	0.76	66	20	28	R 97

PRICE & EQUIPMENT

ACURA CL	2.3CL	3.0CL
Retail price $:	22,310	25,310
Dealer invoice $:	20,159	22,870
Shipping & handling $:	435	435
Automatic transmission:	O	S
Cruise control:	S	S
Power steering:	S	S
Anti-lock brakes:	S	S
Traction control:	-	-
Air conditioning:	SA	SA
Leather:	SH	SH
AM/FM/radio-cassette:	SCD	SCD
Power door locks:	S	S
Power windows:	S	S
Tilt steering:	S	S
Dual adjustable mirrors:	SEH	SEH
Alloy wheels:	S	S
Anti-theft system:	S	S

Colors

Exterior: Black, Titanium, Red, Blue-Green.

Interior: Charcoal, Tan.

AT A GLANCE...

Category: front-wheel drive sports coupes. **Class :** S

HISTORIC
Introduced in: 1997
Made in: East Liberty, Ohio, USA.

DEMOGRAPHICS
Model	Men./Wom.	Age	Married	College	Income
CL	NA				

INDEX
Safety:	80 %	Satisfaction:	85 %
Depreciation:	35 %	Insurance:	$ 935-1 050
Cost per mile:	$ 0.44	Number of dealers:	290

SALES
Model	1996	1997	Result
CL	16 740	28 939	+ 72.9 %

MAIN COMPETITORS
BMW 3-Series coupe, CHRYSLER Sebring, DODGE Avenger, HONDA Prelude, Accord 2dr., MERCURY Cougar, OLDSMOBILE Alero 2dr., PONTIAC Grand Am 2dr., TOYOTA Celica.

MAINTENANCE REQUIRED BY WARRANTY
First revision:	Frequency:	Diagnostic plug:
3 000 miles	6 000 miles	Yes

SPECIFICATIONS

Model	Version Trim	Body/ Seats	Interior volume cu ft	Trunk volume cu ft	Cd	Wheel base in	Lght x Wdgth x Hght in x in x in	Curb weight lb	Susp. ft/rr	Brake ft/rr	Steering type	Turning diameter ft	Steer. turns nber.	Fuel tank gal	tire size	Standard tires make	model	Standard powertrain
ACURA		General warranty: 4 years / 50 000 miles: powertrain: 5 years / 60 000 miles; surface rust: 5 years/ unlimited.																
CL	2.3	2dr.cpe.2+2	84.7	12.0	NA	106.9	190.0x70.1x54.7	3002	ih/ih	dc/ABS	pwr.r&p.	39.4	3.0	17.2	205/55R16	Michelin	MXV4	L4/2.3/M5
CL	3.0	2dr.cpe.2+2	84.7	12.0	NA	106.9	190.0x70.1x54.7	3232	ih/ih	dc/ABS	pwr.r&p.	39.4	3.0	17.2	205/55R16	Michelin	MXV4	V6/3.0/A4

Rich Man Civic's...

In Canada the Acura EL has brought a whole new light on the potential of a luxury approach in the subcompact popular car market segment. The automaker was rewarded for his bold move since the EL is a good seller and appeals to clients who like Honda's but would like something that's a bit more out of the humdrum ordinary. Based on the four-door Civic, the EL has good looks, a neat design and more elaborate equipment at a price that's quite affordable, all things considered.

MODEL RANGE

The EL is a four-door sedan offered in base SE, Sport and Premium. The car is driven by a 1.6L engine associated with a 5-speed manual transmission. The base model has standard power steering, cruise control, power windows, locks and exterior mirrors, tilt steering column and a theft-deterrent system. The Sport version gets added antilock braking, air conditioning and light alloy rims. The Premium also receives leather seat covers and sunroof, but in all cases, the 4-speed automatic transmission is sold as an extra.

TECHNICAL FEATURES

The steel monocoque body only benefits from only reasonable aerodynamic efficiency. Its style is quite different from the Civic look, since its front and rear extremities sport unique headlamps and taillamps. The four-wheel independent suspension consists of a double wishbone setup and stabilizer bar on both axles. The suspension has been designed to achieve a nice blend of cushy comfort and clean handling. All models are equipped with disc and drum brakes, but ABS is standard equipment only on the Sport and Premium. The Acura EL models are driven by a 1.6L SOHC 16-valve engine that delivers 127 hp, thanks to electronic valve timing and lift (VTEC) that also equips the Civic Si sports coupe. All three versions are fitted with the same size and type of tires.

PROS

+ PRICE. The base and Sport versions are attractively priced for the buyer can get a well-reputed small car that's practical, well equipped, all at a reasonable price. The Premium version isn't as affordable.

+ HANDLING. It benefits from the good-quality original tires on the 15-inch tires. Thanks to the two standard stabilizer bars, the EL models can turn into curves with assurance and they're quite nimble on slalom runs.

+ RIDE COMFORT. The ride is super-smooth for such a trim little car, since the suspension takes care of main road faults in a smooth, imperceptible manner. Engine noise and vibration are well muffled, but the same doesn't apply to the wheels that tend to thump on the least little bump. Thump, bump, thump, bump. Seats provide adequate support, whether they're covered with fabric or leather, but upholstery is quite firm.

+ DRIVING. It's pleasant, even if performances aren't really sporty due to an only average power to weight ratio. As is always the case on VTEC engines, power peaks at high r.p.m. but the manual transmission, with its neat shifter, lets you get better yield than the automatic. Controls are smooth and steering is well nigh perfect, although it does suffer from a tad poor reduction ratio.

+ FUEL EFFICIENCY. The VTEC engine is frugal for gas consumption is reasonable, given its performances.

+ CONVENIENCE FEATURES. The trunk is adequate when the rear seats are occupied, but it can also be extended towards the cabin by folding down the rear seatbench. There are enough storage compartments for front seat passengers, but they're pretty skimpy, size-wise.

+ QUALITY. Assembly and finish job are just as clean and tight as on the Civic. Trim materials are attractive, especially the seat covers. This car has inherited some admirable Civic traits such as ergonomics, instrument panel design, good visibility and the straightforward controls and dials are really neat.

+ CAR DESIGN. It's quite fetching, in spite of the body design that isn't too fresh and new. In some shades, the EL looks like a little gem and the cabin on the Premium takes on TL airs.

CONS

- DISAPPOINTING. The SE and Sport versions aren't really posh cars and only their richer equipment makes them different from the humble Civic.

- PERFORMANCES. They're only average, due to heavy vehicle weight due both to a surplus of equipment items and the more rigid body that provides better passenger protection.

- BRAKES. Without ABS, front wheels lock in no time in emergency situations and stops take forever to achieve and car path is less stable than on other models.

- BUILD. The bodywork looks and feels light when you shut the doors, hood and trunk lid and the plastic stuff that decorates the instrument panel is the same, identical plastic you find on the Civic, and after all, this is supposed to be a classy model.

- SILHOUETTE. It's far from ugly, but it's just as blah as that of the Civic with which it's easy to mix up, for its personality hasn't been well enough defined.

- NOISE LEVEL. It's quite uncivilized, for the high-pitched engine song is heard every time your toe touches the accelerator.

- AUTOMATIC GEARBOX. The shifter is jerky at times and it cuts off a bit of the precious horsepower from the small engine, especially when the air conditioning is on.

- TO BE IMPROVED UPON: The instruments are hard to read in the daytime because of the dark orange colors. There's no center armrest or storage compartments in the rear seat area.

CONCLUSION

The initial idea of making a mini-Rolls Royce out of a Civic was a good one, but we regret that Acura didn't go all the way, since, with the exception of the Premium, the EL is only a Super Civic. Why can't the rich and famous be seen in such a humble little carriage? ☺

RATING ACURA EL

CONCEPT :		70%
Technology	80	
Safety :	90	
Interior space :	50	
Trunk volume:	50	
Quality/fit/finish :	80	
DRIVING:		**66%**
Cockpit :	80	
Performance :	60	
Handling :	60	
Steering :	80	
Braking :	50	
ORIGINAL EQUIPMENT:		**78%**
Tires :	85	
Headlights :	80	
Wipers :	75	
Rear defroster :	70	
Radio :	80	
COMFORT :		**70%**
Seats :	75	
Suspension :	75	
Sound level:	50	
Conveniences :	75	
Air conditioning :	75	
BUDGET :		**70%**
Price :	60	
Fuel economy :	80	
Insurance :	70	
Satisfaction :	85	
Depreciation :	55	
Overall rating:		**70.8%**

NEW FOR 1999

- **New-design folding exterior mirrors.**
- **Touched up front grille.**
- **New 6-position shifter on the automatic gearbox.**
- **A new base SE model.**
- **Equipment details on the Sport and Premium versions.**

ENGINES

Model/ version	Type / timing valve / fuel system	Displacement cu in	Power bhp @ rpm	Torque lb-ft @ rpm
1.6EL	L4 1.6 SOHC-16-IEP	97	127 @ 6600	107 @ 5500

TRANSMISSIONS

Compres. ratio	Driving wheels / transmission	Final ratio
9.6 :1	front - M5*	4.25
	front - A4	4.36

PERFORMANCES

Acceler. 0-60 mph s	Standing 1/4 & 5/8 mile s	Acceler. 50-75 mph s	Braking 60-0 mph f	Top speed mph	Lateral acceler. G	Noise level dBA	Fuel economy mpg City	Highway	Fuel type Octane
8.8	16.2 29.8	6.5	131	128	0.78	67	28	36	R 87
10.0	17.0 30.6	6.9	138	112	0.78	68	25	34	R 87

PRICE & EQUIPMENT

ACURA 1.6EL	SE	Sport	Premium
Retail price $:	-	-	-
Dealer invoice $:	-	-	-
Shipping & handling $:	-	-	-
Automatic transmission:	O	O	O
Cruise control:	S	S	S
Power steering:	S	S	S
Anti-lock brakes:	-	S	S
Traction control:	-	-	-
Air conditioning:	S	S	S
Leather:	-	-	SH
AM/FM/radio-cassette:	SCD	SCD	SCD
Power door locks:	S	S	S
Power windows:	S	S	S
Tilt steering:	S	S	S
Dual adjustable mirrors:	SEH	SEH	SEH
Alloy wheels:	-	S	S
Anti-theft system:	S	S	S

Colors

Exterior: Silver, Green, Black, Titanium, Red.

Interior: Charcoal, Gray, Ivory.

AT A GLANCE...

Category: front-wheel drive compact sedans.   **Class :** 3S

HISTORIC

Introduced in: 1996
Made in: Alliston, Ontario, Canada

DEMOGRAPHICS

Model	Men./Wom.	Age	Married	College	Income
1.6EL	NA				

INDEX

Safety:	90 %	Satisfaction:		87%
Depreciation:	30 %	Insurance:		$ 800
Cost per mile:	$ 0.35	Number of dealers:		290

SALES

Model	1996	1997	Result
1.6EL	Not available in USA		

MAIN COMPETITORS

HONDA Civic, MAZDA Protegé, TOYOTA Corolla, VOLKSWAGEN Golf, Jetta.

MAINTENANCE REQUIRED BY WARRANTY

First revision:	Frequency:	Diagnostic plug:
3 000 miles	6 000 miles	Yes

SPECIFICATIONS

Model	Version Trim	Body/ Seats	Interior volume cu ft	Trunk volume cu ft	Cd	Wheel base in	Lght x Wdgth x Hght in x in x in	Curb weight lb	Susp. ft/rr	Brake ft/rr	Steering type	Turning diameter ft	Steer. turns nber.	Fuel tank gal	tire size	Standard tires make	model	Standard powertrain
ACURA		General warranty: 4 years / 50 000 miles: powertrain: 5 years / 60 000 miles; surface rust: 5 years/ unlimited.																
1.6EL	SE	4dr.sdn.4	89.8	11.9	0.32	103.1	176.3x67.1x54.9	2478	ih/ih	dc/dr	pwr.r&p.	32.8	3.6	13.2	195/55R15	Michelin	XGT-V4	L4/1.6/M5
1.6EL	Sport	4dr.sdn.4	89.8	11.9	0.32	103.1	176.3x67.1x54.9	2522	ih/ih	dc/dr/ABS	pwr.r&p.	32.8	3.6	13.2	195/55R15	Michelin	XGT-V4	L4/1.6/M5
1.6EL	Premium	4dr.sdn.4	89.8	11.9	0.32	103.1	176.3x67.1x54.9	3812	ih/ih	dc/dr/ABS	pwr.r&p.	32.8	3.6	13.2	195/55R15	Michelin	XGT-V4	L4/1.6/M5

Way back when, the Integra was the car behind the success of the deluxe Honda brand, but it now seems to be forgotten and left by the wayside, and a redesign is sorely needed. Sales have dropped and there doesn't seem to be an up and coming replacement model. Sporting cars have fewer and fewer fans these days, but the Integra is a fun way to get around with a certain flair without having to burn the asphalt at every traffic light. Lots of similar models have gone the way of all flesh, but the Integra has survived, but for how long?

MODEL RANGE

The Integra is a hatchback coupe sold in RS/SE, GS, GS-R and the limited edition Type R models. They're powered by a 1.8L 16-valve DOHC 4-cylinder engine that develops 139 hp on the RS and GS, 170 hp on the GS-R, thanks to a VTEC valve intake control system and 195 hp on the Type R. The original transmission is a 5-speed manual or an optional 4-speed automatic, except for the Type R that can only receive a manual. Standard equipment on the RS/SE includes air conditioning, power windows, locks and mirrors, light alloy rims, tilt steering column, theft-deterrent system and radio with tape deck and CD player. The GS is also equipped with cruise control and antilock braking. The GS-R has a more muscular engine and different-design light alloy rims. As for the Type R version, its engine develops 25 more hp and it sports a leather-wrapped steering wheel, bucket seats and carbon fiber trim on the dashboard. In all cases, the automatic transmission, leather seat covers and sunroof are sold as extras.

TECHNICAL FEATURES

Integra models have a steel unibody that yields average aerodynamics, with a drag coefficient of 0.32. The fully independent suspension consists of unequal length A-arms at each corner and stabilizer bars for both front and rear axles. Brakes are four-wheel disc and the RS/SE, GS and GS-R versions are fitted with ABS, while the Type R model benefits from yet a more sophisticated antilock braking system. The all-aluminum engine that equips the GS-R and Type R versions is unique, since it has a dual-stage intake manifold and a VTEC distribution sys-

Dusty...

tem, namely an electronic variable valve timing and lift, so the engine doesn't strain as much at high r.p.m. The Type R now has a more robust body, beefier disc brakes, thicker anti-roll bars and a lower center of gravity. Too bad the tires that equip the Type R aren't any bigger than on other models in the lineup.

PROS

+ **STYLE.** It's quite fetching with the lens-shaped headlamps that really distinguish this car from its main rivals.

+ **DRIVING.** It's a blast with such slick, spontaneous moves warranted by accurate steering that benefits from a good reduction ratio, so young drivers really love to get behind the wheel of one of these coupes. The manual speed shifter is quick on the draw and gears are nicely spaced, so you can really milk the engine power. Neat-design seats, clear visibility and good instrument panel layout create a sporty ambience.

+ **PERFORMANCES.** The VTEC engines really pump out the power beyond 3,000 r.p.m., so accelerations and pickup have quite a surge, but you often have to drive beyond legal speeds to get the best out of these engines.

+ **HANDLING.** Thanks to the sophisticated suspension, these cars take curves with great aplomb as long as anti-roll bars are thick enough, for there's moderate sway and wavering. The Type R suspension is more competent still, for it benefits from a lower center of grav-

ity and is less sensitive to understeer.

+ **QUALITY.** Typical to Japanese products, construction and finish details are very rigorous and assembly tolerances are super-tight.

+ **CONVENIENCE FEATURES.** They haven't been overlooked, since the trunk is convertible and storage compartments are a good size and scattered throughout the cabin.

+ **RELIABILITY.** The owner satisfaction rate is very high (90%), which explains the good resale value and the scarcity of models on the used car market.

CONS

- **SAFETY.** The Integra models don't benefit from resistance to impact on a par with more recent models and according to test scores, passengers don't seem to enjoy as much protection as the driver.

- **BRAKES.** The base model isn't equipped with ABS, so front wheel lock is a common occurrence, which is hard on tires and affects car stability, especially since «threshold» braking is hard to apply with any precision on this model.

- **QUALITY.** Some construction materials are rather chintzy, bodywork and seat fabrics are thin and the plastic trim on the dashboard looks far from ritzy.

- **ENGINES.** The multivalve engines develop only low torque below 3,000 r.p.m., so pickup at low r.p.m. is pretty frustrating, especially with the automatic gearbox that simply strips this car of its sporty side.

- **RIDE COMFORT.** It's no great shakes with the firm seat upholstery, snug head and leg room in the rear seats, brutal suspension response on poorly maintained roads and loud noise interference that just doesn't let up.

- **CABIN DESIGN.** It's looking a bit dusty and the instrument panel needs to be spruced up to better reflect this car's character...

- **ACCESS.** The rear end has been reinforced, so the high trunk threshold complicates luggage loading and unloading.

CONCLUSION

The Integra coupes aren't really passé, they benefit from lots of good technical features and engine performances are fine, but they'll need a good dusting off to give sales a new boost, for sales have slumped dramatically over the last two years.

RATING
ACURA Integra

CONCEPT :		62%
Technology	80	
Safety :	65	
Interior space :	30	
Trunk volume:	55	
Quality/fit/finish :	80	
DRIVING:		70%
Cockpit :	80	
Performance :	65	
Handling :	70	
Steering :	80	
Braking :	55	
ORIGINAL EQUIPMENT:		76%
Tires :	75	
Headlights :	80	
Wipers :	75	
Rear defroster :	75	
Radio :	75	
COMFORT :		71%
Seats :	75	
Suspension :	75	
Sound level :	55	
Conveniences :	70	
Air conditioning :	80	
BUDGET :		63%
Price :	50	
Fuel economy :	80	
Insurance :	45	
Satisfaction :	90	
Depreciation :	50	
Overall rating:		**68.4%**

NEW FOR 1999

- RS model replaces the ES «Special Edition» model, equipped with light alloy wheels, rear spoiler and color-coordinated exterior mirrors.

ENGINES

Model/ version	Type / timing valve / fuel system	Displacement cu in	Power bhp @ rpm	Torque lb-ft @ rpm
RS/SE, GS	L4 1.8 DOHC-16-MPFI	112	139 @ 6300	122 @ 5200
GS-R	L4 1.8 DOHC-16-MPFI	109	170 @ 7600	128 @ 6200
Type R	L4 1.8 DOHC-16-MPFI	109	195 @ 8000	130 @ 7500

TRANSMISSIONS

Compres. ratio	Driving wheels / transmission	Final ratio
9.2 :1	front - M5*	4.27
	front - A4	4.36
10.0 :1	front - M5	4.40
10.6 :1	front - M5	4.40

PERFORMANCES

Acceler. 0-60 mph s	Standing 1/4 & 5/8 mile s	Acceler. 50-75 mph s	Braking 60-0 mph f	Top speed mph	Lateral acceler. G	Noise level dBA	Fuel economy mpg City	Fuel economy mpg Highway	Fuel type Octane
8.8	17.2 29.7	6.4	134	124	0.82	68	25	31	R 87
9.6	18.0 30.5	6.9	148	116	0.82	68	24	31	R 87
7.8	16.8 29.0	5.2	131	131	0.85	67	25	30	S 91
7.0	16.2 28.5	4.8	134	137	0.90	70	24	31	S 91

PRICE & EQUIPMENT

ACURA Integra	RS/SE	GS	GS-R	Type R
Retail price $:	16,200	20,850	21,600	23,500
Dealer invoice $:	14,475	18,630	19,300	20.998
Shipping & handling $:	435	435	435	435
Automatic transmission:	O	O	-	-
Cruise control:	-	S	S	S
Power steering:	S	S	S	S
Anti-lock brakes:	-	S	S	S
Traction control:	-	-	-	S
Air conditioning:	S	S	S	S
Leather:	O	O	O	-
AM/FM/radio-cassette:	SCD	SCD	SCD	SCD
Power door locks:	S	S	S	S
Power windows:	S	S	S	S
Tilt steering:	S	S	S	S
Dual adjustable mirrors:	SE	SE	SE	SE
Alloy wheels:	S	S	S	S
Anti-theft system:	S	S	S	S

Colors

Exterior: Silver, White, Red, Green, Black.

Interior: Black.

AT A GLANCE...

Category: front-wheel drive compact sports coupes. **Class :** 3

HISTORIC
Introduced in: 1987-1993
Made in: Suzuka, Japan.

DEMOGRAPHICS

Model	Men./Wom.	Age	Married	College	Income
Integra	61/39 %	36	55 %	56 %	$ 40 000

INDEX
Safety: 65 %   **Satisfaction:** 90 %
Depreciation: 40 %   **Insurance:** $ 1 135
Cost per mile: $ 0.40   **Number of dealers:** 290

SALES

Model	1996	1997	Result
Integra	46 966	38 331	- 18.4 %

MAIN COMPETITORS
CHEVROLET Cavalier Z24, FORD ZX2, HONDA Prelude, Civic SiR, HYUNDAI Tiburon FX, PONTIAC Sunfire GT, SATURN SC2, TOYOTA Celica.

MAINTENANCE REQUIRED BY WARRANTY
First revision: 3 000 miles   **Frequency:** 6 000 miles   **Diagnostic plug:** Yes

SPECIFICATIONS

Model	Version Trim	Body/ Seats	Interior volume cu ft	Trunk volume cu ft	Cd	Wheel base in	Lght x Wdgth x Hght in x in x in	Curb weight lb	Susp. ft/rr	Brake ft/rr	Steering type	Turning diameter ft	Steer. turns nber.	Fuel tank gal	tire size	Standard tires make	model	Standard powertrain
ACURA		General warranty: 4 years / 50 000 miles: powertrain: 5 years / 60 000 miles; surface rust: 5 years/ unlimited.																
Integra	RS/SE	3dr.cpe.4	76.2	13.3	0.32	103.1	178.1x67.3x53.9	2528	ih/ih	dc/dc	pwr.r&p.	34.8	2.98	13.2	195/60R14	Yokohama	Y-376	L4/1.8/M5
Integra	GS	3dr.cpe.4	76.2	13.3	0.32	103.1	178.1x67.3x53.9	2639	ih/ih	dc/ABS	pwr.r&p.	34.8	2.98	13.2	195/55R15	Michelin	XGT-V4	L4/1.8/M5
Integra	GS-R	3dr.cpe.4	76.2	13.3	0.32	103.1	178.1x67.3x53.9	2667	ih/ih	dc/ABS	pwr.r&p.	34.8	2.98	13.2	195/55R15	Michelin	XGT-V4	L4/1.8/M5
Integra	Type R	3dr.cpe..4	76.2	13.3	0.32	103.2	172.4x66.7x51.9	2583	ih/ih	dc/ABS	pwr.r&p.	34.8	2.98	13.2	195/55R15	Bridgestone	RE010	L4/1.8/M5

We're surprised to see that the NSX-T coupe is still listed in the Acura catalogue when we know where sales sit on the charts. Like the Toyota Supra or the defunct Mazda RX-7, exotic coupes just aren't what turns buyers on. Nowadays, macho types drive pickup trucks and fast cars have been left out to pasture and the lone survivors are easy prey to radar nets... This doesn't mean that they won't come back in style, but if there's a sports coupe renaissance, these models will be left far behind in the dust and it's their successors that will get all the glory.

MODEL RANGE

The NSX-T is sold as a 2-seater coupe equipped with a 3.2L V6 mid-engine linked to a 6-speed manual transmission or a 3.0L paired up with a 4-speed automatic with manual "SportShift" speed shifter. Original equipment includes climate control, cruise control, antilock braking-traction control system, stereo sound system, main power accessories, leather-clad seats, light alloy wheels, T-shaped, dual-paneled sunroof and an alarm system.

TECHNICAL FEATURES

Honda spent big bucks when it created the NSX, one of the first limited edition vehicles to have an almost entirely aluminum body, which helped pare down vehicle weight by 300 lb., when compared to an equivalent steel structure. This car looks sleek and streamlined, but its aerodynamics aren't too hot, yielding a coefficient of 0.32 and the underside of the car isn't fitted with any components to redirect ground effect.

The fully independent suspension is borrowed from the competition. It's made up of a double wishbone setup made of forged aluminum and fitted with support springs, steel shock absorbers and steel axle shafts. Weight distribution on this nearly 3 200 lbs car is very good, 42% up front and 58% at the rear, thanks to the mid-engine arrangement.

The V6 engine block is the same as on the former Legend. It benefits from a double camshaft cylinder head with 12 valves per row of cylinders and a valve timing control system called VTEC that Honda has protected with no less than 350 patents. This concept, that's been used on other Honda models, includes three cams and three rocker arms on the intake manifold. Two

No panache...

conventional round cams activate valves up to 5,000 r.p.m. Beyond that, the third cam located between the other two takes over, activated by oil pressure.

PROS

+ STYLE. It's essentially exotic and still attracts curious bystanders who think it's a Ferrari when they see it coming, especially if it's clad in red, but without the same roar, gusto and class, of course...

+ HANDLING. It's very reassuring with the well-distributed weight, comfortable-length wheelbase, low center of gravity and well-honed suspensions that include some really featherweight components.

+ DESIGN. It's highly sophisticated, since it cashes in on Honda's race car experience and high-tech appli-cations such as the use of aluminum for the body and suspension elements.

+ PERFORMANCES. They're more impressive with the manual gear-box than with the automatic and they're almost equivalent to those of their transalpine rivals.

+ DRIVING. It's remarkably civilized for a model in this category. Daily travel is a piece of cake in warm weather, for this car is equipped with a polished engine and it's loaded with niceties, so ride comfort is simply super.

+ QUALITY. It jumps out at you, for the car is solidly built, even with the T-shaped roof, finish touches are finely executed and materials are quite posh.

+ RELIABILITY. It's without doubt the best asset of this model that's

the Maytag of exotic cars, compared with the touchy Ferrari's. In fact, durability stems from the fact that the engine isn't all that exotic, after all it's derived from the one that equipped the former Legend, now called the RL. It's tough and doesn't let poor weather affect its spirits, so you can enjoy driving this car all year long, except in heavy snow belt regions.

+ ACCESS. It isn't too awkward boarding this coupe, even with the low ceiling clearance, since the doors are nice and big and they open wide.

CONS

- BUDGET. The NSX-T isn't a good investment, since retail price is very high and its resale value still fluctuates quite a bit. It would be wiser to buy a used model, if you don't want to lose your shirt, for there aren't scads of people rushing out to buy one.

- ENGINE. It utterly and truly lacks panache, so driving capabilities don't jive with the zippy car appearance.

- STEERING. It doesn't spring back to center and it's sluggish, which isn't wonderful on such a speed-loving car that likes to make quick, slick moves.

- CONVENIENCE FEATURES. As is often the case on this type of car, this aspect has been sacrificed. The trunk is really tiny and there aren't enough storage spots inside the cabin. Oh, there are a few, but they're awfully stingy and don't hold much.

- SOUNDPROOFING. It could be beefed up so as to stifle road noise that takes center stage. Maybe then you could hear the engine growl and roar, but forget the exhaust system, it only purrs away in comparison.

- CABIN DESIGN. The dreary ambience doesn't turn the average jaunt into a thrilling, adventurous experience.

- ACCESS. Getting to the mechanical components is no picnic when it comes to repairs, which is typical of models equipped with a mid-engine.

CONCLUSION

To put it poetically, we could say that the NSX-T won't savor the glory of winning the palm if it enters the fray with such precious little panache. But the responsibility for its destiny lies with its creators who have spoiled its chances by making one compromise too many.

☺

RATING
ACURA NSX-T

CONCEPT :		60%
Technology	100	
Safety :	90	
Interior space :	10	
Trunk volume:	10	
Quality/fit/finish :	90	

DRIVING:		81%
Cockpit :	85	
Performance :	85	
Handling :	85	
Steering :	75	
Braking :	75	

ORIGINAL EQUIPMENT:		81%
Tires :	90	
Headlights :	85	
Wipers :	80	
Rear defroster :	70	
Radio :	80	

COMFORT :		61%
Seats :	80	
Suspension :	70	
Sound level:	40	
Conveniences :	40	
Air conditioning :	75	

BUDGET :		45%
Price :	0	
Fuel economy :	60	
Insurance :	35	
Satisfaction :	90	
Depreciation :	40	

| **Overall rating:** | | **65.6%** |

NEW FOR 1999

- **No major change.**

ENGINES

Model/ version	Type / timing valve / fuel system	Displacement cu in	Power bhp @ rpm	Torque lb-ft @ rpm
NSX-T	V6 3.2 DOHC-24-MPFI	194	290 @ 7100	224 @ 5500
NSX-T	V6 3.0 DOHC-24-MPFI	182	252 @ 6600	210 @ 5300

TRANSMISSIONS

Compres. ratio	Driving wheels / transmission	Final ratio
10.2 : 1	rear - M6	4.06
9.6 : 1	rear - A4	4.43

PERFORMANCES

Acceler. 0-60 mph s	Standing 1/4 & 5/8 mile s	Acceler. 50-75 mph s	Braking 60-0 mph f	Top speed mph	Lateral acceler. G	Noise level dBA	Fuel economy mpg City	Fuel economy mpg Highway	Fuel type Octane
5.4	13.5 24.5	3.6	115	150	0.94	70	18	24	S 91
6.8	14.8 25.5	4.2	125	143	0.90	70	17	24	S 91

PRICE & EQUIPMENT

ACURA NSX-T	man.	autom.
Retail price $:	84 000	-
Dealer invoice $:	73 357	-
Shipping & handling $:	725	-
Automatic transmission:	-	S
Cruise control:	S	S
Power steering:	S	S
Anti-lock brakes:	S	S
Traction control:	S	S
Air conditioning:	SA	SA
Leather:	S	S
AM/FM/radio-cassette:	S	S
Power door locks:	S	S
Power windows:	S	S
Tilt steering:	S	S
Dual adjustable mirrors:	SE	SE
Alloy wheels:	S	S
Anti-theft system:	S	S

Colors

Exterior: Black, Blue, White, Red, Silver, Yellow.

Interior: Leather: Black, Feline.

AT A GLANCE...

Category: rear-wheel drive exotic sports coupes. **Class :** GT

HISTORIC

Introduced in:	1991
Made in:	Tochigi, Japan.

DEMOGRAPHICS

Model	Men./Wom.	Age	Married	College	Income
NSX-T	96/4 %	44	65 %	52 %	$ 130 000

INDEX

Safety:	90 %	**Satisfaction:**	90 %
Depreciation:	53 %	**Insurance:**	$ 2 390
Cost per mile:	$ 1.20	**Number of dealers:**	290

SALES

Model	1996	1997	Result
NSX-T	460	415	- 9.8 %

MAIN COMPETITORS

CHEVROLET Corvette, DODGE Viper GTS, FERRARI 355, PORSCHE 911.

MAINTENANCE REQUIRED BY WARRANTY

First revision:	Frequency:	Diagnostic plug:
3 000 miles	6 000 miles	Yes

SPECIFICATIONS

Model	Version Trim	Body/ Seats	Interior volume cu ft	Trunk volume cu ft	Cd	Wheel base in	Lght x Wdgth x Hght in x in x in	Curb weight lb	Susp. ft/rr	Brake ft/rr	Steering type	Turning diameter ft	Steer. turns nber.	Fuel tank gal	tire size	Standard tires make	model	Standard powertrain
ACURA		General warranty: 4 years / 50 000 miles: powertrain: 5 years / 60 000 miles; surface rust: 5 years/ unlimited.																
NSX-T	man.	2dr.cpe. 2	48.9	5.4	0.32	99.6	174.2x71.3x46.1	3163	ih/ih	dc/ABS	pwr.r&p.	39.4	3.07	18.5	fr.215/45ZR16	Bridgestone	RE010	V6/3.2/M6
NSX-T	autom.	2dr.cpe. 2	48.9	5.4	0.32	99.6	174.2x71.3x46.1	3208	ih/ih	dc/ABS	pwr.r&p.	39.4	3.07	18.5	re. 245/40ZR17	Bridgestone	RE010	V6/3.0/A4

The RL has gained ground bit by bit in its own quiet way and in some parts of the world, it's a better seller than the Lincoln Town Car, which is, after all, a pretty respectable reference. Dropping the name Legend sure didn't help define the car's character, but the biggest drawback is that the last reworking didn't change things any more than other modifications did in the past. By trying to build cars that appeal exclusively to North American tastes, Japanese carmakers have become experts at creating soulless, squeaky-clean models that are nothing special inside, outside, underneath...

MODEL RANGE

The RL is a big four-door sedan equipped with a 3.5L V6 paired up with a 4-speed automatic transmission. It's sold in a single model that's simply loaded with equipment, including all the goodies you usually get spoiled with in a luxury car, namely the usual power accessories, leather seat covers, heated front seats, stereo sound system with CD player and automatic changer, light alloy wheels and theft-deterrent system with engine cut-off switch. Then, of course, there are the heated mirrors and the trunk that connects with the cabin via a ski-sized slot.

TECHNICAL FEATURES

The steel monocoque body includes several galvanized steel panels. The car silhouette has only average aerodynamic finesse, yielding a coefficient of 0.32, even with a wind deflector located behind the front bumper that reduces airflow under the car and directs it towards the sides and roof. This car is a heavyweight, tipping the scales at about 3,750 lbs. curb weight, but at least weight distribution is 60% up front and 40% at the rear. The fully independent suspension consists of a double wishbone arrangement and anti-roll bar both front and rear. The four-wheel disc brakes benefit from a standard antilock braking system associated with a traction control system (TCS) that's linked to brakes and prevents single wheel slippage. The 90-degree 24-valve SOHC V6 is made of aluminum with cast-iron cylinder sleeves. To maximize power and torque, Acura has developed a 3-stage variable-intake system. To reduce the shakes that go with this type of engine, a balance system is mounted on the side

Squealy Clean...

of the engine and driven by the fan belt. The engine is also mounted on an independent cradle via electronically controlled hydraulic supports, thus providing two shock settings, depending on whether the engine is revving above or below 850 r.p.m.

PROS

+ STYLE. The body design is clean and elegant, but it's too much like that of the previous model and there's nothing eye-catching about it whatsoever.

+ PRICE. It isn't too inflated for it sits exactly between those of the Saab 9⁵ and BMW 528, almost equivalent to what you pay for a GS 300.

+ COMFORT. It's pretty impressive, when it comes to the huge trunk, very tough soundproofing, competent suspension and seats

offer nearly ideal lateral and lumbar support.

+ PERFORMANCES. They're honorable for such a heavy car. The engine is brawny, spontaneous and discreet, the transmission does its stuff like a wizard, tires are good-quality and just the right size and the traction control helps control road adherence when things get slick. The engine is also fuel-efficient since gas consumption stays at a reasonable level at all times.

+ HANDLING. It's fine at regular speeds and on silky roads, since the car stays level on straight runs and on curves and it also stays nice and neutral on turns, but the RL is a big, heavy car, so agility isn't one of its strong suits.

+ BRAKES. They're pretty efficient

at first go, since they bring the hefty RL to a complete halt in less than 130 ft. with ABS.

+ COCKPIT. The driver is comfortably seated, enjoys clear visibility and has an ergonomic, neatly organized instrument panel at his or her disposal.

+ QUALITY. Construction is well crafted and fit and finish are carefully rendered, features you're sure to get on a Honda product.

CONS

- SAFETY. It's lacking, since the car isn't equipped with side-impact airbags, powerful headlights or vehicle stability control, a feature found on rivals.

- SIZE. This «in-between» format chosen by Honda is supposed to be roomier than mid-range Lexus models and it's less costly than V8 model cars, but it really doesn't turn anyone's crank.

- DESIGN. Body stylistics are terribly lackluster and the interior has lost the European flavor that graced the former Legend. The main section of the console looks empty and the plastic that it's dressed in is very plain. Lastly, the leather and wood appliqués aren't too classy.

- DRIVING. Being at the wheel of the RL is pretty boring. The engine is frisky and roadability is super, but the car has a squeaky-clean demeanor and lacks definition.

- BRAKES. They're hard to gauge due to the soft pedal and they only have average lasting power when put to the test.

- STEERING. It's over-assisted, crippled by a poor reduction ratio and it's too light and soft when you're gunning it. You sometimes have the awful feeling that the front wheels have lost their grip.

- SUSPENSION. It's too flexible, so it generates lots of wavering, which affects passenger comfort more than handling per se. We're still wondering why the RL, an expensive, high-tech car isn't equipped with a dual-mode adjustable suspension, depending on driving style, as well as an automatic setting.

CONCLUSION

The Acura RL has its merits, but they're submerged in a squeaky-clean over-all design, so much so that we'd tend to opt for a less perfect model that has more spark and spunk, not this anonymous machine that doesn't have much character at all. ☺

RATING
ACURA RL

CONCEPT :		76%
Technology	90	
Safety :	80	
Interior space :	65	
Trunk volume:	60	
Quality/fit/finish :	85	

DRIVING:		68%
Cockpit :	80	
Performance :	65	
Handling :	70	
Steering :	75	
Braking :	50	

ORIGINAL EQUIPMENT:		82%
Tires :	85	
Headlights :	80	
Wipers :	80	
Rear defroster :	75	
Radio :	90	

COMFORT :		79%
Seats :	80	
Suspension :	80	
Sound level :	70	
Conveniences :	80	
Air conditioning :	85	

BUDGET :		49%
Price :	0	
Fuel economy :	65	
Insurance :	45	
Satisfaction :	90	
Depreciation :	45	

Overall rating:　　　**70.8%**

NEW FOR 1999

- Esthetic touches on front and rear extremities, new gas-filled headlamps and built-in fog lamps.
- Beefier brake discs.
- New-design alloy rims and standard Michelin MXV4 tires.
- New «high-tech» front-impact airbags and side-impact airbags.
- Sunvisors with lateral extensions.

ENGINES

Model/ version	Type / timing valve / fuel system	Displacement cu in	Power bhp @ rpm	Torque lb-ft @ rpm
base	V6 3.5 SOHC-24-MPFI	212	210 @ 5200	224 @ 2800

TRANSMISSIONS

Compres. ratio	Driving wheels / transmission	Final ratio
9.6 :1	front - A4	4.18

PERFORMANCES

Acceler. 0-60 mph s	Standing 1/4 & 5/8 mile s	Acceler. 50-75 mph s	Braking 60-0 mph f	Top speed mph	Lateral acceler. G	Noise level dBA	Fuel economy mpg City	Highway	Fuel type Octane
8.5	16.4 29.3	5.7	128	124	0.85	66	19	25	S 91

PRICE & EQUIPMENT

ACURA	3.5RL
Retail price $:	41,200
Dealer invoice $:	35,980
Shipping & handling $:	435
Automatic transmission:	S
Cruise control:	S
Power steering:	S
Anti-lock brakes:	S
Traction control:	S
Air conditioning:	SA
Leather:	SH
AM/FM/radio-cassette:	SDc
Power door locks:	S
Power windows:	S
Tilt steering:	S
Dual adjustable mirrors:	SEH
Alloy wheels:	S
Anti-theft system:	S

Colors

Exterior: Black, White, Gold, Green.

Interior: Black, Parchment, Quartz .

AT A GLANCE...

Category: front-wheel drive luxury sedans.　　**Class :** 7

HISTORIC
Introduced in: 1996
Made in: Sayama, Japan.

DEMOGRAPHICS

Model	Men./Wom.	Age	Married	College	Income
RL	81/19 %	48	86 %	66 %	$ 90 000

INDEX
Safety:	80 %	Satisfaction:	90 %
Depreciation:	50 %	Insurance:	$1 385
Cost per mile:	$ 0.91	Number of dealers:	290

SALES

Model	1996	1997	Result
RL	15 948	16 004	+ 0.4 %

MAIN COMPETITORS
AUDI A6, BMW 5-Series, CHRYSLER 300M, INFINITI Q45, LEXUS GS 300 & LS 400, MERCEDES-BENZ C-280, SAAB 9[5], VOLVO S80.

MAINTENANCE REQUIRED BY WARRANTY
First revision:	Frequency:	Diagnostic plug:
3 000 miles	6 000 miles	Yes

SPECIFICATIONS

Model	Version Trim	Body/ Seats	Interior volume cu ft	Trunk volume cu ft	Cd	Wheel base in	Lght x Wdgth x Hght in x in x in	Curb weight lb	Susp. ft/rr	Brake ft/rr	Steering type	Turning diameter ft	Steer. turns nber.	Fuel tank gal	tire size	Standard tires make	model	Standard powertrain
ACURA RL	3.5	4dr.sdn. 5	96.2	14.8	0.32	114.6	195.1x71.3x54.5	3648	ih/ih	dc/ABS	pwr.r&p.	36.1	3.35	18.0	215/60R16	Michelin	MXV4	V6/3.5/A4

General warranty: 4 years / 50 000 miles: powertrain: 5 years / 60 000 miles; surface rust: 5 years/ unlimited.

ACURA TL
Getting Out of the Doldrums...

Ever since it was first introduced, bearing the name Vigor or TL, this car has only enjoyed relative success, placing far behind the prima donna's in this category, be they the Volvo S70, BMW 3-Series, Audi A4 or Mercedes C-Class, here mentioned according to their sales standing. You have to admit that lost in the midst of such a collection of headstrong and gutsy models, the poor TL didn't have much of a chance of catching buyers' attention and coming out of the sidelines. And offering two different engine models didn't help simplify things for people browsing at the dealerships, since most buyers want a V6 and nothing but. The fact that the RL was equipped with a V6 only added to the confusion.

When it developed the most recent TL model, Acura tried to iron out a few glitches that afflicted the previous models. For starters, the only V6 model sold this year costs the same price as the previous 5-cylinder model. Given that the new model offers loads more equipment, it's a great buy, to say the least. When it comes to style, you can't say the TL is exactly oozing with personality, but it does have an elegant look. The latest TL model is a North American product since it was designed and created in California at the Honda stylistics outfit in Torrance. Designers worked on aerodynamics, so as to give it more finesse than on the previous model. The TL is built at the Honda plant in Marysville, Ohio where the Honda Accord is assembled, since the TL shares the Accord's platform. Its domestic content is 95%, so the EPA will classify it as an American vehicle. Stylists were inspired by the

San Francisco ambience, more specifically the exclusive Nob Hill section of town where they stayed at the famous Fairmont Hotel. At first glance, you may not see how this motley urban architecture could have inspired such flat lines. There are some new, subtle touches on the windshield, front grille and trunk lid that have filled out and firmed up the car silhouette, but haven't added much to the car's general appearance that gets lost in the crowd of models that, in the long run, all look pretty much alike. The reworked body at least benefits from 70% better resistance to torsion and it's 80% more resistant to flexion, which gives you a funny feeling regarding the previous model's structural integrity. Soundproofing required 91 lb. of insulation and the hollow components and roof pillars have been filled with plastic foam. The main structure has been the object of intense studies made with the help of a Cray super-computer to simulate collisions of various impacts and from different directions so as to install reinforcement components in strategic spots. Thus, in the event of a front-impact collision, straight, thick rails direct impact force through the chassis without intermediary reinforcements at the intersections of the transversal sections. So as to go beyond the American federal laws that will go into effect in the year 2003, the TL interior and roof supports have been equipped with shock absorbing linings as well as a roof lining that are all supposed to reduce passenger injuries. Acura also claims to have enhanced active safety features by equipping the new model with an antilock and anti-skid system, a device that will provide better wheel grip on curves and straight-ahead demeanor on straight roads as well as high-intensity gas-filled headlamps.

Since it was first introduced in 1991, the Vigor (as well as the TL since 1996) has always had the second fiddle role. Like stalwart soldiers, these cars had everything it took to succeed, but their utter lack of charisma left them in the shadows, while other models were basking in the limelight. In the automobile industry and in everyday life, we never remember the names of those who came in second, so you have to have a little something that makes you different from the scores of others and the new TL has maybe found its way.

MODEL RANGE

The new Acura TL is a 4-door sedan offered in a single version equipped with a 3.2L V6 that's completely different from the previous model. The electronically controlled four-speed automatic transmission provides for a semi-manual «Sport-Shift» mode. Thus, the driver can move the speed shifter knob in a particular way so as to change gears manually. As far as equipment goes, Acura didn't leave anything to chance and loaded this car with the works. Only the complete «Aero» options package is offered as well as the optional Gold-plated decoration package that's installed by the dealer. In the United States, the navigation system is also sold as an extra.

TECHNICAL FEATURES

The 1999 TL is based on the new universal Honda platform that was used for the first time last year when the Accord was redesigned. The TL wheelbase is 3.7 in shorter, but the over-all vehicle length has stretched to 16.07 ft, that is, 1.4 in more than the previous version. The new TL structure is 70% more torsion-resistant and 80% more flexion-resistant, which yields super-solid road competence. Inside, roof supports are filled with foam buffers and wheel housing extensions are fitted with insulation and there are hermetically mounted hydraulic engine supports, all of which cut down on noise interference.

The front suspension uses a double wishbone arrangement with firmer coil springs and recalibrated shocks to take advantage of the more rigid body structure. The rear suspension is a new independent five-link A-arm arrangement that's more effective and much trimmer, so it allows for more cabin and trunk space. The car is equipped with four-

wheel vented disc brakes with standard ABS and traction control.

PROS

+ PRICE. The new, fully equipped TL costs about seven thousand dollars less than last year. A bargain compared to the stars in the category, like the Lexus ES 300 or the BMW 3-Series. Cars are no longer assembled in Japan, but in the United States and they share 45% of the Honda Accord's parts, which could explain this dramatic reduction in price.

+ EQUIPMENT. Unlike many other deluxe cars, the TL can be driven right off the lot after purchase. Leather-clad seats, ABS braking system, traction control, climate control, theft-deterrent system, power sunroof and heated seats are all included in the initial price. For those who always want more, an Aero options package and Gold Decoration package are available at an extra cost at the dealerships, but they add nothing vital to how the car functions. In the United States, a navigation system is also listed among the options.

+ STEERING. In the past, it was over-assisted and very light and frothy, but now it's accurate and really connects the car to the road. It's a real treat on zigzag country roads.

+ ROADHOLDING. The TL now has a more robust build, more engine power and less weight to haul around, so it's at long last found its sporting soul and it's a real joy to drive. The car stays very neutral on curves and the rear suspension is in there kicking and so this car can truly be called a sports car.

+ CABIN SPACE. It's more spacious, especially up front and front seat passengers have loads of room to breathe and stretch.

+ RIDE COMFORT. Due to the car's rigid structure, the suspension could have been adjusted so as to offer smoother travel, without stepping on the car's sportsy side's toes. All the soundproofing provides a very quiet atmosphere inside the cabin.

+ PERFORMANCES. Acura has finally endowed the TL with the zippy traits that were so sorely lacking, The engine is responsive and never seems to flag. There's just a bit of

torque slump at low r.p.m. and on pickup, which makes it lose some of its fine vitality.

+ QUALITY. As is always the case for Honda products, the car design and build execution are nearly perfect for the car is neat as a pin and the finish job is lovely right down to the finest details. Only a few materials look a bit below-par.

+ TRANSMISSION. The complex gearbox combines several very interesting functions. For example, the hill holder control slows down upshifting when climbing an incline, so as to provide lively pickup. Going downhill, it applies braking effect by automatically downshifting.

CONS

- WEIRD. With all these modifications, engineers also changed the hand brake into a parking brake. The pedal is now engaged/disengaged by pressing a floor pedal. So they'll have to look this item over, if they want it to be easier to use.

- BRAKES. No one really questioned the system's effectiveness, but a few car experts had problems with overheating. A sound very like a pneumatic drill filled the cabin and activated traction control. We discussed this with an Acura engineer who confirmed he was familiar with this phenomenon, but he didn't say anything more about it because this behavior only occured on pre-production models. He confirmed that production models were A-1. Let's hope so.

- SILHOUETTE. The TL looks swish, but it lacks the bit of pizzazz that really grabs your attention. At Acura they say that this car represents social success and potential buyers don't necessarily want to shout their well-heeled status on the rooftops. This explains the TL's low profile, which is maybe too bad. After all, this car does deserve to be noticed.

CONCLUSION

The 1999 TL is supposed to put the wind in Acura's sails. From the very beginning, this carmaker only built run-of-the-mill Honda clones. The TL is a horse of a different color and reflects a whole new attitude. But the people at Acura will have to hustle their buns to rework their lineup, especially the RL, that's going to end up like a white elephant, given that the more up-to-date and more high-performance TL sells for a whole lot less. ☺

RATING ACURA TL

CONCEPT : 76%
Technology	85
Safety :	90
Interior space :	65
Trunk volume:	60
Quality/fit/finish :	80

DRIVING: 67%
Cockpit :	80
Performance :	65
Handling :	50
Steering :	80
Braking :	60

ORIGINAL EQUIPMENT: 80%
Tires :	80
Headlights :	80
Wipers :	75
Rear defroster :	75
Radio :	90

COMFORT : 78%
Seats :	80
Suspension :	80
Sound level:	70
Conveniences :	80
Air conditioning :	80

BUDGET : 59%
Price :	25
Fuel economy :	65
Insurance :	40
Satisfaction :	90
Depreciation :	75

Overall rating: 72.0%

NEW FOR 1999

- New model available in a single TL 3.2 version equipped with a new 3.2L V6 with sequential automatic gearbox.

ENGINES

Model/ version	Type / timing valve / fuel system	Displacement cu in	Power bhp @ rpm	Torque lb-ft @ rpm
3.2TL	V6 3.2 SOHC-24-EFI	196	225 @ 5500	216 @ 5000

TRANSMISSIONS

Compres. ratio	Driving wheels / transmission	Final ratio
9.8 :1	front -A4	4.20

PERFORMANCES

Acceler. 0-60 mph s	Standing 1/4 & 5/8 mile s	Acceler. 50-75 mph s	Braking 60-0 mph f	Top speed mph	Lateral acceler. G	Noise level dBA	Fuel economy mpg City	Highway	Fuel type Octane
8.6	16.8	29.6	6.2 138	137	0.78	66	18	26	S 91

PRICE & EQUIPMENT

ACURA TL	3.2
Retail price $:	29,995
Dealer invoice $:	-
Shipping & handling $:	435
Automatic transmission:	S
Cruise control:	S
Power steering:	S
Anti-lock brakes:	S
Traction control:	S
Air conditioning:	SA
Leather:	SH
AM/FM/radio-cassette:	SCD
Power door locks:	S
Power windows:	S
Tilt steering:	S
Dual adjustable mirrors:	SE
Alloy wheels:	S
Anti-theft system:	S

Colors

Exterior: Black, Silver, Lagoon, Emerald, Red.

Interior: Gray, Beige.

AT A GLANCE...

Category: front-wheel drive luxury sedans. **Class :** 7

HISTORIC
Introduced in: 1999
Made in: Marysville, Ohio, USA.

DEMOGRAPHICS
Model	Men./Wom.	Age	Married	College	Income
TL	80/20 %	43	90 %	60 %	$ 55 000

INDEX
Safety:	75 %	Satisfaction:	90 %
Depreciation:	65 %	Insurance:	$1 100
Cost per mile:	$ 0.65	Number of dealers:	290

SALES
Model	1996	1997	Result
TL	24 700	23 151	- 6.3 %

MAIN COMPETITORS
AUDI A4, BMW 3-Series, INFINITI I30, LEXUS ES 300, MAZDA Millenia, MERCEDES-BENZ C-Class, NISSAN Maxima, TOYOTA Avalon, VOLVO S70.

MAINTENANCE REQUIRED BY WARRANTY
First revision:	Frequency:	Diagnostic plug:
3 000 miles	6 000 miles	Yes

SPECIFICATIONS

Model	Version Trim	Body/ Seats	Interior volume cu ft	Trunk volume cu ft	Cd	Wheel base in	Lght x Wdgth x Hght in x in x in	Curb weight lb	Susp. ft/rr	Brake ft/rr	Steering type	Turning diameter ft	Steer. turns nber.	Fuel tank gal	tire size	Standard tires make	model	Standard powertrain
ACURA					General warranty: 4 years / 50 000 miles: powertrain: 5 years / 60 000 miles; surface rust: 5 years/ unlimited.													
TL	3.2	4dr.sdn. 5	96.5	14.3	0.32	108.1	192.9x70.3x56.1	3450	ih/ih	dc/ABS	pwr.r&p..	36.7	3.5	17.2	205/60R16	Michelin	MXV4	V6/3.2/A4

The Hummer (from HMMWV for High Mobility Multi-purpose Wheeled Vehicle or Humvee), has become a familiar part of the daily life of the rich and famous, since it's yet another way of driving by and being noticed. At least inside a Hummer, you can flee from the paparazzi with more ease than inside a Mercedes... You see this vehicle everywhere, which is a euphemism, since there are few spots on the face of the Earth where it can't make tracks. What we too often forget is that this vehicle is above all a versatile, professional means of transportation.

MODEL RANGE

The Hummer is an all-terrain vehicle that comes with either a soft or hardtop. This pickup truck comes in either a 2 or a 4-door cab model, with short or long wheelbase, whereas the station wagon is equipped with 5 doors.

The 6.5L Diesel V8 engine comes standard, linked to a General Motors 4-speed automatic and a high and low-torque transfer case. The optional 6.5L turbodiesel V8 delivers 195 hp. Standard equipment includes power steering, AM/FM radio and tape deck and intermittent-function wipers.

Other items are also available as extras: air conditioning, cruise control, ABS, power windows and locks and alloy wheels. Depending on your needs, you can also add on a 6-ton winch and a system that regulates tire pressure while travelling, either to compensate for a minor flat or to increase traction on rough terrain.

TECHNICAL FEATURES

The anodized aluminum body is assembled with rivets and Cybond glue and it's mounted on a robust rolled steel-section chassis. The engine is mounted above the longitudinal section so as to offer maximum ground clearance, while the front and rear differential supports are installed symmetrically at both extremities. The hood is made of polyester resin reinforced with fiberglass, whereas the doors are made of steel. The fully independent suspension consists of a double wishbone setup and braking is assured by four discs mounted on the differential extremities. The vehicle is equipped with full-time all-

Tough as a Nail..

wheel drive as well as front and rear Torsen differentials. The tires are unique, for they can be driven in an off-center fashion via a whole series of reduction pinions, to free up the underside of the vehicle as much as possible. The huge tires can be fitted with optional interior tires made of solid rubber to provide greater mobility and reduce external tire damage in the event of a blow-out.

SIMPLY SUPER

++ OFF-ROAD CAPABILITIES. This vehicle is incredibly versatile, since it can climb 42-inch steps, drive around in 27 inches of water or mud and climb very steep hills. It's too big to maneuver nimbly in the bush, but on open terrain, it can get over just about any obstacle in

its way, slowly by surely.

PROS

+ STYLE. This vehicle has a very military look, so it sure gets noticed in urban settings and its sheer hulk gives it center stage, so to speak. The rings up on the hood sure inspire lots of questions from onlookers who have trouble believing they're used when parachuting the vehicle. Its multi-purpose, massive shape isn't exactly graceful, but it's functional and you know it'll never go out of style...

+ VERSATILITY. It's amazing, since besides never going out of style, it can go just about anywhere. Besides American army uses, its mission is to get to really isolated spots, so it's an ideal vehicle for police

forces, rescue teams of all ilks and electric power or telephone companies.

+ DRIVING. It's really easy to drive, so almost anyone can get behind the wheel of this beast. Vehicle demeanor is smooth and predictable and controls are stripped down to a basic minimum.

+ TRACTION. The full-time all-wheel drive makes it the ideal vehicle for hauling heavy loads or trailers.

+ QUALITY. This vehicle is built according to stringent military standards, which explains its awesome reliability and tough durability. The builder doesn't foresee reconditioning these vehicles for another 10 years, according to typical army practice...

CONS

- BUDGET. It costs a mint, due to strict building standards and top-notch quality and so not everyone can own one and gas bills are never cheap.

- VEHICLE SIZE. It's really very wide, so you have to drive it as though it were a tank when getting around in the city and forget about looking for a parking spot. Besides, visibility is problematic in just about every direction with both rooftops, since the roof supports are thick and there are big blind spots.

- PERFORMANCES. They're limited, since accelerations and pickup are very laborious, so you have to drive like a truck driver. Yet, on the highway, it can easily maintain a 75 mph cruising speed that scares compact cars to death...

- CONVENIENCE FEATURES. They're not too hot, since the cabin can only accomodate four passengers in «capsules» of space that are gobbled up by the enormous center console. At the rear, the cargo hold doesn't jive with the humungous dimensions of this beast. There aren't any storage spots and access to the cabin, engine and cargo hold is acrobatic, due to the high ground clearance and there are no standard running boards to make life easier.

CONCLUSION

The Hummer is the ultimate all-terrain vehicle of our era. It doesn't compare with any other vehicle and no other vehicle can match it...

RATING
AMG Hummer

CONCEPT :		81%
Technology	85	
Safety :	80	
Interior space :	80	
Trunk volume:	80	
Quality/fit/finish :	80	
DRIVING:		**38%**
Cockpit :	75	
Performance :	0	
Handling :	30	
Steering :	70	
Braking :	15	
ORIGINAL EQUIPMENT:		**62%**
Tires :	90	
Headlights :	80	
Wipers :	60	
Rear defroster :	0	
Radio :	80	
COMFORT :		**50%**
Seats :	70	
Suspension :	50	
Sound level :	20	
Conveniences :	30	
Air conditioning :	80	
BUDGET :		**43%**
Price :	0	
Fuel economy :	20	
Insurance :	50	
Satisfaction :	85	
Depreciation :	60	
Overall rating:		**54.8%**

NEW FOR 1999

- Improvement of sound-deadening for better comfort.
- Redesigned gearsets and axel ratios so that the engine will rev less.
- Security attachment to the gasoline filler cap so that it will not be lost or fall off the vehicule.

ENGINES / TRANSMISSIONS / PERFORMANCES

Model/ version	Type / timing valve / fuel system	Displacement cu in	Power bhp @ rpm	Torque lb-ft @ rpm	Compres. ratio	Driving wheels / transmission	Final ratio	Acceler. 0-60 mph s	Standing 1/4 & 5/8 mile s	Acceler. 50-75 mph s	Braking 60-0 mph f	Top speed mph	Lateral acceler. G	Noise level dBA	Fuel economy mpg City	Highway	Fuel type Octane
base	V8* 6.5D OHV-16-MI	396	170 @ 3400	290 @ 1700	21.5 :1	all-A4	2.72	20.5	22.0	42.0	NA	60	78	0.65	74	14	18	D
option	V8 6.5TD OHV- 16-MI	396	195 @ 3400	430 @ 1800	21.5: 1	all-A4	2.72	18.5	21.0	39.0	NA	61	81	0.65	72	14	18	D

PRICE & EQUIPMENT

AM GENERAL Hummer	2dr. p-u.	4dr. sdn.	4dr. con.	4dr. wgn.
Retail price $:	-	-	-	-
Dealer invoice $:	-	-	-	-
Shipping & handling $:	-	-	-	-
Automatic transmission:	S	S	S	S
Cruise control:	O	O	O	O
Power steering:	S	S	S	S
Anti-lock brakes:	O	O	O	O
Traction control:	S	S	S	S
Air conditioning:	S	S	S	S
Leather:	-	-	-	-
AM/FM/radio-cassette:	S	S	S	S
Power door locks:	S	S	S	S
Power windows:	S	S	S	S
Tilt steering:	-	-	-	-
Dual adjustable mirrors:	S	S	S	S
Alloy wheels:	S	S	S	S
Anti-theft system:	O	O	O	O

- **Colors** -

Exterior: Red, Black, Yellow, Metallic Silver, Green, White.

Interior: Tan, Gray, Black.

AT A GLANCE...

Category: 4WD all purpose vehicles.   **Class :** utility

HISTORIC
Introduced in: 1985
Made in: South Bend, Indiana, USA.

DEMOGRAPHICS

Model	Men./Wom.	Age	Married	College	Income
Hummer	100/0 %	48	80 %	35 %	$ 110 000

INDEX

Safety:	90 %	Satisfaction:	83 %
Depreciation:	40 %	Insurance:	$ 1 175
Cost per mile:	$1.00	Number of dealers:	40

SALES

Model	1996	1997	Result
Hummer	NA		

MAIN COMPETITORS
CHEVROLET-GMC Suburban-Tahoe, CHEVROLET Silverado, GMC Sierra, DODGE Ram, FORD Expedition.

MAINTENANCE REQUIRED BY WARRANTY

First revision:	Frequency:	Diagnostic plug:
3 000 miles	6 000 miles	No

SPECIFICATIONS

Model	Version Trim	Traction	Body/ Seats	Wheel base in	Lght x Wdgth x Hght in x in x in	Curb weight lb	Susp. ft/rr	Brake ft/rr	Steering type	Turning diameter ft	Steer. turns nber.	Fuel tank gal	tire size	Standard tires make	model	Standard powertrain
AM/GENERAL	General warranty: 3 years / 36 000 miles.															
Hummer	HardTop	4x4	2dr.p-u.2	130.0	184.5x86.5x75.0	6391	ih/ih	dc/dc	pwr.ball	53.1	3.1	25+17	37x12.5R16.5	Goodyear	Wrangler MT	V8/6.5/A4
Hummer	Sedan	4x4	4dr.sdn.4	130.0	184.5x86.5x75.0	6790	ih/ih	dc/dc	pwr.ball	53.1	3.1	25+17	37x12.5R16.5	Goodyear	Wrangler MT	V8/6.5/A4
Hummer	Convertible	4x4	4dr.con.4	130.0	184.5x86.5x76.8	6640	ih/ih	dc/dc	pwr.ball	53.1	3.1	25+17	37x12.5R16.5	Goodyear	Wrangler MT	V8/6.5/A4
Hummer	Wagon	4x4	4dr.wgn.4	130.0	184.5x86.5x76.8	6980	ih/ih	dc/dc	pwr.ball	53.1	3.1	25+17	37x12.5R16.5	Goodyear	Wrangler MT	V8/6.5/A4

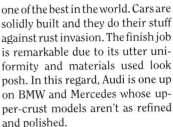

After many years of disregard, if not downright disdain, Audi models look like they're shaping up to become really popular with buyers. The A4 is the first in the lineup to have gained lots of success virtually overnight. The last redesign gave it all the elements necessary to set off a lively wave of enthusiasm: trim-looking and zippy stylistics, more competent engine and more affordable price tag. The upshot has been more interest and appeal for the other models. The people in public relations simply have to keep plugging away in their dialogue with car specialists and give out product information in time...

MODEL RANGE
The A4 is sold in Canada in a single 4-door sedan model, whereas in the United States, a station wagon is also offered. These front-wheel and all-wheel drive cars are equipped with a 1.8 Turbo 4-cylinder engine or a 2.8L V6 inherited from the A6. The original transmission is a 5-speed manual, but a 5-speed automatic is also available as an extra. The quattro all-wheel drive is optional on all A4's. Original equipment includes climate control, power locks, windows and exterior mirrors, traction control linked to antilock braking, light alloy wheels, heated front seats and a theft-deterrent system that's activated by the remote-control door opener. The 2.8 A4 models can receive leather seat covers, but the sunroof and on-board computer are still optional on all versions. Convenience option packages are listed as well: weather package, audio package or sport package.

TECHNICAL FEATURES
The A4's sleek, attractive body design procures good aerodynamic finesse since the drag coefficient is 0.29. The monocoque body is made entirely of galvanized steel, so Audi can provide one of the best guarantees in the world when it comes to the war against rust. The independent front suspension consists of cross struts and the rear suspension is made up of a semi-rigid axle supported by longitudinal control arms. Quattro models benefit from full-time all-wheel drive that includes a Torsen center differential automatically distributing 78% of power between both powertrains, depending on road adherence. The

Multiple Choice...

1.8L turbocharged engine is a 20-valve DOHC, with 5 valves per cylinder, as is the case for the 2.8L V6, one of the most light, trim engine models in its category. The 5-speed automatic transmission is paired up with an electronic control system that shifts into the gear most suited to driving conditions. The four-wheel disc brakes are teamed up with ABS that doubles as electronic traction control.

PROS
+ STYLE. The A4 design is very athletic, one of the best Audi has ever come up with. It makes the car body look trimmer and slimmer than it really is.

+ ALL-WHEEL DRIVE. The quattro system really enhances road competence and fuel efficiency and it's super-safe in the wintertime, as long as you've got the right tires.

+ PERFORMANCES. They're quite adequate thanks to the 2.8L V6's good power to weight ratio. This engine is perfectly at ease with either the manual or automatic gearbox.

+ DRIVING. It's relaxing with the precise, well-assisted steering, though it does exhibit some rather bizarre and bouncy moves. The cockpit provides comfy seating for the driver and the instrument panel is simple and straightforward.

+ PRICE. The base version equipped with the 1.8T engine is more affordable and so it's a good buy, given the resale value that's become more and more substantial...

+ QUALITY. Audi craftsmanship is one of the best in the world. Cars are solidly built and they do their stuff against rust invasion. The finish job is remarkable due to its utter uniformity and materials used look posh. In this regard, Audi is one up on BMW and Mercedes whose upper-crust models aren't as refined and polished.

+ RIDE COMFORT. It's amazing for a car of this size. The flexible suspension is always civilized, front seats are cushy and nicely sculpted and soundproofing takes care of engine and road noise and wind noise is barely perceptible.

+ CONVENIENCE FEATURES. It's super with all the generous storage compartments and the trunk, though it isn't terribly high or deep, can be extended and access is handy.

CONS
- BUDGET. The 2.8 model is less popular (though it's been readjusted), due to costly insurance premiums and gas bills.

- ENGINE. The 1.8T lacks torque at low r.p.m. and the Turbo response time is a bugbear at times. This tendency is more obvious with the automatic since this combination isn't a effective as the V6 when it comes to creamy demeanor.

- CABIN SPACE. Rear seat passengers will feel more cramped than those up front, since the seatbench back cushion is too straight, the upholstery is very hard, the seat cushion is stingy and leg room is really snug. The arched door design doesn't help boarding either.

- CONTROLS. Most of them are rather unusual for North American drivers, so they're confusing and the digital data screen isn't at all legible in the daytime and it's annoying at night with its eternal orange aura.

- TO BE IMPROVED UPON: The twisted wire radio antenna is a bit outdated, since rivals are equipped with antennas built into the window. Rear seat passengers have been overlooked when it comes to storage spots.

CONCLUSION
The Audi A4's success story isn't a mystery by any means. This car is blessed with great looks, the model range is extensive, including various versions and accessories that can meet all kinds of buyers' needs and car budgets... ☺

RATING AUDI A4

CONCEPT : **76%**
Technology	90
Safety :	90
Interior space :	50
Trunk volume:	60
Quality/fit/finish :	90

DRIVING: **64%**
Cockpit :	80
Performance :	50
Handling :	60
Steering :	75
Braking :	55

ORIGINAL EQUIPMENT: **80%**
Tires :	85
Headlights :	80
Wipers :	75
Rear defroster :	80
Radio :	80

COMFORT : **73%**
Seats :	75
Suspension :	75
Sound level:	65
Conveniences :	70
Air conditioning :	80

BUDGET : **56%**
Price :	20
Fuel economy :	75
Insurance :	45
Satisfaction :	85
Depreciation :	55

Overall rating: **69.8%**

NEW FOR 1999

• Information not available before going to press.

ENGINES / TRANSMISSIONS / PERFORMANCES

Model/ version	Type / timing valve / fuel system	Displacement cu in	Power bhp @ rpm	Torque lb-ft @ rpm	Compres. ratio	Driving wheels / transmission	Final ratio	Acceler. 0-60 mph s	Standing 1/4 & 5/8 mile s	Acceler. 50-75 mph s	Braking 60-0 mph f	Top speed mph	Lateral acceler. G	Noise level dBA	Fuel economy mpg City Highway	Fuel type Octane
A4 1.8T	L4T 1.8 DOHC-20-MPSFI	109	150 @ 5700	155 @ 1750	9.5 :1	front - M5*	3.70	8.8	16.5 29.8	6.3	125	131	0.78	67	23 32	R 87
A4 1.8Tqtro	L4T 1.8 DOHC-20-MPSFI	109	150 @ 5700	155 @ 1750	9.5 :1	all - A5	3.73	10.0	17.2 30.5	7.5	137	124	0.80	67	21 29	R 87
A4 2.8	V6 2.8 DOHC-30-MPSFI	169	190 @ 6000	207 @ 3200	10.3 :1	front - M5*	3.70	8.7	15.7 28.5	6.0	137	131	0.78	67	20 29	R 87
						front - A5	3.29	9.7	17.0 29.9	6.8	141	124	0.78	67	18 29	R 87
A4 2.8 qtro	V6 2.8 DOHC-30-MPSFI	169	190 @ 6000	207 @ 3200	10.3 :1	all - M5*	3.89	10.0	16.8 30.2	7.0	144	124	0.80	67	19 28	R 87
						all - A5	3.29	10.5	17.4 31.0	7.2	144	118	0.80	67	17 28	R 87

PRICE & EQUIPMENT

AUDI A4	1.8T FWD	1.8T quattro	2.8 FWD	2.8 quattro	Avant FWD	Avant quattro
Retail price $:	23,790	25,440	28,390	30,040	30,465	31,040
Dealer invoice $:	20,942	22,592	24,944	26,594	26,839	27,464
Shipping & handling $:	500	500	500	500	500	500
Automatic transmission:	O	O	O	O	O	NA
Cruise control:	S	S	S	S	S	S
Power steering:	S	S	S	S	S	S
Anti-lock brakes:	S	S	S	S	S	S
Traction control:	S	S	S	S	S	S
Air conditioning:	SA	SA	SA	SA	SA	SA
Leather:	-H	-H	OH	OH	OH	OH
AM/FM/radio-cassette:	S	S	S	S	S	S
Power door locks:	S	S	S	S	S	S
Power windows:	S	S	S	S	S	S
Tilt steering:	S	S	S	S	S	S
Dual adjustable mirrors:	SEH	SEH	SEH	SEH	SEH	SEH
Alloy wheels:	S	S	S	S	S	S
Anti-theft system:	S	S	S	S	S	S

Colors

Exterior: Black, Silver, White, Red, Mica, Titanium, Emerald, Green, Sand, Blue.

Interior: Anthracite, Neutral, Platinum, Titanium, Blue.

AT A GLANCE...

Category:	FWD or AWD luxury sedans and wagons. Class : 7

HISTORIC
Introduced in:	1973: Fox; 1979: 4000; 1982: 90.
Made in:	Ingolstadt, Germany.

DEMOGRAPHICS
Model	Men./Wom.	Age	Married	College	Income
A4	92/8 %	46	82 %	71 %	$ 70 000

INDEX
Safety:	95 %	Satisfaction:	86 %
Depreciation:	47 %	Insurance:	$ 1 425-1 530
Cost per mile:	$0.67	Number of dealers:	290

SALES
Model	1996	1997	Result
A4	15 319	20 871	+ 36.2 %

MAIN COMPETITORS

ACURA TL, BMW 3-Series, INFINITI I30, LEXUS ES 300, MAZDA Millenia, NISSAN Maxima, SAAB 9³, TOYOTA Avalon, VOLKSWAGEN Passat VR6, VOLVO S70.

MAINTENANCE REQUIRED BY WARRANTY
First revision:	Frequency:	Diagnostic plug:
7 500 miles	7 500 miles	Yes

SPECIFICATIONS

Model	Version Trim	Body/ Seats	Interior volume cu ft	Trunk volume cu ft	Cd	Wheel base in	Lght x Wdgth x Hght in x in x in	Curb weight lb	Susp. ft/rr	Brake ft/rr	Steering type	Turning diameter ft	Steer. turns nber.	Fuel tank gal	tire size	Standard tires make	model	Standard powertrain
AUDI		General warranty: 3 years / 50 000 miles; perforation corrosion: 10 years; free maintenance: 3 years / 50 000 miles; roadside assistance: 3 years.																
A4 1.8T	base	4dr.sdn. 4/5	87.7	13.7	0.29	103.0	179.0x68.2x55.8	2677	ih/sih	dc/ABS	pwr.r&p.	36.4	3.1	16.4	205/60R15	Continental	Supercontact	L4T/1.8/M5
A4 1.8T	quattro	4dr.sdn. 4/5	87.7	13.7	0.29	102.6	178.0x68.2x55.8	3130	ih/ih	dc/ABS	pwr.r&p.	36.4	3.1	16.4	205/60R15	Continental	Supercontact	L4T/1.8/M5
A4 2.8	base	4dr.sdn. 4/5	87.7	13.7	0.29	103.0	178.0x68.2x55.8	3087	ih/sih	dc/ABS	pwr.r&p.	36.4	3.1	16.4	205/55R16	Michelin	Pilot SX	V6/2.8/M5
A4 2.8	quattro	4dr.sdn. 4/5	87.7	13.7	0.29	102.6	178.0x68.2x55.8	3318	ih/ih	dc/ABS	pwr.r&p.	36.4	3.1	16.4	205/55R16	Michelin	Pilot SX	V6/2.8/M5
A4 2.8	avant	4dr.wgn. 4/5	-	-	0.29	103.0	176.8x68.2x56.7	3289	ih/sih	dc/ABS	pwr.r&p.	36.4	3.1	16.4	205/55R16	Michelin	Pilot SX	V6/2.8/M5
A4 2.8 avant	qttro	4dr.wgn. 4/5	-	-	0.29	102.6	176.8x68.2x56.7	3353	ih/ih	dc/ABS	pwr.r&p.	36.4	3.1	16.4	205/55R16	Michelin	Pilot SX	V6/2.8/M5

The A6 sits smack in the middle of the Audi lineup. It was revised last year and its new body stylistics got rave reviews in Europe, but here in North America, comments were more reserved and hesitant. At any rate, with each new generation, the A6 offers pretty awesome driving potential.

MODEL RANGE

The A6 is offered as a 4-door sedan or station wagon equipped with front or all-wheel drive, motivated by a 2.8L V6 with standard sequential automatic transmission. Original equipment is very rich and includes, beside the usual amenities that furbish cars in this price range, climate control with pollen filter, two solar collectors and an optional Cold Weather Package for the Canadian market that includes a heated steering wheel.

TECHNICAL FEATURES

The latest model Audi A6 is still a completely galvanized steel unibody, with some aluminum and magnesium components, like the hood and some suspension parts. So new models are lighter than their predecessors, even though the body is wider and higher, with a longer wheelbase, but is shorter bumper-to-bumper. Aerodynamics are admirable, since they yield an impressive drag coefficient of 0.28. The fully independent suspension consists of four-link, upper and lower control arms mounted on an auxiliary frame up front and at the rear, there's a multi-link system on the front-wheel drive model and unequal-length control arms on the quattro. Both axles are fitted with a stabilizer bar and four-wheel disc brakes are teamed up with ABS that also serves as traction control. The 2.8L V6 still sits longitudinally under the hood. It's both light and compact and is equipped with very unique variable-length intake manifolds controlled by a pressure valve. The long cycle provides good torque at low r.p.m. and the short cycle pumps out the power above 4,000 rpm. The «adaptive» 5-speed automatic gearbox is fitted with an electronic shifter, inspired by the Tiptronic design developed by Porsche. Gear shifting varies with driving style and road conditions, either automatically or manually. Full-time AWD includes three differentials, one for each powertrain and a center Torsen differential that distributes torque to the axle and

Super Touring Car...

wheel lacking adherence.

SIMPLY SUPER

++ SAFETY. Both passive and active safety features are incredibly refined, since the A6 comes equipped with dual front-impact airbags and 4 side-impact airbags housed in the seat backs. The A6 body is one of the most rigid in the world and was awarded one of the top marks in NHTSA collision tests. Driving itself is safer due to the quattro IV system, that's the cat's meow when it comes to traction with its Torsen differential and electronically controlled differential lock, not to mention the EDL-ASR traction control device that provides gutsy, topnotch grip.

PROS

+ QUALITY. The assembly job and trim materials used are clearly a cut above average. The over-all treatment is simply flawless with its superb finish details far ritzier than those on Mercedes and BMW cars.

+ CABIN SPACE. Five passengers will be comfy inside and the longer and wider trunk can also be extended by lowering the rear seatbench back, a rare feature in this category.

+ RIDE COMFORT. You're in for a smooth, comfy ride due to the supple suspension, effective seat design and low noise interference at cruising speed, thanks to the stiff body and impressive soundproofing.

+ TECHNOLOGY. Audi's cars are ahead of their time and the competition in this department, due to avant-garde techniques such as the

completely galvanized body, light alloy components and quattro all-wheel drive.

+ FUEL EFFICIENCY. It's quite economical on the front-wheel drive version that's frugal due in part to a good power to weight ratio and fine aerodynamics.

+ DEPRECIATION. Over the years, Audi's reputation and image have improved, which has affected resale value that isn't as poor as it was at one time.

+ EQUIPMENT. It's very extensive and very posh, which mostly justifies the going price for these models that, contrary to the attitude in Europe, are considered to be out-and-out luxury cars here in North America.

CONS

- PRICE. The Audi A6's aren't within the average buyer's means and the fact that repairs are free during warranty isn't much of a consoling thought.

- TRANSMISSION. The Tiptronic formula doesn't add much zip to this model that can't really pretend to be a true sports car.

- PERFORMANCES. The V6 may be more brawny, but it often strains, especially with the quattro system that's heavier and adversely affects the power to weight ratio.

- DIGITAL SCREEN. It's impossible to read in the daytime, even when it isn't too bright and sunny, which is awkward when you use the Tiptronic function, since you can't really see which gear's engaged.

- SUSPENSION. It's overly flexible, so there's sway which is more annoying than a serious drawback when it comes to handling, especially at regular speeds.

- STEERING. It's lighter on the front-wheel drive model than the quattro and you have to really keep an eye on it in slippery conditions.

- CONTROLS. Some of them are unusual and complex, so it takes a while to to get used to them, so you really have to concentrate on how they work.

- TO BE IMPROVED UPON: Weak-intensity low beam headlamps.

CONCLUSION

The Audi A6 is an almost perfect touring car, for it's competent, safe and comfy at all times. Yet a few dubious compromises adversely affect the over-all vehicle design... ☺

RATING
AUDI A6

CONCEPT : 82%
Technology	90
Safety :	90
Interior space :	60
Trunk volume:	85
Quality/fit/finish :	85

DRIVING: 70%
Cockpit :	85
Performance :	55
Handling :	65
Steering :	80
Braking :	65

ORIGINAL EQUIPMENT: 80%
Tires :	80
Headlights :	80
Wipers :	80
Rear defroster :	80
Radio :	80

COMFORT : 78%
Seats :	80
Suspension :	80
Sound level :	70
Conveniences :	80
Air conditioning :	80

BUDGET : 48%
Price :	0
Fuel economy :	60
Insurance :	45
Satisfaction :	85
Depreciation :	50

Overall rating: 71.6%

NEW FOR 1999

•Information not available before going to press.

ENGINES
Model/version	Type / timing valve / fuel system	Displacement cu in	Power bhp @ rpm	Torque lb-ft @ rpm
A6	V6 2.8 DOHC-30-MPSFI	169	200 @ 6000	207 @ 3200
A6 quattro	V6 2.8 DOHC-30-MPSFI	169	200 @ 6000	207 @ 3200

TRANSMISSIONS
Compres. ratio	Driving wheels / transmission	Final ratio
10.3 :1	front-A5*	3.409
10.3 :1	four-A5*	3.409

PERFORMANCES
Acceler. 0-60 mph s	Standing 1/4 & 5/8 mile s	Acceler. 50-75 mph s	Braking 60-0 mph f	Top speed mph	Lateral acceler. G	Noise level dBA	Fuel economy mpg City	Fuel economy mpg Highway	Fuel type Octane
9.6	16.6 29.5	6.8	138	143	0.80	66	17	28	R 87
11.0	17.8 32.2	7.8	138	140	0.81	66	17	28	R 87

PRICE & EQUIPMENT

AUDI A6	FWD 4dr.sdn.	quattro 4dr.sdn.	quattro 4dr.wgn.
Retail price $:	33,750	35,400	34,400
Dealer invoice $:	29,697	31,347	30,250
Shipping & handling $:	500	500	500
Automatic transmission:	S	S	S
Cruise control:	S	S	S
Power steering:	S	S	S
Anti-lock brakes:	S	S	S
Traction control:	S	S	S
Air conditioning:	SA	SA	SA
Leather:	OH	OH	OH
AM/FM/radio-cassette:	S	S	S
Power door locks:	S	S	S
Power windows:	S	S	S
Tilt steering:	S	S	S
Dual adjustable mirrors:	SEH	SEH	SEH
Alloy wheels:	S	S	S
Anti-theft system:	S	S	S

Colors

Exterior: Black, Silver, White, Mica, Byzance.

Interior: Anthracite, Neutral, Blue, Platinum.

AT A GLANCE...

Category: FWD or AWD luxury sedans & wagons   **Class :** 7

HISTORIC
Introduced in:	1982 (5000), 1998.
Made in:	Neckarsulm, Germany.

DEMOGRAPHICS
Model	Men./Wom.	Age	Married	College	Income
A6	82/18 %	56	89 %	52 %	$ 90 000

INDEX
Safety:	90 %	Satisfaction:	85 %
Depreciation:	48 %	Insurance:	1 475-1 600 $
Cost per mile:	$0.90	Number of dealers:	290

SALES
Model	1996	1997	Result
A6	9 908	9 949	+ 0.4 %

MAIN COMPETITORS
ACURA RL, BMW 5-Series, LEXUS GS 300, MAZDA Millenia, SAAB 9⁵, VOLVO S80.

MAINTENANCE REQUIRED BY WARRANTY
First revision:	Frequency:	Diagnostic plug:
7 500 miles	7 500 miles	Yes

SPECIFICATIONS

General warranty: 3 years / 50 000 miles; perforation corrosion: 10 years; free maintenance: 3 years / 50 000 miles; roadside assistance: 3 years.

Model	Version Trim	Body/Seats	Interior volume cu ft	Trunk volume cu ft	Cd	Wheel base in	Lght x Wdgth x Hght in x in x in	Curb weight lb	Susp. ft/rr	Brake ft/rr	Steering type	Turning diameter ft	Steer. turns nber.	Fuel tank gal	tire size	Standard tires make	model	Standard powertrain
AUDI A6																		
A6	FWD	4dr.sdn.5	98.3	17.2	0.28	108.7	192.0x71.3x57.2	2473	ih/sih	dc/ABS	pwr.r&p.	38.4	2.8	18.5	205/55R16	Goodyear	Eagle RS-A	V6/2.8/A5
A6	quattro	4dr.sdn.5	95.8	15.4	0.28	108.6	192.0x71.3x57.1	3704	ih/ih	dc/ABS	pwr.r&p.	38.4	2.8	18.5	205/55R16	Goodyear	Eagle RS-A	V6/2.8/A5
A6	quattro	4dr.wgn5	99.3	36.4	0.28	108.6	192.0x71.3x58.2	3856	ih/ih	dc/ABS	pwr.r&p.	38.4	2.8	18.5	195/65R15	Goodyear	Eagle RS-A	V6/2.8/A5

The Audi 8 is no doubt the most advanced car of our time. It's the car that integrates the most technological innovations, of which the most sensational is an entirely aluminum body. If you throw in its sophisticated quattro all-wheel drive and latest generation V8 engine, you realize that it constitutes a technological cocktail that's unique on the current market. Yet it sells at a lower price than its main rivals, that only outdo it as to the lush, luxury look of some of their equipment items.

MODEL RANGE

The Audi 8 is a four-door sedan offered in 3.7 and 4.2 versions, equipped with V8 engines paired up with an automatic transmission. The 3.7 equips the front-wheel drive model and the 4.2L powers the quattro IV all-wheel drive model. Both models are equipped with identical and rich items. Options consist of a «Cold Weather Package» that includes heated rear seats and steering wheel and a ski bag in the trunk. For those who live in southerly regions, the «Warm Weather Package» includes insulated glass, sunroof with solar panel that's the energy source for fans when the car is parked in the sun and rear panel and rear window shades. Extras also include radio controls on the steering wheel, chrome wheels, high-fidelity Bose sound system, pearly white paint, hands-free cellular phone and CD changer.

TECHNICAL FEATURES

The A8 is the only mass-produced car in the world that has an all-aluminum alloy unibody. Due to the particular properties of this metal, the structure consists of a space frame made of sectional aluminum on which are attached the body panels, resulting in a much more robust body than is the case for an identical steel-built structure. Aerodynamics are outstanding, yielding a drag coefficient of less than 0.30, even with the wide front, beefy tires and generous orifices. There's a four-link, upper and lower control arm front suspension and the rear suspension consists of trapezoidal control arms. Both axles are fitted with a stabilizer bar. The 3.7 front-wheel drive model is equipped with an electronic anti-slip system (ASR), while the quattro

Good and Bad News...

benefits from automatic locking differentials (EDL). The four-wheel disc brakes are associated with an antilock braking device that adjusts to brake pedal effort, so as to provide optimum vehicle stability. Safety features are in keeping with other A8 attributes, since it's one of the few cars to come equipped with six standard airbags (two front and four side-impact airbags).

PROS

+ TECHNOLOGICAL ADVANCES. Audi was a pioneer in all-wheel drive technology and in the use of aluminum as the main building material for car construction. But the rest of the A8 is also at the cutting edge of technical applications, so it's a car that offers top-of-

the-heap performances and safety features.

+ SAFETY. It's assured by aluminum's resistance to impact, a metal that's much sturdier than steel, as well as six airbags, pretension seatbelts and electronic driving aids.

+ PERFORMANCES. The 4.2L engine achieves high-caliber performances, yet not any zoomier than those of rivals. Accelerations and pickup are lively with such a good power to weight ratio, due to the pared down weight of the aluminum body.

+ HANDLING. Sophisticated suspension components and the overall power flow achieved by this vehicle provide a reassuringly stable and

neutral behavior in most situations. The load-levelling and anti-skid systems are also definite assets in this department. We were amazed at this big car's nimble negotiating of a whole series of curves.

+ FUEL EFFICIENCY. The favorable power to weight ratio allows for amazingly frugal gas consumption, since it's equivalent to that of a V6.

+ RIDE COMFORT. The posh Pullman seats, velvety suspension and superb soundproofing let you make long, fatigue-free trips, making the A8 ideal for long-distance runs.

CONS

- STYLE. It's a shame that such an avant-garde model didn't get blessed with more daring looks in keeping with its innovative character. Audi designers decided to opt for cool anonymity, so the car stays in style for eons.

- BUDGET. You need a hefty cash flow to own this car, for resale value can suffer due to mistrust of all the high tech features. Also, repair jobs to an aluminum structure worry insurance companies and body shop owners.

- DRIVING. The fun at the wheel is really tamed down by this car's squeaky-clean demeanor. This car is maybe too perfect for its own good, that is, it doesn't really get your adrenalin count climbing...

- CABIN DESIGN. The interior is dreary and conventional, a poor reflection of the innovative features that are part of this package. Good old traditional wood trim should have been replaced by carbon fiber components or some other exciting material. There are just too many dull, down-to-earth types at Audi...

- TO BE IMPROVED UPON: Old as the hills radio antenna design that could have been integrated into the rear window, too many controls (40 switches and 3 buttons) that are complicated and easy to mix up, so you almost have to take a driver's initiation course before you get behind the wheel.

CONCLUSION

The Audi 8 is a car that's good news and bad news. Its «under the skin» self is terrific, but driving capabilities and stylistics, both inside and out, are awfully ordinary. ☺

RATING AUDI A8

CONCEPT :		88%
Technology	100	
Safety :	100	
Interior space :	70	
Trunk volume:	80	
Quality/fit/finish :	90	
DRIVING:		**73%**
Cockpit :	85	
Performance :	70	
Handling :	70	
Steering :	80	
Braking :	60	
ORIGINAL EQUIPMENT:		**83%**
Tires :	85	
Headlights :	85	
Wipers :	80	
Rear defroster :	80	
Radio :	85	
COMFORT :		**83%**
Seats :	85	
Suspension :	80	
Sound level:	80	
Conveniences :	80	
Air conditioning :	90	
BUDGET :		**40%**
Price :	0	
Fuel economy :	50	
Insurance :	15	
Satisfaction :	85	
Depreciation :	50	
Overall rating:		**73.4%**

NEW FOR 1999

• Information not available before going to press.

ENGINES

Model/ version	Type / timing valve / fuel system	Displacement cu in	Power bhp @ rpm	Torque lb-ft @ rpm
A8 3.7	V8 3.7 DOHC-32-MPSFI	226	230 @ 5500	235 @ 2700
A8 4.2	V8 4.2 DOHC-32 MPSFI	254	300 @ 6000	295 @ 3300

TRANSMISSIONS

Compres. ratio	Driving wheels / transmission	Final ratio
10.8 :1	front-A5	3.091
10.8: 1	all-A5	2.727

PERFORMANCES

Acceler. 0-60 mph s	Standing 1/4 & 5/8 mile s	Acceler. 50-75 mph s	Braking 60-0 mph f	Top speed mph	Lateral acceler. G	Noise level dBA	Fuel economy mpg City	Highway	Fuel type Octane
8.6	16.8 28.2	6.3	131	131	0.83	65	17	26	R 87
7.5	15.4 27.6	5.4	148	131	0.85	65	17	25	R 87

PRICE & EQUIPMENT

AUDI A8	3.7	4.2
Retail price $:	57,400	65,000
Dealer invoice $:	50,183	56,795
Shipping & handling $:	500	500
Automatic transmission:	S	S
Cruise control:	S	S
Power steering:	S	S
Anti-lock brakes:	S	S
Traction control:	S	S
Air conditioning:	S	S
Leather:	S	SH
AM/FM/radio-cassette:	S	S
Power door locks:	S	S
Power windows:	S	S
Tilt steering:	S	S
Dual adjustable mirrors:	SEH	SEH
Alloy wheels:	S	S
Anti-theft system:	S	S

Colors

Exterior: Aluminum, White, Black, Green, Gray.

Interior: Black, Tan.

AT A GLANCE...

Category: FWD or AWD luxury sedans. **Class :** 7

HISTORIC
Introduced in: 1996
Made in: Ingolstadt, Germany.

DEMOGRAPHICS
Model	Men./Wom.	Age	Married	College	Income
A8	90/10 %	50	91 %	55 %	$ 135 000

INDEX
Safety:	100 %	Satisfaction:	85 %
Depreciation:	50 %	Insurance:	$1 950
Cost per mile:	$1.17	Number of dealers:	290

SALES
Model	1996	1997	Result	
A8	559	2 085	+ 273 %	-

MAIN COMPETITORS
BMW 740iL, INFINITI Q45, LEXUS LS 400, MERCEDES-BENZ Class S.

MAINTENANCE REQUIRED BY WARRANTY
First revision:	Frequency:	Diagnostic plug:
7 500 miles	7 500 miles	Yes

SPECIFICATIONS

Model	Version Trim	Body/ Seats	Interior volume cu ft	Trunk volume cu ft	Cd	Wheel base in	Lght x Wdgth x Hght in x in x in	Curb weight lb	Susp. ft/rr	Brake ft/rr	Steering type	Turning diameter ft	Steer. turns nber.	Fuel tank gal	tire size	Standard tires make	model	Standard powertrain
AUDI A8		General warranty: 3 years / 50 000 miles; perforation corrosion: 10 years; free maintenance: 3 years / 50 000 miles; roadside assistance: 3 years.																
A8 3.7	traction	4dr.sdn.5	99.8	17.6	0.29	113.0	198.2x74.0x56.7	3682	ih/ih	dc/ABS	pwr.r&p.	42.6	2.7	23.8	225/60HR16	Michelin	Pilot SX	V8/3.7/A5
A8 4.2	quattro	4dr.sdn.5	99.8	18.0	0.29	113.0	198.2x74.0x56.7	3902	ih/ih	dc/ABS	pwr.r&p.	42.6	2.7	23.8	225/60HR16	Michelin	Pilot SX	V8/4.2/A5

AUDI TT Coupe
«Petroleum in the Blood»

Audi was aware that its sales and image weren't what they should be in North America, so the carmaker decided to break the ice by grabbing people's attention with a new model that will be introduced on the U.S. market in the fall of 1998 in a front-wheel drive version and in Canada in the spring of 1999 in a quattro version. At first, models will develop 180 hp and buyers will have to wait until the fall of 1999 to take a look at the 225-hp quattro, while the convertible will only be available as of the spring of the year 2000. It's been a long time since Audi included a coupe in its model range and this gutsy comeback is being surrounded with all the due pomp and circumstance. In fact, it's hard not to be wowed by such an original new model derived from the concept car shown for the first time in Frankfurt in 1995.

With its really trim overhangs, its rounded, turtle-shell shape, refined and polished forms and some beautifully wrought sculpted stylistic details, the TT coupe is really mesmeric and it has a solid as a nutshell look. On the exterior, you can see the gas tank filler hole cover that's identical to the one on the former model, cut from an aluminum block and very mod-looking and practical. The TT coupe is a thing of beauty, so it should get rave reviews the world over. The car is simply sensational, but exhibits impeccable taste, a welcome surprise, since Audi is usually so very conservative when it comes to stylistics. The latest Audi model has lots of panache and personality and its massive, muscular silhouette is very akin to other cars, but the TT is the best of the lot, so to speak. The cabin design hasn't been overlooked either, since it has a more classic appearance, yet it's lush as ever. It's inspired by sports cars from the golden days of Tourist Trophy car

races, hence the TT's name, in honor of these races that raised the dust and tore up the tarmac on the roads of Europe. A clever blend of aluminum, fine-ilk plastic and leather give the cabin a clean, cool ambience that exudes class and not one detail is overdone or spoils the over-all effect. But beyond looks, as soon as you're seated inside the TT, you have a feeling of solidity and security, due to the narrow lateral windows. This idea of carapace is everywhere, even in the cockpit where you really feel like you're snug as a bug in a rug, that is, one with this marvellous machine. The car has a massive, solid through and through feeling, especially the heavier quattro model. So come to mind images of this incredibly complex technology, observed on the assembly line in Hungary, that is forgotten in a sense, once the car is put together, but whose effects are felt the instant you're off and running. More than its direct rivals, the TT coupe gives you a sense of being at the wheel of a very sophisticated machine, like a fighter aircraft whose elements are honed for its specific mission. The TT's mission is to give you a thrilling ride and the 225-hp version doesn't hold back, so much so that it was hard to hit the car's limits on the curved Umbrian roads in Italy, so you're aware that the quattro system has evolved even more and is at an all-time peak. What's neat about the TT is that technology doesn't take over and so the driver has absolute control over the machine, even if in the sidelines, the driving aids ensure that everything goes well. And lastly, you get out of this car with a feeling of confidence inspired by this amazing technology whose greatest merit is to expand physical limitations without danger to life or limb.

It's been a few years since Audi listed a sports coupe in its catalogue. The last one hails back to the eighties and was simply called quattro. The Ingolstadt firm wanted to face the competition on an equal footing, namely the Mercedes SLK and Porsche Boxster, so they decided to go ahead and develop the TT prototype that had dazzled everyone at the Frankfurt Auto Show back in 1995. This coupe will soon be joined by a convertible that has the unique advantage of being offered in front-wheel or all-wheel drive, whereas rivals are rear-wheel drive models.

MODEL RANGE

The TT coupe will first be imported as a FWD car, then as a quattro AWD animated by a 1.8L Turbocharged engine developing 180 hp, mated to a 5-speed manual transmission, then later as a 225 hp quattro model with 6-speed manual gearbox. The convertible version will only be introduced on the market afterwards. It's a 2+2 coupe whose original equipment includes most of the current creature comforts such as automatic climate control, major power accessories and an 80-Watt radio and tape deck. For now, no automatic transmission is in the works, but Audi offers option packages like the performance package including Xenon headlamps and 17-inch wheels equipped with summer tires, the comfort package with heated seats and six-function on-board computer as well as the audio package consisting of a Bose sound system and 6-CD changer.

TECHNICAL FEATURES

Due to production costs, the TT's body is made entirely of steel that's galvanized on both sides, but the hood is made of aluminum. In spite of the big tires, large orifices and wide frontal surface, the maximum drag coefficient varies between 0.34 and 0.35. The front suspension is a MacPherson strut setup with A-arms mounted on an independent cradle. The FWD version has a rear tubular torsion axle, while the quattro rear suspension consists of dual transversal A-arms and a longitudinal trailing arm with gas-filled shocks and anti-roll bar in all cases. Diagonal double-circuit brakes are vented discs up font and full discs at the rear with a standard antilock braking-traction control device (FWD)

with electronic power divider of pressure applied. Four-wheel disc brakes are paired up with an ABS 5.3 system including electronic control of pressure on rear wheels.

PROS

+ STYLE. It's been a long time since we've seen such a gorgeous, knock-your-socks-off model. It's startling at first, but you get used to the bulky, but graceful shape of this speedster that looks solid as a rock.

+ SAFETY. The TT coupe benefits from an extremely stiff body, so passengers can be assured good protection in the event of a collision, but it's also equipped with front and side-impact airbags.

+ HANDLING. The quattro version is the most impressive. It seems to be literally glued to the road without any pilot maneuvers or adjustments.

+ PERFORMANCES. The base engine provides reasonably frisky frolic, but it's the 225 hp engine that behaves more like a race car powerplant. It's lively, it emits a lovely roar, in short, the works and this model of the TT seems more

like a true blue sports car.

+ BRAKES. They're easy to adjust, grip just when and how you want and they do so smoothly and progressively. We weren't able to take exact measurements, but «hard» stops were achieved quite quickly and linings hold up well on very serpentine stretches.

+ RIDE COMFORT. Even when the road surface goes awry, the TT is never actually uncomfortable, as is the case for scads of sports cars. The suspension isn't really too flexible, but it's well-adjusted and benefits from enough travel to take a bruising from the bumps, without jostling occupants.

+ CABIN DESIGN. It's gorgeous inside, since the approach is to imitate race car stylistics. The lovely, muted black instrument panel serves as a jewel case for the numerous circular shapes of cast-aluminum, such as the air vents, steering wheel rim, speed shifter, etc. You also find this polished metal on the pedal assembly and footrest.

+ QUALITY. No doubt about it, Audi is one of the best in the indus-

try when it comes to quality. Engineering follows stringent standards, the design is methodically developed, assembly is meticulous and finish job is simply flawless.

+ CONVENIENCE FEATURES. For a sports coupe, the TT provides lots of storage spots such as a big glove compartment, door side-pocket netting, a sort of shelf above the passenger's feet and an open compartment on the transmission tunnel. The trunk isn't huge, but it has a regular shape and the rear seatbench back forms a platform when folded down, so you can store golf bags length-wise.

CONS

- STEERING. The system on the FWD model is no fun. It springs this way and that and it isn't always easy keeping the front end on track when going into curves.

-VISIBILITY. It isn't ideal. You're seated low down, the body belt is high and roof supports are very thick. Exterior mirrors are generous, but they're located too far back, so you have to turn your head to peer into them.

- REAR SEATS. As is always the case on this type of vehicle, they're next to useless and only suited to very small children.

- SHIFTER. The 5-speed gearbox shifter grinds between 2nd and 3rd gear, which is surprising for a German-make car.

- CONSOLE. It gobbles up a lot of space, especially the aluminum bar that forms a handle that you're always hitting your poor knee against.

- ACCESS. It's no picnic climbing aboard in the rear seats, since the front seats don't free up enough space and due to the very arched roof design.

- TO BE IMPROVED UPON: Remote-control switches to open the rear hatch door, gas tank filler hole cap and to deactivate the alarm system are hard to reach, hidden in a compartment at the extremity of the center console.

CONCLUSION

The TT coupe will be sold at a very competitive, tantalizing price that should get things rolling and catapult this car to the same enviable status as the A4 that it's derived from in many respects. ☺

RATING
AUDI TT

CONCEPT :		64%
Technology	90	
Safety :	90	
Interior space :	30	
Trunk volume:	25	
Quality/fit/finish :	85	
DRIVING:		79%
Cockpit :	85	
Performance :	80	
Handling :	70	
Steering :	80	
Braking :	80	
ORIGINAL EQUIPMENT:		81%
Tires :	80	
Headlights :	80	
Wipers :	80	
Rear defroster :	80	
Radio :	85	
COMFORT :		67%
Seats :	80	
Suspension :	75	
Sound level:	40	
Conveniences :	60	
Air conditioning :	80	
BUDGET :		41%
Price :	0	
Fuel economy :	65	
Insurance :	40	
Satisfaction :	75	
Depreciation :	25	
Overall rating:		**66.4%**

Anecdote

To have the privilege of taking the Audi TT coupe out for a three-hour run, we had to take ten planes across four countries, France, Hungary, Austria and Italy, all in six days. A record. But it was worth it, for the road test took place on the roads of Umbria, the part of Italy where the legendary Targa Floria soared and made people swoon.

ENGINES

Model/ version	Type / timing valve / fuel system	Displacement cu in	Power bhp @ rpm	Torque lb-ft @ rpm
FWD	L4T 1.8 DOHC-20-MPSFI	106	180 @ 5500	174 @ 1950
quattro	L4T 1.8 DOHC-20-MPSFI	108	180 @ 5500	174 @ 1950
quattro	L4T 1.8 DOHC-20-MPSFI	108	225 @ 5900	207 @ 2200

* manufacturer's data

TRANSMISSIONS

Compres. ratio	Driving wheels / transmission	Final ratio
9.5 :1	front - M5	3.938
9.5 :1	all - M5	3.938
9.0 :1	all - M6	3.316

PERFORMANCES

Acceler. 0-60 mph s	Standing 1/4 & 5/8 mile s	Acceler. 50-75 mph s	Braking 60-0 mph f	Top speed mph	Lateral acceler. G	Noise level dBA	Fuel economy mpg City Highway	Fuel type Octane
7.4*				142*				S 91
7.4*				142*				S 91
6.4*				151*				S 91

PRICE & EQUIPMENT

AUDI TT 2dr.cpe.	1.8T FWD	1.8T quattro	1.8T 225 quattro
Retail price $:	NA	NA	NA
Dealer invoice $:	-	-	-
Shipping & handling $:	-	-	-
Automatic transmission:	-	-	-
Cruise control:	S	S	S
Power steering:	S	S	S
Anti-lock brakes:	S	S	S
Traction control:	S		
Air conditioning:	SA	SA	SA
Leather:	s	S	S
AM/FM/radio-cassette:	S	S	SCD
Power door locks:	S	S	S
Power windows:	S	S	S
Tilt steering:	S	S	S
Dual adjustable mirrors:	SEH	SEH	SEH
Alloy wheels:	S	S	S
Anti-theft system:	S	S	S

Colors
Exterior: Black, Yellow, Red, Gray, Silver, Blue, Green.

Interior: Black, Gray, Denim blue .

AT A GLANCE...

Category: FWD or AWD sports coupes. **Class :** GT

HISTORIC
Introduced in: 2000
Made in: Győr, Hongria.

DEMOGRAPHICS
Model	Men./Wom.	Age	Married	College	Income
TT	NA				

INDEX
Safety:	90 %	**Satisfaction:**	NA %
Depreciation:	NA %	**Insurance:**	$ 1 485
Cost per mile:	$ 0.69	**Number of dealers:**	290

SALES
Model	1996	1997	Result
TT	Not on the market at that time.		

MAIN COMPETITORS
BMW Z3, MERCEDES-BENZ SLK, PORSCHE Boxster.

MAINTENANCE REQUIRED BY WARRANTY
First revision:	Frequency:	Diagnostic plug:
7 500 miles	7 500 miles	Yes

SPECIFICATIONS

General warranty: 3 years / 50 000 miles; perforation corrosion: 10 years; free maintenance: 3 years / 50 000 miles; roadside assistance: 3 years.

Model	Version Trim	Body/ Seats	Interior volume cu ft	Trunk volume cu ft	Cd	Wheel base in	Lght x Wdgth x Hght in x in x in	Curb weight lb	Susp. ft/rr	Brake ft/rr	Steering type	Turning diameter ft	Steer. turns nber.	Fuel tank gal	tire size	Standard tires make	model	Standard powertrain
AUDI																		
TT	1.8T FWD	2dr.cpe. 2+2	58.9	13.8	0.34	95.3	159.1x69.4x53.0	2656	ih/th	dc/ABS	pwr.r&p.	34.3	2.8	14.5	205/55R16	Michelin	Pilot SX	L4T/1.8/M5
TT	1.8T quattro	2dr.cpe. 2+2	58.9	10.8	0.34	95.6	159.1x69.4x53.0	2910	ih/ih	dc/ABS	pwr.r&p.	34.3	2.8	16.4	205/55R16	Michelin	Pilot SX	L4T/1.8/M5
TT	1.8T quattro 225 hp	2dr.cpe. 2+2	58.9	10.8	0.35	95.6	159.1x69.4x53.0	2910	ih/ih	dc/ABS	pwr.r&p.	34.3	2.8	16.4	225/45ZR17	Michelin	Pilot SX	L4T/1.8/M6

BMW 3-Series
Bette Davis Eye's...

The first thing that you notice when you gaze at the latest BMW 3-Series, is its headlamps that seem to "look" and perhaps wink at you. In fact, it's the front end design that's undergone the most dramatic stylistic changes compared to the previous model and lots of people who aren't in the know won't even notice the difference! Successful models are in a sense prisoners of their image and their attributes, so designers have a tough time changing them, even in the slightest way. Generally speaking, the 3-Series will now be easier to confuse with the 5-Series, since it shares the same high body belt, sculpted rear end and sleeker nose. Main modifications have been made in regard to the smooth suspension response that's more insulated from the body and transmits less undesirable road data and in a very real sense.

This doesn't mean that the car has gone upscale in a drastic way, since the design derives from the traditional refinement typical of these models, yet aims at making these beauties more competent and solid. And after all, the love of comfort isn't a capital sin. You can feel good without having to feel guilty, right? Because BMW's are rear-wheel drive cars and because they have the reputation of being skittish on wet roads, the carmaker wanted to improve vehicle control, especially for non-expert, average drivers. So there are driving aids to take care of vehicle path, slippage, wheel lock and skidding. And the electronic wizard is everywhere, he's always on the lookout and takes care of windshield wiper speed pacing, personal driver adjustments and keeps accessories in good working order. On-board electronics are so sophisticated that we wonder what will soon be left to do for the person who's behind the wheel. All these safety devices may make

sense on more spacious models, but on a compact model like the 3-Series, once you've installed the electric wiring, six airbags and all the rest of the hardware, you mustn't be surprised if cabin space is a bit snug or that the least incident can be costly because it affects everything that's part of this tightly knit arrangement. This exaggerated honing and refining is an indication that BMW is setting out to appeal to a more staid and conservative clientele, rather than a young and restless bunch by offering more comfort than racing capabilities. But then, the driving thrills that you can experience on the highways and roads nowadays aren't what they used to be either, due to different social priorities and values. Speeding and so-called sports car driving are severely criticized and regarded in some states as if they were social evils that had to be eradicated from the face of the earth. The young person on the go doesn't drive a BMW in this day and age,

but a Honda Civic or a Volkswagen Golf, because the 3-Series has become so expensive that only famous folks can own one. So there's a certain logic if these cars are becoming encrusted in the upper class way of life, as did the 5 and 7-Series in the past. After driving these cars, we're seriously wondering if BMW, Mercedes and company shouldn't discard their rear-wheel drive cars and take a look at front-wheel or all-wheel drive as well., so as to be really with the times. This «revolution» was really profitable for Volvo who stifled its classic approach and saw sales soar off the charts throughout the world, without losing its reputation for sports car performances and safe all-season handling...

The 3-Series has had a face-lift. It now sports a style that's similar to that of the 5-Series, without really giving up its format, that remains very compact, in spite of the extension of a few dimensions. Lots of folks don't even notice the difference between the current and previous design, unless they see them side by side. These touch-ups only affect two models, a process that will continue until the year 2001 and in the meantime, current models will still be sold just as they are at the present time.

MODEL RANGE

The 1999 lineup includes the new 4-door 323 and 328 sedans as well as the small 318ti hatchback models, the 2-door coupe sold in a single M trim and convertibles that remain unchanged. Standard equipment includes most of the usual features and accessories on models in this price range, except leather-clad seats and very costly navigation system that doesn't work everywhere...

TECHNICAL FEATURES

The new generation sedans have trimmer overhangs, new-design grille and an air scoop on the hood. Dimensions are more generous, both inside and out, for these cars are now 4 cm longer and wider, which has 2 inches extended cabin and trunk space considerably. These models have a different steel monocoque body, of which 60% of the body work is galvanized and that's coated with a rustproof agent. The body design blends the main traditional BMW touches and has an aerodynamic finesse that's starting to show its age, with a coefficient varying between 0.31 and 0.32. The fully independent suspension consists of a double wishbone construct up front and cross struts at the rear, with a stabilizer bar on both axles. Some of these components are made of lightweight, but robust aluminum. Four-wheel disc brakes, antilock braking, traction and stability control devices are standard on all versions. The technology aimed at improving the 6-cylinder engines' output and to cut down on emissions is called double VANOS. It allows for a more favorable power curve while controlling engine coolant and enhancing the catalytic convertor's efficiency. So these engines

meet current environmental standard and strict California low emission laws (LEV). The automatic transmission, available as an extra for the 323 and 328 models, is an adaptive 5-speed. In other words, it adjusts to the driver's style. Safety-wise, besides the front and side-impact airbags, BMW installs a standard tube-shaped (HPS) airbag that provides head injury protection for front seat passengers. Side-impact airbags located inside the rear doors are also available as an extra. An optional built-in navigation system will also be offered on the new sedans. Power windows are equipped with an automatic stop mechanism if unwanted objects get in the way when closing windows.

PROS

+ DRIVING. It's very creamy due to the chemistry between the rear-wheel drive, engine power ooze and steering that plays a major role in road handling on these models.

+ QUALITY. Finish details are a cut above, notably the lovely instrument panel materials and superb

exterior finish job.

+ HANDLING. It's more competent due to the more lightweight suspension components and this checks out on wet roads, since vehicles are more steady and stable, but the reinforced suspension is more sensitive to divergent demeanor exhibited on poor roads.

+ PERFORMANCES. Only the 6-cylinder engines are worthy of the sports car label, they're versatile and muscular and adapt well to quiet outings or daredevil moves.

+ TRUNK. It's bigger and can be extended by lowering the rear seatbench. Its low threshold makes for easy luggage loading and unloading.

+ RIDE COMFORT. The cabin interior has stretched out. Rear seat passengers will be more at ease and the driver and front seat passenger enjoy more hip and leg room. The driver is very comfortably seated behind the wheel.

+ SAFETY. Only the rear side-impact airbags, built into the doors, are optional. The new protection

tube that provides head protection in the event of a side-impact collision, HPS is now standard equipment and is derived from the technology developed for the 5 and 7-Series.

+ BUDGET. So as to persuade reticent customers to enter the BMW fold, maintenance will be free of charge for three years or 36,000 miles. Only regular parts that need to be replaced will be payed for by the owner (clutch disc and brake linings).

+ BRAKES. They're even better yet, for sudden stops are achieved in shorter stretches thanks to the bigger vented discs on all four wheels.

+ VISIBILITY. It's clear except at the rear due to the high trunk design and the small rear window.

+ INSTRUMENT PANEL. It's regained the typical BMW look and looks less chintzy than was the case on previous generation models.

+ CONVENIENCE FEATURES. Storage compartments are of a more generous size, such as the glove compartment and door side-pockets.

+ NICE FEATURES: The large capacity windshield washer reservoir (1.4 gallon) and the super duper wipers.

CONS

- BUDGET. Well-equipped models cost an arm and a leg and lower-end models don't have the usual niceties thrown in on such expensive cars, so they aren't too appealing.

- SAFETY. The index attributed by the NHTSA to the previous generation cars isn't as favorable as for the latest models.

- CABIN SPACE. The rear seat may be fitted with three seatbelts, but the 3-Series sedans can at no time really accomodate more than four passengers.

-PERFORMANCES. The 4-cylinder engine is a wimp with the automatic transmission and doesn't jive with the idea of a sports car.

CONCLUSION

These models are still the best reference when it comes to sports model cars. They appeal to people who really enjoy driving and like to strut their social status. But these are two things that don't come cheap, especially at BMW... ☺

RATING BMW 3-Series		
CONCEPT :		**69%**
Technology	90	
Safety :	90	
Interior space :	35	
Trunk volume:	50	
Quality/fit/finish :	80	
DRIVING:		**79%**
Cockpit :	85	
Performance :	65	
Handling :	70	
Steering :	90	
Braking :	85	
ORIGINAL EQUIPMENT:		**79%**
Tires :	80	
Headlights :	80	
Wipers :	80	
Rear defroster :	75	
Radio :	80	
COMFORT :		**71%**
Seats :	75	
Suspension :	70	
Sound level:	60	
Conveniences :	70	
Air conditioning :	80	
BUDGET :		**50%**
Price :	10	
Fuel economy :	50	
Insurance :	45	
Satisfaction :	85	
Depreciation :	60	
Overall rating:		**69.6%**

NEW FOR 1999

- Polycarbonate headlamps.
- Remote-control trunk opener.
- Standard radio and cruise control buttons on the steering wheel.
- Full-size spare tire on the 328.
- Different door handles that provide a better grip.

ENGINES / TRANSMISSIONS / PERFORMANCES

Model/ version	Type / timing valve / fuel system	Displacement cu in	Power bhp @ rpm	Torque lb-ft @ rpm	Compres. ratio	Driving wheels / transmission	Final ratio	Acceler. 0-60 mph s	Standing 1/4 & 5/8 mile s	Acceler. 50-75 mph s	Braking 60-0 mph f	Top speed mph	Lateral acceler. G	Noise level dBA	Fuel economy mpg City	Fuel economy mpg Highway	Fuel type Octane
318	L4* 1.9 DOHC-16-EFI	116	138 @ 6000	133 @ 4300	10.0 :1	rear - M5*	3.45	9.8	17.0 31.6	6.8	118	116	0.83	68	23	32	S 91
323	L6* 2.5 DOHC-24-EFI	152	168 @ 5500	181 @ 3500	10.5 :1	rear - M5*1)	3.07	NA							20	30	S 91
328	L6* 2.8 DOHC-24-EFI	170	190 @ 5500	206 @ 3500	10.2 :1	rear - M5*2,3)	2.93	8.0	15.3 28.0	5.6	128	128	0.85	66	20	28	S 91
M3	L6* 3.2 DOHC-24-EFI	195	240 @ 6000	237 @ 3800	10.5 :1	rear - M5*	3.23	7.0	15.2 27.7	4.5	115	137	0.88	68	20	28	S 91

1) Getrag B   2) ZF C   3) optional A5, final ratio 3.46

PRICE & EQUIPMENT

BMW 3-Series	318 ti 3dr.cpe.	323i 2dr.cpe.	323i 2dr.con.	328i 4dr.sdn.	328i 2dr.con.	M3 2dr.cpe.
Retail price $:	21,390	28,700	34,700	33,100	41,500	39,700
Dealer invoice $:	19,225	25,160	30,410	29,010	36,355	34,780
Shipping & handling $:	570	570	570	570	570	570
Automatic transmission:	O	O	O	O	O	-
Cruise control:	O	S	O	S	S	S
Power steering:	S	S	S	S	S	S
Anti-lock brakes:	S	S	S	S	S	S
Traction control:	S	S	S	S	S	S
Air conditioning:	O	SA	S	SA	S	S
Leather:	-	-	O	O	O	S
AM/FM/radio-cassette:	O	S	S	S	S	S
Power door locks:	-	S	S	S	S	S
Power windows:	-	S	S	S	S	S
Tilt steering:	-	S	S	S	S	S
Dual adjustable mirrors:	O	SEH	S	SEH	S	S
Alloy wheels:	O	S	S	S	S	S
Anti-theft system:	-	O	S	O	S	S

Colors
Exterior: White, Black, Blue, Red, Gray, Silver, Violet, Green.
Interior: Anthracite, Gray, Red, Blue, Turquoise. Leather: Black, Beige, Gray, Yellow.

AT A GLANCE...

Category: rear-wheel drive luxury coupes, sedans & conv.   **Class :** 7

HISTORIC
Introduced in: 1982 (320i 2 p.) 1991, 1999.
Made in: Dingolfing, (Münich) Germany.

DEMOGRAPHICS

Model	Men./Wom.	Age	Married	College	Income
3-Series	70/30 %	40	65 %	58 %	$ 60 000

INDEX
Safety: 90 %   **Satisfaction:** 85 %
Depreciation: 40 %   **Insurance:** $ 1 350-1 765
Cost per mile: $ 0.68   **Number of dealers:** 350

SALES

Model	1996	1997	Result
3-Series	46 788	44 530	- 4.8 %

MAIN COMPETITORS
ACURA TL, AUDI A4, HONDA Accord, INFINITI I30, LEXUS ES 300, MAZDA Millenia, MERCEDES-BENZ C-Class, NISSAN Maxima, SAAB 9-3, TOYOTA Camry, VOLVO S80.

MAINTENANCE REQUIRED BY WARRANTY
First revision: 15 000 miles   **Frequency:** 15 000 miles   **Diagnostic plug:** Yes

SPECIFICATIONS

Model	Version Trim	Body/ Seats	Interior volume cu ft	Trunk volume cu ft	Cd	Wheel base in	Lght x Wdgth x Hght in x in x in	Curb weight lb	Susp. ft/rr	Brake ft/rr	Steering type	Turning diameter ft	Steer. turns nber.	Fuel tank gal	tire size	Standard tires make	model	Standard powertrain
BMW		General warranty : 4 years/ 50 000 miles; corrosion: 6 years / unlimited: antipollution: 8 years / 80 000 miles.																
318	ti	3dr.cpe. 4	2322	10.6	0.35	106.3	165.7x66.9x54.8	2778	ih/ih	dc/dr/ABS	pwr.r&p.	34.1	3.4	13.7	185/65SR15	Continental	Eco Plus	L4/1.9/M5
323*	**i**	**4dr.sdn. 4**	**NA**	**15.5**	**0.31**	**107.3**	**176.0x68.5x55.7**	**3152**	**ih/ih**	**dc/ABS**	**pwr.r&p.**	**34.4**	**3.4**	**16.6**	**195/65HR15**	**Michelin**	**Energy MXV4**	**L6/2.8/M5**
323	i	2dr.con. 4	2152	8.1	0.36	106.3	174.5x67.3x53.1	3296	ih/ih	dc/ABS	pwr.r&p.	35.4	3.4	16.4	205/60HR15	Bridgestone	Turanza	L6/2.5/M5
328*	**i**	**4dr.sdn. 4**	**NA**	**15.5**	**0.31**	**107.3**	**176.0x68.5x55.7**	**3197**	**ih/ih**	**dc/ABS**	**pwr.r&p.**	**34.4**	**3.4**	**16.6**	**205/55R16**	**Michelin**	**Energy MXV4**	**L6/2.8/M5**
328	i	2dr.con. 4	2152	8.1	0.36	106.3	174.5x67.3x53.1	3395	ih/ih	dc/ABS	pwr.r&p.	34.1	3.4	16.4	205/60HR15	Dunlop	SP 2000	L6/2.8/M5
M3		2dr.cpe. 4	2322	14.3	0.32	106.3	174.5x67.3x52.6	3175	ih/ih	dc/ABS	pwr.r&p.	38.0	3.4	16.4	225/45ZR17	Michelin	Pilot SX	L6/3.2/M5

* 1999 models

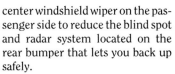

The 5-Series sits in the mid-range of the BMW lineup. It benefits from the 7-Series' engine prowess and from the 3-Series' trim format. But it's the 5-Series' overwhelming single-minded design that's so very impressive and puts it ahead of its closest rivals. Of course, for budget reasons, it can't be the most widespread car on the road, but that doesn't mean that, along with its rival, the Mercedes E320, it isn't one of most accomplished and polished cars currently being built worldwide.

MODEL RANGE

This year, the 5-Series is sold as a 4-door sedan and station wagon in 528i trim, equipped with a 2.8L 6-in-line engine developing 190 hp linked to a standard 5-speed manual gearbox or optional 4-speed automatic, or in 540i trim, driven by a 4.4L V8 that delivers 282 hp, paired up with either a 5-speed manual or automatic gearbox at no extra cost, or an optional 5-speed «Steptronic» borrowed from the 7-Series. Including a list of original equipment items here would be too long, but let's say it's very extensive.

TECHNICAL FEATURES

The steel monocoque body is made up mostly of galvanized panels and it's highly resistant to torsion and flexion. The front surface is quite substantial, but aerodynamic finesse is adequate with a drag coefficient varying between 0.30 and 0.31. To eliminate most exterior noise, doors are fittted with double-pane windows, some flat bodywork has been lined with aluminum and hollow components have been injected with expanding foam. The body itself isn't built of aluminum, but this metal has been used for suspension components, so the car now weighs 145 lbs less. The fully independent suspension consists of double-jointed struts and trailing arms up front and the rear axle is supported by cross struts and longitudinal struts and there's a stabilizer bar for front and rear axles. Four-wheel disc brakes benefit from a standard electronic antilock braking system that serves as traction control. These vehicles are equipped with a residual heat accumulator that provides warm air at 104 degrees Farenheit in less than 30 seconds, even if the car stays parked for two icy minus 4 degrees Farenheit days and it defrosts windows in no time flat. These cars also come equipped with six airbags, two

Perfect Blend...

front-impact and four side-impact airbags located inside the doors. Lastly, cast solid headlights include Xenon gas-discharge high beam lamps that provide excellent visibility without blinding on-coming drivers and they last longer than halogen lamps. The «Steptronic» automatic transmission can be adjusted to function automatically or in manual mode, without having to use a clutch pedal, as is the case for the famous Porsche Tiptronic.

PROS

+ **LOOKS.** This car is a refined thoroughbred that exhibits a perfect and subtle blend of typically BMW attributes and a modern, angular design, with grille integrated into the hood.

+ **RIDE COMFORT.** It's definitely come a long way, thanks to the silky

suspension, nicely shaped and cushy seats and an almost imperceptible noise level, the direct result of efficient soundproofing.

+ **STEERING.** It's smooth and nicely powered, so it provides superb maneuverability, in spite of a slightly high reduction ratio that sometimes makes it seem vague.

+ **PERFORMANCES.** They're above average for both engines that provide very comfortable accelerations and pickup, reassuring for safe travel. The 528's performances are quite adequate, but the 540 benefits from the V8's strength that's dauntless and raring to go.

+ **INNOVATIONS.** The 5-Series has inherited all kinds of gadgets and accessories from the 7, including heated steering wheel, six airbags, residual heat accumulator, off-

center windshield wiper on the passenger side to reduce the blind spot and radar system located on the rear bumper that lets you back up safely.

+ **CONVENIENCE FEATURES.** The trunk is deep and it's modular as well. Access is super due to its tapered opening, and there are lots of generous-size storage compartments throughout the cabin.

CONS

- **BUDGET.** It takes a pretty bundle to own one of these beauties. Purchase price, insurance and upkeep are extremely costly and frequent, expensive trips to the dealership are no reason to jump for joy. Besides, these cars depreciate quite a bit, so there again, you lose out, financially speaking.

- **ACCESS.** It's awkward getting into the rear seats and leg room is tight, especially if the front seats are pushed far back.

- **CABIN SPACE.** Even though it's more generous than on the former generation, it can't really compare with more modest cars that offer roomier passenger space.

- **IN POOR TASTE.** The Zebrano wood appliqués look like bizarre imitation wood and they've been discarded by other automakers for precisely this reason.

- **TRUNK.** It's so deep you have to climb into it to fetch objects that have shifted during transport.

- **CENTER CONSOLE.** It's very wide and less oriented towards the driver and some controls are almost out of reach.

- **REAR MIRRORS.** They're very tiny and don't provide good rear visibility.

- **CONTROLS.** Some of them are rather unusual and complicated, like the radio dials that require a crash course to be able to tune into your favorite station.

- **LEGIBILITY.** Instruments are hard to read at night, since the fluorescent lighting and the small, close-set numbers require real concentration on the part of the driver.

CONCLUSION

The 5-Series isn't the average person's car. It's an exceptional car, designed to appeal to exceptional people with a huge bank account. Only the lucky few will be able to enjoy the perfect blend it offers of zippy sports car temperament and lap of luxury, refined comfort. ☺

RATING
BMW 5-Series

CONCEPT		80%
Technology	90	
Safety :	90	
Interior space :	60	
Trunk volume:	70	
Quality/fit/finish :	90	

DRIVING:		72%
Cockpit :	80	
Performance :	75	
Handling :	60	
Steering :	80	
Braking :	65	

ORIGINAL EQUIPMENT:		85%
Tires :	85	
Headlights :	80	
Wipers :	85	
Rear defroster :	80	
Radio :	95	

COMFORT :		84%
Seats :	90	
Suspension :	90	
Sound level:	70	
Conveniences :	80	
Air conditioning :	90	

BUDGET :		47%
Price :	0	
Fuel economy :	55	
Insurance :	40	
Satisfaction :	85	
Depreciation :	55	

Overall rating: 73.6%

NEW FOR 1999

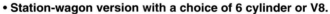

- Station-wagon version with a choice of 6 cylinder or V8.
- Better torque and power for all the powertrains.
- Navigational system available as an option.

ENGINES · TRANSMISSIONS · PERFORMANCES

Model/ version	Type / timing valve / fuel system	Displacement cu in	Power bhp @ rpm	Torque lb-ft @ rpm	Compres. ratio	Driving wheels / transmission	Final ratio	Acceler. 0-60 mph s	Standing 1/4 & 5/8 mile s	Acceler. 50-75 mph s	Braking 60-0 mph f	Top speed mph	Lateral acceler. G	Noise level dBA	Fuel economy mpg City	Fuel economy mpg Highway	Fuel type Octane
528i	L6* 2.8 DOHC-24-EFI	170	190 @ 5300	206 @ 3950	10.2 :1	rear - M5*	2.93	8.0	16.0 28.5	5.8	108	128	0.80	66-72	24.0	37.0	S 91
528iA	L6* 2.8 DOHC-24-EFI	170	190 @ 5300	206 @ 3950	10.2 :1	rear - A4	4.10	8.3	16.3 29.0	6.0	118	128	0.80	66-72	22.0	34.0	S 91
540i	V8* 4.4 DOHC-32-EFI	268	282 @ 5700	310 @ 3900	10.0 :1	rear - M5	2.93	6.7	14.8 26.6	4.8	108	155	0.81	64-70	18.0	31.0	S 91
540iA	V8* 4.4 DOHC-32-EFI	268	282 @ 5700	310 @ 3900	10.0 :1	rear - A5	2.81	7.0	15.2 27.2	5.2	128	128	0.81	64-70	21.0	32.0	S 91

PRICE & EQUIPMENT

BMW 5-Series	528i	540i
Retail price $:	38,900	50,500
Dealer invoice $:	34,490	44,225
Shipping & handling $:	570	570
Automatic transmission:	O	NC
Cruise control:	S	S
Power steering:	S	S
Anti-lock brakes:	S	S
Traction control:	S	S
Air conditioning:	S	S
Leather:	O	S
AM/FM/radio-cassette:	S	S
Power door locks:	S	S
Power windows:	S	S
Tilt steering:	S	S
Dual adjustable mirrors:	S	S
Alloy wheels:	S	S
Anti-theft system:	S	S

Colors
Exterior: White, Red, Green, Black, Silver, Blue, Gray, Beige.

Interior: Black, Gray, Ultramarine, Parchment.

AT A GLANCE...

Category: rear wheel drive luxury sedans   **Class :** 7

HISTORIC
Introduced in: 1972
Made in: Dingolfingen,(Münich) Germany.

DEMOGRAPHICS

Model	Men./Wom.	Age	Married	College	Income
5-Series	89/11 %	45	82 %	75 %	$90 000

INDEX
Safety:	90 %	**Satisfaction:**	85 %
Depreciation:	45 %	**Insurance:**	$ 1 700-1 850
Cost permile:	$ 0.97	**Number of dealers:**	350

SALES

Model	1997	1997	Result
5-Series	22 775	31 347	+ 37.6 %

MAIN COMPETITORS
ACURA RL, AUDI A6, CADILLAC STS, LEXUS GS 300-400, LINCOLN Continental, MERCEDES-BENZ E-Class, OLDSMOBILE Aurora, SAAB 9-5, VOLVO 90.

MAINTENANCE REQUIRED BY WARRANTY
First revision:	Frequency:	Diagnostic plug:
15 000 miles	15 000 miles	Yes

SPECIFICATIONS

Model	Version Trim	Body/ Seats	Interior volume cu ft	Trunk volume cu ft	Cd	Wheel base in	Lght x Wdgth x Hght in x in x in	Curb weight lb	Susp. ft/rr	Brake ft/rr	Steering type	Turning diameter ft	Steer. turns nber.	Fuel tank gal	tire size	Standard tires make	model	Standard powertrain
BMW	General warranty : 4 years/ 50 000 miles; corrosion: 6 years / unlimited: antipollution: 8 years / 80 000 miles.																	
528i		4dr.sdn. 5	91.0	16.2	0.30	111.4	188.0x70.9x56.5	3450	i/idc/dc/ABS	pwr.r&p.	37.1	3.5	18.5	225/60HR15	Michelin	Energy	L6/2.8/M5
540i		4dr.sdn. 5	91.0	16.2	0.31	111.4	188.0x70.9x56.5	3748	i/idc/dc/ABS	pwr.r&p.	37.1	3.5	18.5	225/55HR16	Michelin	Energy	V8/4.4/A5

When BMW reworked its 7-Series in 1995, it came up with a whole new definition of a big luxury car. Its eternal rival, the Mercedes-Benz S-Class, had a more imposing, less graceful format that potential buyers didn't care for and so the carmaker had to keep touching up this model, until it finally made up its mind to replace it earlier than expected by a model of exactly the same size as the current BMW 7-Series. So sales for the big BMW are almost the same as those of its rival, an all-time first...

MODEL RANGE

The 7-Series consists of three 4-door sedans. The 740 equipped with a 4.4L V8 is offered in short (i) or long (iL) wheelbase versions, whereas the 750iL animated by a 5.4L V12 is only available in a long wheelbase version. Besides all the electronic driving aids, equipment on these models is as refined and innovative as it gets, since there's a heated steering wheel where radio and telephone controls are located, while 750 iL rear seat passengers are protected by a privacy curtain and all doors are fitted with individual footrests. This year a navigation system is added to the list of options for all models.

TECHNICAL FEATURES

The 7-Series' success lies in the magic rendered by BMW stylists who succeeded in trimming down its size while refining its overall body design, yielding good aerodynamics, since the drag coefficient is 0.31 even with the wide front end. The body is very resistant to torsion and flexion, which provides a solid base for both powertrains. The fully independent suspension includes struts up front and a multi-arm axle at the rear, including anti-dive and anti-lift geometry. Four-wheel vented disc brakes are paired up with an ABS-traction control system, to which can be added an optional, highly evolved (DSC) antiskid system that makes the car neutral on curves, in the event of driver error or rough fallout from poor road surfaces. Self-adjusting shock absorbers include a rear load-levelling device. Both engines are linked to a 5-speed «Steptronic» automatic gearbox that includes manual or

A New Standard...

automatic shifter and so is coined adaptive, since its programming adjusts to road conditions and to the pilot's driving style by anticipating speed shifts.

PROS

+ TECHNICAL COMPONENTS. They're high-brow sophisticates right down to the last detail, be it in regard to high performance, equipment items or safety features. Several safety devices ensure exceptional passenger protection, such as 6 airbags that provide complete front-impact protection, as well as side-impact protection to offset head, chest and hip injuries. Besides, all the driving aid systems provide remarkable stability, whatever the situation.

+ PERFORMANCES. They're comparable to those of a Grand Tourism coupe, yielding rather high acceleration scores, all achieved in cool comfort and style. Putting this competent and well-honed engine through its paces is a real treat, even with the rather hefty vehicle weight and size.

+ HANDLING. The car is really neutral and stable in reasonable circumstances, since all those electronic parameter controls don't amount to much against an idiotic driver out to prove them wrong.

+ SAFETY. It's at an all-time high, including passive and active passenger protection devices, which makes for relaxed, reassuring driving in tough situations, since the driver has complete control of the vehicle.

+ RIDE COMFORT. It's very refined, with a neither too firm nor too flexible suspension, perfectly shaped front seats, adjustable rear seatbench and truly superb-quality sound dampening.

+ DUAL PERSONALITY. The 750iL is both a creamy, pearls and tux limo or a zoomy sporty car that takes its weight and size in its stride, so driving one of these babies is a real joy, a rare treat in this car class.

+ CABIN DESIGN. The design is more warm and cozy than inside its rival Mercedes S-Class. Finish touches have flair and feeling and are inspired by Jaguar or Maserati traits, like the lovely folds in the leather seat covers, wood appliqués and attractive shades used.

+ QUALITY. It's incredibly impressive: construction, fit and finish job and trim materials are absolutely impeccable.

+ CONVENIENCE FEATURES. The 7-Series is loaded with clever storage compartments scattered throughout the cabin and the trunk can swallow up quite a few Vuitton valises...

CONS

- BUDGET. You have to have above-average income or a very understanding bank manager to buy, maintain, insure and pay gas bills for these models.

- COMPLEXITY. It takes a lot of patience and a comfortable I.Q. to quickly know how to master functions and controls on a 7-Series car. Besides, typically European controls do take some getting used to, especially the sound system or climate control that are a bit of a mystery to non-Germanic minds.

CONCLUSION

The BMW 7-Series sets a new standard for a luxury car that's modern, safe, zippy, competent and refined to the extreme. Not surprising that its success far outstrips that of former models and even has the big Mercedes a bit on edge. ☺

RATING
BMW 7-Series

CONCEPT :		**92%**
Technology	100	
Safety :	100	
Interior space :	80	
Trunk volume:	80	
Quality/fit/finish :	100	
DRIVING:		**78%**
Cockpit :	90	
Performance :	75	
Handling :	75	
Steering :	85	
Braking :	65	
ORIGINAL EQUIPMENT:		**87%**
Tires :	90	
Headlights :	90	
Wipers :	85	
Rear defroster :	80	
Radio :	90	
COMFORT :		**87%**
Seats :	90	
Suspension :	90	
Sound level :	80	
Conveniences :	90	
Air conditioning :	85	
BUDGET :		**38%**
Price :	0	
Fuel economy :	30	
Insurance :	25	
Satisfaction :	85	
Depreciation :	50	
Overall rating:		**76.4%**

NEW FOR 1999

- A few light touches on the front end, including headlamp and grille design and aerodynamic spoiler.
- Navigation system offered as an extra.

ENGINES — TRANSMISSIONS — PERFORMANCES

Model/ version	Type / timing valve / fuel system	Displacement cu in	Power bhp @ rpm	Torque lb-ft @ rpm	Compres. ratio	Driving wheels / transmission	Final ratio	Acceler. 0-60 mph s	Standing 1/4 & 5/8 mile s	Acceler. 50-75 mph s	Braking 60-0 mph f	Top speed mph	Lateral acceler. G	Noise level dBA	Fuel economy mpg City	Highway	Fuel type Octane
740i/iL	V8* 4.4 DOHC-32-MFI	268	282 @ 5700	324 @ 3700	10.0 :1	rear - A5*	2.93	8.0	15.9	28.4	5.7	125	128*	0.82	64-70	17	26	S 91
750iL	V12* 5.4 SOHC-24-MFI	328	322 @ 5000	361 @ 3900	10.0 :1	rear - A5*	2.81	7.0	14 8	27.8	5.0	131	128*	0.81	64-70	15	22	S 91

PRICE & EQUIPMENT

BMW 7-Series	740i/iL	750iL
Retail price $:	61,500 / 65,500	92,100
Dealer invoice $:	54,495 / 57,345	80,100
Shipping & handling $:	570	570
Automatic transmission:	S	S
Cruise control:	S	S
Power steering:	S	S
Anti-lock brakes:	S	S
Traction control:	S	S
Air conditioning:	S	S
Leather:	S	S
AM/FM/radio-cassette:	S	S
Power door locks:	S	S
Power windows:	S	S
Tilt steering:	S	S
Dual adjustable mirrors:	S	S
Alloy wheels:	S	S
Anti-theft system:	S	S

Colors

Exterior: White, Red, Green, Black, Silver, Blue, Gray, Beige, Crimson.

Interior: Black, Gray, Beige, Marine.

AT A GLANCE...

Category:	rear-wheel drive luxury sedans.	Class :	7

HISTORIC
Introduced in: 1986-1997.
Made in: Dingolfing, (Münich) Germany.

DEMOGRAPHICS
Model	Men./Wom.	Age	Married	College	Income
7-Series	92/8 %	56	93 %	66 %	$ 150 000

INDEX
Safety:	100 %	Satisfaction:	87 %
Depreciation:	50 %	Insurance:	$ 2 325-3 650
Cost per mile:	$ 1.60	Number of dealers:	350

SALES
Model	1996	1997	Result
7-Series	17 174	18 273	+ 6.4 %

MAIN COMPETITORS
AUDI A8, CADILLAC Seville STS, INFINITI Q45, JAGUAR XJ8, LEXUS LS 400, MERCEDES -BENZ S-Class.

MAINTENANCE REQUIRED BY WARRANTY
First revision:	Frequency:	Diagnostic plug:
15 000 miles	15 000 miles	Yes

SPECIFICATIONS

Model	Version Trim	Body/ Seats	Interior volume cu ft	Trunk volume cu ft	Cd	Wheel base in	Lght x Wdgth x Hght in x in x in	Curb weight lb	Susp. ft/rr	Brake ft/rr	Steering type	Turning diameter ft	Steer. turns nber.	Fuel tank gal	tire size	Standard tires make	model	Standard powertrain
BMW		General warranty : 4 years/ 50 000 miles; corrosion: 6 years / unlimited: antipollution: 8 years / 80 000 miles.																
740	i	4dr.sdn. 5	105	17.6	0.31	115.4	196.2x73.3x56.5	4255	ih/ih	dc/ABS	pwr.ball	38.1	3.5	22.5	235/60HR16	Michelin	MXV4 XSE	V8/4.4/A5
740	iL	4dr.sdn. 5	105	17.6	0.31	120.9	201.7x73.3x56.1	4288	ih/ih	dc/ABS	pwr.ball	40.0	3.5	22.5	235/60HR16	Michelin	MXV4 XSE	V8/4.4/A5
750	iL	4dr.sdn. 5	105	17.6	0.32	120.9	201.7x73.3x56.1	4559	ih/ih	dc/ABS	pwr.ball	40.0	3.5	25.1	235/60HR16	Michelin	MXV4 XSE	V12/5.4/A5

The Z3 roadster put fresh new wind in the sails of the BMW lineup that had for so long included only cool, conventional sedans and sports coupes that lacked pizzazz. Even the 3-Series convertible hadn't changed much and life followed its untrammelled and quiet course. Since this roadster's really spectacular launch, it has become solidly established among popular, high-performance models and has gained more and more attention with each more muscular version that hits the market.

MODEL RANGE

The 1999 Z3 is available in four versions: a special-order coupe and three roadsters: the base model equipped with the 323's 2.5L 6-cylinder engine, the 2.8 powered by the 328's 2.8L engine or the M animated by the M3 engine, with 5-speed manual transmission. Original equipment on the base model includes power steering, anti-lock braking system, power locks, windows and mirrors, radio-cassette player, light alloy rims and anti-roll bars that offer better passenger protection if ever the car flips over. The 2.8 and M are also fitted with power roof device, air conditioning, cruise control, traction control, leather trim, heated seats, CD changer and theft-deterrent system.

TECHNICAL FEATURES

The Z3 is built on the pared down 318i convertible platform. Models differ according to rim design and some exterior accessories or flared touches on the body. The body consists of a steel monocoque shell with some panels that are galvanized on both sides. Build is super solid and fairly light. The windshield frame acts as a roll bar up front and there are also the very same self-deploying roll bars that equip the 3-Series convertibles. Suspensions are inspired by those of the latest M3 model. Up front there are MacPherson struts and arc-shaped lower arms, while there's a rear classic semi-trailing arm setup, with various-design coil springs, shock absorbers, anti-roll bars and links according to model. Four-wheel disc brakes are paired up with a standard ABS device. Traction control distributes torque to the wheel offering the best grip, according to accelerations and braking maneuvers.

Traditional Treat

PROS

+ STYLE. It's sleek yet it's a BMW beauty. Its design is a clever blend of modern and retro touches, a mix of current technical musts and traditional roadster attributes.

+ PERFORMANCES. The 2.8 and M versions are brawnier than the base model, but the V6 engine doesn't achieve the performances you get in a Miata, at least technically speaking. Accelerations and pickup range from normal to zoomy. The M model's 240-hp engine is so lively that you have to keep an eye on things if you don't want to get tracked down by radar... The best compromise is still the 2.8 model that's motivated by a smooth, slick engine that doesn't burn too much petrol.

+ DRIVING PLEASURE. It's just great with the low-slung driver's seat, exhaust roar and wind effect that makes you feel like you're in a road rocket. And the manual shifter is a real treat...

+ STEERING. It's nearly perfect. It's right-on precise, benefits from ideal assistance and reduction ratio and a short steer angle diameter really makes for clean moves.

+ HANDLING. Competent thanks to the sophisticated suspension and great-grip tires that perform like champions even on poor road surfaces. On slalom runs, the car exhibits agility and aplomb and handles curves beautifully, but watch your foot on the accelerator on damp roads, otherwise the rear end tends to slide even with traction control.

+ BRAKES. Easy to gauge, they achieve very short emergency stops and they're stable and tough as nails.

+ RIDE COMFORT. The suspension and seats are firm, but not unpleasant in the long run and the optional air deflector shunts wind nicely when the top is down.

+ CONVENIENCE FEATURES. They're pretty good, really. The trunk may be fairly small, but it holds two suitcases and a travel bag and the cabin includes enough storage spots.

CONS

- ROOFTOP. It's pretty basic, it isn't lined, doesn't hold up against the wet outdoors (above the side windows) and it's fitted with a plastic rear window, incredible when the one on the less pricey Miata is made of glass and includes an electric defroster. Lastly, the roof cover is hell to install and its design is pretty homespun, nothing like what you'd expect from a factory-made item.

- NOISE. Noise becomes a real pain on the highway because the rooftop isn't lined and body soundproofing is pretty thin.

- CONTROLS. Some switches are poorly located, like the power window switches on the center console and especially the steering column that isn't adjustable and doesn't budge one bloody bit.

- ROAD AUTONOMY. With a meager 13 gallon gas tank, the Z3 can cover 250 miles or less, which is pretty tight for highway hauls.

- QUALITY. Finish details and trim material texture are spiffier on the 2.8 and M than on the base model. The lower end model is a poor church mouse in comparison.

- TO BE IMPROVED UPON: low beam headlights are less effective than high beam, poorly located battery that's hard to remove.

CONCLUSION

The Z3 offers three types of driving thrills, depending on the various V6 models. BMW provides driving pleasure in a less austere and pretty swanky-looking roadster. But we wonder if the wide model choice is a wise move, given the slim market segment?... 😐

RATING
BMW Z3

CONCEPT :		57%
Technology	85	
Safety :	80	
Interior space :	20	
Trunk volume:	20	
Quality/fit/finish :	80	

DRIVING:		82%
Cockpit :	80	
Performance :	75	
Handling :	75	
Steering :	90	
Braking :	90	

ORIGINAL EQUIPMENT:		64%
Tires :	85	
Headlights :	75	
Wipers :	80	
Rear defroster :	0	
Radio :	80	

COMFORT :		64%
Seats :	80	
Suspension :	60	
Sound level :	50	
Conveniences :	50	
Air conditioning :	80	

BUDGET :		54%
Price :	10	
Fuel economy :	70	
Insurance :	45	
Satisfaction :	80	
Depreciation :	65	

Overall rating: **64.2%**

NEW FOR 1999

- The special-order coupe.
- The new 2.5L engine replacing the 1.9L on the Z3 base model.
- A navigation system offered as an extra.

ENGINES / TRANSMISSIONS / PERFORMANCES

Model/ version	Type / timing valve / fuel system	Displacement cu in	Power bhp @ rpm	Torque lb-ft @ rpm	Compres. ratio	Driving wheels / transmission	Final ratio	Acceler. 0-60 mph s	Standing 1/4 & 5/8 mile s		Acceler. 50-75 mph s	Braking 60-0 mph f	Top speed mph	Lateral acceler. G	Noise level dBA	Fuel economy mpg City	Highway	Fuel type Octane
Z3 2.3	L6* 2.5 DOHC-24-EFI	152	168 @ 5500	181 @ 3950	10.5 :1	rear - M5*	2.93	8.0	15.7	27.0	6.8	121	125	0.86	68-75	22	32	S 91
						rear - A4	2.93	8.9	16.5	28.4	7.0	125	118	0.86	68-76	19	29	S 91
Z3 2.8	L6* 2.8 DOHC-24-EFI	170	189 @ 5300	203 @ 3950	10.2 :1	rear - M5*	3.15	7.0	15.4	28.0	5.6	121	131	0.87	67-74	19	27	S 91
						rear - A4	4.10	7.8	16.0	28.4	6.0	125	124	0.87	67-74	18	27	S 91
Z3 M	L6* 3.2 DOHC-24-EFI	192	240 @ 6000	236 @ 3800	10.5 :1	rear - M5*	3.23	6.6	15.0	26.2	4.8	121	137	0.88	68-75	20	30	S 91

PRICE & EQUIPMENT

BMW Z3	2.3	2.8	M
Retail price $:	29,425	35,900	42,200
Dealer invoice $:	26,015	31,555	37,065
Shipping & handling $:	570	570	570
Automatic transmission:	O	O	-
Cruise control:	O	S	S
Power steering:	S	S	S
Anti-lock brakes:	S	S	S
Traction control:	O	S	S
Air conditioning:	O	S	S
Leather:	O	S	S
AM/FM/radio-cassette:	S	S CD	S CD
Power door locks:	S	S	S
Power windows:	S	S	S
Tilt steering:	-	S	-
Dual adjustable mirrors:	S	S	S
Alloy wheels:	S	S	S
Anti-theft system:	O	S	S

Colors
Exterior: Violet-Red, Red, Green, Black, White, Silver, Blue.

Interior: Cloth : Anthracite-black, Blue-black, Green-black. Leatherette :Black-Gray
Leather : Black, Violet-black, Red-black, Green-beige, 2 tone beige.

AT A GLANCE...

Category: rear-wheel drive sports convertible & coupes.   **Class :** 3S

HISTORIC
Introduced in: 1997
Made in: Spartanburg (North Carolina) USA.

DEMOGRAPHICS
Model	Men./Wom.	Age	Married	College	Income
Z3	NA				

INDEX
Safety:	80 %	Satisfaction:	80 %
Depreciation:	35% (2 years)	Insurance:	$1300-1500
Cost per mile:	$ 0.72-80	Number of dealers:	350

SALES
Model	1996	1997	Result
Z3	Not on the market at that time		

MAIN COMPETITORS
BMW 318i, MAZDA Miata, MERCEDES-BENZ SLK, PORSCHE Boxster.

MAINTENANCE REQUIRED BY WARRANTY
First revision:	Frequency:	Diagnostic plug:
15 000 miles	15 000 miles	Yes

SPECIFICATIONS

General warranty : 4 years/ 50 000 miles; corrosion: 6 years / unlimited: antipollution: 8 years / 80 000 miles.

Model	Version Trim	Body/ Seats	Interior volume cu ft	Trunk volume cu ft	Cd	Wheel base in	Lght x Wdgth x Hght in x in x in	Curb weight lb	Susp. ft/rr	Brake ft/rr	Steering type	Turning diameter ft	Steer. turns nber.	Fuel tank gal	tire size	Standard tires make	model	Standard powertrain
BMW																		
Z3	2.3	2dr.con. 2	NA	5.8	0.41	96.3	158.5x66.6x50.7	2689	i/i	dc/ABS	pwr.r&p.	32.8	3.0	13.5	225/50ZR16	Michelin	Pilot MXM	L6/2.3/M5
		2dr.con. 2	NA	5.8	0.41	96.3	158.5x66.6x50.7	2766	i/i	dc/ABS	pwr.r&p.	32.8	3.0	13.5	225/50ZR16	Michelin	Pilot MXM	L6/2.3/A4
Z3	2.8	2dr.con. 2	NA	5.8	0.42	96.3	158.5x68.5x50.9	2778	i/i	dc/ABS	pwr.r&p.	34.1	3.0	13.5	225/45ZR17	Dunlop	SP 8000	L6/2.8/M5
		2dr.con. 2	NA	5.8	0.42	96.3	158.5x68.5x50.9	2866	i/i	dc/ABS	pwr.r&p.	34.1	3.0	13.5	re.245/40ZR17	Dunlop	SP 8000	L6/2.8/A4
Z3	M	2dr.con. 2	NA	5.8	0.42	96.3	158.5x68.5x50.9	2976	i/i	dc/ABS	pwr.r&p.	34.1	3.0	13.5	same	Dunlop	SP 8000	L6/3.2/M5

Now that a full year has run its course, we can say that General Motors made the right bid. This year, the Century-Regal siblings have had the same success as the Oldsmobile Intrigue and the Pontiac Grand Prix. This North American automaker has always favored the midsize model range, up until Ford launched the Taurus. Since then, the cards have changed hands and the Century-Regal combination presently held by GM seems to be more promising.

MODEL RANGE

The Century has really become the lower end model in the Buick line since the demise of the Skylark, but it's especially suited to the fleet car and car rental market niche. The Regal is more geared to scoring against the Camry and Accord, its more obviously targeted rivals. These four-door sedans are offered in Custom or Limited trim for the Century and in LS or GS for the Regal. The first two models are equipped with a 160 hp 3.1L V6 engine, while the third model gets the umpteenth version of the legendary 3.8L conventional gas engine delivering 195 hp or the supercharged version that pumps out 240 hp. Standard equipment on these cars is quite lush, even on the low end version, since it includes automatic transmission, power steering, ABS linked to traction control, climate control, power windows and locks, tilt steering wheel and theft deterrent system.

TECHNICAL FEATURES

The Century-Regal models are built on the latest revamped W platform and are equipped with a steel monocoque body fitted with numerous panels galvanized on both sides except for the roof panel. These cars are sleek, but aerodynamics aren't record-shattering by any means, not with a drag coefficient of 0.32. The fully independent suspension is made up of a MacPherson strut setup up front and struts at the rear with a stabilizer bar on both powertrains. The Century is equipped with disc/drum brakes, whereas the Regal comes with four-wheel disc brakes; yet ABS linked to traction control is standard on both models. The front wheel drive feature has been around for many years. Yet it's the 3.8L engine that's the outstanding element because of its well-reputed reliability and sheer muscle, in either conventional or supercharged format. Climate con-

A Winning Hand...

trol includes a dust and pollen filter system, the battery has an anti-discharge control switch, a device prevents the starter from working when the engine is running and variable assist steering comes standard on the Regal but as an extra on the Century Limited.

PROS

+ VALUE. The fact that so much equipment comes at such an affordable price makes even the most basic car very appealing indeed and explains why the car manages to maintain an above-average resale value.

+ STYLE. The Century and Regal are elegant and very much in keeping with a classic approach, with no added frills, so they shouldn't go out of style for many a moon.

+ RIDE COMFORT. The roomy

BUICK Century Custom
BUICK Century Custom

cabin comfortably seats five passengers. Seats are nicely shaped and upholstered and the noise level is decent, since discreet.

+ FUEL ECONOMY. These engines have been around for quite a while, yet fuel intake is frugal considering engine performance range. The zippy 3.8L supercharged engine accelerates better than several so-called sporty cars and gives it the few precious seconds' edge, yet this powerplant is known for its pristine reliability.

+ ROADHANDLING. Thanks to firmer suspensions and good-quality shocks, the Regal handles well in most circumstances.

+ BRAKES. The Regal, equipped with four-wheel disc brakes, stops in a reassuring way, since panic stops at 60 mph are achieved on average in slightly more than 135ft.

The brake pedal is clean and gradual, so brake control is easy to manage.

+ CONVENIENCE FEATURES. This is a great car for practical, everyday use. There are loads of storage compartments and the trunk is really roomy and easy to get to with the nice and wide trunk lid.

+ NICE FEATURES. For once it's a pleasure to point out that headlights really cut it either on low or high beam, that rather quick and slick windshield wipers clean most of the window surface and that climate control is quick on the draw in providing heat or cold, although the blower is a bit weak.

CONS

- QUALITY. Interior design and trim materials have come a long way, but these car models are still far below Japanese products when it comes to assembly and finish standards and component reliability. This is the result of a long and difficult process that North American car builders have been up against for a number of years.

- SUSPENSION. The suspension that equips the Century is so spongy that it reminds you of those dreamboats of yore. The ride is smooth on the ribbon of highway, but elsewhere you're in for a rough trip, since there's a whole lot of swaying going on, which ends up affecting handling and comfort level on curved roads or rough surfaces. Seasickness guaranteed.

- BRAKES. Rear drum brakes on the Century don't provide for really effective stops compared to those achieved by the four-wheel disc brakes on the Regal. Emergency stops stretch out and linings just don't hold up to intensive use.

- TIRES. The original General tires that equip the Century aren't the perfect fit for this car, since grip gets pretty wishy washy on slippery surfaces.

- TO BE IMPROVED UPON. The Century's hohum cabin interior, air vents, multi-control shifter that's so complicated it's a real pain to use, stubby speed shifter, no center armrest in the rear seat nor a convertible trunk on the Century.

CONCLUSION

By deciding to opt for a new way of designing and fitting the product to market demands (an approach initiated mostly by Japanese automakers), General Motors has come up with a winning hand, since it tried to offer a product with a winning personality and real intrinsic value. ☺

RATING
BUICK Century - Regal

CONCEPT:		80%
Technology :	75	
Safety :	90	
Interior space :	80	
Trunk volume:	75	
Quality/fit/finish :	80	

DRIVING:		65%
Cockpit :	80	
Performance :	70	
Handling :	50	
Steering :	80	
Braking :	45	

ORIGINAL EQUIPMENT:		79%
Tires :	75	
Headlights :	85	
Wipers :	80	
Rear defroster :	75	
Radio :	80	

COMFORT :		74%
Seats :	75	
Suspension :	80	
Sound level :	60	
Conveniences :	75	
Air conditioning :	80	

BUDGET :		60%
Price :	45	
Fuel economy :	65	
Insurance :	65	
Satisfaction :	75	
Depreciation :	50	

Overall rating:		71.6%

NEW FOR 1999

- Main control unit for ABS and traction control.
- New added shade: Auburn Nightmist Pearl.
- Standard tire pressure control system.
- Concert Sound III sound system (Century).
- Sportier suspension on the base model Regal LS.
- More efficient coolant fan.

ENGINES / TRANSMISSIONS / PERFORMANCES

Model/ version	Type / timing valve / fuel system	Displacement cu in	Power bhp @ rpm	Torque lb-ft @ rpm	Compres. ratio	Driving wheels / transmission	Final ratio	Acceler. 0-60 mph s	Standing 1/4 & 5/8 mile s		Acceler. 50-75 mph s	Braking 60-0 mph f	Top speed mph	Lateral acceler. G	Noise level dBA	Fuel economy mpg City	Highway	Fuel type Octane
Century	V6* 3.1 OHV-12-SFI	191	160 @ 5200	185 @ 4000	9.6:1	front - A4	3.29	9.8	17.6	32.0	7.7	167	106	0.75	66	20	30	R 87
Regal LS	V6* 3.8 OHV-12-SFI	231	200 @ 5200	225 @ 4000	9.4:1	front - A4	3.05	8.3	16.2	29.4	5.9	151	109	0.77	64-68	19	32	R 87
Regal GS	V6C* 3.8 OHV-12-SFI	231	240 @ 5200	280 @ 3600	8.5:1	front - A4	2.93	7.7	15.7	28.5	5.3	138	115	0.77	64-67	17	29	S 91

PRICE & EQUIPMENT

BUICK Century	Custom	Ltd		
BUICK Regal			**LS**	**GS**
Retail price $:	18,415	19,775	21,045	23,790
Dealer invoice $:	17,218	18,731	19,256	21,768
Shipping & handling $:	550	550	550	550
Automatic transmission:	S	S	S	S
Cruise control:	O	S	S	S
Power steering:	S	S	S	S
Anti-lock brakes:	S	S	S	S
Traction control:	S	S	S	S
Air conditioning:	SM	SM	S	S
Leather:	-	O	O	S
AM/FM/radio-cassette:	O	S	S	S
Power door locks:	S	S	S	S
Power windows:	S	S	S	S
Tilt steering:	S	S	S	S
Dual adjustable mirrors:	O	SE	SE	SE
Alloy wheels:	O	O	O	S
Anti-theft system:	S	S	S	S

Colors
Exterior: Gray, White, Blue, Black, Red, Green, Sand, Auburn.

Interior: Gray, Blue, Red, Taupe.

AT A GLANCE...

Category:	front-wheel drive mid-size sedans.			Class : 5

HISTORIC
Introduced in:	Century: 1981, Regal: 1987 renewed in 1997
Made in:	Oshawa, Ontario, Canada

DEMOGRAPHICS
Model	Men./Wom.	Age	Married	College	Income
Century	72/28 %	70	68 %	26 %	$27 000
Regal	82/18 %	64	80 %	31 %	$34 000

INDEX
Safety:	C:NA-R:NA	Satisfaction:	-
Depreciation:	C:50%-R:55%	Insurance:	$825-950
Cost per mile:	C:$0.45-R:$0.58	Number of dealers:	3 000

SALES
Model	1996	1997	Result
Century	72 433	91 232	+ 26.0 %
Regal	86 847	50 691	- 41.6 %

MAIN COMPETITORS
CHEVROLET Lumina, CHRYSLER Concorde-Intrepid, FORD Taurus, HONDA Accord, HYUNDAI Sonata V6, MAZDA 626, MERCURY Sable, NISSAN Maxima, OLDSMOBILE Intrigue, PONTIAC Grand Prix, TOYOTA Camry, VW Passat.

MAINTENANCE REQUIRED BY WARRANTY
First revision:	Frequency:	Diagnostic plug:
3 000 miles	6 000 miles	Yes

SPECIFICATIONS

Model	Version Trim	Body/ Seats	Interior volume cu ft	Trunk volume cu ft	Cd	Wheel base in	Lght x Wdgth x Hght in x in x in	Curb weight lb	Susp. ft/rr	Brake ft/rr	Steering type	Turning diameter ft	Steer. turns nber.	Fuel tank gal	tire size	Standard tires make	model	Standard powertrain
BUICK	General warranty: 3 years / 40 000 miles; antipollution: 5 years / 50 000 miles; perforation corrosion: 6 years / 100 000 miles. Road assistance.																	
Century	Custom	4dr.sdn. 6	102	16.7	0.32	109.0	194.6x72.7x56.6	3335	ih/ih	dc/dr/ABS	pwr.r&p.	37.5	3.04	17.5	205/70R15	General	Ameri G4S	V6/3.1/A4
Century	Limited	4dr.sdn. 6	102	16.7	0.32	109.0	194.6x72.7x56.6	3371	ih/ih	dc/dr/ABS	pwr.r&p.	37.5	3.04	17.5	205/70R15	General	Ameri G4S	V6/3.1/A4
Regal	LS	4dr.sdn. 5	102	16.7	0.33	109.0	196.2x72.7x56.6	3439	ih/ih	dc/ABS	pwr.r&p.	37.5	2.39	17.5	215/70R15	GoodYear	Eagle LS	V6/3.8/A4
Regal	GS	4dr.sdn. 5	102	16.7	0.33	109.0	196.2x72.7x56.6	3543	ih/ih	dc/ABS	pwr.r&p.	37.5	2.39	17.5	225/60R16	GoodYear	Eagle LS	V6C/3.8/A4

The Buick LeSabre is a classic example of extreme conservatism in the automobile industry. For years it's been one of the top sellers and so when GM began updating this model, it did so with minor hesitant touches, so as not to displease its particular group of buyers. This model still rakes in 40% of sales in this market segment and is still a crowd pleaser because of its traditional looks, performance and maintenance budget.

MODEL RANGE
This midsize classic car is sold as a four-door sedan in Custom and Limited trim, as well as a set of options called Grand Touring that includes a shorter axle ratio allowing for zippier acceleration. The car is powered by a 3.8L Series II V6, one of the best on the market when it comes to fuel economy. Standard equipment is rich since it includes just about everything even on the lower end Custom model, except for traction control, leather trim seats, radio-tapedeck and light allow rims.

TECHNICAL FEATURES
The LeSabre shares the Oldsmobile 88 and Pontiac Bonneville H-series platform, as well as most of the same mechanical components and a few body and window stylistic features. Its steel monocopque body, fitted with some panels that are galvanized on both sides, is now stiffer and sturdier to meet current safety standards, especially in regard to side impact protection. Even with a sleeker silhouette, the drag coefficient is still average. The fully independent suspension includes MacPherson struts up front and a Chapman strut with coil springs and stabilizer bar at the rear. The disc-drum brake system is linked to ABS on all models, even on the slightly more powerful Grand Touring model.

PROS
+ STYLE. The car is definitely very conventional when it comes to looks, but with such predictable and familiar stylistic touches, it no doubt appeals to the target market.

+ CABIN VOLUME. The cabin and trunk on this model car are a tad less generous than those on the defunct Roadmaster. Theoretically you're supposed to be able to accomodate six travellers, but in fact, four passengers will be infinitely more comfy.

+ PERFORMANCE. Pretty impressive all-round, since accelerations

Retromobile...

and pickup are unusual for this type of vehicle. This is due to a favorable 17 lbs/hp power to weight ratio, worthy of more exotic models.

+ MECHANICAL FEATURES
The good old 3.8L engine is of simple and straightforward design and it does its stuff, yielding good power and torque with ease and fuel consuption that's still within a reasonable range, if you don't gun it too often. It's linked to one of the best transmissions on the market, driven by a smooth shifter that downshifts beautifully.

+ RIDE COMFORT. It's what you get mostly due to the velvety powderpuff suspension and low noise level, so you feel in a kind of dreamy state on long hauls.

+ CONTROLS. Controls located on the steering wheel on the upper end models are convenient since there aren't too many of them and they're simple to use.

+ EQUIPMENT. It includes all the trimmings even on the base trim model and includes many accessories that are usually offered as options.

+ NICE FEATURES. Bright and powerful high and low beam headlamps and rather impressive maneuverability for a vehicle of this size, as well as climate control fitted with individual controls for driver and front seat passenger.

CONS

- HANDLING. The super cushy suspension that hails back to a bygone era generates a lot of unpleasant sway and it goes haywire on poor pavement.

- TIRES. The Goodyear Eagle GA tires on our test car aren't the greatest choice for this model, since their grip is far from perfect even on dry surfaces, and they're noisy as heck.

- STEERING. It's over-assisted so you don't have any road feel and besides it's vague at the center.

- BRAKES. Brake efficiency is only average with those ever so long telltale stopping distances and linings that kick up a fuss when put to the test. The simplistic ABS system doesn't control wheel lock as it should and the elastic pedal makes it tough to control braking.

- INSTRUMENT PANEL. You can't get much more retro stylistically speaking, this instrument panel looks like a museum piece with its flattened out shape and rather weird and dusty ergonomics. Those big switches at either end aren't exactly in good taste.

- SEATS. They too hail back to another time and place, since they offer no lateral or lumbar support whatsoever, both for front and rear seat passengers.

- OUTWARD VIEW. It's far from ideal for the driver's seat's is lowslung, the body belt is high, roof pillars are thick and those tiny exterior mirrors are something of a joke.

- FIT & FINISH. Some trim materials aren't up to snuff, for example, those flashy fake wood appliqués or that cheap plastic stuff that graces the instrument panel.

- SHIFTER. Whether it's located under the steering wheel or on the floor, the speed shifter is no picnic because it's short and stubby and not anywhere near accurate.

- TOO BAD. Traction control isn't part of the original equipment, which would sure make for safer driving on slippery roads, especially in the wild and wooly winter.

- TO BE IMPROVED UPON:
Impractical storage space, too skimpy and inconveniently located, ergonomics of some of the controls located on the driver's door, and those pretty awful windshield wipers.

CONCLUSION
The overall performance that the LeSabre can muster up proves with each passing year that this model is outstripped by other current models. As for comfort, it isn't the cat's meow either and even a long list of lush accessories can't make up for this glaring lack. This car will be replaced next year by a completely revamped model. ☺

RATING
BUICK LeSabre

CONCEPT :		79%
Technology	75	
Safety :	80	
Interior space :	85	
Trunk volume:	80	
Quality/fit/finish :	75	

DRIVING:		65%
Cockpit :	70	
Performance :	70	
Handling :	60	
Steering :	70	
Braking :	55	

ORIGINAL EQUIPMENT:		74%
Tires :	70	
Headlights :	80	
Wipers :	60	
Rear defroster :	80	
Radio :	80	

COMFORT :		69%
Seats :	75	
Suspension :	70	
Sound level :	70	
Conveniences :	50	
Air conditioning :	80	

BUDGET :		52%
Price :	35	
Fuel economy :	50	
Insurance :	55	
Satisfaction :	80	
Depreciation :	40	

Overall rating:		**67.8%**

NEW FOR 1999

- Two new exterior shades: Silver and Bronze.
- Improved clean emission system.

ENGINES

Model/ version	Type / timing valve / fuel system	Displacement cu in	Power bhp @ rpm	Torque lb-ft @ rpm
base	V6* 3.8 OHV-12-SFI	231	205 @ 5200	230 @ 4000
G. Touring	V6* 3.8 OHV-12-SFI	231	205 @ 5200	230 @ 4000

TRANSMISSIONS

Compres. ratio	Driving wheels / transmission	Final ratio
9.4 :1	front - A4	2.86
9.4 :1	front - A4	3.05

PERFORMANCES

Acceler. 0-60 mph s	Standing 1/4 & 5/8 mile s	Acceler. 50-75 mph s	Braking 60-0 mph f	Top speed mph	Lateral acceler. G	Noise level dBA	Fuel economy mpg City	Fuel economy mpg Highway	Fuel type Octane
8.5	16.3 29.8	6.1	144	115	0.76	67-70	19	31	R 87
8.2	15.8 29.0	5.8	148	112	0.77	67-70	19	31	R 87

PRICE & EQUIPMENT

BUICK LeSabre	Custom	Limited
Retail price $:	22,465	25,790
Dealer invoice $:	20,555	23,598
Shipping & handling $:	605	605
Automatic transmission:	S	S
Cruise control:	S	S
Power steering:	S	S
Anti-lock brakes:	S	S
Traction control:	-	-
Air conditioning:	S	S
Leather:	O	O
AM/FM/radio-cassette:	O	S
Power door locks:	S	S
Power windows:	S	S
Tilt steering:	S	S
Dual adjustable mirrors:	S	S
Alloy wheels:	O	S
Anti-theft system:	S	S

Colors
Exterior: Silver, White, Blue, Emerald, Black, Bordeaux, Red, Green, Bronze, Beige.

Interior: Gray, Blue, Red, Taupe.

AT A GLANCE...

Category: Front-wheel drive full-size sedans.   **Class :** 6

HISTORIC
Introduced in: 1969.
Made in: Buick City, Flint, Michigan, USA.

DEMOGRAPHICS

Model	Men./Wom.	Age	Married	College	Income
LeSabre	85/15 %	67	89 %	26 %	$ 34 000

INDEX

Safety:	80 %	Satisfaction:	80 %
Depreciation:	58 %	Insurance:	$950
Cost per mile:	$0.56	Number of dealers:	3 000

SALES

Model	1996	1997	Result
LeSabre	131 316	150 744	+ 14.8 %

MAIN COMPETITORS
CHRYSLER Concorde-Intrepid, FORD Crown Victoria, MERCURY Grand Marquis, PONTIAC Bonneville, OLDSMOBILE 88.

MAINTENANCE REQUIRED BY WARRANTY

First revision:	Frequency:	Diagnostic plug:
3 000 miles	6 000 miles	Yes

SPECIFICATIONS

BUICK General warranty: 3 years / 40 000 miles; antipollution: 5 years / 50 000 miles; perforation corrosion: 6 years / 100 000 miles. Road assistance.

Model	Version Trim	Body/ Seats	Interior volume cu ft	Trunk volume cu ft	Cd	Wheel base in	Lght x Wdgth x Hght in x in x in	Curb weight lb	Susp. ft/rr	Brake ft/rr	Steering type	Turning diameter ft	Steer. turns nber.	Fuel tank gal	tire size	Standard tires make	model	Standard powertrain
LeSabre	Custom	4dr.sdn.6	108.5	17.0	0.34	110.8	200.8x74.4x55.6	3444	ih/ih	dc/dr/ABS	pwr.r&p.	40.7	2.97	18.0	205/70R15	Goodyear	Eagle GA	V6/3.8/A4
LeSabre	Limited	4dr.sdn.6	108.5	17.0	0.34	110.8	200.8x74.4x55.6	3468	ih/ih	dc/dr/ABS	pwr.r&p.	39.4	2.97	18.0	205/70R15	Goodyear	Eagle GA	V6/3.8/A4

The Park Avenue is the biggest and most luxurious car in the Buick lineup. It's about the same size as the Cadillac de Ville or the Oldsmobile Aurora, but it's the most discreet of the three.

MODEL RANGE

This four-door sedan is offered in a base model driven by a 3.8L V6 conventional engine or in the Ultra that's animated by a supercharger. Original equipment is quite complete, since it includes automatic transmission, ABS, climate control, cruise control, radio-tape deck, power windows, door locks and mirrors, light alloy wheels and the theft deterrent Pass-Key III keyless entry system. The Ultra is also equipped with traction control, leather trimmed, heated seats and a sportier suspension.

TECHNICAL FEATURES

Built on the same C platform as the Cadillac Seville, Eldorado and Oldsmobile Aurora, the Park Avenue has a monocoque steel body yielding rather ordinary aerodynamics with a drag coefficient of 0.34. Independent chassis cradles support the front and rear powertrains that support the engine and four-wheel independent suspension. Up front, there are MacPherson type struts up front and double wishbones with cross struts at the rear. The brake system includes four disc brakes linked to state-of-the-art ABS, also enhanced by standard traction control on the Ultra.

PROS

+ STYLE. The nicely rounded curves of this model are classic and distinguished looking, touches very typical of Buick beauties. The car has clean, classic lines but when it comes into your line of vision, you know at once that it's a Buick.

+ USEFUL SPACE. The cabin and trunk can easily accomodate five passengers and all their luggage. A sixth passenger would be welcome on board, but only for short jaunts, since space is a bit snug for six passengers.

+ OVERALL DESIGN. The design blend is almost perfect with the sturdy body, effective suspension and fairly muscular drivetrain, so the ride is interesting even on the base model.

+ RIDE COMFORT. The Park Avenue and the Ultra are real winners with such a velvety suspension, plush seats and soundproofing that cuts noise down to a whisper at

High Society...

highway cruising speed. And the really impressive climate control system can roast your buns in the winter and put frost on your nose in the good old summertime...

+ EQUIPMENT. The base model car has lots and lots of accessories and features, since the Ultra only has added leather trim, heated front seats and traction control.

+ PERFORMANCE. The 3.8L V6 supercharger gives the Ultra a unique drive feel, since accelerations and pickup are crisper and gutsier than those of the base model Park Avenue, thanks to a more favorable power to weight ratio. Going from 0 to 60 mph in 8.5 seconds is pretty downright impressive for a middle class car that weighs in at 3,858 pounds... The gearbox really enhances overall performance, since

it's silky smooth, precise and well calibrated.

+ ROADHOLDING. The Park Avenue Ultra is less affected by swish and sway than its base model counterpart equipped with softer, more comfort-oriented springs and shock absorbers and less beefy stabilizer bars. The car approaches curves in a more gingerly fashion, but it's nice and dependable in everyday circumstances.

+ BRAKES. Rear disc brakes have cut down on stopping distances and have improved resilience to overheating.

+ FUEL ECONOMY. Both 3.8L V6 engines deliver a lot of power and torque, but this still doesn't affect the relatively frugal fuel consumption for this type of car, since it sits above 18 mpg.

+ FIT & FINISH. Over the years, this car is getting better and better. It boasts of an ever sturdier body build, more careful craftsmanship and lusher trim materials.

+ CABIN DESIGN. The interior is neat with its modern instrument panel and very practical main console with scads of storage compartments and convenient armrest.

+ NICE FEATURES. The pollen filter climate control and tilt mirrors when in reverse.

CONS

- HANDLING. The Park Avenue is sometimes tricky when it comes to maneuvers and parking because of its wide steering diameter.

- SUSPENSION. The spongy suspension on the base model really affects body control and provokes a lot of sway, so you have to slow down on serpentine stretches.

- TRANSMISSION. Untypical of GM products, the transmission doesn't provide enough braking effect when you downshift manually to slow down.

- SEATS. Designed for more mature, elderly folk, they don't provide enough lateral and lumbar support, since they're quite flat and too soft when covered with fabric.

- OUTWARD VIEW. Rear view at quarterback is crippled by the thick C pillar that creates a large blind spot.

- NOISE LEVEL. The Ultra powerplant roars at the least acceleration or pickup, which isn't too appropriate for a car that's blessed with such a plush, discreet interior and style.

- TIRES. The Goodyear Eagle GA tires perform quite well on other model cars, but they're less suited to the Park Avenue since they suffer from weight transfer on turns. Bigger-diameter tires would also make for more stable brake performance.

- TO BE IMPROVED UPON: the skimpy-sized ashtray, shallow, totally useless door side-pockets and crummy ergonomics on the middle section of the instrument panel.

CONCLUSION

The Park Avenue models are growing old gracefully and continue to offer luxury space, comfort and accessories of a definitely discreet character. The conventional and supercharged engines offer two distinct driving styles and enjoy a solid, well-reputed reliablity. This car will be the choice of those who want to strut their success without upsetting the boss... ☺

RATING
BUICK Park Avenue

CONCEPT :   **78%**
Technology	80
Safety :	80
Interior space :	85
Trunk volume:	70
Quality/fit/finish :	75

DRIVING: **65%**
Cockpit :	80
Performance :	70
Handling :	55
Steering :	70
Braking :	50

ORIGINAL EQUIPMENT: **75%**
Tires :	75
Headlights :	80
Wipers :	70
Rear defroster :	75
Radio :	75

COMFORT :   **72%**
Seats :	75
Suspension :	80
Sound level :	70
Conveniences :	50
Air conditioning :	85

BUDGET :   **51%**
Price :	20
Fuel economy :	60
Insurance :	50
Satisfaction :	80
Depreciation :	45

Overall rating: **68.2%**

NEW FOR 1999

- Five new exterior shades: Silver, Blue, Gold, Bronze, White.
- Interior electrochemical rearview mirror and standard high-performance battery on the Ultra version.
- Improved hood lid seal and taillights.

ENGINES / TRANSMISSIONS / PERFORMANCES

Model/ version	Type / timing valve / fuel system	Displacement cu in	Power bhp @ rpm	Torque lb-ft @ rpm	Compres. ratio	Driving wheels / transmission	Final ratio	Acceler. 0-60 mph s	Standing 1/4 & 5/8 mile s		Acceler. 50-75 mph s	Braking 60-0 mph f	Top speed mph	Lateral acceler. G	Noise level dBA	Fuel economy mpg City	Highway	Fuel type Octane
Park Ave.	V6* 3.8 OHV-12-MPSFI	231	205 @ 5200	230 @ 4000	9.4 :1	front - A4*	3.05	9.5	16.7	30.5	6.7	151	112	0.75	65-68	18	29	R 87
Ultra	V6* C 3.8 OHV-12-MPSFI	231	240 @ 5200	280 @ 3600	8.5 :1	front - A4*	2.93	8.5	16.4	29.5	6.2	144	124	0.77	65-68	17	28	S 91

PRICE & EQUIPMENT

BUICK Park Avenue	Park Avenue	Ultra
Retail price $:	30,675	35,550
Dealer invoice $:	27,761	32,173
Shipping & handling $:	665	665
Automatic transmission:	S	S
Cruise control:	S	S
Power steering:	S	S
Anti-lock brakes:	O	S
Traction control:	O	S
Air conditioning:	SA	SA
Leather:	O	S
AM/FM/radio-cassette:	S	S CD
Power door locks:	S	S
Power windows:	S	S
Tilt steering:	S	S
Dual adjustable mirrors:	S	S
Alloy wheels:	S	S
Anti-theft system:	S	S

Colors

Exterior: Silver, White, Blue, Green, Black, Bordeaux, Red, Gold, Bronze, Beige.

Interior: Gray, Blue, Red, Taupe.

AT A GLANCE...

Category: front-wheel drive luxury sedans.   **Class :** 7

HISTORIC
Introduced in: 1971
Made in: Wentzville, Missouri, USA.

DEMOGRAPHICS
Model	Men./Wom.	Age	Married	College	Income
Park Avenue	87/13 %	67	89 %	28 %	$ 40 000

INDEX
Safety:	80 %	Satisfaction:	82 %
Depreciation:	55 %	Insurance:	$1 050-1 155
Cost per mile:	$0.58	Number of dealers:	3 000

SALES
Model	1996	1997	Result
Park Avenue	47 732	68 777	+ 44.1 %

MAIN COMPETITORS
ACURA RL, CHRYSLER LHS & 300M, OLDSMOBILE Aurora, LEXUS ES & GS 300, MAZDA Millenia, PONTIAC Bonneville, TOYOTA Avalon, VOLVO S80.

MAINTENANCE REQUIRED BY WARRANTY
First revision:	Frequency:	Diagnostic plug:
3 000 miles	6 000 miles	Yes

SPECIFICATIONS

Model Version Trim	Body/ Seats	Interior volume cu ft	Trunk volume cu ft	Cd	Wheel base in	Lght x Wdgth x Hght in x in x in	Curb weight lb	Susp. ft/rr	Brake ft/rr	Steering type	Turning diameter ft	Steer. turns nber.	Fuel tank gal	tire size	Standard tires make	model	Standard powertrain
BUICK	General warranty: 3 years / 40 000 miles; antipollution: 5 years / 50 000 miles; perforation corrosion: 6 years / 100 000 miles. Road assistance.																
Park Avenue	4dr.sdn.5/6	112	19.1	0.34	113.8	206.8x74.7x57.4	3779	ih/ih	dc/ABS	pwr.r&p. l	39.4	2.93	18.5	225/60R16	Goodyear	Eagle LS	V6/3.8/A4
Park Avenue Ultra	4dr.sdn.5/6	112	19.1	0.34	113.8	206.8x74.7x57.4	3884	ih/ih	dc/ABS	pwr.r&p. r	40.0	3.15	18.5	225/60R16	Goodyear	Eagle LS	V6C/3.8/A4

Right from the beginning, the Riviera coupe has been the favorite of a very particular clientele, namely folks who are looking for a vehicle of the same ilk and dimensions as their family yacht. Since its homologue the Lincoln Mark VIII went the way of all flesh, the Riviera, along with the Eldorado, is one of the rare specimens of the luxury coupe breed that was the rage some thirty odd years ago. But things have changed, today the means of transportation has to be a multipurpose vehicle that can go to the ends of the earth, rain or shine and sheer brute force has replaced finesse and good taste.

MODEL RANGE
The Riviera is now only offered in a single trim level animated by a 3.8 V6 supercharger that develops 240 hp. Equipment is pretty ritzy indeed, since the only extras available are front heated seats and sunroof.

TECHNICAL FEATURES
The monocoque body is built of double-sided galvanized steel, except for the roof and the engine hood is made of aluminum as well, yielding a rather average drag coefficient of 0.34, even with that very clean, chic silhouette. In its last redesign workover, the body gained a definitely tougher structural integrity so as to assure crisper handling, lower noise level and fewer vibrations from the running gear. The car is fitted with independent cradles fore-and-aft to support mechanical and suspension components. The fully independent suspension consists of MacPherson struts up front and a double wishbone and transverse control arms setup at the rear. The four-wheel disc brakes are aided by a standard ABS system. Since last year, the finely tuned 3.8 L V6 engine is linked to an automatic transmission equipped with bigger, sturdier drive pinions and propeller shaft to improve over-all durability and to handle all the torque the supercharger pumps out.

PROS
+ SILHOUETTE. The Riviera's curvaceous form always gets admiring glances, since it does make one think of a boat keel or an airpane fuselage. Besides having a certain elegance, it boasts of very original looks.

+ USEFUL SPACE. Leg and head room aren't as generous in the rear seats as they are up front, yet the

Endangered Species...

cabin isn't cramped and can seat five passengers and the trunk can accomodate all their luggage.

+ COMFORT. On smooth roads, the suspension is smooth and relaxing, thickly padded seats are nice and comfy and noise is kept to a discreet minimum at cruising speed.

+ PERFORMANCES. They're a pleasant surprise with such a get up and go 3.8L V8 supercharger that provides this hefty car with accelerations and pickup worthy of a sports car, without guzzling gallons of gas, for fuel consumption sits at about 18 mpg.

+ QUALITY. Assembly, finish details and trim materials are of good quality, but they can't really compete with what you get in European or Japanese counterparts.

+ RIDE. You might not expect this in such a car, but you can really get a kick out of being at the wheel of this big Buick coupe. Controls are silky smooth and neat as a pin and the powerplant really has pizzazz and good manners as well.

+ HANDLING. The firmer suspension provides better balance on curves and it controls sway nicely and is amazingly solid for a vehicle of such a hefty size.

+ EQUIPMENT. Top of the line, it includes luxury and comfort accessories that you enjoy inside an imported car.

+ CONVENIENCE FEATURES. Unusual for this type of car, there are all kinds of handy spots to store your stuff.

CONS
- MANEUVERABILITY. The curved shape of the Riviera tends to make it look smaller than it actually is. Its cumbersome size cripples slick moves in city traffic and on curved, snaky roads, it's no champion.

- OUTWARD VIEW. It's limited up front and thick roof supports affect rearward visibility, along with the high body and low driver's seat. Also, those round extremities make it tough to gauge parking maneuvres with accuracy.

- STEERING. You have to keep a grip on the wheel, for it's over-assisted and so it's light and sensitive at center. When the wind is blowing, you have to play with the rudder to stay on course.

- BRAKES. Such an impressive vehicle weight does affect brake endurance, since linings quickly lose vitality with intensive use. On emergency stops, we noticed lots of wheel lock but it was more of a hassle than a hazard. Also, the new transmission provides no braking effect when you're downshifting manually.

- INSTRUMENT PANEL. No doubt about it, it is an original design, but the layout is more stylish than ergonomic. Some controls are beyond the driver's reach and all those round instrument gauges are rather tiring, visually speaking.

- ACCESS. The heavy doors are quite long, but climbing aboard the rear seats is tricky with such skimpy head and leg room. The trunk lid is high as blazes, so luggage handling can be quite a chore.

- TO BE IMPROVED UPON: Rear windows that don't open, the adjustable steering column that doesn't make much of a difference for the guy or gal at the wheel and nerve-wracking wind noise that sweeps around such a sleek body.

CONCLUSION
The Riviera coupe is more geared to comfort than to zippy driving. Yet it doesn't really mind burning a bit of rubber when the asphalt is perfect and on straight stretches, but you can feel a bit seasick on curves. Its ever so elegant style and luxury items explain why it's one of the rare survivors of its species. But its days are numbered because buyers are disappearing fast... ☺

RATING
BUICK Riviera

CONCEPT :		**75%**
Technology	75	
Safety :	80	
Interior space :	70	
Trunk volume:	70	
Quality/fit/finish :	80	
DRIVING:		**66%**
Cockpit :	80	
Performance :	75	
Handling :	50	
Steering :	75	
Braking :	50	
ORIGINAL EQUIPMENT:		**74%**
Tires :	75	
Headlights :	75	
Wipers :	70	
Rear defroster :	70	
Radio :	80	
COMFORT :		**76%**
Seats :	75	
Suspension :	75	
Sound level :	80	
Conveniences :	70	
Air conditioning :	80	
BUDGET :		**49%**
Price :	15	
Fuel economy :	55	
Insurance :	45	
Satisfaction :	80	
Depreciation :	50	
Overall rating:		**68.0%**

NEW FOR 1999

- Four-wheel traction control.
- New 125-amp. alternator.
- Four new body shades: Silver, Blue, Gold and Bronze.

ENGINES / TRANSMISSIONS / PERFORMANCES

Model/ version	Type / timing valve / fuel system	Displacement cu in	Power bhp @ rpm	Torque lb-ft @ rpm	Compres. ratio	Driving wheels / transmission	Final ratio	Acceler. 0-60 mph s	Standing 1/4 & 5/8 mile s	Acceler. 50-75 mph s	Braking 60-0 mph f	Top speed mph	Lateral acceler. G	Noise level dBA	Fuel economy mpg City	Highway	Fuel type Octane
Riviera	V6C 3.8 OHV-12-MPSFI	231	240 @ 5200	280 @ 3600	8.5:1	front - A4	2.93	7.8	15.7	28.5	5.0	144	112	0.75	67-69	17	28	S 91

PRICE & EQUIPMENT

BUICK Riviera	**base**
Retail price $:	32,500
Dealer invoice $:	29,413
Shipping & handling $:	665
Automatic transmission:	S
Cruise control:	S
Power steering:	S
Anti-lock brakes:	S
Traction control:	S
Air conditioning:	SA
Leather:	S
AM/FM/radio-cassette:	S CD
Power door locks:	S
Power windows:	S
Tilt steering:	S
Dual adjustable mirrors:	S
Alloy wheels:	S
Anti-theft system:	S

Colors

Exterior: Silver, White, Blue, Emerald, Black, Bordeaux, Gold, Beige, Bronze.

Interior: Gray, Blue, Green, Red, Taupe.

AT A GLANCE...

Category: Front-wheel drive mid-size coupes. **Class :** 7

HISTORIC
Introduced in: 1949 designation. 1963 first model; 1993 actual model.
Made in: Lake Orion, Michigan, USA.

DEMOGRAPHICS

Model	Men./Wom.	Age	Married	College	Income
Riviera	80/20 %	56	81 %	37 %	$ 55 000

INDEX

Safety:	80 %	Satisfaction:	78 %
Depreciation:	52 %	Insurance:	$1 250
Cost per mile:	$0.57	Number of dealers:	3 000

SALES

Model	1996	1997	Result
Riviera	20 641	14 097	- 31.7 %

MAIN COMPETITORS

CADILLAC Eldorado.

MAINTENANCE REQUIRED BY WARRANTY

First revision:	Frequency:	Diagnostic plug:
3 000 miles	6 000miles	Yes

SPECIFICATIONS

Model	Version Trim	Body/ Seats	Interior volume cu ft	Trunk volume cu ft	Cd	Wheel base in	Lght x Wdgth x Hght in x in x in	Curb weight lb	Susp. ft/rr	Brake ft/rr	Steering type	Turning diameter ft	Steer. turns nber.	Fuel tank gal	tire size	Standard tires make	model	Standard powertrain
BUICK Riviera Supercharged		2dr.cpe.5	99.5	17.4	0.34	113.8	207.2x75.0x54.6	3705	ih/ih	dc/ABS	pwr.r&p.	39.1	3.15	18.5	225/60R16	Goodyear	Eagle GA	V6C/3.8/A4

General warranty: 3 years / 40 000 miles; antipollution: 5 years / 50 000 miles; perforation corrosion: 6 years / 100 000 miles. Road assistance.

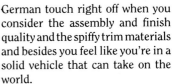

General Motors may have taken some dubious short cuts to catch up in the affordable compact luxury car segment, but we have to admit that for once it payed off. Over the last ten years, this type of car built by European and Japanese automakers has been more and more popular with buyers. Up until quite recently, American car companies didn't have a single model to compete with the BMW 3-Series, Nissan Maxima or Lexus ES 300.

MODEL RANGE

The Catera is a four-door sedan sold in a single loaded luxury model that can be furbished with a handful of options. It's powered by a 3.0L V6 engine linked to an automatic transmission, it's equipped with dual-zone climate control, power seats, ABS and traction control and a sophisticated theft deterrent system. Main options are aluminum chrome rims, remote garage door opener, glass sunroof and a CD player located in the trunk.

TECHNICAL FEATURES

Built by Opel in Germany, the Catera is inspired by the Omega MV6 and its components hail from the four corners of the globe. The body is built in Germany, the automatic transmission in France, the engine in England and some final trim items in the United States. Its steel unibody is as rigid as it gets. Its architecture is a real classic. The Catera is a rear-wheel drive car. Its main mechanical features are affixed to two independent cradles that support same away from the main frame. Up front the suspension is of MacPherson design with some hydraulic links in order to maximize accurate handling and stability on emergency stops; at the rear there's a constant load levelling device. Four-wheel disc brakes are equipped with standard ABS and traction control. The 3.0L V6 engine has its cylinder rows set at 54 degrees. Spark plugs are fitted with triple electrodes, the belt and coolant are made to last, so you can put off your first tuneup to 100,000 miles.

PROS

+ DESIGN. Dignity is what exudes from such a classic and elegant appearance that belies its Cadillac vintage. Inside the cabin, things are quite posh, seats are roomy and the instrument panel is richly equipped.

+VALUE. The price-package com-

The Empire Strikes Back

bination is relatively good compared to some of its direct rivals, since you're blessed with heated adjustable seats both up front and in the rear, but it's rather strange that leather trim is an extra.

+SAFETY FEATURES. This German-built car is loaded with passenger-protection devices and it's as heavy and stalwart as an army tank. Outward view is great any which way, in spite of the rather high body belt. The driver is right at home with the myriad seat adjustments available Night driving is a breeze with such remarkably bright and powerful headlamps, either on high or low beam.

+ RIDE COMFORT. It's superb with such a voluminous cabin where passengers have all kinds of room to breathe and stretch, such a cushy

suspension that filters out road faults, such thickly upholstered seats that provide excellent support and with a low noise level due to very effective soundproofing.

+ HANDLING. On winter roads, the Catera sometimes has serious trouble managing curves even with the sophisticated ABS system, but generally this model holds the road beautifully, yet the rear-wheel drive feature, geared to sporty maneuvers, doesn't really add much, given the rather sluggish engine under the hood.

+ BRAKES. They're powerful and balanced, so you can achieve a whole series of emergency stops without any sign of brake fatigue and the brake pedal is right on.

+ QUALITY. You can sense the

German touch right off when you consider the assembly and finish quality and the spiffy trim materials and besides you feel like you're in a solid vehicle that can take on the world.

+ MANEUVERABILITY. Steering benefits from an only average reduction ratio, but it has a really short turn angle diameter so parking is no problem at all. Response is quick on the draw, precise and nicely calibrated to allow for optimum control in all circumstances.

+ CONVENIENCE FEATURES. Several storage compartments are scattered throughout the cabin and the trunk really holds a lot of luggage and can be extended by lowering the entire or partial rear seatback.

CONS

- LOOKS. You can't really say that the car has much charisma, you can drive by and nobody will even blink. GM designers are usually very innovative, but they missed the boat on this car, since they tried to keep a maximum of the original stylistic features and the look is getting pretty dusty.

- PERFORMANCES. For a car in this price range and class, accelerations and pickup are humdrum, which is an understatement, due to hefty vehicle weight. This sure affects driving pleasure and when the car is loaded, driving is no fun at all.

- INSTRUMENT PANEL. Another side-effect of the old car design, the dashboard is high and massive and really eats up the space surrounding front seat passengers.

-REAR-WHEEL DRIVE. Even with good traction control and tires, you don't have the same assurance as with a front-wheel drive vehicle, especially in winter conditions. You really have to keep an eye on things to stay on track in the snowy season.

CONCLUSION

The Catera shows signs of some compromises based on ecomomics, but it isn't a bad car. Yet its design is getting out-of-date and it doesn't put out performances on a par with its closest rivals. ☺

RATING CADILLAC Catera		
CONCEPT :		78%
Technology	85	
Safety :	90	
Interior space :	70	
Trunk volume :	60	
Quality/fit/finish :	85	
DRIVING:		68%
Cockpit :	80	
Performance :	60	
Handling :	60	
Steering :	80	
Braking :	60	
ORIGINAL EQUIPMENT:		78%
Tires :	80	
Headlights :	80	
Wipers :	75	
Rear defroster :	75	
Radio :	80	
COMFORT :		79%
Seats :	80	
Suspension :	80	
Sound level :	80	
Conveniences :	75	
Air conditioning :	80	
BUDGET :		44%
Price :	15	
Fuel economy :	60	
Insurance :	45	
Satisfaction :	50	
Depreciation :	50	
Overall rating:		**69.4%**

NEW FOR 1999

- Improved main control for power locks.
- More extended memory to record four separate drivers' styles.
- OnStar system available as an extra.

ENGINES / TRANSMISSIONS / PERFORMANCES

Model/ version	Type / timing valve / fuel system	Displacement cu in	Power bhp @ rpm	Torque lb-ft @ rpm	Compres. ratio	Driving wheels / transmission	Final ratio	Acceler. 0-60 mph s	Standing 1/4 & 5/8 mile s	Acceler. 50-75 mph s	Braking 60-0 mph f	Top speed mph	Lateral acceler. G	Noise level dBA	Fuel economy mpg City Highway	Fuel type Octane
base	V6*3.0 DOHC-24-MPSFI	181	200 @ 6000	192 @ 3600	10.0 :1	rear - A4	3.9	9.0	16.6	29.8	6.3	131	124	0.80	65-69	18 26	S 91

PRICE & EQUIPMENT

CADILLAC Catera	base
Retail price $:	29,995
Dealer invoice $:	28,880
Shipping & handling $:	640
Automatic transmission:	S
Cruise control:	S
Power steering:	S
Anti-lock brakes:	S
Traction control:	S
Air conditioning:	S
Leather:	S
AM/FM/radio-cassette:	S
Power door locks:	S
Power windows:	S
Tilt steering:	S
Dual adjustable mirrors:	SE
Alloy wheels:	S
Anti-theft system:	S

Colors

Exterior: Black, White, Beige.

Interior: Beige, Gray, Black.

AT A GLANCE...

Category: rear-wheel drive luxury sedans. **Class :** 7

HISTORIC
Introduced in: 1997
Made in: Ruesselsheim, Germany

DEMOGRAPHICS

Model	Men./Wom.	Age	Married	College	Income
Catera	NA				

INDEX

Safety:	85 %	Satisfaction:	NA
Depreciation:	30 %	Insurance:	$1 250
Cost per mile:	$0.65	Number of dealers:	1 600

SALES

Model	1996	1997	Result
Catera	1 676	25 411	

MAIN COMPETITORS

ACURA TL, AUDI A4, BMW 3-Series, INFINITI I30, LEXUS ES 300 & GS 300, MAZDA Millenia, NISSAN Maxima, SAAB 9-3 & 9.5, VOLVO S70.

MAINTENANCE REQUIRED BY WARRANTY

First revision:	Frequency:	Diagnostic plug:
3 000 miles	6 months / 6 000miles	Yes

SPECIFICATIONS

Model	Version Trim	Body/ Seats	Interior volume cu ft	Trunk volume cu ft	Cd	Wheel base in	Lght x Wdgth x Hght in x in x in	Curb weight lb	Susp. ft/rr	Brake ft/rr	Steering type	Turning diameter ft	Steer. turns nber.	Fuel tank gal	tire size	Standard tires make	model	Standard powertrain
CADILLAC General warranty: 4 years/ 50 000 miles; antipollution: 5 years / 50 000 miles; perforation corrosion: 6 years / 100 000 miles. Road assistance.																		
Catera	base	4dr.sdn.5	98.2	14.5	0.33	107.4	194.0x70.3x56.3	3770	ih/ih	dc/ABS	pwr.bal.	33.5	3.0	16	225/55HR16	Goodyear	Eagle RS-A	V6/3.0/A4

Ford seems to do everything it can to help out the competition. After having botched its success with the Taurus, now it's making customers squirm with the new Lincoln Town Car design, so much so that regulars aren't buying. In the meantime, the questionable "Edge Design" is gracing the Cadillac that's keeping its lead in North American luxury car sales (with Mercedes-Benz as a close second), thanks to a more conservative approach that doesn't exclude high performance or sophisticated technical features.

MODEL RANGE

The DeVille is only sold as a four-door sedan in base, Concours or d'Elegance trim, all powered by a 4.6L Northstar V8 engine that develops 275 hp on the lower end model and 300 hp on the Concours. Original niceties include traction and ABS, light alloy wheels and automatic climate control. Leather-clad trim (on the base model), heated front seats, sunroof and OnStar communication system via satellite are offered as extras.

TECHNICAL FEATURES

The steel monocoque build of these model cars boasts of a remarkable drag coefficient (0.35), given the wide frontal surface. The self-adjusting suspension, coined «Road Sensing Suspension II», is fully independent on all four wheels. Up front, there's a MacPherson strut arrangement, at the rear, there's a double wishbone and cross strut setup and an anti-roll bar both front and rear. The four-wheel disc brakes are linked to a Bosch ABS-traction control system and power steering fluid pressure is controlled by a magnetic device called Magnasteer. Safety-wise, the car is now equipped with side-impact air bags for front seat passengers.

PROS

+ **LOOKS.** The DeVille is a pretty big car, but it has a very dignified, discreet and balanced body design, the perfect symbol of the success of the American middle class.

+ **CABIN SPACE.** Cabin dimensions are proportional to vehicle size, so five passengers can be comfortably seated for long trips.

+ **COMFORT.** The Deville loves the smooth ribbon of highway where it cruises along, thanks to a smooth suspension, sumptuous seats, superb soundproofing and efficient climate control.

+ **TECHNICAL TOUCHES.** The De Ville has conservative styling, but

Royal...

it's equipped with pretty amazing high tech features. Front-wheel drive is super in winter weather and this car is swimming in electronic devices of Star Wars caliber...

+ **ENGINE.** The Northstar is one of the most refined engines of its generation. The acceleration and pickup capabilities it bestows on the Concours (300 hp) are awesome and compare well with those of true grit sports coupes. Performances on the lower end or d'Elegance models are really quite impressive as well.

+ **HANDLING.** The Concours handles like a dream, thanks to its electronically controlled suspension that keeps the car path straight and sure, more so than on the other models that may be dreamboats, but are clumsy in comparison.

+ **QUALITY.** Over-all quality has dramatically improved over the years, be it build craftsmanship, finish details and trim fabrics and such, which explains why more than 85% of owners are very satisfied with their purchase. After all, such a high satisfaction rate used to be the pride and joy of Japanese carmakers.

+ **BRAKES.** The brake system is gutsy and stable, but linings show signs of strain when put to the test.

+ **FUEL ECONOMY.** Fuel consumption isn't as greedy as you'd expect, considering the sheer hulk of these vehicles. On average, it sits at about 18 mpg for the 275-hp engine. On the more zoomy model, it varies according to the weight and thrust of the driver's right foot.

+ **NICE FEATURES:** Wipers that automatically operate when they

detect rain and especially the OnStar communication system via satellite that offers an interesting array of safety features, such as notifiying the authorities in the event of an accident, remote control unlocking of doors if you've forgotten the key inside, or tracking down the vehicle if it's been stolen. Besides, the OnStar system offers scads of info to help you arrive at any given destination, be it a recommended hotel or restaurant.

CONS

- **STEERING.** The car is loaded with high-tech goodies, but you can't adjust power steering assistance that's too strong and makes the system light and sensitive and robs you of all road feel. It takes some getting used to if you want to stay on the straight and narrow in crosswinds.

- **MANEUVERABILITY.** Besides the usual driver's license, you need ship captain's papers to manage this juggernaut. It's absolutely huge and the wide steer angle makes some moves pretty tricky...

- **SUSPENSION.** The overly spongy suspension on the base and d'Elegance models really causes a heck of a lot of sway, which can create seasickness on poor surfaces and sure complicate taking those tight curves which the De Ville really has a time of it negociating.

- **OUTWARD VIEW.** The car has lots of window surfaces, but the rearward view at quarterback isn't ideal due to the thick C pillar.

- **TOO BAD!** The OnStar system, like other tracking sytems, isn't available everywhere in North America, and it does make for safer motoring all-round.

- **SEATS.** They've definitely improved, but they still offer only mediocre lateral and lumbar support for front and rear passengers.

- **COCKPIT.** It would be more comfy if the steering column were less long and if the steering wheel were closer to the dashboard.

CONCLUSION

Until it's completely revamped next year, the DeVille remains the American luxury car par excellence. Traditionally roomy and comfortable, it does muster pretty amazing performances. Fuel consumption is reasonable and some of the technical features are state-of-the-art. ☺

RATING CADILLAC DeVille		
CONCEPT :		**89%**
Technology	90	
Safety :	90	
Interior space :	95	
Trunk volume :	90	
Quality/fit/finish :	80	
DRIVING:		**67%**
Cockpit :	85	
Performance :	70	
Handling :	50	
Steering :	80	
Braking :	50	
ORIGINAL EQUIPMENT:		**78%**
Tires :	80	
Headlights :	80	
Wipers :	80	
Rear defroster :	70	
Radio :	80	
COMFORT :		**80%**
Seats :	80	
Suspension :	80	
Sound level:	80	
Conveniences :	70	
Air conditioning :	90	
BUDGET :		**47%**
Price :	0	
Fuel economy :	55	
Insurance :	45	
Satisfaction :	85	
Depreciation :	50	
Overall rating:		**72.2%**

NEW FOR 1999

- Standard equipment: theft-deterrent sound alarm and inside electrochemical rearview mirror with compass.
- Optional equipment: OnStar system with warning of side-impact air bag deployment.
- Three new body shades.

ENGINES / TRANSMISSIONS / PERFORMANCES

Model/ version	Type / timing valve / fuel system	Displacement cu in	Power bhp @ rpm	Torque lb-ft @ rpm	Compres. ratio	Driving wheels / transmission	Final ratio	Acceler. 0-60 mph s	Standing 1/4 & 5/8 mile s	Acceler. 50-75 mph s	Braking 60-0 mph f	Top speed mph	Lateral acceler. G	Noise level dBA	Fuel economy mpg City	Highway	Fuel type Octane
1)	V8* 4.6 DOHC-32-MPSFI	278	275 @ 5600	300 @ 4000	10.3 :1	front - A4*	3.11	8.8	16.3	30.0	4.8	148	124	0.78	64-70	17.0	28.0	S 91
2)	V8* 4.6 DOHC-32-MPSFI	278	300 @ 6000	295 @ 4400	10.3 :1	front - A4*	3.71	8.0	15.8	28.6	4.5	138	137	0.80	65-70	17.0	27.0	S 91

1) DeVille & d'Elegance   2) DeVille Concours

PRICE & EQUIPMENT

CADILLAC DeVille	Sedan	Concours	d'Elegance
Retail price $:	-	-	-
Dealer invoice $:	-	-	-
Shipping & handling $:	-	-	-
Automatic transmission:	S	S	S
Cruise control:	S	S	S
Power steering:	S	S	S
Anti-lock brakes:	S	S	S
Traction control:	S	S	S
Air conditioning:	SA	SA	SA
Leather:	O	S	S
AM/FM/radio-cassette:	S	S	S
Power door locks:	S	S	S
Power windows:	S	S	S
Tilt steering:	S	S	S
Dual adjustable mirrors:	SE	SE	SE
Alloy wheels:	S	S	S
Anti-theft system:	S	S	S

Colors

Exterior: Green, White, Black, Beige, Garnett, Red, Mocha, Amethyst, Blue, Argyle, Sand, Carmin.
Interior: Black, Red, Blue, Beige.

AT A GLANCE...

Category: front-wheel drive luxury sedans.   **Class :** 7

HISTORIC
Introduced in: 1970.
Made in: Hamtramck-Detroit, Michigan, USA.

DEMOGRAPHICS
Model	Men./Wom.	Age	Married	College	Income
DeVille	82/18 %	66	87 %	29 %	$ 70 000

INDEX
Safety:	90 %	Satisfaction:	85 %
Depreciation:	52 %	Insurance:	$1 425
Cost per mile:	$0.75	Number of dealers:	1 600

SALES
Model	1996	1997	Result
DeVille	103 730	104 743	+1.0 %

MAIN COMPETITORS
LEXUS LS 400, LINCOLN Continental & Town Car, OLDSMOBILE Aurora.

MAINTENANCE REQUIRED BY WARRANTY
First revision:	Frequency:	Diagnostic plug:
3 000 miles	6 000 miles	Yes

SPECIFICATIONS

CADILLAC — General warranty: 4 years / 50 000 miles; antipollution: 5 years / 50 000 miles; perforation corrosion: 6 years / 100 000 miles. Road assistance.

Model	Version Trim	Body/ Seats	Interior volume cu ft	Trunk volume cu ft	Cd	Wheel base in	Lght x Wdgth x Hght in x in x in	Curb weight lb	Susp. ft/rr	Brake ft/rr	Steering type	Turning diameter ft	Steer. turns nber.	Fuel tank gal	tire size	Standard tires make	model	Standard powertrain
DeVille	Sedan	4dr.sdn.6	117	20	0.35	113.8	209.8x76.5x56.0	4012	ih/ih	dc/ABS	pwr.r&p.	41.0	2.65	20.0	225/60R16	Michelin	XW4	V8/4.6/A4
DeVille	Concours	4dr.sdn.5	117	20	0.35	113.8	209.8x76.5x56.0	4063	ih/ih	dc/ABS	pwr.r&p.	41.0	2.83	20.0	225/60R16	Goodyear	Eagle RS-A	V8/4.6/A4
DeVille	d'Elegance	4dr.sdn.6	117	20	0.35	113.8	209.8x76.5x56.0	4052	ih/ih	dc/ABS	pwr.r&p.	41.0	2.65	20.0	225/60R16	Michelin	XW4	V8/4.6/A4

Strange that General Motors, the first carmaker to realize that the big all-terrain deluxe vehicle market was about to explode, didn't add a product to its Cadillac lineup that would be able to match the Lincoln Navigator. Of course, the sensational success story of this vehicle, along with that of the Ford Expedition, took everybody by surprise, including the folks in Dearborn. The popularity of this type of vehicle is so irrational that no one could have imagined that sales figures would climb so quickly. So Cadillac came up with a last-ditch effort to transform the GMC Denali into what is known as the Escalade...

MODEL RANGE

The Escalade is a bulky four-door SUV equipped with a 5.7L V8 engine with 4-speed automatic transmission, sold in a single trim model. Equipment is pretty impressive. Standard equipment includes five leather-trim «Nuance» seats, electrically powered and heated front seats, a Bose sound system that allows front and rear seat passengers to listen to different programs, fog lamps, a hitch that can haul a 3-ton trailer and chrome aluminum rims.

TECHNICAL FEATURES

The Escalade is the direct descendant of the GMC Denali that was already furbished with equipment and trim details a cut above those of the Yukon. This new vehicle has the very same body and mechanical features, including Auto Trak, a system that provides for either rear or all-wheel drive on demand or in permanent mode. The steel body is mounted on a galvanized steel H-frame fitted with five cross-members, borrowed from former generation GM pickup trucks. The independent front suspension consists of a double wishbone setup with torsion bars; the rigid rear suspension is equipped with leaf springs. In comparison with that of its Chevrolet and GMC counterparts, the suspension is less firm and soundproofing is so good you get cushy Cadillac comfort inside. The body design isn't too sleek, yielding a drag coefficient of 0.45. All models are equipped with variable assist power steering, disc and drum brakes and standard four-wheel ABS.

PROS

+ CABIN SPACE. The cabin interior

Fire Sale...

and luggage compartment aren't as long as those of the Suburban, but five occupants and all their gear can be nicely accomodated.

+ CABIN DESIGN. It's very lush with its soft leather seats, Zebrano wood appliqués and steering wheel clad in leather and wood. Cadillac customers will be right at home since they'll find all the usual creature comforts in the Escalade.

+ RIDE COMFORT. The Escalade runs smoothly on the highway, since the suspension is really flexible and noise is kept to a minimum, with only the wind noise around the windshield and exterior mirrors troubling the quiet ambience.

+ DRIVE. Drivers who like to be at the wheel of a big vehicle will enjoy handling this big truck-size model. Controls are smooth and the nicely

designed interior with its super ergonomic instrument panel that's not too big, yet has a plethora of gauges and convenient features like the storage compartment located between the front seats and that even includes a writing tablet...

+ SEATS. They're incredibly comfy and include adjustable headrests and fold-up armrests up front.

+ OUTWARD VIEW. It's great in all directions for the cockpit is perched high, there are lots of big windows and rearview mirrors are nice and big.

+ ONSTAR SYSTEM. You can be in touch with a help center almost at once, so you can get travel directions, make reservations at a hotel or restaurant, ask for assistance in an emergency and even open doors from outside if you've

forgotten your key inside the vehicle...

CONS

- TECHNICAL FEATURES. They're already out-of-date since the Escalade won't benefit from the latest improvements on GM SUV's for another three years.

- FUEL ECONOMY. The V8 is no lightweight, since it drinks about 10 mpg and the huge gas tank allows for road autonomy up to 300 miles...

- TOWING CAPABILITIES. The Escalade is equipped with a standard hitch that can haul only a 6,600 lb trailer, whereas most big trailers weigh 2,000 lbs more...

- HANDLING. The soft suspension, vague steering and high ground clearance all add up to a feeling of apprehension when going into tight curves that this vehicle doesn't manage with much aplomb.

- OFF-ROAD MANEUVERS. The front filler above the bumper is humungous, so it really hampers getting around on rough turf, so much so that we weren't able to get out of a shallow ditch without running into snags.

- MANEUVERABILITY. Vehicle size and weight are handicaps so this vehicle isn't at ease in narrow city streets, due to a wide steer angle; it's definitely not a city slicker.

- COMFORT. The going gets rough as soon as the asphalt isn't as smooth as glass. The Escalade sways and rolls to its heart's content and the thumping wheels give away its humble, utility vehicle ancestry...

- REAR SEATS. They're no fun at all, tough to get to via those narrow doors and seat cushions are short and provide no lateral support whatsoever.

- HATCHBACK. The only one available is split in two horizontal sections that lift and lover, which sure complicates luggage handling.

CONCLUSION

Is the Escalade sophisticated enough to really compete with the more mod Ford product? We have our doubts and the price tag will be a major sales factor that will determine whether Cadillac customers stay with their dealer or look elsewhere...

RATING
CADILLAC Escalade

CONCEPT :		80%
Technology	75	
Safety :	85	
Interior space :	85	
Trunk volume:	75	
Quality/fit/finish :	80	

DRIVING:		55%
Cockpit :	80	
Performance :	40	
Handling :	40	
Steering :	75	
Braking :	40	

ORIGINAL EQUIPMENT:		75%
Tires :	75	
Headlights :	80	
Wipers :	75	
Rear defroster :	70	
Radio :	75	

COMFORT :		74%
Seats :	80	
Suspension :	75	
Sound level:	60	
Conveniences :	75	
Air conditioning :	80	

BUDGET :		39%
Price :	0	
Fuel economy :	20	
Insurance :	45	
Satisfaction :	80	
Depreciation :	50	

Overall rating:		**64.6%**

NEW FOR 1999

• New model based on the GMC Denali and spiffed up according to Cadillac standards.

ENGINES / TRANSMISSIONS / PERFORMANCES

Model/ version	Type / timing valve / fuel system	Displacement cu in	Power bhp @ rpm	Torque lb-ft @ rpm	Compres. ratio	Driving wheels / transmission	Final ratio	Acceler. 0-60 mph s	Standing 1/4 & 5/8 mile s	Acceler. 50-75 mph s	Braking 60-0 mph f	Top speed mph	Lateral acceler. G	Noise level dBA	Fuel economy mpg City	Highway	Fuel type Octane
base	V8* 5.7 OHV-16-SFI	350	255 @ 4600	330 @ 2800	9.4 :1	four -A4	3.73	11.0	18.0 32.2	7.8	168	109	0.70	66	13.0	18.0	R 87

PRICE & EQUIPMENT

CADILLAC	Escalade
Retail price $:	NA
Dealer invoice $:	NA
Shipping & handling $:	665
Automatic transmission:	S
Cruise control:	S
Power steering:	S
Anti-lock brakes:	S
Traction control:	S
Air conditioning:	S
Leather:	S
AM/FM/radio-cassette:	S-CD
Power door locks:	S
Power windows:	S
Tilt steering:	S
Dual adjustable mirrors:	S
Alloy wheels:	S
Anti-theft system:	S

Colors

Exterior: White, Black, Silver, Bordeaux.

Interior: Tan.

AT A GLANCE...

Category: 4x4 all purpose vehicle. **Class :** utility

HISTORIC
Introduced in: 1999
Made in: Arlington, Texas, USA.

DEMOGRAPHICS
Model	Men./Wom.	Age	Married	College	Income
Escalade	85/15 %	65	85 %	30 %	$ 60 000

INDEX
Safety:	90 %	Satisfaction:	NA
Depreciation:	NA	Insurance:	$1 100
Cost per mile:	$0.65	Number of dealers:	1600

SALES
Model	1996	1997	Result
Escalade	Not on the market at that time		

MAIN COMPETITORS
CHEVROLET-GMC Tahoe-Denali-Suburban, FORD Expedition, LEXUS LX 470, LINCOLN Navigator, MERCEDES-BENZ M-Class.

MAINTENANCE REQUIRED BY WARRANTY
First revision:	Frequency:	Diagnostic plug:
3 000 miles	6 months / 6 000 miles	Yes

SPECIFICATIONS

Model	Version Trim	Traction	Body/ Seats	Wheel base in	Lght x Wdgth x Hght in x in x in	Curb weight lb	Susp. ft/rr	Brake ft/rr	Steering type	Turning diameter ft	Steer. turns nber.	Fuel tank gal	tire size	Standard tires make	model	Standard powertrain
CADILLAC	General warranty: 4 years / 50 000 miles; antipollution: 5 years / 50 000 miles; perforation corrosion: 6 years / 100 000 miles. Road assistance.															
Escalade	base	4x4	4dr.wgn. 6	117.5	201.2x77.0x74.3	5573	it/rl	dc/dr/ABS	pwr.bal.	40.7	3.0	30	265/70R16	Firestone	Firehawk LS	V8/5.7/A4

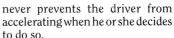
Cadillac did give the Seville a makeover in 1998, but it didn't try to wow potential buyers, but rather to hone the only model in its lineup that it could really export as a worthy ambassador of American technology, without making any drastic stylistic modifications. Cadillac really wanted to make it more compact (-12 in. for the Asian and European markets), more competent as far as handling went, more refined in terms of ride comfort and richer yet in its furbishings.

MODEL RANGE

The Seville is a four-door deluxe sedan offered in two models: the luxurious SLS and the sporty STS. The Eldorado coupe is available in two similar models, namely the base and ETC versions. All models are powered by a 4.6L V8 Northstar engine linked to an electronically controlled 4-speed automatic transmission. The engine delivers 275 hp on the SLS and Eldorado and 300 hp on the STS and ETC versions. Standard equipment includes leather seats, a sophisticated sound system, front seats equipped with side-impact air bags and built-in safety belts, a theft deterrent system and anti-skid device called StabiliTrak. But the OnStar communication and assistance system via satellite is only offered as an extra.

TECHNICAL FEATURES

The Seville and Eldorado share the Oldsmobile Aurora G platform. The structure has undergone umpteen improvements. In comparison with last year's model, it's 58% more rigid in regard to flexion and 53% more torsion-resistant. We'd like to point out that the Seville models exported to Europe and Asia are slightly shorter than those sold on our North American market. In these countries where space is a rare commodity, laws favor vehicles less than 16.5 ft in length, which explains the trimmer export model size. These precious inches were nibbled at on the front and rear bumper stone deflectors. The unibody is built of galvanized steel and includes two subframes, both front and rear. Hydroformed reinforcing tubes create a safety cage to assure high resistance in the event of a collision. The front suspension made up of MacPherson struts is similar to that on the former model, but the rear suspension now includes a dual wishbone linkage of forged aluminum supported by adjustable cross-struts, stabilizer bar and air suspension levelling control. Four-wheel disc brakes are

International Market

fitted with a four-channel system and ABS-anti-skid control. Magnetically controlled Rack-and-pinion variable assist steering is identical to that on the Aurora. The Seville is literally loaded with electronic gadgetry; a Multiplex system oversees the transmission of data for all control systems. A noteworthy detail: the on-board computer can deliver information in five languages, making a distinction between standard and French Canadian French. A subtle touch!

PROS

+ RIDE COMFORT. The suspension provides a cushy ride, even on the STS. Wheel travel has been increased by 20% in comparison with the suspension on the former Seville. Adaptive and heated seats are listed among the options; they automatically adjust

to fit the occupants' body shape and offer superb support. Effective sound dampening muffles any noise coming from the engine or chassis.

+ PERFORMANCES. The Northstar engine yields pretty amazing accelerations and pickup, which ensures really safe driving in emergency situations.

+ STYLE. This car has cool, clean looks both inside and out for an American car. Besides, there's a lovely leather scent, a pleasure you don't experience too often in this antiseptic, squeaky-clean age!

+ HANDLING. On the highway, the Seville exhibits smooth, predictable behavior, whether the driver is relaxed or raring to go. In difficult maneuvers, this is pretty reassuring. Besides, the StabiliTrak system, designed to control vehicle attitude, is really appealing since it's more adaptable than on Seville rivals. It

never prevents the driver from accelerating when he or she decides to do so.

+ CONVENIENCE FEATURE. That sliding drawer, albeit optional, that you can install in the trunk and that facilitates unloading parcels, especially those stored at the trunk bottom. Lincoln already came up with the idea for the Continental...

CONS

- TIRES. The Z-rated tires included in the «Autobahn» option package are well adapted to the vehicle, but the regular LS tires that equip the STS and ETC don't let you to hit the high speeds this car is capable of safely, for these tires make steering very touchy to control. Drivers who'd like to hit the accelerator a tad just to see, beware...

- FUEL ECONOMY. The STS and ETC engines are gas-thirsty, since it's commonplace to see the on-board computer indicating 12 mpg when high speeds are maintained.

- MANEUVERABILITY. The STS is clumsy in the city and on curved roads and on slalom runs, wheel lock sometimes occurs. Not surprising with a bod that weighs slightly more than 2 tons...

- SOME CONTROLS. The new instrument panel is elegant and relatively well organized, but the cruise control is inconveniently located, since it's outside the driver's line of vision. It's a good idea to try it out before setting out on a trek.

- NOISE. Sound dampening is effective when dealing with road or engine noise, so much so that wind whistling around the windshield roars away as soon as you hit 50 mph.

- TO BE IMPROVED UPON. Some finish and equipment details are disappointing, like the exterior weatherproofing around the doors, that tends to buckle; the flat pancake spare tire, the old-design seatbelts up front and the trunk lining that's of Cavalier vintage...

CONCLUSION

Cadillac is betting on the Seville to get in on the international car sales game. But to get there, the automaker will have to correct some of the annoying items that keep the Seville a bit behind in the race against its European and Japanese rivals. ☺

RATING
CADILLAC Seville-Eldorado

CONCEPT :		**84%**
Technology	100	
Safety :	90	
Interior space :	80	
Trunk volume:	70	
Quality/fit/finish :	80	
DRIVING:		**68%**
Cockpit :	80	
Performance :	75	
Handling :	50	
Steering :	80	
Braking :	55	
ORIGINAL EQUIPMENT:		**80%**
Tires :	80	
Headlights :	80	
Wipers :	75	
Rear defroster :	75	
Radio :	90	
COMFORT :		**82%**
Seats :	80	
Suspension :	80	
Sound level :	80	
Conveniences :	80	
Air conditioning :	90	
BUDGET :		**47%**
Price :	0	
Fuel economy :	50	
Insurance :	45	
Satisfaction :	90	
Depreciation :	50	
Overall rating:		**72.2%**

NEW FOR 1999

- Optional OnStar communication and assistance system.
- Optional adaptive heated seats.
- Power adjustable seats with lumbar massage supports offered on the STS.
- Three new body shades.

ENGINES / TRANSMISSIONS / PERFORMANCES

Model/ version	Type / timing valve / fuel system	Displacement cu in	Power bhp @ rpm	Torque lb-ft @ rpm	Compres. ratio	Driving wheels / transmission	Final ratio	Acceler. 0-60 mph s	Standing 1/4 & 5/8 mile s	Acceler. 50-75 mph s	Braking 60-0 mph f	Top speed mph	Lateral acceler. G	Noise level dBA	Fuel economy mpg City	Highway	Fuel type Octane
SLS-base	V8*4.6 DOHC-32-SFI	279	275 @ 5600	300 @ 4000	10.3 :1	front - A4	3.11	7.8	15.8	29.0	5.0	135	112	0.77	65-70	17	28	S 91
STS-ETC	V8*4.6 DOHC-32-SFI	279	300 @ 6000	295 @ 4400	10.3 :1	front - A4	3.71	7.5	15.5	28.5	4.5	138	150	0.79	65-71	17	27	S 91

PRICE & EQUIPMENT

CADILLAC Seville	SLS	STS		
CADILLAC Eldorado			**base**	**ETC**
Retail price $:	42,495	46,995	38,495	42,695
Dealer invoice $:	39,038	43,155	35,378	39,221
Shipping & handling $:	665	665	665	665
Automatic transmission:	S	S	S	S
Cruise control:	S	S	S	S
Power steering:	S	S	S	S
Anti-lock brakes:	S	S	S	S
Traction control:	S	S	S	S
Air conditioning:	SA	SA	SA	SA
Leather:	S	S	S	S
AM/FM/radio-cassette:	S	S	S	S
Power door locks:	S	S	S	S
Power windows:	S	S	S	S
Tilt steering:	S	S	S	S
Dual adjustable mirrors:	S	S	S	S
Alloy wheels:	S	S	S	S
Anti-theft system:	S	S	S	S

Colors

Exterior: Green, White, Black, Beige, Garnet, Red, Mocha, Blue, Clay, Sand, Carmine.

Interior: Black, Cappuccino, Dark cherry, Dark blue, Beige.

AT A GLANCE...

Category:	front-wheel drive luxury coupes & sedans.
Class :	**7**

HISTORIC

Introduced in:	1976-1998
Made in:	Hamtramck-Detroit, Michigan, USA.

DEMOGRAPHICS

Model	Men./Wom.	Age	Married	College	Income
Seville	87/13%	53	83%	44%	$ 70 000

INDEX

Safety:	100 %	Satisfaction:	92 %
Depreciation:	51 %	Insurance:	$1500-1650
Cost per mile:	$0.85	Number of dealers:	1 600

SALES

Model	1996	1997	Result
Seville	33 809	29 837	-11.7 %
Eldorado	20 964	20 609	- 1.7 %

MAIN COMPETITORS

BMW 5-Series, INFINITI Q45, JAGUAR XJ8, LEXUS GS-LS 400, LINCOLN Continental, MERCEDES-BENZ E-Class, OLDSMOBILE Aurora.

MAINTENANCE REQUIRED BY WARRANTY

First revision:	Frequency:	Diagnostic plug:
3 000 miles	6 000 miles	Yes

SPECIFICATIONS

Model	Version Trim	Body/ Seats	Interior volume cu ft	Trunk volume cu ft	Cd	Wheel base in	Lght x Wdgth x Hght in x in x in	Curb weight lb	Susp. ft/rr	Brake ft/rr	Steering type	Turning diameter ft	Steer. turns nber.	Fuel tank gal	tire size	Standard tires make	model	Standard powertrain
CADILLAC	General warranty: 4 years / 50 000 miles; antipollution: 5 years / 50 000 miles; perforation corrosion: 6 years / 100 000 miles. Road assistance:																	
Seville	SLS	4dr.sdn. 5	104.2	15.7	0.31	112.2	201.0x75.0x55.7	3970	ih/ih	dc/ABS	pwr.r&p.	40.5	2.40	18.5	235/60R16	Goodyear	Integrity	V8/4.6/A4
Seville	STS	4dr.sdn. 5	104.2	15.7	0.31	112.2	201.0x75.0x55.4	4001	ih/ih	dc/ABS	pwr.r&p.	40.5	2.40	18.5	235/60R16	Goodyear	Eagle LS	V8/4.6/A4
Eldorado	base	2dr.cpe. 5	99.5	15.3	0.33	108.0	200.6x75.5x53.6	3843	ih/ih	dc/ABS	pwr.r&p.	40.3	2.65	20.0	225/60R16	Michelin	XW4	V8/4.6/A4
Eldorado	ETC	2dr.cpe. 5	99.5	15.3	0.33	108.0	200.6x75.5x53.6	3876	ih/ih	dc/ABS	pwr.r&p.	40.3	2.83	20.0	225/60R16	Goodyear	Eagle RS-A	V8/4.6/A4

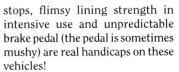

The Astro and the Safari are the only vehicles in a unique market segment, namely rear-wheel drive mid-size vans. These vehicles sit between front-wheel drive minivans and big rear-wheel drive delivery trucks. In spite of seriously dubious quality and reliability, they're still popular with some drivers with special transportation needs.

MODEL RANGE

Since 1995, the only body style available is the extended version. Yet GM offers 4X2 and 4X4 models in three trim levels: base, LS and LT at Chevrolet as well as SLX, SLE and SLT at GMC. A 4.3L V6 engine powers these vans, linked to a 4-speed electronically controlled automatic transmission.

TECHNICAL FEATURES

The Astro and Safari are almost identical twins, except for a few minor variants. These minivans are pretty boxy-looking, yet they yield a drag coefficient of 0.38, which is pretty respectable given the considerable vehicle hulk. The steel monocoque body has an ancillary H-frame up front that adds to overall structural rigidity. The independent front suspension uses cross-struts on the 4X2 versions and torsion bars on the 4X4's. At the rear, the rigid axle suspension of Salisbury design is supported by dual leaf springs. The vehicle is equipped with variable assist recirculating ball steering. The front disc brakes and rear drum brakes are linked to standard ABS. These vans have a hauling capacity of 1765 pounds and a towing capacity of 5 500 lbs. This kind of prowess is often the reason behind the purchase, since there isn't a single front-wheel drive minivan on the road that can boast of such brawn.

PROS

+ VERSATILITY. The Astro and the Safari have a dual personality: they can seat up to eight passengers, then be converted into work vehicles capable of hauling a heavy load or pulling a hefty trailer. Load volume is up to 170 cu.ft.

+ SIZE The midsize body of these vans places them in a category midway between minivans and bulky delivery vans.

+ ENGINE. Interior and exterior design features are more nicely crafted than before and the instrument panel is more ergonomic.

Utility Wagon

+ COCKPIT. Broad windows, generous rearview mirrors and a big rear window (on models with triple-panel Dutch doors in the rear) provide excellent visibility in all directions. And the transmission shifter located behind the steering wheel is really handy. Lastly, the transmission downshifts quickly while shifting gears and offers good braking effect.

+ CONSOLE. The console near the engine hood is really neat and compensates for the missing glove compartment.

+ STEERING. The 4X2's maneuver better than the 4X4's due to a smaller turn angle diameter. The 4X4's also have more direct steering, which makes for more agile moves.

+ NICE FEATURES: 80% of owners are very satisfied with the reliability of their vehicle. The triple-panel Dutch rear doors are very practical and they're fitted with a windshield wiper and electric defroster, features you don't get on conventional swing doors.

CONS

- SAFETY FEATURES. Collision tests run by the United States N.H.T.S.A. infer low-level passenger safety. These tests indicate that serious bodily harm could occur in some types of accidents.

- FUEL CONSUMPTION. We recorded one of the highest gas consumption levels in the minivan category. A V8 engine of low displacement would no doubt be a better choice and it would provide more torque.

- BRAKES. Long stretching stopping distances on emergency stops, flimsy lining strength in intensive use and unpredictable brake pedal (the pedal is sometimes mushy) are real handicaps on these vehicles!

- STEERING. At low speeds, it's too sensitive, whereas for normal driving, it's sometimes too firm, and it's vague at the center. Definitely not a showpiece in the genre.

-HANDLING. This really depends mostly on tire quality. Besides, the high-perched center of gravity on these vans requires some prudence, especially on tight curves. In winter conditions, it would be wise to equip these vehicles with good-quality tires so as to avoid some clumsy pas de deux.

- LACK OF SPACE. Rear seat passengers enjoy more leg room than the driver and front seat passenger, because the engine protrudes inside the cabin, as do the front wheel wells, so you end up with a far from flat floor. Besides, these rear-wheel drive vehicles come equipped with the usual drive gear, so the floor is very high and it's hard to climb aboard both up front and at the rear.

- TO BE IMPROVED UPON: The front door opening angle is too narrow. As well, the front seat adjustment controls are so inconveniently located that you have to open the door to use them!

-RIDE COMFORT. The rather rough and ready suspension isn't a friend of uneven road surfaces. The seat cushions are very short and stingy. And there sure is a lot of resounding noise at certain speeds. If you're looking for comfort, best to shop elsewhere!

- HANDICAP. These vans are so high that you can't park them in a regular garage or in an inside parking lot.

CONCLUSION

The Astro and Safari vans are «work vehicles». They're nothing like minivans and not at all like cars. On the other hand, for transporting or pulling heavy loads, they're ideal...if their insatiable gas appetite doesn't bother you too much!

RATING
CHEVROLET-GMC Astro-Safari

CONCEPT :		72%
Technology	70	
Safety :	50	
Interior space :	100	
Trunk volume:	70	
Quality/fit/finish :	70	

DRIVING:		52%
Cockpit	80	
Performance :	35	
Handling :	35	
Steering :	75	
Braking :	35	

ORIGINAL EQUIPMENT:		65%
Tires :	70	
Headlights :	70	
Wipers :	70	
Rear defroster :	40	
Radio :	75	

COMFORT :		69%
Seats :	75	
Suspension :	70	
Sound level :	50	
Conveniences :	70	
Air conditioning :	80	

BUDGET :		54%
Price :	50	
Fuel economy :	40	
Insurance :	60	
Satisfaction :	75	
Depreciation :	45	

Overall rating: **62.4%**

NEW FOR 1999

- Keys with a larger grasp end offer a better grip.
- New overhead console.
- Improved automatic transmission.
- Transfer box on the all-wheel drive model.
- Two new body shades.

ENGINES / TRANSMISSIONS / PERFORMANCES

Model/ version	Type / timing valve / fuel system	Displacement cu in	Power bhp @ rpm	Torque lb-ft @ rpm	Compres. ratio	Driving wheels / transmission	Final ratio	Acceler. 0-60 mph s	Standing 1/4 & 5/8 mile s	Acceler. 50-75 mph s	Braking 60-0 mph f	Top speed mph	Lateral acceler. G	Noise level dBA	Fuel economy mpg City	Fuel economy mpg Highway	Fuel type Octane
4x2	V6 4.3 OHV-12-SFI	262	190 @ 4400	250 @ 2800	9.2 :1	rear - A4*	3.73	11.0	17.9 32.3	7.8	158	106	0.67	68	16	22	R 87
4x4	V6 4.3 OHV-12-SFI	262	190 @ 4400	250 @ 2800	9.2 :1	rear/4 - A4*	3.73	11.7	18.5 33.0	8.5	164	103	0.67	68	16	21	R 87

PRICE & EQUIPMENT

CHEVROLET Astro	base	LS	LT
GMC Safari	**SLX**	**SLE**	**SLT**
Retail price $:	20,174	23,510	25,696
Dealer invoice $:	18,257	21,126	23,023
Shipping & handling $:	585	585	585
Automatic transmission:	S	S	S
Cruise control:	O	S	S
Power steering:	S	S	S
Anti-lock brakes:	S	S	S
Traction control:	-	-	-
Air conditioning:	SM	SM	SM
Leather:	-	-	O
AM/FM/radio-cassette:	O	O	O
Power door locks:	O	S	S
Power windows:	O	S	S
Tilt steering:	O	S	S
Dual adjustable mirrors:	SM	SE	SE
Alloy wheels:	-	O	S
Anti-theft system:	S	S	S

Colors
Exterior: White, Silver, Lime, Gray, Blue, Black, Green, Copper, Red, Bronze.

Interior: Medium Gray, Blue, Red, Neutral.

AT A GLANCE...

Category: rear-wheel drive or AWD midsize vans. **Class :** utility.

HISTORIC
Introduced in: 1986
Made in: Baltimore, Maryland, USA.

DEMOGRAPHICS
Model	Men./Wom.	Age	Married	College	Income
Astro	77/23 %	45	87 %	30 %	$36 000
Safari	80/20 %	45	93 %	32 %	$36 000

INDEX
Safety:	50 %	Satisfaction:	75 %
Depreciation:	53 %	Insurance:	$825-1000
Cost per mile:	$0.51	Number of dealers:	4 466

SALES
Model	1996	1997	Result
Astro	125 962	111 390	- 11.6 %
Safari	39 999	35 787	- 10.5 %

MAIN COMPETITORS
CHEVROLET Venture, DODGE Caravan/ Grand Caravan, FORD Villager & Windstar, HONDA Odyssey, MAZDA MPV, MERCURY Villager, NISSAN Quest, PLYMOUTH Voyager/Grand Voyager, PONTIAC Trans Sport, TOYOTA Sienna, VW EuroVan.

MAINTENANCE REQUIRED BY WARRANTY
First revision:	Frequency:	Diagnostic plug:
3 000 miles	6 000 miles	Yes

SPECIFICATIONS

Model	Version Trim	Traction	Body/ Seats	Wheel base in	Lght x Wdgth x Hght in x in x in	Curb weight lb	Susp. ft/rr	Brake ft/rr	Steering type	Turning diameter ft	Steer. turns nber.	Fuel tank gal	tire size	Standard tires make	model	Standard powertrain
CHEVROLET / GMC	General warranty: 3 years / 36 000 miles; antipollution: 5 years / 50 000 miles; perforation corrosion: 6 years / 100 000 miles. Road assistance:															
Astro / Safari base / SLX 4x2			4dr.van 2/8	111.2	189.8x77.5x74.9	4195	ih/rldc/dr/ABS		pwr.ball	38.3	3.10	25	215/75R15	Uniroyal	Tiger Paw	V6/4.3/A4
Astro / Safari LS / SLE 4x2			4dr.van 5/8	111.2	189.8x77.5x74.9	-	ih/rtdc/dr/ABS		pwr.ball	38.3	3.10	25	215/75R15	Uniroyal	Tiger Paw	V6/4.3/A4
Astro / Safari LT / SLT 4x2			4dr.van 5/8	111.2	189.8x77.5x74.9	-	ih/rtdc/dr/ABS		pwr.ball	38.3	3.10	25	215/75R15	Uniroyal	Tiger Paw	V6/4.3/A4
Astro / Safari base / SLX 4x4			4dr.van 2/8	111.2	189.8x77.5x74.9	4442	ih/rtdc/dr/ABS		pwr.ball	41.7	2.70	25	215/75R15	Uniroyal	Tiger Paw	V6/4.3/A4
Astro / Safari LS / SLE 4x4			4dr.van 5/8	111.2	189.8x77.5x74.9	-	ih/rtdc/dr/ABS		pwr.ball	41.7	2.70	25	215/75R15	Uniroyal	Tiger Paw	V6/4.3/A4
Astro / Safari LT / SLT 4x4			4dr.van 5/8	111.2	189.8x77.5x74.9	-	ih/rtdc/dr/ABS		pwr.ball	41.7	2.70	25	215/75R15	Uniroyal	Tiger Paw	V6/4.3/A4

A new luxury variant joins the Chevrolet Blazer and GMC Jimmy cohort for 1999: it's called the GMC Envoy. GM wanted to keep its 4X4 midsize SUV's at the top of the heap in this category. Better still, since 1997, their combined North American sales have placed them in second place behind the Ford Explorer and ahead of the Jeep Grand Cherokee. So the added new model surely won't increase sales dramatically, but will help consolidate the popularity of the whole lineup.

MODEL RANGE
GM offers the Blazer-Jimmy in either 2 or 4-door models, with either rear or all-wheel drive. The Envoy, on the other hand, is only sold in a 4-door 4X4 version. Chevrolet is offering three trim levels: base, LS and LT. At GMC, the equivalent versions are called: SL, SLS and SLT. The Envoy is a cream of the crop model exclusive to the GMC lineup. Generally speaking, these vehicles are richly equipped and goodies include standard automatic gearbox, climate control, cruise control, tilt steering wheel (except the lower end versions), four-wheel ABS and a PASS-Lock theft deterrent system.

TECHNICAL FEATURES
The central tube chassis is welded onto the body that's clad in dual-side galvanized sheet metal, except for the roof. «Insta-Trac» all-wheel drive that equips the 4X4's isn't in constant mesh, but can be activated by shift-on-the-fly. A new permanent «AutoTrac» system is available as an option for 1999 (standard on the Envoy). On the 4X4's, torque is distributed 35/65% to front and rear respectively. The independent front suspension consists of A-arms and cross-struts, with coil springs for the 4X2's and torsion bars for the 4X4's. At the rear, the rigid axle is suspended from semi-elliptic leaf springs. An anti-roll bar completes each setup. There are three shock absorber modes: the first is geared to ride comfort with a negative effect on pulling force; the second is firmer, so it helps when hauling heavy trailers; the third is super firm and maximizes trailering capabilities. Since 1998, the vehicle is equipped with four-wheel disc brakes linked to standard ABS. But since last year, the 4.3L V6 Vortec engine develops 15 hp less than the 4.0L V6 that drives the Explorer and GM doesn't offer a V8 model engine, unlike the competition.

PROS
+ **PERFORMANCES.** The V6

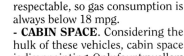

Always Popular

engine provides top-notch accelerations and pickup; in 4X2 mode, performances are akin to those of an average family sedan. On off-the-road maneuvres, the muscular torque is a welcome traveller.

+ **RIDE COMFORT.** Highway driving is very comfy, except with the reinforced suspension. Road irregularities are well disguised and the big tires act in quite a civilized manner.

+ **HANDLING.** With a tougher chassis and frame, road handling on these SUV's seems more reassured, especially on rough surfaces. But don't go thinking it's perfect.

+ **BRAKES.** The four-wheel brakes provide powerful and never-die braking. It cuts down on the stopping distances and ABS stabilizes vehicle path. But brakes

are hard to apply, since the pedal is spongy.

+**QUALITY.** In comparison with the first Blazer models, the new generation is definitely better crafted. Even finish and trim materials seem plusher.

+ **INTERESTING.** Insta-Trac lets you engage the rear wheels while driving, at whatever speed. It's easy to apply, thanks to an electronically controlled transfer box.

+ **DESIGN DETAILS.** The interior is both elegant and ergonomic. Controls and accessories are generally conveniently located and easy to reach and the instrument panel has a neat lay-out.

+ **SEATS.** Nicely shaped seats provide quite a bit of lateral support and lots more lumbar support. The cockpit is easy to adjust to. The rear seatbench cushion is low-slung, but upholstery is cushy.

+ **STORAGE COMPARTMENTS.** The glove compartment isn't too roomy, but front and rear side-pockets on the upper end models make up for this stingy feature.

CONS
- **FUEL CONSUMPTION.** These vehicles are juggernauts (4 045 lbs) and the V6 displacement is pretty respectable, so gas consumption is always below 18 mpg.

- **CABIN SPACE.** Considering the hulk of these vehicles, cabin space is disappointing. Only four travellers can be comfortably seated, due to the really narrow body; a fifth passenger would only want to climb aboard in a pinch.

-**SOUNDPROOFING.** Road noise coming from the chassis and engine roars at the slightest touch of the accelerator, proof positive that sound dampening isn't what it could be.

- **ACCESS.** It's limited in the rear seats, whether it's a 2 or 4-door vehicle and rear seats are tough to get to due to a narrow door opening angle and poorly located handles.

-**HATCHBACK.** Some models come with a small hatch door linked to a swing door, a design combination that limits access to the luggage hold. The single-panel rear door with lifting rear window is more convenient. You can even stash away small parcels by simply raising the rear window.

- **OUTWARD VIEW.** It's awfully limited towards the rear. The 2-door versions are pretty crummy in this regard, yielding some major blind spots.

- **TO BE IMPROVED UPON.** Some controls are so bloody complicated that the engineers should go back to the drawing board, such as the shifter located to the left of the steering wheel and we noticed that some models aren't equipped with rear seat headrests.

CONCLUSION
In this vehicle segment that's literally crowded with models, the Blazer, Jimmy and Envoy are average. Yet the Ford Explorer and Jeep Grand Cherokee are still more appealing for a number or reasons, such as a wider engine model choice.

RATING
CHEVROLET-GMC Blazer-Jimmy

CONCEPT :		73%
Technology	75	
Safety :	75	
Interior space :	65	
Trunk volume:	75	
Quality/fit/finish :	75	

DRIVING:		58%
Cockpit :	80	
Performance :	55	
Handling :	45	
Steering :	70	
Braking :	40	

ORIGINAL EQUIPMENT:		74%
Tires :	80	
Headlights :	80	
Wipers :	70	
Rear defroster :	60	
Radio :	80	

COMFORT :		67%
Seats :	75	
Suspension :	70	
Sound level :	50	
Conveniences :	60	
Air conditioning :	80	

BUDGET :		52%
Price :	45	
Fuel economy :	40	
Insurance :	50	
Satisfaction :	75	
Depreciation :	50	

Overall rating:		**64.8%**

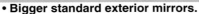

NEW FOR 1999
- Bigger standard exterior mirrors.
- Warning lamp for poorly closed windows.
- Autotrac transmission available as an option.
- Six-way adjustable power driver's seat as an option.
- Sophisticated Bose sound system as an option.
- New CD changer that holds 6 CD's.
- Luxury version Envoy in the Jimmy lineup.

ENGINES / TRANSMISSIONS / PERFORMANCES

Model/ version	Type / timing valve / fuel system	Displacement cu in	Power bhp @ rpm	Torque lb-ft @ rpm	Compres. ratio	Driving wheels / transmission	Final ratio	Acceler. 0-60 mph s	Standing 1/4 & 5/8 mile s	Acceler. 50-75 mph s	Braking 60-0 mph f	Top speed mph	Lateral acceler. G	Noise level dBA	Fuel economy mpg City	Fuel economy mpg Highway	Fuel type Octane
4x2	V6 4.3 OHV-12-SFI	262	190 @ 4400	250 @ 2800	9.2 :1	rear-M5	3.42	9.0	16.7	29.8	6.5	144	115	0.72	69	16	24	R 87
						rear-A4*	3.42	9.4	17.2	30.6	6.8	157	118	0.72	69	16	22	R 87
4x4	V6 4.3 OHV-12-SFI	262	190 @ 4400	250 @ 2800	9.2 :1	four-M5	3.42	9.6	17.2	30.4	7.0	148	109	0.72	69	15	21	R 87
						four-A4*	3.42	9.9	17.5	30.6	7.7	153	115	0.72	69	13	22	R 87

PRICE & EQUIPMENT

CHEVROLET Blazer	base	LS	ZR2	LT	TrailBlazer
GMC Jimmy	**SL**	**SLS**	**SLE**	**SLT**	
Retail price $:	21,663	25,219	23,513	27,342	NA
Dealer invoice $:	19,605	22,663	21,196	24,489	NA
Shipping & handling $:	515	515	515	515	515
Automatic transmission:	S	S	S	S	S
Cruise control:	O	S	S	S	S
Power steering:	S	S	S	S	S
Anti-lock brakes:	S	S	S	S	S
Traction control:	-	-	-	-	-
Air conditioning:	SM	SM	SM	SA	SA
Leather:	-	-	-	S	S
AM/FM/radio-cassette:	O	S	S	S	SCD
Power door locks:	O	S	S	S	S
Power windows:	O	S	S	S	S
Tilt steering:	O	S	S	S	S
Dual adjustable mirrors:	SM	SE	SE	SE	SE
Alloy wheels:	O	S	S	S	S
Anti-theft system:	S	S	S	S	S

Colors
Exterior: White, Black Blue, Gold, Green, Red, Copper, Beige, Pewter.

Interior: Graphite, Medium Gray, Beige.

AT A GLANCE...

Category: rear-wheel drive or 4WD all-terrain vehicle. **Class :** utility

HISTORIC
Introduced in: 1983: Blazer S-10/Jimmy.
Made in: Moraine, OH, Linden NJ, USA.

DEMOGRAPHICS
Model	Men./Wom.	Age	Married	College	Income
Blazer/Jimmy	80/20 %	46	75 %	28 %	$39 000

INDEX
Safety:	75 %	Satisfaction:	75 %
Depreciation:	50 %	Insurance:	$955 -1 065
Cost per mile:	$0.55	Number of dealers:	4 466

SALES
Model	1996	1997	Result
Blazer	246 307	221 400	- 10.1 %
Jimmy	77 838	75 817	- 2.6 %

MAIN COMPETITORS
DODGE Durango FORD Explorer, ISUZU Rodeo & Trooper, JEEP Cherokee & Grand Cherokee, NISSAN Pathfinder, TOYOTA 4Runner.

MAINTENANCE REQUIRED BY WARRANTY
First revision:	Frequency:	Diagnostic plug:
3 000 miles	6 months/ 6 000 miles	Yes

SPECIFICATIONS

Model	Version Trim	Traction	Body/ Seats	Wheel base in	Lght x Wdgth x Hght in x in x in	Curb weight lb	Susp. ft/rr	Brake ft/rr	Steering type	Turning diameter ft	Steer. turns nber.	Fuel tank gal	tire size	Standard tires make	model	Standard powertrain
CHEVROLET / GMC				General warranty: 3 years / 36 000 miles; antipollution: 5 years / 50 000 miles; perforation corrosion: 6 years / 100 000 miles. Road assistance.											
Blazer-Jimmy base		4x2	2dr.wgn.4	100.5	176.8x67.8x64.9	3519	ih/rl	dc/ABS	pwr.bal	34.8	3.38	19.0	205/75R15	Michelin	XW4	V6/4.3/A4
Blazer-Jimmy base		4x2	4dr.wgn.5	107.0	183.3x67.8x64.3	3673	ih/rl	dc/ABS	pwr.bal	36.6	3.38	18.0	205/75R15	Michelin	XW4	V6/4.3/A4
Blazer-Jimmy base		4x4	2dr.wgn.4	100.5	176.8x67.8x64.5	3849	it/rl	dc/ABS	pwr.bal	35.2	2.97	19.0	205/75R15	Michelin	XW4	V6/4.3/A4
Blazer-Jimmy base		4x4	4dr.wgn.5	107.0	183.3x67.8x64.2	4041	it/rl	dc/ABS	pwr.bal	39.5	2.97	18.0	205/75R15	Michelin	XW4	V6/4.3/A4

Plummeting Camaro sales are a bad sign. This car's future remains far from a sure thing; its disappearance from the landscape is being suggested, along with the demise of its twin the Firebird. This phenomenon was to be expected, after all. If GM hadn't limited modifications to esthetic touch up jobs and a more rigid platform way back in 1993, maybe things would have been different today, even if this market segment is experiencing a certain disfavor with the public.

MODEL RANGE

The Camaro and Firebird have different exterior stylistic details, but they're built on the same platform and are equipped with identical mechanical features. The Chevrolet model range is made up of coupes and convertibles that vary according to equipment level: base, RS and Z28. A 3.8L V6 engine paired up with a 5-speed manual transmission animates the lower end and RS models. As for the Z28 versions, they borrow the 5.7L LS1 V8 from the Corvette. It's zoomy with its 305 hp (320 hp for the SS option package) and is linked to a 4-speed automatic gearbox or an optional 6-speed manual gearbox. Chevrolet sells «performance» sets of options for the V6 (RPO Y87) and the Z28 (RPO 1LE).

TECHNICAL FEATURES

This sleek-looking body yields good aerodynamics, with a drag coefficient of 0.32 for the coupe and 0.36 for the convertible. The body is built of galvanized steel (rear fenders and hood) and composite polymer (door panels, front fenders, roof, trunk lid and rear spoiler). Compared to former models that it replaced in 1993, this Camaro benefits from a more rigid structure due to reinforcements and longitudinal beams running under the doors. The front suspension consists of uneven transverse control arms, while the rear suspension is made up of a rigid axle suspended by multi-link Salisbury components and a torque arm. There are anti-roll bars of various diameters at the front and rear, depending on the model. Four-wheel disc brakes are listed among standard equipment items, as is the Bosch ABS system. Each year the rack-and-pinion power steering keeps undergoing some ajustments geared to improve performance and its reduction ratio is better on the Z28 versions.

Borrowed Time ?

PROS

+ STYLE. The Camaro looks like an arrow in flight. Simply spectacular! It still makes heads turn even after all these years, especially the Z28 and the SS dressed in flashy-colored metal.

+ PERFORMANCES. With the new LS1 Corvette engine, acceleration time and pickup on the Z28 are pretty well the same as on the leader of the pack Chevrolet model car.

+ RIDE FEEL. Push the accelerator to the floor and the Z28 will fill you with its V8 surge and feline roar, a sensation that's really thrilling!

+VALUE. The price/performance ratio is still appealing to drivers who want to really feel alive at the wheel, especially those who talk about 0-60 mph take-off time from dawn till dusk.

+ HANDLING. Driving pleasure is directly proportional to road surface quality. The new stiffer frame helps keep the car right on track and cuts down on sway effect. So you can hit a pretty good lateral acceleration speed, albeit less sensational than that achieved in a Corvette, a model that benefits from a lower center of gravity and tires that have more grit grip.

+ INTERIOR DESIGN. The instrument panel was given a face-lift in 1997 and is now ergonomic and definitely less flashy and gawdy-looking. It looks swish, now that trim materials don't include that tacky plastic stuff that it sported not so long ago.

+ CONVERTIBLE MODEL. The device to remove the convertible roof is super efficient and the rear window is made of glass.

+ TRACTION CONTROL. It comes standard on all models, and so accelerating on wet roads is more solid and stable, which should make for safer street races...

CONS

- SIZE. Is there still a market niche for the Camaro? It's so bulky and cumbersome and so very heavy and it's equipped with really out-of-date technology!

- OUTWARD VIEW. Visibility sure wasn't a priority for the people who designed this vehicle. The instrument panel is very high and the seats swing low in this chariot so even the view out front isn't the greatest; lateral outward view is blocked by the high frame; towards the back, the thick B pillar and the sharply slanted rear window blot out the view.

- V6 ENGINE. With such a poor power to weight ratio, the V6 engine is more geared to quiet Sunday drives than to bold and brassy moves.

- V8 ENGINE. Not everyone can drive a Z28! Its responses are almost brutal: with such a potentially high-performance engine and such a firm suspension, you're in for a bucking bronco ride on poor pavement.

-RIGIDITY. The convertibles lack structural stiffness. Frame torsion makes driving somewhat haphazard, so much so that a driver who guns it beyond his own capabilities... will be in a cold sweat!

- NOT TOO CONVENIENT. Given the size of this car, getting aboard is pretty tricky and involves a series of acrobatic moves even with those huge doors. Rear seats, storage space and trunk are so stingy they're something of a joke.

- TO BE IMPROVED UPON: The catalytic converter impinges on cabin space up front and it causes passenger discomfort due to a misshapen floor; the arduous speed shifter with the manual transmission; the convertible top protective cover that's a pain to use.

CONCLUSION

The Camaro's diminishing success proves beyond a doubt that it's a vehicle of a bygone era. You can try to cling to a myth but potential buyers' needs and expectations have changed. GM would have better sales in the case of a versatile hybrid with all-wheel drive equipped with a relatively muscular engine. After all, even Porsche will soon be launching an all-terrain vehicle soon! ☺

RATING
CHEVROLET Camaro

CONCEPT : 62%
Technology	75
Safety :	90
Interior space :	35
Trunk volume:	40
Quality/fit/finish :	70

DRIVING: 70%
Cockpit :	80
Performance :	70
Handling :	70
Steering :	70
Braking :	60

ORIGINAL EQUIPMENT: 78%
Tires :	80
Headlights :	80
Wipers :	80
Rear defroster :	70
Radio :	80

COMFORT : 58%
Seats :	60
Suspension :	60
Sound level:	40
Conveniences :	50
Air conditioning :	80

BUDGET : 50%
Price :	45
Fuel economy :	40
Insurance :	40
Satisfaction :	75
Depreciation :	50

Overall rating: 63.6%

NEW FOR 1999

- Zexel Torsen differential for all non-slip differentials.
- Indicator lamp for engine oil life.
- Monsoon sound system available as an extra.
- Traction control now available on V6 models.
- Plastic 16.8 gallons gas tank.
- Three new exterior shades.

ENGINES / TRANSMISSIONS / PERFORMANCES

Model/ version	Type / timing valve / fuel system	Displacement cu in	Power bhp @ rpm	Torque lb-ft @ rpm	Compres. ratio	Driving wheels / transmission	Final ratio	Acceler. 0-60 mph s	Standing 1/4 & 5/8 mile s	Acceler. 50-75 mph s	Braking 60-0 mph f	Top speed mph	Lateral acceler. G	Noise level dBA	Fuel economy mpg City	Fuel economy mpg Highway	Fuel type Octane
base L36	V6* 3.8 OHV-12-SFI	231	200 @ 5200	225 @ 4000	9.4 :1	rear - M5*	3.23	9.0	15.8 29.7	6.2	131	115	0.85	68	20	33	R 87
						rear - A4	3.08	9.8	17.0 30.8	6.7	138	112	0.85	68	20	32	R 87
Z28 LS1	V8* 5.7 OHV-16-SFI	346	305 @ 5200	335 @ 4000	10.1 :1	rear - M6	3.42	5.5	14.0 25.4	3.7	125	143	0.87	72	17	29	S 91
						rear - A4*	2.73	6.0	14.5 26.0	4.0	131	137	0.87	72	17	26	S 91
Z28 SS	V8 5.7 OHV-16-SFI	346	320 @ 5200	340 @ 4400	10.1 :1	rear -M6	3.42	5.4	13.8 25.2	3.6	125	149	0.88	72	16	26	S 91

PRICE & EQUIPMENT

CHEVROLET Camaro	cpe	conv.	cpe. Z28	conv. Z28
Retail price $:	16,625	22,125	20,470	27,450
Dealer invoice $:	15,212	20,244	18,730	25,117
Shipping & handling $:	525	525	525	525
Automatic transmission:	O	O	S	S
Cruise control:	O	O	S	S
Power steering:	S	S	S	S
Anti-lock brakes:	S	S	S	S
Traction control:	O	O	O	O
Air conditioning:	SM	SM	SM	SM
Leather:	O	O	O	O
AM/FM/radio-cassette:	S	S	S	S
Power door locks:	O	O	O	O
Power windows:	O	O	O	S
Tilt steering:	S	S	S	S
Dual adjustable mirrors:	SM	SM	SM	SE
Alloy wheels:	O	O	S	S
Anti-theft system:	S	S	S	S

Colors
Exterior: Black, Red, Teal, White, Gold, Blue, Green, Orange, Pewter.

Interior: Cloth : Neutral, Dark Gray, Red.
Leather : White, Dark Gray, Neutral.

AT A GLANCE...

Category: rear-wheel drive sport coupes & convertibles.   **Class :** S

HISTORIC
Introduced in:	1967-1993
Made in:	Ste-Thérèse, Quebec, Canada.

DEMOGRAPHICS
Model	Men./Wom.	Age	Married	College	Income
Camaro	70/30 %	39	48 %	39 %	$42 000

INDEX
Safety:	90 %	Satisfaction:	75 %
Depreciation:	50 %	Insurance:	$1 385 -1 475
Cost per mile:	$0.45	Number of dealers:	4 466

SALES
Model	1996	1997	Result
Camaro	66 866	55 973	- 16.3%

MAIN COMPETITORS
ACURA Integra, CHRYSLER Sebring, DODGE Avenger, FORD Mustang, HONDA Prelude, MITSUBISHI Eclipse & 3000 GT, TOYOTA Supra..

MAINTENANCE REQUIRED BY WARRANTY
First revision:	Frequency:	Diagnostic plug:
3 000 miles	6 000 miles	Yes

SPECIFICATIONS

Model	Version Trim	Body/ Seats	Interior volume cu ft	Trunk volume cu ft	Cd	Wheel base in	Lght x Wdgth x Hght in x in x in	Curb weight lb	Susp. ft/rr	Brake ft/rr	Steering type	Turning diameter ft	Steer. turns nber.	Fuel tank gal	tire size	Standard tires make	model	Standard powertrain
CHEVROLET		General warranty: 3 years / 36 000 miles; antipollution: 5 years / 50 000 miles; perforation corrosion: 6 years / 100 000 miles. Road assistance.																
Camaro	base	2dr.cpe. 2+2	81.9	12.9	0.32	101.1	193.2x74.1x51.3	3300	ih/rh	dc/ABS	pwr.r&p.	40.8	2.67	16.8	215/60R16	BF Goodrich	Comp T/A	V6/3.8/M5
	base	2dr.con. 2+2	80.6	7.6	0.36	101.1	193.2x74.1x52.0	3500	ih/rh	dc/ABS	pwr.r&p.	40.8	2.67	16.8	215/60R16	BF Goodrich	Comp T/A	V6/3.8/M5
	Z28	2dr.cpe. 2+2	81.9	12.9	0.32	101.1	193.2x74.1x51.3	3439	ih/rh	dc/ABS	pwr.r&p.	40.1	2.28	16.8	235/55R16	Goodyear	Eagle GS-C	V8/5.7/A4
	Z28	2dr.con. 2+2	80.6	7.6	0.36	101.1	193.2x74.1x52.0	3574	ih/rh	dc/ABS	pwr.r&p.	40.1	2.28	16.8	235/55R16	Goodyear	Eagle GS-C	V8/5.7/A4

CHEVROLET-GMC
Silverado-Sierra

Back in Full Force

It's about time General Motors got its pickup trucks in shape so as to be able to really be serious contenders in the market ring. Since the earth-shattering arrival of the Dodge Ram in 1994 and the Ford F-150 in 1997, the C/K pickup trucks have really fallen behind. The do-or-die motto that helped give these utility vehicles a face-lift was: bigger, faster, brawnier and brighter...

Nothing too spectacular, technically speaking, was applied to liven up this typically North American product that's one of the best-sold on the continent, but Chevrolet and GMC that sell respectively the Silverado and Sierra, really wanted to clean up their act and add elements that were missing on the old multi-purpose utility vehicles. The first task was to seriously beef up chassis solidity. To do so, they decided to borrow from the Ram

design, that is to divide up the chassis into three sections rivetted rather than welded together. This approach not only makes the chassis more modular, but makes it easier to construct so as to really increase torsion and flexion resistance at a more affordable production price. This is also an added bonus for all components mounted on the chassis, like suspensions, steering and drive gear and it sure improves handling and roadability that have really been refined as well. Engineers brag that it's by far the most intelligently built chassis ever produced by GM in terms of durability and dependability. The front suspension has been modified to procure more precision at center and to reduce the steer angle diameter. So, control arms are longer to increase load capacity. At the rear, the main modification consists of a wider

wheel track for greater stability. Recirculating ball steering has been replaced by rack-and-pinion steering on the rear-wheel drive models whose full load weight is less than 3 tons, so as to improve accuracy and behavior with an empty box. Another dramatic modification for the better, vehicles are now equipped with standard four-wheel disc brakes linked to ABS. Brake linings should last three or four times longer due to more robust calipers and discs. The 4.3L V6 gas engine and 6.5L V6 turbocharged diesel engine are still available, but it's the new 4.8L, 5.3L and 6.0L V8 powerplants that steal the show. These engines represent the ultimate technological development the folks at Chevrolet, who have been around for forty years, have ever come up with. Of Vortec design, they pump out the most power in their category thanks to new-design pistons and valves and an engine-block setup that makes them super solid. The lubrication system, the coolant system and seal joints have been dramatically improved so as to increase reliability. The transmission offers a mode allowing for greater hauling capabilities on rough terrain, while the optional AutoTrack on the 4X4's automatically engages the front axle when rear wheels lose their grip. The electrical system has been simplified, streamlined and is more reliable and stronger headlights provide better visibility. The trailer hitch arrangement has been completely revamped so as to achieve greater pulling power, the new cabin has been widened to provide for more passenger comfort and the third door is now standard equipment. Finally, build quality and fit and finish are a notch above what they were.

In terms of individual model sales, the Chevrolet Silverado and GMC Sierra pickup trucks place second behind the Ford F-150. (780,838 for Ford and combine sales of 725,403 for GMC-Chevrolet). The struggle to the top to get to first place on the podium is going to be even tougher when seriously reworked models hit the market. It's interesting to point out that 75% of pickup trucks sold have a load capacity of a half-ton, 60% have an extended cabin and 56% are 4X4's...

MODEL RANGE

Chevrolet-GMC pickup trucks are technically identical and only differ according to some stylistic details and equipment items. There are lots and lots of models divided up into two main families of 1/2 and 3/4-ton load capacity vehicles: the 4X2's (C 1500-2500) or 4X4's (K 1500-2500) with regular box and cabin or extended cabin in 2 or 3-door versions, with shortened box and flare side fenders called Sportside and short or long box with straight sides called Fleetside, with single or double rear wheels. The bulky 3500's will be revamped as well during the coming year, but in the meantime they'll be just as they were in 1998. Besides the 4.3L V6 and the 6.5L V8 turbocharged diesel identical to former models, you can choose between three new V8 engines: 4.8L, 5.3L and 6.0L. The Chevrolet Silverado's are sold in base, LS and LT trim levels and the GMC Sierra comes in SL, SLE and SLT models. Standard equipment on all these vehicles includes power steering and four-wheel disc brakes paired up to ABS.

TECHNICAL FEATURES

These pickup trucks are built on a galvanized steel H-frame including 9 cross-members. It's built in three sections; the front section is of hydroformed construction. The main section is U-shaped and is available in 4 lengths so as to be able to accomodate two wheelbase lengths and two cabin sizes. In fact, this new approach provides 65% more structural integrity than was the case with the former chassis, yet it's 27% lighter. The rear end common to all models was designed to dramatically reduce the number of hookup links needed on former trailer hitches. The independent

front suspension is made up of a double wishbone and added torsion bars on the 4X4's, while at the rear, the rigid rear axle is supported by leaf springs. Four-wheel disc brakes and ABS are standard equipment, as is the new rack-and-pinion steering on rear-wheel drive models with a half-ton load capacity. The body design has been completely renewed, it's wider and more spacious all round, more so than is the case for most of the competition and the third door now comes standard on the extended cabin. Lateral panels on the Sportside box are of composite material, so they're rust-proof and dent and scratch-proof. Seats and dashboard have really come a long way as far as ergonomics go and the climate control system is more effective and powerful.

PROS

+ HANDLING. The new super-solid chassis, along with the enhanced suspension have dramatically improved roadholding on the latest generation GM pickup trucks. This adds up to crisper follow-through

and more stability so you can easily negociate all kinds of curves.

+ BRAKES. Four-wheel disc brakes with ABS, new-design linings, improved coolant system and balanced pressure application on rear wheels have really cut down on stopping distances by up to 30%.

+ QUALITY. It's better all-round, in terms of technical features, build, materials and finish details, so as to offer a product comparable if not superior to the competition.

+ PERFORMANCES. These pickup trucks can now receive the most powerful V8 engines in their class, so accelerations are a lot zoomier than before.

+ FINISH DETAILS. The cabin interior isn't really too different from what it was last year, but it's more refined and rounded out in the automobile sense of the term, with notably new thin-lens headlights. Inside the cabin, everything looks less like a utility vehicle, even on the lower end models fitted with more attractive-looking seats.

+ CONVENIENCE FEATURES

The cabin is roomier and is crammed with storage spots (the number varies with the trim level) and a running board step on the passenger side to facilitate boarding.

+ DRIVING PLEASURE. It's smoother than before, you feel more like you're at the wheel of a car, especially inside the half-ton load capacity models. Steering is silkier and more precise, brakes are easier to apply and the suspension behaves in a much more genteel fashion, since it benefits from beefier chassis rigidity. To all this, add excellent visibility offered by big, wide windows, nicely-sized mirrors and more powerful headlights.

+ RIDE COMFORT. The more flexible suspension, nicely shaped seats and more effective soundproofing have really added to cabin comfort, but it's more obvious inside the rear-wheel drive long-wheelbase models.

+ LOAD AND TRAILERING. Both have improved due to the more rigid chassis, roomier boxes, a whole range of new more powerful engines as well as more effective trailer hitch systems more suited to owners' needs.

CONS

- FUEL CONSUMPTION. It gets sky-high with the V8 gas engines and forces you to consider buying the turbocharged diesel engine if you're on the road a lot.

- MANEUVERABILITY. These bulky utility vehicles are tricky to put through certain maneuvers, which takes getting used to.

- RIDE COMFORT. In the short-wheelbase or 4X4's, the ride gets pretty bumpy as soon as the pavement goes awry and the turbocharged diesel engine makes the optional added sound dampening a must if you really want to be comfortable.

CONCLUSION

General Motors did what it had to do to put its pickup trucks on a par with rivals. It must be noted that GM listened to customers when it was renewing these models that are so vital to future sales performance and to a rosy future for the company. When you know that 80% of pickup truck owners remain loyal to their vehicle brand, you can understand why Chevrolet and GMC moved mountains to keep their clients who just might have strayed elsewhere. Mission accomplished...

RATING
CHEVROLET Silverado-GMC Sierra 1500

CONCEPT :		67%
Technology	80	
Safety :	90	
Interior space :	60	
Trunk volume:	25	
Quality/fit/finish :	80	

DRIVING:		56%
Cockpit :	80	
Performance :	40	
Handling :	40	
Steering :	80	
Braking :	40	

ORIGINAL EQUIPMENT:		63%
Tires :	75	
Headlights :	80	
Wipers :	80	
Rear defroster :	-	
Radio :	80	

COMFORT :		70%
Seats :	75	
Suspension :	65	
Sound level :	55	
Conveniences :	75	
Air conditioning :	80	

BUDGET :		56%
Price :	50	
Fuel economy :	30	
Insurance :	70	
Satisfaction :	80	
Depreciation :	50	

| **Overall rating:** | | **62.4%** |

NEW FOR 1999

- Completely revamped models with a very rigid chassis, more spacious and comfortable cabin, more powerful brakes and the choice of three new V8 Vortec engines: 4.8L, 5.3L and 6.0L.

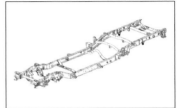

ENGINES / TRANSMISSIONS / PERFORMANCES

Model/ version	Type / timing valve / fuel system	Displacement cu in	Power bhp @ rpm	Torque lb-ft @ rpm	Compres. ratio	Driving wheels / transmission	Final ratio	Acceler. 0-60 mph s	Standing 1/4 & 5/8 mile s	Acceler. 50-75 mph s	Braking 60-0 mph f	Top speed mph	Lateral acceler. G	Noise level dBA	Fuel economy mpg City Highway	Fuel type Octane
base	V6 4.3 OHV-12-SFI	262	200 @ 4600	260 @ 2800	9.4 :1	rear - M5	3.08	11.7	18.0 33.0	7.6	183	90	0.63	68	16 22	R 87
options	V8 4.8 OHV-16-SFI	293	255 @ 5200	285 @ 4000	9.5 :1	rear/4 - M5	3.42	NA								R 87
	V8 5.3 OHV-16-SFI	325	270 @ 5000	315 @ 4000	9.5 :1	rear/4 - A4	3.42	NA								R 87
	V8 6.0 OHV-16-SFI	364	300 @ 4800	355 @ 4000	9.4 :1	rear/4 - M5	4.10	NA								R 87
	V8 TD 6.5 OHV-16-MI	394	215 @ 3400	440 @ 1800	19.5 :1	rear/4 - M5	3.73	NA								D

PRICE & EQUIPMENT

CHEVROLET Silverado	base	LS	LT
GMC Sierra	LS	SLE	SLT
Retail price $:	22,726	24,261	-
Dealer invoice $:	19,885	21,205	-
Shipping & handling $:	-	-	-
Automatic transmission:	O	O	S
Cruise control:	O	S	S
Power steering:	S	S	S
Anti-lock brakes:	S	S	S
Traction control:	-	-	-
Air conditioning:	O	S	S
Leather:	-	O	S
AM/FM/radio-cassette:	O	SCD	SCD
Power door locks:	-	S	S
Power windows:	-	S	S
Tilt steering:	S	S	S
Dual adjustable mirrors:	SM	SE	SE
Alloy wheels:	O	S	S
Anti-theft system:	S	S	S

Colors
Exterior: Green, Gray, Gold, Red, Copper, Blue, Pewter, Black, White.

Interior: Neutral, Blue, Gray, Red.

AT A GLANCE...

Category:	rear-wheel drive and 4x4 pickups. **Class :** utility

HISTORIC
Introduced in:	1936-1992
Made in:	Fort Wayne, Indiana, Pontiac, Michigan, USA. Oshawa, Ont., Canada.

DEMOGRAPHICS
Model	Men./Wom.	Age	Married	College	Income
Silverado	96/4 %	49	65 %	15 %	$ 33 000
Sierra	96/4 %	47	61 %	18 %	$ 32 000

INDEX
Safety:	90 %	**Satisfaction:**	82 %
Depreciation:	50 %	**Insurance:**	$845-990
Cost per mile:	$0.58	**Number of dealers:**	4466

SALES
Model	1996	1997	Result
C/K	550 594	553 729	+ 0.6 %

MAIN COMPETITORS
DODGE Ram, FORD F-Series, TOYOTA T150.

MAINTENANCE REQUIRED BY WARRANTY
First revision:	Frequency:	Diagnostic plug:
3 000 miles	6 months/10 000 miles	Yes

SPECIFICATIONS

Model Version Trim	Traction	Body/ Seats	Wheel base in	Lght x Wdgth x Hght in x in x in	Curb weight lb	Susp. ft/rr	Brake ft/rr	Steering type	Turning diameter ft	Steer. turns nber.	Fuel tank gal	tire size	Standard tires make	model	Standard powertrain
CHEVROLET / GMC 1500-Series			General warranty: 3 years / 36 000 miles; antipollution: 5 years / 50 000 miles; perforation corrosion: 6 years / 100 000 miles. Road assistance.												
Silverado-Sierra reg.cab.short bed	2dr.p-u.3	4x2	119.0	203.1x78.5x71.2	3920	ih/rl	dc/ABS	pwr.r&p.	43.6	3.04	26.0	235/75R16	Uniroyal	Tiger Paw	V6/4.3/M5
Silverado-Sierra reg.cab.long bed	2dr.p-u.3	4x2	133.0	222.0x78.5x71.0	4032	ih/rl	dc/ABS	pwr.r&p.	40.4	3.04	34.0	235/75R16	Uniroyal	Tiger Paw	V6/4.3/M5
Silverado-Sierra long cab short bed.	2dr.p-u.3/5	4x2	143.5	227.6x78.5x71.2	4235	ih/rl	dc/ABS	pwr.r&p.	46.6	3.04	26.0	235/75R16	Uniroyal	Tiger Paw	V6/4.3/M5
Silverado-Sierra long cab & bed	2dr.p-u.3/5	4x2	157.5	246.5x78.5x70.8	4442	ih/rl	dc/ABS	pwr.r&p.	50.5	3.04	34.0	235/75R16			V6/4.3/M5
Silverado-Sierra reg.cab.short bed	2dr.p-u.3	4x4	119.0	203.3x78.5x73.8	4248	it/rl	dc/ABS	pwr.ball	43.6	2.88	26.0	245/75R16	GoodyearWrangler RT/S		V6/4.3/M5
Silverado-Sierra reg.cab.long bed	2dr.p-u.3	4x4	133.0	222.2x78.5x73.8	4365	it/rl	dc/ABS	pwr.ball	44.6	2.88	34.0	245/75R16	GoodyearWrangler RT/S		V6/4.3/M5
Silverado-Sierra long cab short bed.	2dr.p-u.3/5	4x4	143.5	227.6x78.5x73.9	4621	it/rl	dc/ABS	pwr.ball	47.2	2.88	26.0	245/75R16	GoodyearWrangler RT/S		V6/4.3/M5
Silverado-Sierra long cab & bed	2dr.p-u.3/5	4x4	157.5	246.7x78.5x73.8	4749	it/rl	dc/ABS	pwr.ball	51.2	2.88	34.0	245/75R16			V6/4.3/M5

The Cavalier's success rests on a few very simple, basic ideas: attractive content, good looks, practical size and convincing prices. So no wonder it was the best sold car in Canada in 1997. In the United States, it arrived in 9th place with 302,161 units sold right behind the Honda Civic. The 1999 Cavalier hasn't been modified much, which shouldn't affect its appeal.

MODEL RANGE

Simplified to the extreme, it only comes in five versions: a base sedan and coupe, an LS sedan furbished with richer equipment, as well as a Z24 coupe and convertible with a more obvious sports feel. The base engine is a 2.2L 4-cylinder model assisted by a 5-speed manual gearbox or a 3-speed automatic. A 2.4L 150-hp double camshaft multivalve engine motivates the Z24 versions and it's listed as an option for the LS sedan. This model also receives a standard 4-speed electronically controlled automatic gearbox. This transmission is offered as an extra for the other versions.

TECHNICAL FEATURES

The Cavalier's steel monocoque body is robust and yields sure and steady roadability, besides assuring enhanced passenger protection. Road noise and vibration are well blotted out as well. But that clean, slinky silhouette hides rather poor aerodynamics, as the drag coefficient of 0.38 to 0.42 attests to. The front suspension consists of MacPherson struts and at the rear, there's a tubular semi-rigid axle. Front disc brakes and rear drum brakes are linked to standard ABS. Power steering is also part of the original equipment items. The LS sedan gets added standard traction control, an optional feature on models equipped with a 4-speed automatic transmission.

VERY NICE FEATURES

++ ESTHETICS. To appeal to so many buyers, this car's style had to be very attractive... and it is! About half of Cavalier sedan owners are men, but the situation is the opposite for the coupes and convertibles.

PROS

+ VALUE. This car's main drawing card is still its generous standard equipment, offered at an affordable price. But watch out, those sets of optional accessory items tend to

Widespread !

inflate the initial price.

+ RIDE COMFORT. Long trips are very pleasant and fatigue-free when you're travelling in such a roomy cabin, either in the front or rear seats, carried along on such an effective suspension and front seats are the cat's meow.

+ SIZE The Cavalier is blessed with a convenient format and cabin space is proportional to vehicle size. The numerous storage areas are handy to get to, the glove compartment is very roomy and the trunk is accessible and can be extended on all models by lowering the rear seatbench.

+ TRIM FEATURES. Compared with former Cavalier models, the new generation car looks more spiffy thanks to bright and youthful trim shades.

+ CHASSIS. On the road, the Cavalier is super solid and there's not much sway effect. This really makes for accurate steering on curves and for generally predictable behavior. Of course, road handling depends on tire quality.

+ ENGINE. This zippy 2.4L multivalve engine pumps out crisper accelerations and pickup than does the base 4-cylinder version. Yet it isn't as smooth as the V6 that graced the former Cavalier generation. It doesn't develop as much torque either.

CONS

- QUALITY. Some components or finish details give away the reason behind this car's affordability. You get what you pay for and even though reliability has come a long way, there's still room for improvement.

- 2.2L ENGINE. It lacks vim and vigor when paired up with the old 3-speed automatic. It's even more sluggish when you turn on the air conditioning.

- TIRES. The lower end models are equipped with poor-quality tires. On curves, they squeal. On dry roads, they offer little grip and are even more slippery on wet surfaces. When you consider that our very life, when we're travelling, depends on a few square inches of rubber...

- STEERING. Steering benefits from a good reduction ratio, but it's poorly assisted. It's too light and airy fairy at the center. In bad weather, you sure have to keep an eye and a grip on things.

- BRAKES. Brakes hold up well, but they're only fair to midling when it comes to effectiveness. The pedal is too soft, which makes it hard to apply brakes as required. Stopping distances stretch out to the horizon and the simplistic ABS system often kicks in too soon and it doesn't iron out all the wheel lock either!

- NOISE. Neither engine is great when it comes to discretion or smoothness. And soundproofing isn't really what it should be, especially on the base models.

- HOOD. The wide gap between the bumper and the hood lid is annoying because you get the impression that the hood is partially open. All it would take is a simple rubber sealing strip to correct this stylistic flaw.

- TRANSMISSION. The old 3-speed gearbox puts a strain on the engine and imposes high r.p.m. levels, which translates into hefty gas bills.

CONCLUSION

If the Cavalier keeps on basking in popularity, it's simply because the product meets buyers' basic expectations, but especially because the content/price combination is favorable. GM seems to have got the message. So as long as the recipe works, the Cavalier runs the risk of remaining just as it is at the present time. ☺

RATING
CHEVROLET Cavalier

CONCEPT : **66%**
Technology	75
Safety :	75
Interior space :	55
Trunk volume:	55
Quality/fit/finish :	70

DRIVING: **63%**
Cockpit :	75
Performance :	60
Handling :	55
Steering :	70
Braking :	55

ORIGINAL EQUIPMENT: **74%**
Tires :	70
Headlights :	80
Wipers :	80
Rear defroster :	70
Radio :	70

COMFORT : **69%**
Seats :	75
Suspension :	70
Sound level :	50
Conveniences :	70
Air conditioning :	80

BUDGET : **67%**
Price :	70
Fuel economy :	75
Insurance :	60
Satisfaction :	75
Depreciation :	55

Overall rating: **67.8%**

NEW FOR 1999

- Refined 2.4L Twin Cam engine.
- Body color radiator grille shade for the RS and LS versions.
- Two new exterior shades.
- Fabric-clad seats.

ENGINES / TRANSMISSIONS / PERFORMANCES

Model/ version	Type / timing valve / fuel system	Displacement cu in	Power bhp @ rpm	Torque lb-ft @ rpm	Compres. ratio	Driving wheels / transmission	Final ratio	Acceler. 0-60 mph s	Standing 1/4 & 5/8 mile s	Acceler. 50-75 mph s	Braking 60-0 mph f	Top speed mph	Lateral acceler. G	Noise level dBA	Fuel economy mpg City	Highway	Fuel type Octane
1)	L4* 2.2 OHV-8-SFI	134	115 @ 5000	135 @ 3600	9.0 :1	front - M5*	3.58	10.5	17.6	31.5	7.3	141	103	0.75	68	23	39	R 87
						front - A3	3.18	11.5	18.4	32.7	7.8	144	100	0.75	68	22	33	R 87
2)	L4* 2.4 DOHC-16-SFI	146	150 @ 5600	155 @ 4400	9.5 :1	front - M5*	3.94	8.0	16.1	28.5	5.8	144	112	0.78	70	22	36	R 87
						front - A4	3.91	8.8	16.4	30.3	6.3	148	109	0.78	70	22	36	R 87

1) base cpe., sedan, RS cpe., sedan LS.   2) base Z24 cpe. & con., option sedan LS.

PRICE & EQUIPMENT

CHEVROLET Cavalier	base sdn/cpe	RS cpe	LS sdn	Z24 cpe	Z24 cabrio
Retail price $:	-	-	-	-	-
Dealer invoice $:	-	-	-	-	-
Shipping & handling $:	-	-	-	-	-
Automatic transmission:	O	O	S	O	O
Cruise control:	O	S	S	S	S
Power steering:	S	S	S	S	S
Anti-lock brakes:	O	O	O	O	O
Traction control:	O	O	O	O	O
Air conditioning:	O	O	S	S	S
Leather:	-	-	-	-	-
AM/FM/radio-cassette:	O	S	S	S	S
Power door locks:	O	O	O	S	S
Power windows:	-	O	O	S	S
Tilt steering:	-/O	S	S	S	S
Dual adjustable mirrors:	SM	SM	SE	SE	SE
Alloy wheels:	-	O	O	S	S
Anti-theft system:	S	S	S	S	S

Colors
Exterior: Metallic green, White, Red, Black, Green, Gold, Cayenne, Blue, Sand.

Interior: Neutral, Graphite, Medium Gray, White (convertible).

AT A GLANCE...

Category:	front-wheel drive compacts	**Class :**	3

HISTORIC
Introduced in: 1982-1995
Made in: Ramos Arizpe, Mexico, Lordstown, Ohio, Lansing, Michigan, USA.

DEMOGRAPHICS
Model	Men./Wom.	Age	Married	College	Income
Z24	42/58 %	33	48 %	31 %	$29 000
coupe	45/55 %	38	50 %	43 %	$31 000
sedan	60/40 %	42	72 %	39 %	$27 000

INDEX
Safety:	75 %	Satisfaction:	75 %
Depreciation:	45 %	Insurance:	$835 to 1 150
Cost per mile:	$0.42	Number of dealers:	4 466

SALES
Model	1996	1997	Result
Cavalier	277 222	302 161	+ 9.0 %

MAIN COMPETITORS
DODGE-PLYMOUTH Neon, FORD Escort, HONDA Civic, HYUNDAI Elantra, MAZDA Protegé, SATURN, SUBARU Impreza, TOYOTA Corolla, VOLKSWAGEN Golf/Jetta.

MAINTENANCE REQUIRED BY WARRANTY
First revision:	Frequency:	Diagnostic plug:
3 000 miles	6 000 miles	Yes

SPECIFICATIONS

Model	Version Trim	Body/ Seats	Interior volume cu ft	Trunk volume cu ft	Cd	Wheel base in	Lght x Wdgth x Hght in x in x in	Curb weight lb	Susp. ft/rr	Brake ft/rr	Steering type	Turning diameter ft	Steer. turns nber.	Fuel tank gal	tire size	Standard tires make	model	Standard powertrain
CHEVROLET		General warranty: 3 years / 36 000 miles; antipollution: 5 years / 50 000 miles; perforation corrosion: 6 years / 100 000 miles. Roadside assistance.																
Cavalier	base	2dr.cpe.4	87.3	13.2	0.39	104.1	180.7x68.7x53.0	2619	ih/sihdc/dr/ABS	pwr.r&p.	35.7	2.6	15.0	195/70R14	Goodyear	Conquest	L4/2.2/M5
Cavalier	RS	2dr.cpe.4	87.3	13.2	0.39	104.1	180.7x68.7x53.0	2626	ih/sihdc/dr/ABS	pwr.r&p.	35.7	2.6	15.0	195/65R15	BF Goodrich	Touring T/A	L4/2.2/M5
Cavalier	Z24	2dr.cpe.4	87.3	13.2	0.39	104.1	180.7x68.7x53.0	2749	ih/sihdc/dr/ABS	pwr.r&p.	35.7	2.8	15.0	205/55R16	Goodyear	Eagle RS-A	L4/2.4/M5
Cavalier	Z24	2dr.con.4	83.0	10.5	0.42	104.1	180.7x68.7x54.1	2840	ih/sihdc/dr/ABS	pwr.r&p.	35.7	2.6	15.0	195/65R15	Goodyear	Eagle RS-A	L4/2.4/M5
Cavalier	base	4dr.sdn.5	91.7	13.6	0.38	104.1	180.7x67.9x54.7	2676	ih/sihdc/dr/ABS	pwr.r&p.	35.7	2.6	15.0	195/70R14	BF Goodrich	Touring T/A	L4/2.2/M5
Cavalier	LS	4dr.sdn.5	91.7	13.6	0.38	104.1	180.7x67.9x54.7	2722	ih/sihdc/dr/ABS	pwr.r&p.	35.7	2.6	15.0	195/65R15	BF Goodrich	Touring T/A	L4/2.2/A4

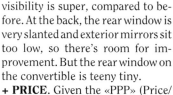

The new "C5" Corvette has got rave reviews but it's also been panned by the critics. The ultimate American sports car has been completely re-designed technically speaking, and for the better. But the exterior shell has kept some ultra-conservative stylistic elements. At least it's proved to be a champion on the test course. So for Corvette purists and enthusiasts, the model range is more attractive since it gets a hard-top coupe this year.

MODEL RANGE

The Chevrolet standard bearer is now available in three distinct versions: there's a coupe convertible equipped with a fixed panel, a classic convertible and the new «Hard Top» coupe. Each model is animated by a 5.7L V8 that delivers 345 hp. This gutsy powerplant is paired up with a standard 4-speed automatic transmission. A 6-speed manual transmission is offered as an extra.

TECHNICAL FEATURES

The dashing body is made of composite polymer (fiberglass). The aerodynamic drag coefficient is only 0.29! The body is mounted on a surrounding chassis with tubular steel frame siderails. The chassis vibrates at 23 Hz when the roof is installed and at 21 Hz with the roof removed. The main chassis consists of components made of hydroformed galvanized steel. An aluminum cradle up front receives the main mechanical elements. The fully independent suspension uses, both front and rear, double unequal-length trailing control arms, transverse leaf springs made of composite materials and an anti-roll bar. The windshield is lodged in an aluminum structure that solidifies the instrument panel sector. A steel roll bar is built into the rear roof section. Steering, of magnetic design, is variable assist. Over-sized disc brakes incorporate standard ABS and traction control. By integrating the transmission into the rear axle, along with the differential, an almost perfect weight distribution of 51.5/48.5% was achieved.

PROS

+ DRIVING FEEL. The engine never seems to be short of power surge and the low growl it lets out when it's coaxed is really thrilling!

+ BRAKES. Our braking measurements for the Corvette are among the best we've ever seen. You can

High Flying Trio !

stop the Corvette at 60 mph within 110 feet . The average for the car industry is 140 feet.

+ PERFORMANCES. With a power to weight ratio of 9.4 lbs/hp, you're in for brawny accelerations and pickup. The surge is simply spectacular and thanks to the non-slip differential, car path is straight-ahead perfect.

+ HANDLING. The stiff chassis and the Goodyear Eagle F1 tires that bite the tarmac ensure remarkable handling on dry surfaces. Even on the «comfort» mode of the adaptive suspension, body sway is kept to a minimum. We hit almost 1 G in lateral acceleration, a record for a mass-produced car.

+RIDE COMFORT. Forget the old Corvette. The ride in the C5, blessed with «supple» or «average» adap-

tive suspension modes, is neither too rocky, nor too rough. You won't have to make an appointment with your chiropractor after each jaunt. But when you set the suspension to «sport» mode, expect a very firm, hard ride, especially on poor road surfaces!

+ FUEL ECONOMY. At the end of our road test, we calculated an average 19 mpg gas consumption, which seems almost reasonable given the circumstances...

+ CONVENIENCE FEATURES. You now have outside access to the trunk. It holds a fair amount, for example two suitcases, two totebags and the hard top roof panel. This panel is so light, that one person can handle it like a charm.

+ OUTWARD VIEW. The coupe has lots of wide windows, so front

visibility is super, compared to before. At the back, the rear window is very slanted and exterior mirrors sit too low, so there's room for improvement. But the rear window on the convertible is teeny tiny.

+ PRICE. Given the «PPP» (Price/Power/Performance) ratio, the Corvette is pretty reasonably priced.

CONS

- FRONT END. It's loaded down with the engine, so it tends to do Olympic dives and needs to be put back on track. The rougher the road, the rougher the ride!

- SIZE. Parking maneuvers in the 15 ft.Corvette are no picnic. Ironically, even aboard, space is skimpy. Hulky, tall folks will feel terribly cramped.

- ROAD CLEARANCE. The thin rubber flap located on the front bumper sits at 2 inches from the ground, so it gets scratched and scuffed up in no time!

- NOISE. Between 40 and 50 mph, once the roof is off, car passengers are exposed to lots of wind interference.

- A MISSING FEATURE. There's no indicator on the dashboard for the automatic transmission, so you don't know which gear you're in. As a result, you have to keep looking down to check it out.

- HEADLIGHTS. This car is definitely not equipped with powerful enough headlights. This type of car should be fitted with halogen headlamps. And windshield wipers are awfully sluggish.

- STORAGE SPACE. The glove compartment is too small and there's not a door side-pocket in sight. As for the console compartment, it holds next to nothing: you can stash two roadmaps or a glasses case and that's about it!

VERY POOR FEATURES

- STYLE. The rear body extremity is humungous and brutish-looking compared to the neat front end stylistic touches. The stylists seemed to have finished their task once they designed the front end!

CONCLUSION

The C-5 is clearly more comfortable and occupant-friendly, and it puts out much better performances, but who in the world can really benefit from all that muscle (and still follow the laws of the land)? We'll have to wait and see if buyers will flock to the dealers and keep this American car myth alive. ☺

RATING
CHEVROLET Corvette

CONCEPT :   **65%**
Technology   90
Safety :   90
Interior space :   15
Trunk volume: 50
Quality/fit/finish :   80

DRIVING: **86%**
Cockpit :   80
Performance :   85
Handling :   90
Steering :   75
Braking :   100

ORIGINAL EQUIPMENT: **79%**
Tires :   90
Headlights :   75
Wipers :   75
Rear defroster :   75
Radio :   80

COMFORT :   **55%**
Seats :   80
Suspension :   60
Sound level :   20
Conveniences :   30
Air conditioning :   85

BUDGET :   **43%**
Price :   0
Fuel economy :   40
Insurance :   35
Satisfaction :   80
Depreciation :   60

Overall rating: **65.6%**

NEW FOR 1999

- The Hardtop version equipped with original Goodyear Eagle F1 tires, Z51 suspension, 3.42 non-slip differential and a 6-speed manual gearbox.
- Windshield display system (Head-Up Display).
- Power adjustable steering column.
- New Magnetic Red Metallic body shade.

ENGINES / TRANSMISSIONS / PERFORMANCES

Model/ version	Type / timing valve / fuel system	Displacement cu in	Power bhp @ rpm	Torque lb-ft @ rpm	Compres. ratio	Driving wheels / transmission	Final ratio	Acceler. 0-60 mph s	Standing 1/4 & 5/8 mile s	Acceler. 50-75 mph s	Braking 60-0 mph f	Top speed mph	Lateral acceler. G	Noise level dBA	Fuel economy mpg City	Highway	Fuel type Octane
base	V8* 5.7 OHV-16-SFI	346	345 @ 5600	350 @ 4400	10.1 :1	rear-A4*	2.73	5.3	14.0	25.3	3.5	115	167	0.95	72-80	17	27	S 91
						rear-M6*1	3.42	5.0	13.8	24.8	3.2	108	170	0.95	72	18	29	S 91

1)standard Hardtop with no options

PRICE & EQUIPMENT

CHEVROLET Corvette	cpe	HT	cabrio
Retail price $:	-	-	-
Dealer invoice $:	-	-	-
Shipping & handling $:	-	-	-
Automatic transmission:	S	NA	S
Cruise control:	S	S	S
Power steering:	S	S	S
Anti-lock brakes:	S	S	S
Traction control:	S	S	S
Air conditioning:	SM	SM	SM
Leather:	S	S	S
AM/FM/radio-cassette:	S	S	S
Power door locks:	S	S	S
Power windows:	S	S	S
Tilt steering:	S	S	S
Dual adjustable mirrors:	SEC	SEC	SEC
Alloy wheels:	S	S	S
Anti-theft system:	S	S	S

Colors
Exterior: Black, White, Red, Pewter, Silver, Blue.

Interior: Black, Light Gray, Red, Oak.

AT A GLANCE...

Category: rear-wheel drive sports coupes & convertibles   **Class :** S & GT.

HISTORIC
Introduced in: 1953, 1963, 1968, 1984, 1997.
Made in: Bowling Green, Kentucky, USA.

DEMOGRAPHICS
Model	Men./Wom.	Age	Married	College	Income
Corvette	75/25 %	45	66 %	36 %	$100 000

INDEX
Safety:	90 %	Satisfaction:	80 %
Depreciation:	40 %	Insurance:	$2 150
Cost per mile:	$0.85	Number of dealers:	4 466

SALES
Model	1996	1997	Result
Corvette	17 805	22 724	+ 27.6%

MAIN COMPETITORS
BMW M roadster , DODGE Viper, PORSCHE 911 & Boxster, MERCEDES-BENZ CLK 430, TOYOTA Supra.

MAINTENANCE REQUIRED BY WARRANTY
First revision: 3 000 miles   **Frequency:** 6 months/6 000 miles   **Diagnostic plug:** Yes

SPECIFICATIONS

Model	Version Trim	Body/ Seats	Interior volume cu ft	Trunk volume cu ft	Cd	Wheel base in	Lght x Wdgth x Hght in x in x in	Curb weight lb	Susp. ft/rr	Brake ft/rr	Steering type	Turning diameter ft	Steer. turns nber.	Fuel tank gal	tire size	Standard tires make	model	Standard powertrain
CHEVROLET	General warranty: 3 years / 36 000 miles; antipollution: 5 years / 50 000 miles; perforation corrosion: 6 years / 100 000 miles. Roadside assistance.																	
Corvette	coupe	2dr.cpe.2	51.4	24.8	0.29	104.5	179.7x73.6x47.8	3245	il/il	dc/ABS	pwr.r&p.	40.0	2.32	20.0	fr.245/45ZR17	Goodyear	Eagle F1	V8/5.7/A4
Corvette	Hardtop	2dr.cpe.2	NA	NA	0.29	104.5	179.7x73.6x47.9	3152	il/il	dc/ABS	pwr.r&p.	40.0	2.32	20.0		Goodyear	Eagle F1	V8/5.7/M6
Corvette	convertible	2dr.con.2	NA	13.9	0.32	104.5	179.7x73.6x47.7	3247	il/il	dc/ABS	pwr.r&p.	40.0	2.32	20.0	re.275/40ZR18	Goodyear	Eagle F1	V8/5.7/A4

Generic Vehicle

The Chevrolet Lumina and Monte Carlo are as anonymous as it gets. Their lackluster looks are terribly blah. So much so that you could say they're "generic" cars: just your usual means of getting around, nothing more. Of course, they do their job perfectly — they get you from point A to point B — but that's about it. Even the so-called sports models can't fool you. When GM will replace these cars next year under the new Impala name, they'll easily fall into oblivion.

MODEL RANGE

The Lumina sedan and Monte Carlo coupe are the oldest members in the GM midsize W-Series, a family that also includes the Buick Century and Regal, the Oldsmobile Intrigue and the Pontiac Grand Prix. Chevrolet is offering the Lumina in three trim levels: base, LS and LTZ, but the Monte Carlo only comes in two versions: the LS and Z34. The 3.1L 160-hp V6 is the original engine for both the Lumina sedan and the Monte Carlo LS coupe. The LTZ sedan can receive, on request, the 3.8L 200-hp V6 that animates the Monte Carlo Z34. The only transmission available is the four-speed automatic.

TECHNICAL FEATURES

The same platform is basic to all W-Series models. The same applies to mechanical organs, that are almost identical for all cars. The Lumina and Monte Carlo benefit from a steel unibody that's clearly stiffer than was formerly the case. But with a drag coefficient of only 0.34 to brag about, their aerodynamic prowess is nothing to write home about. The fully independent suspension consists of MacPherson struts up front and three trailing arms linked to a MacPherson strut at the rear. Cars are equipped with four-wheel disc brakes and standard ABS.

PROS

+ PRICE. Potential customers will be impressed by the attractive price tags on the base models that are a pretty good buy. But standard equipment is rather basic and once you add on a few options, the price looks a lot less affordable.

+ ENGINE. The «big» V6 engine is a real beauty. Performances are zoomy and it's fuel-efficient, since it doesn't guzzle gallons and gallons of gas.

+ CABIN SPACE. These two cars were designed to seat up to six passengers. But five passengers will be a lot more comfy, especially inside the coupe. Both trunks are quite roomy and the rather low trunk opening really lightens the task of stashing stuff away.

+ RIDE COMFORT. The silky suspension on the lower end models is quite good, especially for highway driving and noise is kept to a decent minimum.

+ TRANSMISSION. The four-speed automatic gearbox is one of the best on the market. It's smooth and shifting is a breeze. Besides, it procures more braking effect than you get in a rival Ford or Chrysler.

+ HANDLING. The «sports» LTZ and Z34 versions are equipped with a firmer suspension and better-grip tires. You stay right on track.

+ DRIVING PLEASURE. Driving along at cruising speed is very pleasurable with such modern and well-designed mechanical features.

+ CABIN DESIGN. Compared to the former generation Lumina and Monte Carlo, these cars sport classy instrument panels that are more ergonomic and better organized.

+ OUTWARD VIEW. The relatively thin B pillars and indented C pillar on the sedan don't hamper visibility. But on the coupe, the ever so wide C pillar obstructs rear view at quarterback.

+ NICE FEATURES: Easy-to-use instrument panel and radio controls and optional dual-zone climate control.

CONS

- SWAY. The suspension on the base models really provokes heavy swish and sway on curves and during lane changes at high speeds. So the vehicle is put off-balance, which makes taking curves rather tricky.

- ESTHETICS. The Lumina and Monte Carlo go by and no one really notices...except for the Lumina models equipped with those police package emergency rotating lights! No wonder they never quite compete with other mid-sized cars. Some stylistic changes are a must.

- SEATS. Seats on the base models make you want to spend the least amount of time aboard. Lumbar support is at a bare minimum and seat cushions are far too soft.

- BRAKES. They're only average, even on the Monte Carlo Z34 that's equipped with four-wheel disc brakes. The proof? These models need more than the average 130 ft. to come to a full stop.

- STEERING. It's very light and frothy since it suffers from chronic over-assistance. The driver really has to be cautious in cross-winds.

- FINISH DETAILS. None of these cars would win a beauty contest, not with the botched up finish job they're inflicted with and some of the chintzy-looking trim components inside the cabin.

- POOR FEATURES. The lower end models look stripped down with their skimpy handful of instrument gauges. And storage space inside the cabin seems to be have been ridiculously overlooked by the designers. Headlamps aren't too bright and the windshield wipers and air ventilation system need to be improved upon.

CONCLUSION

There, we've said what we had to say, but will GM really take these comments seriously? Surely not. The Lumina and Monte Carlo are condemned to stay just as they are. They're stuck with a dreary generic design that keeps them far from the spotlight; they'll just go on living like ghosts in the shadows, especially the Lumina, which is too bad for a car whose name indicates that it would like to shine... ☺

RATING
CHEVROLET Lumina-Monte Carlo

CONCEPT : 76%
Technology	75
Safety :	90
Interior space :	70
Trunk volume:	70
Quality/fit/finish :	75

DRIVING: 63%
Cockpit :	70
Performance :	60
Handling :	60
Steering :	70
Braking :	55

ORIGINAL EQUIPMENT: 71%
Tires :	70
Headlights :	75
Wipers :	70
Rear defroster :	70
Radio :	70

COMFORT : 72%
Seats :	65
Suspension :	75
Sound level :	70
Conveniences :	70
Air conditioning :	80

BUDGET : 57%
Price :	50
Fuel economy :	60
Insurance :	50
Satisfaction :	75
Depreciation :	50

Overall rating: 67.8%

NEW FOR 1999

• New Purple body shade.

ENGINES

Model/ version	Type / timing valve / fuel system	Displacement cu in	Power bhp @ rpm	Torque lb-ft @ rpm
1)	V6* 3.1 OHV-12-SFI	191	160 @ 5200	185 @ 4000
2)	V6 3.8 OHV-12-SFI	231	200 @ 5200	225 @ 4000

1) base, LS   2) LTZ & Z34

TRANSMISSIONS

Compres. ratio	Driving wheels / transmission	Final ratio
9.6 :1	front - A4*	3.29
9.4 :1	front - A4*	3.29

PERFORMANCES

Acceler. 0-60 mph s	Standing 1/4 & 5/8 mile s	Acceler. 50-75 mph s	Braking 60-0 mph f	Top speed mph	Lateral acceler. G	Noise level dBA	Fuel economy mpg City	Fuel economy mpg Highway	Fuel type Octane
9.8	17.0	30.8	6.8	141	103	0.77	67	19	30	R 87
8.6	16.4	29.6	6.1	144	109	0.78	66	19	31	R 87

PRICE & EQUIPMENT

CHEVROLET Lumina CHEVROLET Monte Carlo	base	LS LS	LTZ	Z34
Retail price $:	17,395	19,395	19,745	20,295
Dealer invoice $:	15,916	17,746	18,067	18,570
Shipping & handling $:	550	550	550	550
Automatic transmission:	S	S	S	S
Cruise control:	O	O	O	S
Power steering:	S	S	S	S
Anti-lock brakes:	O	S	S	S
Traction control:	-	-	-	-
Air conditioning:	S	S	S	S
Leather:	-	O	O	O
AM/FM/radio-cassette:	O	S	S	S
Power door locks:	S	S	S	S
Power windows:	O	S	S	S
Tilt steering:	S	S	S	S
Dual adjustable mirrors:	SM	SE	SE	SE
Alloy wheels:	O	S/O	S	S
Anti-theft system:	S	S	S	S

Colors
Exterior: White, Blue, Black, Jade, Driftwood, Red, Auburn, Pewter.

Interior: Blue, Medium Gray, Neutral, Ruby red.

AT A GLANCE...

Category: front-wheel drive midsize coupes & sedans.   **Class :** 5

HISTORIC
Introduced in: 1995
Made in: Oshawa, Ontario, Canada.

DEMOGRAPHICS
Model	Men./Wom.	Age	Married	College	Income
Lumina	75/25%	59	82%	23%	$ 30 000
Monte Carlo	70/30%	46	68%	35%	$ 48 000

INDEX
Safety: L : 90 % MC: 80 %   **Satisfaction:** 77 %
Depreciation: 50 %   **Insurance:** L : 835$ MC : $965
Cost per mile: L : $0.43 MC : $0.45   **Number of dealers:** 4 466

SALES
Model	1996	1997	Result
Lumina	237 973	228 451	- 4.0 %
Monte Carlo	79 593	71 543	- 10.1%

MAIN COMPETITORS
Lumina : CHRYSLER Concorde & Intrepid, FORD Taurus, MERCURY Sable, TOYOTA Camry.
Monte Carlo : CHRYSLER Sebring, DODGE Avenger.

MAINTENANCE REQUIRED BY WARRANTY
First revision:	Frequency:	Diagnostic plug:
3 000 miles	6 000 miles	Yes

SPECIFICATIONS

Model	Version Trim	Body/ Seats	Interior volume cu ft	Trunk volume cu ft	Cd	Wheel base in	Lght x Wdgth x Hght in x in x in	Curb weight lb	Susp. ft/rr	Brake ft/rr	Steering type	Turning diameter ft	Steer. turns nber.	Fuel tank gal	tire size	Standard tires make	model	Standard powertrain
CHEVROLET	General warranty: 3 years / 36 000 miles; antipollution: 5 years / 50 000 miles; perforation corrosion: 6 years / 100 000 miles. Roadside assistance.																	
Lumina	base	4dr.sdn.6	100.5	15.5	0.33	107.5	200.9x72.5x55.2	3330	ih/ih	dc/dr	pwr.r&p.	36.7	2.60	16.6	205/70R15	BF Goodrich	Touring T/A	V6/3.1/A4
Lumina	LS	4dr.sdn.6	100.5	15.5	0.33	107.5	200.9x72.5x55.2	3372	ih/ih	dc/dr/ABS	pwr.r&p.	36.7	2.26	16.6	225/60R16	BF Goodrich	Touring T/A	V6/3.1/A4
Lumina	LTZ	4dr.sdn.6	100.5	15.5	0.33	107.5	200.9x72.5x55.2	3420	ih/ih	dc/dr/ABS	pwr.r&p.	39.0	2.26	16.6	225/60R16	Goodyear	Eagle RS-A	V6/3.8/A4
Monte Carlo	LS	2dr.cpe.5	96.1	15.5	0.34	107.5	200.7x72.5x53.8	3306	ih/ih	dc/dr/ABS	pwr.r&p.	36.7	2.60	16.6	205/70R15	BF Goodrich	Touring T/A	V6/3.1/A4
Monte Carlo	Z34	2dr.cpe.5	96.1	15.5	0.34	107.5	200.7x72.5x53.8	3436	ih/ih	dc/ABS	pwr.r&p.	39.0	2.26	16.6	225/60R16	Goodyear	Eagle RS-A	V6/3.8/A4

The Malibu design is supposed to knock the socks off potential Camry and Accord buyers, nothing less. Compared to the Lumina, it's like day and night! This practical down-to-earth sedan is modern and richly equipped. The name may not be new, but it has nothing in common with the former Malibu of old, nor with the Chevrolet Corsica that it replaced, for that matter. The Malibu's arrival on the car market scene launched a new GM era that's characterized by more up-to-date products geared to beat the pants off the Asian competition.

MODEL RANGE

The Malibu is a four-door sedan that comes in two versions: the base and LS. The 2.4L Twin Cam 4-cylinder engine that powers the Cavalier Z24 models, equips the base model Malibu. The Malibu LS, on the other hand, is animated by a 3.1L V6 that develops as much brawn as the 4-cylinder engine (150-hp), but is far smoother. A four-speed electronically controlled automatic transmission rounds out this car's technical portrait. The base model has loads of equipment items, including 15-in. wheels, manually controlled climate control, adjustable steering column and ABS. The LS gets added fog lamps, remote-control door locks, cruise control, adjustable power mirrors, power windows, six-way adjustable driver's seat, alloy rims, front bucket seats and a 60/40 split-folding rear seatbench.

TECHNICAL FEATURES

The Malibu is built on the new «P90» platform that it shares with the new GM N-Series models, the Grand Am and Alero. The Malibu's exterior tire size are about the same as those of the Toyota Camry, so cabin space sits between that of the Ford Taurus and Camry. Yet the Malibu isn't a big compact car, but a midsize model! Its monocoque body is fitted with dual-side galvanized steel panels and build is really very solid. But even with those clean sweeping lines, the drag coefficient is only an average 0.32. The suspension is fully independent. Up front, it benefits from MacPherson struts and at the rear, three trailing arms do the job. There are anti-roll bars both front and rear. The disc and drum brake system is linked to fourth-generation ABS on both versions. Both engines develop 150 hp, but the V6

Anti-Japanese

pumps out 25 lb.ft more torque at low r.p.m.

PROS

+ VALUE. The Malibu offers lots of niceties for the going price, so it's very competitive with Asian cars that are often less well-equipped and cost more. But equipment items are unique and chosen to demonstrate that this car is different from other models on the market.

+ LOOKS. This sedan has a distinguished and modern body design that compares favorably with Japanese and North American rival counterparts.

+ CABIN AND TRUNK SPACE. The spacious cabin can easily accomodate up to five passengers who'll be more than comfy inside. Besides, the big convertible trunk can really gobble up the luggage.

+ PERFORMANCES. Given this sedan's weight, engines procure zoomy accelerations and pickup. Yet both engine models develop different torque levels. The V6 is, of course, more lively and motivates the Malibu quite nicely.

+ RIDE COMFORT. The suspension really irons out road wrinkles, and the seats provide good support. The noise level at cruising speed is fine as well. Who could ask for anything more?

+ HANDLING. The Malibu enjoys predictable roadability in spite of its mid-quality tires. It takes curves without leaning into them and can handle sudden emergency moves with ease.

+ CONVENIENCE FEATURES. Contrary to the Lumina, the Malibu

has scads of storage spots up front: a generous glove compartment, door side-pockets, a center console compartment and cup-holders, including one to the left of the steering wheel.

+ FINISH DETAILS. They're meticulous and trim materials are very attractive for the most part, especially in comparison with other same-brand products. Chevrolet obviously wanted to put together a car that could compete on an even footing with well-crafted rivals.

CONS

- NOISE. Sound dampening could be more refined, since there's an audible roar from the old-design engines on accelerations and suspension component noise when driving over poor-quality pavement.

- BRAKES. They're gutsy and easy to gauge, but stopping distances are much longer than average for this category. Poor-quality brake pads seem to be behind this crummy performance, since they wear out quickly.

- TRANSMISSION. The automatic transmission is sometimes jumpy while changing gears; this occurs with both engines. It seems to hesitate between gears, so you're in for some unpleasant jolts.

- STORAGE SPACE. They're sadly lacking in the rear; rear seat passengers have two meagre cup-holders at their disposal.

- TO BE IMPROVED UPON: The plastic trim on door panels and the imitation wood on the dashboard that jar with the ritzy quality of other cabin trim materials. There are no assist grips on the roof and no foot-rest for the driver, which comes across as being a bit cheap.

CONCLUSION

General Motors has come up with a whole new way of doing things. By attempting to imitate Asian car products, the people at GM are hoping to place the Malibu among the shining lights in the compact car category, a class that's the rage these days. It's reassuring to know that the American giant is still capable of coming up with some pleasant surprises in these troubled times of its history. ☺

RATING
CHEVROLET Malibu

CONCEPT :   **74%**
Technology	75
Safety :	80
Interior space :	70
Trunk volume:	70
Quality/fit/finish :	75

DRIVING: **60%**
Cockpit :	80
Performance :	50
Handling :	50
Steering :	80
Braking :	40

ORIGINAL EQUIPMENT: **79%**
Tires :	75
Headlights :	80
Wipers :	80
Rear defroster :	80
Radio :	80

COMFORT :   **70%**
Seats :	75
Suspension :	75
Sound level:	50
Conveniences :	65
Air conditioning :	85

BUDGET :   **65%**
Price :	55
Fuel economy :	70
Insurance :	70
Satisfaction :	80
Depreciation :	50

Overall rating: **69.6%**

NEW FOR 1999

- New Bronze exterior shade.

ENGINES
Model/version	Type / timing valve / fuel system	Displacement cu in	Power bhp @ rpm	Torque lb-ft @ rpm
base	L4* 2.4 DOHC-16-SFI	146	150 @ 6000	155 @ 4400
LS	V6* 3.1 OHV-12-SFI	191	150 @ 4800	180 @ 3200

TRANSMISSIONS
Compres. ratio	Driving wheels / transmission	Final ratio
9.5 :1	front - A4	3.42
9.6 :1	front - A4	3.05

PERFORMANCES
Acceler. 0-60 mph s	Standing 1/4 & 5/8 mile s	Acceler. 50-75 mph s	Braking 60-0 mph f	Top speed mph	Lateral acceler. G	Noise level dBA	Fuel economy mpg City	Highway	Fuel type Octane
10.0	17.2	31.0	6.9	138	106	0.75	68	22	32	R 87
9.5	16.5	30.4	6.6	144	112	0.75	67	20	30	R 87

PRICE & EQUIPMENT

CHEVROLET Malibu	base	LS
Retail price $:	15,670	18,620
Dealer invoice $:	14,338	17,037
Shipping & handling $:	525	525
Automatic transmission:	S	S
Cruise control:	O	S
Power steering:	S	S
Anti-lock brakes:	S	S
Traction control:	-	-
Air conditioning:	SM	SM
Leather:	-	O
AM/FM/radio-cassette:	O	S
Power door locks:	O	S
Power windows:	O	S
Tilt steering:	S	S
Dual adjustable mirrors:	O	S
Alloy wheels:	O	S
Anti-theft system:	S	S

Colors
Exterior: White, Metallic silver, Blue, Black, Cherry, Beige, Sand, Jade, Malachite Bronze.
Interior: Neutral, Oak, Medium Gray, Light Gray.

AT A GLANCE...
Category: front-wheel drive compact.   **Class :** 4

HISTORIC
Introduced in: 1997
Made in: Wilmington, Delaware & Oklahoma City, Oklahoma, USA.

DEMOGRAPHICS
Model	Men./Wom.	Age	Married	College	Income
Malibu	NA				

INDEX
Safety:	80%	Satisfaction:	82%
Depreciation:	50 %	Insurance:	$835
Cost per mile:	$0.43	Number of dealers:	4 466

SALES
Model	1996	1997	Result
Malibu	2 274	164 654	-

MAIN COMPETITORS
CHRYSLER Cirrus, DODGE Stratus, FORD Contour, HONDA Accord, HYUNDAI Sonata, MAZDA 626, MERCURY Mystique, NISSAN Altima, PLYMOUTH Breeze, SUBARU Legacy, TOYOTA Camry & VOLKSWAGEN Passat.

MAINTENANCE REQUIRED BY WARRANTY
First revision:	Frequency:	Diagnostic plug:
3 000 miles	6 000 miles	Yes

SPECIFICATIONS

Model	Version Trim	Body/Seats	Interior volume cu ft	Trunk volume cu ft	Cd	Wheel base in	Lght x Wdgth x Hght in x in x in	Curb weight lb	Susp. ft/rr	Brake ft/rr	Steering type	Turning diameter ft	Steer. turns nber.	Fuel tank gal	tire size	Standard tires make	model	Standard powertrain
CHEVROLET	General warranty: 3 years / 36 000 miles; antipollution: 5 years / 50 000 miles; perforation corrosion: 6 years / 100 000 miles. Roadside assistance.																	
Malibu	base	4dr.sdn. 4/5	98.6	16.4	0.32	107.0	190.4x69.4x56.4	3051	ih/ih	dc/dr/ABS	pwr.r&p.	36.4	2.9	15.0	215/60R15	Firestone	Affinity	L4/2.4/A4
Malibu	LS	4dr.sdn. 4/5	98.6	16.4	0.32	107.0	190.4x69.4x56.4	3077	ih/ih	dc/dr/ABS	pwr.r&p.	36.4	2.9	15.0	215/60R15	Firestone	Affinity	V6/3.1/A4

Nowadays, the car market doesn't have much room or respect for super-economical minicars. It's a sign of the times! Attractive long-term rental plans make big 4X4 vehicles and minivans a heck of a lot more appealing than these flea-size cars. Rumor has it, by the way, that GM is on the verge of dropping Metro-Firefly models from its lineup, given the poor sales results. Will Suzuki follow in their footsteps?

MODEL RANGE

The Metro (formerly the Geo), and Swift are basically identical. They differ in trim detail and engine models available. The Swift is now only sold in the DLX 3-door hatchback version driven by a 1.3L 4-cylinder engine. But GM still offers 3-door hatchback models and 4-door sedans, both in the Chevrolet and Pontiac model range. The hatchback is still equipped with the 1.0L 3-cylinder engine, whereas the sedan gets a 1.3L 4-cylinder engine. But this engine is also available on the hatchback. A 5-speed manual transmission comes standard, but the 3-speed automatic is listed among the options. Due to their basically economic character, these vehicles don't have much standard equipment, but they are nevertheless equipped with dual air bags and intermittent wipers. The radio, air conditioning and ABS are extras for all models, whereas power steering can be added to the Metro sedans.

TECHNICAL FEATURES

These tiny cars with a monocoque steel body are of course light as a feather. They're slim and trim, but aerodynamic finesse is only average, which in the long run doesn't matter much, given vehicle weight and performances. The four-wheel independent suspension is made up of MacPherson struts with A-arms and a stabilizer bar up front. At the rear, there's a MacPherson strut setup linked to oblique A-arms, transverse control arms and stabilizer bar. Stopping is achieved by a disc and drum brake system, but it's deprived of ABS. Rack-and-pinion steering doesn't benefit from power assistance and tiny 13-in tires cover the steel wheel rims. The engines on these cars are the smallest

Fly Traps...

displacement engines on the North American market.

PROS

+ FUEL ECONOMY. These tiny cars are cheap to operate. Fuel consumption is the lowest of all vehicles sold here. Yet insurance premiums are just about the same as for a subcompact car that's roomier, after all.

+ BUILD. The car structure is more solid than before. Doors are now fitted with reinforcement beams and dual air bags come as standard equipment.

+ ROADHOLDING. The latest models are equipped with 13-in tires and weigh more, so roadability has improved, which is reassuring.

+ STYLE. These cars have a mischievous, yet classic look, so they're quite appealing, especially the sedan that looks bigger than it really is.

+ CABIN SPACE. Four adults can be seated inside the sedan and travel in relative comfort.

+ MANEUVERABILITY. Driving one of these cars is a lot of fun. These minicars can go just about anywhere and they're wonderful in downtown traffic jams, since they can get out of any pinch and they're a breeze to park.

CONS

- SAFETY. Such a small car is vulnerable in the event of a collision with a heavier vehicle, because of its size, thin metal bodywork and fairly fragile structure.

- BRAKES. In emergencies, brakes tend to seize up. Strange that ABS is only an option! Also, brake linings are rather flimsy and don't hold up with intensive use, so stops take forever to achieve. As for the tires, they grip pretty well but they can act up on poor road surfaces.

- ENGINE. The 1.0L 3-cylinder engine that animates the Metro models is a bit of a wimp. The same goes for the 1.3L engine when linked to the automatic transmission that siphons off a lot of juice. Accelerations and pickup are far from lively and so the driver has to be on the lookout and really anticipate other drivers' moves. With four passengers and their luggage aboard, lots of prudence is a must.

- STEERING. These cars are supersensitive to cross-winds. Steering is already a bit whimsical and it does kick up a fuss when up against road faults, especially longitudinal ruts left by heavy trucks.

- RIDE COMFORT. Needless to say, the suspension on these cars is rather stiff and so it gets jumpy at times. The sedan cabin can accomodate four adults, but it is narrow. You can't be shy about rubbing shoulders with your fellow-travellers. Getting into the rear seats, especially in the hatchback, isn't a strong suit for these fly traps...

- MODEL CHOICE. The model range has been stripped down to essentials and cars are only offered in a single trim level.

- LOOKS. Finish details are pretty basic, more so for the Chevrolet and Pontiac models. Cabin trim looks terribly chintzy as is the case with some other items, such as tires.

- TRUNK. The loading area in the hatchback is very tiny when the rear seatbench is occupied. On the other hand, you can triple its size by lowering the rear seatbench.

CONCLUSION

These are urban cars par excellence. The sedan cabin is great and the hatchback is really versatile. These cars are fuel-frugal and they maneuver like magic. But all you have to do is drive alongside a tractor-trailer to realize that the degree of safety provided in cars such as this is really very relative... ☹

RATING
Metro

CONCEPT :		62%
Technology	75	
Safety :	80	
Interior space :	50	
Trunk volume:	35	
Quality/fit/finish :	70	

DRIVING:		46%
Cockpit :	70	
Performance :	20	
Handling :	45	
Steering :	65	
Braking :	30	

ORIGINAL EQUIPMENT:		69%
Tires :	65	
Headlights :	75	
Wipers :	75	
Rear defroster :	70	
Radio :	60	

COMFORT :		57%
Seats :	60	
Suspension :	60	
Sound level:	40	
Conveniences :	50	
Air conditioning :	75	

BUDGET :		72%
Price :	90	
Fuel economy :	70	
Insurance :	80	
Satisfaction :	70	
Depreciation :	50	

Overall rating:	61.2%

NEW FOR 1999

• Two new body shades: Dark Green Metallic and Silver Metallic.

ENGINES / TRANSMISSIONS / PERFORMANCES

Model/ version	Type / timing valve / fuel system	Displacement cu in	Power bhp @ rpm	Torque lb-ft @ rpm	Compres. ratio	Driving wheels / transmission	Final ratio	Acceler. 0-60 mph s	Standing 1/4 & 5/8 mile s	Acceler. 50-75 mph s	Braking 60-0 mph f	Top speed mph	Lateral acceler. G	Noise level dBA	Fuel economy mpg City	Fuel economy mpg Highway	Fuel type Octane
1)	L3* 1.0 SOHC-6-EFI	61	55 @ 5700	58 @ 3300	9.5 :1	front - M5*	4.39	14.3	19.3	37.2	13.5	151	90	0.75	70	43	55	R 87
2)	L4* 1.3 SOHC-16-MPFI	79	79 @ 6000	75 @ 3000	9.5 :1	front - M5*	3.79	13.2	18.8	36.4	11.8	160	100	0.75	68	37	48	R 87
						front - A3	3.61	14.0	19.5	37.5	13.0	157	93	0.75	68	31	38	R 87

1) Metro 2dr.   2) Metro 2 dr. LSi & 4 dr.LSi

PRICE & EQUIPMENT

CHEVROLET Metro	2dr.	2dr. LSi	4dr. LSi
Retail price $:	8,755	9,555	10,155
Dealer invoice $:	8,247	8,905	9,464
Shipping & handling $:	340	340	340
Automatic transmission:	-	O	O
Cruise control:	-	-	-
Power steering:	-	-	O
Anti-lock brakes:	O	O	O
Traction control:	-	-	-
Air conditioning:	O	O	O
Leather:	-	-	-
AM/FM/radio-cassette:	O	O	O
Power door locks:	-	-	O
Power windows:	-	-	-
Tilt steering:	-	-	-
Dual adjustable mirrors:	SM	SM	SM
Alloy wheels:	-	-	-
Anti-theft system:	-	-	-

Colors
Exterior: Black, White, Red, Blue, Green, Gold, Silver.

Interior: Gray.

AT A GLANCE...

Category: front-wheel drive sub compact coupes & sedans. **Class :** 2

HISTORIC
Introduced in: 1987,1995.
Made in: Ingersoll, Ontario, Canada.

DEMOGRAPHICS

Model	Men./Wom.	Age	Married	College	Income
Metro	53/47 %	36	46 %	28 %	$ 23 000

INDEX
Safety:	70 %	Satisfaction:	82 %
Depreciation:	47 %	Insurance:	$750
Cost per mile:	$0.35	Number of dealers:	4 466

SALES

Model	1996	1997	Result
Metro	88 763	55 629	- 37.3 %

MAIN COMPETITORS
HYUNDAI Accent 3 dr.

MAINTENANCE REQUIRED BY WARRANTY
First revision:	Frequency:	Diagnostic plug:
3 000 miles	6 000 miles	No

SPECIFICATIONS

Model Version Trim	Body/ Seats	Interior volume cu ft	Trunk volume cu ft	Cd	Wheel base in	Lght x Wdgth x Hght in x in x in	Curb weight lb	Susp. ft/rr	Brake ft/rr	Steering type	Turning diameter ft	Steer. turns nber.	Fuel tank gal	tire size	Standard tires make	model	Standard powertrain
CHEVROLET	General warranty: 3 years / 36 000 miles; perforation corrosion:5 years / unlimited. 24 hrs Roadside assistance.																
Metro base	3dr.cpe. 4	85.8	8.4	0.33	93.1	149.4x62.6x54.7	1895	ih/ih	dc/dr	r&p.	31.5	3.7	10.3	155/80R13	Goodyear	Invicta GL	L3/1.0/M5
Metro LSi	4dr.sdn. 4	90.4	10.3	0.34	93.1	164.0x62.6x55.4	1984	ih/ih	dc/dr	r&p.	31.5	3.7	10.3	155/80R13	Goodyear	Invicta GL	L4/1.3/M5

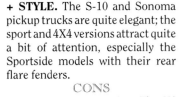

The new Dodge Dakota made its debut in 1997 and it caused a slump in S-10 and Sonoma sales. Now these vehicles are in third place, since the Ford Ranger and Dakota have taken the lead in this vehicle category. Yet the real rock-bottom slump occurred after the unveiling of updated versions that now had, among other goodies, a third door for the extended cabin. It seems that the comparable price and midsize format of the Dakota and especially its winsome looks are factors GM will have to take into account.

MODEL RANGE

The S-10 and Sonoma are almost identical twins. They're available in 4X2 and 4X4 versions, with regular or extended cabin, a long, short or «Sportside» box with running boards. Chevrolet and GMC offer them in three trim levels: base, LS and SS/ZR2 for the first vehicle; SL, SLS and SLE for the second. The 4X2 models are driven by a 2.2L 120-hp 4-cylinder base model engine; the 4X4's are powered by the 4.3L 180-hp Vortec V6. There are other engine models available, including a 190-hp powerplant for the 4X4's and another that develops 175 hp for the 4X2's. These pickup trucks aren't particularly loaded with equipment. The 4X2's are equipped with standard power steering, four-wheel ABS and intermittent wipers. The 4X4's also get four-wheel disc brakes.

TECHNICAL FEATURES

The body is made of steel that's galvanized on both sides, except for the roof panel and front frame panel. It rests on a ladder chassis with 5 crossmembers. The «InstaTrac» transfer box isn't in permanent mode, but it can be engaged via shift-on-the-fly. Engine torque is thus distributed at 35% to front wheels and at 65% to rear wheels. The independent front suspension consists of coil springs for the 4X2 models and torsion bars for the 4X4's. At the back, the rigid rear axle is supported by leaf springs. The 4X2 versions are equipped with disc and drum brakes, while the 4X4's benefit from four-wheel disc brakes. Moreover, recirculating ball steering has a variable assist system.

PROS

+ CHOICE. The wide variety of vehicles and trim levels is sure to meet each and every buyer's needs.

+ V6 ENGINE. The V6 engine packs more of a wallop than its coun-

Losing Steam

terparts that power rival brands. Accelerations and pick-up are car-like.

+ RIDE COMFORT. Thanks to a well-honed suspension, even with an empty box, this pickup truck provides a pleasant ride. Even the 4X4 suspension is less nervous and jittery, yes, even with those big tires. Inside, you're in for a treat with those thickly upholstered, hip-hugger bucket seats. And sound-proofing is quite adequate. The extended cabin seats two adults and two children in the rear fold-up auxiliary seats.

+ HANDLING. The rigid chassis and frame provide competent roadability on smooth pavement. But things get out of line quickly, so you have to keep taking your foot off the accelerator, especially on the 4X4

versions equipped with a firmer suspension and more generous tires.

+ CONVENIENT. The «InstaTrac» system automatically distributes available power to wheels with the best grip, which is a boon on difficult, uneven turf.

+ QUALITY. Compared with models in former years, over-all quality has climbed up a few notches. Build quality seems more consistent, finish details are rendered more carefully and trim materials are on the up and up.

+ THE 3RD DOOR! The third door on the driver's side is listed among original equipment items on extended cabin models. It sure helps boarding and loading stuff inside.

+ PRICE. These vehicles are sold at tempting prices. Yet original equipment is often limited.

+ STYLE. The S-10 and Sonoma pickup trucks are quite elegant; the sport and 4X4 versions attract quite a bit of attention, especially the Sportside models with their rear flare fenders.

CONS

- FUEL CONSUMPTION. The V6 engines aren't particularly economical to run because of their hefty displacement and weight (3 638 lbs). If fuel consumption is an issue or a priority for you, the 4-cylinder engine would maybe better suit your needs. But don't forget that this engine was designed for light tasks.

- NOISE LEVEL. The 4-cylinder models don't have appropriate sound dampening. Occupants are exposed to an unpleasant (and forever unfinished) symphony made up of road noise and squeals and such from the engine, when speeding up.

- GROUND CLEARANCE. The S-10/Sonoma 4X4's are more limited on off-road maneuvers, more so than some rivals. In some cases, ground clearance is barely 8 inches.

- BRAKES. Braking isn't nice and gradual and it's only average on sudden stops. Luckily, ABS compensates by achieving greater vehicle stability. Besides, brake linings seem to hold up better than on former models.

- SEATS. Base models with regular cabin offer a pretty uncomfortable seat to occupants; they get no lateral or lumbar support when aboard this vehicle. As for the auxiliary seats, think of them as emergency tools. You don't always need them, but they're nice to have on hand when you're in a pinch.

- CONVENIENCE FEATURES. Vehicles are equipped with a very tiny glove compartment and only the more expensive members of the lineup have the right to door side-pockets and console compartment.

- TO BE IMPROVED UPON: GM should rethink a few accessories, such as the multifunction shifter to the left of the steering wheel that holds far too many controls.

CONCLUSION

A brand new product always enjoys a certain notoriety when it comes to compact pickup trucks, as is demonstrated by the sales slump of these models, since the arrival on the scene of the new-generation Dodge Dakota. After all, this type of vehicle's success depends on fashion trends... 😐

RATING
CHEVROLET-S-10 GMC-Sonoma

CONCEPT : **61%**
Technology	75
Safety :	60
Interior space :	60
Trunk volume:	40
Quality/fit/finish :	70

DRIVING: **54%**
Cockpit :	80
Performance :	45
Handling :	40
Steering :	75
Braking :	30

ORIGINAL EQUIPMENT: **71%**
Tires :	70
Headlights :	75
Wipers :	70
Rear defroster :	-
Radio :	70

COMFORT : **62%**
Seats :	65
Suspension :	70
Sound level:	45
Conveniences :	50
Air conditioning :	80

BUDGET : **52%**
Price :	45
Fuel economy :	40
Insurance :	45
Satisfaction :	75
Depreciation :	55

Overall rating: **60.0%**

NEW FOR 1999

- New Xtreme trim level.
- Improved automatic transmission.
- Bigger exterior mirrors that can be folded.
- Safety system is now standard equipment.
- Three new body shades: Gold, Green and Red.

ENGINES / TRANSMISSIONS / PERFORMANCES

Model/ version	Type / timing valve / fuel system	Displacement cu in	Power bhp @ rpm	Torque lb-ft @ rpm	Compres. ratio	Driving wheels / transmission	Final ratio	Acceler. 0-60 mph s	Standing 1/4 & 5/8 mile s	Acceler. 50-75 mph s	Braking 60-0 mph f	Top speed mph	Lateral acceler. G	Noise level dBA	Fuel economy mpg City	Fuel economy mpg Highway	Fuel type Octane
4x2*	L4 2.2 OHV-8-SFI	134	120 @ 5000	140 @ 3600	9.0 :1	rear-M5*	2.73	12.5	18.5 35.7	10.7	148	91	0.75	70	22	32	R 87
						rear-A4	4.11	13.7	19.2 36.4	11.2	154	87	0.75	71	19	27	R 87
4x2 option	V6 4.3 OHV-12-SFI	262	175 @ 4400	240 @ 2800	9.2 :1	rear-M5*	3.42	8.0	15.8 28.2	5.8	148	103	0.77	69	16	24	R 87
			180 @ 4400	245 @ 2800	9.2 :1	rear-A4	3.42	8.5	16.4 29.5	6.0	144	109	0.77	69	16	22	R 87
4x4	V6 4.3 OHV-12-SFI	262	180 @ 4400	245 @ 2800	9.2 :1	rear/4-M5*	3.42	9.2	16.8 30.6	6.5	157	100	0.77	69	15	21	R 87
			190 @ 4400	250 @ 2800	9.2 :1	rear/4-A4	3.42	9.5	17.2 30.8	6.7	151	106	0.78	69	16	22	R 87

PRICE & EQUIPMENT

CHEVROLET S-10-Series GMC Sonoma	base SL	LS SLS	Xtreme SLS	ZR2 SLS
Retail price $:	11,998	13,179	17,923	20,082
Dealer invoice $:	11,338	11,927	16,220	18,174
Shipping & handling $:	510	510	510	510
Automatic transmission:	O	O	O	O
Cruise control:	-	O	O	O
Power steering:	S	S	S	S
Anti-lock brakes:	S	S	S	S
Traction control:	-	-	-	-
Air conditioning:	O	O	O	O
Leather:	-	-	-	-
AM/FM/radio-cassette:	O	O	O	O
Power door locks:	O	O	O	S
Power windows:	O	O	O	S
Tilt steering:	O	O	S	S
Dual adjustable mirrors:	-	O	S	S
Alloy wheels:	-	O	S	O
Anti-theft system:	S	S	S	S

Colors

Exterior: White, Onyx, Black, Blue, Green, Red, Copper, Silver, Gold.

Interior: Medium Gray, Graphite, Beige.

AT A GLANCE...

Category: 4x2 or 4x4 pickups   **Class :** utility

HISTORIC
Introduced in: 1982,1994
Made in: Linden NJ, Shreveport, LO, USA

DEMOGRAPHICS
Model	Men./Wom.	Age	Married	College	Income
S-10/Sonoma	88/12 %	44	59 %	28 %	$ 31 000

INDEX
Safety:	90 %	Satisfaction:	75 %
Depreciation:	45 %	Insurance:	$775
Cost per mile:	$0.38	Number of dealers:	4 466

SALES
Model	1996	1997	Result
S-10	190 178	192 314	+ 1.1 %
Sonoma	44 629	41 714	- 6.5 %

MAIN COMPETITORS
DODGE Dakota, FORD Ranger, ISUZU Hombre, MAZDA B, NISSAN Frontier, TOYOTA Tacoma.

MAINTENANCE REQUIRED BY WARRANTY
First revision:	Frequency:	Diagnostic plug:
3 000 miles	6 months/ 10 000 miles	Yes

SPECIFICATIONS

Model Version Trim	Traction	Body/ Seats	Wheel base in	Lght x Wdgth x Hght in x in x in	Curb weight lb	Susp. ft/rr	Brake ft/rr	Steering type	Turning diameter ft	Steer. turns nber.	Fuel tank gal	tire size	Standard tires make	model	Standard powertrain
CHEVROLET-GMC		*General warranty: 3 years / 36 000 miles; antipollution: 5 years / 50 000 miles; perforation corrosion: 6 years / 100 000 miles. Roadside assistance.*													
S-10-Sonoma short bed	4x2	2dr.p-u.2/3	108.3	190.1x67.9x62.0	3031	ih/rldc/dr/ABS	pwr.bal.	34.8	2.75	19.0	205/75R15	Uniroyal	Tiger Paw	L4/2.2/M5
S-10-Sonoma long bed	4x2	2dr.p-u.2/3	117.9	206.1x67.9x62.9	3102	ih/rldc/dr/ABS	pwr.bal.	36.7	2.75	19.0	205/75R15	Uniroyal	Tiger Paw	L4/2.2/M5
S-10-Sonoma extd cab	4x2	2dr.p-u.4/5	122.9	204.7x67.9x62.7	3240	ih/rldc/dr/ABS	pwr.bal.	41.7	2.75	19.0	205/75R15	Uniroyal	Tiger Paw	V6/4.3/M5
S-10-Sonoma short bed	4x4	2dr.p-u.2/3	108.3	190.1x67.9x63.4	3564	ih/rl	dc/ABS	pwr.bal.	34.8	2.75	19.0	205/75R15	Uniroyal	Tiger Paw	L4/2.2/M5
S-10-Sonoma long bed	4x4	2dr.p-u.2/3	117.9	206.1x67.9x64.4	3653	ih/rl	dc/ABS	pwr.bal.	36.7	2.75	19.0	205/75R15	Uniroyal	Tiger Paw	L4/2.2/M5
S-10-Sonoma extd cab	4x4	2dr.p-u.4/5	122.9	204.7x67.9x63.4	3757	ih/rl	dc/ABS	pwr.bal.	41.7	2.75	19.0	205/75R15	Uniroyal	Tiger Paw	V6/4.3/M5

GM was the first automaker to develop the big all-purpose vehicle market segment with its impressive Suburban. The current model's ancestry actually goes back to the end of the 1980's! As for the Tahoe and Yukon, they're derived from the Suburban and designed to cash in on the rage for big 4X4 vehicles. The appearance of the GMC Yukon Denali and Cadillac Escalade is part of the same phenomenon, what we're seeing is a race to carve out a niche in the deluxe 4X4 vehicle market, a segment that's growing by leaps and bounds nowadays.

MODEL RANGE

GM now offers five variants of these big station wagons. The Tahoe, Yukon and Suburban remain unchanged. Besides the rather stripped-down-to-essentials base versions, Chevrolet offers three other trim levels for the Tahoe: LS, LT and Sport and two others for the Suburban: SL, SLE and SLT. Yet two new luxury models are now part of this already wide range of products: the GMC Yukon Denali and the Cadillac Escalade, the first mass-produced truck bearing the GM cream of the crop division crest. These two vehicles are lavishly furbished clones of the 4-door Tahoe-Yukon's. They share the same 5.7L 255-hp V8 gas engine. The Denali and Escalade are all-wheel drive vehicles and they're equipped with an AutoTrac transfer box with a 4X4 automatic mode. The Tahoe-Yukon and Suburban 4X4's come with a conventional transfer box with floor shifter, except on the LT and SLT equipped with standard AutoTrac. 4X2 Tahoe-Yukon and Suburban versions are also available, as well as 2-door versions. The Tahoe-Yukon and Suburban can also receive a 6.5L turbocharged diesel engine, while the awesome 7.4L V8 is exclusive to the Suburban. These vehicles are equipped with a 4-speed automatic transmission, variable assist power steering, dual air bags, ABS system and intermittent wipers. More elaborate models benefit from climate control, cruise control, power windows, tilt steering wheel, remote-control mirrors and alloy rims.

TECHNICAL FEATURES

These utility vehicles share the platform inspired by the former C/K pickup trucks. The Tahoe, Yukon, Denali and Escalade have a body 12 inches shorter than that of the Suburban. The galvanized steel body sits on a ladder chassis made up of side-frames and 5 crossmembers. They're very boxy-looking and the air displacement surface is huge,

Clash of the Titans

yielding a telltale drag coefficient of 0.45. The fully independent suspension consists of A-arms up front and, for the 4X2's, coil springs, while 4X4's are fitted with torsion bars. At the rear, the rigid rear axle is suspended from semi-elliptic leaf springs. There are front disc brakes and rear drum brakes, linked to ABS.

PROS

+ CABIN AND LUGGAGE SPACE. These vehicles are really spacious. The Tahoe can welcome six passengers aboard, and the Suburban, up to nine...not to mention their luggage!

+ PRICE. Some versions of these vehicles are offered at competitive prices compared to more modest vehicles like the Blazer, Grand Cherokee or Explorer.

+ PERFORMANCES. With 255 hp under the hood, the Yukon-Tahoe's

achieve performances akin to those of big passenger car sedans. That's why GM created a model for police fleets, to replace the defunct Caprice.

+ RIDE COMFORT. These big beauties are comfy on the highway at cruising speed, since the suspension is civilized in such circumstances and the noise level is acceptable.

+ DRIVING PLEASURE. These truck-like vehicles will appeal to true-blue truck fans, with their smooth controls and neat-design cabin interior. The dashboard isn't a model of ergonomics, but it holds a lot of instruments and storage compartments, not to mention the big compartment between the front seats that even includes a writing tablet!

+ CAPABILITIES. These utility vehicles can boast of impressive load

and trailering capabilities (7 000 lbs), when equipped with hitching devices recommended by the automaker.

+ FINISH DETAILS. The upper-crust models have a tight, clean look and fit, but you have to check off a lot of items on the options list if you want to have a complete array of equipment.

+ OUTWARD VIEW. The driver sits nice and high, the frame belt is low and there are big mirrors, so over-all visibility is super.

+ HANDLING. These vehicles are safe, but they don't handle like a car, not with the high perched center of gravity and more sluggish personality.

CONS

- FUEL CONSUMPTION. The V8 engines are gas-guzzlers. Even the diesel engine can't seem to slake its thirst.

- MANEUVERABILITY. The imposing hulk of these vehicles and especially the wide steer angle are definite drawbacks in city streets.

- SEATS. Cushions are short and they don't provide much lateral support because they're terribly flat. With the leather trim seats on some models, there's even less support!

- DISCOMFORT. These vehicles can't hide their humble origins on poor road surfaces. The rear end slips and slides quite a bit and road noise from the frame builds up over the miles.

- TO BE IMPROVED UPON: The two side swing doors are standard equipment and really make luggage hold access easy, but they do block rearward view. But on the other hand, the optional rear door with swing panel isn't much better, since once it's open, it cuts you off from the luggage loading area. But it does provide better visibility.

CONCLUSION

Cadillac came up with the right name for its 4X4 vehicle. Its arrival coincides with...the escalation of choices available in this Titans' club, including the Escalade, of course. And it isn't over. Ford had a smashing success with the Expedition and Navigator, but it's about to launch another Titan, the Excursion, a future Suburban rival, while Dodge is putting the final touches on another mastodon so as to grab some of the Tahoe-Yukon sales. Stay tuned... :|

RATING
CHEVROLET-GMC Tahoe-Yukon, Suburban

CONCEPT :		**77%**
Technology	75	
Safety :	75	
Interior space :	85	
Trunk volume:	75	
Quality/fit/finish :	75	

DRIVING:		**57%**
Cockpit :	80	
Performance :	40	
Handling :	40	
Steering :	75	
Braking :	50	

ORIGINAL EQUIPMENT:		**75%**
Tires :	75	
Headlights :	80	
Wipers :	75	
Rear defroster :	70	
Radio :	75	

COMFORT :		**68%**
Seats :	70	
Suspension :	70	
Sound level :	50	
Conveniences :	70	
Air conditioning :	80	

BUDGET :		**46%**
Price :	20	
Fuel economy :	20	
Insurance :	55	
Satisfaction :	80	
Depreciation :	55	

Overall rating:		**64.6%**

NEW FOR 1999

- The 5.7L Vortec V8 starter and the more durable radiator.
- Improvements on the 4L60-E automatic transmission.
- Three new metallic body shades: Charcoal Gray, Gold and Prairie Green.

ENGINES / TRANSMISSIONS / PERFORMANCES

Model/ version	Type / timing valve / fuel system	Displacement cu in	Power bhp @ rpm	Torque lb-ft @ rpm	Compres. ratio	Driving wheels / transmission	Final ratio	Acceler. 0-60 mph s	Standing 1/4 & 5/8 mile s	Acceler. 50-75 mph s	Braking 60-0 mph f	Top speed mph	Lateral acceler. G	Noise level dBA	Fuel economy City	Fuel economy Highway	Fuel type Octane
base	V8*5.7 OHV-16-SFI	350	255 @ 4600	330 @ 2800	9.4 :1	rear/4 - A4*	3.42	9.3	16.8	30.5	6.6	151	109	0.68	68	13	18	R 87
option.Sub	V8TD 6.5 OHV-16-MI	395	195 @ 3400	430 @ 1800	19.5 :1	rear/4 - A4*	NA	13.5	19.2	36.0	10.8	170	93	0.66	71	15	22	D
option. Sub	V8 7.4 OHV-16-SFI	454	290 @ 4000	410 @ 3200	8.9 :1	rear/4 - A4*	NA	12.0	18.2	33.6	8.5	157	112	0.67	68	12	19	R 87

PRICE & EQUIPMENT

CHEVROLET Tahoe	base	LS	LT
GMC Yukon		**SLE**	**SLT**
Retail price $:	23,900	29,700	35,419
Dealer invoice $:	20,913	25,988	30,906
Shipping & handling $:			
Automatic transmission:	S	S	S
Cruise control:	O	S	S
Power steering:	S	S	S
Anti-lock brakes:	S	S	S
Traction control:	-	S	-
Air conditioning:	O	S	S
Leather:	-	-	S
AM/FM/radio-cassette:	O	S	SCD
Power door locks:	O	O	O
Power windows:	-	S	S
Tilt steering:	O	S	S
Dual adjustable mirrors:	SM	SE	SE
Alloy wheels:	O	S	S
Anti-theft system:	S	S	S

Colors
Exterior: Black, White, Red, Blue, Pewter, Copper, Green, Gray, Gold.

Interior: Neutral, Gray, Blue, Red.

AT A GLANCE...

Category: 4x2 or 4x4 all purpose vehicle.   **Class :** utility

HISTORIC
Introduced in: 1936: Suburban; 1970: Blazer; 1995 : Yukon, Tahoe.
Made in: Arlington Texas, Janesville, WI, USA, Silao, Mexico.

DEMOGRAPHICS
Model	Men./Wom.	Age	Married	College	Income
Suburban	80/20 %	42	75 %	45 %	$ 60 000
Tahoe	60/40 %	38	61 %	30 %	$ 44 000
Yukon	85/15 %	43	66 %	44 %	$ 48 000

INDEX
Safety:	75 %	Satisfaction:	80 %
Depreciation:	45 %	Insurance:	$965
Cost per mile:	$0.65	Number of dealers:	4 466

SALES
Model	1996	1997	Result
Tahoe	124 061	124 125	+ 0.1 %
Suburban	137 171	142 205	+ 3.7 %
Yukon	36 566	41 072	+12.3%

MAIN COMPETITORS
Tahoe/Yukon : FORD Expedition, LEXUS LX470, ISUZU Trooper, LINCOLN Navigator, Land ROVER, Range ROVER, TOYOTA Land Cruiser.
Suburban: none

MAINTENANCE REQUIRED BY WARRANTY
First revision:	Frequency:	Diagnostic plug:
3 000 miles	6 mois/6 000 miles	No

SPECIFICATIONS

Model	Version Trim	Traction	Body/ Seats	Wheel base in	Lght x Wdgth x Hght in x in x in	Curb weight lb	Susp. ft/rr	Brake ft/rr	Steering type	Turning diameter ft	Steer. turns nber.	Fuel tank gal	tire size	Standard tires make	model	Standard powertrain
CHEVROLET-GMC 1500-Series			General warranty: 3 years / 36 000 miles; antipollution: 5 years / 50 000 miles; perforation corrosion: 6 years / 100 000 miles. Roadside assistance.													
Tahoe-Yukon	4x2		2dr.wgn.5/6	111.5	188.0x77.1x70.8	4526	ih/rldc/dr/ABS		pwr.bal.	38.1	3.0	30.0	235/75R15	BF Goodrich	Long Trail	V8/5.7/A4
Tahoe-Yukon	4x4		2dr.wgn.5/6	111.5	188.0x77.1x71.4	4876	it/rldc/dr/ABS		pwr.bal.	39.0	3.0	30.0	245/75R16	BF Goodrich	Long Trail	V8/5.7/A4
Tahoe-Yukon	4x2		4dr.wgn.5/6	117.5	199.6x76.8x70.7	4420	ih/rldc/dr/ABS		pwr.bal.	39.8	3.0	30.0	235/75R15	BF Goodrich	Long Trail	V8/5.7/A4
Tahoe-Yukon	4x4		4dr.wgn.5/6	117.5	199.6x76.8x72.8	5332	it/rldc/dr/ABS		pwr.bal.	40.7	3.0	30.0	245/75R16	BF Goodrich	Long Trail	V8/5.7/A4
Suburban	C1500	4x2	4dr.wgn.6/9	131.5	219.5x76.7x72.5	4821	ih/rldc/dr/ABS		pwr.bal.	43.7	3.0	42.0	235/75R15	Uniroyal	Laredo	V8/5.7/A4
Suburban	K1500	4x4	4dr.wgn.6/9	131.5	219.5x76.7x72.4	5297	it/rldc/dr/ABS		pwr.bal.	44.7	3.0	42.0	245/75R16	Uniroyal	Laredo	V8/5.7/A4

The Japanese automaker Suzuki was the forerunner in producing light all-terrain vehicles, but it rested on its laurels and so it was open season for new competitors who grabbed first place and ran. Now that the Honda CR-V is doing wheelies and squealing for joy since it's way way ahead in the sales race, followed by the Toyota RAV4, the GM associate has finally woken up and is out to conquer lost ground. One thing is certain, the Vitara and its clone the Tracker are good vehicles, but will they have what it takes to regain customer confidence?

MODEL RANGE

The Chevrolet Tracker is identical to the Suzuki Vitara and Grand Vitara that take after the Sidekick, except for a few finish details and equipment items. In Canada, the only model sold is equipped with all-wheel drive and comes in a 2-door convertible or 4-door station wagon in a single trim level. The convertible is driven by a 1.6L 4-cylinder engine and the station wagon gets a new 2.0L engine derived from the former 1.8L with a standard manual gearbox, as well as four-wheel ABS and power steering.

TECHNICAL FEATURES

The steel unibody is now mounted on a separate, much beefier chassis. Aerodynamic yield isn't as efficient as that of a small car, but it's been refined and is pretty impressive. The wheelbase lengths haven't changed, but the vehicle itself is longer and wider. The front suspension is independent and is made up of struts with upper A-arms and rigid axle supported by longitudinal control arms and reactive A-arm, whereas the rear axle is maintained by five trailing arms and suspended by coil springs. The transmission can only shift from rear-wheel to all-wheel drive on demand, by engaging the transfer box that activates the front wheels via shift-on-the-fly, but front wheel hubs kick in automatically. Steering is now powered and of rack-and-pinion design and the disc and drum brakes are linked to ABS.

PROS

+ LOOKS. These neat, compact utility vehicles are spiffy-looking and quite appealing with their more refined silhouette. As always, they're sure to please the customers, who are mostly ladies.

+ CABIN SPACE. Both models are

Finally at long last...

roomier because they're longer and wider.

+ PRICE. Both models are sold at affordable prices, which explains why they aren't loaded with equipment. But it's nice to be able to buy a convertible or station wagon without wincing.

+ 2.0L ENGINE. It may not be as brawny as the V6 offered by Suzuki, but the new engine that animates the station wagon puts out adequate performances. Too bad they didn't give the same engine to the convertible that simply doesn't have much get up and go.

+ HANDLING. On the road we noticed that major improvements have been achieved in regard to roadability. It's a lot more competent with the more rigid platform

and more accurate rack-and-pinion steering.

+ MANEUVERABILITY. The rack-and-pinion steering has cut down on the steer angle diameter for both vehicles, so they can squeeze into tight spots, both in the city and in the bush.

+ FINISH DETAILS. The cabin has a whole new look that's modern and functional; it feels more like a car than a SUV. We're sorry that some trim material still looks a bit cheap...

+ CONVENIENCE FEATURES. The Tracker's are very versatile. Well-planned storage compartments and the baggage compartment on the 4-door wagon can be extended by lowering the rear seatbench. A nice touch: the rear door is a single swing panel, so

luggage access is handier, but it's too bad the hinges are on the right, as is the case with the competition, since the vehicle is designed for export markets to countries where you drive on the left side of the road...

CONS

- STABILITY. It still really depends on the road surface, wind and tire grip for on poorly maintained roads, even experienced drivers will get some unpleasant surprises with the short wheelbase on the convertible.

-FUEL ECONOMY. The 1.6L engine yield is crippled by a poor power to weight ratio (28 lb/hp), which means high gas consumption for such scrawny engine displacement.

- QUESTIONABLE. Off-the-road capabilities of these vehicles is even more dubious than on former models, because entrance and exit angles as well as ground clearance have been reduced and the original tires really aren't up to treks in the wild.

- DISCOMFORT. The ride is far from comfy with such a sensitive suspension that reacts badly to the least road flaw, seat upholstery is pretty hard and sound dampening is next to nil.

-BRAKES. They're still not up to par, yielding the same long stretches on sudden stops. But vehicle path is more predictable with standard ABS assistance.

-AUTOMATIC GEARBOX. It's rough and noisy with such a stop-and-start shifter and it siphons off a lot of juice from the engines, especially the 1.6L that doesn't amount to a hill of beans.

-ACCESS. It's still a bit of a task getting to the rear seats inside the convertible because of lack of space and missing running boards.

-TO BE IMPROVED UPON: The very jittery suspension on the two-door soft top model, the near-stingy heater, cramped rear seats and inadequate baggage compartment,

CONCLUSION

The Tracker's face-lift has sure taken some time, but the new model is pretty good and technical features are markedly improved. Yet we'll always gripe about the wimpy engines and somewhat haphazard handling. Too bad the all-wheel drive Tracker isn't more competent on off-the-road maneuvers... ☹

RATING
CHEVROLET Tracker

CONCEPT :		**60%**
Technology :	80	
Safety :	75	
Interior space :	40	
Trunk volume :	30	
Quality/fit/finish :	75	
DRIVING:		**53%**
Cockpit :	80	
Performance :	25	
Handling :	50	
Steering :	75	
Braking :	35	
ORIGINAL EQUIPMENT:		**75%**
Tires :	80	
Headlights :	75	
Wipers :	80	
Rear defroster :	70	
Radio :	70	
COMFORT :		**61%**
Seats :	75	
Suspension :	60	
Sound level:	25	
Conveniences :	70	
Air conditioning :	75	
BUDGET :		**63%**
Price :	60	
Fuel economy :	70	
Insurance :	50	
Satisfaction :	80	
Depreciation :	55	
Overall rating:		**62.4%**

NEW FOR 1999

- Brand new body design.
- 2.0L engine replacing the 1.8L.
- Rear suspension consisting of five trailing arms.
- Rack-and-pinion steering that replaces the recirculating ball steering.
- A whole new interior design make-over.

ENGINES / TRANSMISSIONS / PERFORMANCES

Model/ version	Type / timing valve / fuel system	Displacement cu in	Power bhp @ rpm	Torque lb-ft @ rpm	Compres. ratio	Driving wheels / transmission	Final ratio	Acceler. 0-60 mph s	Standing 1/4 & 5/8 mile s	Acceler. 50-75 mph s	Braking 60-0 mph f	Top speed mph	Lateral acceler. G	Noise level dBA	Fuel economy mpg City	Highway	Fuel type Octane
2 dr.	L4*1.6 SOHC-16-MPFI	97	97 @ 5200	100 @ 4000	9.5:1	rear/4 - M5*	5.12	12.2	18.7	34.2	10.2	144	103	0.75	70	27	33	R 87
						rear/4 - A4	4.87	NA										
4 dr. & opt.	L4*2.0 DOHC-16-MPFI	122	127 @ 6000	134 @ 3000	9.3:1	rear/4 - M5*	4.62	NA										
						rear/4 - A4	4.87	NA										

PRICE & EQUIPMENT

CHEVROLET Tracker	2 dr.	4 dr.
Retail price $:	NA	NA
Dealer invoice $:	NA	NA
Shipping & handling $:	-	-
Automatic transmission:	O	O
Cruise control:	O	O
Power steering:	S	S
Anti-lock brakes:	O	O
Traction control:	-	-
Air conditioning:	O	O
Leather:	-	-
AM/FM/radio-cassette:	O	O
Power door locks:	-	O
Power windows:	-	O
Tilt steering:	O	O
Dual adjustable mirrors:	SM	SM
Alloy wheels:	O	O
Anti-theft system:	-	-

Colors

Exterior: White, Black, Silver, Green, Red, Violet, Blue.

Interior: Medium Gray.

AT A GLANCE...

Category: rear-wheel drive or 4WD all purpose vehicles. **Class :** utility

HISTORIC

Introduced in: 1990
Made in: Ingersoll, Ontario, Canada.

DEMOGRAPHICS

Model	Men./Wom.	Age	Married	College	Income
Tracker	45/55 %	39	56 %	33 %	$32 000

INDEX

Safety:	75 %	Satisfaction:	80 %
Depreciation:	45 %	Insurance:	$1 075
Cost per mile:	$0.50	Number of dealers:	4 466

SALES

Model	1996	1997	Result
Tracker	47 188	33 354	- 29.3 %

MAIN COMPETITORS

HONDA CR-V, JEEP Cherokee & TJ, SUBARU Forester, TOYOTA RAV4.

MAINTENANCE REQUIRED BY WARRANTY

First revision:	Frequency:	Diagnostic plug:
-	-	-

SPECIFICATIONS

Model Version Trim	Traction	Body/ Seats	Wheel base in	Lght x Wdgth x Hght in x in x in	Curb weight lb	Susp. ft/rr	Brake ft/rr	Steering type	Turning diameter ft	Steer. turns nber.	Fuel tank gal	tire size	Standard tires make	model	Standard powertrain
CHEVROLET	General warranty: 3 years / 50000 miles. 24 hrs roadside assistace														
Tracker 2 door	4x4	2dr.con.4	86.6	148.8x66.7x66.5	2717	ih/rh	dc/dr	pwr.r&p.	31.5	3.5	14.8	205/75R15	-	-	L4/1.6/M5
Tracker 4 door	4x4	4dr.wgn.5	97.6	159.8x66.7x66.5	2891	ih/rh	dc/dr	pwr.r&p.	34.8	3.5	17.4	205/75R15	-	-	L4/2.0/M5

The arrival of the Venture minivan and its twins the Pontiac Trans Sport and Oldsmobile Silhouette should help GM become a serious contender against the champions in this category, namely, the Chrysler minivans. In comparison with the former models clad in plastic, these vehicles are more conventional and also more practical. Not to mention the fact that GM had the bright idea of integrating new, up-to-date touches like long wheelbase and sliding doors on both sides that can receive an optional power feature.

MODEL RANGE
The Venture is available in regular or extended body format. Both models can be equipped with the optional second sliding side door. Only two trim levels are listed: the base and LS versions (the latter isn't available for the commercial model Venture). Automatic transmission, manually controlled climate control, power steering and ABS come as standard equipment. Extras include side-impact air bags built into the front seats and linked to the front-impact air bag system. Among the options, we'd like to mention a traction control system, power sliding passenger-side door and an auxiliary system combining air conditioning and heating for the rear seat area.

TECHNICAL FEATURES.
The Venture has a monocoque chassis clad in steel metal work that's galvanized on both sides, except for the roof panel. The engine hood is made of aluminum. The chassis rests on an H-subframe that adds to structural integrity. The independent front suspension consists of MacPherson struts and stabilizer bar. At the rear, the semi-independent suspension is made up of a torsion axle suspended by coil springs. The rear suspension also includes a stabilizer bar. A «Tourism» suspension adds pneumatic self-levelling devices. The 3.4L V6, a tried and tested engine, develops 180 hp and 205 lb.ft. of torque, which makes it the gutsiest original engine in the minivan market. It's mounted on an independent cradle affixed to the body via rubber components. The 4-speed electronically controlled automatic transmission sends power to the front wheels. Braking is taken care of via a disc/drum system and four-wheel ABS. Power steering is rack-and-pinion.

Almost There !

Chevrolet offers four setups for the rear section of the vehicle: individual seats (the ultra-light 35 lb seats on last year's model), full or split seatbenches, or captain's chair seats. Depending on the type of seating, the Venture can accomodate six to eight passengers.

PROS
+ RIDE COMFORT. The Venture is a spoiler on the highway. Its silky smooth suspension, nicely crafted and cushy front seats and effective soundproofing prove that highway driving is its forte. As far as noise level goes, you only hear tire hum, depending on the condition of the road surface.

+PERFORMANCES. The Venture needs about 11 seconds to climb to 60 mph and pickup is adequate for passing, at least with half a load. It isn't too gas-thirsty, since average consumption is about 22 mpg.

+ DRIVING PLEASURE. The automatic gearbox is, without a doubt, this minivan's strong suit. It shifts gears without a hitch and provides lots of braking effect when shifting from 3rd to 2nd gear.

+ HANDLING. In most cases, the vehicle stays nice and stable. You can go into tight curves with ease.

+ GREAT FEATURES. We really liked the remote-control for the sliding passenger-side door, all the spots to stash stuff, the rear bumper that doubles as a step and brisk wipers that clear a large section of the windshield.

CONS
- SEATS. Seat cushions are too low. Seats aren't as comfortable as they should be, especially the intermediate seatbench. Rear seats are hard and flat and headrests are pretty simplistic.

- FINISH DETAILS. The vehicles we tested didn't exhibit a top-notch engineering job. Wires, ducts and electrical harnesses (in the engine compartment) were hanging every which way because the supports had given out. In the winter, windshield wipers and climate control air vents located at the base of the windshield under the hood are forever freezing up, so they're non-functional. Lastly, the chassis on the extended model lacks rigidity, a conclusion we arrived at due to the racket coming from the frame when on poor roads.

- BRAKES. The brake pedal is spongy and hard to gauge just right. Stopping distances are awfully long, proof positive that braking is mediocre.

- COMPLICATED. The control unit that oversees turn signal lights, windshield wipers and washer, cruise control and dimming of headlights (wow!) is tough to use. European counterparts of this minivan (Opel Sintra) have different controls that are a heck of a lot more user-friendly. What's all this talk about making the grade on the world market?

- SUSPENSION. On uneven pavement or roads, the suspension gets ornery when the front wheels get thrust power. There just isn't enough suspension travel.

- ACCESS. Set in way back, almost under the windshield and instrument panel, the engine isn't easy to get to when you want to do routine maintenance checkups.

- FINISH DETAILS. The Venture interior trim isn't too nice with such a bland palette and bargain basement plastic.

CONCLUSION
At first glance, the Venture minivan seems to have all the attributes needed to gain popularity. But when you take a second, closer look, you see that a below par fit and finish job and not too comfy seats aren't going to convince potential buyers. As if GM didn't have the bucks to back a better assembly job, at least so it's on an even footing with Chrysler products... ☺

RATING
CHEVROLET Venture

CONCEPT : **67%**
Technology	75
Safety	40
Interior space :	80
Trunk volume :	70
Quality/fit/finish :	70

DRIVING: **52%**
Cockpit :	75
Performance :	35
Handling :	45
Steering :	70
Braking :	35

ORIGINAL EQUIPMENT: **81%**
Tires :	70
Headlights :	80
Wipers :	90
Rear defroster :	85
Radio :	80

COMFORT : **70%**
Seats :	70
Suspension :	75
Sound level:	50
Conveniences :	75
Air conditioning :	80

BUDGET : **65%**
Price :	50
Fuel economy :	65
Insurance :	70
Satisfaction :	80
Depreciation :	60

Overall rating: **67.0%**

NEW FOR 1999

- Standard theft-deterrent Pass-Key II system.
- Standard heated exterior mirrors.
- OnStar system available as an extra.

ENGINES / TRANSMISSIONS / PERFORMANCES

Model/ version	Type / timing valve / fuel system	Displacement cu in	Power bhp @ rpm	Torque lb-ft @ rpm	Compres. ratio	Driving wheels / transmission	Final ratio	Acceler. 0-60 mph s	Standing 1/4 & 5/8 mile s	Acceler. 50-75 mph s	Braking 60-0 mph f	Top speed mph	Lateral acceler. G	Noise level dBA	Fuel economy mpg City Highway	Fuel type Octane
regular	V6* 3.4 OHV-12-SFI	205	185 @ 5200	210 @ 4000	9.6 :1	front-A4	3.29	11.0	17.7 32.2	8.6	148	106	0.72	67	16 23	R 87
long	V6* 3.4 OHV-12-SFI	205	185 @ 5200	210 @ 4000	9.6 :1	front-A4	3.29	11.7	18.4 33.5	9.2	171	103	0.71	68	16 23	R 87

PRICE & EQUIPMENT

CHEVROLET Venture	base 3dr.reg	LS 4dr.long	LT 4dr.long
Retail price $:	20,249	23,899	-
Dealer invoice $:	18,325	21,558	-
Shipping & handling $:	570	570	570
Automatic transmission:	S	S	S
Cruise control:	O	S	S
Power steering:	S	S	S
Anti-lock brakes:	S	S	S
Traction control:	-	O	S
Air conditioning:	SM	SM	SM
Leather:	-	O	O
AM/FM/radio-cassette:	O	S	SDc
Power door locks:	O	S	S
Power windows:	O	S	S
Tilt steering:	S	S	S
Dual adjustable mirrors:	SE	SE	SE
Alloy wheels:	O	S	S
Anti-theft system:	S	S	S

Colors
Exterior: White, Green, Red, Sand, Silver, Blue, Teal.
Interior: Gray, Beige, Brown, Teal.

AT A GLANCE...

Category: front-wheel drve minivans. **Class :** utility

HISTORIC
Introduced in: 1997
Made in: Doraville, Georgia, USA.

DEMOGRAPHICS
Model	Men./Wom.	Age	Married	College	Income
Venture	82%/18%	46	95%	33%	$ 35 000

INDEX
Safety:	60 %	Satisfaction:	75 %
Depreciation:	45 %	Insurance:	$ 800
Cost per mile:	$ 0.51	Number of dealers:	4 466

SALES
Model	1996	1997	Result
Venture	31 230	77 414	+ 147.9 %

MAIN COMPETITORS
DODGE Caravan-Grand Caravan, FORD Windstar, HONDA Odyssey, MAZDA MPV, MERCURY Villager, NISSAN Quest, OLDSMOBILE Silhouette, PLYMOUTH Voyager-Grand Voyager, PONTIAC Trans Sport, TOYOTA Sienna, VW EuroVan.

MAINTENANCE REQUIRED BY WARRANTY
First revision: 3 000 miles   Frequency: 6 months/6 000 miles   Diagnostic plug: Yes

SPECIFICATIONS

Model	Version Trim	Traction	Body/ Seats	Wheel base in	Lght x Wdgth x Hght in x in x in	Curb weight lb	Susp. ft/rr	Brake ft/rr	Steering type	Turning diameter ft	Steer. turns nber.	Fuel tank gal	tire size	Standard tires make	model	Standard powertrain
CHEVROLET	General warranty: 3 years / 36 000 miles; antipollution: 5 years / 50 000 miles; perforation corrosion: 6 years / 100 000 miles. Roadside assistance.															
Venture	regular	4x2	4dr.van 7	112.0	186.9x72.0x67.4	3699	ih/rh	dc/dr/ABS	pwr.r&p.	37.4	3.0	20.0	215/70R15	General	XP 2000 GT	V6/3.4/A4
Venture	long	4x2	4dr.van 7	120.0	200.9x72.0x68.1	3838	ih/rh	dc/dr/ABS	pwr.r&p.	39.7	3.0	25.0	215/70R15	General	XP 2000 GT	V6/3.4/A4

We were anxiously awaiting the introduction of the multi-purpose vehicle that would be derived from the Dakota pickup truck. Enthusiasts dreamed about its alluring style and great performances and they thought it would be the be-all and end-all, that is the perfect specimen in this category. But the miracle didn't happen, for in spite of its neat design, the Durango isn't a brisk seller. Actually, you don't see many of them on the road compared to some competitive models that are saturating the market.

MODEL RANGE

This midsize multipurpose all-terrain vehicle is available in a four-door wagon in SLT or SLT+ models, the latter being an option package. It's sold equipped with a standard 3.9L V6 engine that can be replaced by two optional V8 engines, either the 5.2L or the 5.9L LEV (low emission). The transmission can be either rear or all-wheel drive on demand thanks to a manual transfer case and 4-speed automatic transmission. Original equipment is quite rich, for it includes all the frills you find on this type of vehicle, except ABS and a theft-deterrent system. Pretty stingy when you check out the price...

TECHNICAL FEATURES

The Durango is a direct descendant of the Dakota pickup truck. It has the same chassis, main mechanical features and front end design including the same dashboard and controls. The steel unibody is mounted via twelve insulator components to a robust H-chassis integrating five crossmembers and providing high-level torsion rigidity. The chassis is painted with an electrostatic technique for better rust resistance. The front suspension on the rear-wheel versions consists of uneven-length control arms and a MacPherson strut. This layout has enhanced the steer angle diameter, back to center positioning and stability on curves. The suspension on the all-wheel drive versions still includes torsion bars, whereas the rear suspension includes a more sophisticated rear axle supported by leaf springs for more ride comfort and more competent handling on all versions. RWD vehicles are equipped with rack-and-pinion steering, the AWD's are fitted with recirculating ball steering. Brakes are disc and drum, but they don't benefit from a standard ABS system.

PROS

+ STYLE. This vehicle has smashing looks. Its big bold, muscular form is appropriate for a utility ve-

First In Its Class..!

hicle. It sits high and looks ready to pounce and overcome any obstacle on its path. The over-all look is simple, even austere, which gives it a serious down-to-brass-tacks character that suits such a practical vehicle. A very unique design.

+ CABIN SPACE. The Durango is the only vehicle in its category to seat eight passengers inside a cabin that really doesn't look as spacious as that. The baggage compartment is no Scrooge either when it comes to space, since load capacity is 1 453 liters.

+ STRENGTH. Right off, Dodge equipped the Durango with a muscular V8 that works like a charm on the Dakota. With such a powerplant, it has a pretty awesome load capacity and trailering prowess, and it's almost on a par with the Expedition since it can handle up to 7,300 lb.

+ SIZE. All that engine power motivating a compact SUV impresses just about everyone that's not quite up to tackling a Yukon, Expedition or Suburban. A short steer diameter and good reduction ratio ensure good maneuverability of this brute.

+ TRACTION. Whether you're pulling heavy loads with the RWD vehicle or carving a path through rough terrain in a 4X4, the Durango offers competent and balanced traction.

+ SOLID AS A ROCK. This is the first impression you get when you climb aboard this vehicle. You get a sense of the awesome vehicle weight and you know there's a lot of beef on the bone.

+ INSTRUMENT PANEL. It may not be one of the most splashy or lavish ones around, but at least it's logical and has a nice, let's-get-down-to-business look. But radio

controls are located out of the driver's reach.

+ SUSPENSION. You could say this vehicle is somewhat rustic, especially at the rear, but it provides pretty amazing ride comfort compared to the roughing up you get in same brand minivans equipped with leaf springs that are radiocarbon dated...

+ CLEVER TOUCHES. The compartment located under the luggage floor pan can hide all kinds of stuff out of sight. And you can consider the seats as being modular, given how easily you can fold down both seatbenches, either entirely or partially.

CONS

- FUEL CONSUMPTION. When it was first sold, this newcomer was available unit by unit and only with the 5.2L V8 engine that's a real gas glutton, the kind that easily throws back 12 mpg and even more on off-the-road treks...

- BRAKES. They don't kick in with much gusto and they're not too effective or balanced, since they're not linked up to any ABS system, which isn't too safe in emergencies. Brakes are hard to gauge as well, due to a rather spongy pedal.

- SEATS. They're terribly disappointing, they're quite flat up front and don't offer enough lateral support, and the seatbenches are thinly upholstered.

- STEERING. It lacks spontaneity on the 4X4, so driving is blurry. This is due in part to the big bouncy tires, but especially because of the recirculating ball steering. After all, the 4X2 has rack-and-pinion steering.

- TECHNICAL FEATURES. They're pretty simplistic, really, since there isn't a transmission system that can automatically transfer power to wheels adhering to the road surface. Most of the competitors benefit from this feature.

CONCLUSION

The Durango is by far the best student in the class, since it's the toughest and the brightest. But it'll need a few refinements to be more than just a utility vehicle and to compete better with the Grand Cherokee that, for the time being, pushes it into the sidelines. ☺

RATING
DODGE Durango

CONCEPT :		79%
Technology	75	
Safety :	80	
Interior space :	80	
Trunk volume:	80	
Quality/fit/finish :	80	

DRIVING:		56%
Cockpit :	75	
Performance :	45	
Handling :	50	
Steering :	70	
Braking :	40	

ORIGINAL EQUIPMENT:		77%
Tires :	75	
Headlights :	75	
Wipers :	75	
Rear defroster :	80	
Radio :	80	

COMFORT :		74%
Seats :	75	
Suspension :	80	
Sound level:	55	
Conveniences :	80	
Air conditioning :	80	

BUDGET :		49%
Price :	20	
Fuel economy :	20	
Insurance :	50	
Satisfaction :	80	
Depreciation :	75	

Overall rating:		**67.0%**

NEW FOR 1999

- Rear-wheel drive model is available.
- Engine model including a 3.9L V6, a 5.2L V8 and a 5.9L LEV.
- New overhead console.
- New body shades: Silver and Blue.
- Fresh stylistic touches on the hatchback door.
- Rotary headlight switch.

ENGINES / TRANSMISSIONS / PERFORMANCES

Model/version	Type / timing valve / fuel system	Displacement cu in	Power bhp @ rpm	Torque lb-ft @ rpm	Compres. ratio	Driving wheels / transmission	Final ratio	Acceler. 0-60 mph s	Standing 1/4 & 5/8 mile s	Acceler. 50-75 mph s	Braking 60-0 mph f	Top speed mph	Lateral acceler. G	Noise level dBA	Fuel economy mpg City	Fuel economy mpg Highway	Fuel type Octane
4x2	V6* 3.9 OHV-12-MPSFI	238	175 @ 4800	225 @ 3200	9.1:1	rear/ 4 - A4*	3.92	NA									
	V8 5.2 OHV-16-MPSFI	318	230 @ 4400	300 @ 3200	9.1:1	rear/ 4 - A4*	3.55	9.0	17.0 30.8	7.0	167	115	0.73	67	-	-	R 87
	V8 5.9 OHV-16-MPSFI	360	245 @ 4000	335 @ 3200	8.9:1	rear/ 4 - A4	3.55	NA									
4x4	V6* 3.9 OHV-12-MPSFI	238	175 @ 4800	225 @ 3200	9.1:1	rear/ 4 - A4*	3.92	12.0	18.7 33.8	9.9	180	93	0.70	67	14	19	R 87
	V8 5.2 OHV-16-MPSFI	318	230 @ 4400	300 @ 3200	9.1:1	rear/ 4 - A4*	3.92	9.5	17.2 31.1	7.0	190	115	0.70	68	13	18	R 87
	V8 5.9 OHV-16-MPSFI	360	245 @ 4000	335 @ 3200	8.9:1	rear/ 4 - A4*	3.92	NA									

PRICE & EQUIPMENT

DODGE Durango	SLT 4x2	SLT+ 4x4
Retail price $:	26,540	29,790
Dealer invoice $:	23,960	26,723
Shipping & handling $:	525	525
Automatic transmission:	S	S
Cruise control:	S	S
Power steering:	S	S
Anti-lock brakes:	S re.	S re.
Traction control:	-	-
Air conditioning:	S	S
Leather:	-	S
AM/FM/radio-cassette:	S	SCD
Power door locks:	S	S
Power windows:	S	S
Tilt steering:	S	S
Dual adjustable mirrors:	SE	SE
Alloy wheels:	S	S
Anti-theft system:	O	S

Colors

Exterior: Silver, Blue, Green, Red, White, Driftwood.

Interior: Pebble, Beige, Gray.

AT A GLANCE...

Category: 2WD or 4WD sport-utility. **Class :** utility

HISTORIC
Introduced in: 1998
Made in: Newark, Delaware, USA.

DEMOGRAPHICS

Model	Men./Wom.	Age	Married	College	Income
Durango	75/25%	42	76 %	30 %	$32 000

INDEX
Safety:	80 %	Satisfaction:	78 %
Depreciation:	25 %	Insurance:	$ 825-975
Cost per mile:	$0.52	Number of dealers:	1 887 (Dod)

SALES

Model	1996	1997	Result
Durango		20 263	

MAIN COMPETITORS
CHEVROLET Blazer, FORD Explorer, GMC Jimmy, ISUZU Rodeo & Trooper, JEEP Cherokee & Grand Cherokee, NISSAN Pathfinder, TOYOTA 4Runner.

MAINTENANCE REQUIRED BY WARRANTY
First revision	Frequency:	Diagnostic plug:
5 000 miles	6 months / 6 000 miles	Yes

SPECIFICATIONS

Model	Version Trim	Traction	Body/Seats	Wheel base in	Lght x Wdgth x Hght in x in x in	Curb weight lb	Susp. ft/rr	Brake ft/rr	Steering type	Turning diameter ft	Steer. turns nber.	Fuel tank gal	tire size	Standard tires make	model	Standard powertrain
DODGE		General warranty: 3 years / 36 000 miles; surface rust: 3 years; perforation: 7 years / 100 000 miles; roadside assistance: 3 years /36 000 miles.														
Durango	SLT	4x2	4dr.wgn.5-6	115.9	193.3X71.5X71.0	4259	ih/rl	dc/dr/ABSrerpwr.r&p.		39.0	3.15	25.0	235/75R15	Goodyear Wrangler RT/S		V6/3.9/A4
Durango	SLT	4x2	4dr.wgn.5-6	115.9	193.3X71.5X71.0	4394	ih/rl	dc/dr/ABSre pwr.r&p.		39.0	3.15	25.0	235/75R15	Goodyear Wrangler RT/S		V8/5.2/A4
Durango	SLT	4x4	4dr.wgn.5-7	115.9	193.3X71.5X72.9	4512	it/rl	dc/dr/ABSre pwr.ball		39.0	3.15	25.0	235/75R15	Goodyear Wrangler RT/S		V6/3.9/A4
Durango	SLT	4x4	4dr.wgn.5-7	115.9	193.3X71.5X72.9	4656	it/rl	dc/dr/ABSre pwr.ball		39.0	3.15	25.0	235/75R15	Goodyear Wrangler RT/S		V8/5.2/A4
Durango	SLT	4x4	4dr.wgn.5-7	115.9	193.3X71.5X72.9	4678	it/rl	dc/dr/ABSre pwr.ball		39.0	3.15	25.0	235/75R15	Goodyear Wrangler RT/S		V8/5.9/A4

The Sebring convertible replaced the former LeBaron, but the Sebring and Avenger coupes don't exactly represent true replacement models for the defunct Daytona. These cars are neither luxurious or sportcar-like, they're devoid of even an ounce of originality and performances are ho-hum. Luckily the convertible comes to the rescue of this lackluster lot by adding a tonic holiday feeling. In fact, the Sebring is the most popular convertible in North America, no wonder it eclipses the two coupes of more or less dubious ancestry.

MODEL RANGE

The Avenger is only offered in a base or ES coupe at Dodge, the Sebring is sold as a JX and Jxi convertible, or an LX or Lxi coupe at Chrysler. Coupes are equipped with a standard 2.0L 4-cylinder engine borrowed from the Neon associated with a manual 5-speed gearbox and the convertible is driven by the 2.4L 4-cylinder Cirrus-Stratus engine linked to a 4-speed automatic transmission, whereas the 2.5L V6 is available as an option on both these models, linked to a 4-speed automatic. Equipment on base models does include power steering, radio cassette player and tilt steering wheel.

TECHNICAL FEATURES.

These three cars don't share the same ancestry. The coupes are look-alike cousins, except for a few cosmetic touches. They were built on the Eagle Talon platform, a model that's just like the Mitsubishi Eclipse...from which they borrow their main mechanical components such as suspensions, engines, transmission as well as the instrument panel design. They're still built by Mitsubishi, as is the optional 2.5L V6 engine. The convertible is built in Mexico. It's directly inspired by the Cirrus-Stratus-Breeze platform and shares these models' features, like some front end design details and instrument panel. Their silhouette is sweeping, but it only yields very midling aerodynamic efficiency. The steel monocoque body is equipped with four-wheel independent suspensions. They're made up of unequal-length upper and lower control arms on the convertible and double wishbone front and rear on the coupes. All suspensions include coil springs and stabilizer bars. Steering is rack-and-pinion and disc brakes benefit from standard ABS on some versions.

BONUS POINTS

+ **LOOKS.** The Sebring convertible exudes charm with the top up or down. The convertible top is a breeze

Not Much Enthusiasm...

to manipulate and includes a glass rear window fitted with a defroster. It's one of the most weatherproof designs on the market and it's lined with a canopy to mask the arches. The BMW Z3 doesn't even compete...

PROS

+ **STYLE.** With all the touch-ups, the coupes finally do have a rather lovely design. The convertible body is more sleek and fluid with its deeply slanted windshield and its rear extremity that is very akin to the Camaro-Firebird rear end design.

+ **CABIN SPACE.** A rare commodity for this type of vehicle, it's as generous inside the coupes as it is in the convertible. Four adults can be comfortably seated, provided passengers in the rear seats aren't too chunky or spindly. There's sufficient head and leg room, but the seatbench back slants quite a bit, so even short trips can be tiring.

+ **DRIVING PLEASURE.** It comes mostly from the right-on steering and well-honed suspension, so handling is competent.

+ **PERFORMANCES.** The 2.4L engine is better suited to these vehicles, even with the automatic transmission that could be better calibrated.

+ **ACCESS.** Thanks to those long doors that open wide, getting aboard is easy and natural for both models, both front and rear. Rear seat passengers have good leg room.

+ **TRUNK.** Coupes have a roomier trunk than does the convertible, since the trunk on the latter model can't be extended and has to hold the car top as well.

+ **BRAKES.** The brake system is more effective and accurate and the

pedal is less mushy, especially on the heavier convertible. Latest-generation ABS really makes a difference.

CONS

- **RIGIDITY.** It's pretty iffy, since these cars emit a lot of strange noises when driving on less than perfect secondary roads.

- **ANONYMITY.** The coupes haven't got an ounce of charisma, especially the Avenger that doesn't get any benefit from the aura surrounding the Viper monster sold in the same division.

- **PERFORMANCES.** The V6 engine is a terrible disappointment. It just doesn't have the punch or pizzazz of its popular counterpart at Mazda. As for the 2.0L engine borrowed from the Neon, well, it's afflicted with a crummy power to weight ratio, so it performs like a slug.

- **FINISH DETAILS.** The coupes' interior design is so dull, it's a crying shame and the imitation wood trim inside the Sebring doesn't help one bit. Instrument panels are very lackluster on the coupes and the convertible's dashboard, inherited from the Cirrus, is crippled by a too low-slung center console.

- **OUTWARD VIEW.** It' just as poor on both types of models. You're seated at rock bottom up front and the trunk lid is so bloody high that rearward view is poor. The thick C pillar on the coupes and the teeny rear window on the convertible top form a big blind spot at quarterback and the inside rearview mirror is minuscule.

- **CONVENIENCE FEATURES.** Storage space wasn't a priority when the designers drew up plans for these cars. All you get are tiny glove compartments and hard to get at door side-pockets.

- **TO BE IMPROVED UPON:** the simplistic cabin design and cheap components on some models; weak blower that doesn't cool things down on hot, scorching days; rear windows that don't open on the coupes and the totally unacceptable headlight quality that seems to be the blight of Chrysler brand products. Not too bright...

CONCLUSION

The Sebring convertible is by far the star of this motley trio that aren't a thrill to drive and all things considered, nothing much to look at. ☺

RATING CHRYSLER FG

CONCEPT :		**71%**
Technology	80	
Safety :	90	
Interior space :	60	
Trunk volume:	50	
Quality/fit/finish :	75	
DRIVING:		**60%**
Cockpit :	70	
Performance :	40	
Handling :	50	
Steering :	80	
Braking :	60	
ORIGINAL EQUIPMENT:		**69%**
Tires :	75	
Headlights :	50	
Wipers :	80	
Rear defroster :	60	
Radio :	80	
COMFORT :		**68%**
Seats :	75	
Suspension :	80	
Sound level:	50	
Conveniences :	60	
Air conditioning :	75	
BUDGET :		**68%**
Price :	50	
Fuel economy :	75	
Insurance :	60	
Satisfaction :	80	
Depreciation :	75	
Overall rating:		**67.2%**

NEW FOR 1999

- Latest-generation driver's air bag.
- Refinements in equipment offered.
- Two new body shades: Inferno Red and Cypress Green (soft top) or Plum and Shark Blue (coupes).
- Some trim details.

ENGINES / TRANSMISSIONS / PERFORMANCES

Model/ version	Type / timing valve / fuel system	Displacement cu in	Power bhp @ rpm	Torque lb-ft @ rpm	Compres. ratio	Driving wheels / transmission	Final ratio	Acceler. 0-60 mph s	Standing 1/4 & 5/8 mile s	Acceler. 50-75 mph s	Braking 60-0 mph f	Top speed mph	Lateral acceler. G	Noise level dBA	Fuel economy mpg City	Highway	Fuel type Octane
1)	L4*2.0 DOHC-16-MPSFI	122	140 @ 6000	130 @ 4800	9.6 : 1	front - M5*	3.94	10.5	18.0 31.7	8.5	141	103	0.76	69	21	34	R 87
						front - A4	3.91	11.8	18.6 32.8	8.5	134	100	0.76	70	20	31	R 87
2)	L4*2.4 DOHC-16-MPSFI	148	150 @ 5200	167 @ 4000	9.4 : 1	front - A4	3.91	10.7	17.8 31.6	7.5	141	106	0.78	69	20	32	R 87
3)	V6 2.5 SOHC-24-MPSFI	152163-168 @ 5500		170 @ 4350	9.4 : 1	front - A4	3.91	10.2	17.3 31.4	7.0	148	109	0.78	68	18	29	R 87

1) base coupe   2) base convertible   3) option base, cabriolet JXi & JXi Ltd.

PRICE & EQUIPMENT

CHRYSLER Sebring DODGE Avenger	JX con.	JXi con.	LX cpe.	LXi cpe.	base cpe.	ES cpe.
Retail price $:	20,700	25,965	17,065	21,150	15,310	17,585
Dealer invoice $:	19,003	23,689	15,698	19,334	14,076	16,101
Shipping & handling $:	535	535	535	535	535	535
Automatic transmission:	S	S	O	O	O	O
Cruise control:	O	S	O	S	O	S
Power steering:	S	S	S	S	S	S
Anti-lock brakes:	O	S	O	S	O	-
Traction control:	-	-	-	-	-	-
Air conditioning:	S	S	S	S	O	S
Leather:	-	S	-	O	-	O
AM/FM/radio-cassette:	SCD	SCD	S	SCD	S	S
Power door locks:	O	S	O	S	O	O
Power windows:	S	S	O	S	O	O
Tilt steering:	S	S	S	S	S	S
Dual adjustable mirrors:	SM	SE	SM	SE	SM	SM
Alloy wheels:	O	S	O	S	O	S
Anti-theft system:	O	S	-	-	-	-

Colors

Exterior: White, Amethyst, Champagne, Green, Red, Silver, Blue, Slate, Coffee, Black, Plum, Paprika.

Interior: Gras, Red, Pebble, Beige, White-Black, Gray-Black, Black-Beige.

AT A GLANCE...

Category: front-wheel drive compact coupes & convertibles. **Class :** 4

HISTORIC

Introduced in: 1995.
Made in: coupes : Normal, Illinois, USA. convertible : Toluca, Mexico.

DEMOGRAPHICS

Model	Men./Wom.	Age	Married	College	Income
Avenger	72/28 %	35	46 %	47 %	$ 35 000
Sebring	82/18 %	47	56 %	53 %	$ 41 000

INDEX

Safety:	coupé 100 %, con 75%	**Satisfaction:**	80 %
Depreciation:	coupé 50%, con 42 %	**Insurance:**	$ 835-960
Cost per mile:	$0.46	**Number of dealers:**	1 887 (Dod)

SALES

Model	1996	1997	Result
Sebring	85 633	88 419	+ 3.3 %
Avenger	35 774	31 943	- 10.7 %

MAIN COMPETITORS

CHEVROLET Camaro, FORD Mustang, HONDA Prelude, PONTIAC Firebird.

MAINTENANCE REQUIRED BY WARRANTY

First revision:	Frequency:	Diagnostic plug:
3 000 miles	6 months or 6 000 miles	Yes

SPECIFICATIONS

Model	Version Trim	Body/ Seats	Interior volume cu ft	Trunk volume cu ft	Cd	Wheel base in	Lght x Wdgth x Hght in x in x in	Curb weight lb	Susp. ft/rr	Brake ft/rr	Steering type	Turning diameter ft	Steer. turns nber.	Fuel tank gal	tire size	Standard tires make	model	Standard powertrain
CHRYSLER	General warranty: 3 years / 36 000 miles; surface rust: 3 years; perforation: 7 years / 100 000 miles; roadside assistance: 3 years /36 000 miles.																	
Sebring	LX	2dr.cpe. 4	91.1	13.1	0.36	103.7	190.9x69.7x53.0	2967	ih/ih	dc/dr	pwr.r&p.	39.4	2.4	15.9	195/70R14	Michelin	XW4	L4/2.0/M5
Sebring	LXi	2dr.cpe. 4	91.1	13.1	0.36	103.7	190.9x69.7x53.3	3203	ih/ih	dc/dc	pwr.r&p.	40.7	2.35	15.9	215/50R17	Goodyear	Eagle GT	V6/2.5/A4
Sebring	JX	2dr.con. 4	89.1	11.3	0.36	106.0	192.6x70.1x54.8	3331	ih/ih	dc/dr	pwr.r&p.	40.0	2.8	15.9	205/65R15	Michelin	MX4	L4/2.4/A4
Sebring	JXi	2dr.con. 4	89.1	11.3	0.36	106.0	192.6x70.1x54.8	3382	ih/indc/dr/ABS	pwr.r&p.	40.0	2.8	15.9	215/55R16	Michelin	XGT4	V6/2.5/A4
Sebring	JXi Limited	2dr.con. 4	89.1	11.3	0.36	106.0	192.6x70.1x54.8	3406	ih/ih	dc/ABS	pwr.r&p.	40.0	2.8	16.0	215/55R16	Michelin	XGT4	V6/2.5/A4
DODGE	General warranty: 3 years / 36 000 miles; surface rust: 3 years; perforation: 7 years / 100 000 miles; roadside assistance: 3 years /36 000 miles.																	
Avenger	base	2dr.cpe. 4	91.1	13.1	0.36	103.7	1/90.2x69.1x51.0	2897	ih/ih	dc/dr	pwr.r&p.	39.4	2.4	15.9	195/70R14	Michelin	XW4	L4/2.0/M5
	ES	2dr.cpe. 4	91.1	13.1	0.36	103.7	1/90.2x69.1x51.4	2996	ih/ih	dc/dc	pwr.r&p.	40.7	2.4	15.9	215/50R17	Goodyear	Eagle GT	L4/2.4/M5

In the upper echelon of compact cars, the Chrysler Cirrus, Stratus and Breeze are at the top of the sales charts, ahead of the GM N-Series and the Ford Contour-Mystique. This isn't just due to chance, for these models are furbished with serious attributes. The first and not the least is a flattering design both inside and out, but these cars are also more spacious and more comfortable than their close rivals. Unfortunately, when it comes to engine choice, they're not any better than their counterparts.

MODEL RANGE.

The Chrysler Cirrus is sold in a single Lxi model equipped with a standard 2.5L V6 engine and 4-speed automatic transmission. The Dodge Stratus is offered in a base or ES version with the 2.0L Neon engine and a 5-speed manual gearbox. The Plymouth Breeze gets similar equipment to that of the Stratus and it's only available in a unique base model. The Stratus can receive as an extra either the 2.4L 4-cylinder engine or the 2.5L V6 as well as a 4-speed automatic transmission. All three car models are equipped with power steering, adjustable steering column, climate control and remote-control exterior mirrors.

TECHNICAL FEATURES

These compact cars have a steel unibody. It offers an excellent degree of rigidity, be it torsion or flexion resistance and aerodynamic finesse is great thanks to a favorable 0.31 drag coefficient. The four-wheel independent suspension uses MacPherson struts up front with unequal-length arms whose joints isolate the frame from wheel vibration and shake. At the rear, there are unequal-length adjusting control arms with induced directional effect. Anti-roll bars are mounted on front and rear suspensions and cars are equipped with variable assist steering. Brakes are disc and drum, except for the Cirrus animated by a V6, which is easy to understand given the plump weight of these vehicles. Modifications for 1999 consist of making adjustments so as to improve the vehicle's directional integrity and procure more reassuring and crisp handling. Another point: sound dampening has been refined and some suspension components honed for a smoother ride.

PROS

+ **PRICE.** Chrysler manages to offer a well-equipped model at a very

As if on a Cloud...

competitive price thanks to a lower cost price than elsewhere.

+ **ESTHETICS**. After being on the market for four years, these cars still look fresh and lovely. They're blessed with original, yet classic looks. The cab forward principle gives them a familiar look, since they resemble other Chrysler family members and this design has a unique, swish appearance.

+ **HANDLING**. It's very effective. These cars handle like European imports, they provide good roadability, but without sacrificing comfort. The car behaves predictably and stays right on track and shock absorbers perform their magic.

+ **FUEL ECONOMY.** The 2.4L 4-cylinder engine performs almost as well as the V6 and it's just as smooth,

but it's more fuel-efficient and thus more economical.

+ **RIDE COMFORT.** The ride is super due to the flexible, but not too much so, suspension, nicely sculpted and cushioned front seats that provide good hip and back support. Besides, road noise is well muffled without having to revert to costly independent cradles to support both vehicle extremities.

+ **CABIN & TRUNK SPACE.** It's chiefly rear seat passengers that have more toe and head room than is the case for rival models. The trunk is huge and nicely shaped and it can be extended by lowering the seatbench back.

+ **BRAKES.** Sudden stops are achieved over a shorter distance, at a little more than 130 ft, especially with the Cirrus that really needed

rear disc brakes and it's the only model equipped with standard ABS.

CONS

- **BRAKES.** Without ABS or rear disc brakes, the Stratus and Breeze brake pads and linings can't take the heat. The brake pedal is too soft and hard to adjust just right.

- **SAFETY.** It's surprising to see the mediocre scores achieved by the structure of these modern cars according to American N.H.T.S.A. collision tests.

- **AUTOMATIC GEARBOX.** It's one of the worst designs Chrysler has come up with over the last few years. It's horrible to use with its poorly spaced gears, downshifting is as slow as molasses and there's no braking effect at all when you downshift manually.

- **PERFORMANCES.** The V6 engine isn't wonderful and it lacks enthusiasm compared to its Mazda 626 counterpart of the same displacement, that's a joy to drive with its muscular powerplant. The 2.0L Stratus-Breeze base model engine may be fuel-frugal but it's timid, besides being noisy and shaky as hell.

- **OUTWARD VIEW.** As is the case for all Chrysler products, visibility is hampered by the high trunk lid and the narrow rear window, so parking maneuvers are tricky business.

- **STORAGE COMPARTMENTS.** There aren't enough of them, for the glove compartment and door side-pockets don't hold much at all.

- **FRONT SUSPENSION.** When the car is loaded at full capacity, the flexible front suspension pays its dues and takes one nosedive after another on less than perfect surfaces.

- **SEATBENCH.** It isn't as comfy as the front seats, since it's flat and the uneven upholstery job is somewhat botched. Could it be that there are two classes of travellers?

- **QUALITY.** Some trim components on the instrument panel and inner door panels are far from ritzy.

- **TO BE IMPROVED UPON:** The system that holds the trunk open doesn't work too well and terribly insufficient headlight brilliance.

CONCLUSION

These cars really do deserve to be at the top of the sales hit parade, for they offer, each in its own way, an attractive package at an affordable price. The only wrinkle is the V6 engine that is far from thrilling...

RATING CHRYSLER JA

CONCEPT : 69%
Technology	80
Safety :	50
Interior space :	65
Trunk volume:	75
Quality/fit/finish :	75

DRIVING: 62%
Cockpit :	75
Performance :	45
Handling :	60
Steering :	75
Braking :	55

ORIGINAL EQUIPMENT: 70%
Tires :	75
Headlights :	60
Wipers :	60
Rear defroster :	75
Radio :	80

COMFORT : 64%
Seats :	75
Suspension :	75
Sound level :	55
Conveniences :	50
Air conditioning :	65

BUDGET : 69%
Price :	60
Fuel economy :	70
Insurance :	75
Satisfaction :	80
Depreciation :	60

Overall rating: 66.8%

NEW FOR 1999

- Suspension more geared to comfort.
- Standard four-wheel disc brakes on the Cirrus.
- Better soundproofing.
- A few new stylistic touches.
- Two new body shades.
- Theft-deterrent system available as an extra (Stratus-Btreeze).

ENGINES / TRANSMISSIONS / PERFORMANCES

Model/ version	Type / timing valve / fuel system	Displacement cu in	Power bhp @ rpm	Torque lb-ft @ rpm	Compres. ratio	Driving wheels / transmission	Final ratio	Acceler. 0-60 mph s	Standing 1/4 & 5/8 mile s	Acceler. 50-75 mph s	Braking 60-0 mph f	Top speed mph	Lateral acceler. G	Noise level dBA	Fuel economy mpg City	Fuel economy mpg Highway	Fuel type Octane
1)	L4* 2.0-SOHC-16-MPSFI	122	132 @ 6000	128 @ 5000	9.8 :1	front - M5*	3.94	11.3	17.6 31.8	7.8	151	103	0.80	68	26	39	R 87
						front - A4	4.08	12.0	18.0 32.2	8.1	144	100	0.80	68	22	34	R 87
2)	L4 2.4-DOHC-16-MPSFI	148	150 @ 5200	167 @ 4000	9.4 :1	front - A4	3.91	10.4	17.5 31.1	7.1	137	109	0.81	68	20	32	R 87
3)	V6* 2.5-SOHC-24-MPSFI	152	168 @ 5800	170 @ 4350	9.4 :1	front - A4*	3.91	9.7	17.0 30.4	6.7	141	112	0.83	67	18	30	R 87

1) base Stratus-Breeze   2) option Stratus-Breeze   3) base Cirrus, option Stratus

PRICE & EQUIPMENT

	CHRYSLER Cirrus LXi	DODGE Stratus base	ES	PLYMOUTH Breeze base
Retail price $:	19,460	14,965	17,790	14,800
Dealer invoice $:	17,794	13,749	16,263	13,587
Shipping & handling $:	535	535	535	535
Automatic transmission:	S	O	S	O
Cruise control:	S	O	S	O
Power steering:	S	S	S	S
Anti-lock brakes:	S	O	O	O
Traction control:	-	-	-	-
Air conditioning:	S	S	S	S
Leather:	O	-	O	-
AM/FM/radio-cassette:	S	O	S	O
Power door locks:	S	O	S	O
Power windows:	S	O	S	O
Tilt steering:	S	S	S	S
Dual adjustable mirrors:	SEH	SM	SEH	SE
Alloy wheels:	O	-	S	-
Anti-theft system:	O	-	O	O

Colors
Exterior: White, Red, Blue, Green, Amethyst, Cranberry, Platinum, Champagne, Slate.
Interior: Pebble, Beige, Silver.

AT A GLANCE...

Category: front-wheel drive compact sedans.   **Class :** 4

HISTORIC
Introduced in: 1995, 1996 pour Breeze.
Made in: Sterling Heights, MI, USA.

DEMOGRAPHICS
Model	Men./Wom.	Age	Married	College	Income
Cirrus	76/24 %	54	74 %	32 %	$ 32 000
Stratus	57/43 %	51	78 %	30 %	$ 34 000

INDEX
Safety:	50 %	Satisfaction:	80 %
Depreciation:	45 %	Insurance:	$ 765-825
Cost per mile:	$ 0.41-0.45	Number of dealers:	148

SALES
Model	1996	1997	Result
Cirrus	36 007	31 549	- 12.1 %
Stratus	98 065	99 040	+ 1.0 %
Breeze	64 500	72 499	+ 12.5 %

MAIN COMPETITORS
FORD Contour, HONDA Accord, HYUNDAI Sonata, MAZDA 626, MERCURY Mystique, NISSAN Altima, OLDSMOBILE Alero, PONTIAC Grand Am, SUBARU Legacy, TOYOTA Camry, VW Passat.

MAINTENANCE REQUIRED BY WARRANTY
First revision:	Frequency:	Diagnostic plug:
5 000 miles	6 months	Yes

SPECIFICATIONS

Model	Version Trim	Body/ Seats	Interior volume cu ft	Trunk volume cu ft	Cd	Wheel base in	Lght x Wdgth x Hght in x in x in	Curb weight lb	Susp. ft/rr	Brake ft/rr	Steering type	Turning diameter ft	Steer. turns nber.	Fuel tank gal	tire size	Standard tires make	model	Standard powertrain
CHRYSLER	General warranty: 3 years / 36 000 miles; surface rust: 3 years; perforation: 7 years / 100 000 miles; roadside assistance: 3 years /36 000 miles.																	
Cirrus	LXi	4dr.sdn. 5	95.9	15.7	0.31	108.0	187.0x71.7x54.3	3146	ih/ih	dc/ABS	pwr.r&p.	37.0	3.10	16.0	195/65R15	Michelin	MX4	V6/2.5/A4
DODGE	General warranty: 3 years / 36 000 miles; surface rust: 3 years; perforation: 7 years / 100 000 miles; roadside assistance: 3 years /36 000 miles.																	
Stratus	base	4dr.sdn. 5	95.5	15.7	0.31	108.0	186.0x71.7x54.3	2921	ih/ih	dc/dr	pwr.r&p.	37.1	3.09	16.0	195/70R14	Michelin	XW4	L4/2.0/M5
Stratus	ES	4dr.sdn. 5	95.5	15.7	0.31	108.0	186.0x71.7x54.4	3067	ih/ihdc/dr/ABS		pwr.r&p.	37.1	3.09	16.0	195/65R15	Michelin	MX4	L4/2.4/A4
PLYMOUTH	General warranty: 3 years / 36 000 miles; surface rust: 3 years; perforation: 7 years / 100 000 miles; roadside assistance: 3 years /36 000 miles.																	
Breeze	base	4dr.sdn. 5	95.9	15.7	0.31	108.0	186.0x71.7x54.3	2925	ih/ih	dc/dr	pwr.r&p.	37.1	3.09	16.0	195/70R14	Michelin	XW4	L4/2.0/M5

Chrysler is the automaker that has been the most successful worldwide in the minivan and all-terrain sport-utility vehicles. Yet the folks at Chrysler still believe in the conventional automobile, especially the mid-priced class. The latest model Concorde has a different vocation than the former model that was so typically North American in design and that only enjoyed average sales, since its reputation was tainted by all kinds of reliability glitches. The new replacement model has a more international flair and its front end design is inspired by prestigious automobile classics.

MODEL RANGE
The latest model Concorde and Intrepid are still four-door mid-luxury sedans offered in LX and Lxi trim levels for the Concorde and base or ES for the Intrepid. They're powered by two new V6 engines assisted by an automatic transmission: a 2.7L model for the base versions and a 3.2L model for the Lxi and ES. Original equipment items include automatic transmission, power steering, climate control, cruise control, radio cassette player, power locks, windows and exterior mirrors and adjustable steering column. The Lxi and ES receive standard ABS-traction control, light alloy wheels, a theft-deterrent system and CD changer.

TECHNICAL FEATURES
The most recent Concorde is built very much like the prototype unveiled at the Detroit Auto Show in January 1997. It incorporates the cab forward concept that consists of thrusting the wheels out towards the four corners of the cabin so as to maximize interior space. This car has really spectacular looks but its clean lines yield impressive aerodynamics as well, namely a drag coefficient of 0.29. The chassis has been improved when it comes to structural rigidity, but it's the two new engines that are the most remarkable. These two V6 beauties are at the cutting edge of present-day technology. They're made entirely of aluminum with a cast iron liner and they're 10% more powerful yet they emit 30% less air pollution. They're paired up to the adaptive electronically controlled automatic transmission that equipped the former models, which isn't the best news, at least not for many disgruntled

Scottish Shower...

owners. There's a fully independent suspension and four-wheel high-performance disc brakes. The engine and front suspension of MacPherson strut design are installed on an independent cradle built of hydroformed elements. The rear suspension is made up of a multi-link Chapman setup with aluminum crossmember to lighten and rigidify the whole.

PROS
+ SILHOUETTE. It's very dynamic especially at the swishy front end. The grille is reminiscent of the one that graced prestigious models in the sixties such as the Aston Martin, Ferrari and company.

+ CABIN & TRUNK SPACE. The cabin and trunk are very roomy. Three passengers can be

accomodated in the rear seats.

+ HANDLING. Compared to the preceding model, roadholding is more of a sure thing with the more rigid structure that assures crisper directional movement. The shock absorber system really paves the way to a smooth ride while maintaining a straight-ahead course.

+ MANEUVERABILITY. It's superb for such a big car, so parking in the city or doing a U-turn on narrow roads is easy to manage. Power steering is super smooth and accurate.

+ CONVENIENCE FEATURES. This facet hasn't been forgotten, for most of the storage compartments are generous both up front and in the rear. Rear seat passengers can store things in the seat pocket or inside the huge storage compart-

ment in the centre armrest and there are two cup-holders as well. The trunk is big, but it isn't convertible, yet you have access to it via a ski-sized pass-through.

+ HEADLAMPS. They're definitely a cut above what they were before. They're much brighter and reach further into the dark.

CONS
- NOISE. It's pretty poor for a such a new model car. You can hear engine, road and wind noise, signs that a good drag coefficient isn't everything...

- QUALITY. Plastic trim components on the instrument panel are chintzier-looking than on former models. The over-all effect isn't what you'd expect on such a classy car.

- PERFORMANCES. Accelerations and pickup mustered by the new V6 engines are nothing out of the ordinary and scores achieved were lower than before.

- BRAKES. They're only average, in spite of refinements, since most stops take an average of 165 ft at 60 mph and brakes really don't bite in when applied.

- SUSPENSION. It bottoms out when the car is at full load capacity due to low-level travel that cuts down on ride comfort.

- A FEW MISSING FEATURES. There aren't any headrests to speak of in the rear seats and the front headrests can't be adjusted. The remote door lock system is sluggish and the control could be more conveniently located.

- AUTOMATIC GEARBOX. Just as before, there is no braking effect whatsoever when you downshift manually, so brakes take a beating on long descents with the Concorde. The «AutoStick» shifter on the Intrepid ES solves this glitch but switching gears is sometimes rough as blazes if you want to hit higher speeds.

CONCLUSION
The latest models Concorde-Intrepid's are gorgeous to look at and they provide a comfy ride, but they don't shine when it comes to aerodynamic finesse, performances and especially in regard to the cabin appearance, since finish details and some trim materials are very run-of-the-mill. Trying to cut corners on production costs can sometimes lead to risky compromises. ☺

RATING CHRYSLER LH		
CONCEPT :		83%
Technology	80	
Safety :	90	
Interior space :	80	
Trunk volume:	90	
Quality/fit/finish :	75	
DRIVING:		66%
Cockpit :	80	
Performance :	55	
Handling :	60	
Steering :	80	
Braking :	55	
ORIGINAL EQUIPMENT:		82%
Tires :	80	
Headlights :	80	
Wipers :	80	
Rear defroster :	80	
Radio :	90	
COMFORT :		76%
Seats :	80	
Suspension :	80	
Sound level :	70	
Conveniences :	70	
Air conditioning :	80	
BUDGET :		61%
Price :	50	
Fuel economy :	75	
Insurance :	45	
Satisfaction :	85	
Depreciation :	50	
Overall rating:		**73.6%**

NEW FOR 1999
- Smoother suspension and less noise and vibration.
- Ignition cut-out device added to the theft-deterrent system.
- Low-emission V6 engine model.
- Two new body shades.
- Retainer net in the trunk (Concorde).
- New type of leather seat trim.

ENGINES / TRANSMISSIONS / PERFORMANCES

Model/ version	Type / timing valve / fuel system	Displacement cu in	Power bhp @ rpm	Torque lb-ft @ rpm	Compres. ratio	Driving wheels / transmission	Final ratio	Acceler. 0-60 mph s	Standing 1/4 & 5/8 mile s	Acceler. 50-75 mph s	Braking 60-0 mph f	Top speed mph	Lateral acceler. G	Noise level dBA	Fuel economy mpg City	Fuel economy mpg Highway	Fuel type Octane
1)	V6* 2.7 DOHC-24-MPSFI	167	200 @ 5800	190 @ 4850	9.7 :1	front - A4	3.89	10.5	17.5 30.2	7.2	157	112	0.76	68	20	31	R 87
2)	V6* 3.2 SOHC-24-MPSFI	197	225 @ 6300	225 @ 3800	9.5 :1	front - A4	3.66	9.3	17.2 30.0	6.4	164	118	0.78	68	18	30	R 87

1) Concorde LX & Intrepid   2) Concorde LXi & Intrepid ES

PRICE & EQUIPMENT

CHRYSLER Concorde DODGE Intrepid	LX	LXi	base	ES
Retail price $:	21,305	24,685	19,865	22,465
Dealer invoice $:	19,511	22,519	18,050	20,524
Shipping & handling $:	550	550	550	550
Automatic transmission:	S	S	S	S
Cruise control:	S	S	S	S
Power steering:	S	S	S	S
Anti-lock brakes:	O	S	O	S
Traction control:	O	O	-	O
Air conditioning:	SM	SA	SM	SM
Leather:	-	S	-	-
AM/FM/radio-cassette:	S	SCD	S	S
Power door locks:	S	S	S	S
Power windows:	S	S	S	S
Tilt steering:	S	S	S	S
Dual adjustable mirrors:	SE	SE	SE	SE
Alloy wheels:	-	S	-	S
Anti-theft system:	-	S	-	O

Colors
Exterior: Green, Platinum, Red, Champagne, Amethyst, Cranberry, Slate, White.
Interior: Quartz, Pebble, Beige.

AT A GLANCE...
Category: front-wheel drive full-size sedans.   **Class :** 6

HISTORIC
Introduced in: 1993
Made in: Bramalea, Ontario, Canada.

DEMOGRAPHICS

Model	Men./Wom.	Age	Married	College	Income
Concorde	82/18 %	62	85 %	27 %	$ 35 000
Intrepid	77/23 %	49	84 %	42 %	$ 35 000

INDEX
Safety: 90 %   **Satisfaction:** 85 %
Depreciation: 47-54 %   **Insurance:** $ 850
Cost per mile: $ 0.46   **Number of dealers:** 1 822 (Chrys)

SALES

Model	1996	1997	Result
Concorde	52 106	38 772	- 25.6 %
Intrepid	145 402	118 537	- 18.5 %

MAIN COMPETITORS
CHEVROLET Lumina, BUICK Century-Regal-LeSabre, FORD Taurus, HONDA Accord, MERCURY Sable, NISSAN Maxima, OLDSMOBILE Intrigue, PONTIAC Bonneville-Grand Prix, TOYOTA Camry.

MAINTENANCE REQUIRED BY WARRANTY
First revision: 5 000 miles   **Frequency:** 6 months / 6 000 miles   **Diagnostic plug:** Yes

SPECIFICATIONS

Model	Version Trim	Body/ Seats	Interior volume cu ft	Trunk volume cu ft	Cd	Wheel base in	Lght x Wdgth x Hght in x in x in	Curb weight lb	Susp. ft/rr	Brake ft/rr	Steering type	Turning diameter ft	Steer. turns nber.	Fuel tank gal	tire size	Standard tires make	model	Standard powertrain
CHRYSLER		General warranty: 3 years / 36 000 miles; surface rust: 3 years; perforation: 7 years / 100 000 miles; roadside assistance: 3 years /36 000 miles.																
Concorde	LX	4dr.sdn.5	107.6	530	0.30	113.0	209.1x74.4x55.9	3446	ih/ih	dc/dc	pwr.r&p.	37.7	3.11	16.9	205/70R15	Goodyear	Conquest GA	V6/2.7/A4
Concorde	LXi	4dr.sdn.5	107.6	530	0.30	113.0	209.1x74.4x55.9	3556	ih/ih	dc/ABS	pwr.r&p.	37.7	3.11	16.9	225/60R16	Goodyear	Eagle GA	V6/3.2/A4
DODGE		General warranty: 3 years / 36 000 miles; surface rust: 3 years; perforation: 7 years / 100 000 miles; roadside assistance: 3 years /36 000 miles.																
Intrepid		4dr.sdn.5	104.5	521	0.30	113.0	203.7x74.7x55.9	3422	ih/ih	dc/dc	pwr.r&p.	37.7	3.11	16.9	205/70R15	Goodyear	Conquest GA	V6/2.7/A4
Intrepid	ES	4dr.sdn.5	104.5	521	0.30	113.0	203.7x74.7x55.9	3519	ih/ih	dc/ABS	pwr.r&p.	37.7	3.11	16.9	225/60R16	Goodyear	Eagle GA	V6/3.2/A4

CHRYSLER LHS et 300M
More Spirit Than Skill..

CHRYSLER LHS

The Eagle Vision's demise and the LHS make-over have given Chrysler the chance to begin a new era and be in the running in market segments where it was poorly represented thus far. In the luxury car class, the first LHS scored quite well, sometimes selling more than the Cadillac Seville over given monthly periods. But its cushy luxury has never really made it a candidate for exportation to Europe where car fans prefer sport sedans. The 300M's mission will be to replace the Eagle Vision on North American markets and to try to woo buyers across the Atlantic.

The name 300M refers to high-performance sedans that Chrysler put through the paces to beat the clock back in the sixties, in the Pony Car era.

Several generations of the 300 model beat some pretty enviable records and thus proved that Chrysler was capable of belonging to the fast car club. Today things have changed and you can't race to the next intersection whenever you please, but the spirit is still there and gunning the accelerator doesn't hurt once in a while, provided you don't get caught.

The LHS is directly inspired by the Concorde and borrows its body design and main mechanical attributes, whereas the 300M shares its stylistics with the Intrepid. So, in both cases, only the front and rear extremities have been touched up so as to give these two models a personality to call their own. But the door and window design is perfectly identical. The 300M is less than 5m long, so it fits perfectly into the big European sedan class, keeping

CHRYSLER LHS

CHRYSLER 300M

CHRYSLER 300M

company with the Audi A6, Mercedes-Benz 320, BMW 5-Series and 7-Series and the XJ6 models, cars that are most frequently seen on the road. Here in North America, the LHS will try to outperform the Park Avenue, Aurora and Continental, not to mention the loyal Lexus ES 300 and more recently the Cadillac Catera that's starting to create a wave of enthusiasm.

Unlike the Concorde and Intrepid, these newcomers receive an exclusive new 3.5L V6 engine extrapolated from the latest 3.2L, at least in North America, for in Europe the 2.7L is available. Beyond cosmetic touches and wheel drive type, Chrysler wanted to refine what was lacking on the former LHS and Vision, namely the suspension. Both cars, each in their own way, lacked polish and pizzazz. Compared to the Concorde and Intrepid, a new

front cradle has been designed, made up of three rigorously rigid hydroformed reinforcing tubes. The geometry has been revised so as to better control rear end lift on accelerations and nose-dives when braking. Springs have been insulated as well and shock absorbers are more powerful. At the rear, an aluminum crossmember produces a smoother ride without adversely affecting handling. On our continent, these two models will be fitted with Goodyear Eagle LS (like the Seville), but the sports versions will get Michelin XGTV4 tires included in a «handling» options package on the 300M, but these items will be standard equipment on versions exported to Europe... The cabin design is practically identical for both models, except for a few different instruments, but the 300M is the only one to receive a standard «AutoStick» sequential shifter.

When it comes to spinning drivers' dreams, Chrysler has no equal. This super formula is tried and true and it works every time. Two years before a model is launched, it's shown at the Detroit Auto Show in a spectacular prototype form. The design is very down-to-earth, but the bold, modern silhouette makes car journalists and car buffs drool. When the time comes to reveal the model in question, things are orchestrated in such a way that there are the fewest spy photos possible in car magazines so that the surprise effect is perfect, then the car is unveiled in due grand style and everyone falls in love with it, because it's even more gorgeous and refined than the prototype, so it gets excellent reviews and chances are good that these cars will sell like hot cakes. The LHS is geared to a more mature clientele, but the 300M is going to try to win over younger buyers between 35 and 45 years of age of whom 40% will be women, customers with an average annual income of $ 50,000 The marketing gurus at Chrysler see this new buyer segment as articulate, athletic, cultured and looking for a car with a unique personality. Anyone can dream...

MODEL RANGE

The 300M and LHS are four-door luxury sedans offered in a single trim level, but they can be furbished with a «sports handling» package in the case of the 300M. They're powered by the latest 3.5L V6 linked to an electronically controlled automatic transmission with standard «AutoStick» sequential shifter on the 300M. Original equipment includes all the usual luxury items found in this car class, as well as fine leather seats, automatic climate control, CD changer and trip computer.

TECHNICAL FEATURES

The LHS is a spin-off of the Concorde body design, whereas the 300M is inspired by the Intrepid. But they're different from their mentors, since they're equipped with a more rigid front cradle supporting the engine and suspension. This body design in sensational and its aerodynamics are simply super, since the drag coefficient is an impressive 0.31. Structural integrity has been improved by 40% in flexion and by 20% in torsion and an

aluminum crossmember solidifies the rear end. The suspensions are the same as those found on other LH models, but springs and shock absorbers have been carefully calibrated according to net weight, so as to achieve a creamier ride and more precise handling. Cars are equipped with four-wheel disc brakes with standard ABS and traction control. The V6 engine common to both models is a 3.5L derived from the LH 3.2L powerplant. It's made entirely of aluminum with a cast iron liner and it develops 253 hp and 255 lb.ft. torque. Emissions are 30% cleaner as well. In order to cut down on noise, a second resonator has been added. The transmission is an electronically controlled adaptive automatic. It's the transmission that equipped the old models, which isn't really good news.

PROS

+LOOKS. The Concorde's 300M-LHS's very dynamic front end is reminiscent of that on legendary cars of the sixties, such as the Aston Martin, Ferrari and such.

+ RIDE COMFORT. The cabin is spacious and the trunk is generous, five passengers and all their luggage can be easily accomodated. The ride is velvety smooth without being soft and syrupy, as is the lot of other classy American cars in this class. The suspension handles road faults like a champion and soundproofing dampens most noise. Compared to last year's LHS, there's far much less wind noise around the windshield and windows.

+ ROADABILITY. It's more solid thanks to the more rigid car architecture and to modifications aimed at making handling as competent as possible. Specially calibrated shock absorbers are flexible but don't cause sway that would affect levelling. This car doesn't tend to buck and nosedive like the Concorde-Intrepid.

+ MANEUVERABILITY. It's great for such substantial cars, so city parking or U-turns on narrow roads are no problem at all. Steering is smooth and accurate, a real plus.

+ CONVENIENCE FEATURES. Most storage spots are roomy both front and rear. In the rear seat, travellers have access to a seat pocket and the center armrest hold a huge storage compartment and two cupholders. The absolutely hug trunk connects to the cabin via a ski slot.

+ HEADLAMPS. Definitely better than before. They hae more reach and brilliance so you can drive with confidence.

+ INSTRUMENT PANEL. It's generally a lot like the LH dashboard and the layout is pretty much the same. But it's a lot more spiffy with its lush trim and remarkable instruments, especially inside the 300M with black on white gauges. The look is classy and finish details are exquisite.

CONS

-PERFORMANCES. The 3.5L engine's accelerations and pickup left us unsatisfied, especially on the 300M, since performances don't match the character that the name evokes. They lack piquant and scores achieved prove it.

- BRAKES. They're only average even with all the elaborate refinements. Most stops were achieved at about 150 ft at 60 mph and they don't bite in when applied.

- AUTOMATIC GEARBOX. It doesn't provide any braking effect when downshifting manually, so brakes get no relief on long descending slopes with the LHS. The «AutoStick» sequential shifter that equips the 300M takes care of this matter, but shifting is sometimes pretty rough and ready if you want to speed up.

- A FEW MISSING FEATURES. There aren't any headrests worthy of the name in the rear seats and up front they can't be adjusted. The remote control for the door locks is slow and the control isn't too handy.

CONCLUSION

The LHS is a better buy than the 300M, since it's come a long way in terms of ride comfort and handling is much more precise. The 300M just doesn't accomplish its mission of being the sporty car in this duo, since a heck of a lot of other less pricy cars perform better. A supercharger would give this car just the edge it needs to be what it was meant to be. ☺

RATING CHRYSLER LHS

CONCEPT :   84%
Technology	80
Safety :	90
Interior space :	80
Trunk volume:	90
Quality/fit/finish :	80

DRIVING: 67%
Cockpit :	80
Performance :	65
Handling :	55
Steering :	80
Braking :	55

ORIGINAL EQUIPMENT: 82%
Tires :	80
Headlights :	80
Wipers :	80
Rear defroster :	80
Radio :	90

COMFORT :   74%
Seats :	80
Suspension :	80
Sound level:	60
Conveniences :	70
Air conditioning :	80

BUDGET :   52%
Price :	20
Fuel economy :	60
Insurance :	50
Satisfaction :	85
Depreciation :	45

Overall rating: 71.8%

Anecdote

These two models were unveiled on the top balcony of an Atlanta hotel. The cars were transported there by helicopter! There was magic in the air as we gazed at this duo dangling high in the air with the wind blowing us every which way. John Erlich, the designer for these beauties, was pretty disshevelled. A ritual that wasn't at all down-to-earth, believe me...

ENGINES

Model/version	Type / timing valve / fuel system	Displacement cu in	Power bhp @ rpm	Torque lb-ft @ rpm
base	V6 3.5 SOHC-24-MPSFI	215	253 @ 6400	255 @ 3950

TRANSMISSIONS

Compres. ratio	Driving wheels / transmission	Final ratio
10.1 :1	front - A4	3.66

PERFORMANCES

Acceler. 0-60 mph s	Standing 1/4 & 5/8 mile s	Acceler. 50-75 mph s	Braking 60-0 mph f	Top speed mph	Lateral acceler. G	Noise level dBA	Fuel economy mpg City	Highway	Fuel type Octane
8.5	16.3 29.4	6.1	154	137	0.77	67	17	25	M 89

PRICE & EQUIPMENT

CHRYSLER	300M	LHS
Retail price $:	28,300	28,400
Dealer invoice $:	25,942	26,041
Shipping & handling $:	595	595
Automatic transmission:	S	S
Cruise control:	S	S
Power steering:	S	S
Anti-lock brakes:	S	S
Traction control:	S	S
Air conditioning:	SA	SA
Leather:	S	S
AM/FM/radio-cassette:	SCD	SCD
Power door locks:	S	S
Power windows:	S	S
Tilt steering:	S	S
Dual adjustable mirrors:	SEH	SEH
Alloy wheels:	S	S
Anti-theft system:	S	S

Colors
Exterior: Green, Platinum, Red, Champagne, Cinnamon, Amethyst, Cranberry, Slate, White.
Interior: Pebble, Beige.

AT A GLANCE...

Category: front-wheel drive luxury sedans.   **Class :** 7

HISTORIC
Introduced in: 1994-1999
Made in: Bramalea, Ontario, Canada.

DEMOGRAPHICS
Model	Men./Wom.	Age	Married	College	Income
300M	60/40 %	40	78 %	41 %	$ 52 000
LHS	92/8 %	60	87 %	37 %	$ 54 000

INDEX
Safety:	90 %	Satisfaction:	78 %
Depreciation:	45 %	Insurance:	$ 1 100
Cost per mile:	$0.55	Number of dealers:	1 887 (Dod)

SALES
Model	1996	1997	Result
300M	Not on the market at that time.		
LHS	37 213	30 189	- 18.9 %

MAIN COMPETITORS
LHS : BUICK Park Avenue, CADILLAC Catera, INFINITI I30, LEXUS ES & GS 300, LINCOLN Continental, OLDSMOBILE Aurora.

300M : AUDI A6, BMW 5-Series, JAGUAR XJ8, MERCEDES-BENZ E320.

MAINTENANCE REQUIRED BY WARRANTY
First revision:	Frequency:	Diagnostic plug:
5 000 miles	6 months / 6 000 miles	Yes

SPECIFICATIONS

Model	Version Trim	Body/Seats	Interior volume cu ft	Trunk volume cu ft	Cd	Wheel base in	Lght x Wdgth x Hght in x in x in	Curb weight lb	Susp. ft/rr	Brake ft/rr	Steering type	Turning diameter ft	Steer. turns nber.	Fuel tank gal	tire size	Standard tires make	model	Standard powertrain
CHRYSLER	General warranty: 3 years / 36 000 miles; surface rust: 3 years; perforation: 7 years / 100 000 miles; roadside assistance: 3 years /36 000 miles.																	
300M	base	4dr.sdn. 5	105.1	476	0.31	113.0	197.7x74.4x56.0	3567	ih/ih	dc/ABS	pwr.r&p.	37.7	3.11	16.9	225/55R17	Goodyear	Eagle LS	V6/3.5/A4
LHS	base	4dr.sdn. 5	107.3	530	0.31	2870	207.7x74.4x56.0	3578	ih/ih	dc/ABS	pwr.r&p.	37.7	3.11	16.9	225/55R17	Goodyear	Eagle LS	V6/3.5/A4

Two years ago the Dakota got a complete face-lift and ever since it's been getting better and better sales results. Not bad when you remember that this model was considered a bit of a marginal maverick not terribly long ago. In fact, such handsome looks are half the reason behind its success story, but the big V8 powerplant and intermediate size make it super-versatile and it's such a practical compact pickup truck.

MODEL RANGE

The Dakota comes in either rear or four-wheel drive with regular or extended cabin, but it's still only fitted with two doors. Load capacity is 2,600 lb. and it can haul a trailer weighing up to 6,800 lb. Inside the extended cabin, there's a three-seater fold up seatbench facing frontwards. Trim levels are base, Sport and SLT for the regular cabin version, and base, Sport, Plus, SLT and SLT Plus for the Club Cab version. Standard equipment on all models includes power steering, rear-wheel ABS, radio, adjustable exterior mirrors and intermittent wipers.

TECHNICAL FEATURES

The steel unibody is mounted onto a robust steel H-frame chassis made up of five crossmembers boasting of tough torsion resistance. The chassis is painted via an electrostatic technique to improve rustproofing. The front suspension on the RWD models consists of unequal-length control arms and MacPherson strut. This helps reduce the steer angle diameter, control the tendency to spring back to center and improve stability on curves. The AWD models' suspension is still based on torsion bars, but at the rear the rigid axle supported by leaf springs has been modified so as to provide for smoother travel and better roadhandling. This revised rear axle suspension equips all models. Steering is rack-and-pinion on the RWD vehicles and recirculating ball on the AWD's; both types of steering are powered. Disc and drum brakes are associated with standard rear-wheel ABS. The base engine on the RWD version is a 2.5L 4-cylinder that only comes with a 5-speed manual gearbox, while the 3.9L V6 is standard on the Club Cab versions and the 5.2L V8 is optional for RWD and AWD pickups fitted with a standard 5-speed manual gearbox. For 1999, the 5.9L V8 engine is only available on the 4X2 R/T model.

Originality Pays...

PROS

+ STYLE. It's inspired by the Ram, but it's cleaner, crisper and the body is longer. What you have is a great-looking pickup that's raring to go. No wonder it's so gosh darn popular.

+ VERSATILITY. The Dakota pickup truck is a great second vehicle, since it can tackle tasks when things have to get done and it can be a great companion when your're enjoying leisure activities. It can do all this due to a load capacity and trailering capabilities far superior to those of the average compact pickup, especially with a 5.2L V8 under the hood.

+ SIZE. You feel less cramped inside the Dakota cabin than when you climb aboard the main rivals. And don't forget that the extended cabin model truck can transport 4'X8' sheets of plywood without having to mount any special attachments.

+ V8 ENGINES. They pump out the power and torque it takes to really move this pickup and these engines provide exceptional load capacity and traction for this category.

+ CABIN SPACE. The Club Cab is equipped with a full-width seatbench facing the front that can accomodate three passengers more comfortably than the auxiliary seats on the competition or else it can hold quite a bit of luggage.

+ RIDE COMFORT. It's above average thanks to finely adjusted suspensions, thicker seat cushions and super soundproofing for a utility vehicle.

+ HANDLING. It's noticeably better with more precise directional prowess at the front end and the bigger-diameter tires keep things a lot more stable.

+ QUALITY. Compared to before, it's much more obvious. You get a nice solid feel both inside and out. The cabin interior is more carefully crafted and trim materials and touches really look great.

+ STEERING. It's more accurate on the RWD models since shorter steer angle diameters sure help make the moves you want. But the steering on the AWD versions isn't too responsive or precise at center and sometimes it seems to be dead or on hold.

CONS

- BRAKES. Stopping distances stretch out, a telltale sign of ineffective brakes. Brakes don't dig in when applied either. Besides, four-wheel ABS would really make for more stability, something this vehicle doesn't have much of in wet weather or when the box is empty...

- ACCESS. The Club Cab doesn't have the rear half-doors that make the competition shine and so climbing aboard or stashing stuff in the rear seat is a bit of a task.

- FUEL CONSUMPTION. It's never frugal with the V6 and much less so with the V8 engines. On the 4X4, it can easily go as low as 12 mpg when on rough terrain... An optional Diesel or natural gas engine would be attractive to some owners.

- SAFETY. Rear seat passengers don't benefit from headrests, so they tend to knock their skulls against the rear window whenever the driver's toe touches the accelerator.

- FINISH DETAILS. The cabin design isn't at all like the flamboyant body style. Such a dull, dreary look isn't the fruit of a lively imagination, especially the instrument panel that's very bare-bones basic.

CONCLUSION

The Dakota pickup is a popular vehicle, a well-deserved reward for the Chrysler engineers who had the guts and know-how to be original and offer other alternatives to consumers. In this case, originality has won the day over more routine ways of doing things. At Chrysler, creative innovations are more important than following fashion trends, an approach that's given new life to this firm and that's the envy of the competition.

DODGE Dakota — CHRYSLER N -Series

RATING DODGE Dakota

CONCEPT : 62%
- Technology 80
- Safety : 75
- Interior space : 40
- Trunk volume: 40
- Quality/fit/finish : 75

DRIVING: 57%
- Cockpit : 70
- Performance : 40
- Handling : 55
- Steering : 70
- Braking : 50

ORIGINAL EQUIPMENT: 64%
- Tires : 80
- Headlights : 75
- Wipers : 85
- Rear defroster : 0
- Radio : 80

COMFORT : 71%
- Seats : 75
- Suspension : 70
- Sound level : 60
- Conveniences : 70
- Air conditioning : 80

BUDGET : 60%
- Price : 65
- Fuel economy : 30
- Insurance : 70
- Satisfaction : 80
- Depreciation : 55

Overall rating: 62.8%

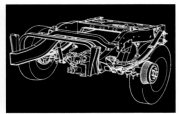

NEW FOR 1999
- The 5-speed manual gearbox linked up to the 2.5L in-line 4 engine.
- Sport and Performance option package tires.
- Improved: brakes, remote control door locks, noise and vibration levels.
- Rotary headlight switch.
- New load capacities.

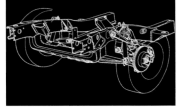

ENGINES / TRANSMISSIONS / PERFORMANCES

Model/version	Type / timing valve / fuel system	Displacement cu in	Power bhp @ rpm	Torque lb-ft @ rpm	Compres. ratio	Driving wheels / transmission	Final ratio	Acceler. 0-60 mph s	Standing 1/4 & 5/8 mile s	Acceler. 50-75 mph s	Braking 60-0 mph f	Top speed mph	Lateral acceler. G	Noise level dBA	Fuel economy mpg City	Highway	Fuel type Octane
1)	L4* 2.5 OHV-8-MPSFI	150	120 @ 5200	145 @ 3250	9.2 :1	rear - M5*	3.92	13.6	19.0 37.0	14.2	154	103	0.75	68	18	26	R 87
2)	V6* 3.9 OHV-12-MPSFI	238	175 @ 4800	225 @ 3200	9.1 :1	rear/ 4 - M5*	3.21	11.8	18.7 35.0	12.0	164	100	0.77	68	14	23	R 87
						rear/ 4 - A4	3.55	12.6	19.3 35.8	11.5	167	93	0.77	68	14	22	R 87
3)	V8 5.2 OHV-16-MPSFI	318	230 @ 4400	300 @ 3200	9.1 :1	rear/ 4 - A4	3.55	8.0	15.7 27.2	5.7	148	112	0.78	67	13	18	R 87
4)	V8 5.9 OHV-16-MPSFI	360	250 @ 4400	345 @ 3200	8.9 :1	rear - A4*	3.92	7.5	15.5 26.8	5.4	144	118	0.83	69	12	18	R 87

1) * 4x2   2) * 4x4, option 4X2   3) option 4X2, 4x4   4) R/T 4X2

PRICE & EQUIPMENT

DAKOTA regular cab.	Base 4x2 long	Sport 4x2 long	SLT 4x2 Base	Club Cab 4x2 Sport	4x4 SLT	4x4 SLT +
Retail price $:	13,585	14,760	16,225	17,955	22,575	23,245
Dealer invoice $:	12,355	13,745	14,599	16,187	20,251	20,821
Shipping & handling $:	510	510	510	510	510	510
Automatic transmission:	O	O	O	O	O	O
Cruise control:	-	O	O	-	O	O
Power steering:	S	S	S	S	S	S
Anti-lock brakes:	S	S	S	S	S	S
Traction control:	-	-	-	-	-	-
Air conditioning:	-	O	S	O	S	S
Leather:	-	-	-	-	-	-
AM/FM/radio-cassette:	S	S	S	S	S	S
Power door locks:	-	O	O	-	O	S
Power windows:	-	O	O	-	O	S
Tilt steering:	O	O	S	O	O	S
Dual adjustable mirrors:	SM	SM	SM	SM	SM	SM
Alloy wheels:	-	S	S	-	S	S
Anti-theft system:	-	O	O	-	O	S

Colors

Exterior: Black, White, Amethyst, Green, Red, Blue, Driftwood, Yellow.

Interior: Pebble, Gray.

AT A GLANCE...

Category: 2WD or 4WD pickups.   **Class :** utility.

HISTORIC
- Introduced in: 1986, modèle 1987
- Made in: Dodge City, (Warren, Michigan)

DEMOGRAPHICS

Model	Men./Wom.	Age	Married	College	Income
Dakota 4x2	94/ 6 %	53	83 %	23 %	$ 34 000
Dakota 4x4	89/11 %	46	70 %	25 %	$ 32 000

INDEX
- Safety: 75 %   Satisfaction: 80 %
- Depreciation: 45 %   Insurance: $ 775 -835
- Cost per mile: $ 0.41 - 0.45   Number of dealers: 1 887

SALES

Model	1996	1997	Result
Dakota	104 754	131 961	+ 26.0 %

MAIN COMPETITORS
FORD Ranger, CHEVROLET S-10, GMC Sonoma, MAZDA B, NISSAN Frontier, TOYOTA Tacoma & T150.

MAINTENANCE REQUIRED BY WARRANTY
- First revision: 5 000 miles
- Frequency: 6 months
- Diagnostic plug: Yes

SPECIFICATIONS

Model	Version Trim	Traction	Body/Seats	Wheel base in	Lght x Wdgth x Hght in x in x in	Curb weight lb	Susp. ft/rr	Brake ft/rr	Steering type	Turning diameter ft	Steer. turns nber.	Fuel tank gal	tire size	Standard tires make	model	Standard powertrain
DODGE	General warranty: 3 years / 36 000 miles; surface rust: 3 years; perforation: 7 years / 100 000 miles; roadside assistance: 3 years /36 000 miles.															
Dakota	reg.	4x2	2dr.p-u.2	111.9	195.8x71.5x65.6	3353	ih/rl	dc/dr/ABS*	pwr.r&p.	36.1	2.86	15.0	215/75R15	Goodyear	Wrangler ST	L4/2.5/M5
Dakota	long	4x2	2dr.p-u.2	123.9	215.2x71.5x65.3	3571	ih/rl	dc/dr/ABS*	pwr.r&p.	39.4	2.86	15.0	215/75R15	Goodyear	Invicta GL	V6/3.9/M5
Dakota	Club Cab	4x2	2dr.p-u.5	131.0	214.8x71.5x65.6	3876	ih/rl	dc/dr/ABS*	pwr.r&p.	41.3	2.86	15.0	235/75R15	Goodyear	Invicta GL	V6/3.9/M5
Dakota	reg.	4x4	2dr.p-u.2	112.0	195.8x71.5x67.9	3807	ih/rl	dc/dr/ABS*	pwr.ball	35.7	3.83	15.0	215/75R15	Goodyear	Wrangler RT/S	V6/3.9/M5
Dakota	Club Cab	4x4	2dr.p-u.5	131.0	214.8x71.5x68.5	4030	ih/rl	dc/dr/ABS*	pwr.ball	41.0	3.83	15.0	235/75R15	Goodyear	Wrangler RT/S	V8/5.2/M5

* ABS on rear wheels

Year after year, as time goes by, more and more minivans are hitting the market and the more Chrysler continues to keep its monopoly on this type of vehicle it invented in 1984. Intelligent designing, never-ending exploring of new ideas and on-going refinements have helped the Town and Country, Caravan and Voyager stay in the lead for sales in this category where twice the number of Chrysler minivans are sold for every one sold by the competition...

MODEL RANGE

The Caravan-Voyager (short version) are available in base, SE and LE trim levels and the Grand Caravan-Grand Voyager (long version) are sold in SE, LE and sporty ES. Chrysler offers the Town & Country in LX and Lxi models in two wheelbase lengths. The short versions are equipped with the base 2.4L 4-cylinder engine, the SE versions with a 3.0L V6, the long versions are driven by a 3.3L V6 and the Town & Country and AWD vehicles, by a 3.8L engine that now develops 180 hp. The second sliding door on the driver's side is still only available as an extra, but even lower-end models have standard automatic transmission, power steering, ABS and now all passengers can benefit from headrests.

TECHNICAL FEATURES

The new models are longer and wider than before and fitted with bigger windows. The latest-generation Chrysler minivans are the most modern of the three most popular models sold. The steel unibody is much beefier and aerodynamic performance is near car-like. The front suspension includes a cast-aluminum crossmember that adds precision to the geometry and cuts down on vehicle weight and steer angle diameter. The rear suspension consists of a tubular rigid axle suspended by two single-leaf springs along with a torque bar to avoid rear end zizag effect. Disc and drum brakes paired up with ABS are standard equipment for all models. All-wheel drive model benefits from a transfer box and viscous coupling that distributes 10% of the power to the rear wheels when there's less adherence. Chrysler should dust off its power trains since they aren't as gutsy as those of the competition, even if power to weight ratios are still favorable.

The Measuring Stick...

PROS

+ ESTHETICS. The body design is appealing, functional and benefits from good aerodynamic efficiency. The monochrome paint finishes are just gorgeous (Town & Country and Sport), but some years there doesn't seem to offer much choice of color.

+ RIDE COMFORT. The ride is superb. The suspension is cushy, front seats provide effective support and noise and vibration are kept to a minimum even on the lower-end models.

+ CABIN SPACE. It's now 10% roomier for both body styles. There's more legroom, hip and shoulder room and the space between seats is wider and the doors are set lower.

+ HANDLING. A rigid aluminum crossmember has improved front end aim, so you can negotiate curves with ease, especially with the 16-inch tires that are highly recommended. The rear end is more civilized on poor pavement and roads and the vehicle stays on an even keel, in spite of the rather rustic design.

+ QUALITY. Engineering, assembly, fit and finish as well as trim materials have moved up a notch and the over-all look doesn't have «utility-vehicle» written all over it, not like before.

+ FUEL ECONOMY. The Chrysler V6 engines aren't the newest kids on the block, but they're among the most frugal when it comes to gas, since consumption is always below average for this type of displacement.

+ ACCESS. It's handier with the lowered door threshholds, the op-

tional second sliding door and the outside handle on the rear hatch.

+ NICE FEATURES: The rear seat headrests that now come as standard equipment, the defroster that gets rid of ice build-up at the base of the windshield, wiper blades that keep on going even in extremely cold temperatures and the little wheels on the seatbenches that help shifting the furniture around as needed.

CONS

- AUTOMATIC GEARBOX. The 4-speed electronically controlled gearbox offers practically no braking effect when downshifting, gear changes are sometimes iffy and the shifter isn't too reliable. A real pain.

- HEADLIGHTS. They're nowhere bright enough, a feature that's totally unacceptable and unworthy of the progressive Chrysler image. They're the worst around. Ridiculous.

- STORAGE COMPARTMENTS. They're downright skimpy. The glove compartment is tiny, the storage drawer under the seat is way out of reach and the storage bin is located way down on the console. There aren't any nice, big side-pockets on the doors and no storage shelves in the rear seat area (Kia came up with this item). We still miss the little storage tub under the dashboard on the old model that was so darn handy...

- INSTRUMENT PANEL. It looks great, but it isn't too practical or ergonomic, for some controls are hard to reach and the center console is way too low.

- SEATBENCHES. They're hard, seat and back cushions are short and they're horribly heavy and hard to handle. They aren't modular at all, so if you want to store stuff, you have to slip it under one of the seats...

- REAR HATCH DOOR. Hard to close because the hydraulic jacks are poorly balanced. Which means you have to make several attempts before you succeed.

- TO BE IMPROVED UPON: No step built into the rear bumper and coat hooks that can't hold a clothes hanger...

CONCLUSION

The introduction of new rivals and the rage for all-terrain SUV's haven't really affected sales. These Chrysler minivans are still the best reference, the best measuring stick in the field... ☺

RATING
CHRYSLER NS-Series

CONCEPT : 79%
Technology	80
Safety :	80
Interior space :	90
Trunk volume:	65
Quality/fit/finish :	80

DRIVING: 59%
Cockpit :	75
Performance :	35
Handling :	40
Steering :	80
Braking :	65

ORIGINAL EQUIPMENT: 74%
Tires :	80
Headlights :	40
Wipers :	80
Rear defroster :	80
Radio :	90

COMFORT : 78%
Seats :	90
Suspension :	80
Sound level :	80
Conveniences :	60
Air conditioning :	80

BUDGET : 64%
Price :	50
Fuel economy :	75
Insurance :	60
Satisfaction :	85
Depreciation :	50

Overall rating: 70.8%

NEW FOR 1999
- The ES version of the Grand Caravan, equipped with a 3.8L engine, AutoStick sequential shifter and 17-in aluminum wheels.
- A new body shade: Cypress Green.
- New arrangement for the rear floor pan and spare tire, so as to improve exit angle.
- Standard headrests for seatbenches on all models.

ENGINES

Model/ version	Type / timing valve / fuel system	Displacement cu in	Power bhp @ rpm	Torque lb-ft @ rpm
1)	L4* 2.4 DOHC-16-MPSFI	148	150 @ 5200	167 @ 4000
2)	V6* 3.0 SOHC-12-MPSFI	181	150 @ 5200	176 @ 4000
3)	V6* 3.3 OHV-12-MPSFI	201	158 @ 4850	203 @ 3250
4)	V6* 3.8 OHV-12-MPSFI	231	180 @ 4400	240 @ 3200
5)	V6* 3.8 OHV-12-MPSFI	231	180 @ 4400	240 @ 3200

TRANSMISSIONS

Compres. ratio	Driving wheels / transmission	Final ratio
9.4 :1	front - A3	3.19
8.9 :1	front - A3*/A4	3.19
8.9 :1	front - A4*	3.62
9.6 :1	front - A4*	3.45
9.6 :1	all - A4*	3.45

PERFORMANCES

Acceler. 0-60 mph s	Standing 1/4 & 5/8 mile s		Acceler. 50-75 mph s	Braking 60-0 mph m	Top speed mph	Lateral acceler. G	Noise level dBA	Fuel economy mpg City	Highway	Fuel type Octane
NA								21	28	R 87
12.0	18.6	34.8	9.7	148	103	0.70	68	19	26	R 87
11.7	18.2	32.8	8.3	131	106	0.70	68	18	26	R 87
11.0	17.8	32.0	7.6	137	109	0.70	67	17	26	R 87
11.5	18.3	32.7	8.2	157	103	0.70	67	16	25	R 87

1) std Car-Voy 2) std Gd Car-Voy & SE, Car-Voy SE, opt base 3) std Car-Gd Car LE,T&C SX & LX, opt all models 4) std T&C LXi, option Car LE- Gd CarLE-SE, T&C LX 5) standard AWD

PRICE & EQUIPMENT

DODGE Caravan	base	SE	LE	ES	FWD long	AWD long
PLYMOUTH Voyager	base	SE			SX	LXi/Ltd
CHRYSLER Town & Country	reg	reg	reg	extd		
Retail price $:	17,450	21,415	25,155	26,730	26,805	35,910
Dealer invoice $:	15,955	19,365	22,656	24,082	24,328	32,341
Shipping & handling $:	580	580	580	580	580	580
Automatic transmission:	S	S	S	S	S	S
Cruise control:	O	S	S	S	S	S
Power steering:	S	S	S	S	S	S
Anti-lock brakes:	O	O	S	S	S	S
Traction control:	-	-	O	S	S	S
Air conditioning:	O	SM	SM	SA	SA	SA
Leather:	-	-	O	O	O	S
AM/FM/radio-cassette:	O	S	S	S	S	SDc
Power door locks:	O	O	S	S	S	S
Power windows:	O	O	S	O	S	S
Tilt steering:	O	S	S	S	S	S
Dual adjustable mirrors:	SM	SEC	SEC	SEC	SEC	SEC
Alloy wheels:	-	O	O	S	S	S
Anti-theft system:	O	O	O	O	O	O

Colors
Exterior: Gray, Green, Red, Amethyst, White, Teal, Cranberry, Taupe, Champagne, Slate.
Interior: Beige, Gray, Silver.

AT A GLANCE...

Category:	front-wheel drive or AWD vans.
Class :	utility.

HISTORIC
Introduced in:	1984: regular; 1987: extended.
Made in:	Windsor, Ontario, Canada & St-Louis, Missouri, USA.

DEMOGRAPHICS
Model	Men./Wom.	Age	Married	College	Income
Caravan/Voy.	78/22 %	42	87 %	42 %	$ 35 500
T & Country	60/40 %	44	65 %	61 %	$ 51 000

INDEX
Safety:	85 %	Satisfaction:	85 %
Depreciation:	45-52 %	Insurance:	$ 770-1 150
Cost per mile:	$ 0.50	Number of dealers:	1822 (C)

SALES
Model	1996	1997	Result
Caravan	300 117	285 736	- 4.8 %
Town & Country	84 228	76 653	- 9.0 %
Voyager	153 862	156 056	+ 1.4 %

MAIN COMPETITORS
CHEVROLET Astro & Venture, FORD Windstar, HONDA Odyssey, MAZDA MPV, MERCURY Villager, NISSAN Quest, OLDSMOBILE Silhouette, PONTIAC Trans Sport, TOYOTA Sienna, VW EuroVan.

MAINTENANCE REQUIRED BY WARRANTY
First revision:	Frequency:	Diagnostic plug:
5 000 miles	6 months / 6 000 miles	Yes

SPECIFICATIONS

Model	Version Trim	Body/ Seats	Wheel base in	Lght x Wdgth x Hght in x in x in	Curb weight lb	Susp. ft/rr	Brake ft/rr	Steering type	Turning diameter ft	Steer. turns nber.	Fuel tank gal	tire size	Standard tires make	model	Standard powertrain
CHRYSLER	General warranty: 3 years / 36 000 miles; surface rust: 3 years ; perforation: 7 years / 100 000 miles; roadside assistance: 3 years / 36 000 miles.														
Town & Country	SX	4dr.van.7	113.3	186.4x76.8x68.7	3957	ih/rldc/dr/ABS		pwr.r&p.	37.7	3.14	20.0	215/65R16	Michelin	MX4	V6/3.3/A4
Town & Country	LX/LXi AWD	4dr.van.7	119.3	199.7x76.8x68.7	4345	ih/rldc/dr/ABS		pwr.r&p.	37.7	3.14	20.0	215/65R16	Michelin	MX4	V6/3.8/A4
DODGE-PLYMOUTH	General warranty: 3 years / 36 000 miles; surface rust: 3 years ; perforation: 7 years / 100 000 miles; roadside assistance: 3 years / 36 000 miles.														
Caravan-Voyager	base	4dr.van.5/7	113.3	186.3x76.8x68.5	3516	ih/rl	dc/dr	pwr.r&p.	37.7	3.14	20.0	205/75R14	Goodyear	Conquest	L4/2.4/A3
Caravan-Voyager	SE	4dr.van.5/7	113.3	186.3x76.8x68.5	3708	ih/rl	dc/dr/ABS	pwr.r&p.	37.7	3.14	20.0	215/65R15	Goodyear	Conquest	V6/3.0/A4
Caravan	LE	4dr.van.7	113.3	186.3x76.8x68.5	3966	ih/rl	dc/dr/ABS	pwr.r&p.	37.7	3.14	20.0	215/65R15	Goodyear	Conquest	V6/3.3/A4
Gd- Caravan-Voyager	base	4dr.van.7	119.3	199.6x76.8x68.5	3684	ih/rl	dc/dr/ABS	pwr.r&p.	39.4	3.14	20.0	215/70R15	Goodyear	Conquest	V6/3.0/A4
Gd- Caravan-Voyager	SE	4dr.van.7	119.3	199.6x76.8x68.5	3812	ih/rl	dc/dr/ABS	pwr.r&p.	39.4	3.14	20.0	215/70R15	Goodyear	Conquest	V6/3.0/A4
Gd- Caravan	ES	4dr.van.7	119.3	199.6x76.8x68.5	4050	ih/rl	dc/dr/ABS	pwr.r&p.	39.4	3.14	20.0	215/60R17	Goodyear	Conquest	V6/3.8/A4

We could never thank Chrysler enough for having the guts (or the intelligence) to design vehicles like the Viper or the Prowler. Not only does it add zest to conversation, but it adds a bit of flamboyant color to our city streets that would otherwise be devoid of any frolic or fun. In short, I felt like something of a Good Samaritan as I drove by in a Prowler. Sleepy drivers' faces lit up when I was bringing the car back to the garage, in morning traffic on a gray Monday morn...

MODEL RANGE

The Prowler roadster only comes in a single two-door convertible model animated by the latest 3.5L V6 and 4-speed automatic gearbox with «AutoStick» sequential shifter. The car looks rather simplistic in design, but it's loaded with standard equipment, well, at least you get the basics to be comfortable, such as air conditioning, CD player and power locks, windows and mirrors. But the spare tire and ABS-traction control system are unknown in this cohort, which is surprising when you think of the expensive low-profile tires that equip this car. How in the world could you drive to a garage without causing damage if you get a flat?...

TECHNICAL FEATURES

The body design hails back to the hot-rods of the fifties, but the car's features are at the cutting edge of automobile technology. This rear-wheel drive roadster has a chassis and body made of aluminum panels that are glued and rivetted together. Some components like the fenders are built of composite materials. There's really no point in going on and on about the drag coefficient of this beauteous bod. In this case, it doesn't really matter, does it?...

The four-wheel independent suspension is composed of transverse A-arms and rear axle supported by longitudinal, transverse and oblique control arms. Most of the elements are made of forged aluminum just like on race cars. The suspension is completed by stabilizer bars, coil springs and telescopic shocks. Brakes are four-wheel disc but deprived of any ABS-traction control system. Rack-and-pinion steering benefits from variable assist power.

SIMPLY SUPER

+ **STYLE.** This fabulous car is just irresistible and everyone is drawn by its magnetism. Of all the cars

Being Seen And Not See..

we've had the chance to try out, this one is way ahead when it comes to an innate power to attract attention. It's a great concept. The body design is exquisite right down to minor touches like the headlamps, bumpers and grille.

+ **DRIVING PLEASURE.** Getting behind the wheel of this vehicle is a rare thrill. The car responds beautifully. There are all kinds of great growls and squeals when you accelerate so you get quite an adrenalin rush. Besides, it sure is unusual nowadays to be able to drive a car whose wheels and front suspension are visible, which really adds to the experience.

+ **STEERING.** It's almost perfect, it's smooth, precise and well powered without getting any negative feedback from the wheels.

PROS

+ **TECHNICAL FEATURES.** Chrysler wasn't cheap when it put this baby together. Aluminum chassis, body and suspension elements aren't exactly items that are commonly used in the automobile industry. The suspension geometry is inspired by that of race cars and the automatic transmission with sequential shifter are proof of same.

+ **PRICE.** You could say that it's almost reasonable, but fat chance of paying the suggested retail price when this car is worth so much nowadays because of the great demand. Gas consumption is pretty reasonable as well, it's about 20 mpg and maintenance costs are affordable since so many parts are

borrowed from mass-produced cars.

+ **PERFORMANCES.** The Prowler doesn't exactly tear up the tarmac, but accelerations are vigorous and the noise it emits is a feast for the ears of car fanatics. Pickup isn't quite as dramatic, but this engine has enough juice to scare you a bit on serpentine roads.

+ **QUALITY.** For a limited edition car, the assembly, trim materials and fit and finish are very much like those of mass-produced cars, even better than similar attributes on the Viper.

+ **THE LIGHT RETRO TOUCH.** The old-style tachometer on the steering column and the other instrument gauges exude real retro charm...

CONS

- **OUTWARD VIEW.** It's very limited when the roof is up because of the high frame, high dashboard and teeny rear window.

- **BRAKES.** They don't benefit from ABS, so stops are pretty haphazard and take long stretches to achieve. The small wheels up front tend to lock up in no time, so stopping on a dime is out of the question.

- **RIDE COMFORT.** The ride isn't bad on smooth surfaces, but the Prowler really shakes up passengers on poor roads and the suspension is without pity. Finally, the lovely roar that thrilled you during the first 30 or so miles is no thrill at all on long jaunts.

- **CONVENIENCE FEATURES.** They're non-existent, for storage compartments and trunk are purely symbolic and the mini-trailer offered as an option for luggage is far from being a gadget.

- **TO BE IMPROVED UPON:** Location of some controls (headlamps), flimsy retainer fixtures for the roof top, poor vehicle rigidity when the top is down and yes, even the clattering door hinges. No fun at all.

CONCLUSION

Driving a Prowler is something of a task, for you have to struggle against the elements: scores of curious onlookers, controls and the beastly behavior of the engine on poor road surfaces. What you won't do to be seen without noticing?... ☹

RATING
PLYMOUTH Prowler

CONCEPT :		48%
Technology	90	
Safety :	75	
Interior space :	0	
Trunk volume:	0	
Quality/fit/finish :	75	

DRIVING:		70%
Cockpit :	50	
Performance :	80	
Handling :	70	
Steering :	90	
Braking :	60	

ORIGINAL EQUIPMENT:		72%
Tires :	90	
Headlights :	75	
Wipers :	70	
Rear defroster :	50	
Radio :	75	

COMFORT :		40%
Seats :	80	
Suspension :	40	
Sound level :	0	
Conveniences :	10	
Air conditioning :	70	

BUDGET :		50%
Price :	0	
Fuel economy :	70	
Insurance :	30	
Satisfaction :	50	
Depreciation :	100	

Overall rating:		56.0%

NEW FOR 1999

- The 3.5L that equips the Chrysler LHS and 300M.
- Latest generation air bags.
- Switch for the passenger air bag.
- New body shades.

ENGINES / TRANSMISSIONS / PERFORMANCES

Model/ version	Type / timing valve / fuel system	Displacement cu in	Power bhp @ rpm	Torque lb-ft @ rpm	Compres. ratio	Driving wheels / transmission	Final ratio	Acceler. 0-60 mph s	Standing 1/4 & 5/8 mile s	Acceler. 50-75 mph s	Braking 60-0 mph f	Top speed mph	Lateral acceler. G	Noise level dBA	Fuel economy mpg City Highway	Fuel type Octane
Prowler	V6* 3.5 SOHC-24-MPSFI	215	253 @ 6400	255 @ 3950	10.1 :1	rear - A4	3.89	7.0	14.3 26.0	4.6	151	124	0.85	78-82	19 27	S 91

PRICE & EQUIPMENT

PLYMOUTH Prowler	base 2dr.con.
Retail price $:	39,300
Dealer invoice $:	36,773
Shipping & handling $:	700
Automatic transmission:	S
Cruise control:	S
Power steering:	S
Anti-lock brakes:	-
Traction control:	-
Air conditioning:	SM
Leather:	S
AM/FM/radio-cassette:	SCD
Power door locks:	S
Power windows:	S
Tilt steering:	-
Dual adjustable mirrors:	SE
Alloy wheels:	S
Anti-theft system:	S
Colors	

Exterior: Purple, Yellow, Red, Black.

Interior: Pebble.

AT A GLANCE...

Category: rear-wheel drive hot-rod.   Class : GT

HISTORIC
Introduced in: 1997
Made in: Conner Avenue Detroit, Michigan, USA.

DEMOGRAPHICS
Model	Men./Wom.	Age	Married	College	Income
Prowler	NA				

INDEX
Safety:	NA	Satisfaction:	NA
Depreciation:	NA	Insurance:	$1 850
Cost per mile:	$0.55	Number of dealers:	1822- Plym

SALES
Model	1996	1997	Result
Prowler		120	-

MAIN COMPETITORS
BMW Z3 2.8 & M, MERCEDES-BENZ SLK, PORSCHE Boxster.

MAINTENANCE REQUIRED BY WARRANTY
First revision:	Frequency:	Diagnostic plug:
5 000 miles	6 months/ 6 000 miles	No

SPECIFICATIONS

Model	Version Trim	Body/ Seats	Interior volume cu ft	Trunk volume cu ft	Cd	Wheel base in	Lght x Wdgth x Hght in x in x in	Curb weight lb	Susp. ft/rr	Brake ft/rr	Steering type	Turning diameter ft	Steer. turns nber.	Fuel tank gal	tire size	Standard tires make	model	Standard powertrain
PLYMOUTH																		
Prowler	base	2dr.con. 2	47.9	1.8	NA	113.3	165.3x76.5x50.9	2838	ih/ih	dc/dc	pwr.r&p.	38.4	3.1	12.0	fr.225/45R17	Goodyear	Eagle GS-D	V6/3.5/A4
															re.295/40R20	Goodyear	Eagle GS-D	

General warranty: 3 years / 36 000 miles; surface rust: 3 years ; perforation: 7 years / 100 000 miles; roadside assistance: 3 years / 36 000 miles.

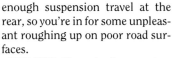

As is often the case, now that the Neon has been completely re-worked, it seems to have come into its own. After a rocky career start, it never has sold as well as the automaker predicted. In fact, as far as sales go, it's in fourth place behind the Cavalier-Sunfire, Corolla and Escort. But Chrysler has never stopped refining this car in terms of ride comfort and equipment, so as to make it more and more of a worthwhile buy. The replacement model will be introduced in the year 2000.

MODEL RANGE
The Neon is sold at Dodge and Plymouth. It's offered in base trim two-door coupes and four-door sedans that can receive two option packages: Sport and R/T at Dodge and Expresso or Style at Plymouth. Both body style models are equipped with a standard 2.0L 132-hp SOHC engine, but only the coupe can receive the optional DOHC that delivers 150 hp. The manual transmission and power steering are standard on all versions. The automatic 3-speed gearbox and ABS are sold as extras.

TECHNICAL FEATURES
The Neon body is inspired by the cab forward design. Its steel structure is more sturdily built so as to offer good passenger protection in the event of an accident and to provide more competent handling. Aerodynamics are good, since the drag coefficient is 0.33. The four-wheel suspension is fully independent, using MacPherson struts up front and a Chapman arrangement at the rear. The Neon is equipped with power rack-and-pinion steering and disc and drum brakes on all models except for the R/T coupe that benefits from four-wheel disc brakes, a firmer sporty suspension and high-performance tires. In order to cut down on production costs, Chrysler has experimented with unusual assembly techniques that even impressed, yes, Japanese carmarkers... The 2.0L engine is modern, but it's never been as refined at that of Nipponese rivals.

PROS
+ STYLE. The Neon's front end has rather frog-like traits, due to the headlamp design, but inside the trim palette is fresh and lovely.

+ VALUE. Lower-end models are a good buy for the going price. Equipment isn't super-lavish, but it does include vital features such as climate control, power steering, ad-

Fully Mature...

justable mirrors and power locks.

+ HANDLING. It's very confident on smooth road surfaces, since sway is under control and shock absorbers do their stuff. But in some circumstances, the suspension may seem to be a bit firm for a family sedan.

+ DRIVING PLEASURE. It's super with such gutsy engine power and torque. Accelerations have a nice surge and direct, right-on steering yields high-level competence.

+ CABIN & TRUNK SPACE. It's fairly generous with such a relatively wide body, but head and legroom in the rear seat area is less comfortable. The trunk holds quite a bit and it can be extended by lowering the back cushion on the rear seatbench.

+ COUPES. They're fun to drive. They've got that sportscar feel and flow aimed to please young buyers who can test their pilot skills at an affordable price.

CONS
- OUTWARD VIEW. It's limited towards the rear due to the high trunk lid and the sharply slanted rear window that darkens at the first sign of rain.

- HEADLIGHTS. As is the case on other Chrysler models, they lack reach and luminosity.

- ENGINE. It's rough, noisy and it has the shakes, sort of like its rough and ready counterparts at GM and Saturn. Power isn't too impressive, given the displacement, and there's not much difference between the SOHC and DOHC engines.

- SUSPENSION. There isn't

enough suspension travel at the rear, so you're in for some unpleasant roughing up on poor road surfaces.

- BRAKES. These brakes are simply awful. They're wishy washy when you need them, car path is unstable without ABS and the mushy pedal is hard to regulate. Four-wheel disc brakes and ABS would make you feel a lot more safe.

- CONVENIENCE FEATURES. Storage compartments are super skimpy and poorly designed. There isn't a footrest for the driver and rustic seat belts make long trips tiring.

- QUALITY. You could say that things are getting more and more consistent in regard to construction, finish touches and trim materials. But the doors and hood still make a hollow sound when you close them.

- ERGONOMICS. The cabin design isn't the best around, especially for tall travellers who'll feel cramped. The steering wheel isn't convenient, the center console is slung way down low and the dashboard reflects into the windshield, which is a pain in bright conditions.

- SEATBENCH. It's been trimmed down to give the illusion of more space. Seat cushions are too short and the terribly flat seat backs don't provide any support whatsoever. Getting aboard the two-door models is no picnic either.

- AUTOMATIC GEARBOX. It's old as the hills with its 3 speeds that sure don't cut down on fuel consumption. But at least it provides braking effect when downshifting. The manual gearbox is smoother, but the shifter is vague, so it's no fun, really.

CONCLUSION
The new Neon will arrive soon. But in the meantime, this car has earned its stripes as a popular car, even if it did take some wrist wrenching. Generally speaking, owners don't complain too much and Chrysler promises to do a better job on the next-generation Neon that'll be more compact and economic to run, so as to be able to compete with rivals here and in other parts of the world where it will be exported. ☺

RATING
DODGE-PLYMOUTH Neon

CONCEPT :		**69%**
Technology	80	
Safety :	80	
Interior space :	50	
Trunk volume:	60	
Quality/fit/finish :	75	
DRIVING:		**62%**
Cockpit :	70	
Performance :	60	
Handling :	60	
Steering :	75	
Braking :	45	
ORIGINAL EQUIPMENT:		**68%**
Tires :	80	
Headlights :	60	
Wipers :	60	
Rear defroster :	70	
Radio :	70	
COMFORT :		**59%**
Seats :	70	
Suspension :	70	
Sound level :	65	
Conveniences :	30	
Air conditioning :	60	
BUDGET :		**72%**
Price :	75	
Fuel economy :	85	
Insurance :	75	
Satisfaction :	75	
Depreciation :	50	
Overall rating:		**66.0%**

NEW FOR 1999

• **Latest-generation air bags.**

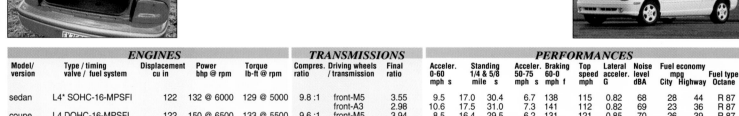

ENGINES

Model/ version	Type / timing valve / fuel system	Displacement cu in	Power bhp @ rpm	Torque lb-ft @ rpm
sedan	L4* SOHC-16-MPSFI	122	132 @ 6000	129 @ 5000
coupe	L4 DOHC-16-MPSFI	122	150 @ 6500	133 @ 5500

TRANSMISSIONS

Compres. ratio	Driving wheels / transmission	Final ratio
9.8 :1	front-M5	3.55
	front-A3	2.98
9.6 :1	front-M5	3.94
	front-A3	3.19

PERFORMANCES

Acceler. 0-60 mph s	Standing 1/4 & 5/8 mile s		Acceler. 50-75 mph s	Braking 60-0 mph f	Top speed mph	Lateral acceler. G	Noise level dBA	Fuel economy mpg City	Highway	Fuel type Octane
9.5	17.0	30.4	6.7	138	115	0.82	68	28	44	R 87
10.6	17.5	31.0	7.3	141	112	0.82	69	23	36	R 87
8.5	16.4	29.5	6.2	131	121	0.85	70	26	39	R 87
9.4	16.6	30.4	6.6	134	118	0.85	70	24	33	R 87

PRICE & EQUIPMENT

DODGE-PLYMOUTH Neon

	base 2dr.cpe.	base 4d.sdn.	Sport 2dr.cpe.	R/T 2dr.cpe.
Retail price $:	11,100	11,300	11,480	11,680
Dealer invoice $:	10,497	10,681	10,617	10,797
Shipping & handling $:	500	500	500	500
Automatic transmission:	O	O	O	O
Cruise control:	O	O	O	O
Power steering:	S	S	S	S
Anti-lock brakes:	O	O	O	O
Traction control:	-	-	-	-
Air conditioning:	O	O	S	S
Leather:	-	-	-	-
AM/FM/radio-cassette:	O	O	O	S
Power door locks:	S	S	S	S
Power windows:	O	O	O	-
Tilt steering:	O	O	O	O
Dual adjustable mirrors:	S	S	S	S
Alloy wheels:	O	O	O	S
Anti-theft system:	-	-	-	-

Colors

Exterior: Platinum, Green, White, Blue, Red, Champagne, Slate, Cranberry, Black, Amethyst.
Interior: Pebble, Tan.

AT A GLANCE...

Category: front-wheel drive coupes & sedans.   **Class :** 3S

HISTORIC
Introduced in: January 1994 as 1995 model
Made in: Belvidere, Illinois, USA & Toluca, Mexico.

DEMOGRAPHICS

Model	Men./Wom.	Age	Married	College	Income
sedan	57/43%	41	63 %	52 %	$ 31 000
coupe	48/52%	36	51 %	46 %	$ 31 000

INDEX

Safety:	80 %	**Satisfaction:**	78 %
Depreciation:	48 %	**Insurance:**	$765
Cost per mile:	$0.36	**Number of dealers:**	1 887 (Dod)

SALES

Model	1996	1997	Result
Neon	245 403	208 552	- 15.0 %

MAIN COMPETITORS

sedan : CHEVROLET Cavalier, FORD Escort, HONDA Civic 4dr., HYUNDAI Elantra, NISSAN Sentra, PONTIAC Sunfire, SATURN SL, SUBARU Impreza, TOYOTA Corolla, VW Golf.
Coupe : HONDA Civic Si, SATURN SC.

MAINTENANCE REQUIRED BY WARRANTY

First revision:	Frequency:	Diagnostic plug:
5 000 miles	6 months	Yes

SPECIFICATIONS

Model	Version Trim	Body/ Seats	Interior volume cu ft	Trunk volume cu ft	Cd	Wheel base in	Lght x Wdgth x Hght in x in x in	Curb weight lb	Susp. ft/rr	Brake ft/rr	Steering type	Turning diameter ft	Steer. turns nber.	Fuel tank gal	tire size	Standard tires make	model	Standard powertrain
DODGE-PLYMOUTH	General warranty: 3 years / 36 000 miles; surface rust: 3 years ; perforation: 7 years / 100 000 miles; roadside assistance: 3 years / 36 000 miles.																	
Neon		2dr.cpe. 5	91.2	11.8	0.33	104.0	171.8x67.4x54.9	2469	ih/ih	dc/dr	pwr.r&p.	35.4	3.2	12.5	185/65R14	Goodyear	Eagle GA	L4/2.0/M5
Neon	Sport	2dr.cpe. 5	91.2	11.8	0.33	104.0	171.8x67.4x54.9	2469	ih/ih	dc/dr	pwr.r&p.	35.4	3.2	12.5	185/65R14	Goodyear	Eagle GA	L4/2.0/M5
Neon	R/T	2dr.cpe. 5	91.2	11.8	0.33	104.0	171.8x67.4x54.9	2469	ih/ih	dc/dc	pwr.r&p.	35.4	2.8	12.5	185/65HR14	Goodyear	Eagle RS-A	L4/2.0/M5
Neon		4dr.sdn. 5	90.0	11.8	0.33	104.0	171.8x67.2x54.9	2507	ih/ih	dc/dr	pwr.r&p.	35.4	3.2	12.5	185/65R14	Goodyear	Eagle GA	L4/2.0/M5

No doubt about it, it was the introduction of the latest Ram pickup truck that gave the needed spurt it took to trigger the renewal of pickup trucks that are the # 1 vehicle sold in North America. Ford followed suit two years ago and GM did so this year. The Ram is in third place behind its two rivals, but it did improve its score in a truly spectacular way with 350,000 units sold last year on our continent, that is, three times more than was the case the year before.

MODEL RANGE

Ram pickups are offered in 1500, 2500 and 3500 versions with rear or all-wheel drive, equipped with short or long boxes and cabins. The extended cabin called Club Cab can now be equipped, as an option package coined Quad Cab with four doors, that is, two rear doors allowing for easier boarding and loading. The 3.9L V6 base engine drives the 1500, a 5.2L and 5.9L V8 engine animate the 2500 and 3500, to which can be added a Cummins turbocharged diesel engine and an 8.0L V10 powerplant. Standard transmission is a 5-speed manual or a 4-speed automatic as an extra. Original equipment is rather stingy on the lower-end model that's a lowly workhorse, whereas the SLT can practically compete with thoroughbred luxury vehicles.

TECHNICAL FEATURES

The Ram has a steel H-frame chassis consisting of five crossmembers and numerous reinforcements as to procure optimum rigidity. The side-frames on the front part of the chassis are welded and at the rear they're rivetted for easier maintenance. The nicely rounded body design yields an acceptable aerodynamic efficiency for a vehicle of this type. It's mounted onto the chassis via rubber insulators so as to reduce noise and vibration.

The independent front suspension consists of an asymmetrical double wishbone system on the 4X2 1500 and 2500 and rigid axle maintained by multiple bars on the 4X2 3500 and the 4X4's. The rear suspension is made up of a rigid axle and leaf springs. All models are equipped with disc and drum brakes and standard rear-wheel ABS, but all-wheel ABS is available as an extra.

SIMPLY SUPER

+ STYLE. Very manly, so to speak, which has no doubt affected a lot of buyers' choice, for it's modern, yet

The Trigger...

a tad retro, reminiscent of the famous Dodge trucks that participated in the Second World War. It's pretty hard not recognizing this pickup that was the ancestor of the Dakota and Durango.

PROS

+ RIDE COMFORT. It's one of the Ram's top assets for the suspension response is smooth, more obviously so on the 4X2's than on the 4X4's, always more nervous. Seats offer more support than before and soundproofing is almost car-like.

+ SOLIDITY. This pickup inspires confidence due to its extremely robust build. Some techniques used in chassis construction and cabin mounts have since been borrowed by the competition.

+ CHOICE. Besides the really wide range of model choice, depending on aspects that define each version, there's a remarkable choice of engines. With a range going from a V6 to a V10, including two V8's and a turbocharged Diesel, power and torque can be ordered à la carte.

+ VALUE. The Ram is a good investment either for work or leisure purposes. Rivals have caught up on the technical level, but this vehicle has a charm all its own that gives it an amazing resale value.

+ QUAD CAB. The four-door extended cab can seat up to six people quite comfortably. Or the rear section can be converted into a pretty roomy luggage hold, even though the layout isn't as clever as on the Ford F-150.

+ INSTRUMENT PANEL. It has a serious, well organized look. It's logical and ergonomic.

+ NICE FEATURE. The center part of the front seatbench has a fold-down armrest that can double as a desk...

CONS

- FUEL CONSUMPTION. You have to plan for a big gas budget, for the Ram (like its counterparts) doesn't run on water. The V8 engines does 12 to 14 mpg, so you're forever filling up.

- NOISE. The Diesel engine produces a lot of muscular power and torque, but it does have its drawbacks. It's awfully noisy both inside and out. It's unbelievable that Dodge hasn't found a solution, since comfort really suffers.

- BRAKES. Emergency stops stretch out a heck of a long way and brakes don't have much bite when applied. The soft pedal doesn't make for precise braking. Brakes can dig in too much on sudden stops, causing some unpleasant surprises on wet roads and without ABS.

- MANEUVERABILITY. It could be better on the extended cab and Club Cab versions due to the huge steer angle diameter and it takes a lot of elbow grease to make a simple U-turn.

- ACCESS. Not too great on the 4X4's due to high ground clearance. Dodge should be able to come up with an original way of integrating a running board or step that wouldn't affect travel on rough terrain...

- BAGGAGE COMPARTMENT. Usually carmakers aren't shy about stealing ideas from the competition. What's Dodge waiting for? Why not give the rear seatbench in the Club Cab a fold-up feature as bright as the one designed by Ford for its F-150?

CONCLUSION

The Ram pickup is one of the blue chips on the current utility vehicle market. A few details still need work and reliability wrinkles need to be ironed out. Then this pickup would be on a par with rivals. After all, the Ram's been roughing up the competition for the last five years... ☺

RATING
DODGE Ram 1500

CONCEPT :		70%
Technology	80	
Safety :	70	
Interior space :	60	
Trunk volume:	65	
Quality/fit/finish :	75	

DRIVING:		55%
Cockpit :	75	
Performance :	50	
Handling :	35	
Steering :	75	
Braking :	40	

ORIGINAL EQUIPMENT:		62%
Tires :	75	
Headlights :	75	
Wipers :	80	
Rear defroster :	0	
Radio :	80	

COMFORT :		68%
Seats :	80	
Suspension :	50	
Sound level:	60	
Conveniences :	70	
Air conditioning :	80	

BUDGET :		55%
Price :	50	
Fuel economy :	30	
Insurance :	60	
Satisfaction :	80	
Depreciation :	55	

Overall rating:		62.0%

NEW FOR 1999

- Standard all-wheel ABS on the 3500 versions.
- Sport version body design.
- Rotary headlight switch.
- A Yellow shade for the Sport version and Agate for the leather trim version.

ENGINES

Model/ version	Type / timing valve / fuel system	Displacement cu in	Power bhp @ rpm	Torque lb-ft @ rpm
1500 4x2	V6* 3.9 OHV-12-MPSFI	238	175 @ 4800	230 @ 3200
1500 4X4	V8* 5.2 OHV-16-MPSFI	318	230 @ 4400	300 @ 3200
2500/3500	V8* 5.9 OHV-16-MPSFI	360	245 @ 4000	335 @ 3200
option	L6DT 5.9 OHV-24-MI	359	215 @ 2700	420 @ 1600
option	V10 8.0 OHV-20-MPSFI	488	300 @ 4000	450 @ 2800

TRANSMISSIONS

Compres. ratio	Driving wheels / transmission	Final ratio
9.1 :1	rear- M5*	3.21
9.1 :1	rear/4 - M5*	3.55
8.9 :1	rear - M5*	3.54
17.5 :1	rear/4 - M5*	3.54
8.6 :1	rear/4 - M5*	3.54

PERFORMANCES

Acceler. 0-60 mph s	Standing 1/4 & 5/8 mile s	Acceler. 50-75 mph s	Braking 60-0 mph f	Top speed mph	Lateral acceler. G	Noise level dBA	Fuel economy mpg City	Fuel economy mpg Highway	Fuel type Octane
12.0	18.6 33.2	8.4	157	100	0.71	68	14	22	R 87
11.5	18.2 32.6	8.0	194	106	0.74	67	12	20	R 87
9.0	16.5 31.5	6.5	184	103	0.75	67	12	20	R 87
14.0	19.5 33.0	12.0	174	93	0.72	72	16	23	D
8.5	16.6 30.4	6.5	184	109	0.73	69	10	14	R 87

PRICE & EQUIPMENT

DODGE Ram 1500 4x2	WS reg	ST extd	SLT Club Cab
Retail price $:	14,560	16,620	25,335
Dealer invoice $:	13,298	14,612	22,095
Shipping & handling $:	640	640	640
Automatic transmission:	O	O	O
Cruise control:	O	O	S
Power steering:	S	S	S
Anti-lock brakes:	re. S	S	S
Traction control:	-	-	-
Air conditioning:	O	O	S
Leather:	-	-	O
AM/FM/radio-cassette:	O	S	S
Power door locks:	-	O	S
Power windows:	-	-	S
Tilt steering:	O	O	S
Dual adjustable mirrors:	SM	SM	SE
Alloy wheels:	-	O	S
Anti-theft system:	-	-	O

Colors

Exterior: Red, Driftwood brown, Green, Blue, Black, White.

Interior: Gray, Beige, Pebble.

AT A GLANCE...

Category: 4x2 or 4x4 full size pickups.   **Class :** utility

HISTORIC

Introduced in: 1994

Made in: Dodge City (Warren, Michigan), St-Louis, Missouri, USA. Largo Alberto & Saltillo, Mexico (Club Cab).

DEMOGRAPHICS

Model	Men./Wom.	Age	Married	College	Income
Ram 1500	92/8 %	48	81 %	19 %	$ 35 000

INDEX

Safety:	70 %	Satisfaction:	80 %
Depreciation:	45 %	Insurance:	$ 850 -950
Cost per mile:	$0.62	Number of dealers:	1887 (Dod)

SALES

Model	1996	1997	Result
Ram	383 960	350 257	-8.8 %

MAIN COMPETITORS

CHEVROLET-GMC Silverado-Sierra, FORD F-Series, TOYOTA T-150.

MAINTENANCE REQUIRED BY WARRANTY

First revision:	Frequency:	Diagnostic plug:
5 000 miles	6 months	Yes

SPECIFICATIONS

Model	Version Trim	Traction	Body/ Seats	Wheel base in	Lght x Wdgth x Hght in x in x in	Curb weight lb	Susp. ft/rr	Brake ft/rr	Steering type	Turning diameter ft	Steer. turns nber.	Fuel tank gal	tire size	Standard tires make	model	Standard powertrain
DODGE Ram 1500-Series		General warranty: 3 years / 36 000 miles; surface rust: 3 years ; perforation: 7 years / 100 000 miles; roadside assistance: 3 years / 36 000 miles.														
1500	Reg. cab short bed	4x2	2dr.p-u.3	118.7	204.2x79.4x71.9	4224	ih/rl	dc/dr/ABS*	pwr.ball	40.9	3.2	25.9	225/75R16	Goodyear Wrangler APc		V6/3.9/M5
2500	Reg. cab extd bed	4x2	2dr.p-u.3	134.7	224.1x79.4x72.1	4334	ih/rl	dc/dr/ABS*	pwr.ball	45.7	3.9	34.9	245/75R16	Michelin LTX		V6/3.9/M5
3500	Cab/Quad extd bed	4x2	4dr.p-u.6	154.7	244.1x79.3x72.8	4665	ih/rl	dc/dr/ABS*	pwr.ball	52.4	3.9	34.9	215785R16	Michelin LTX		V8/5.2/M5
1500	Reg. cab. short bed	4x4	2dr.p-u.3	118.7	204.2x79.4x74.7	4672	rt/rl	dc/dr/ABS*	pwr.ball	40.9	3.0	25.9	225/75R16	Goodyear Wrangler APc		V8/5.2/M5
2500	Reg cab. extd bed	4x4	2dr.p-u.3	134.7	224.1x79.4x75.1	4746	rt/rl	dc/dr/ABS*	pwr.ball	45.6	3.7	34.9	245/75R16	Michelin LTX		V8/5.2/M5
3500	Cab/Quad extd bed	4x4	4dr.p-u.6	154.7	244.1x79.3x77.2	5020	rt/rl	dc/dr/ABS*	pwr.ball	52.4	3.7	34.9	215785R16	Michelin LTX		V8/5.2/M5

* ABS on rear wheels

The Viper is without a doubt the number-one North American-built exotic car. Its performances at the last 24-hour Le Mans race have only added to its prestige that now eclipses that of the Corvette. This model has also given Chrysler the unique status of being an innovative automaker who can set buyers' imaginations on fire by creating such a monster or a hot-rod like the Prowler for the sheer fun of it...

MODEL RANGE

The Viper is an exotic car that's available as an RT/10 convertible or in a three-door GTS coupe. Both models are powered by an 8.0L V10 engine that develops a whopping 450 hp and is linked exclusively to a 6-speed manual gearbox. Original equipment on both versions is quite elaborate since it includes air conditioning, power windows, locks and mirrors, power steering and luxury items such as leather-clad seats and a sophisticated sound system. Yet we notice that there isn't any ABS-traction control system offered, even as an extra. We'd like to mention that during the course of 1998, the RT/10 traded its sliding lateral panels for power windows and was even furbished with real genuine door locks...

TECHNICAL FEATURES

The Viper has a rolled steel chassis reinforced with a tubular structure. The independent four-wheel suspension has some forged aluminum components and consists of an arrangement of unequal-length A-arms with adjustable spring-shock ensembles and stabilizer bar both front and rear. The car is equipped with power rack-and-pinion steering and huge vented disc brakes. Body panels are built of forced injection synthetic composite materials. The frame around the windshield including the top of the instrument panel serves as a roll bar up front. This design was patented and really beefs up vehicle structure. The limited slip differential uses a disc system, but no automatic transmission is available. The pedal assembly is adjustable lengthwise so an ideal pilot position can be achieved.

SIMPLY SUPER

+ GTS COUPE. This thrilling car is wonderfully like the Cobra Daytona that participated in the Le Mans 24-hour race in the golden days of yore. Its closed body design makes it prac-

Fatal Bite..

tical for everyday use, even in poor weather, since visibility and trunk size are much better than these same features are on the convertible that really isn't as down-to-earth a car.

+ DRIVING PLEASURE. All that engine power really moves this baby and wheel response is as direct as it gets. So It's you against this amazing machine with the roaring rev of this V10 beauty in the background. With a car such as this, the sky is literally the limit. But under rainy skies, the driver will have to be a bit diplomatic if he or she wants to stay on the road.

PROS

+ LOOKS. The Viper isn't blessed with the Prowler's handsome flamboyance, but its giant, oversized nose sure evokes power to burn.

+ V10 ENGINE. It puts out awesome power and torque, so you're in for rocket accelerations and pickup and you take off in a thunderous roar. But you do need quite a bit of room to express yourself, so city driving is more frustrating than thrilling.

+ HANDLING. With such minimal sway, well-honed suspension and humungous tires, the Viper is literally rivetted to the road and is in perfect balance, a rare feat, on dry roads. In the rain, it's a good idea to drive with an egg under your right foot, so to speak, and to be careful when accelerating on curves...

+ BRAKES. They're brawny brutes, easy to apply as needed and quite balanced even without ABS. The tires cost an arm and a leg, so it's

wise to avoid wild stops.

+ COCKPIT. The adjustable pedal assembly is a real plus when it comes to driver comfort. You're also less distracted when changing gears.

+ SAFETY. Air bags, the hard top on the GTS coupe and the roll bar on the roadster ensure good passenger protection.

+ TECHNICAL FEATURES. When Chrysler built the Viper, it went all out and used state-of-the-art technology to match its engineering ambitions and at no time do you get the impression of being in a Kit-Car. The small inconveniences you run across are typical of this type of vehicle.

CONS

- BUDGET. You have to have money to burn in order to acquire, feed and maintain this fast car, not to mention the many small snags that come up when you're behind the wheel of such a vehicle...

- RIDE COMFORT. The bucket seats are well upholstered, but cabin space is snug and the suspension doesn't spare passengers on rough surfaces. Engine heat and noise are hard to take on long trips.

- CONVENIENCE FEATURES. There isn't much storage space inside the roadster cabin and the trunk is very small, so you'd better travel light (but a credit card is a must).

- MANEUVERABILITY. The Viper doesn't do a U-turn on a dime. It's crippled by a big steer angle diameter, hulky bod and big tires. You need patience to be a Viper pilot.

REALLY POOR FEATURES.

- OUTWARD VIEW. It's still the roadster's biggest handicap. The rear and side windows are very narrow and the roll bar creates a big blind spot at rear quarterback. Visibility is even worse when the top is up. Best not to have claustrophobic tendencies...

CONCLUSION

Even the most indifferent on-looker is impressed by the Viper. It's hard not to be impressed by its sheer might, thunderous sound and muscular moves. It takes a real car pilot to handle this brute and a real banker to back you when you make such an investment... ☺

RATING
DODGE Viper RT/10 & GTS

CONCEPT :		61%
Technology	90	
Safety :	90	
Interior space :	20	
Trunk volume:	30	
Quality/fit/finish :	75	

DRIVING:		88%
Cockpit :	80	
Performance :	100	
Handling :	100	
Steering :	80	
Braking :	80	

ORIGINAL EQUIPMENT:		78%
Tires :	90	
Headlights :	80	
Wipers :	70	
Rear defroster :	70	
Radio :	80	

COMFORT :		46%
Seats :	75	
Suspension :	50	
Sound level :	10	
Conveniences :	20	
Air conditioning :	75	

BUDGET :		43%
Price :	0	
Fuel economy :	20	
Insurance :	40	
Satisfaction :	85	
Depreciation :	70	

Overall rating:	63.2%

NEW FOR 1999

- Chrome-plated aluminum wheels with Michelin Pilot tires.
- Remote-control adjustable exterior mirrors.
- Connolly leather seats available as an extra.
- Satin finish aluminum accents inside the cabin.
- New transmission shifter design.
- Exterior finish details: black with silver stripes.

ENGINES / TRANSMISSIONS / PERFORMANCES

Model/ version	Type / timing valve / fuel system	Displacement cu in	Power bhp @ rpm	Torque lb-ft @ rpm	Compres. ratio	Driving wheels / transmission	Final ratio	Acceler. 0-60 mph s	Standing 1/4 & 5/8 mile s	Acceler. 50-75 mph s	Braking 60-0 mph f	Top speed mph	Lateral acceler. G	Noise level dBA	Fuel economy mpg City	Highway	Fuel type Octane
base	V10*8.0 OHV-20-MPSFI	488	450 @ 5200	490 @ 3700	9.6:1	rear - M6	3.07	4.3	12.4 21.5	2.8	131	165	1.00	75	13	20	S 91

PRICE & EQUIPMENT

DODGE Viper	RT/10 2dr.con.	GTS 2dr.cpe.
Retail price $:	64,000	66,500
Dealer invoice $:	57,720	59,720
Shipping & handling $:	700	700
Automatic transmission:	-	-
Cruise control:	-	-
Power steering:	S	S
Anti-lock brakes:	-	-
Traction control:	-	-
Air conditioning:	S	S
Leather:	S	S
AM/FM/radio-cassette:	SCD	SCD
Power door locks:	S	S
Power windows:	S	S
Tilt steering:	S	S
Dual adjustable mirrors:	SE	SE
Alloy wheels:	S	S
Anti-theft system:	-	-

Colors

Exterior: Silver, Red, Black.

Interior: Gray & black.

AT A GLANCE...

Category: rear-wheel drive exotic coupes & roadsters. **Class :** GT

HISTORIC
Introduced in: 1992 roadster 2 seats.
Made in: Conner Avenue, Detroit, Michigan, USA.

DEMOGRAPHICS
Model	Men./Wom.	Age	Married	College	Income
Viper	94/6%	54	57 %	58 %	$ 100 000

INDEX
Safety:	90 %	Satisfaction:	86 %
Depreciation:	30 %	Insurance:	$2 100
Cost per mile:	$1.42	Number of dealers:	1887 (Dod)

SALES
Model	1996	1997	Result
Viper	1 597	1 458	- 8.7 %

MAIN COMPETITORS
CHEVROLET Corvette, Porsche 911 Turbo, Acura NSX, MERCEDES-BENZ SL 600.

MAINTENANCE REQUIRED BY WARRANTY
First revision:	Frequency:	Diagnostic plug:
5 000 miles	6 months	Yes

SPECIFICATIONS

Model	Version Trim	Body/ Seats	Interior volume cu ft	Trunk volume cu ft	Cd	Wheel base in	Lght x Wdgth x Hght in x in x in	Curb weight lb	Susp. ft/rr	Brake ft/rr	Steering type	Turning diameter ft	Steer. turns nber.	Fuel tank gal	tire size	Standard tires make	model	Standard powertrain
DODGE		General warranty: 3 years / 36 000 miles; corrosion: 10 years; roadside assistance: 3 years / 36 000 miles.																
Viper	RT/10	2dr.con. 2	NA	6.8	0.46	96.2	175.1x75.7x44.0	3318	ih/ih	dc/dc	pwr.r&p.	12.34	2.4	19.0	fr.275/35ZR18 re.335/30ZR18	Michelin Pilot Michelin Pilot	Sport MXX3 Sport MXX3	V10/8.0/M6
Viper	GTS	2dr.cpe. 2	NA	9.2	0.35	96.2	176.7x75.7x47.0	3383	ih/ih	dc/dc	pwr.r&p.	12.34	2.4	19.0				V10/8.0/M6

For its last production year before being replaced around the year 2000, the F355 lineup now includes an F1 version that, as the name indicates, is equipped with a feature borrowed from Formula 1 race cars. This new exotic element is the sequential shifter that drives the transmission, allowing the driver to change speeds without having to take his or her hands off the wheel. So the lucky owner of such a car can do the Schumacher bit all day long if he or she so pleases, or simply drive a super-efficient car.

MODEL RANGE

The F355 is offered in a number of versions: the Targa TS coupe, the TB or F1 coupe and the Spider that's fitted with a semi-automatic roof device. All share the 3.5L V8 engine associated with a 6-speed manual gearbox, except the F1 that benefits from a sequential shifter.

TECHNICAL FEATURES

The F355 replaces the 348 of somewhat ill repute, since the former model was a bit of a mishmash of various elements, the perfect image of the automaker's approach at the time. The F355's monocoque structure, equipped with two metallic cradles supporting the front and rear end, is much more robust. The floor pan underside has been streamlined to form two tunnels to provide ground effect, so this car literally sticks to the road without having to revert to chunky spoilers. The hood and brake calipers are made of cast-aluminum, while door frames are built of composite materials and wheel rims, of magnesium. The electronically controlled suspension allows for shock adjustments according to road surface quality or driving style. The longitudinally-set engine is a 3.5L V8 with 40 valves (5 per cylinder) that develops 380 hp at 8,250 r.p.m., which confers an awesome 7.8 lb/hp power to weight ratio to the F355. Power steering is variable assist and brakes are linked to an ABS system that can be deactivated on demand.

PROS

+ STYLE. Pininfarina's creations are absolutely unique. His body designs are veritable sculptures in movement on which light and wind play to their heart's content. The 355 is a bit more squarish-looking than its sisters, but it has the same chromosomes in its genetic code.

+ PERFORMANCES. Ferrari has finally succeeded in proving that there's life beyond the V12 engine, the mascot, so to speak, associated with this carmaker. The 355 engine pumps out wondrous power and

V8 Arrabiata..

torque, but it's smooth and so very refined with such short transmission gear ratios. It's just raring to go and wants to forget the small stuff. So you can literally catapult this car at almost 185 mph at top speed and accelerate from 0 to 60 mph in 5.0 seconds flat.

+ HANDLING. It's superbly and amazingly balanced, thanks to the much sturdier tubular structure, active suspension, ground effect and bigger tires that keep the car remarkably on keel. With such an agile car, you can take one curve after another with not a care in the world, without having to be a seasoned pilot. The dragfoiler located underneath the floor (an approach borrowed from the competiton) is incredibly efficient, for the resulting ground effect keeps this baby solid as a rock, so curves are literally a breeze.

+ TRANSMISSION. The sequential shifter adds a whole new dimension to the F1 version, the only car benefitting from such a wonder at the present time. Plates located behind the steering wheel let you upshift (to the right) or downshift (to the left) without having to even touch a clutch pedal. The small switch for reverse located on the center console is another kettle of fish, it's no fun at all.

+ BRAKES. Easy to apply when slowing down in normal circumstances and effective as well as sturdy, but the ABS system that stabilizes car path also lengthens stopping distances, but you can cut down on same by 10 to 15% by deactivating ABS.

+ DRIVING PLEASURE. Driving a Ferrari is something of an out-of-this-world experience and the 355 is no exception. It's not that we're scared stiff, but we have to admit that each and every time we get behind the wheel and turn on the ignition, something unusual happens. The pilot's challenge is to be a match for this rocket in all situations, which is no mean feat. Music lovers will enjoy the voice range of the revving engine.

+ SAFETY. It's been dramatically improved with the more robust structure, air bags and ABS system that can be deactivated as needed.

CONS

- QUALITY. It's come a long way, but it's still not up to industry standards. We notice that there are still a few missing finish details, a few weird aspects and some fragile elements that tend to break, which owners find annoying, but they don't really complain much. Could it be due to masochistic tendencies?

- ERGONOMICS. Some controls aren't too logical and they're out of reach since located on the center console. Not to mention that the cockpit slants and there's a big blind sport at rear quarterback, factors that are no fun.

- RIDE COMFORT. It's getting better, but it isn't what it could be. Seats are firm, the suspension goes haywire on poor roads and exhaust noise is, well, exhausting.

- CONVENIENCE FEATURES. This aspect is by no means incompatible with pleasant travel, but it's below par on this car. The trunk is tiny and storage compartments amount to a small glove compartment, console compartment and a bit of space behind the seats.

- TO BE IMPROVED UPON: A traction control clutch would make for safer driving on wet roads. In wet conditions, stepping on the gas is still risky business.

CONCLUSION

Who would have believed it? Times have changed and so has Ferrari. Under Luca Di Montezzemollo's leadership, this upper-crust Fiat brand has acquired a sense of responsiblity. The Italian carmaker is now less arrogant and has developed more refined technical features, thus scoring points in the car industry, not only in championship car races. This 355 has become a car in its own right, not a sub-Ferrari, but another kind of Ferrari equipped with a V8 that gives it a unique character. We're not used to this approach and it was sure worth the detour...

RATING
FERRARI F355

CONCEPT : **63%**
Technology	90
Safety :	80
Interior space :	40
Trunk volume:	25
Quality/fit/finish :	80

DRIVING: **88%**
Cockpit :	80
Performance :	100
Handling :	90
Steering :	80
Braking :	90

ORIGINAL EQUIPMENT: **82%**
Tires :	90
Headlights :	85
Wipers :	85
Rear defroster :	70
Radio :	80

COMFORT : **51%**
Seats :	70
Suspension :	60
Sound level :	65
Conveniences :	20
Air conditioning :	40

BUDGET : **37%**
Price :	0
Fuel economy :	25
Insurance :	10
Satisfaction :	75
Depreciation :	75

Overall rating: **64.2%**

NEW FOR 1999

• The F1 version equipped with a sequential shifter, activated by two plates under the steering wheel.

ENGINES / TRANSMISSIONS / PERFORMANCES

Model/version	Type / timing valve / fuel system	Displacement cu in	Power bhp @ rpm	Torque lb-ft @ rpm	Compres. ratio	Driving wheels / transmission	Final ratio	Acceler. 0-60 mph s	Standing 1/4 & 5/8 mile s	Acceler. 50-75 mph s	Braking 60-0 mph f	Top speed mph	Lateral acceler. G	Noise level dBA	Fuel economy mpg City	Fuel economy mpg Highway	Fuel type Octane
F355	V8* 3.5 DOHC-40 MPFI	213	375 @ 8250	268 @ 6000	11.0 :1	rear-M6*	4.3	5.0	13.5 24.8	3.0	118	183	0.98	74	10	16	S 91

PRICE & EQUIPMENT

FERRARI	F355
Retail price $:	-
Dealer invoice $:	-
Shipping & handling $:	-
Automatic transmission:	O (F1)
Cruise control:	S
Power steering:	S
Anti-lock brakes:	S
Traction control:	S
Air conditioning:	S
Leather:	S
AM/FM/radio-cassette:	S
Power door locks:	S
Power windows:	S
Tilt steering:	S
Dual adjustable mirrors:	S
Alloy wheels:	S
Anti-theft system:	S

Colors
Exterior: Red, Black, White, Gray, Yellow, Blue.
Interior: Black, White, Tan, Blue.

AT A GLANCE...

Category: rear-wheel drive exotic coupes & convertibles. **Class :** GT

HISTORIC
Introduced in: 1995: GTS & Spider F355.
Made in: Maranello, Modena, Italy.

DEMOGRAPHICS
Model	Men./Wom.	Age	Married	College	Income
F355	98/2 %	48	80 %	80 %	$160 000

INDEX
Safety:	80 %	Satisfaction:	75 %
Depreciation:	35 %	Insurance:	$5 750
Cost per mile:	$1.65	Number of dealers:	36

SALES
Model	1996	1997	Result
Ferrari		NA	

MAIN COMPETITORS
ACURA NSX-T, MERCEDES-BENZ 500 SEC-SL, PORSCHE 911.

MAINTENANCE REQUIRED BY WARRANTY
First revision:	Frequency:	Diagnostic plug:
300 miles	3 000 miles	Yes

SPECIFICATIONS

Model	Version Trim	Body/ Seats	Interior volume cu ft	Trunk volume cu ft	Cd	Wheel base in	Lght x Wdgth x Hght in x in x in	Curb weight lb	Susp. ft/rr	Brake ft/rr	Steering type	Turning diameter ft	Steer. turns nber.	Fuel tank gal	tire size	Standard tires make	model	Standard powertrain
FERRARI		Total warranty : 2 years / unlimited mileage with roadside assistance.																
F355	GTS	2dr.cpe. 2	NA	7.8	0.32	96.5	167.3x74.8x46.1	2976	ih/ih	dc/ABS	pwr.r&p.	39.7	3.25	21.7				V8/3.5/M6
F355	GTB	2dr.cpe. 2	NA	7.8	0.32	96.5	167.3x74.8x46.1	2976	ih/ih	dc/ABS	pwr.r&p.	39.7	3.25	21.7	fr.225/40ZR18	Pirelli	Pzero	V8/3.5/M6
															re.265/40ZR18	Pirelli	Pzero	
F355	F1	2dr.cpe. 2	NA	7.8	0.32	96.5	167.3x74.8x46.1	2976	ih/ih	dc/ABS	pwr.r&p.	39.7	3.25	21.7		Pirelli	Pzero	V8/3.5/M6
F355	Spider	2dr.con. 2	NA	NA	0.34	96.5	167.3x74.8x46.1	2976	ih/ih	dc/ABS	pwr.r&p.	39.7	3.25	21.7				V8/3.5/M6

Just as a sculptor puts some final touches on a perfect work of art, Pininfarina has polished a few stylistic touches on the body of this star car that has won many a heart in just a few short years. Ferrari experts already agree that the 456 is one of the best cars ever built by this company and wearing the rearing horse crest. It can seat four passengers and it's really the only Ferrari that just about anyone can drive, so it's the Ferrari family car par excellence, the one that causes some family quarrels, since everyone insists on being the one who'll take it for a spin to get some milk at the local store...

MODEL RANGE

The 456 is a 2+2 coupe animated by a 5.5L V12 engine and is available in two models: the GT with 6-speed manual transmission and the GTA with 4-speed automatic gearbox. Equipment on these babies is very lavish and includes everything you'd ever want or expect on such a very (let's face it) expensive car, except a true traction control system and heated seats.

TECHNICAL FEATURES.

Pininfarina has outdone himself by coming up with the 456 design, and it's perfectly understandable that Sergio the boss uses it as a company car...The aluminum alloy body is mounted on a tubular steel chassis so the car structure is very rigid. The doors are made of aluminum alloys and the hood and hidden headlamp covers are made of carbon fibers. The silhouette has super aerodynamics, thanks to the movable flap built into the rear bumper that reduces rear end lift according to speed. The four-wheel independent suspension consists of transverse double A-arms. The suspension has three different settings: firm, normal or flexible and includes a rear load-levelling device. The car is equipped with variable assist power steering and disc brakes benefit from double calipers and an ATE antilock braking system. The all-aluminum engine has 12 cylinders opposed in a V shape at 65°, 4 overhead camshafts and 48 valves. Ignition and gas injection are controlled by a Bosch 5.2 Motronic system. This year, the firing order has been reversed so as to acquire a few more horsepower digits. Lastly, the gearbox is built into the rear axle and rear wheels are linked to traction control.

Ferrari Family Car...

PROS

+ STYLE. Pininfarina created a real masterpiece when he came up with such a discreet, elegant yet absolutely sensational body design. You get a glimpse of it and you know at once it's a Ferrari.

+ PERFORMANCES. They're amazing, since this engine is simply oozing with power and torque no matter what the r.p.m., so much so that you can accelerate in fifth gear while driving at 30 mph. Each time you touch the accelerator, there's a sweet guttural song, so you get a real adrenalin rush.

+ ROADHOLDING. The 456 GT is a big, heavy car, but it exhibits great agility and precision in any situation thanks to an exceptional weight distribution (56/44%). Wheel travel is perfect even on tight curves with

the limited slip differential and tires that grip like champions.

+ DRIVING PLEASURE. It's guaranteed with such responsive and right-on steering so you can put this car just where you want it and the fine-design transmission doesn't take the thrill out of driving, but makes city traffic a lot less stressful. What strikes the most about the 456 is its dual personality. It can be a raging bull when pushed to the limit, but it can be as gentle as a lamb. Incredible, but true: the car adjusts beautifully to any situation.

+ BRAKES. A perfect match for such a high-performance car. Stops can be achieved in no time and in a nice, gradual fashion, even with ABS and brakes know how to take the heat.

+ CABIN SPACE. The generous,

spacious cabin offers all kinds of leg and head room, especially in the rear seats that are quite practical and more than purely symbolic.

+ RIDE COMFORT. It's simply magnificent. Seats are very posh and provide good support, the adjustable suspension does its job beautifully, and engine noise is loud enough to enjoy but not so loud as to tire travellers out.

+ QUALITY. Some trim materials and equipment items have really been spiffed up and the Fiat switches are nowhere in sight.

+ CONVENIENCE FEATURES. Surprise, there are enough storage spots inside and they're convenient as well. The trunk is easy to get to with such a tapered trunk lid. The spare tire is no longer stored inside the trunk, so there's quite a bit of space, enough to hold the made to measure set of suitcases that can be acquired as an extra.

CONS

- FINISH DETAILS. There's still work ahead in this department if this aspect is to be anywhere in keeping with the astronomical sum needed to become a proud owner of such a car. Ferrari should steal Lexus' secret plastic component formula.

- GAUGES. Those located in the middle of the instrument panel are almost illegible and some controls are too far out of the driver's reach.

- RELIABILITY. It's less iffy than it once was, but you still have to take these cars to the garage for many visit in order to to keep them in shape.

VERY POOR FEATURES

- BUDGET. We hesitate broaching the topic, but as the saying goes: «Everything has its price, especially the good things in life». Obviously, those who can afford to make such an acquisition won't have any trouble spoiling their car and paying the mechanic who pampers it. Let's just say that the price attached to this type of creature comfort seems a bit exaggerated.

CONCLUSION

The 456 is a real work of art, which explains why the going price is beyond what all Ferrari aficionados can afford. Such style and such refined, brilliant performances give this car a unique status in the automobile industry worldwide. In this model, you can't go for a solo spin, since you have to share it with three other, albeit hand-picked passengers. When will this family-style car include a four-door model? ☺

RATING
Ferrari 456 GT

CONCEPT :		71%
Technology	90	
Safety :	90	
Interior space :	50	
Trunk volume:	45	
Quality/fit/finish :	80	

DRIVING:		82%
Cockpit :	80	
Performance :	95	
Handling :	85	
Steering :	80	
Braking :	70	

ORIGINAL EQUIPMENT:		82%
Tires :	90	
Headlights :	90	
Wipers :	80	
Rear defroster :	70	
Radio :	80	

COMFORT :		71%
Seats :	75	
Suspension :	80	
Sound level :	75	
Conveniences :	60	
Air conditioning :	65	

BUDGET :		32%
Price :	0	
Fuel economy :	10	
Insurance :	10	
Satisfaction :	80	
Depreciation :	60	

Overall rating: 67.6%

NEW FOR 1999

- Stylistic touches on the front and rear bumpers designed to create an aerodynamic lift effect and foglamps now built into the grille.
- Redesigned instrument panel with built-in air vents borrowed from the 550, fewer gauges but seams on the leather trim do stick out like a sore thumb.

ENGINES

Model/version	Type / timing valve / fuel system	Displacement cu in	Power bhp @ rpm	Torque lb-ft @ rpm
GT	V12* 5.5 DOHC-48-EFI	334	436 @ 6250	407 @ 4500
GTA				

TRANSMISSIONS

Compres. ratio	Driving wheels / transmission	Final ratio
10.6 :1	rear-M6	3.28
	rear-A4	3.53

PERFORMANCES

Acceler. 0-60 mph s	Standing 1/4 & 5/8 mile s	Acceler. 50-75 mph s	Braking 60-0 mph f	Top speed mph	Lateral acceler. G	Noise level dBA	Fuel economy mpg City	Highway	Fuel type Octane
5.5	13.4 23.4	3.4	118	186	0.90	68	8	16	S 91
5.7	13.6 23.7	3.2	121	186	0.90	68	7	17	S 91

PRICE & EQUIPMENT

FERRARI 456	GT	GTA
Retail price $:	-	-
Dealer invoice $:	-	-
Shipping & handling $:	-	-
Automatic transmission:	-	S
Cruise control:	S	S
Power steering:	S	S
Anti-lock brakes:	S	S
Traction control:	S	S
Air conditioning:	SA	SA
Leather:	S	S
AM/FM/radio-cassette:	S	S
Power door locks:	S	S
Power windows:	S	S
Tilt steering:	S	S
Dual adjustable mirrors:	S	S
Alloy wheels:	S	S
Anti-theft system:	S	S

Colors

Exterior: Red, Black, White, Gray, Yellow, Blue.

Interior: Black, White, Tan, Blue.

AT A GLANCE...

Category:	rear-wheel drive exotic.	Class :	GT

HISTORIC
Introduced in: 1993.
Made in: Grugliasco (body) & Maranello (powertrain), Italy.

DEMOGRAPHICS

Model	Men./Wom.	Age	Married	College	Income
456 GT	95/5 %	58	90 %	80 %	$250 000

INDEX
Safety:	90 %	Satisfaction:	80 %
Depreciation:	30 %	Insurance:	$7 950
Cost per mile:	$2.17	Number of dealers:	36

SALES

Model	1996	1997	Result
Ferrari	NA		

MAIN COMPETITORS
ASTON MARTIN Virage, MERCEDES-BENZ 600 SEC-SL.

MAINTENANCE REQUIRED BY WARRANTY
First revision:	Frequency:	Diagnostic plug:
300 miles	3 000 miles	Yes

SPECIFICATIONS

Model	Version Trim	Body/ Seats	Interior volume cu ft	Trunk volume cu ft	Cd	Wheel base in	Lght x Wdgth x Hght in x in x in	Curb weight lb	Susp. ft/rr	Brake ft/rr	Steering type	Turning diameter ft	Steer. turns nber.	Fuel tank gal	tire size	Standard tires make	model	Standard powertrain
FERRARI		Total warranty : 2 years / unlimited mileage with roadside assistance.																
456	GT	2dr.cpe.2+2	-	11.1	0.34	102.4	186.2x75.6x51.2	3726	ih/ih	dc/ABS	pwr.r&p.	38.7	3.1	29	fr.255/45ZR17 re.285/40ZR17			V12/5.5/M6
456	GTA	2dr.cpe.2+2	-	11.1	0.34	102.4	186.2x75.6x51.2	3902	ih/ih	dc/ABS	pwr.r&p.	38.7	3.1	29				V12/5.5/A4

The 550 Maranello isn't as exotic as the latest Testarossa heir. Over-all design is more classic: the body design is more sensible and size has been trimmed down, so the 550 can go unnoticed, which is a no minor insult for such an expensive car. It may better suit its well-heeled clientele, but it really lacks the panache you'd expect to see on the prize car of the automaker the most directly involved in the fastest and highest-caliber car races in the world.

MODEL RANGE

The 550 Maranello is a two-seater coupe that's offered in a single version motivated by a 5.5L V12 paired up with a six-speed manual gearbox. Ritzy equipment includes most luxury items and creature comforts found inside cream of the crop vehicles.

TECHNICAL FEATURES

The Maranello coupe is built on a tubular welded steel chassis on which is mounted the aluminum body. The underside of the vehicle is streamlined to improve air flow and ensure efficient ground effect for greater stability, without all those rather frumpy-looking flaps. The fully independent suspension consists of transverse levers and unequal-length A-arms with anti-roll bar front and rear. Dual-caliper vented disc brakes are controlled by a Bosch antilock system. Adjustable traction control with clutch control comes as standard equipment, as does the adaptive suspension that procures a whole range of driving styles, inversely proportional to ride comfort. The V12 engine is that of the 456 GT: it has the same engine block design, the same cylinder heads with DOHC and four valves per cylinder.

SIMPLY SUPER

+ ENGINE. This is a typical Ferrari fireball, it's responsive and loves revving up, drowning you in a unique musical sound blend. Its considerable muscle and torque offer all the more versatility and the feeling at the wheel is absolutely awesome. With 485 hp available to pull a load capacity of about 4 200 lbs., this translates into a 8.6 lbs/hp power to weight ratio, whereas the average sits just below 22 lbs/hp!

+ HANDLING. The stiff structure, the well-honed, neat as a pin suspension and steering control add up to relaxed and reassuring driving, even at speeds that would make

More Down-to-earth..

a North American police officer's hair stand on end... Actually, things look so simple that the average driver may not anticipate danger if the car swerves a bit or hits a bump while going over rough pavement, for example.

+ SAFETY. Ferrari neglected this aspect for quite a while and kept concentrating its efforts on sheer speed, but now safety features include air bags as well as an antilock braking system and traction control, so as to provide better vehicle stability when wheel grip is less than perfect. But Ferrari has a long road ahead before it'll ever attain Mercedes standards...

PROS

+ STYLE. Pininfarina, exclusive couturier at the house of Modena,

has once again created a classic outfit that has woven-in traditional elements, but the designer has achieved a modern, down-to-earh look.

+ AMBIENCE. The cabin is filled with a lovely leather scent and has a very Italian flavor, in other words, it's classic and very refined.

+ DRIVING PLEASURE. The feeling at the wheel of the 550 is a lot like the sensation of driving its 456 predecessor. What strikes you, right off, is the ease with which an ordinary driver can handle such a horde of fast-speed horses. But we do have one reservation about being able to deactivate the clutch for traction control, which makes for dangerous moves in some cases. Accelerating properly while coming out a

curve is crucial on damp surfaces, since car path can be seriously affected. Power and torque are so feisty that you can skip gears and even «forget» to downshift...

+ CONVENIENCE FEATURES. The 550 is nothing like the latest model F512M in this department. The trunk is quite roomy, the glove compartment is a good size, door side-pockets actually hold stuff and you can stash cassettes and CD's in the compartment located on the center console.

+ EFFICIENCY. Even if it almost seems sacrilegious to say so, we'd like to point out that headlamps and windshield wipers are very efficient, which wasn't always the case on some Ferrari models in the past.

+ LUXURY. The Italian automaker has really tried to raise the equipment level on its upper-crust models to be on a par with German rivals that are less expensive and much more sophisticated. So now seats are equipped with super-quick power adjustments (typical for a Ferrari...), such as a lateral support adjustment, a feature that isn't seen too often as of yet. But all these posh accessories do add pounds and liras.

CONS

- STYLE. The body design is a bit too conservative compared to the loaded, over-worked instrument panel.

- WEIGHT. It's way up there, in spite of all the lightweight materials such as aluminum, magnesium and titanium. Even with the near-perfect weight distribution (53/47%), there's a bit of sluggishness felt on tight curves where the least swerve can wreak havoc if it isn't perfectly under control.

- RIDE COMFORT. With such high performances, the suspension is without pity even on the flexible mode and engine noise blots out all others, especially wind noise that's almost as tiring as big band tire hum. The 550 isn't really the ideal carriage if you want to go for a romantic drive...

CONCLUSION

The 550 Maranello is less exotic than its predecessor and attracts more buyers who were no longer crazy about getting on their knees to climb aboard. We often forget that it isn't enough to create dream cars. You also have to sell them... ☺

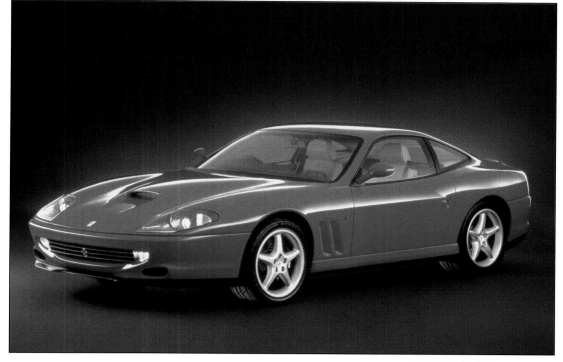

RATING
FERRARI 550 Maranello

CONCEPT :		61%
Technology	90	
Safety :	90	
Interior space :	20	
Trunk volume:	15	
Quality/fit/finish :	90	

DRIVING:		88%
Cockpit :	90	
Performance :	100	
Handling :	100	
Steering :	90	
Braking :	60	

ORIGINAL EQUIPMENT:		88%
Tires :	100	
Headlights :	90	
Wipers :	85	
Rear defroster :	75	
Radio :	90	

COMFORT :		60%
Seats :	90	
Suspension :	50	
Sound level :	20	
Conveniences :	60	
Air conditioning :	80	

BUDGET :		37%
Price :	0	
Fuel economy :	0	
Insurance :	5	
Satisfaction :	80	
Depreciation :	100	

Overall rating:	66.8 %

NEW FOR 1999

- No major change.

ENGINES

Model/ version	Type / timing valve / fuel system	Displacement cu in	Power bhp @ rpm	Torque lb-ft @ rpm
550	V12*5.5DOHC-48-EFI	334	479 @ 7000	421 @ 5000

TRANSMISSIONS

Compres. ratio	Driving wheels / transmission	Final ratio
10.8 :1	rear-M6*	3.91

PERFORMANCES

Acceler. 0-60 mph s	Standing 1/4 & 5/8 mile s	Acceler. 50-75 mph s	Braking 60-0 mph f	Top speed mph	Lateral acceler. G	Noise level dBA	Fuel economy City mpg	Highway	Fuel type Octane
4.5	12.7 22.5	3.2	131	199	1.00	72	7	14	S 91

PRICE & EQUIPMENT

FERRARI 550 Maranello	coupe
Retail price $:	-
Dealer invoice $:	-
Shipping & handling $:	included
Automatic transmission:	O (F1)
Cruise control:	S
Power steering:	S
Anti-lock brakes:	S
Traction control:	S
Air conditioning:	SA
Leather:	S
AM/FM/radio-cassette:	S
Power door locks:	S
Power windows:	S
Tilt steering:	S
Dual adjustable mirrors:	SE
Alloy wheels:	S
Anti-theft system:	S

Colors
Exterior: Red, Black, White, Gray, Yellow, Blue.

Interior: Black, White, Tan, Blue.

AT A GLANCE...

Category:	rear-wheel drive exotic.		Class : GT

HISTORIC
Introduced in:	1996
Made in:	Maranello (Italy)

DEMOGRAPHICS
Model	Men./Wom.	Age	Married	College	Income
Ferrari 550	98/2%	64	90%	85%	$ 300 000

INDEX
Safety:	80%	Satisfaction:	NA
Depreciation:	NA	Insurance:	$7 900
Cost per mile:	$2.17	Number of dealers:	36

SALES
Model	1996	1997	Result
Ferrari	NA		

MAIN COMPETITORS
ASTON-MARTIN DB7, JAGUAR XKR, LAMBORGHINI Diablo, MERCEDES-BENZ SEC & SL600.

MAINTENANCE REQUIRED BY WARRANTY
First revision:	Frequency:	Diagnostic plug:
300 miles	3 000 miles	Yes

SPECIFICATIONS

Total warranty : 2 years / unlimited mileage with roadside assistance.

Model	Version Trim	Body/ Seats	Interior volume cu ft	Trunk volume cu ft	Cd	Wheel base in	Lght x Wdgth x Hght in x in x in	Curb weight lb	Susp. ft/rr	Brake ft/rr	Steering type	Turning diameter ft	Steer. turns nber.	Fuel tank gal	tire size	Standard tires make	model	Standard powertrain
FERRARI																		
F550	base	2dr.cpe. 2	-	6.5	0.33	98.4	179.1x76.2x50.3	3726	ih/ih	dc/ABS	pwr.r&p.	38.1	2.7	30	fr.255/40ZR18 re.295/35ZR18	-	-	V12/5.5/M6

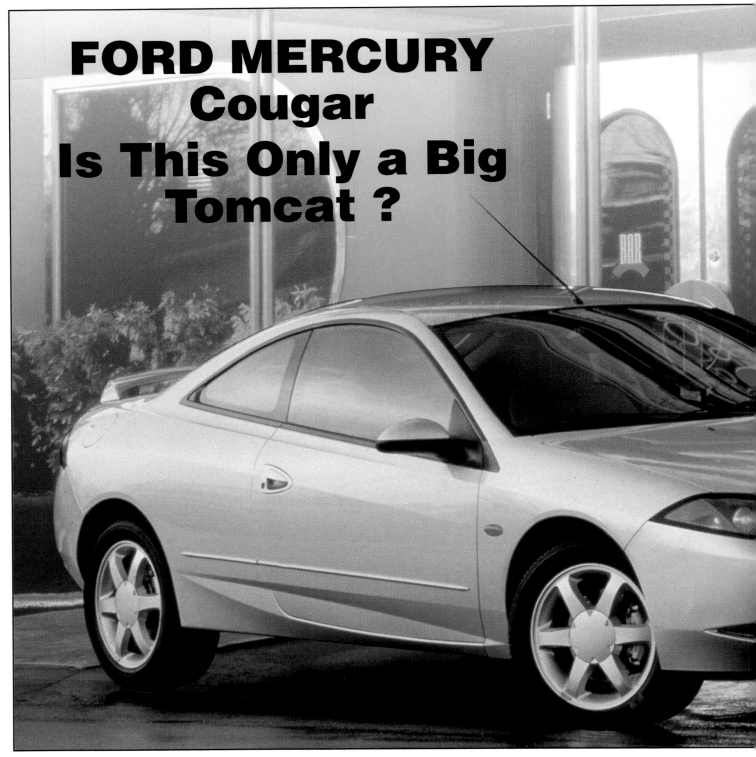

FORD MERCURY
Cougar
Is This Only a Big Tomcat ?

The ways of God are inscrutable, and so are those of some automakers. Last year Ford yanked the Probe coupe, a car with an honorable track record, off the market, along with the Thunderbird and Cougar. A year later, a vehicle with Probe-like stylistics reappeared at Mercury and was called the Cougar. Where's the logic?

Obviously, Ford didn't want to brush up the Probe, since it was already established and built by Mazda, and because the Thunderbird and Cougar, specimens of a dying species, just didn't cut it anymore and especially because the Mercury division really had to find a new clientele in a hurry, otherwise its traditional clientele would drag it to its grave... The other question is: why put so much energy on a vehicle that just doesn't sell nowadays? The answer is simple. When the carmaker decided to design a coupe based on the Contour-Mystique platform, the Expedition and Navigator hadn't as yet been such smashing successes and no one could have dreamed or foreseen that the 4X4 fever would spread overnight and at such a pitch that it would affect just about every living soul.

The «new» Cougar is a 2+2 sports coupe with a definitely modern body design, sporting lens-shaped headlamps, very elaborate ports and some rather exotic accents. Actually, 72% of the Cougar's attributes hail from the Contour-Mystique. This isn't a bad thing in itself, when you know that this platform was established in Europe for the Mondeo design and that it's well-known for its rugged architecture and rational powertrain layout.

The new Mercury Cougar is nothing at all like the old model bearing the same name. Even a brief glance at the new Cougar lets you know that Ford only wanted to keep this popular name in its catalogue. Good looks are the most appealing feature of this small coupe derived from the Mystique. It's obvious that Claude Lobbo, head designer at Ford, keeps using more and more «Edge Design» applications on all models. Bio body design is taut and full of flowing folds. Designers really let loose and came up with a finely styled Cougar right down to the last detail. Absolutely everything is very original and stylish, from door handles to headlights and taillights, including minute touches on the dashboard. In some ways, a few details seem to be a bit far-fetched, even ridiculously so, since they'll go out of style in a

hurry and give a dusty look to this vehicle. Other touches are super, like the built-in rear spoiler, rocker panel folds, neat port and headlamp design and the semicircular cockpit layout surrounding the driver, very much like what you see in single-seater race cars. The inner door design is quite lovely, another item that adds spice to this package. Mechanical features are less flamboyant, but they're modern since the car is equipped with sophisticated suspensions and engines were first used on the Contour-Mystique four years ago now. Safety-wise, the Cougar coupe is the first Ford-built vehicle to be equipped with side-impact airbags providing head and chest protection.

Going headlong against current market trends that reflect the 4X4 pickup and minivan rage, Ford is launching a new compact sports coupe aimed to appeal to young at heart, adventurous drivers. This is a pretty daring move, especially for a Mercury! The new Cougar isn't at all like those ultra-conservative, clumsy vehicles that bore this classy division name not too many years ago. In fact, this Cougar shares more common traits with the original luxury alternative to the Ford "Pony Car", the Mustang!

MODEL RANGE
The Cougar is a 3-door coupe. Its style is inspired by the «Edge Design» approach that blends curves and tight, sleek lines. The Cougar borrows the Contour/Mystique sedans' engines: the 2.0L DOHC Zetec 4-cylinder and 2.5L DOHC Duratec V6. The first comes with a 5-speed manual gearbox only, while the second can be linked up to an optional 4-speed automatic. Standard equipment includes, among other items, a remote powered rear door opener, 15-inch rims and anti-theft cut-off switch and alarm. The Cougar V6 model's equipment is a cut above, so it also includes climate control and chrome tailpipe extension.

TECHNICAL FEATURES
The Cougar is a direct spin-off of the Contour/Mystique/Mondeo platform but wheelbase and wheel track design are a bit different. Yet it shares almost 70% of the three sedans' components. Besides, the Cougar chassis is now 20% more rigid than that of the Contour! Its steel body is mounted on a unitized frame and yields an average drag coefficient of 0.32. The fully independent suspension is mounted on subframes via rubber insulator joints. Up front, it uses MacPherson struts, whereas the rear axles are suspended on four control arms. There are anti-roll bars both front and rear. Both models are equipped with disc and drum brakes. Disc brakes are available, but only as an extra, as are ABS and traction control.

PROS
+ LOOKS. This modern, daring coupe design is really different from typically easy-going, cushy Mercury products, usually geared to a more seasoned clientele. You can't not notice this car, it's both bold and beauteous, but younger folk like it

more than sensible drivers. Exactly what Mercury had in mind...

+ MEMORY SEATS. Not every 2-door car has them, but the Cougar does, neat! The passenger seat has a memory device that lets the seat return to exactly the same position as before reclining it.

+ REAR DOOR. It's light and doesn't lift too high up. It has a neat handle, so it's easy to close shut. There's also a removable luggage-covering shelf.

+ CONVENIENCE FEATURES. This is a sports car, but it's also versatile thanks to its modular trunk, since the 50/50 split-fold rear that can be lowered as needed.

+ RIDE COMFORT. Front seats are beautifully sculpted and they offer wonderful lateral and lumbar support. Front seat passengers have loads of leg room and the driver even has a footrest. Simply super!

+ INSTRUMENT PANEL. The Cougar's dashboard isn't as daring as that on the Escort ZX2, but it's very nicely styled and it's really ergonomic.

+ HANDLING. Derived from the

European Mondeo, the suspension is a great compromise between comfort and roadholding, so you can hit lateral speeds worthy of the most speedy and expensive cars out there. But on our test model, the front end was unstable and dealing with torque was a bit tricky on wet surfaces.

+ EXHAUST SYSTEM. Not all noise is unpleasant. For example, the Cougar's exhaust has a gutsy growl and you don't mind at all, but it's too bad performances aren't as impressive as all this sound and fury...

CONS
- STYLE. It's pretty unique, but it's overdone both inside and out and will tend to go out of fashion in no time. Some accessories are just gadgets, really, and seem a bit silly.

- PERFORMANCES. They're disappointing, compared to those of the former Ford Probe that was a heck of a lot more fun to drive. The 4-cylinder engine puts out more power, when motivated along, more so than the V6 that's a bore in comparison.

- STEERING. It's quite quick and

nicely powered, but it just isn't crisp and clean enough when you feel like heading in another direction.

- EQUIPMENT. This sports coupe, bearing the muscular Mercury crest, can't really boast of rich equipment, since four-wheel disc brakes, rear wiper, cruise control and 16-inch tires mounted on alloy rims are all extras, each and every one.

- NOISE. With a rear hatch door, noise is always more pervasive than in a two or four-door vehicle. Our sound-level meter recorded noise levels inside the Cougar that were the highest among all cars we tested this year!

- REAR SEATS. Automakers say that rear seats on a coupe are never used. In that case, why install such minuscule seats, when a big trunk would be just as useful?

- VISIBILITY. With such a sharp, angular body design that requires a rather high rear end, backing up is tricky due to reduced rear outward view.

- STEERING WHEEL. You have a good grip, but it's so ridiculously huge and jars with the modern interior design. The Momo steering wheel installed as standard equipment on the latest Miata is proof that designers can come up with a nice blend of practical elegance and safety features, since it holds a latest-generation airbag as well.

- OPENING THE TRUNK. The remote control for the rear door opener is located in a rather strange spot, that is at floor level, near the hood lid switch. Why not have installed it inside the door instead, or on the instrument panel, where it would be more within reach?

- ACCESS. The convertible trunk is huge, but the opening is so bloody high that you could end up with a sore back from loading or unloading heavy luggage!

CONCLUSION
The Cougar is more of a looker than a performer. Nothing's perfect, when you make so many compromises. This car is more geared to ride comfort than to speedy, slick moves. It may roar like a wildcat and look like it's ready to pounce, but this Cougar is nothing more than a very sedate, rather plump tomcat... ☺

RATING
MERCURY Cougar

CONCEPT :		66%
Technology	80	
Safety :	80	
Interior space :	35	
Trunk volume:	60	
Quality/fit/finish :	75	

DRIVING:		64%
Cockpit :	75	
Performance :	45	
Handling :	65	
Steering :	75	
Braking :	60	

ORIGINAL EQUIPMENT:		78%
Tires :	75	
Headlights :	75	
Wipers :	80	
Rear defroster :	80	
Radio :	80	

COMFORT :		64%
Seats :	75	
Suspension :	75	
Sound level:	30	
Conveniences :	60	
Air conditioning :	80	

BUDGET :		60%
Price :	70	
Fuel economy :	70	
Insurance :	60	
Satisfaction :	50	
Depreciation :	50	

Overall rating:	66.4%

NEW FOR 1999

• New model built on the Contour-Mystique platform and sharing their mechanical features, also borrowing the 2.0L Zetec 4-cylinder and 2.5L Duratec V6 engines.

ENGINES / TRANSMISSIONS / PERFORMANCES

Model/version	Type / timing valve / fuel system	Displacement cu in	Power bhp @ rpm	Torque lb-ft @ rpm	Compres. ratio	Driving wheels / transmission	Final ratio	Acceler. 0-60 mph s	Standing 1/4 & 5/8 mile s	Acceler. 50-75 mph s	Braking 60-0 mph f	Top speed mph	Lateral acceler. G	Noise level dBA	Fuel economy mpg City	Highway	Fuel type Octane
I-4	L4* 2.0 DOHC-16-MPSFI	121	125 @ 5500	130 @ 4000	9.6 :1	front - M5	3.82	11.0	17.8	32.0	7.4	131	109	0.80	67	24	28	R 87
V-6	V6 2.5 DOHC-24-MPSFI	155	170 @ 6250	165 @ 4250	9.7 :1	front - M5	4.06	9.0	16.7	30.5	6.6	134	115	0.82	67	19	29	R 87
						front - A4	3.77	10.4	17.5	32.0	7.2	128	112	0.82	68	20	32	R 87

PRICE & EQUIPMENT

MERCURY Cougar	I-4	V-6
Retail price $:	16,195	16,695
Dealer invoice $:	14,814	15,259
Shipping & handling $:	400	400
Automatic transmission:	-	O
Cruise control:	O	O
Power steering:	S	S
Anti-lock brakes:	O	O
Traction control:	-	O
Air conditioning:	SM	SM
Leather:	-	-
AM/FM/radio-cassette:	S	S
Power door locks:	S	S
Power windows:	S	S
Tilt steering:	S	S
Dual adjustable mirrors:	SEC	SEC
Alloy wheels:	S	S
Anti-theft system:	S	S

Colors
Exterior: Orange, Gold, Red, Green, Blue, Silver, Black, White.

Interior: Silk, Black, Brown.

AT A GLANCE...

Category: front-wheel drive sport coupes. **Class :** 3S

HISTORIC
Introduced in: 1999
Made in: Flat Rock, Michigan, USA.

DEMOGRAPHICS
Model	Men./Wom.	Age	Married	College	Income
Cougar	NA				

INDEX
Safety:	80 %	**Satisfaction:**	NA %
Depreciation:	NA %	**Insurance:**	$800-950
Cost per mile:	$0.42	**Number of dealers:**	5 200

SALES
Model	1996	1997	Result
Cougar	Not on the market at that time.		

MAIN COMPETITORS
ACURA Integra, BMW M3, EAGLE Talon, CHEVROLET Camaro, CHRYSLER Sebring, DODGE Avenger, FORD Mustang, HONDA Prelude, NISSAN 240SX, PONTIAC Firebird, TOYOTA Celica.

MAINTENANCE REQUIRED BY WARRANTY
First revision:	Frequency:	Diagnostic plug:
5 000 miles	6 months	Yes

SPECIFICATIONS

Model	Version Trim	Body/ Seats	Interior volume cu ft	Trunk volume cu ft	Cd	Wheel base in	Lght x Wdgth x Hght in x in x in	Curb weight lb	Susp. ft/rr	Brake ft/rr	Steering type	Turning diameter ft	Steer. turns nber.	Fuel tank gal	tire size	Standard tires make	model	Standard powertrain
MERCURY		Total warranty, antipollution & battery: 3 years / 36 000 miles; corrosion perforation: 5 years / unlimited.																
Cougar	I-4	2dr.cpe.2+2	84.2	14.5	0.32	106.4	185.0x69.6x52.2	2892	ih/ih	dc/dr	pwr.r&p.	37.0	3.28	15.5	205/60R15	Firestone	Firehawk GTA	L4/2.0/M5
Cougar	V-6	2dr.cpe.2+2	84.2	14.5	0.32	106.4	185.0x69.6x52.2	3005	ih/ih	dc/dr	pwr.r&p.	37.0	3.28	15.5	205/60R15	Firestone	Firehawk GTA	V6/2.5/M5

Ford hoped to gain the same brisk sales with the Contour and Mystique as was the case for the Tempo-Topaz. Potential buyers were expecting replacement models to be sold at the same prices! But there you have it, the #2 American carmaker just forgot to mention that the Escort would replace the Tempo-Topaz models and that the Contour-Mystique models were designed to get in the race against other models like the Integra, Malibu, Grand Am, Breeze, Stratus, Accord and 626. The anonymous traits of these "world cars" got a face-lift in 1998, but the Achilles' heal V6 engine is still the same old bugbear it always was.

MODEL RANGE

The Ford Contour and Mercury Mystique have slightly different stylistic touches (grille and rear end design) and cabin layout. These four-door sedans are offered in two trim levels: LX and SE at Ford and GS and LS at Mercury. The Contour GL and base model Mystique are no longer sold. Both brand cars are equipped with a standard 2.0L Zetec 4-cylinder engine, associated with a 5-speed manual gearbox. A 4-speed automatic transmission is sold as an extra for all versions. On the other hand, the optional 2.5L Duratec V6 engine can only equip the Contour SE and Mystique LS versions. The Ford lineup also includes a high-performance model called the Contour SVT that's powered by a V6 that now develops 200 hp (5 more than last year).

TECHNICAL FEATURES

The Contour-Mystique duo was developed at the same time as the Ford Mondeo that's built and sold across Europe, thus they're called "world cars". The steel monocoque body is very sleek, as the 0.31 drag coefficient indicates. The four-wheel independent suspension uses MacPherson struts up front and a multi-link directional effect setup at the rear. There are anti-roll bars both front and rear. The more sporty versions, the V6-powered Contour SE, Mystique LS and Contour SVT, are equipped with stiffer shocks and bigger-diameter stabilizer bars. These models also benefit from rear disc brakes rather than drum brakes. All models are equipped with power steering, but SE, SVT and LS models have super-quick steering to match their slick moves. Ford states that its engines are at the cutting edge of current technology and will

Under-estimated..

require no major maintenance for 100,000 miles, except for oil and filter changes!

PROS

+ THE SVT MODEL. This unique car performs like a champion and with a lot of flair and the engine sure roars beautifully!

+ STYLE. New touches rendered in 1998 added a lot of character to these sedans. The grille design is simply gorgeous, especially the Mystique's classy, upper-crust grille.

+ TECHNICAL FEATURES. Ford designed these models on the European Mondeo platform, in other words, it pulled out all the stops, technically speaking, so cars have a very robust build and are equipped with a well-honed suspension and modern Zetec and Duratec engines.

+ TEMPERAMENT. The Contour SVT has more gusto and handles beautifully, much more so than the SE/LS models.

+ QUALITY. Assembly and finish details exhibit great craftsmanship. There's no interference heard even on poor roads and trim materials and accessories are spiffy.

+ BRAKES. Brakes on the SE/LS and SVT have a lot of brawn, given the car category. They bite the tarmac, they grip like champions, apply power gradually and in a nice, balanced way with ABS.

+ PERFORMANCES. The 4-cylinder engine puts out more impressive power than the V6 that equips the SE/LS. Acceleration and pickup response time are very close for both engines, which is disappointing. But the SVT benefits from a more brilliant powerplant, so

accelerations and pickup are achieved in a second less.

+ RIDE COMFORT. The Contour/Mystique's are blessed with a cushy suspension that eliminates road surface irregularities and seats are thick and nicely designed. Noise level is low, even on the SVT that zips along without being impolite to passengers.

+ HANDLING. On the highway, these sedans are neutral and steering is straight-on predictable. On curved stretches, the SE/LS are more fun to drive since there's less sway, but not as much fun as being at the wheel of the SVT equipped with a still firmer suspension and high-performance tires that really grab the gravel.

+ TRUNK. It's absolutely huge and with the wide, low opening, luggage handling is a breeze. The 60/40 split-fold seatbench (optional) really opens out a lot of storage space.

+ NICE FEATURES: Touches like illuminated inner door handles (at night), a control to lower the seatbench back located in the trunk and the pollen filter climate control system.

CONS

-PASSENGER PROTECTION. In the event of a collision, passenger protection isn't as effective as for the driver who benefits from optimum protection.

- STEERING. The SVT steering is over assisted, so it's light on acceleration and precision suffers from pronounced torque fallout.

- INTERIOR DESIGN. Rear seat leg room is snug even with the new-design seating and so tall passengers will feel cramped.

- V6 ENGINE. Performance scores are too close to those of the 4-cylinder engine, that's definitely more frugal. It just doesn't make any sense!

- MANUAL GEARBOX. Except on the SVT, the shifter is wishy washy and gears take forever to get their act together.

- MANEUVERABILITY. The V6-powered versions suffer from a bigger steer angle diameter than the 4-cylinder versions.

CONCLUSION

The Contour-Mystique's aren't as popular as they should be. The fault lies with Ford that didn't come up with refined and classy enough cars, proving once again that the concept of a world car is still something of a utopian dream. ☺

RATING
FORD-MERCURY Contour-Mystique

CONCEPT :		69%
Technology	80	
Safety :	75	
Interior space :	50	
Trunk volume:	60	
Quality/fit/finish :	80	

DRIVING:		66%
Cockpit :	80	
Performance :	50	
Handling :	60	
Steering :	75	
Braking :	65	

ORIGINAL EQUIPMENT:		76%
Tires :	75	
Headlights :	80	
Wipers :	80	
Rear defroster :	70	
Radio :	75	

COMFORT :		66%
Seats :	75	
Suspension :	75	
Sound level:	50	
Conveniences :	50	
Air conditioning :	80	

BUDGET :		72%
Price :	60	
Fuel economy :	75	
Insurance :	65	
Satisfaction :	85	
Depreciation :	75	

Overall rating:	69.8%

NEW FOR 1999
- Reworked front seats to allow for more space in the rear.
- Contour GL and base model Mystique no longer offered.
- Redefined front suspension.
- Modified instrument panel.
- Gas tank now having a 15 gallon capacity.
- Engine delivering 5 hp more power on the Contour SVT.
- Better-performance tires on the Contour SVT.

ENGINES / TRANSMISSIONS / PERFORMANCES

Model/ version	Type / timing valve / fuel system	Displacement cu in	Power bhp @ rpm	Torque lb-ft @ rpm	Compres. ratio	Driving wheels / transmission	Final ratio	Acceler. 0-60 mph s	Standing 1/4 & 5/8 mile s	Acceler. 50-75 mph s	Braking 60-0 mph f	Top speed mph	Lateral acceler. G	Noise level dBA	City	Highway	Fuel type Octane
base	L4* 2.0 DOHC-16-MPSFI	121	125 @ 5500	130 @ 4000	9.6 :1	front- M5	3.84	10.0	17.2 31.5	6.8	131	109	0.78	67	24	38	R 87
						front-A4	3.92	11.1	17.8 32.2	7.8	137	106	0.78	68	23	35	R 87
option	V6 2.5 DOHC-24-MPSFI	155	170 @ 6250	165 @ 4250	9.7 :1	front-M5	4.06	8.8	16.7 29.0	6.5	125	112	0.82	67	21	32	R 87
						front-A4	3.77	9.4	17.0 30.6	6.7	128	109	0.82	68	22	32	R 87
SVT	V6 2.5 DOHC-24-MPSFI	155	200 @ 6700	167 @ 5625	10.0 :1	front-M5	4.06	7.7	16.4 28.5	5.0	125	137	0.85	68	20	28	S 91

PRICE & EQUIPMENT

FORD Contour / MERCURY Mystique	LX	SE	SVT	GS	LS
Retail price $:	14,460	15,955	22,405	16,390	17,745
Dealer invoice $:	13,544	14,585	20,325	14,982	16,188
Shipping & handling $:	535	535	535	535	535
Automatic transmission:	O	O	-	O	O
Cruise control:	O	S	S	S	S
Power steering:	S	S	S	S	S
Anti-lock brakes:	O	O	S	O	O
Traction control:	-	-	-	-	-
Air conditioning:	SM	SM	SM	SM	SM
Leather:	-	O	S	-	S
AM/FM/radio-cassette:	O	S	S	S	S
Power door locks:	O	S	S	S	S
Power windows:	-	S	S	S	S
Tilt steering:	S	S	S	S	S
Dual adjustable mirrors:	SE	SE	SE	SE	SE
Alloy wheels:	-	O	S	O	S
Anti-theft system:	S	S	S	S	S

Colors
Exterior: Blue, Brown, Red, Green, Silver, Black, White.

Interior: Blue, Brown, Silk.

AT A GLANCE...
Category: front-wheel drive compact sedans. Class : 4

HISTORIC
Introduced in: 1995
Made in: Kansas City, MI, USA & Cuautitlan, Mexico.

DEMOGRAPHICS

Model	Men./Wom.	Age	Married	College	Income
Contour	65/35 %	48	71 %	44 %	$ 35 000
Mystique	72/28 %	52	82 %	46 %	$ 33 700

INDEX
Safety:	75 %	Satisfaction:	85 %
Depreciation:	27 %	Insurance:	$ 800 - 935
Cost per mile:	$0.40	Number of dealers:	5 200

SALES
Model	1996	1997	Result
Contour	174 187	151 060	- 13.3 %
Mystique	57 102	41 038	- 28.1 %

MAIN COMPETITORS
ACURA Integra 4dr., CHEVROLET Malibu, CHRYSLER Cirrus, DODGE Stratus, HONDA Accord, MAZDA 626, NISSAN Altima, OLDSMOBILE Alero, PLYMOUTH Breeze, PONTIAC Grand Am, SUBARU Legacy, VW Passat.

MAINTENANCE REQUIRED BY WARRANTY
First revision:	Frequency:	Diagnostic plug:
5 000 miles	6 months	Yes

SPECIFICATIONS

Model	Version Trim	Body/ Seats	Interior volume cu ft	Trunk volume cu ft	Cd	Wheel base in	Lght x Wdgth x Hght in x in x in	Curb weight lb	Susp. ft/rr	Brake ft/rr	Steering type	Turning diameter ft	Steer. turns nber.	Fuel tank gal	tire size	Standard tires make	model	Standard powertrain
FORD		Total warranty, antipollution & battery: 3 years / 36 000 miles; corrosion perforation: 5 years / unlimited.																
Contour	LX	4dr.sdn. 5	90.2	13.9	0.31	106.5	184.6x69.1x54.5	2769	ih/ih	dc/dr	pwr.r&p.	36.5	2.78	15.0	185/70R14	Firestone	Firehawk GTA	L4/2.0/M5
Contour	SE	4dr.sdn. 5	90.2	13.9	0.31	106.5	184.6x69.1x54.5	2833	ih/ih	dc/dr	pwr.r&p.	37.3	2.71	15.0	185/70R14	Firestone	Firehawk GTA	V6/2.5/M5
Contour	SVT	4dr.sdn. 5	89.4	13.9	0.31	106.5	183.8x69.1x54.5	3069	ih/ih	dc/ABS	pwr.r&p.	40.0	2.71	15.0	215/50ZR16BF	Goodrich	G-Force T/A	V6/2.5/M5
MERCURY		Total warranty, antipollution & battery: 3 years / 36 000 miles; corrosion perforation: 5 years / unlimited.																
Mystique	GS	4dr.sdn. 5	89.6	13.9	0.31	106.5	184.8x69.1x54.4	2808	ih/ih	dc/dr	pwr.r&p.	36.5	2.78	15.0	185/70R14	Firestone	Firehawk GTA	L4/2.0/M5
Mystique	LS	4dr.sdn. 5	90.2	13.9	0.31	106.5	184.8x69.1x54.4	2808	ih/ih	dc/dc	pwr.r&p.	37.3	2.71	15.0	205/60R15	Firestone	Firehawk GTA	V6/2.5/M5

The Crown Victoria and Grand Marquis sedans hail back to the bygone era of the "big" traditional American automobile. An endangered species, since these cars are the last specimens alive of this kind since the Chevrolet Caprice and Buick Roadmaster disappeared from the landscape. These big bod cars do have their fans, mainly among older citizens and public service enterprises, such as police forces, taxi companies and commercial fleets, etc. Ford has a monopoly on this market niche, so these limos should survive, at least for now.

MODEL RANGE

The Crown Victoria and Grand Marquis are four-door sedans offererd in two trims: base and LX at Ford and GS and LS at Mercury. They're designed to accomodate five or six adults. The 4.6L SOHC V8 engine that equips models is linked to a 4-speed automatic transmission. The body design got a makeover in 1998, which included mostly stylistic touches. These models are still based on a platform first introduced in the fall of 1978.

TECHNICAL FEATURES

Both rather generously sized sedans are identical but for a few exterior stylistic touches and cabin design details. These cars are sleek and well-proportioned but none can claim having great aerodynamics, not with a telltale 0.37 drag coefficient . In each case, the steel body is mounted on a surrounding chassis equipped with an independent front suspension made up of unequal-length control arms and a rear rigid axle supported by four control arms and a Watt suspension parallelogram. Suspensions also include coil springs and gas-filled shocks, with anti-roll bars. Cars are equipped with variable assist recirculating ball steering and benefit from four-wheel disc brakes. An antilock braking system is now standard equipment on these models, but traction control is still only offered as an extra. The dual-valve per cylinder V8 engine doesn't just equip the Crown Victoria and Grand Marquis. It's also under the hood of the 1998 Lincoln Town Car and Mustang GT.

PROS

+ RIDE COMFORT. It's hard to

Retro Driving Pleasure...

debunk the cushy ride inside these two cars. On super smooth expressways, they seem to float on a cloud, in utter and complete silence. But their suspension doesn't like bumps too much, since it really acts up when faced with such nonsense. The 50/50 split-fold seatbenches provide more lateral and lumbar support than in the past, but they're still too flat.

+ CABIN DESIGN. The cabin can easily seat five or six occupants. Head, shoulder and toe room is generous and doors open nice and wide, so boarding and unboarding is no problem.

+ FUEL CONSUMPTION. Even with the big engine and such hefty vehicle size and weight, gas consumption sits at around 19 mpg, which is pretty surprising.

+ BRAKES. Four-disc wheel brakes can be applied gradually, they're accurate and tough. The 1999 models are now equipped with standard ABS.

+ DRIVING PLEASURE. These cars are pretty unique and they offer a nice, old-fashioned driving feel. You're carried along, you're in a sort of quiet bubble and sometimes you feel like you're at the helm of a big ship. Oh, the good old days!

+ QUALITY. Over the last twenty years, build quality has really improved. Component refinements and assembly reflect current-day standards. Trim material quality has come a long way as well. The most

dramatic difference is how much sturdier the chassis is, since almost all structural squeaks and groans have been eliminated.

CONS

- VEHICLE SIZE. Naturally, with such a big bod car, you have to bone up on your driving skills when it comes to maneuvering or parking on narrow downtown streets. The steer angle radius is smaller than it once was, but it's still an impressive size, as are the front and rear overhangs that are definitely bigger than average.

- REAR AXLE. It makes its presence known as soon as you drive over an expansion joint on a curve, exhibiting a sliding effect characteristic of these cars. Which does affect ride comfort. And we strongly recommend the optional traction control and a good set of winter tires for the snowy season, to offset rear-wheel drive hassles.

- TRUNK. It may be humungous, but it's weirdly shaped and then there's the spare tire and the deep, cavernous bottom, so it isn't convenient nor easy to use and the high opening makes luggage handling a chore.

- INSTRUMENT PANEL. It's been spruced up over the years, but it looks old-fashioned by today's standards. Controls are well located, but the sound system dials are way out of the driver's reach! The faux-bois trim that was supposed to add class to the dashboard has the opposite effect: it looks awfully cheap.

- TRAILERING CAPABILITIES. These sedans are big cars, but they can't pull trailers weighing more than a ton. Camping and boating enthusiasts might be disappointed.

- CONVENIENCE FEATURES. There aren't loads and loads of storage spots, neither up front nor in the rear; there aren't even any cupholders, for Pete's sake.

CONCLUSION

The Crown Victoria and Grand Marquis are bygone beauty queens, but they do have their appealing traits: cushy ride, good safety features and reasonable performance scores. Yet the rigid rear axle and stingy convenience features give away their age! ☺

RATING
Crown Victoria-Grand Marquis

CONCEPT :		83%
Technology	70	
Safety :	90	
Interior space :	90	
Trunk volume:	90	
Quality/fit/finish :	75	

DRIVING:		55%
Cockpit :	50	
Performance :	60	
Handling :	60	
Steering :	75	
Braking :	30	

ORIGINAL EQUIPMENT:		77%
Tires :	75	
Headlights :	80	
Wipers :	75	
Rear defroster :	80	
Radio :	75	

COMFORT :		75%
Seats :	75	
Suspension :	70	
Sound level:	70	
Conveniences :	70	
Air conditioning :	90	

BUDGET :		57%
Price :	40	
Fuel economy :	40	
Insurance :	70	
Satisfaction :	85	
Depreciation :	50	

Overall rating:		**69.4%**

NEW FOR 1999

- Standard antilock braking device.
- New exterior shades.

ENGINES

	Model/ version	Type / timing valve / fuel system	Displacement cu in	Power bhp @ rpm	Torque lb-ft @ rpm
1)	V8* 4.6 SOHC-16-MPFI		281	200 @ 4250	275 @ 3000
2)	V8* 4.6 SOHC-16-MPFI		281	215 @ 4500	285 @ 3000
3)	V8* 4.6 SOHC-16-MPFI		281	175 @ 4500	235 @ 3500

1) base 2) double exhaust 3) NGV

TRANSMISSIONS

Compres. ratio	Driving wheels / transmission	Final ratio
9.0 :1	rear - A4*	2.73
9.0 :1	rear - A4*	3.27
10.0 :1	rear - A4*	3.27

PERFORMANCES

Acceler. 0-60 mph s	Standing 1/4 & 5/8 mile s	Acceler. 50-75 mph s	Braking 60-0 mph f	Top speed mph	Lateral acceler. G	Noise level dBA	Fuel economy mpg City	Fuel economy mpg Highway	Fuel type Octane
9.0	16.5 30.2	6.5	158	109	0.75	65-72	17	26	R 87
8.8	16.2 30.0	6.3	154	109	0.75	65-72	17	26	R 87
NA									

PRICE & EQUIPMENT

FORD Crown Victoria	base	LX		
MERCURY Grand Marquis			GS	LS
Retail price $:	21,135	23,335	22,090	23,990
Dealer invoice $:	19,748	21,750	20,637	22,366
Shipping & handling $:	605	605	605	605
Automatic transmission:	S	S	S	S
Cruise control:	S	S	S	S
Power steering:	S	S	S	S
Anti-lock brakes:	S	S	S	S
Traction control:	O	O	O	O
Air conditioning:	SM	SM	SM	SM
Leather:	-	O	O	O
AM/FM/radio-cassette:	S	S	S	S
Power door locks:	S	S	S	S
Power windows:	S	S	S	S
Tilt steering:	S	S	S	S
Dual adjustable mirrors:	SE	SE	SE	SE
Alloy wheels:	O	O	O	O
Anti-theft system:	S	S	S	S

Colors

Exterior: Gold, Red, Green, Blue, Gray, Silver, Black, White.

Interior: Blue, Parchment, Brown, Graphite, White-Graphite.

AT A GLANCE...

Category:	rear-wheel drive full size sedans.	Class :	6

HISTORIC
Introduced in:	1979
Made in:	St-Thomas, Ontario, Canada.

DEMOGRAPHICS
Model	Men./Wom.	Age	Married	College	Income
Crown Victoria	82/18 %	67	87 %	25 %	$ 32 500
Grand Marquis	90/10 %	67	87 %	17 %	$ 32 600

INDEX
Safety:	90 %	Satisfaction:	85 %
Depreciation:	50 %	Insurance:	$ 850
Cost per mile:	$ 0.58	Number of dealers:	5 200

SALES
Model	1996	1997	Result
Crown-Vic	108 798	107 872	- 0.8 %
Gd- Marquis	99 770	109 539	+ 9.8 %

MAIN COMPETITORS
BUICK LeSabre, OLDSMOBILE 88, PONTIAC Bonneville, TOYOTA Avalon.

MAINTENANCE REQUIRED BY WARRANTY
First revision:	Frequency:	Diagnostic plug:
5 000 miles	6 months	Yes

SPECIFICATIONS

Model	Version Trim	Body/ Seats	Interior volume cu ft	Trunk volume cu ft	Cd	Wheel base in	Lght x Wdgth x Hght in x in x in	Curb weight lb	Susp. ft/rr	Brake ft/rr	Steering type	Turning diameter ft	Steer. turns nber.	Fuel tank gal	tire size	Standard tires make	model	Standard powertrain
FORD		Total warranty, antipollution & battery: 3 years / 36 000 miles; corrosion perforation: 5 years / unlimited.																
Crown Victoria base	4dr.sdn.6		111.4	20.6	0.37	114.7	212.0x78.2x56.8	3915	ih/rh	dc/ABS	pwr.ball	40.3	3.4	19.0	225/60SR16	Goodyear	Eagle LS	V8/4.6/A4
Crown Victoria LX	4dr.sdn.6		111.4	20.6	0.37	114.7	212.0x78.2x56.8	3926	ih/rh	dc/ABS	pwr.ball	40.3	3.4	19.0	225/60SR16	Goodyear	Eagle LS	V8/4.6/A4
MERCURY		Total warranty, antipollution & battery: 3 years / 36 000 miles; corrosion perforation: 5 years / unlimited.																
Gd Marquis GS	4dr.sdn.6		109.3	20.6	0.37	114.7	212.0x78.2x56.8	3918	ih/rh	dc/ABS	pwr.ball	40.3	3.4	19.0	225/60SR16	Goodyear	Eagle LS	V8/4.6/A4
Gd Marquis LS	4dr.sdn.6		109.3	20.6	0.37	114.7	212.0x78.2x56.8	3951	ih/rh	dc/ABS	pwr.ball	40.3	3.4	19.0	225/60SR16	Goodyear	Eagle LS	V8/4.6/A4

The Ford Escort has undergone a lot of modifications over the years, so much so that it's one of the most covetted cars in its category. Constantly improved reliability and a practical cabin design are definite assets in this regard. Borrowing some mechanical features from the Mazda 323 and Protegé seem to have ironed out some technical wrinkles. Yet this Escort model is coming towards the end of its career, since it will be replaced by a new compact car called Focus in the fall of 1999.

MODEL RANGE

The Ford catalogue now lists three Escort versions: a four-door sedan and station wagon and since 1998, the ZX2 coupe that has a life of its own (we'll talk about this model in another section later on). The sedan is sold in two models, LX and SE and the station wagon comes in a single SE model. There are two clones in the Mercury lineup for American customers: the GS and LS Tracer. The only engine available is a 2.0L in-line 4. It's paired up with a standard 5-speed manual gearbox or an optional 4-speed automatic. Presented as an economy car, the Escort LX has rather rustic original equipment, but it at least includes power steering and a 60/40 split-fold rear seatbench, so trunk space can be extended. But to really equip this model, you have to check off items on the long list of options. The LX model isn't even equipped with standard intermittent wipers!

TECHNICAL FEATURES

The steel unibody was reworked in 1997. The car has a clean, crisp silhouette, but aerodynamics aren't too hot, since the drag coefficient is 0.34. But compared with former Escort models, the new one benefit from greater rigidity and resistance to torsion and there's less secondary engine noise and vibration. And they're treated to better hold up against rust. Cars are equipped with front disc brakes and rear drum brakes and an ABS system is available as an extra.

The suspension is fitted with stiffer shocks and big stabilizer bars. Wider 14-inch tires add to ride comfort and driving pleasure. The manual transmission is right-on, but the automatic is linked to a torque converter that optimizes performance and cuts down on fuel consumption. This 2.0L engine, derived from the former 1.9L

Near Retirement...

engine, has a dual intake manifold that regulates fuel intake according to r.p.m., which makes for a more efficient engine. This powerplant is 25% more muscular than its predecessor and it's one of the cleanest burning engines in its category. And there are platinum-tipped spark plugs that don't have to be replaced for 100,000 miles!

PROS

+ FUEL EFFICIENCY. The 2.0L engine is fuel-frugal. It burns an average of 30 mpg, which yields a 400 mile road autonomy.

+ HANDLING. The Escort is fun to drive. It's more solid on its feet than before and there's less swish and sway. Handling is very predictable on straight runs or while taking curves.

+ RIDE COMFORT. The suspension earns some points when it comes to comfort. It handles road faults with competence, but it does vibrate on bigger bumps. Seats are firm and provide enough support to offset fatigue. But the seatbench is flat and offers only minimum comfort where it counts.

+ DRIVING PLEASURE. It's enjoyable being behind the wheel of an Escort; accurate steering makes it easy to maneuver. And the engine is more brawny than its predecessors.

+ SIZE. Given its exterior fairly modest size, the cabin and trunk offer suitable space. The luggage compartment on the station wagon, a bit roomier than before, provides lots of space over a nearly flat sur-

face, once the 60/40 split-fold seatbench is lowered.

+ COCKPIT. The instrument panel layout is neat and handy and there's excellent visibility in all directions, with all those windows.

+ FIT AND FINISH. Compared to former Escort's, assembly and finish detail quality is definitely much better than it was. Trim and component fit seems neat and tight inside and out and seat fabric looks good.

CONS

- PERFORMANCES. Accelerations and pickup aren't what they should be for a 2.0L engine, but they're perfectly suited to a family car.

- CABIN DESIGN. One thing hasn't changed over the years: the interior design is just as dull and dreary as ever. The shiny gray or black plastic trim, used just about everywhere, isn't much to look at.

- BRAKES. Braking distances are long for a small car and without ABS, car path is far from a sure thing.

- NOISE. At more than 60 mph, noise gets really pervasive. You hear all kinds of nonsense: engine noise at certain r.p.m.'s, road noise that doesn't go away and some whistling wind depending on road quality.

- ACCESS. Doors are really rounded at the top, so you have to lower your head if you don't want to get bonked while boarding.

- TO BE IMPROVED UPON: Headlights aren't too bright. And wipers really don't clear enough of the windshield. Inside the cabin, there are only minuscule storage compartments.

CONCLUSION

The Escort is still one of the top sellers in the North American economy compact car market. It's not at all like the models of yesteryear that we'd all like to forget. It's convenient and economical to run, which are downright admirable traits, even if they aren't the most muscular and most splashy-looking cars on the road. Let's hope that the Focus that'll replace it next year will go even further, but in the same direction!

RATING
FORD-MERCURY Escort-Tracer

CONCEPT :	**67%**
Technology	80
Safety :	80
Interior space :	50
Trunk volume :	50
Quality/fit/finish :	75
DRIVING:	**59%**
Cockpit :	75
Performance :	50
Handling :	50
Steering :	70
Braking :	50
ORIGINAL EQUIPMENT:	**75%**
Tires :	75
Headlights :	70
Wipers :	75
Rear defroster :	75
Radio :	80
COMFORT :	**64%**
Seats :	75
Suspension :	75
Sound level :	50
Conveniences :	50
Air conditioning :	70
BUDGET :	**73%**
Price :	75
Fuel economy :	90
Insurance :	70
Satisfaction :	80
Depreciation :	50
Overall rating:	**67.6%**

NEW FOR 1999

- Standard remote power trunk opener on the sedans.
- Standard luggage-covering canvas, roof luggage rack and rear wipers on the SE station wagon.
- Bolted-on 14-inch hub caps.
- New seat fabric for low-back seats.
- Standard driver's vanity mirror.

ENGINES

Model/version	Type / timing valve / fuel system	Displacement cu in	Power bhp @ rpm	Torque lb-ft @ rpm
base	L4* 2.0 SOHC-8-MPSFI	121	110 @ 5000	125 @ 3750

TRANSMISSIONS

Compres. ratio	Driving wheels / transmission	Final ratio
9.2 :1	front - M5*	3.85
	front - A4	3.74

PERFORMANCES

Acceler. 0-60 mph s	Standing 1/4 & 5/8 mile s	Acceler. 50-75 mph s	Braking 60-0 mph f	Top speed mph	Lateral acceler. G	Noise level dBA	Fuel economy mpg City	Highway	Fuel type Octane
10.0	17.5 31.5	9.3	141	109	0.70	68	28	41	R 87
11.0	18.2 32.8	9.5	151	106	0.70	68	25	37	R 87

PRICE & EQUIPMENT

FORD Escort MERCURY Tracer	LX 4dr.sdn.	SE 4dr.sdn.	SE 4dr.wgn.	GS 4dr.sdn.	LS 4dr.sdn.	LS 4dr.wgn.
Retail price $:	11,430	12,730	13,930	11,505	12,860	14,355
Dealer invoice $:	10,721	11,904	12,996	10,789	12,023	13,383
Shipping & handling $:	415	415	415	415	415	415
Automatic transmission:	O	O	O	O	O	O
Cruise control:	-	O	O	O	O	O
Power steering:	S	S	S	S	S	S
Anti-lock brakes:	O	O	O	O	O	O
Traction control:	-	-	-	-	-	-
Air conditioning:	OM	SM	SM	OM	SM	SM
Leather:	-	-	-	-	-	-
AM/FM/radio-cassette:	O	S	S	S	S	S
Power door locks:	-	O	O	O	O	O
Power windows:	-	O	O	O	O	O
Tilt steering:	-	O	O	O	O	O
Dual adjustable mirrors:	SM	SE	SE	SM	SE	SE
Alloy wheels:	O	O	O	O	O	O
Anti-theft system:	O	O	O	O	O	O

Colors

Exterior: Mocha, Red, Blue, Seaweed, Green, Silver, Amber, Gold, Ebony, White.

Interior: Medium graphite , Blue, Brown.

AT A GLANCE...

Category: front-wheel drive compact sedans and wagons. **Class :** 3

HISTORIC
Introduced in: 1980, 1990, 1997.
Made in: Wayne, Michigan, USA & Hermosillo, Mexico.

DEMOGRAPHICS

Model	Men./Wom.	Age	Married	College	Income
Escort LX	55/45 %	44	62 %	41 %	$ 28 000
Escort SE	50/50 %	44	55 %	39 %	$ 26 000

INDEX
Safety:	80 %	Satisfaction:	80 %
Depreciation:	48 %	Insurance:	$690-950
Cost per mile:	$0.32	Number of dealers:	5 200

SALES

Model	1996	1997	Result
Escort	284 644	283 898	- 0.3 %
Tracer	47 797	43 589	- 8.8 %

MAIN COMPETITORS

CHEVROLET Cavalier, DODGE-PLYMOUTH Neon, HONDA Civic , HYUNDAI Elantra, MAZDA Protegé, NISSAN Sentra, PONTIAC Sunfire, SATURN SL, SUBARU Impreza, TOYOTA Corolla, VOLKSWAGEN Golf-Jetta.

MAINTENANCE REQUIRED BY WARRANTY
First revision:	Frequency:	Diagnostic plug:
5 000 miles	6 months	Yes

SPECIFICATIONS

Model	Version Trim	Body/Seats	Interior volume cu ft	Trunk volume cu ft	Cd	Wheel base in	Lght x Wdgth x Hght in x in x in	Curb weight lb	Susp. ft/rr	Brake ft/rr	Steering type	Turning diameter ft	Steer. turns nber.	Fuel tank gal	tire size	Standard tires make	model	Standard powertrain
FORD-MERCURY		Total warranty, antipollution & battery: 3 years / 36 000 miles; corrosion perforation: 5 years / unlimited.																
Escort	LX	4dr.sdn. 4	87.2	12.8	0.34	98.4	174.3x67.0x53.3	2467	ih/ih	dc/dr	pwr.r&p.	31.5	3.1	12.8	185/65R14	Uniroyal	Tiger Paw	L4/2.0/M5
Escort	SE	4dr.sdn. 4	87.2	12.8	0.34	98.4	174.3x67.0x53.3	2471	ih/ih	dc/dr	pwr.r&p.	31.5	3.1	12.8	185/65R14	Uniroyal	Tiger Paw	L4/2.0/M5
Escort	SE	5dr.wgn. 4	93.8	26.3	0.36	98.4	172.7x67.0x53.9	2531	ih/ih	dc/dr	pwr.r&p.	31.5	3.1	12.8	185/65R14	Uniroyal	Tiger Paw	L4/2.0/M5
Tracer	GS	4dr.sdn. 4	87.2	12.8	0.34	98.4	174.7x67.0x53.3	2467	ih/ih	dc/dr	pwr.r&p.	31.5	3.1	12.8	185/65R14	Uniroyal	Tiger Paw	L4/2.0/M5
Tracer	LS	4dr.sdn. 4	87.2	12.8	0.34	98.4	174.4x67.0x53.3	2471	ih/ih	dc/dr	pwr.r&p.	31.5	3.1	12.8	185/65R14	Uniroyal	Tiger Paw	L4/2.0/M5
Tracer	LS	5dr.wgn. 4	93.8	26.3	0.36	98.4	172.7x67.0x53.9	2531	ih/ih	dc/dr	pwr.r&p.	31.5	3.1	12.8	185/65R14	Uniroyal	Tiger Paw	L4/2.0/M5

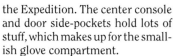

The tremendous success of Ford's most recent all-purpose vehicle, the Expedition, has proven that there's an insatiable appetite out there for this type of big SUV. Otherwise, how can you explain why so many drivers could do without such a beast for so long? Especially since GM has been producing the Suburban for some 40 years! At any rate, Ford is cashing in on the current situation and has a lot of tricks up its sleeve. First it cloned the Expedition to create the Lincoln Navigator and now it's about to launch a new juggernaut that's even bigger than the Super Duty pickup truck...

MODEL RANGE

This big four-door wagon comes in RWD or AWD. It's sold in two trim levels, XLT and Eddie Bauer, and can accomodate from 5 to 8 passengers, depending on cabin layout. The standard engine is a 4.6L V8 paired up with a 4-speed automatic transmission. A 5.4L V8 powerplant is available as an option. The Expedition's original equipment is, in a nutshell, reasonable considering the going price. Ford has even added standard cruise control on the XLT, a feature it didn't benefit from in 1998. Illuminated running boards are listed among the options.

TECHNICAL FEATURES

Just as the Chevrolet Tahoe is inspired from the former C/K pickup, the Expedition is a «spin-off» from the F-150 pickup. It has the F-150 ladder chassis frame and front end design, right up to the B pillar. The steel unibody is mounted to the chassis via rubber insulator components. The front suspension is identical to that of the F-150 and uses a combination of unequal-length control arms fitted with coil springs on the RWD models and torsion bars on the AWD models. But the rear suspension is different since the rigid rear axle is supported by five control ams and suspended on coil springs. An air suspension with ground clearance control is sold as an extra on the AWD models. Four-wheel disc brakes benefit from all-wheel ABS. The driver can switch from RWD to AWD by touching a power switch located on the dash. There are various settings: RWD, AWD H, AWD L and Auto. The automatic mode sends power to the front wheels as soon as there's rear wheel slippage, without any interference from the driver.

PROS

+ **STYLE.** The Expedition has a

Extreme Wagon...

bold and beautiful appearance. The neat, well-proportioned body design makes the vehicle seem trimmer than it actually is. From a distance, without a scale reference, it's easy to think you're looking at an Explorer, especially from the rear, since both vehicles have a similar rear end design.

+ **CABIN SPACE.** From five to eight passengers can climb aboard an Expedition. Naturally, luggage space becomes more limited depending on how many occupants there are, but let's say, you have a more than comfortable margin...

+ **RIDE COMFORT.** This SUV is super comfy. The rear end is less jumpy than that on its rivals that have bouncier leaf springs. The AWD version has a bit more firm demeanor, but it doesn't really af-

fect comfort. Nice-design seats are really comfortable and sound dampening does the trick quite nicely.

+ **MANEUVERABILITY.** The Expedition has a steer angle diameter that's 3 ft less than the F-150, so it handles well. Ford engineers put a lot of thought into this, after hearing female buyers speak up and state how important this feature is.

+ **HANDLING.** The front suspension really keeps this beauty on track, even in crosswinds or on poorly kept-up roads.

+ **REAR DOOR.** It's a breeze to open or close with the well-adjusted door jacks and hinged window that provides access to the luggage hold without having to lift the hatch door.

+ **STORAGE SPACE.** There are lots of handy storage spots inside

the Expedition. The center console and door side-pockets hold lots of stuff, which makes up for the smallish glove compartment.

+ **NICE FEATURES:** We really liked the simple, easy-to-use control that engages wheel traction, now offering an automatic AWD mode. Also, we'd like to mention two neat options: illuminated running boards that provide safe boarding and the new adjustable pedal.

CONS

- **BUDGET.** It takes a lot of cash to buy and operate this vehicle, since average fuel consumption is about 13 mpg. In fact, only the insurance premium seems fairly reasonable in this budget bonanza of more or less expensive items.

- **VEHICLE SIZE.** The big, brawny Expedition isn't easy to maneuver on narrow downtown streets and parking in those tiny allotted spots is no picnic.

- **PERFORMANCES.** The 4.6L V8 feels wimpy, due to hefty vehicle weight. Accelerations and pickup are more of a chore and if you have a lot of people to take here and there or if you have to pull heavy loads, the 5.4L V8 is a better choice.

- **FIT AND FINISH.** Some finish details could be neater. For example, some of the plastic inserts in the inner door panels seem to fit rather poorly.

- **ACCESS.** Climbing aboard 4X4 versions is no easy matter, even with all the handles and such, since the vehicle sits so high. Which makes the optional runningboards a real must.

- **THE THIRD SEATBENCH.** Passengers who have to sit on the remote rear seatbench won't be any too comfy. It's tough getting there, the seatbench is less thickly upholstered than the middle seatbench and it's flat as a pancake.

- **NO DIESEL?** Ford should offer a diesel engine as an option for this big brute. It would increase sales in parts of the world where gas doesn't come cheap.

CONCLUSION

The Expedition is geared to folks who need lots of cabin space or good trailering capabilities, but it also targets buyers who want to show off at the wheel of a big vehicle. Two clienteles with different goals in mind... ☺

RATING
FORD Expedition

CONCEPT :		85%
Technology	80	
Safety :	75	
Interior space :	100	
Trunk volume:	90	
Quality/fit/finish :	80	

DRIVING:		53%
Cockpit :	80	
Performance :	45	
Handling :	35	
Steering :	75	
Braking :	30	

ORIGINAL EQUIPMENT:		78%
Tires :	85	
Headlights :	70	
Wipers :	80	
Rear defroster :	70	
Radio :	85	

COMFORT :		71%
Seats :	75	
Suspension :	75	
Sound level :	50	
Conveniences :	75	
Air conditioning :	80	

BUDGET :		46%
Price :	0	
Fuel economy :	20	
Insurance :	70	
Satisfaction :	80	
Depreciation :	60	

Overall rating:	66.6%

NEW FOR 1999

- New-design grille and wheels.
- Optional adjustable pedal assembly.
- Standard electronically controlled climate control on the Eddie Bauer model.
- Sound system with volume leveller.
- Seatbench equipped with wheels for easier manipulation.

ENGINES

Model/ version	Type / timing valve / fuel system	Displacement cu in	Power bhp @ rpm	Torque lb-ft @ rpm
base	V8*4.6 SOHC-16-SFI	281	240 @ 4750	293 @ 3500
option	V8 5.4 SOHC-16-SFI	330	260 @ 4500	345 @ 2300

TRANSMISSIONS

Compres. ratio	Driving wheels / transmission	Final ratio
9.0 :1	rear/4 - A4	3.31
9.0 :1	rear/4 - A4	3.31

PERFORMANCES

Acceler. 0-60 mph s	Standing 1/4 & 5/8 mile s	Acceler. 50-75 mph s	Braking 60-0 mph f	Top speed mph	Lateral acceler. G	Noise level dBA	Fuel economy mpg City	Fuel economy mpg Highway	Fuel type Octane
11.5	18.5 33.4	9.0	148	106	0.70	68	14	21	R 87
11.0	18.0 32.8	8.0	157	109	0.70	68	13	19	R 87

PRICE & EQUIPMENT

FORD Expedition	XLT 4x2 4 dr.	XLT 4x4 4 dr.	E.Bauer 4x2 4 dr.	E.Bauer 4x4 4 dr.
Retail price $:	28,225	30,825	32,055	34,690
Dealer invoice $:	24,737	26,947	27,993	30,233
Shipping & handling $:	640	640	640	640
Automatic transmission:	S	S	S	S
Cruise control:	S	S	S	S
Power steering:	S	S	S	S
Anti-lock brakes:	S	S	S	S
Traction control:	-	-	-	-
Air conditioning:	SM	SM	SA	SA
Leather:	-	-	S	S
AM/FM/radio-cassette:	S	S	SDc	SDc
Power door locks:	S	S	S	S
Power windows:	S	S	S	S
Tilt steering:	S	S	S	S
Dual adjustable mirrors:	SE	SE	SE	SE
Alloy wheels:	O	O	S	S
Anti-theft system:	S	S	S	S

Colors

Exterior: Gold, Green, Red, Blue, Silver, White, Black.

Interior: Medium graphite, Dark graphite, Brown.

AT A GLANCE...

Category: 2WD or 4WD all purpose vehicles.   **Class :** utility

HISTORIC
Introduced in: 1997
Made in: Wayne, Michigan, USA.

DEMOGRAPHICS

Model	Men./Wom.	Age	Married	College	Income
Expedition	68/32%	42	72%	40 %	$ 55 000

INDEX
Safety: 75 %   **Satisfaction:** 78 %
Depreciation: 38 % (2 years)   **Insurance:** $ 950
Cost per mile: $0.64   **Number of dealers:** 5 200

SALES

Model	1996	1997	Result
Expedition	82 807	214 524	+ 159.1 %

MAIN COMPETITORS
CADILLAC Escalade, DODGE Durango, CHEVROLET Tahoe- GMC Yukon, CHEVROLET Suburban, JEEP Grand Cherokee, LEXUS RX 300 & LX 470, LINCOLN Navigator. MERCEDES-BENZ M-Class.

MAINTENANCE REQUIRED BY WARRANTY
First revision: 5 000 miles   **Frequency:** 6 months / 5 000 miles   **Diagnostic plug:** Yes

SPECIFICATIONS

Model	Version Trim	Traction	Body/ Seats	Wheel base in	Lght x Wdgth x Hght in x in x in	Curb weight lb	Susp. ft/rr	Brake ft/rr	Steering type	Turning diameter ft	Steer. turns nber.	Fuel tank gal	tire size	Standard tires make	model	Standard powertrain
FORD	General warranty, antipollution & battery: 3 years / 36 000 miles; corrosion perforation: 5 years / unlimited.															
Expedition	XLT	4x2	4dr.wgn.6	119.1	204.6x78.6x74.3	4848	ih/rh	dc/ABS	pwr.ball	40.4	3.3	26.0	255/70R16	Goodyear Wrangler RT/S		V8/4.6/A4
Expedition	Eddie Bauer	4x2	4dr.wgn.6	119.1	204.6x78.6x74.3	-	ih/rh	dc/ABS	pwr.ball	40.4	3.3	26.0	255/70R16	Goodyear Wrangler RT/S		V8/4.6/A4
Expedition	XLT	4x4	4dr.wgn.6	119.1	204.6x78.6x76.6	-	ih/rh	dc/ABS	pwr.ball	40.5	3.3	30.0	255/70R16	Goodyear Wrangler RT/S		V8/4.6/A4
Expedition	Eddie Bauer	4x4	4dr.wgn.6	119.1	204.6x78.6x76.6	-	ih/rh	dc/ABS	pwr.ball	40.5	3.3	30.0	265/70R17	Goodyear Wrangler RT/S		V8/4.6/A4

How do you keep a champion in first place on the podium? By giving it better and better attributes. Ford did just that by equipping the Explorer with a more supple five-speed automatic transmission, a brawnier V6, a high-performance V8 and sophisticated all-wheel drive. Add to this a well-furbished and posh cabin and there you have the main ingredients needed to maintain this SUV's appeal. Now all North American Lincoln-Mercury dealers will be selling the equivalent Mountaineer.

MODEL RANGE

Ford offers a whole range of Explorer models: 2 and 4-door models, RWD and AWD vehicles as well as full-time all-wheel drive versions. There is now only a single 2-door version called Sport, but there are, in all, four 4-door versions sold: XL, XLT, Eddie Bauer and Limited. A standard 4.0L OHV V6 engine animates the Sport, XL and XLT models with either a 5-speed manual transmission or an optional 5-speed automatic (the latter comes standard on the XLT). A 4.0L SOHC V6 equips the Eddie Bauer and Limited models, but comes as an option on the other models. The 5.0L Thunderbolt V8 powerplant can also equip the XLT, Eddie Bauer and Limited. Both engines are linked to a 5-speed automatic transmission.

TECHNICAL FEATURES

The Explorer's steel body is mounted on an H frame and bolted down via rubber insulator components. Aerodynamics have gone up a notch since the 1998 reworked design; now the drag coefficient is 0.41 due to a more rounded-out grille design. The front suspension is independent. It uses a combination of unequal-length control arms with torsion bars and the rigid rear axle is supported by leaf springs. The base model V6 develops 160 hp compared to 210 hp for the SOHC V6. The V8 that's been on the circuit for quite a while is well-liked for its impressive torque output. The electronically controlled all-wheel drive «Control Trac» system is regulated via a button located on the dashboard. It has an «Auto» mode that shifts power to the front wheels when rear wheels lose their grip. The 5-speed automatic transmission is a variant of the former 4-speed automatic, to which a fifth gear called «Swap Shift» has been added.

#1 on the Podium...

PROS

+ LOOKS. The Explorer is a winner and handsome looks have a lot to do with it, even if the newest touch up job wasn't everyone's cup of tea.

+ CHOICE. This is an important factor, since the wide model range lets all kinds of buyers find just the vehicle they need and can afford.

+ CABIN SPACE. The 4-door version is roomier due to a 9.8 inches longer wheelbase. Five occupants and all their effects can be nicely accomodated.

+ ENGINES. The mighty 205-hp 4.0L V6 and the 5.0L V8 really pump out the power, considering the Explorer's power to weight ratio. These engines have what it takes to pull pretty hefty loads.

+ ROADABILITY. The front suspension, first introduced in 1995, has enhanced vehicle competence and adds to steering precision.

+ CABIN LAYOUT. The owner of a luxury car will be right at home aboard an Eddie Bauer or Limited. Actually, their respective equipment is lush and includes lots of accessories geared to spoiling travellers.

+ RELIABILITY. The Explorer is known for its darn good dependability, a definite asset, as proven by J.D. Power studies and the high owner satisfaction rate. This trait gives it a real edge over the main competition.

+ RIDE COMFORT. The load-levelling air suspension sure adds to comfy ride feel. It's now available on the XLT, Eddie Bauer and Limited versions. These vehicles are blessed with really cushy seats and superb soundproofing, so long-distance travellers will enjoy the ride.

+ INSTRUMENT PANEL. It's ergonomic, classy-looking and very user-friendly and the center console has loads of storage space.

+ CONVENIENCE FEATURES. The 4-door version offers more amenities. Access is easier, but there's also another neat feature, namely the rear door that's fitted with a hinged window that can be opened independently to stash stuff.

CONS

- BUDGET. This vehicle is a pricey purchase and is by no means cheap to run, since even insurance premiums are costly. What a sheer waste of money when you know that Explorer owners only use 30% of its potential!

- BASE V6 ENGINE. It's terribly sluggish. Accelerations and pickup are lazy, which can be downright dangerous when passing on the highway, for instance. We think the 210-hp SOHC V6 engine is a better choice.

- BRAKES. It isn't the greatest, not with those long stretches required to come to a full stop, even with four-wheel disc brakes. Brake pad resistance to intensive use is only fair to midling, but sudden stops are nice and straight, thanks to standard ABS.

- RWD MODELS. The base RWD model is far from cushy. Poor seat design, jumpy suspension and simplistic sound dampening don't make for what you'd call a pleasure trip.

- TO BE IMPROVED UPON: Low ground clearance on the lower-end models and tough rear seat access due to skimpy space on the 2-door model and due to narrow doors on the 4-door versions.

CONCLUSION

The Explorer's popularity derives from engineers' on-going efforts to make it a better vehicle and of course, its top-notch reliability. As for the rest, it's a winner more due to current fashion trends than to real daily, nitty-gritty needs.

Explorer - Mountaineer — FORD-MERCURY

RATING Explorer-Mountaineer

CONCEPT: 77%
- Technology: 80
- Safety: 90
- Interior space: 65
- Trunk volume: 75
- Quality/fit/finish: 75

DRIVING: 55%
- Cockpit: 75
- Performance: 60
- Handling: 40
- Steering: 70
- Braking: 30

ORIGINAL EQUIPMENT: 77%
- Tires: 75
- Headlights: 75
- Wipers: 70
- Rear defroster: 75
- Radio: 90

COMFORT: 66%
- Seats: 75
- Suspension: 75
- Sound level: 60
- Conveniences: 40
- Air conditioning: 80

BUDGET: 53%
- Price: 30
- Fuel economy: 40
- Insurance: 65
- Satisfaction: 80
- Depreciation: 50

Overall rating: 65.6%

NEW FOR 1999

- Reworked front bumper and foglamps.
- Side mouldings on the Eddie Bauer and Limited versions.
- Rear air suspension offered as an extra.
- Optional rear radar detection device.
- New-design seats, roof luggage rack and 16-inch wheels on the Limited version.

ENGINES / TRANSMISSIONS / PERFORMANCES

Model/ version	Type / timing valve / fuel system	Displacement cu in	Power bhp @ rpm	Torque lb-ft @ rpm	Compres. ratio	Driving wheels / transmission	Final ratio	Acceler. 0-60 mph s	Standing 1/4 & 5/8 mile s	Acceler. 50-75 mph s	Braking 60-0 mph f	Top speed mph	Lateral acceler. G	Noise level dBA	Fuel economy mpg City	Highway	Fuel type Octane
1)	V6* 4.0 OHV-12-MPSFI	244	160 @ 4200	225 @ 2750	9.0 :1	rear/all-M5	3.27	9.0	16.6 30.6	6.6	180	106	0.72	68	16	22	R 87
						rear/all-A5	3.27	NA									
2)	V6* 4.0 SOHC-12-MPSFI	244	210 @ 5250	240 @ 3250	9.7 :1	rear/all-A5	3.55	8.5	16.4 29.5	6.1	187	109	0.73	68	16	22	R 87
3)	V8 5.0 OHV-16-MPSFI	302	215 @ 4200	288 @ 3300	9.0 :1	rear/all-A4	3.73	10.0	17.2 30.7	6.8	177	109	0.72	70	13	21	R 87

1) Std Explorer XL, Sport 4X2, XLT. 2) Std Eddie Bauer, Limited & Mountaineer; opt. XL, Sport 4X2, XLT. 3) opt. Mountaineer, XLT, Eddie Bauer & Limited.

PRICE & EQUIPMENT

FORD Explorer	XL 4 dr. 4x2	Sport 2 dr. 4x4	XLT 4 dr. 4x4	EB 4 dr. AWD	Limited 4 dr. AWD
Retail price $:	21,560	22,725	26,745	30,465	33,270
Dealer invoice $:	19,598	20,623	24,160	27,434	29,903
Shipping & handling $:	525	525	525	525	525
Automatic transmission:	O	O	S	S	S
Cruise control:	O	O	S	S	S
Power steering:	S	S	S	S	S
Anti-lock brakes:	S	S	S	S	S
Traction control:	-	-	-	S	S
Air conditioning:	SM	SM	SM	SA	SA
Leather:	-	-	-	S	S
AM/FM/radio-cassette:	S	S	SDc	SDc	SDc
Power door locks:	O	S	S	S	S
Power windows:	O	O	S	S	S
Tilt steering:	S	S	S	S	S
Dual adjustable mirrors:	SM	SE	SE	SE	SEC
Alloy wheels:	-	S	S	S	S
Anti-theft system:	S	S	S	S	S

Colors

Exterior: Gold, Green, Orange, Brown, Red, Blue, Platinum, White, Black.

Interior: Medium graphite, Dark graphite, Brown.

AT A GLANCE...

Category: 2WD or 4WD all purpose vehicles. **Class:** utility.

HISTORIC
Introduced in: 1991: Explorer, 1997 Mountaineer
Made in: Louisville, Kentucky, & St-Louis, Missouri, USA.

DEMOGRAPHICS

Model	Men./Wom.	Age	Married	College	Income
Explorer 4x2	76/24 %	42	90 %	44 %	$ 44 500
Explorer 4x4	74/26 %	47	80 %	50 %	$ 55 200
Mountaineer	NA				

INDEX
Safety:	85 %	Satisfaction:	80 %
Depreciation:	50 %	Insurance:	$ 850-975
Cost per mile:	$0.55	Number of dealers:	5 200

SALES

Model	1996	1997	Result
Explorer	402 663	383 852	- 4.7 %
Mountaineer	26 700	45 363	+ 69.9%

MAIN COMPETITORS
CHEVROLET Blazer, GMC Jimmy, ISUZU Rodeo & Trooper, JEEP Cherokee & Grand Cherokee, LAND ROVER Discovery, LEXUS RX 300, MERCEDES-BENZ M-Class, NISSAN Pathfinder, OLDSMOBILE Bravada, TOYOTA 4Runner.

MAINTENANCE REQUIRED BY WARRANTY
First revision:	Frequency:	Diagnostic plug:
5 000 miles	6 months/ 5 000 miles	Yes

SPECIFICATIONS

Model	Version Trim	Traction	Body/ Seats	Wheel base in	Lght x Wdgth x Hght in x in x in	Curb weight lb	Susp. ft/rr	Brake ft/rr	Steering type	Turning diameter ft	Steer. turns nber.	Fuel tank gal	tire size	Standard tires make	model	Standard powertrain
FORD	Total warranty, antipollution & battery: 3 years / 36 000 miles; corrosion perforation: 5 years / unlimited.															
Explorer	Sport	4x2	2dr.wgn.4/5	101.7	180.8x70.2x67.1	3675	it/rl	dc/ABS	pwr.r&p.	34.7	3.5	17.5	235/75R15	Firestone	Wilderness	V6/4.0/M5
Explorer	XL	4x2	5dr.wgn.4/5	111.5	190.7x70.2x67.1	3891	it/rl	dc/ABS	pwr.r&p.	37.3	3.5	21.0	225/70R15	Firestone	Wilderness	V6/4.0/A5
Explorer	Eddie Bauer	4x4	5dr.wgn.4/5	111.5	190.7x70.2x67.5	4145	it/rl	dc/ABS	pwr.r&p.	37.3	3.5	21.0	255/70R16	Firestone	Wilderness	V6/4.0/A5
Explorer	Limited	4x4	5dr.wgn.4/5	111.5	190.7x70.2x67.5	4244	it/rl	dc/ABS	pwr.r&p.	37.3	3.5	21.0	255/70R16	Firestone	Wilderness	V6/4.0/A5
Mountaineer		4x2	5dr.wgn.4/5	111.5	190.7x70.2x67.5	3929	it/rl	dc/ABS	pwr.r&p.	37.3	3.5	21.0	255/70R16	Firestone	Wilderness	V6/4.0/A5
Mountaineer		4x4	5dr.wgn.4/5	111.5	190.7x70.2x67.5	4149	it/rl	dc/ABS	pwr.r&p.	37.3	3.5	21.0	255/70R16	Firestone	Wilderness	V6/4.0/A5

The F-150 virtually revolutionized the pickup market. It's a robust but comfy vehicle, two elements that don't seem compatible for this type of tough as nails vehicle. The Dodge Ram played on the public's nostalgic heartstrings, but Ford opted for a modern approach that seems to have worked, given the latest-generation SUV's huge success since it was first introduced on the market. For 1999, Ford has upgraded convenience features by equipping SuperCab models with two rear doors.

MODEL RANGE

By mixing and matching various elements vital to the F-150's character, we come up with about a hundred different versions, depending on rear or four-wheel drive, one of the six various wheelbase lengths, a Styleside or Flareside box and a regular or extended SuperCab. A noteworthy item: now SuperCab versions have two rear doors that open opposite to the front doors and only when the latter are open. These additional doors free up a huge opening and provide super access to the rear seatbench, either for climbing aboard or for storing luggage on the platform created by the folded down bench. The F-150 comes in four equipment levels: «Work», XL, XLT and Lariat. Three Triton engines are listed in the catalogue: the 4.2L V6 that comes standard on the Work, XL and XLT versions; the 4.6L V8 that equips the Lariat but can be ordered as an extra on the other models; last of all, an optional 5.4L V8 than can equip all models. The Work, XL and XLT models come with a standard 5-speed manual gearbox or an optional 4-speed automatic. But the Lariat is equipped with a standard automatic gearbox. For 1999, Ford is also offering a dual fuel V8 engine that can run on natural gas. All engines are fitted with a device that prevents overheating, so the engine can keep running temporarily even if you're out of coolant.

TECHNICAL FEATURES

The F-150's steel body is set on a steel H frame consisting of 8 crossmembers. It's mounted onto the frame via rubber insulator pads that absorb secondary vibrations and other nonsense. Aerodynamics are quite good, due to the sleek front end, yielding a fairly low 0.37 drag coefficent. The front suspen-

Something For Everyone

sion is like that of the Expedition, that is, it consists of MacPherson struts and unequal-length control arms linked to coil springs on the RWD models and torsion bars on the AWD models. The rear rigid axle is supported by leaf springs. Vehicles are equipped with disc and drum brakes, with standard rear-wheel ABS. A four-wheel ABS system is listed among the options.

SIMPLY SUPER

+ OVERALL DESIGN. This super solid vehicle can go just about anywhere and do just about anything. Yet it's blessed with an elegant body design and provides real cabin comfort, so it's the ideal vehicle for everyday use.

PROS

+ SOLID BUILD. Brand name fanatics state the F-150's robust build and reliability as the main reasons for their purchase. Yet the high owner satisfaction rate seems to contradict data on the still high problem rate per 100 vehicles.

+ MODEL CHOICE. With such a panoply of models, each and every customer can find what he or she is looking for.

+ LOOKS. The F-150 is a real looker with such classy, well-proportioned stylistic lines that don't make it seem any less robust and muscular. Actually, the rounded edges make the vehicle look smaller than it is.

+ RIDE COMFORT. For a heavy-duty vehicle, the ride is pretty darn comfy. Longer wheelbase models are equipped with a less jittery suspension. On the other hand, the

AWD models with a short, high chassis do rough up passengers on bumpy roads.

+ REAR DOORS. The standard two rear doors on the SuperCab versions make a dramatic difference when it comes to convenience.

+ THE FEEL AT THE WHEEL. The independent front suspension has elimated wavering in crosswinds and on rutted roads, something that took the fun out of driving former F-150 pickup models.

+ STORAGE COMPARTMENTS. Upper-end models have more storage spots than do the lowly base models. The center armrest compartment can hold all the stuff that tends to hang around and make the cabin look messy.

+ ENGINE EFFICIENCY. Engines are pretty efficient. They're smooth and gutsy. Even the V6's performances are a pleasant surprise. But these vehicles are heavyweights, so you can't really say they're fuel-efficient.

+ NICE FEATURES. The shifter that lets you go from RWD to AWD is really neat, as is the automatic AWD function that only kicks in when needed.

CONS

- BUDGET. These vehicles cost an arm and a leg. Purchase price and gas bills aren't within everyone's budget.

- FUEL CONSUMPTION. None of these conventional gas engines is fuel-frugal and unfortunately Ford doesn't offer a diesel as an alternative.

- ACCESS. You literally «climb» aboard the F-150 4X4 and even all those handles and assist grips don't compensate for the high floor threshold. Running boards look pretty essential as a purchase.

- STEERING. Steering is light and you have to have your wits about you when parking the really long models, no thanks to the big steer angle diameter.

CONCLUSION

Now that GM has put its new pickups on the market, the race is on and it's anybody's guess as to whether the Silverado-Sierra or the F-150 will be in the lead next year in this North American top of the charts vehicle category... ☺

RATING
FORD F-150

CONCEPT : **75%**
Technology	80
Safety :	90
Interior space :	75
Trunk volume:	50
Quality/fit/finish :	80

DRIVING: **56%**
Cockpit :	80
Performance :	40
Handling :	35
Steering :	75
Braking :	50

ORIGINAL EQUIPMENT: **79%**
Tires :	85
Headlights :	75
Wipers :	80
Rear defroster :	70
Radio :	85

COMFORT : **64%**
Seats :	70
Suspension :	60
Sound level :	50
Conveniences :	60
Air conditioning :	80

BUDGET : **52%**
Price :	40
Fuel economy :	30
Insurance :	60
Satisfaction :	80
Depreciation :	50

Overall rating: **65.2%**

NEW FOR 1999

- **Standard fourth door for SuperCab models.**
- **New-design grille, rocker panel mouldings, 16-inch alloy rims, front seats and door trim.**
- **The more muscular 5.4L V8.**
- **The barrel-shaped box cover.**
- **GVWR of 6,000 lb. with the 4.6L V8.**

ENGINES

Model/ version	Type / timing valve / fuel system	Displacement cu in	Power bhp @ rpm	Torque lb-ft @ rpm
base	V6* 4.2 OHV-12-MPSFI	256	205 @ 4750	250 @ 3000
option	V8 4.6 SOHC-16-MPSFI	281	220 @ 4500	290 @ 3250
option	V8 5.4 SOHC-16-MPSFI	330	260 @ 4500	345 @ 2300

TRANSMISSIONS

Compres. ratio	Driving wheels / transmission	Final ratio
9.3 :1	rear/4 - M5	3.08
	rear/4 - A4	3.31
9.0 :1	rear/4 - M5	3.08
	rear/4 - A4	3.08
9.0 :1	rear/4 - A4	3.08

PERFORMANCES

Acceler. 0-60 mph s	Standing 1/4 & 5/8 mile s	Acceler. 50-75 mph s	Braking 60-0 mph f	Top speed mph	Lateral acceler. G	Noise level dBA	Fuel economy mpg City	Highway	Fuel type Octane
12.0	18.3 33.7	9.8	154	100	0.68	68	14	21	R 87
13.0	18.8 34.8	10.6	161	97	0.68	68	16	22	R 87
11.0	17.5 33.2	8.0	151	103	0.68	68	14	20	R 87
11.7	18.1 33.4	8.5	157	100	0.68	68	14	21	R 87
10.0	17.2 32.4	7.4	157	106	0.68	68	13	20	R 87

PRICE & EQUIPMENT

FORD F-150	Work 4x2 reg.cab.	XL 4x2 Sup.cab.	XLT 4x4 reg.cab.	Lariat 4x4 Sup.cab.
Retail price $:	14,835	18,380	21,940	26,730
Dealer invoice $:	13,565	16,133	19,159	23,231
Shipping & handling $:	640	640	640	640
Automatic transmission:	O	O	O	O
Cruise control:	O	O	S	S
Power steering:	S	S	S	S
Anti-lock brakes:	S	S	S	S
Traction control:	-	-	-	-
Air conditioning:	-	-	SM	SM
Leather:	-	-	-	S
AM/FM/radio-cassette:	O	O	S	SCD
Power door locks:	-	-	S	S
Power windows:	-	-	S	S
Tilt steering:	O	O	S	S
Dual adjustable mirrors:	SM	SM	SE	SE
Alloy wheels:	O	O	S	S
Anti-theft system:	-	-	-	-

Colors
Exterior: Gold, Red, Blue, Green, Teal, Black, Silver, White.

Interior: Medium graphite, Brown, Blue, Dark graphite.

AT A GLANCE...

Category: 4x2 & 4x4 pickups. **Class :** utility

HISTORIC
Introduced in: 1996 (F-150) 1997 (F-250)
Made in: Kansas City, Missouri; Wayne, Michigan; Norfolk, Virginia; Louisville, Kentucky, USA. Oakville, Ontario, Canada.

DEMOGRAPHICS
Model	Men./Wom.	Age	Married	College	Income
F-150 4x2	94/6 %	43	74 %	16 %	$ 29 500
F-150 4x4	94/6 %	39	60 %	25 %	$ 30 000

INDEX
Safety:	90 %	Satisfaction:	70 %
Depreciation:	50 %	Insurance:	$ 850-975
Cost per mile:	$ 0.52	Number of dealers:	5 200

SALES
Model	1996	1997	Result
F-Series	780 838	746 111	- 4.4%

MAIN COMPETITORS
CHEVROLET Silverado, DODGE Ram, GMC Sierra, TOYOTA T150.

MAINTENANCE REQUIRED BY WARRANTY
First revision:	Frequency:	Diagnostic plug:
5 000 miles	6 months/ 5 000 miles	Yes

SPECIFICATIONS

Model	Version Trim	Traction	Body/ Seats	Wheel base in	Lght x Wdgth x Hght in x in x in	Curb weight lb	Susp. ft/rr	Brake ft/rr	Steering type	Turning diameter ft	Steer. turns nber.	Fuel tank gal	tire size	Standard tires make	model	Standard powertrain
FORD			Total warranty, antipollution & battery: 3 years / 36 000 miles; corrosion perforation: 5 years / unlimited.													
F-150	Reg. cab.short bed.Work	4x2	2dr.p-u.3	119.9	202.2x78.4x72.4	3849	ih/rldc/dr/ABS/re.		pwr.ball	40.5	3.3	25.0	235/70R16	Firestone	Wilderness	V6/4.2/M5
F-150	Reg. cab. extd. bed Work	4x2	2dr.p-u.5	138.5	220.8x78.4x75.3	4235	ih/rldc/dr/ABS/re.		pwr.ball	40.4	3.3	25.0	235/70R16	Firestone	Wilderness	V6/4.2/M5
F-150	Sup.Cab.short bedt.XL	4x2	2dr.p-u.5	138.5	220.8x78.4x72.6	4045	ih/rldc/dr/ABS/re.		pwr.ball	45.9	3.3	25.0	235/70R16	Firestone	Wilderness	V6/4.2/M5
F-150	Sup.Cab.extd. bed XLT	4x2	2dr.p-u.5	157.1	239.4x78.4x72.4	4200	ih/rldc/dr/ABS/re.		pwr.ball	51.3	3.3	30.0	235/70R16	Firestone	Wilderness	V6/4.2/M5
F-150	Reg. cab. extd. bed. Work	4x4	2dr.p-u.3	120.2	203.7x79.5x72.1	3959	it/rldc/dr/ABS.		pwr.ball	45.9	3.3	24.5	235/70R16	Goodyear	Wrangler RT/S	V6/4.2/M5
F-150	Reg. cab. extd. bed. Work	4x4	2dr.p-u.3	138.8	222.3x79.5x72.1	4339	it/rldc/dr/ABS		pwr.ball	45.8	3.3	25.0	235/70R16	Goodyear	Wrangler RT/S	V6/4.2/M5
F-150	Sup.Cab.short bed.XL	4x4	2dr.p-u.5	138.8	222.3x79.5x75.3	4478	it/rldc/dr/ABS		pwr.ball	45.8	3.3	25.0	235/70R16	Goodyear	Wrangler RT/S	V6/4.2/M5
F-150	Sup.Cab.extd. bed. XLT	4x4	2dr.p-u.5	157.4	240.9x79.5x75.1	4605	it/rldc/dr/ABS		pwr.ball	51.2	3.3	30.0	235/70R16	Goodyear	Wrangler RT/S	V6/4.2/M5

The next totally redesigned Mustang will be launched in the year 2002, but until then the present model is getting a new wardrobe to celebrate its 35th birthday with class. Body panels have a new look in keeping with "Edge Design" tailoring, engines have more muscle, the chassis is beefier and roadholding is more competent, aspects lacking on models available up until now. The instrument panel hasn't changed an iota, but seats have a better structural feel and they're more finely clad.

MODEL RANGE
The 1999 Mustang will be available in coupe and convertible versions in two trim levels: base or GT. The base model Mustang is equipped with a 3.8L V6 and the GT is powered by a 4.6L SOHC V8. The 5-speed manual gearbox comes standard and the 4-speed automatic is sold as an extra. Convertibles are equipped with a power droptop control and can receive an optional polymer hard top. Standard equipment is just about the same, but options include high-performance traction control that's effective at all speeds and that's activated by ABS sensors, ABS also being an option.

TECHNICAL FEATURES
The 1999 Mustang bod is inspired by the 1964 1/2 model. It has a nice folded flowing look similar to that of the original model and there's even the authentic emblem and grille motif to boot. Headlights and taillights sport a new design as do ports and rims. The steel unibody is much more rigid and robust on both versions, especially the convertible that thus improves roadholding and resistance to impact. The independent front suspension is made up of MacPherson struts, but at the rear, the rigid axle design is as old as the hills! It's suspended by four trailing arms and is fitted with an anti-roll bar.

The V8 models are equipped with bigger-diameter anti-roll bar and the rear axle is fitted with four shock absorbers. All versions benefit from four-wheel disc brakes. Both available engines have a lot more gusto and get-up-and-go. The 3.8L V6 delivers 40 more hp and the 4.6L V8 puts out 25 more hp, thanks to a number of refinements such as a more balanced crankshaft, reinforced engine blocks and new aluminum bearings.

Thirty-five Candles...

PROS
+ STYLISTICS. The 1999 Mustang has an appearance akin to that of the very first model, which will sure please all those Mustang nostalgia fans out there.

+ SUCCESS. Trim size and competitive price, given the reasonable array of equipment, add up to a successful recipe, so this car remains popular even at a time when this type of vehicle isn't exactly in the limelight.

+ PERFORMANCES. The V6 can boast of 40 more hp, so it's zippier than before. The V8's accelerations and pickup scores were about the same as for the Cobra that we're told won't be available this year, at least that's the scoop as we write these lines.

+ HANDLING. With each passing year and with each new generation, the Mustang exhibits more competent handling due to a stiffer chassis and better-quality tires.

+ DRIVING PLEASURE. It's simply great, especially when it comes to revving the lively 4.6L V8 that's smooth as silk and has power to burn. Steering is quick and benefits from a good reduction ratio, transmissions are well-synchronized and gears are nicely adjusted. You can do what you darn well please inside this car, you can go for a quiet, relaxing drive or you can take this wild horse out for a thrilling run.

+ RIDE COMFORT. It's much better than in the past. The suspension is more civilized, seats are more comfy, noise level is more appropriate, yet this car still boasts of being on the wild side and rear seats, get this, are almost useful!

+ THE SOUND AND THE FURY. The V8's low growl is an absolutely vital part of the Mustang experience. Nonetheless, when at cruising speed, things quiet down, you're in for a generally more comfortable spin!

+ NICE FEATURES: The much more sturdy build, especially noticeable on the convertibles, the lined easy-to-use soft top that's equipped with a glass rear window and defroster, which isn't the case for the snooty BMW Z3...

CONS
-QUALITY. There have been some glitches in regard to build quality and reliability. Owners are supposed to be crazy about their car, but the owner satisfaction rate is never higher than 75%!

- RIGID AXLE. It's still this car's major flaw, it swings on rough surfaces and generates a lot of annoying jostling about, but luckily it isn't dangerous per se. It looks like Ford just doesn't have the technical know-how to be able to come up with an independent suspension.

-BRAKES. Without ABS, they're inaccurate and unstable and this feature would sure make for safer driving if it were included as standard equipment.

- TRACTION. The rear end often slips and slides, especially with the gutsy V8 engines. Once again, too bad Ford can't come up with a better idea and include standard traction control.

-STEERING. It's a bit vague on the convertibles that don't have as rigid a frame and body as the coupes.

- REAR SEATS. They're uncomfortable. Space is snug and the flat seatbench offers no lateral or lumbar support.

- ROAD AUTONOMY. The GT animated by a V8 has very limited road autonomy that isn't more than 215 miles at continuous speeds, so you have to make a lot of stops at the pumps along the way if you're on a long trip.

-SEATS. The base model offers passengers pretty crummy, poor-design seating, while seats on the GT don't offer the support you'd expect in a zoomy sports car!

CONCLUSION
The Mustang remains the most popular North American sports coupe, since it's a fun car to zip around in and it's sold at a competitive price. Sales are higher than for its closest rivals, the Camaro-Firebird, coupes afflicted with a very uncertain future... ☺

RATING
FORD Mustang

CONCEPT :   **61%**
Technology : 75
Safety : 90
Interior space : 30
Trunk volume: 35
Quality/fit/finish : 75

DRIVING: **75%**
Cockpit : 80
Performance : 75
Handling : 70
Steering : 80
Braking : 70

ORIGINAL EQUIPMENT: **75%**
Tires : 80
Headlights : 75
Wipers : 75
Rear defroster : 65
Radio : 80

COMFORT :   **65%**
Seats : 75
Suspension : 70
Sound level : 50
Conveniences : 50
Air conditioning : 80

BUDGET :   **57%**
Price : 50
Fuel economy : 60
Insurance : 50
Satisfaction : 75
Depreciation : 50

Overall rating: **66.6%**

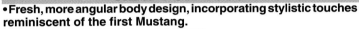

NEW FOR 1999
- **Fresh, more angular body design, incorporating stylistic touches reminiscent of the first Mustang.**
- **Higher output 3.8L V6 and 4.6L V8.**
- **New standard 3.27 differential for all models.**
- **Significantly reduced steer angle diameter.**
- **New design and fabric for front seats.**

ENGINES / TRANSMISSIONS / PERFORMANCES

Model/ version	Type / timing valve / fuel system	Displacement cu in	Power bhp @ rpm	Torque lb-ft @ rpm	Compres. ratio	Driving wheels / transmission	Final ratio	Acceler. 0-60 mph s	Standing 1/4 & 5/8 mile s	Acceler. 50-75 mph s	Braking 60-0 mph f	Top speed mph	Lateral acceler. G	Noise level dBA	Fuel economy mpg City	Highway	Fuel type Octane
base	V6* 3.8 OHV-12-SFI	232	190 @ 5250	220 @ 3000	9.36 :1	rear-M5*	3.27	8.2	16.2 28.8	6.3	131	106	0.80	67	19	31	R 87
						rear-A4	3.27	9.0	17.0 30.2	6.7	137	103	0.80	67	18	30	R 87
GT	V8* 4.6 SOHC-16-SFI	281	250 @ 5000	295 @ 4000	9.0 :1	rear-M5*	3.27	6.7	14.8 26.8	4.8	125	118	0.85	68	16	27	R 87
						rear-A4	3.27	7.5	15.2 27.5	5.6	131	112	0.85	68	16	26	R 87

PRICE & EQUIPMENT

FORD Mustang	base 2dr.cpe.	2dr.con.	GT 2dr.cpe.	2dr.con.
Retail price $:	16,150	20,650	20,150	24,150
Dealer invoice $:	14,819	18,824	18,279	21,939
Shipping & handling $:	525	525	525	525
Automatic transmission:	O	O	O	O
Cruise control:	O	O	O	O
Power steering:	S	S	S	S
Anti-lock brakes:	O	O	O	O
Traction control:				
Air conditioning:	SM	SM	SM	SM
Leather:	O	O	O	O
AM/FM/radio-cassette:	S	S	S	S
Power door locks:	O	S	O	S
Power windows:	O	S	O	S
Tilt steering:	S	S	S	S
Dual adjustable mirrors:	SE	SE	SE	SE
Alloy wheels:	O	O	S	S
Anti-theft system:	S	S	S	S

Colors
Exterior: Orange, Red, Blue, Green, Black, Silver, White.

Interior: Brown, Medium graphite, Black, Parchment.

AT A GLANCE...

Category: rear-wheel drive sport coupes & convertibles **Class :** 3S

HISTORIC
Introduced in: 1994
Made in: Dearborn, Michigan, USA.

DEMOGRAPHICS

Model	Men./Wom.	Age	Married	College	Income
Mustang	60/40 %	35	42 %	43 %	$ 35 000

INDEX
Safety: 90 %   **Satisfaction:** 75 %
Depreciation: 48 %   **Insurance:** $ 950 & 1 150
Cost per mile: $ 0.48   **Number of dealers:** 5 200

SALES

Model	1996	1997	Result
Mustang	122 674	116 610	- 4.9 %

MAIN COMPETITORS
ACURA Integra, CHEVROLET Camaro, CHRYSLER Sebring, DODGE Avenger, HONDA Prelude, PONTIAC Firebird, TOYOTA Celica.

MAINTENANCE REQUIRED BY WARRANTY
First revision: 5 000 miles
Frequency: 6 months/ 5 000 miles
Diagnostic plug: Yes

SPECIFICATIONS

Model	Version Trim	Body/ Seats	Interior volume cu ft	Trunk volume cu ft	Cd	Wheel base in	Lght x Wdgth x Hght in x in x in	Curb weight lb	Susp. ft/rr	Brake ft/rr	Steering type	Turning diameter ft	Steer. turns nber.	Fuel tank gal	tire size	Standard tires make	model	Standard powertrain
FORD		Total warranty, antipollution & battery: 3 years / 36 000 miles; corrosion perforation: 5 years / unlimited.																
Mustang		2dr.cpe.4	93.9	10.9	0.33	101.3	183.2x73.1x53.1	3069	ih/rh	dc/dc	pwr.r&p.	37.0	2.38	15.7	205/65R15	Goodyear	Eagle GA	V6/3.8/M5
Mustang		2dr.con.4	83.0	7.7	0.38	101.3	183.2x73.1x53.2	3210	ih/rh	dc/dc	pwr.r&p.	37.0	2.38	15.7	205/65R15	Goodyear	Eagle GA	V6/3.8/M5
Mustang	GT	2dr.cpe.4	93.9	10.9	0.36	101.3	183.2x73.1x53.3	3274	ih/rh	dc/dc	pwr.r&p.	38.0	2.38	15.7	225/55R16	BF.Goodrich	-	V8/4.6/M5
Mustang	GT	2dr.con.4	83.0	7.7	0.38	101.3	183.2x73.1x53.3	3428	ih/rh	dc/dc	pwr.r&p.	38.0	2.38	15.7	225/55R16	BF.Goodrich	-	V8/4.6/M5

The Ranger puts Ford at the top of the heap for North American compact pickup sales, ahead of the Dodge Dakota and the Chevrolet S-10 and GMC Sonoma duo, that come in second and third place respectively. So, since the F-150 is also leader of the pack when it comes to big format pickups, Ford dominates the very popular (and very lucrative) pickup truck market. Ford equipped the SuperCab with two rear doors rather than one, to be sure to keep the Ranger's #1 status in this category.

MODEL RANGE

The Ranger comes in regular cabin and short or long box or in the extended SuperCab model with short box. The SuperCab cabin is now equipped with two rear doors that open opposite to the front doors, when these are open. There are two trim levels available: XL and XLT, with Flareside and Styleside boxes and RWD or AWD. Rear-wheel drive versions are fitted with a standard 2.5L 4-cylinder engine or with an optional 3.0L or 4.0L V6. All-wheel drive models are animated by a standard 3.0L V6. The 5-speed manual transmission comes standard on all models. An optional 4-speed automatic can be linked to the 3.0L V6 and a 5-speed automatic can be paired up with the 4.0L V6.

TECHNICAL FEATURES

These utility vehicles have a steel body set on a seven-crossmember H frame (eight for the SuperCab) via rubber insulator units. The front suspension is like that of the F-150, consisting of unequal-length control arms linked to coil springs on RWD models and torsion bars on the AWD models. The rear rigid axle is supported by very conventional leaf springs. Vehicles benefit from rack-and-pinion steering and disc and drum brakes associated with standard rear-wheel ABS or optional four-wheel ABS. On the 4X4's, front wheels get the go-ahead via a power switch located on the dashboard. This simplistic system doesn't include a main differential and can only be engaged on slippery road surfaces and at low speeds, otherwise it really deteriorates.

PROS

+ RELIABILITY. The owner satisfaction rate confirms this vehicle's dependability and tried-and-true technical features. The Ranger is known for its super-solid

Junior Size...

build and clean finish job that really add to its appeal and value.

+ ON THE ROAD. The front suspension is now less sensitive to road faults and provides competent moves and contributes to right-on steering.

+ MANUAL GEARBOX. It's easy to use with its smooth, accurate gears. And pedal travel and effort are well-calibrated.

+ V6 ENGINES. They have terrific load hauling and trailering capabilities, so they're the best choice for these utility vehicles.

+ EXTENDED CABIN. The 1999 extended cabin versions are equipped with a second rear door and you can cancel the original auxiliary seats if you so wish on the SuperCab versions.

+ NICE FEATURES. Windshield wipers that sweep a large span at a good clip, so visibility is good even in driving rain and bucket seats or 60/40 split-folding seatbench that offer good support.

CONS

-PERFORMANCES. The 2.5L 4-cylinder engine is fine for light tasks, but it delivers more sluggish accelerations and pickup and burns more gas with a full load and the air conditioner on. The V6 engines lack gusto at low r.p.m., they're far from smooth and they're real gas guzzlers. As is the case for Dodge, Ford should consider equipping the Ranger with a small V8, so as to satisfy buyers looking for power and torque in a vehicle without having to purchase an F-150.

-RIDE COMFORT. These pickups

are out to get the job done, not pamper passengers. With an empty load, the suspension is jumpy and bounces constantly and you have to be pretty tough to take the rough ride as soon as the road surface gets the least bumpy.

-BRAKES. They're not impressive on the RWD models, since brakes only benefit from rear-wheel ABS and they're not too great, especially with a full load.

-HANDLING. Getting around on wet or damp surfaces is a hassle. The base model is equipped with a pretty flexible suspension and undersize tires, whereas the AWD models have the opposite handicap: their suspension is too hard and tires are too big.

- STEERING. Vehicles are equipped with rack-and-pinion steering, but it suffers from a poor reduction ratio and it's springy as heck, so it's no picnic. And the wide steer angle diameter really cripples maneuverability.

- ALL-WHEEL DRIVE. It's a far-from-perfect simplistic system that isn't too versatile and can only really be used on slippery roads, which limits vehicle use and safety features.

-FUEL CONSUMPTION. The V6's burn a lot of gas, especially for rough all-terrain use.

- NO V8 AVAILABLE. If the Ranger were powered by a V8 engine, it would be more versatile and could handle loads like a champion and benefit from gutsier traction, desirable traits on all-purpose vehicles, Naturally, there's the Dodge Dakota...

-POOR FEATURE: The base model seatbench is rather rudimentary. It provides no lateral or lumbar support. Why do you have to put yourself through such an ordeal?

CONCLUSION

The Ranger pickup is a solid utility vehicle that can get the job done, but you shouldn't think it's a car, because you might be disappointed. It's a dependable and hard-working beast, but it isn't super comfy and road demeanor isn't too refined, which shouldn't be too much to ask... ☺

RATING
FORD Ranger

CONCEPT :		60%
Technology	80	
Safety :	70	
Interior space :	40	
Trunk volume:	35	
Quality/fit/finish :	75	

DRIVING:		51%
Cockpit :	70	
Performance :	30	
Handling :	40	
Steering :	75	
Braking :	40	

ORIGINAL EQUIPMENT:		54%
Tires :	70	
Headlights :	80	
Wipers :	70	
Rear defroster :	0	
Radio :	50	

COMFORT :		56%
Seats :	65	
Suspension :	50	
Sound level :	50	
Conveniences :	40	
Air conditioning :	75	

BUDGET :		62%
Price :	60	
Fuel economy :	60	
Insurance :	65	
Satisfaction :	75	
Depreciation :	50	

Overall rating:		**56.6%**

NEW FOR 1999

- The optinal fourth door on the SuperCab.
- Standard air conditioner on the XLT models.
- Splash version no longer available.
- The option of not including auxiliary seats on SuperCab versions.

ENGINES / TRANSMISSIONS / PERFORMANCES

Model/version	Type / timing valve / fuel system	Displacement cu in	Power bhp @ rpm	Torque lb-ft @ rpm	Compres. ratio	Driving wheels / transmission	Final ratio	Acceler. 0-60 mph s	Standing 1/4 & 5/8 mile s	Acceler. 50-75 mph s	Braking 60-0 mph f	Top speed mph	Lateral acceler. G	Noise level dBA	Fuel economy mpg City	Highway	Fuel type Octane
1)	L4* 2.5 SOHC-8-MPSFI	153	119 @ 5000	146 @ 3000	9.37 :1	rear - M5*	-	12.8	18.8 34.3	10.5	138	91	0.69	70-76	22	28	R 87
						rear - A4	-	13.6	19.5 35.2	11.2	147	88	0.69	69-75	20	27	R 87
2)	V6* 3.0 OHV-12-MPSFI	182	150 @ 5000	185 @ 3750	9.14 :1	rear/4 - M5*	-	12.0	18.8 33.8	9.8	151	97	0.71	68-75	16	24	R 87
						rear/4 - A4	-	13.2	19.4 34.5	10.6	170	93	0.71	68-75	16	24	R 87
3)	V6* 4.0 OHV-12-MPSFI	244	160 @ 4200	225 @ 2750	9.0 :1	rear/4 - M5	-	11.0	18.2 33.5	9.5	157	100	0.73	68-74	16	22	R 87
						rear/4 - A5	-	11.8	19.7 34.2	10.0	164	97	0.73	68-74	15	22	R 87

1) * Reg.Cab. & SuperCab. 2)* Reg. Cab. & SuperCab 4x4. 3) option on all models.

PRICE & EQUIPMENT

FORD Ranger	XL 4X2 short	XL 4x4 short	XLT 4x2 long	XLT 4x4 long
Retail price $:	11,485	15,765	15,445	18,880
Dealer invoice $:	10,927	14,684	13,951	16,974
Shipping & handling $:	510	510	510	510
Automatic transmission:	O	O	O	O
Cruise control:	O	O	O	O
Power steering:	S	S	S	S
Anti-lock brakes:	S	S	S	S
Traction control:	-	-	-	-
Air conditioning:	O	O	O	O
Leather:	-	-	-	-
AM/FM/radio-cassette:	-	-	O	O
Power door locks:	O	O	O	O
Power windows:	O	O	O	O
Tilt steering:	-	-	-	-
Dual adjustable mirrors:	SM	SM	SM	SM
Alloy wheels:	-	-	S	S
Anti-theft system:	-	-	-	-

Colors

Exterior: Gold, Red, Blue, Green, Orange, Platinum, Black, White.

Interior: Medium graphite, Brown, Dark graphite.

AT A GLANCE...

Category: 4x2 & 4x4 compact pickups. **Class :** utility

HISTORIC
Introduced in: 1983
Made in: Louisville, Kentucky, Twin Cities, Minnesota, Edison, New Jersey, USA.

DEMOGRAPHICS

Model	Men./Wom.	Age	Married	College	Income
Ranger	89/11 %	44	57 %	32 %	$ 27 000

INDEX
Safety:	75 %	Satisfaction:	75 %
Depreciation:	47 %	Insurance:	$ 835-950
Cost per mile:	$ 0.43	Number of dealers:	5 200

SALES

Model	1996	1997	Result
Ranger	288 393	298 796	+ 3.6 %

MAIN COMPETITORS
DODGE Dakota, CHEVROLET S-10, GMC Sonoma, ISUZU, NISSAN Frontier, TOYOTA Tacoma.

MAINTENANCE REQUIRED BY WARRANTY

First revision:	Frequency:	Diagnostic plug:
5 000 miles	6 months/ 5 000 miles	Yes

SPECIFICATIONS

Model	Version Trim	Traction	Body/Seats	Wheel base in	Lght x Wdgth x Hght in x in x in	Curb weight lb	Susp. ft/rr	Brake ft/rr	Steering type	Turning diameter ft	Steer. turns nber.	Fuel tank gal	tire size	Standard tires make	model	Standard powertrain
FORD																
Ranger	short XL	4x2	2dr.p-u.2	111.6	187.5x69.4x64.9	2961	ih/rldc/dr/ABS*		pwr.r&p.	-	-	16.5	205/75R14	Firestone	Radial ATX	L4/2.5/M5
Ranger	long XL	4x2	2dr.p-u.2	117.5	200.7x69.4x64.9	3366	ih/rldc/dr/ABS*		pwr.r&p.	-	-	20.0	205/75R14	Firestone	Radial ATX	L4/2.5/M5
Ranger	SuperCab XL	4x2	2dr.p-u.3	125.7	202.9x69.4x64.8	3236	ih/rldc/dr/ABS*		pwr.r&p.	-	-	20.0	205/75R14	Firestone	Radial ATX	L4/2.5/M5
Ranger	short XL	4x4	2dr.p-u.2	111.6	188.7x70.3x64.9	3329	ih/rldc/dr/ABS		pwr.r&p.	-	-	16.5	215/75R15	Firestone	Wilderness HT	V6/3.0/M5
Ranger	long XL	4x4	2dr.p-u.2	117.5	199.5x70.3x64.9	3366	ih/rldc/dr/ABS		pwr.r&p.	-	-	20.0	215/75R15	Firestone	Wilderness HT	V6/3.0/M5
Ranger	SuperCab XL	4x4	2dr.p-u.3	125.9	201.7x70.3x64.8	3646	ih/rldc/dr/ABS		pwr.r&p.	-	-	20.0	215/75R15	Firestone	Wilderness HT	V6/3.0/M5

Total warranty, antipollution & battery: 3 years / 36 000 miles; corrosion perforation: 5 years / unlimited.

* on rear wheelsr.

Second-generation Taurus-Sable models haven't generated the same enthusiasm as did the first models. After having lost their title as the best sold car in North America, thanks to the Toyota Camry, the Ford Taurus and its twin, the Mercury Sable pursue their comet course following a major face-lift job in 1998. Ford put all its eggs in the style basket without worrying about practical features, while rivals opted for a conservative approach.

MODEL RANGE

Ford has renamed the 1999 Taurus versions. These sedans are sold in three trim levels: LS and SE as well as the amazing high-performance SHO that's a unique kind of vehicle. The station wagon now only comes in an SE version. Mercury offers sedans and station wagons in two trim levels: GS and LS. In 1999, the 3.0L V6 Vulcan engine becomes the standard engine for the Taurus and Sable and of course, for the SHO as well. The 3.0L DOHC Duratec V6, delivering 55 more hp than the Vulcan, is avalaible as an extra. The Taurus SHO remains unchanged, since it's animated by a 3.4L V8 designed by Yamaha. All models are equipped with a 4-speed automatic transmission, including the SHO. Power steering, climate control, power windows and remote power exterior mirrors come as standard items.

TECHNICAL FEATURES

The Taurus' clean, sleek silhouette improves air flow. The Taurus sedan yields a drag coefficient of 0.30, two points better than the Sable sedan - proof that more traditional, angular body design can sometimes cut down on aerodynamic finesse - while the station wagons have a coefficient of 0.34. The sedans are quite different from one another, due to lots of distinctive stylistic touches, but station wagons are more than close cousins. Vehicles have a steel unibody that's one of the most rigid in the category; this feature was a top priority during the recent reworking of these cars. The fully independent suspension consists of MacPherson struts. The front suspension was designed to maximize stability and directional prowess, while eliminating noise and vibration interference. The Taurus LX/SE and Sable GS/LS sedans are equipped with disc and drum brakes, while station wagons

Style is Pricey..?

and the SHO benefit from four-wheel disc brakes. The SHO is the only version with a standard antilock braking system.

SIMPLY SUPER

+ SHO VERSION. The term "hot rod for business executives" best describes the essence of the SHO's personality: it's a civilized sedan, but it's equipped with a highly refined and powerful engine that purrs away nicely until you unleash it by stepping on the gas.

PROS

+ FINISH JOB. Construction quality is top-notch, both inside and out. Components are tightly assembled and trim materials are more refined than they were before.
+ CABIN SPACE. These models are a few inches wider, so they're roomier and can now accomodate five passengers.
+ RIDE COMFORT. The suspension does its magic trick when dealing with road nonsense, but it is a bit firm. Seats provide good hip and back support and sound dampening is good too.
+ FUEL EFFICIENCY. The V8 that motivates the SHO is brawny, yet quite economic with a 21 mpg average.
+ VERSATILITY. The SHO is a zoomy, yet super practical car, a definite plus. The rear seatbench even has a 60/40 split-folding back, so the trunk can be extended!
+ NICE FEATURES. The center console on the 6-passenger versions that serves as an armrest and storage compartment. A neat and original

item that also compensates for limited storage space on the 5-passenger models. And of course, the gorgeous SHO V8's growl that gets the adrenalin going. The SHO cabin is lush-looking and the leather seats are lovely.

CONS

-THE DURATEC V6. It's still a snail, since the venerable OHV Vulcan delivers almost equivalent performances. Hefty vehicle weight seems to make these engines really sweat and strain when carrying a heavy load.
- TIRES. Original tires (except for the SHO) don't really help driving demeanor for they don't grip well on damp surfaces.
- BRAKES. They're not up to snuff and take quite a stretch before achieving a full stop and you wonder what Ford is waiting for to equip sedans with rear-wheel disc brakes and a standard ABS that's worth its salt.
- STEERING. When really gunning it, the SHO's front end lacks adherence. Torque is nicely under control, but the vehicle tends to waver off course, so steering gets vague. The steer angle radius is far bigger than for other Taurus models, which explains why some moves are far from slick.
- SHO SUSPENSION. This suspension doesn't like bumpy roads. It lacks suspension travel and bottoms out in no time.
- TO BE IMPROVED UPON: Stingy storage space, even if Ford added small door side-pockets for front seat travellers in 1999 and limited view at rear quarterback inside sedans and station wagons both, because of the rear window design.

CRUMMY FEATURES

-THE "PIZZA". The oval control unit located in the middle of the dashboard that contains confusing sound system and climate control dials, is pretty awful. A more conventional setup would be in order.

CONCLUSION

You can lose your shirt if you're too greedy. Ford took the fast track stylistically speaking, but in so doing, it just may have jeopardized these star models' appeal, which could put their crown in peril. You can't win every single time... ☺

RATING
FORD Taurus MERCURY Sable

CONCEPT : **78%**
Technology	85
Safety :	90
Interior space :	70
Trunk volume:	70
Quality/fit/finish :	75

DRIVING: **58%**
Cockpit :	75
Performance :	55
Handling :	50
Steering :	70
Braking :	40

ORIGINAL EQUIPMENT: **73%**
Tires :	75
Headlights :	75
Wipers :	70
Rear defroster :	70
Radio :	75

COMFORT : **70%**
Seats :	70
Suspension :	75
Sound level :	75
Conveniences :	50
Air conditioning :	80

BUDGET : **60%**
Price :	50
Fuel economy :	60
Insurance :	60
Satisfaction :	80
Depreciation :	50

Overall rating: **67.8%**

NEW FOR 1999

• Standard 5-passenger and 6-passenger cabin design.
• New-design speedometer.
• Fresh look for hub caps.
• Front door side-pockets.

ENGINES / TRANSMISSIONS / PERFORMANCES

Model/ version	Type / timing valve / fuel system	Displacement cu in	Power bhp @ rpm	Torque lb-ft @ rpm	Compres. ratio	Driving wheels / transmission	Final ratio	Acceler. 0-60 mph s	Standing 1/4 & 5/8 mile s	Acceler. 50-75 mph s	Braking 60-0 mph f	Top speed mph	Lateral acceler. G	Noise level dBA	Fuel economy mpg City	Highway	Fuel type Octane
LX/SE/GS	V6* 3.0 OHV-12-MPSFI	182	145 @ 5250	170 @ 3250	9.3 :1	front - A4	3.77	10.6	18.0	31.8	7.2	144	103	0.78	68-72	18	29	R 87
SE/LS	V6 3.0 DOHC-24-MPSFI	181	200 @ 5750	200 @ 4500	10.0 :1	front - A4	3.98	9.4	16.7	30.4	6.7	157	109	0.78	66-72	18	27	R 87
SHO	V8* 3.4 DOHC-32-MPSFI	207	235 @ 6100	230 @ 4800	10.0 :1	front - A4	3.77	8.0	15.9	28.5	5.3	134	124	0.80	66-72	16	26	S 91

PRICE & EQUIPMENT

FORD Taurus MERCURY Sable	LX 4dr.sdn.	SE 4dr.wgn.	SE 4dr.sdn.	SHO 4dr.sdn.	GS 4dr.sdn.	LS 4dr.sdn.
Retail price $:	18,445	21,285	19,525	29,000	19,525	20,575
Dealer invoice $:	17,055	19,399	17,833	26,265	17,853	18,787
Shipping & handling $:	550	550	550	550	550	550
Automatic transmission:	S	S	S	S	S	S
Cruise control:	O	S	S	S	S	S
Power steering:	S	S	S	S	S	S
Anti-lock brakes:	O	O	O	S	O	O
Traction control:	-	-	-	S	-	-
Air conditioning:	SM	SM	SM	SA	SM	SM
Leather:	-	-	-	S	-	-
AM/FM/radio-cassette:	O	S	S	S	S	S
Power door locks:	S	S	S	S	S	S
Power windows:	S	S	S	S	S	S
Tilt steering:	S	S	S	S	S	S
Dual adjustable mirrors:	SE	SE	SE	SEC	SE	SE
Alloy wheels:	O	O	O	S	S	O
Anti-theft system:	O	O	O	S	O	O

Colors
Exterior: Gold, Red, Green, Blue, Silver, Black, White.
Interior: Medium graphite, Brown, Blue.

AT A GLANCE...

Category: front-wheel drive mid size sedans & wagons. **Class :** 5

HISTORIC
Introduced in: 1996.
Made in: Atlanta, Georgia & Chicago, Illinois, USA.

DEMOGRAPHICS
Model	Men./Wom.	Age	Married	College	Income
Taurus	73/27 %	61	85 %	39 %	$ 32 000
Sable	77/23 %	63	85 %	31%	$ 34 000

INDEX
Safety:	90 %	Satisfaction:	80 %
Depreciation:	50-54 %	Insurance:	$ 855 -1 150
Cost per mile:	$ 0.45-0.55	Number of dealers:	5 200

SALES
Model	1996	1997	Result
Taurus	401 049	357 162	- 10.9 %
Sable	114 164	112 400	- 1.5 %

MAIN COMPETITORS
BUICK Century-Regal, CHEVROLET Lumina, DODGE Intrepid, CHRYSLER Concorde, HONDA Accord V6, HYUNDAI Sonata, NISSAN Maxima, OLDSMOBILE Cutlass, PONTIAC Grand Prix, TOYOTA Camry V6.

MAINTENANCE REQUIRED BY WARRANTY
First revision:	Frequency:	Diagnostic plug:
5 000 miles	6 months/ 5 000 miles	Yes

SPECIFICATIONS

Model	Version Trim	Body/ Seats	Interior volume cu ft	Trunk volume cu ft	Cd	Wheel base in	Lght x Wdgth x Hght in x in x in	Curb weight lb	Susp. ft/rr	Brake ft/rr	Steering type	Turning diameter ft	Steer. turns nber.	Fuel tank gal	tire size	Standard tires make	model	Standard powertrain
FORD		Total warranty, antipollution & battery: 3 years / 36 000 miles; corrosion perforation: 5 years / unlimited.																
Taurus	LX	4dr.sdn.5	101.5	15.8	0.30	108.5	197.5x73.0x55.1	3329	ih/ih	dc/dr	pwr.r&p.	38.0	2.96	16.0	205/65R15	General	Ameri G45	V6/3.0/A4
Taurus	SE	4dr.wgn.5	104.5	38.4	0.34	108.5	199.6x73.0x57.6	3481	ih/ih	dc/dc	pwr.r&p.	38.0	2.96	16.0	205/65R15	General	Ameri G45	V6/3.0/A4
Taurus	SE	4dr.sdn.5	101.5	15.8	0.30	108.5	197.5x73.0x55.1	3353	ih/ih	dc/dc	pwr.r&p.	38.0	2.96	16.0	205/65R15	Goodyear	Eagle GS-C	V6/3.0/A4
Taurus	SHO	4dr.sdn.5	101.5	15.8	0.30	108.5	198.4x73.0x57.8	3316	ih/ih	dc/ABS	pwr.r&p.	42.4	2.66	16.0	225/55ZR16	Goodyear	Eagle RS-A	V8/3.4/A4
MERCURY		Total warranty, antipollution & battery: 3 years / 36 000 miles; corrosion perforation: 5 years / unlimited.																
Sable	GS	4dr.sdn.5	101.8	16.0	0.32	108.5	199.7x73.0x55.4	3302	ih/ih	dc/dr	pwr.r&p.	38.0	2.96	16.0	205/65R15	General	Ameri G45	V6/3.0/A4
Sable	GS	4dr.wgn.5	104.1	38.4	0.34	108.5	199.1x73.0x57.6	3470	ih/ih	dc/dc	pwr.r&p.	38.0	2.96	16.0	205/65R15	General	Ameri G45	V6/3.0/A4

In a sense, the Mercury Villager plays second violin. Classified as being a "luxury" vehicle and more compact than the Windstar, it occupies a marginal position in the minivan market. New 1999 design modifications bring this vehicle up to par with the competition, without affecting its eternal alternative vehicle status, that of course, guarantees only relative success. Its twin, the Nissan Quest, gives the builder a pretty good piece of the market pie.

MODEL RANGE

The Villager/Quest duo was created by Nissan in the United States, yet these minivans are built by Ford at the Ohio plant. They're virtual clones that only differ as to cabin layout and exterior stylistic touches. Compared to former models, the new arrivals are 4.7 inches longer, 1.2 inches wider and the rear overhang has been extended by 3.2 inches, which has allowed for more leg room for middle seatbench passengers. The Villager comes in base, Estate and Sport versions and the Quest is sold in GXE, SE and GLE. They're powered by a 3.3L Nissan V6 that delivers 170 hp, that is 19 more hp than its predecessor, associated with a 4-speed automatic transmission.

TECHNICAL FEATURES

These newcomers still have the former Maxima platform. But the engine is the Pathfinder powerplant, with some refinements to better suit these vehicles. So it's imported from Japan and constitutes the only component hailing from outside the United States. The independent front suspension is made up of MacPherson struts and the rear rigid axle is suspended by a new Hotchkiss single-leaf spring. A disc and drum brake duo equips all models, with optional antilock system for the Mercury versions and standard ABS for Nissan counterparts!

The Villager/Quest models are the only minivans boasting of a modular seat arrangement coined "Quest Trac". It consists of middle and rear seatbenches mounted on longitudinal tracks, so they can slide and be positioned as desired. This design really helps optimize use of all available space without having to remove the seats that are heavy. A great idea that unfortunately hasn't as yet been taken up by the competition.

PROS

+ CABIN DESIGN. These two

Second Fiddle...

minivans have pretty gorgeous cabins furbished with luxury accessories, so they're geared to appeal to buyers who want to replace their luxury car rather than to commercial delivery types!

+ MODULAR SEATS. The convenient Quest Trac seat design is still one of a kind. It's really surprising that not a single other automaker has borrowed this idea for their minivans, not even Ford for its Windstar!

+ RIDE COMFORT. The cushy suspension, thick seats and competent soundproofing make for fatigue-free long-distance trips.

+ PERFORMANCES. Thanks to the new 3.3L engine, accelerations and pickup are a cut above what they were with the former 3.0L model, so overall performances are

now average, but of course, higher fuel consumption goes with the territory! At least now these vehicles can pull trailers weighing up to 3,500 lb. when using the proper hookup equipment.

+ ROADHANDLING. These vehicles handle nice and safely, in spite of the sway generated by the flexible suspension. The Quest SE is more competent with its stiffer suspensions, rear antiroll bar and 16-inch tires.

+ QUALITY. Here we have an exception that deserves mention: an American product assembled in Ohio is on a par with Japanese assembly standards. Which shows that a little cooperation can go a long way...

+ EQUIPMENT. The Quest is more richly equipped than the Mercury,

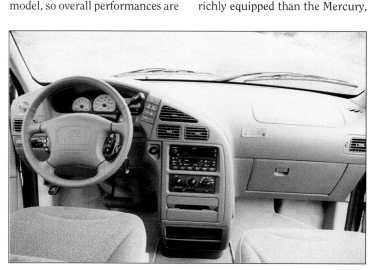

since the latter has only optional antilock braking system and theft-deterrent system.

+ INSTRUMENT PANEL. It has a fresh, new look and looks really neat. It's ergonomic and well-organized, but some controls are still tricky to use.

+ NICE FEATURES. The shelf with holding net installed in the luggage compartment that lets you stack heavy items, front door side-pockets and rear window that opens.

CONS

- SAFETY FEATURES. Nissan still has some work ahead as far as safety goes. Even with the rigid frame, airbags, standard headrests for all passengers and standard ABS brake system for the Nissan models (optional on the Ford models!), these minivans have thus far only earned rather low scores when it comes to passenger protection.

- BRAKES. They aren't too powerful. They don't dig in when applied and don't hold up too well and without ABS, front wheels tend to lock at the drop of a hat in emergency situations.

- CABIN SPACE. Even with the new-design body, cabin space is insufficient for the 7-passenger layout, since remote rear occupants have to put up with cramped leg room. The narrow cabin interior makes it tough getting around inside. Lastly, it would be tricky stuffing seven passengers' luggage into the cargo hold!

- FRONT SUSPENSION. The front suspension is overloaded and tends to bottom out on bumpy surfaces, so you have to slow down to maintain a reasonable comfort level.

- STEERING. It's over-assisted and gets light and vague. The steer angle diameter is wide as well, which doesn't help maneuvering, not with the short wheelbase.

- COCKPIT. Tall drivers feel cramped and would appreciate being able to push the seat back more.

- TO BE IMPROVED UPON. The center console that's slung too low and you almost have to bend over to adjust the air conditioning controls.

CONCLUSION

The Villager/Quest minivans are more refined and comfy, but they're still quite compact and a bit snug with the 7-passenger setup. With only four or five occupants aboard, they provide the same travel comfort as a luxury sedan. ☺

RATING
MERCURY Villager NISSAN Quest

CONCEPT :		76%
Technology	80	
Safety :	80	
Interior space :	80	
Trunk volume:	60	
Quality/fit/finish :	80	

DRIVING:		61%
Cockpit :	80	
Performance :	40	
Handling :	50	
Steering :	75	
Braking :	60	

ORIGINAL EQUIPMENT:		76%
Tires :	80	
Headlights :	80	
Wipers :	75	
Rear defroster :	70	
Radio :	75	

COMFORT :		70%
Seats :	75	
Suspension :	75	
Sound level:	50	
Conveniences :	70	
Air conditioning :	80	

BUDGET :		58%
Price :	40	
Fuel economy :	50	
Insurance :	60	
Satisfaction :	85	
Depreciation :	55	

Overall rating:		**68.2%**

NEW FOR 1999

- Redesigned body with second sliding door.
- 3.3L V6 engine.
- Reworked instrument panel.
- Modified cabin layout.

ENGINES / TRANSMISSIONS / PERFORMANCES

Model/ version	Type / timing valve / fuel system	Displacement cu in	Power bhp @ rpm	Torque lb-ft @ rpm	Compres. ratio	Driving wheels / transmission	Final ratio	Acceler. 0-60 mph s	Standing 1/4 & 5/8 mile s	Acceler. 50-75 mph s	Braking 60-0 mph f	Top speed mph	Lateral acceler. G	Noise level dBA	Fuel economy mpg City	Highway	Fuel type Octane
base	V6* 3.3 SOHC12-MPSFI	200	170 @ 4800	200 @ 2800	8.9 :1	front - A4	3.86	11.0	17.8	32.6	8.0	148	112	0.75	67-71	16	26	R 87

PRICE & EQUIPMENT

MERCURY Villager	base	Estate	Sport			
NISSAN Quest				GXE	SE	GLE
Retail price $:	20,805	25,075	26,905	26,049	-	-
Dealer invoice $:	18,843	22,601	24,211	23,186	-	-
Shipping & handling $:	580	580	580	490	490	490
Automatic transmission:	S	S	S	S	S	S
Cruise control:	S	S	S	O	S	S
Power steering:	S	S	S	S	S	S
Anti-lock brakes:	O	O	O	S	S	S
Traction control:	-	-	-	-	-	-
Air conditioning:	SM	SM	SM	SM	SM	SA
Leather:	-	O	S	O	O	S
AM/FM/radio-cassette:	S	S	S	S	S	SDc
Power door locks:	S	S	S	SM	S	S
Power windows:	S	S	S	S	S	S
Tilt steering:	S	S	S	S	S	S
Dual adjustable mirrors:	SE	SEC	SEC	SM	SEC	SEC
Alloy wheels:	O	S	S	-	S	S
Anti-theft system:	O	O	O	O	S	S

Colors

Exterior: Red, Blue, Green, Silver, Black, White, Gray, Gold.

Interior: Mink, Gray, Green.

AT A GLANCE...

Category: front-wheel drive compact vans.   **Class :** utility

HISTORIC
Introduced in:	1993
Made in:	Avon Lake, Ohio, USA.

DEMOGRAPHICS
Model	Men./Wom.	Age	Married	College	Income
Villager/Quest	79/21 %	41	88 %	55 %	$ 45 000

INDEX
Safety:	80 %	Satisfaction:	85 %
Depreciation:	46 %	Insurance:	$ 845
Cost per mile:	$ 0.51	Number of dealers:	5 200

SALES
Model	1996	1997	Result
Villager	65 587	55 168	- 15.9 %
Quest	46 636	46 858	+ 0.5 %

MAIN COMPETITORS
CHEVROLET Venture, CHRYSLER T&C, DODGE Caravan, HONDA Odyssey, PONTIAC Trans Sport, OLDSMOBILE Silhouette, PLYMOUTH Voyager, MAZDA MPV, TOYOTA Sienna, VW EuroVan.

MAINTENANCE REQUIRED BY WARRANTY
First revision:	Frequency:	Diagnostic plug:
5 000 miles	6 months/ 5 000 miles	Yes

SPECIFICATIONS

Model	Version Trim	Body/ Seats	Interior volume cu ft	Trunk volume cu ft	Cd	Wheel base in	Lght x Wdgth x Hght in x in x in	Curb weight lb	Susp. ft/rr	Brake ft/rr	Steering type	Turning diameter ft	Steer. turns nber.	Fuel tank gal	tire size	Standard tires make	model	Standard powertrain
MERCURY	Total warranty, antipollution & battery: 3 years / 36 000 miles; corrosion perforation: 5 years / unlimited.																	
Villager		4dr.wgn. 7	NA	NA	0.36	112.2	194.7x74.9x70.1	NA	ih/rl	dc/dr	pwr.r&p.	38.7	3.0	20.0	215/70R15	-	-	V6/3.3/A4
Villager	Estate	4dr.wgn. 7	NA	NA	0.36	112.2	194.7x74.9x70.1	NA	ih/rl	dc/dr	pwr.r&p.	38.7	3.0	20.0	225/60R16	-	-	V6/3.3/A4
Villager	Sport	4dr.wgn. 7	NA	NA	0.36	112.2	194.7x74.9x70.1	NA	ih/rl	dc/dr	pwr.r&p.	38.7	3.0	20.0	225/60R16	-	-	V6/3.3/A4
NISSAN	Total warranty, antipollution & battery: 3 years / 36 000 miles; corrosion perforation: 5 years / unlimited.																	
Quest	GXE	4dr.wgn. 7	NA	NA	0.36	112.2	194.8x74.9x67.3	NA	ih/rldc/dr/ABS		pwr.r&p.	38.7	3.0	20.0	215/70R15	Goodyear	Eagle LS	V6/3.3/A4
Quest	SE	4dr.wgn. 7	NA	NA	0.36	112.2	194.8x74.9x67.3	NA	ih/rldc/dr/ABS		pwr.r&p.	38.7	3.0	20.0	225/60R16	-	-	V6/3.3/A4
Quest	GLE	4dr.wgn. 7	NA	NA	0.36	112.2	194.8x74.9x67.3	NA	ih/rldc/dr/ABS		pwr.r&p.	38.7	3.0	20.0	215/70R15	Goodyear	Eagle LS	V6/3.3/A4

The Windstar is now finally equipped with a fourth door and still boasts of five-star safety features, so it's ready to tackle the second «round»...Ford was the pioneer for multiple doors on pickups, but it never imagined that minivan customers would request a driver's side second door as well. The new Windstar's are now equipped with one. Besides, in its revised form, the Windstar is furbished with unusual equipment items such as a rear radar detection device.

MODEL RANGE

The Windstar still comes in a single long-wheelbase model. The new model is almost the same size as before, but it's 0.4 inch shorter, 1.2 inches wider and sits 2.2 inches lower. The front overhang has been trimmed down as well. Ford offers four versions: 3.0L, LX, SE and SEL. Only the 3.0L version receives the 3.0L V6. The three other versions are animated by a 3.8L V6. All models are equipped with a 4-speed automatic transmission. There are umpteen equipment item variations, but all models are equipped with power steering, antilock braking system, rear wiper and a 6-passenger seating setup. The new driver's side sliding door isn't available on the 3.0L model; it's manually operated on the LS and SE, but has a power function on the SEL.

TECHNICAL FEATURES

The 1999 Windstar platform resembles that of the former Taurus. The steel monocoque body is very stiff, which explains high safety scores awarded by the NHTSA. Which also explains why the Windstar is more of a heavyweight than its rivals. The independent front suspension consists of MacPherson struts, while the rear torsion axle acting as a stabilizer bar is fitted with coil springs. The new body design hasn't affected aerodynamics any, since the drag coefficient is the same. The Windstar is unique because of its very spacious interior and a floor height that's lower than average, to facilitate access. For 1999, the two engines aren't any more powerful, but torque is much more muscular.

PROS

+ **SAFETY FEATURES.** Ford was bent on keeping Windstar's hard-

Rising Star...

earned five-star safety collision scores, which proves that the body is super-robust, even with the second sliding door opening. We also took note that side-impact airbags with head and chest protection assure front seat passenger protection.

+ **ENGINE POWER.** The 200-hp V6 now develops more torque, so it's ahead of the competition at GM and Chrysler (180 hp). It procures crisp acceleration and pickup surge, thanks to the favorable power to weight ratio.

+ **CABIN SPACE.** The really roomy interior can accomodate up to seven passengers and all their luggage. The cargo hold can be extended by removing the two rear seatbenches now equipped with wheels for easier

manipulation (a Chrysler idea that was first introduced three years ago!)

+ **RIDE COMFORT.** The Windstar ride is comfy with such a well-honed suspension, thick, plush seats and effective sound dampening.

+ **BRAKES.** They're nice and gradual and have a lot of bite, no doubt they're the best in this vehicle category. Emergency stops are achieved in less than 135 ft, no mean feat even with ABS.

+ **DRIVE FEEL.** The ride is so cushy and civilized that you feel like you're at the wheel of a big sedan rather than inside an SUV.

+ **ROBUST BUILD.** The super-stiff chassis is great for starters with such a big vehicle, the fit and finish job is well rendered and trim material is quite nice.

+ **NICE FEATURES:** The parking brake lever located to the right of the driver's seat, handy rear radar detection device, good-design hatch door handle and intermittent rear wiper. Even the base model has a middle seatbench fitted with headrests!

CONS

- **CHOICE.** There isn't much engine, body format and cabin layout choice (it's not really modular), which is a handicap.

- **LOOKS.** No doubt about it, Ford is having a hard time with its design team that can't seem to come up with a coherent approach for these vehicles, since they don't really have any recognizable family traits other than the famous oval grille...

- **SWAY.** The super-cushy suspension causes a heck of a lot of swish and sway, which causes serious understeer that the poor-quality tires can't offset.

- **INSTRUMENT PANEL.** It's been reworked but it still isn't too ergonomic. The main section is too low and its irregular shape doesn't make for good use of available space.

- **SEATBENCHES.** The middle and rear seatbenches are afflicted with short cushions and the rear one is hell to get to. They're heavy and hard to lug about. Too bad Ford is unaware of the Nissan track design that's so neat on the Quest/Villager duo. It makes the cabin so marvellously modular.

- **CONVENIENCE FEATURES.** Storage space is terribly sparce for a minivan. The glove compartment doesn't hold much and the console compartment is too low and hard to reach. At least this year, front doors are fitted with side-pockets on some trim levels!

- **TO BE IMPROVED UPON:** Off-center rear wiper that only sweeps a tiny section of the window...and not where you need it!

CONCLUSION

The Windstar has undergone some modifications and refinements to get a better crack at beating its main rivals. If it's sold at competitive prices and if it includes an economic lower-end model that isn't so just on paper (!), it has a good chance of getting a bigger piece of the pie.

RATING
FORD Windstar

CONCEPT :		84%
Technology	80	
Safety :	100	
Interior space :	85	
Trunk volume:	80	
Quality/fit/finish :	75	

DRIVING:		61%
Cockpit :	80	
Performance :	50	
Handling :	35	
Steering :	70	
Braking :	70	

ORIGINAL EQUIPMENT:		74%
Tires :	75	
Headlights :	75	
Wipers :	75	
Rear defroster :	70	
Radio :	75	

COMFORT :		72%
Seats :	75	
Suspension :	70	
Sound level:	75	
Conveniences :	60	
Air conditioning :	80	

BUDGET :		62%
Price :	50	
Fuel economy :	50	
Insurance :	70	
Satisfaction :	85	
Depreciation :	55	

Overall rating:		70.6%

NEW FOR 1999
- New body design with sliding door on the driver's side.
- Fresh-look cabin layout.
- Seatbenches equipped with wheels for easier manipulation.
- Reworked instrument panel.
- Higher torque developed by V6 engines.
- Optional side-impact airbags.
- Rear radar detection device.

ENGINES

Model/version	Type / timing valve / fuel system	Displacement cu in	Power bhp @ rpm	Torque lb-ft @ rpm
3.0L	V6* 3.0 OHV-12-MPSFI	182	150 @ 5000	186 @ 3750
LX, SE, SEL	V6* 3.8 OHV-12-MPSFI	232	200 @ 4900	240 @ 3600

TRANSMISSIONS

Compres. ratio	Driving wheels / transmission	Final ratio
9.3 :1	front-A4	NA
9.3 :1	front-A4	3.37

PERFORMANCES

Acceler. 0-60 mph s	Standing 1/4 & 5/8 mile s	Acceler. 50-75 mph s	Braking 60-0 mph f	Top speed mph	Lateral acceler. G	Noise level dBA	Fuel economy mpg City	Fuel economy mpg Highway	Fuel type Octane
9.8	16.9 30.6	6.8	128	109	0.67	68	17	24	R 87

PRICE & EQUIPMENT

FORD Windstar	3.0L	LX	SE	SEL
Retail price $:	19,380	26,405	29,705	-
Dealer invoice $:	17,977	23,771	26,675	-
Shipping & handling $:	580	580	580	580
Automatic transmission:	S	S	S	S
Cruise control:	O	S	S	S
Power steering:	S	S	S	S
Anti-lock brakes:	S	S	S	S
Traction control:	-	-	-	-
Air conditioning:	O	SM	SA	SA
Leather:	-	-	-	S
AM/FM/radio-cassette:	O	S	S	SDc
Power door locks:	-	S	S	S
Power windows:	-	S	S	S
Tilt steering:	-	S	S	S
Dual adjustable mirrors:	SM	SE	SEC	SEC
Alloy wheels:	O	O	S	S
Anti-theft system:	S	S	S	S

Colors

Exterior: Red, Blue, Gold, Green, Brown, White, Silver, White.

Interior: Blue, Graphite, Parchment.

AT A GLANCE...

Category: front-wheel drive compact vans.   **Class:**

HISTORIC
Introduced in: 1995-1999
Made in: Oakville, Ontario, Canada.

DEMOGRAPHICS
Model	Men./Wom.	Age	Married	College	Income
Windstar	79/21 %	42	94 %	42 %	$ 38 000

INDEX
Safety: 100 %   **Satisfaction:** 85 %
Depreciation: 46 %   **Insurance:** $ 850
Cost per mile: $ 0.51   **Number of dealers:** 5 200

SALES
Model	1996	1997	Result
Windstar	209 033	205 356	- 1.8%

MAIN COMPETITORS
CHEVROLET Venture, CHRYSLER T&C, DODGE-PLYMOUTH Caravan-Voyager, HONDA Odyssey, PONTIAC Trans Sport, MAZDA MPV, MERCURY Villager, NISSAN Quest, OLDSMOBILE Silhouette, TOYOTA Sienna, VOLKSWAGEN EuroVan.

MAINTENANCE REQUIRED BY WARRANTY
First revision: 5 000 miles   **Frequency:** 6 months   **Diagnostic plug:** Yes

SPECIFICATIONS

Model	Version Trim	Body/Seats	Interior volume cu ft	Trunk volume cu ft	Cd	Wheel base in	Lght x Wdgth x Hght in x in x in	Curb weight lb	Susp. ft/rr	Brake ft/rr	Steering type	Turning diameter ft	Steer. turns nber.	Fuel tank gal	tire size	Standard tires make	model	Standard powertrain
FORD		Total warranty, antipollution & battery: 3 years / 36 000 miles; corrosion perforation: 5 years / unlimited.																
Windstar	3.0	3dr.wgn. 7	NA	NA	0.35	120.7	200.9x76.6x66.1	NA	ih/srh	dc/dr/ABS	pwr.r&p.	40.7	2.8	26.0	205/70R15	-	-	V6/3.0/A4
Windstar	LX	4dr.wgn. 7	NA	NA	0.35	120.7	200.9x76.6x65.8	NA	ih/srh	dc/dr/ABS	pwr.r&p.	40.7	2.8	26.0	215/70R15	-	-	V6/3.8/A4
Windstar	SE	4dr.wgn. 7	NA	NA	0.35	120.7	200.9x76.6x65.8	NA	ih/srh	dc/dr/ABS	pwr.r&p.	40.7	2.8	26.0	215/70R15	-	-	V6/3.8/A4
Windstar	SEL	4dr.wgn. 7	NA	NA	0.35	120.7	200.9x76.6x65.8	NA	ih/srh	dc/dr/ABS	pwr.r&p.	40.7	2.8	26.0	225/60R16	-	-	V6/3.8/A4

Ford decided to add an affordable and distinctive sports car version to its Escort lineup at a time when the demand for this type of vehicle is plummetting dramatically. The ZX2 has unique looks and personality. But it shares the same catalogue spread where Ford lists all products... from the Escort family! A sleek body design isn't always enough to transform a compact car into a revvy racer. At any rate, young drivers like it.

MODEL RANGE

The ZX2 coupe is sold in two versions called «Cool» and «Hot», depending on small variations in equipment items. The first, less expensive version has manually operated mirrors and AM/FM radio, whereas the second benefits from power mirrors, color-coordinated protective mouldings, AM/FM radio-cassette player, air conditioning and power locks. Besides these two versions, there's a «Sport» options package that adds 15-inch alloy rims, fog lamps, «sport» seats, rear spoiler and a chrome tailpipe extension. A single engine model is listed: the 2.0L DOHC Zetec 4-cylinder, linked to a standard manual gearbox or optional automatic.

TECHNICAL FEATURES

This coupe had a steel unibody yielding average aerodynamics with a drag coefficient of 0.33. It's based on a slightly modified Escort platform. So it shares the Escort's wheelbase as well as several of its vital mechanical features. The fully independent suspension consists of MacPherson struts up front and at the rear, each axle is supported by four control arms. There are antiroll bars both front and rear. The multivalve 2.0L Zetec engine develops 130 hp, that's 20 more than the Escort, thanks to its DOHC cylinder head. A total weight of 2,478 lb. gives this coupe a favourable power to weight ratio, compared to that of the Neon! To get more juice when you need it, there's a device that cuts out the air conditioning function when accelerating or speeding up. Besides, this engine benefits from variable camshaft timing that increases torque output (127 lb/ft.). Disc and drum brakes can be paired up with optional ABS. Ford still doesn't offer any traction control system.

Sportscar Image...

PROS

+ LOOKS. The ZX2 has a winsome face. It has neat, clean lines, even if aerodynamics aren't too hot.

+ HANDLING. The ZX2 handles well, thanks to its 15-inch wheels that give a nice clean edge to steering and let you take curves with aplomb. Steering is a bit stiffer than that on the sedan, but the suspension generates less sway and takes the wrinkles out of poorly maintained roads.

+ DRIVING PLEASURE. Being behind the wheel of the ZX2 is a nice feeling. The responsive engine has good power output and you even feel like you're driving a much zippier car!

+ USEFUL SPACE. The cabin seats four and the trunk is quite roomy even before lowering the 60/40 split-folding rear seatbench cushion. But doing so yields even more space for storing luggage.

+ RIDE COMFORT. The ride is pretty creamy for such a compact, affordable car. The nicely-coordinated suspension procures good shock absorption. And the bucket seats are wonderfully firm. At cruising speed on the highway, the noise level remains reasonably low.

+ MANEUVERABILITY. The ZX2 maneuvers really well, due to a small steer angle diameter.

CONS

- PERFORMANCES. A stopwatch indicates that the ZX2's performances aren't as impressive as you might think. Even with its added 20 hp, it doesn't perform any better than the Escort sedan!

- STEERING. The ZX2 borrows many major sedan components, such as its «simplistic» steering, so it suffers from a slow reduction ratio.

- TORQUE. When you push the accelerator to the floor, you'd better keep both hands firmly on the wheel, for there's a heck of a lot of torque.

-BRAKES. Brakes are accurate and nicely balanced, but they're less powerful and lose their stamina when put to the test. Sudden stops are achieved within above average distances (141 ft for 60-0 mph). That's quite a stretch for a lightweight car. Four-wheel disc brakes would iron out this problem.

- INSTRUMENT PANEL. It looks simply horrible! The angular shape of the instrument cluster panel towards the left is unpleasant and the «pizza» in the middle that holds the sound system and ventilation system controls, like the Taurus design, is terribly distracting. Please give this a bit of thought!

-CABIN SPACE. With four adults on board, space is a bit tight. Up front, you rub elbows with your travelling companion and with the awkward position of the transmission clutch, you have to keep your legs straight!

-MANUAL GEARBOX. The shifter is vague and mushy, which doesn't exactly fit the so-called sporty profile of this model.

-REAR SEATS. Rear seat passengers will have to settle for a flat, thinly upholstered seatbench. Besides, head clearance is limited, so only children will be really comfy back there.

-ORIGINAL EQUIPMENT. There's no footrest and you have to check out the long list of extras to «dress up» this car appropriately! Not too many storage areas either...

- NOISE LEVEL. On poor roads, noise level is high, coming from roaring road noise and from the engine that makes a lot of racket at the least acceleration.

CONCLUSION

The ZX2 is fun to drive; it's predictable and safe. But it's far from having the sporty temperament of the former Escort GT models, for it doesn't perform or handle at all the same. When you get right down to it, it's nothing but a sweet little Escort with distinctive, slightly more winsome looks... ☺

RATING FORD ZX2

CONCEPT :		62%
Technology	75	
Safety :	80	
Interior space :	30	
Trunk volume:	50	
Quality/fit/finish :	75	

DRIVING:		60%
Cockpit :	70	
Performance :	55	
Handling :	55	
Steering :	70	
Braking :	50	

ORIGINAL EQUIPMENT:		75%
Tires :	80	
Headlights :	75	
Wipers :	70	
Rear defroster :	75	
Radio :	75	

COMFORT :		63%
Seats :	70	
Suspension :	75	
Sound level:	40	
Conveniences :	50	
Air conditioning :	80	

BUDGET :		71%
Price :	70	
Fuel economy :	85	
Insurance :	70	
Satisfaction :	80	
Depreciation :	50	

Overall rating:	66.2%

NEW FOR 1999

- Standard power function to open trunk.
- New-design seat fabric.
- Optional leather-clad steering wheel included in the Sport group of options.

ENGINES / TRANSMISSIONS / PERFORMANCES

Model/ version	Type / timing valve / fuel system	Displacement cu in	Power bhp @ rpm	Torque lb-ft @ rpm	Compres. ratio	Driving wheels / transmission	Final ratio	Acceler. 0-60 mph s	Standing 1/4 & 5/8 mile s	Acceler. 50-75 mph s	Braking 60-0 mph f	Top speed mph	Lateral acceler. G	Noise level dBA	Fuel economy mpg City	Highway	Fuel type Octane
base	L4* 2.0 DOHC-16-MPSFI	121	130 @ 5750	127 @ 4250	9.6 :1	front - M5*	4.10	9.5	17.0 31.0	6.9	141	112	0.78	70	25	34	R 87
						front - A4	3.74	10.0	17.5 31.8	7.3	154	109	0.78	70	25	34	R 87

PRICE & EQUIPMENT

FORD ZX2	Cool	Hot
Retail price $:	11,580	13,080
Dealer invoice $:	10,857	12,222
Shipping & handling $:	415	415
Automatic transmission:	O	O
Cruise control:	O	O
Power steering:	S	S
Anti-lock brakes:	O	O
Traction control:	-	-
Air conditioning:	O	SM
Leather:	-	O
AM/FM/radio-cassette:	O	S
Power door locks:	O	O
Power windows:	O	O
Tilt steering:	O	O
Dual adjustable mirrors:	SM	SE
Alloy wheels:	O	O
Anti-theft system:	O	S

Colors
Exterior: Mocha, Gold, Green, Red, Blue, Silver, Black, White, Seaweed.
Interior: Medium gray, Blue, Brown.

AT A GLANCE...

Category: front-wheel drive coupes. Class : 3S

HISTORIC
Introduced in: 1998
Made in: Hermosillo, Mexico

DEMOGRAPHICS

Model	Men./Wom.	Age	Married	College	Income
ZX2	50/50 %	35	50%	30%	$ 24 000

INDEX
Safety:	80 %	Satisfaction:	80 %
Depreciation:	40 %	Insurance:	$ 835
Cost per mile:	$0.33	Number of dealers:	5 200

SALES
Model	1996	1997	Result
ZX2	Not on the market at that time.		

MAIN COMPETITORS
CHEVROLET Cavalier, DODGE-PLYMOUTH Neon, HONDA Civic, HYUNDAI Tiburon, PONTIAC Sunfire, SATURN SC.

MAINTENANCE REQUIRED BY WARRANTY
First revision:	Frequency:	Diagnostic plug:
5 000 miles	6 months	Yes

SPECIFICATIONS

Model	Version Trim	Body/ Seats	Interior volume cu ft	Trunk volume cu ft	Cd	Wheel base in	Lght x Wdgth x Hght in x in x in	Curb weight lb	Susp. ft/rr	Brake ft/rr	Steering type	Turning diameter ft	Steer. turns nber.	Fuel tank gal	tire size	Standard tires make	model	Standard powertrain
FORD Escort	ZX2	2dr.cpe. 4	80.6	11.8	0.33	98.4	175.2x67.4x52.3	2478	ih/ih	dc/dr	pwr.r&p.	31.5	3.1	12.8	185/65R14	Goodyear	Eagle RS-A	L4/2.0/M5

Total warranty, antipollution & battery: 3 years / 36 000 miles; corrosion perforation: 5 years / unlimited.

The Accord is Honda's near-perfect world car, in the sense that it's without doubt the car that's best suited to meeting current needs everywhere on the planet. This tremendous success springs from the exceptional design blend of this vehicle, a car that doesn't seem to suffer from any major flaws since its concept, refinements and construction are nearly impeccable. This new model is out of this world, but there are still a few details to refine even further, but let's say that you can't really go wrong if you acquire one of these models.

MODEL RANGE
The Honda Accord is sold as a 2-door coupe in LX, EX and EX V6 trim levels and as a 4-door sedan in DX, LX, EX and EX V6 trim. The DX, LX and EX are driven by an original 135 or 150-hp 2.3L 4-cylinder engine, whereas the EX V6 versions are animated by a 200-hp 3.0L V6. Standard equipment for all models includes torque-sensitive power steering, particulate filter climate control, cruise control, AM/FM radio and tape deck, tilt steering wheel, adjustable exterior mirrors and remote trunk and fuel filler door release.

TECHNICAL FEATURES
Last year, the Accord's steel monocoque body got a complete overhaul and gained in resistance to torsion (+ 40%) and flexion (+ 60%). Aerodynamic finesse sits at a comfortable average with a drag coefficient varying between 0.31 and 0.32. Suspensions are mounted on two independent frames so as to isolate the body from powertrain noise and vibration. They consist of a double wishbone design, which includes 5 trailing arms at the rear. The DX and LX versions are equipped with disc and drum brakes, the LX, EX and EX V6 benefit from four-wheel disc brakes and an antilock braking system comes standard on all models except the base DX sedan. Rack-and-pinion steering is torque-sensitive. The 2.3L 4-cylinder engine is an enhanced version of the former 2.2L, but the V6 is entirely new. This new-design powerplant has its cylinder rows set at 60° and benefits from VTEC technology that provides for optimum cylinder intake thanks to electronically controlled variable valve timing. A theft-deterrent system that equips all models consists of an ignition key (without battery) that emits a magnetic code activating the microprocessor that controls ignition and engine fuel feed. This coding allows for literally millions of different combinations.

Almost Perfect...

SIMPLY SUPER
+ VALUE. It's one of the best on the current market, because of the meticulous design, careful assembly and well-known reliability.

+ SINGLE-MINDED DESIGN. This is the overwhelming impression you get when you look at this car that's so well put together, since its elements are in perfect accord, so to speak, and aimed at optimum performance and use.

+ QUALITY. Construction and fit and finish are simply exquisite, since tolerance points and adjustments are so tight. Trim materials look more noble, especially the plastic components, lovely to look at and to touch.

PROS
+ STYLE. The coupe has a fresh, zippy look and is blessed with a truly classy, original design. The sedan has a more elegant appearance and has undergone a few minor changes but has remained its graceful, composed self.

+ PERFORMANCES. They're not sensational, since scores obtained are conservative. The V6 is a beautiful specimen blending muscle and silky demeanor and the 4-cylinder engine is lively and responsive even with the manual gearbox that's nicely calibrated and provides effective braking effect.

+ TECHNOLOGY. Honda is still in the lead when it comes to building engines that emit low and very low pollution levels and that already meet tough California clean emission laws.

+ CABIN & TRUNK SPACE. Honda went out of its way to maximize cabin space so as to really and truly accomodate three average-height rear seat passengers in both coupes and sedans. The good-size trunk can be extended by lowering the rear seatbench cushion.

+ DRIVING PLEASURE. Controls are smooth and precise, for example the brake pedal and steering system, both being well calibrated and benefitting from a good reduction ratio. The suspension is crisp and competent, providing perfect directional flow, so driving one of these beauties is a real treat, with any engine under the hood.

+ RIDE COMFORT. The Accord's suspension is a well-nigh perfect blend between roadhandling and passenger comfort; it's civilized at all times, even when the asphalt goes awry.

+ CONVENIENCE FEATURES. It's definitely better on the new models, since there are all kinds of generous and convenient spots to stash stuff away.

CONS
- BRAKES. They're stable and tough, but they're rather fair to midling when it comes to making sudden stops, since emergency stopping distances are longer than average.

- SEATS. They could be more comfy, for generally speaking, seat cushions are short, lateral support fair and upholstery is a tad too firm, except for leather-covered seats.

- NOISE LEVEL. Sound dampening could be more effective, since there's engine roar on accelerations and while downshifting and tires thump heavily along over expansion joints.

- ADHERENCE. Wheel grip is far from perfect, especially since no traction control device is included for these models, not even as an extra.

- THE DX VERSION. It isn't a good buy since resale is tough due to minimal equipment that doesn't even include ABS and it's equipped with tiny, crummy-quality tires.

- POOR FEATURES: Inverted sound system and air conditioning controls, light paint shades sensitive to streaking, front center armrest that's awkward with the manual gearbox and too narrow interior rearview mirror.

CONCLUSION
The Accord is one of the five best-built and best-loved cars in the world, along with the Mercedes-Benz E320, the Toyota Camry and Corolla and the Honda Civic. As long as you opt for the right model, you really can't go wrong, except maybe on the color choice... ☺

RATING
HONDA Accord

CONCEPT : **77%**
Technology	85
Safety :	90
Interior space :	65
Trunk volume:	60
Quality/fit/finish :	85

DRIVING: **66%**
Cockpit :	80
Performance :	60
Handling :	50
Steering :	80
Braking :	60

ORIGINAL EQUIPMENT: **78%**
Tires :	80
Headlights :	80
Wipers :	75
Rear defroster :	75
Radio :	80

COMFORT : **74%**
Seats :	75
Suspension :	75
Sound level :	60
Conveniences :	80
Air conditioning :	80

BUDGET : **66%**
Price :	50
Fuel economy :	75
Insurance :	65
Satisfaction :	90
Depreciation :	50

Overall rating: **72.2%**

NEW FOR 1999
- Easier to read clock.
- Exterior mirrors that can be folded down.
- Seat fabric on the DX and LX models.
- Standard antilock braking system on the LX.
- Standard leather trim on the EX, also including heated front seats, wood appliqués and power-adjustable driver's seat.

ENGINES / TRANSMISSIONS / PERFORMANCES

Model/ version	Type / timing valve / fuel system	Displacement cu in	Power bhp @ rpm	Torque lb-ft @ rpm	Compres. ratio	Driving wheels / transmission	Final ratio	Acceler. 0-60 mph s	Standing 1/4 & 5/8 mile s	Acceler. 50-75 mph s	Braking 60-0 mph f	Top speed mph	Lateral acceler. G	Noise level dBA	Fuel economy mpg City	Fuel economy mpg Highway	Fuel type Octane
DX	L4* 2.3 SOHC-16-MPFI	138	135 @ 5400	145 @ 4700	8.8 :1	front - M5*	4.062	9.8	17.2 30.6	6.5	151	109	0.75	67-75	24	33	R 87
						front - A4	4.466	10.6	17.5 31.5	7.8	157	106	0.75	67-74	22	32	R 87
LX-EX	L4* 2.3 SOHC-16-MPFI	138	150 @ 5700	152 @ 4900	9.3 :1	front - M5	4.062	9.4	16.8 30.6	6.4	141	112	0.75	68-76	24	34	R 87
						front - A4*	4.466	10.0	17.2 31.2	7.5	157	109	0.75	66-74	22	31	R 87
EX-V6	V6* 3.0 SOHC-24-MPFI	183	200 @ 5500	195 @ 4700	9.4 :1	front - A4	4.200	8.0	15.7 28.8	5.2	138	124	0.77	65-72	20	29	R 87

PRICE & EQUIPMENT

HONDA Accord sedans	DX	LX	EX	EX-V6			
HONDA Accord coupes					**LX**	**EX**	**EX-V6**
Retail price $:	15,100	18,290	20,800	24,150	18,290	20,800	24,150
Dealer invoice $:	13,343	16,182	18,380	21,340	16,182	18,380	21,340
Shipping & handling $:	395	395	395	395	395	395	395
Automatic transmission:	O	O	O	O	O	O	O
Cruise control:	S	S	S	S	S	S	S
Power steering:	S	S	S	S	S	S	S
Anti-lock brakes:	-	S	S	S	S	S	S
Traction control:	-	-	-	S	-	-	S
Air conditioning:	SM	SM	SM	SA	SM	SA	SA
Leather:	-	-	-	S	-	-	S
AM/FM/radio-cassette:	S	S	S	SCD	S	S	S CD
Power door locks:	-	S	S	S	S	S	S
Power windows:	-	S	S	S	S	S	S
Tilt steering:	S	S	S	S	S	S	S
Dual adjustable mirrors:	SM	SE	SE	SE	SE	SE	SE
Alloy wheels:	-	-	S	S	-	S	S
Anti-theft system:	-	-	S	S	-	S	S

Colors
Exterior: White, Black, Blue, Emerald, Pink, Silver, Raisin, Blackcurrent.

Interior: Lapis, Gray, Ivory.

AT A GLANCE...
Category: front-wheel drive compact coupes & sedans.   **Class :** 4

HISTORIC
Introduced in:	1986-1998
Made in:	Marysville, Ohio, USA.

DEMOGRAPHICS
Model	Men./Wom.	Age	Married	College	Income
Accord	73/27 %	47	85 %	47 %	$ 37 000

INDEX
Safety:	80 %	Satisfaction:	90 %
Depreciation:	42 %	Insurance:	$ 835-950
Cost per mile:	$ 0.46	Number of dealers:	1 000

SALES
Model	1996	1997	Result
Accord	382 298	384 609	+ 0.6 %

MAIN COMPETITORS
CHRYSLER Cirrus, DODGE Stratus, FORD Contour, MAZDA 626, MERCURY Mystique, NISSAN Altima & Maxima, OLDSMOBILE Alero, PLYMOUTH Breeze, PONTIAC Grand Am, SUBARU Legacy, TOYOTA Camry, VOLKSWAGEN Passat.

MAINTENANCE REQUIRED BY WARRANTY
First revision:	Frequency:	Diagnostic plug:
4 000 miles	4 000 miles	Yes

SPECIFICATIONS

Model	Version Trim	Body/ Seats	Interior volume cu ft	Trunk volume cu ft	Cd	Wheel base in	Lght x Wdgth x Hght in x in x in	Curb weight lb	Susp. ft/rr	Brake ft/rr	Steering type	Turning diameter ft	Steer. turns nber.	Fuel tank gal	tire size	Standard tires make	model	Standard powertrain
HONDA		General warranty: 3 years / 36 000 miles; powertrain: 5 years / 60 000 miles.																
Accord	LX	2dr.cpe. 5	92.7	13.6	0.32	105.1	186.8x70.3x55.1	2965	ih/ihdc/dr/ABS		pwr.r&p.	36.1	3.05	17.0	195/65HR15	Bridgestone	Turanza	L4/2.3/M5
Accord	EX	2dr.cpe. 5	92.7	13.6	0.32	105.1	186.8x70.3x55.1	3009	ih/ih	dc/ABS	pwr.r&p.	36.1	3.05	17.0	195/65HR15	Bridgestone	Potenza E241	L4/2.3/M5
Accord	EX-V6	2dr.cpe. 5	92.7	13.6	0.32	105.1	186.8x70.3x55.1	3263	ih/ih	dc/ABS	pwr.r&p.	36.1	3.05	17.0	205/60VR16	Michelin	MXV4	V6/3.0/A4
Accord	DX	4dr.sdn. 5	101.7	14.1	0.33	106.9	188.8x70.3x56.9	2877	ih/ih	dc/dr	pwr.r&p.	38.7	3.11	17.2	195/70SR14	Dunlop	SP40	L4/2.3/M5
Accord	LX	4dr.sdn. 5	101.7	14.1	0.33	106.9	188.8x70.3x56.9	2976	ih/ihdc/dr/ABS		pwr.r&p.	38.7	3.11	17.2	195/65HR15	Michelin	MXV4	L4/2.3/M5
Accord	EX	4dr.sdn. 5	101.7	14.1	0.33	106.9	188.8x70.3x56.9	2877	ih/ih	dc/ABS	pwr.r&p.	38.7	3.11	17.2	195/65HR15	Michelin	MXV4	L4/2.3/M5
Accord	EX-V6	4dr.sdn. 5	101.7	14.1	0.33	106.9	188.8x70.3x56.9	2976	ih/ih	dc/ABS	pwr.r&p.	38.7	3.11	17.2	205/60VR16	Michelin	MXV4	L4/2.3/M5

The Honda Civic is the ideal all-round car for first-time owners. It's compact and nicely designed, so it's already won the hearts of several generations of young drivers who were easy to spot, wearing their baseball caps backwards. These customers have become older, but they've remained loyal to models hailing back to their youth and these cars have evolved along with them, gaining in volume and comfort so as to satisfy their needs. Finally, Honda has beefed up safety features, but this aspect has increased vehicle weight and thus cut down on performance.

MODEL RANGE

The Civic is sold in three body designs: the three-door hatchback in CX or DX trim, the two-door coupe in DX or Si and the four-door sedan in LX or EX versions. Equipment on the lower-end CX hatchback doesn't amount to much, but it does have an engine, four wheels and an airbag! The DX entry-level coupe is just as poorly attired, but it's at least equipped with dual airbags. The Si coupe and sedans are a bit more richly equipped, but the automatic transmission, cruise control (except on the Si-EX), antilock braking system (not available on the hatchback) and air conditioning are extras on all models.

TECHNICAL FEATURES

Civic models have a steel monocoque body. It's been seriously rigidified during the last reworking and vehicle dimensions have been extended to increase cabin and trunk space. Cars are heavier as a result and aerodynamics are very conservative. The fully independent suspension is made up of a double wishbone setup and the rear axle is supported by trailing arms. All versions are equipped with rack-and-pinion steering and disc and drum brakes, but ABS is offered as an extra on all models except for both hatchbacks. The Civic's are motivated by two 16-valve 1.6L SOHC engines. The engine under the hood of the CX, DX, LX and EX develops 106 hp and the model that motivates the Si coupe develops 127 hp, thanks to an electronically controlled variable valve timing system, called VTEC. For the last two years, Honda has sold engines with low and very low pollution emissions (LEV and ULEV) that

Driving School..

meet stringent California emission laws that will go into effect as of next year.

PROS

+ CABIN & TRUNK SPACE. It's now roomier, especially in the rear of the hatchback with the higher interior ceiling clearance and bigger-volume trunk.

+ HANDLING. It depends essentially on tire quality that's really very poor on base models. The Civic's are fun to drive, because they're compact and quick as bunnies. They're competent and safe, exhibit good roadability and zip in and out of city traffic with great agility.

+ RIDE COMFORT. It's quite good, considering vehicle price and format. The suspension is smooth when tackling road faults and engine and road noise and vibration are

well-muffled.

+ DRIVING PLEASURE. It's great with such accurate and silky controls, a manual transmission that's easy to use and super power steering, although it does suffer from a bit of over-assistance.

+ FUEL ECONOMY. For regular runs, the 1.6L engine is amazingly economical, since fuel consumption sits at around 30 mpg, even with the whole performance range it's capable of.

+ QUALITY. It's more obvious in terms of engineering, assembly and finish job, but the bodywork still looks a bit «light».

CONS

- PERFORMANCES. With the beefier body, vehicle weight has been plumped up to almost a ton, thus affecting power to weight ratio, so

engine performances and braking suffer. Accelerations and pickup on the sedans have suffered the most due to these modifications.

- BRAKES. They still lack gripping power and emergency stopping distances are too long and car path is very uncertain on models without ABS.

- THE CX HATCHBACK. This vehicle isn't the best choice, due to manual steering that's vague and crippled by a poor reduction ratio, a soft suspension and Spartan equipment items, at a higher price than that of the competition.

- LOOKS. Civic fans find the recent make-over more attractive than past attempts.

- SPACE. It's limited in the coupe and hatchback rear seat area and getting aboard the rear seats is awfully tricky, due to low head clearance and reclining front seats on some models that don't free up enough leg room for tallish passengers.

- SEATS. They're not a perfect example of what a seat should offer in terms of comfort. Upholstery is thin and hard and the seatbench provides less support than do front seats. Not the best choice of vehicle to take on a world tour...

- CABIN DESIGN. It's terribly blah either in light or dark gray trim and some components look very bargain basement. It shouldn't cost millions to use patterned fabrics like the ones that dressed up the last del Sol coupe...

- QUALITY. It's really not too great when you consider some materials like the plastic door trim, seat fabric or crummy radio that's unworthy of a Japanese product.

- TRUNK. It's smallish on the hatchback when the rear seatbench is occupied, but it can be extended by lowering the seatbench.

CONCLUSION

The Civic is the first car must for scads of young drivers who like this car's looks, temperament, performances and economical side. But it's mostly reliability and good resale value that appeal to them and so buying a Civic is less risky business than is the case for its rivals, even if they do cost less initially. ☺

RATING
HONDA Civic

CONCEPT :   **69%**
- Technology : 80
- Safety : 100
- Interior space : 35
- Trunk volume : 50
- Quality/fit/finish : 80

DRIVING :   **62%**
- Cockpit : 70
- Performance : 50
- Handling : 70
- Steering : 80
- Braking : 40

ORIGINAL EQUIPMENT :   **74%**
- Tires : 80
- Headlights : 80
- Wipers : 75
- Rear defroster : 70
- Radio : 65

COMFORT :   **65%**
- Seats : 65
- Suspension : 75
- Sound level : 50
- Conveniences : 60
- Air conditioning : 75

BUDGET :   **73%**
- Price : 75
- Fuel economy : 70
- Insurance : 75
- Satisfaction : 85
- Depreciation : 60

Overall rating: **68.6%**

NEW FOR 1999
- Stylistic touches on both front and rear ends as well as on the main section of the instrument panel.
- Six-position shifter.
- SiR version powered by a 160-hp engine and equipped with 15-in. tires, four-wheel disc brakes, sporty suspension, height-adjustable driver's seat, heated exterior mirrors, map lights and CD player.

ENGINES / TRANSMISSIONS / PERFORMANCES

Model/ version	Type / timing valve / fuel system	Displacement cu in	Power bhp @ rpm	Torque lb-ft @ rpm	Compres. ratio	Driving wheels / transmission	Final ratio	Acceler. 0-60 mph s	Standing 1/4 & 5/8 mile s	Acceler. 50-75 mph s	Braking 60-0 mph f	Top speed mph	Lateral acceler. G	Noise level dBA	Fuel economy City	Fuel economy Highway	Fuel type Octane
base	L4* 1.6 SOHC-16-MPFI	97	106 @ 6200	103 @ 4600	9.4 :1	front - M5*	3.72	11.0	17.6 32.7	7.8	141	109	0.78	68	30	40	R 87
						front - A4	4.35	12.2	18.4 34.5	10.0	144	106	0.78	68	27	37	R 87
Si	L4* 1.6 SOHC-16-MPFI	97	127 @ 6600	107 @ 5500	9.6 :1	front - M5*	4.25	9.0	16.2 28.8	6.6	151	118	0.80	68	28	36	R 87
						front - A4	4.35	10.8	17.6 31.5	7.2	148	112	0.80	68	25	34	R 87
SiR	L4* 1.6 DOHC-16-MPFI	97	160 @ 7600	110 @ 7000	10.2 :1	front - M5*	4.27	NA									

PRICE & EQUIPMENT

HONDA Civic Hbk	CX	DX				
HONDA Civic Coupe			DX	EX-SiR		
HONDA Civic sedan					LX	EX
Retail price $:	10,650	12,100	12,580	15,250	14,750	16,480
Dealer invoice $:	9,990	10,856	11,287	13,682	12,988	14,786
Shipping & handling $:	395	395	395	395	395	395
Automatic transmission:	O	O	O	O	O	O
Cruise control:	-	-	-	S	-	S
Power steering:	O	O	S	S	S	S
Anti-lock brakes:	-	-	O	O	O	O
Traction control:	-	-	-	-	-	-
Air conditioning:	O	O	O	O	O	O
Leather:	-	-	-	-	-	S
AM/FM/radio-cassette:	O	O	O	SDc	O	S
Power door locks:	-	-	-	S	-	S
Power windows:	-	-	S	S	-	S
Tilt steering:	O	S	S	S	S	S
Dual adjustable mirrors:	SM	SM	SM	SEH	SM	SEH
Alloy wheels:	-	-	-	S	-	-
Anti-theft system:	-	-	O	O	O	O

Colors
Exterior: Coupe & Hatchbacks : Black, Silver, Red, Amethyst.
Sedans : Black, Silver, Green, Red, White, Teal.
Interior: Gray, Dark gray.

AT A GLANCE...
Category: front-wheel drive sub-compact coupes&sedans&hbk. **Class :** 3S

HISTORIC
Introduced in: 1996.
Made in: Alliston, Ontario, Canada.

DEMOGRAPHICS
Model	Men./Wom.	Age	Married	College	Income
Hatch/Coupe	52/48 %	30	34 %	48 %	$ 30 000
Berline	58/42 %	38	78 %	55 %	$ 35 500

INDEX
Safety:	100 %	Satisfaction:	90 %
Depreciation:	42 %	Insurance:	$ 780-850
Cost per mile:	$ 0.32	Number of dealers:	1 000

SALES
Model	1996	1997	Result
Civic	281 781	315 546	+ 12.0 %

MAIN COMPETITORS
CHEVROLET Cavalier, DODGE-PLYMOUTH Neon, FORD Escort, HYUNDAI Accent, MAZDA Protegé, NISSAN Sentra, PONTIAC Sunfire, TOYOTA Tercel, VOLKSWAGEN Golf.

MAINTENANCE REQUIRED BY WARRANTY
First revision:	Frequency:	Diagnostic plug:
4 000 miles	4 000 miles	Yes

SPECIFICATIONS

Model	Version Trim	Body/ Seats	Interior volume cu ft	Trunk volume cu ft	Cd	Wheel base in	Lght x Wdgth x Hght in x in x in	Curb weight lb	Susp. ft/rr	Brake ft/rr	Steering type	Turning diameter ft	Steer. turns nber.	Fuel tank gal	tire size	Standard tires make	model	Standard powertrain
HONDA		General warranty: 3 years / 36 000 miles; powertrain: 5 years / 60 000 miles.																
Civic	CX	3dr.hbk.4/5	72.7	13.4	0.31	103.2	164.6x67.1x54.1	2286	ih/ih	dc/dr	r&p.	35.4	3.6	11.9	185/65R14	Dunlop	-	L4/1.6/M5
Civic	DX	3dr.hbk.4/5	72.7	13.4	0.31	103.2	164.6x67.1x54.1	2286	ih/ih	dc/dr	r&p.	35.4	3.6	11.9	185/65R14	-	-	L4/1.6/M5
Civic	DX	2dr.cpe.4/5	73.2	11.9	0.31	103.2	175.2x67.1x54.1	2346	ih/ih	dc/dr	pwr.r&p.	35.4	3.6	11.9	185/65R14	-	-	L4/1.6/M5
Civic	Exi	2dr.cpe.4/5	73.2	11.9	0.31	103.2	175.2x67.1x54.1	2463	ih/ih	dc/dr	pwr.r&p.	35.4	3.6	11.9	185/65R14	-	-	L4/1.6/M5
Civic	SiR	2dr.cpe.4/5	73.2	11.9	0.31	103.2	175.2x67.1x54.1	2480	ih/ih	dc/dc	pwr.r&p.	35.4	3.6	11.9	195/60R15	-	-	L4/1.6/M5
Civic	LX	4dr.sdn.4/5	78.0	11.9	0.32	103.2	175.2x67.1x54.7	2337	ih/ih	dc/dr	pwr.r&p.	35.4	3.6	11.9	185/65R14	-	-	L4/1.6/M5
Civic	EX	4dr.sdn.4/5	78.0	11.9	0.32	103.2	175.2x67.1x54.7	2390	ih/ih	dc/dr	pwr.r&p.	35.4	3.6	11.9	185/65R14	-	-	L4/1.6/M5

In some parts of the world, the Honda CR-V has beat sales records to shreds, far surpassing its pursuers including the Toyota RAV4 and the Subaru Forester. Of course, it must be said that Honda has come up with a sure thing when it designed a truly versatile vehicle that's competent and easy to drive, inspired by the renowned Honda Civic platform. By setting aside allterrain capabilities and concentrating on safety features inherent to all-wheel drive, this Japanese automaker has hit the target right on.

MODEL RANGE
The CR-V is a 4-door multi-purpose all-wheel drive vehicle offered in LX with manual transmission or EX with an automatic. Both models are powered by a 128-hp 2.0L 4-cylinder engine that's already been used on other Honda models. Original equipment is rich for both trim levels and includes in all cases: power steering, antilock braking system, cruise control, climate control and main power functions.

TECHNICAL FEATURES
The CR-V steel unitized body yields an unpublished drag coefficient. In spite of its rather high ground clearance (8.25 in.), this vehicle can't really be classified as having a genuine all-terrain temperament, since it isn't equipped with the transfer case that would give it a range of short gear ratios, nor with true-grit tires and protective plates to keep major organs out of harm's way are nowhere in sight.

The four-wheel independent suspension consists of a double wishbone setup with coil springs and stabilizer bars. Vehicles are equipped with power rack-and-pinion steering and disc and drum brakes linked to a standard ABS device. The all-wheel drive requires no intervention on the part of the driver. When road adherence is picture perfect, the front wheels do the work, but when things get slick, both powertrains are fitted with a hydraulic pump that turns along with the wheels. As soon as wheel rotation speed fluctuates, the increased pressure deploys a multi-disc clutch that distributes torque to rear wheels in a proportion that can vary between 100% up front and 0% at the rear to 50-50% on both extremities. This device acts, as the name indicates, in real time.

PROS

+ SIZE. The CR-V is unique because

Right on Target...

it constitutes the intelligent synthesis of features found on several vehicles. All-wheel drive allows for safe driving on all kinds of surfaces, seats are very straight and you can get around inside the cabin a bit as if you were inside a minivan. The vehicle has four swing doors as on a station wagon, it's easy to drive and handles like a regular car and boasts of car-like performances and safety features.

+ DRIVING PLEASURE. Driving this vehicle is straightforward and not the least bit complicated. Controls are smooth and right-on, visibility is super in all directions and the engine has enough pep to spice up the ride.

+ CONVENIENCE FEATURES. The CR-V is very versatile. You can climb aboard the cabin with no trouble at all and there are loads of handy storage spots. The fold-away shelf located between the front seats, along with the picnic table that also serves as a floor in the luggage hold are indications of how innovative Honda stylists can be. The luggage compartment volume can easily be extended by lowering the 40/60 split-folding rear seat. The dual-section hatch door is easy to use and makes for easy cargo hold access.

+ ROADHOLDING. In spite of impressive wheel travel, roll and sway are well under control and wheels grip like champions when taking curves and the CR-V is very agile in such circumstances.

+ QUALITY. Body components look rather flimsy and some trim materials aren't too great, but assembly and finish are very clean

and dependability seems to be on a level with other Honda vehicles, according to new owners.

+ PERFORMANCES. The small 2.0L engine provides accelerations and pickup equivalent to those achieved by vehicles powered by bigger and greedier engines.

+ MANEUVERABILITY. The short steer angle diameter, reasonable reduction ratio and excellent visibility make getting around in the concrete jungle less of a task.

+ PRICE. It's reasonable considering the extensive equipment included. It's quite competitive in comparison with the 4-cylinder Cherokee to which you have to add a few options to arrive at an equivalent equipment level.

+ FUEL ECONOMY. The 2.0L engine yields a decent 23 lbs/hp power to weight ratio and does an honest 20 mpg.

CONS

- STEERING. It's a bit over-assisted, but more important, response is springy which isn't always fun and coming back to center isn't automatic.

- BRAKES. They could be more effective, they don't dig in when applied and emergency stops are very long to achieve. But brakes are nice and gradual and very accurate and the vehicle stays right on course thanks to ABS that works like a Trojan to do the job right.

- NOISE LEVEL. It's pervasive no matter what, because of the cabin layout and lack of soundproofing that doesn't dampen engine and road noise as it should. Bodywork is light and the doors and hood sound hollow when you close them shut.

- LIMITATIONS. The CR-V isn't a true-grit all-terrain beast, but rather an «all-road» beauty. Poorly protected mechanical components discourage rambles in the wild, for only the gas tank has a protective plate.

- TO BE IMPROVED UPON: Some poorly located controls, shifter and hand brake that are both hassles to use, teeny tiny wheels and rear wiper that doesn't have an intermittent function.

CONCLUSION
By using a tried and true platform for starters to come up with a vehicle that's perfectly suited to most potential buyers in the new compact SUV market, Honda has aimed just right and is already cashing in on the benefits of its shrewd move.

☺

RATING
HONDA CR-V

CONCEPT :		74%
Technology	85	
Safety :	80	
Interior space :	70	
Trunk volume:	55	
Quality/fit/finish :	80	

DRIVING:		58%
Cockpit :	75	
Performance :	50	
Handling :	50	
Steering :	75	
Braking :	40	

ORIGINAL EQUIPMENT:		75%
Tires :	80	
Headlights :	85	
Wipers :	80	
Rear defroster :	70	
Radio :	60	

COMFORT :		73%
Seats :	75	
Suspension :	80	
Sound level :	40	
Conveniences :	90	
Air conditioning :	80	

BUDGET :		64%
Price :	40	
Fuel economy :	70	
Insurance :	55	
Satisfaction :	90	
Depreciation :	65	

Overall rating: 68.8%

NEW FOR 1999

• A new «Gold» body paint.

ENGINES

Model/ version	Type / timing valve / fuel system	Displacement cu in	Power bhp @ rpm	Torque lb-ft @ rpm
LX	L4* 2.0 DOHC-16 IEMP	120	128 @ 5500	137 @ 4300
EX	L4* 2.0 DOHC-16 IEMP	120	128 @ 5500	137 @ 4300

TRANSMISSIONS

Compres. ratio	Driving wheels / transmission	Final ratio
9.2 :1	all - M5	NA
9.2 :1	all - A4	4.36

PERFORMANCES

Acceler. 0-60 mph s	Standing 1/4 & 5/8 mile s	Acceler. 50-75 mph s	Braking 60-0 mph f	Top speed mph	Lateral acceler. G	Noise level dBA	Fuel economy mpg City	Highway	Fuel type Octane
11.0	17.7	32.0	7.6	138	97	0.75	69	18	28	R 87

PRICE & EQUIPMENT

HONDA CR-V	LX	EX
Retail price $:	18,750	20,250
Dealer invoice $:	17,014	18,375
Shipping & handling $:	395	395
Automatic transmission:	O	S
Cruise control:	S	S
Power steering:	S	S
Anti-lock brakes:	S	S
Traction control:	-	-
Air conditioning:	S	S
Leather:	-	-
AM/FM/radio-cassette:	O	SCD
Power door locks:	S	S
Power windows:	S	S
Tilt steering:	S	S
Dual adjustable mirrors:	S	S
Alloy wheels:	-	S
Anti-theft system:	-	-

Colors

Exterior: Black, Red, Silver, Green, Blue, Gold.

Interior: Gray.

AT A GLANCE...

Category: 2WD or 4WD all purpose vehicles. **Class :** utility

HISTORIC
Introduced in: 1997
Made in: Saima, Japon.

DEMOGRAPHICS

Model	Men./Wom.	Age	Married	College	Income
CR-V	NA				

INDEX
Safety:	80 %	Satisfaction:		88 %
Depreciation:	35 %	Insurance:		975 $
Cost per mile:	$ 0.47	Number of dealers:		1 001

SALES

Model	1996	1997	Result
CR-V	-	66 752	

MAIN COMPETITORS
CHEVROLET Tracker, JEEP Cherokee, SUBARU Forester, SUZUKI Sidekick, TOYOTA RAV4.

MAINTENANCE REQUIRED BY WARRANTY

First revision:	Frequency:	Diagnostic plug:
3 000 miles	3 000 miles	Yes

SPECIFICATIONS

Model	Version Trim	Body/ Seats	Interior volume cu ft	Trunk volume cu ft	Cd	Wheel base in	Lght x Wdgth x Hght in x in x in	Curb weight lb	Susp. ft/rr	Brake ft/rr	Steering type	Turning diameter ft	Steer. turns nber.	Fuel tank gal	tire size	Standard tires make	model	Standard powertrain
HONDA		General warranty: 3 years / 36 000 miles; powertrain: 5 years / 60 000 miles.																
CR-V	LX	4dr.wgn. 5	97.9	29.6	NA	103.2	177.6x68.9x65.9	2943	ih/ih	dc/dr/ABS	pwr.r&p.	34.8	3.0	15.3	205/70R15	Bridgestone	Dueler H/T	L4/2.0/M5
CR-V	EX	4dr.wgn. 5	97.9	29.6	NA	103.2	177.6x68.9x65.9	2976	ih/ih	dc/dr/ABS	pwr.r&p.	34.8	3.0	15.3	205/70R15	Bridgestone	Dueler H/T	L4/2.0/A4

HONDA Odyssey
Big Time...

Honda is the last carmaker to have become a contender in the minivan market. In the past, Honda tried to cut a few corners by improvising a hybrid vehicle, half-car, half-minivan, that in the long run didn't impress anyone, but now the carmaker is back on track and producing a model specially adapted to the North American market, of the same caliber as those beauteous beasts making record-breaking sales over the last fifteen years, namely the Grand Caravan-Voyager. The new Odyssey directly borrows from them as well as from the Windstar that hasn't done too badly on the market over the last few years. Yet the market niche for this product sits in the middle, between well-equipped models like the Dodge Sport and luxury versions like the Oldsmobile Silhouette.

Since the minivan was introduced in 1983, the market has evolved and undergone some pretty major changes. Sales have kept increasing, but they're going to level off at about the year 2000. At any rate, this vehicle is the ideal family vehicle, so there isn't a carmaker who can really not include one in its popular model range. The target clientele is very well defined, but Honda wanted not only to appeal to these folks, but to come up with a vehicle that would really tickle their fancy. Honda researchers thus observed that customers use their minivans in a very unique way, not like other vehicle owners. The first criterion is space, because if the vehicle is nice and roomy, it's very versatile. And the design should be modular, so as to meet everyone's particular needs. This modular concept isn't new, but not all carmakers are equal in this regard. Chrysler and Ford don't even

want to discuss this factor, whereas General Motors has included it in the specifications for the Venture, Trans Sport and Silhouette when it was a matter of redesigning the vehicle. The cabin is marvellously multi-purpose, since it can transport a mini-league baseball team, sheets of plywood, antique furniture or hunting dogs, the sky's the limit. This aspect wasn't an issue ten years ago, but today this vehicle has to be constantly updated so as to keep regular customers happy. Yet there are some essential traits that can't be tampered with. The minivan has to be spacious, but you have to be able to park in the city and inside a regular car garage. The V6 engine has become the norm, because it's frugal and very effective when paired up with an automatic transmission, another intangible element. When it came to improving this type of vehicle up another notch, Honda decided to concen-

trate on the engine, suspension and safety features, areas that this carmaker is known for in car design. That's why the 3.5L V6 is the most brawny on the market and the suspension is the first to be independent, just like on a car. So, while you're at it, it's a good idea to improve handling by getting around the center of gravity problem and getting vehicle sway under control and improving the braking system. Honda did all of this, and brilliantly. The new Odyssey is a real achievement, it reflects a new approach, treating the vehicle design less like an SUV and giving it car-like traits. This will, of course, force the competition to follow suit.

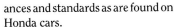

After the relative failure of the first Odyssey that was only a dressed-up Accord station wagon, Honda decided to take a high risk and play big by launching this truly competitive vehicle in this dog-eat-dog market segment. To do so, the carmaker imitated Ford's approach and opted for a single extended wheelbase model, limiting the model range to a single sports-utility vehicle. Honda took the approach "If you want to tackle a major problem, start with the easy stuff". Which meant adapting the minivan concept to its general product philisophy, by trying to get a handle on what would incite new customers to become part of the family and would keep existing customers in the fold...

MODEL RANGE

The «big Odyssey» is a full-blown minivan, offered in a single 7-passenger, extended wheelbase model and equipped with two sliding doors. It's sold in LX and EX versions, both receiving the same mechanical components, namely a 3.5L V6 with electronically controlled 4-speed automatic transmission. Original equipment on the LX includes air conditioning, antilock braking system, power windows, locks and quarter windows, cruise control, tilt steering column, radio and tape deck and theft-deterrent system with engine shut-off function. The EX is equipped with added features, namely power sliding doors, traction control, power multi-ajustable driver's seat, stereo sound system including a CD player, keyless entry system, automatic climate control, 16-inch light alloy rims and power mirrors.

TECHNICAL FEATURES

The new Odyssey's steel unitized body comes with its most vulnerable panels galvanized. The body is based on a very rigid framework integrated into the platform. The frame itself includes four circles that form roof pillars and that reinforce the structure as a whole. There are no official figures on the drag coefficient, but the vehicle's flowing lines should yield pretty good aerodynamics. The suspension is fully independent, a rare feature for a minivan. Up front, it consists of MacPherson struts with a cast-metal lower A-arm, while at the rear, there's a Honda-design double-

wishbone arrangement. Up front, generous rubber bushing reduces road interference and at the rear, a slight wheel toe has been integrated into the transverse control arms to provide a steering effect so as to withstand lateral pressure such as wind. Vehicles are equipped with disc and drum brakes and standard antilock braking device that benefits from an electronic distribution control unit that lightens rear wheel pressure when approaching wheel lock threshold. The EX is the only model that can receive standard electronic traction control that's hooked up to ABS sensors.

PROS

+ CABIN SPACE. By opting for the big format, Honda has given the latest model minivan every possible chance of appealing to the greatest number of potential buyers. You can convert the cabin interior according to specific needs thanks to the removable individual seats and the rear seatbench that can fold down into the floor.

+ HANDLING. It derives from that

of Honda car models and is enhanced by the reasonably low center of gravity that keeps the vehicle level on curves, especially with the wheel tracks that are the widest in the category. Vehicle sway is moderate and nicely under control, so the Odyssey takes all kinds of curves with aplomb.

+ PERFORMANCES. The 210-hp engine that powers the most recent Honda minivan puts it ahead of the Windstar when it comes to muscle. The Odyssey achieves brisk accelerations and goes from 0-60 m/hr in less than 10 seconds, which is remarkable for a vehicle animated by 3.5L V6 and weighing more than two tons with one passenger aboard...

+ EQUIPMENT. It' very generous, even on the LX, which explains why the Odyssey is in the upper echelon, in direct competition with American luxury versions.

+ QUALITY. It was a vital ingredient at every step of the way, in regard to engineering, assembly and finish details, since this new vehicle exhibited the same topnotch toler-

ances and standards as are found on Honda cars.

+ CONVENIENCE FEATURES. The modular cabin makes the Odyssey super-versatile. The cabin is loaded with storage areas, such as the generous glove compartment, the compartment located at the base of the console, door side-pockets and the fold-up tablet located between the front seats, borrowed from the CR-V.

+ MAGIC SEAT. What a super idea to have integrated this rear seatbench that equipped the original Odyssey. It folds down into the cargo hold floor. And when the seatbench is occupied, the base prevents luggage from shifting around.

+ NICE FEATURES: Neat details, such as the driver's footrest, a rare item on a minivan, as well as standard headrests for all passengers.

CONS

- INSTRUMENT PANEL. It's really hulky and high. It blocks the frontward view in the front seats, which is contrary to current practice.

- POWER DOORS. This is quite a nice feature, but it's more of a gadget compared to how complex the doors are themselves.

- RIDE COMFORT. Travel isn't really uncomfortable, but you don't get the velvety sensation as you do inside a Grand Caravan or Windstar. Besides, seats could be more contoured and cushier in the rear since the seatbenches are terribly flat, but even the front seats aren't wonderful.

-CABIN DESIGN. It's rather blah and depending on color combinations, it's very run-of-the-mill, so you don't get the impression of being inside a luxury, top-of-the-line product, given the current price.

- SPARE TIRE. It isn't too handy, since it's hidden in a compartment located under the floor behind the driver's seat. But at least it stays nice and clean and it's out of sight...

CONCLUSION

If you wanted to come up with a description in a nutshell, we'd say that the new Odyssey is without doubt the minivan that exhibits the most car-like demeanor and performances, very close to what you get on a Honda Accord... ☺

RATING
HONDA Odyssey

CONCEPT :   79%
Technology	80
Safety :	80
Interior space :	90
Trunk volume:	65
Quality/fit/finish :	80

DRIVING: 63%
Cockpit :	75
Performance :	50
Handling :	50
Steering :	80
Braking :	60

ORIGINAL EQUIPMENT: 78%
Tires :	80
Headlights :	80
Wipers :	75
Rear defroster :	80
Radio :	75

COMFORT :   70%
Seats :	75
Suspension :	70
Sound level:	50
Conveniences :	80
Air conditioning :	75

BUDGET :   66%
Price :	40
Fuel economy :	70
Insurance :	55
Satisfaction :	90
Depreciation :	75

Overall rating: 71.2%

NEW FOR 1999

- Brand new design minivan that's bigger, equipped with two sliding doors and powered by a 210-hp 3.5L V6.

ENGINES / TRANSMISSIONS / PERFORMANCES

Model/ version	Type / timing valve / fuel system	Displacement cu in	Power bhp @ rpm	Torque lb-ft @ rpm	Compres. ratio	Driving wheels / transmission	Final ratio	Acceler. 0-60 mph s	Standing 1/4 & 5/8 mile s	Acceler. 50-75 mph s	Braking 60-0 mph f	Top speed mph	Lateral acceler. G	Noise level dBA	Fuel economy mpg City	Highway	Fuel type Octane
LX, EX	V6 3.5 SOHC-24-MPSFI	212	210 @ 5200	229 @ 4300	9.4 :1	front - A4	3.91	9.6	17.0 31.0	6.8	138	118	0.75	68	19	25	R 87

PRICE & EQUIPMENT

HONDA Odyssey	LX	EX
Retail price $:	24,000	25,500
Dealer invoice $:	-	-
Shipping & handling $:	395	395
Automatic transmission:	S	S
Cruise control:	S	S
Power steering:	S	S
Anti-lock brakes:	S	S
Traction control:	-	S
Air conditioning:	SM	SA
Leather:		
AM/FM/radio-cassette:	S	SCD
Power door locks:	S	S
Power windows:	S	S
Tilt steering:	S	S
Dual adjustable mirrors:	SE	SE
Alloy wheels:		S
Anti-theft system:	S	S

Colors

Exterior: Blue, Green, Beige, Silver.

Interior: Gray, Ivory, Green.

AT A GLANCE...

Category: front-wheel drive compact minivan.   **Class :** 4

HISTORIC
Introduced in: 1999
Made in: Alliston, Ontario, Canada

DEMOGRAPHICS
Model	Men./Wom.	Age	Married	College	Income
Odyssey	78/22 %	48	91 %	51 %	$ 42 000

INDEX
Safety:	90 %	Satisfaction:	87 %
Depreciation:	25 %	Insurance:	$975
Cost per mile:	$ 0.49	Number of dealers:	1 001

SALES
Model	1996	1997	Result
Odyssey	27 025	20 333	- 24.8 %

MAIN COMPETITORS
CHEVROLET Venture, DODGE Caravan, MAZDA MPV, MERCURY Villager, NISSAN Quest, PLYMOUTH Voyager, PONTIAC Montana, TOYOTA Sienna, VW EuroVan.

MAINTENANCE REQUIRED BY WARRANTY
First revision:	Frequency:	Diagnostic plug:
3 000 miles	3 000 miles	Yes

SPECIFICATIONS

Model	Version Trim	Body/ Seats	Interior volume cu ft	Trunk volume cu ft	Cd	Wheel base in	Lght x Wdgth x Hght in x in x in	Curb weight lb	Susp. ft/rr	Brake ft/rr	Steering type	Turning diameter ft	Steer. turns nber.	Fuel tank gal	tire size	Standard tires make	model	Standard powertrain
HONDA		General warranty: 3 years / 36 000 miles; powertrain: 5 years / 60 000 miles.																
Odyssey	LX	4dr.wgn.6/7	134.6	25.1	NA	118.1	201.2x65.6x68.5	4211	ih/ih	dc/dr/ABS	pwr.r&p.	37.7	3.0	20.0	215/65R16	Goodyear	Conquest	V6/3.5/A4
Odyssey	EX	4dr.wgn.6/7	134.6	25.1	NA	118.1	201.2x65.6x68.5	4288	ih/ih	dc/dr/ABS	pwr.r&p.	37.7	3.0	20.0	215/65R16	Goodyear	Conquest	V6/3.5/A4

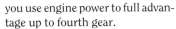

The Prelude coupe isn't the most popular model out there, but since its redesign two years ago, sales have been brisker and more akin to those of its days of glory. One of the reasons behind this is the demise of numerous models in this category, because they weren't updated significantly or quickly enough, so they could no longer cut it... By correcting the previous model's flaws, Honda chose to equip the car with sophisticated mechanical components so as to end up with a unique sports vehicle that was really worth its salt. And the original front end design was added to catch people's attention.

MODEL RANGE

The Honda Prelude is sold in two versions, base and Type SH, equipped with the same mechanical organs including a 2.2L engine with standard 5-speed manual transmission. Strangely enough, only the base model can receive an optional 4-speed automatic with sequential shifter. Original equipment items include disc brakes with antilock braking device and 16-inch wheels fitted with light alloy rims. Interior features include climate control, cruise control, tilt steering wheel, power locks, windows and mirrors, sunroof and theft-deterrent system. The Type SH version gets added leather-clad shifter lever knob and ATTS system, that is, Active Torque Transfer System.

TECHNICAL FEATURES

The most recent Prelude's body is longer and higher so as to provide more generous rear seat and trunk space. It's a steel unibody that's stiffer to provide crisper road handling, while really cutting down on noise, vibration and shakes. The new structure is 55% more torsion-resistant and 40% more flexion-resistant. Compared to the previous model, this has lowered the noise level by 3.5 decibels when travelling over rough pavement. To further keep noise interference down, the exhaust and intake systems have had a going over and wheel housings are covered with sandwich panels to reduce road roar. The new automatic transmission with sequential shifter, called «Sport-Shift», is controlled by a more powerful processor that allows you to engage the clutch in a

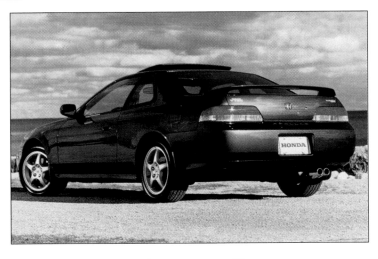

Saturday Night Fever...

linear fashion, so it's more progressive. The shifter is unique, for besides moving in parallel, it also shifts laterally so you can change gears manually without engaging the clutch. An indicator on the dashboard tells the driver what mode and gear have been selected. The Type SH model is equipped with ATTS. This system allows you to vary rotation speed and torque on the inside wheel when taking a curve, so there's no floating wheel effect and there's better control of unwanted straight directional pull.

PROS

+ PERFORMANCES. They have a bit more character than those on the former model and both versions are equipped with the same engine.

Accelerations and pickup are super thanks to a state-of-the-art engine that only asks to be revved up and you really feel the second breath it gets with the VTEC beyond 5,000 rpm., and gas consumption is quite reassuring.

+ HANDLING. It's beyond a doubt this model's forte. The well-honed suspension really does its stuff since the Prelude goes into even the tightest curves with assurance, and powertrains provide good vehicle flow and sway and body waver are well under control.

+ DRIVING PLEASURE. It's great with such clean, cohesive demeanor due to smooth, direct and nicely assisted steering and the super-quick sequential shifter that lets

you use engine power to full advantage up to fourth gear.

+ BRAKES. They're effective and easy to apply as required, so they're right-on and gradual. ABS works like a charm. Emergency stopping distances are within the average range.

+ CABIN DESIGN. The instrument panel on the current model is light years ahead of the previous one. It's logical, location of controls and dials respects good ergonomics, but it's pretty ordinary-looking, since the only available shade is black... Yet trim materials are a cut above now that plastic components and seat fabric are spiffy-looking.

+ CONVENIENCE FEATURES. The storage compartments inside the Prelude cabin are nicely located and they're a good size. The trunk is high, but it isn't too deep or wide, so it doesn't hold terribly much luggage especially since it connects with the cabin via a ski slot.

CONS

- PRICE. The Prelude is expensive and it doesn't resell as quickly or with as much profit as was the case at one time.

- STEERING. It gets light at times and seems to jerk around its circuit, a problem caused by the power steering pump.

- RIDE COMFORT. It doesn't jive with Sport since the Prelude doesn't really provide seating for four, the suspension is ruthless and noise interference is sometimes pretty pervasive.

- ACCESS. It's tricky boarding into the front seats with the narrow opening angle of the doors and the really slanted windshield, whereas getting to the rear seats is, yes, hazardous with the snugger leg and head room.

-QUALITY. Some accessories like the radio are shamefully deficient for such a swishy car that doesn't come cheap and headlamps and wipers are below par.

CONCLUSION

The Prelude is a fun car, but it's a costly and upper-crust pleasure that can't really be shared with others. It has survived the storm that wiped out lots of other models, but it lacks some assets such as cushy comfort and handy touches to make of it more of a versatile vehicle that fits in with your regular, day-to-day needs. ☺

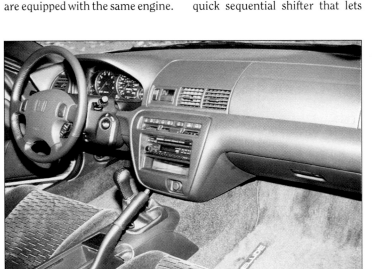

RATING
HONDA Prelude

CONCEPT: 61%
- Technology 85
- Safety: 80
- Interior space: 30
- Trunk volume: 30
- Quality/fit/finish: 80

DRIVING: 72%
- Cockpit 80
- Performance: 70
- Handling: 65
- Steering: 80
- Braking: 65

ORIGINAL EQUIPMENT: 77%
- Tires: 80
- Headlights: 80
- Wipers: 75
- Rear defroster: 70
- Radio: 80

COMFORT: 76%
- Seats: 85
- Suspension: 70
- Sound level: 70
- Conveniences: 80
- Air conditioning: 75

BUDGET: 59%
- Price: 35
- Fuel economy: 70
- Insurance: 45
- Satisfaction: 85
- Depreciation: 60

Overall rating: 69.0%

NEW FOR 1999

- Engine not needing a tune-up for 100,000 miles and whose peak output goes from 195 hp to 200 hp.
- Standard leather seat covers on the Type SH model.
- Keyless entry system.
- Climate control with particulate air filter.
- Honeycomb-shaped grille with Prelude logo.

ENGINES / TRANSMISSIONS / PERFORMANCES

Model/version	Type / timing valve / fuel system	Displacement cu in	Power bhp @ rpm	Torque lb-ft @ rpm	Compres. ratio	Driving wheels / transmission	Final ratio	Acceler. 0-60 mph s	Standing 1/4 & 5/8 mile s	Acceler. 50-75 mph s	Braking 60-0 mph f	Top speed mph	Lateral acceler. G	Noise level dBA	Fuel economy mpg City	Highway	Fuel type Octane
base	L4* 2.2 DOHC-16-MPFI	138	200 @ 7000	156 @ 5250	10.0:1	front - M5*	4.266	7.2	15.2 26.5	5.2	138	137	0.81	70	21	27	S 91
SportShift	L4* 2.2 DOHC-16-MPFI	138	190 @ 6600	156 @ 5250	NA	front - A4	4.785	8.5	16.6 29.5	6.0	134	131	0.81	70	20	29	S 91

PRICE & EQUIPMENT

HONDA Prelude	base	Type SH
Retail price $:	23,300	25,800
Dealer invoice $:	20,667	22,885
Shipping & handling $:	395	300
Automatic transmission:	O	-
Cruise control:	S	S
Power steering:	S	S
Anti-lock brakes:	S	S
Traction control:	-	S
Air conditioning:	S	S
Leather:	-	S
AM/FM/radio-cassette:	S CD	S CD
Power door locks:	S	S
Power windows:	S	S
Tilt steering:	S	S
Dual adjustable mirrors:	SE	SE
Alloy wheels:	S	S
Anti-theft system:	S	S

Colors
Exterior: Black, Red, Blue, White.
Interior: Black.

AT A GLANCE...

Category: front-wheel drive sports coupes. **Class:** S

HISTORIC
- **Introduced in:** 1979-1997.
- **Made in:** Sayama, Japan.

DEMOGRAPHICS
Model	Men./Wom.	Age	Married	College	Income
Prelude	54/46 %	31	32 %	49 %	$ 38 000

INDEX
- **Safety:** 80 %
- **Depreciation:** 38 %
- **Cost per mile:** $ 0.48
- **Satisfaction:** 87 %
- **Insurance:** $ 1 175-1 285
- **Number of dealers:** 1 001

SALES
Model	1996	1997	Result
Prelude	12 063	16 678	+ 38.3 %

MAIN COMPETITORS
ACURA Integra GS-R, CHEVROLET Camaro V6, FORD Mustang, NISSAN 240SX, PONTIAC Firebird V6, TOYOTA Celica.

MAINTENANCE REQUIRED BY WARRANTY
- **First revision:** 3 000 miles
- **Frequency:** 3 000 miles
- **Diagnostic plug:** Yes

SPECIFICATIONS

General warranty: 3 years / 36 000 miles; powertrain: 5 years / 60 000 miles.

Model	Version Trim	Body/Seats	Interior volume cu ft	Trunk volume cu ft	Cd	Wheel base in	Lght x Wdgth x Hght in x in x in	Curb weight lb	Susp. ft/rr	Brake ft/rr	Steering type	Turning diameter ft	Steer. turns nber.	Fuel tank gal	tire size	Standard tires make	model	Standard powertrain
Prelude	base	2dr.cpe. 4	78.3	8.7	-	101.8	178.0x69.0x51.8	2954	ih/ih	dc/ABS	pwr.r&p.	36.1	2.8	15.9	205/50R16	Bridgestone Potenza	R 92	L4/2.2/M5
Prelude	Type SH	2dr.cpe. 4	78.3	8.7	-	101.8	178.0x69.0x51.8	3042	ih/ih	dc/ABS	pwr.r&p.	36.1	2.7	15.9	205/50R16	Bridgestone Potenza	R 92	L4/2.2/M5

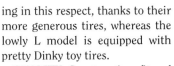

This compact car was the first in the current generation Hyundai models to reflect a radical strategy change for the Korean automaker, as to its world-wide marketing, in competition with Japanese rival companies. In the past, the carmaker didn't mind using technology that was a bit out-dated, since it could sell models at a lower price. This approach was a real fiasco in North America where poor product quality, mediocre reliability and crummy service are unforgivable. Since this car replaced the Excel (poorly named, to say the least), Accent sales have climbed up to the top model sales charts and now it's in good company, behind the Honda Civic and Toyota Tercel...

MODEL RANGE

The Accent 3-door hatchback coupe comes in L and GSi versions and the 4-door sedan is sold exclusively in GL trim. Cars are all equipped with the same direct fuel injected 1.5L SOHC 4-cylinder engine paired up with a 5-speed manual gearbox or with an optional 4-speed automatic. The L base model's equipment is pretty minimal, since it doesn't include much besides intermittent wipers, manually adjustable mirrors and radio with tape deck. The GSi/GL versions also receive power steering. The automatic gearbox, antilock braking system, airbags, air conditioner, sunroof and light alloy wheels are all billed as extras.

TECHNICAL FEATURES

The Accent has a steel monocoque body with a lightly rounded silhouette that procures good aerodynamic yield with a drag coefficient of 0.31. The fully independent suspension consists of MacPherson struts up front and a dual-link at the rear, with stabilizer bar at both extimeties. All models are equipped with disc and drum brakes, but ABS is sold as an extra, as are the two front-seat airbags.

PROS

+ PRICE. It's very competitive, because it doesn't include some vital safety features such as airbags and antilock braking. The base hatchback model gets pretty slim trimmings when it comes to equipment, since it doesn't even come equipped

Mini-Budget...

with standard power steering, a feature that the other models benefit from.

+ CABIN SPACE. The cabin is quite modest, but it can accomodate four adults and all their luggage quite nicely, since there's enough breathing room all-round.

+ PERFORMANCES. They're more thrilling with the manual transmission that warrants livelier accelerations and pickup, whereas the automatic downshifts at the least molehill and siphens off a good part of available juice, not to mention the air conditioning...Here, there isn't an ideal choice.

+ FUEL EFFICIENCY. It's one of the most frugal on the North American market, but not as impressive

as that of some Japanese rivals.

+ STYLE. It's upbeat shape and fun-loving roundish mug look pretty sharp in some of the bright shades and when the car's equipped with light alloy rims.

+ DRIVING. It's definitely more fun with the precise, responsive power steering that makes for slick moves due to a short steer angle diameter and trim body size.

+ RIDE COMFORT. It benefits from the super suspension and nicely shaped front seats that provide pretty good support, depending on the occupants' physique.

+ ROADHOLDING. It's quite impressive, but isn't as competent as that of some Japanese rivals. The GSi/GL versions are more reassur-

ing in this respect, thanks to their more generous tires, whereas the lowly L model is equipped with pretty Dinky toy tires.

+ QUALITY. Construction, fit and finish job and the type of trim materials used have really come a long way and the cabin has a livelier, lovelier look than on some rivals, although the Accent can't really hide its lowly origins.

CONS

- STEERING. Manual steering is absolutely awful, it's all over the map and suffers from a poor reduction ratio, so driving the base model is no fun at all.

- PERFORMANCES. They're very midling, for engines strain on accelerations and pickup, especially with a load.

- FINISH JOB. It could be neater without spending a mint. Some details like the trunk lining are really neglected.

- MANUAL GEARBOX. It's far from perfect, since it's vague and wavering, which makes city driving a bit frustrating, since it often mixes up first and third gears.

- BRAKES. They lack grip and lasting power, so sudden stopping distances stretch out too far for a car of this weight. Car path is rather uncertain without ABS.

- ATTENTION. Road ruts also affect car path for these compact, high-perched vehicles and you really, we mean really, have to watch out for the small tires on the base version that are Soupy shuffle slippery.

-NOISE. It's loud at all times, since the engine roars at the least coaxing, and wind and road noise increase with speed.

- ODOR. Plastic components on the dashboard emit a scent that's really sickening on hot summer days, so you have to leave the windows open to offset it.

CONCLUSION

There aren't too many small, entry-level cars on the market anymore, so the Accent has this huge market all to itself. Some aspects of the Accent will have to be remedied to make it even more competitive, yet without seriously affecting retail price. Customers are getting very fussy, especially when they're on a tight budget. ☺

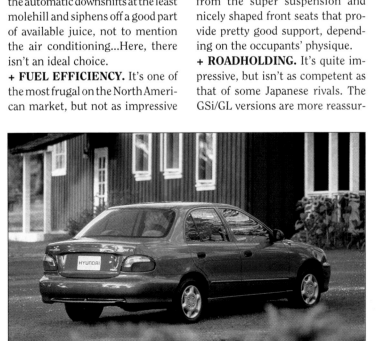

RATING
HYUNDAI Accent

CONCEPT : 61%
Technology	75
Safety :	50
Interior space :	50
Trunk volume:	60
Quality/fit/finish :	70

DRIVING: 59%
Cockpit :	75
Performance :	50
Handling :	50
Steering :	70
Braking :	50

ORIGINAL EQUIPMENT: 70%
Tires :	70
Headlights :	75
Wipers :	70
Rear defroster :	65
Radio :	70

COMFORT : 59%
Seats :	65
Suspension :	60
Sound level:	40
Conveniences :	60
Air conditioning :	70

BUDGET : 79%
Price :	85
Fuel economy :	85
Insurance :	80
Satisfaction :	80
Depreciation :	65

Overall rating: 65.6%

NEW FOR 1999

- Streamlined lineup: 3-door hatchback in L and GSi, 4-door in GL.
- Different-design rims on the GL version.
- A new exterior shade.

ENGINES / TRANSMISSIONS / PERFORMANCES

Model/ version	Type / timing valve / fuel system	Displacement cu in	Power bhp @ rpm	Torque lb-ft @ rpm	Compres. ratio	Driving wheels / transmission	Final ratio	Acceler. 0-60 mph s	Standing 1/4 & 5/8 mile s	Acceler. 50-75 mph s	Braking 60-0 mph f	Top speed mph	Lateral acceler. G	Noise level dBA	Fuel economy mpg City	Highway	Fuel type Octane
base	L4* 1.5 SOHC-12-MPFI	91	92 @ 5500	97 @ 4000	10.0 :1	front - M5*	3.842	11.5	17.7 32.8	7.3	148	109	0.76	70	28	36	R 87
						front - A4	3.656	12.8	18.8 34.8	10.2	151	103	0.76	70	27	35	R 87

PRICE & EQUIPMENT

HYUNDAI Accent	L	GL	GSi
Retail price $:	9,099	10,299	10,699
Dealer invoice $:	8,622	9,547	9,918
Shipping & handling $:	435	435	435
Automatic transmission:	-	O	O
Cruise control:	-	-	-
Power steering:	-	S	S
Anti-lock brakes:	-	O	O
Traction control:	-	-	-
Air conditioning:	-	O	O
Leather:	-	-	-
AM/FM/radio-cassette:	S	S	S
Power door locks:	-	-	-
Power windows:	-	-	S
Tilt steering:	-	-	-
Dual adjustable mirrors:	SM	SM	SE
Alloy wheels:	-	-	S
Anti-theft system:	-	-	-

Colors
Exterior: Green, Silver, Plum, Blue, White, Black, Red.

Interior: Gray-Green.

AT A GLANCE...

Category: front-wheel drive sub-compact coupes & sedans. **Class :** 3S

HISTORIC
Introduced in:	1995
Made in:	Ulsan, South Korea.

DEMOGRAPHICS
Model	Men./Wom.	Age	Married	College	Income
Accent	45/55 %	38	53 %	32 %	$ 24 000

INDEX
Safety:	50 %	Satisfaction:	80 %
Depreciation:	48 %	Insurance:	$725-780
Cost per mile:	$0.33	Number of dealers:	500

SALES
Model	1996	1997	Result
Accent	52 242	40 355	- 24.2 %

MAIN COMPETITORS
CHEVROLET Metro, HONDA Civic, NISSAN Sentra, SATURN SL1, SUZUKI Swift, TOYOTA Tercel.

MAINTENANCE REQUIRED BY WARRANTY
First revision:	Frequency:	Diagnostic plug:
3 000 miles	6 000 miles	No

SPECIFICATIONS

Model	Version Trim	Body/ Seats	Interior volume cu ft	Trunk volume cu ft	Cd	Wheel base in	Lght x Wdgth x Hght in x in x in	Curb weight lb	Susp. ft/rr	Brake ft/rr	Steering type	Turning diameter ft	Steer. turns nber.	Fuel tank gal	tire size	Standard tires make	model	Standard powertrain
HYUNDAI		General warranty: 3 years / 36 000 miles; powertrain: 5 years / 60 000 miles; corrosion perforation: 5 years / 60 000 miles; antipollution: 5 years / 36 000 miles.																
Accent	L	3dr.cpe.4	88.0	16.1	0.31	94.5	161.5x63.8x54.9	2101	ih/ih	dc/dr	r&p.	31.8	3.9	11.9	155/80R13	General	HP 40	L4/1.5/M5
Accent	GSi	3dr.cpe.4	88.0	16.1	0.31	94.5	161.5x63.8x54.9	2114	ih/ih	dc/dr	pwr.r&p.	31.8	3.9	11.9	175/70R14	General	HP 40	L4/1.5/M5
Accent	GL	4dr.sdn.4	88.0	10.7	0.31	94.5	162.1x63.8x54.9	2119	ih/ih	dc/dr	pwr.r&p.	31.8	3.9	11.9	175/70R14	General	HP 40	L4/1.5/M5

The Elantra is a sort of Hyundai Corolla, but when it comes to popularity, there's a world of difference between these two models that share the compact car market segment. Since this small, simple car got a face-lift in 1995, it's more appealing, sales are on the increase and owners' comments are more and more positive. It's no doubt the only way to reconquer lost ground due to poor credibility during the first few years this model was sold in North America. Bit by bit...

MODEL RANGE

The Elantra is sold as a 4-door sedan or station wagon in GL and GLS versions. This year, both models are equipped with the 2.0L engine that powers the Tiburon, associated with a standard 5-speed manual transmission or an optional 4-speed automatic that benefits from dual-mode function, namely sport or normal. As is the case for the Orphan Annie Accent base model, the Elantra GL doesn't come with many goodies, since equipment only includes power steering, intermittent wipers, manually adjustable mirrors, tilt steering wheel and radio with tape deck. The GLS versions are more pampered since they receive standard dual front-impact airbags as well as power windows, locks and mirrors. Optional items are: air conditioning, automatic transmission, four-wheel antilock braking (GLS sedan and wagon), light alloy wheels and sunroof (GLS sedan).

TECHNICAL FEATURES

The Elantra's steel monocoque body benefits from adequate aerodynamic finesse with a drag coefficient varying between 0.32 for the sedan and 0.34 for the station wagon. The four-wheel independent suspension consists of MacPherson struts up front and a dual-link setup at the rear, with stabilizer bars on both axles. Cars are equipped with standard disc and drum brakes and power steering. The new engine is a derivative of the previous one. It's a modern, front-wheel drive 140-hp 16-valve DOHC engine. It only weighs 300 lbs. with its aluminum block and plastic rocker arm cover. Engine and cabin soundproofing have been beefed up to transmit only minimal noise, vibration and rattles.

Handy and Efficient...

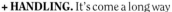

PROS

+ PRICE. It's competitive, since it's about 5 to 8% lower than those of Japanese cars of comparable quality and equipment. But many features found on the options list make the Elantra models look less expensive than their rivals, which isn't always necessarily the case.

+ LOOKS. This is a damn good-looking car. The body design is clean and has nice plump curves, especially the station wagon, one of the rare such models in this category.

+ QUALITY. These vehicles are well-built, component fit is tight and trim materials look and feel lovely. The over-all look is more attractive, so now the Elantra is more on a par with the competition.

+ TECHNOLOGY. It's simple and straightforward, yet works like a charm and it owes nothing to former Mitsubishi products. The engine inherited from the Tiburon is friskier and more competent than the one it replaced and the body structure is more rigid, which gives a solid as a rock feeling that helps vehicle control, but doesn't add much to ride comfort.

+ DRIVING. It's pleasurable due to a willing and eager engine that has good power output, accelerations are brisk and steering is smooth, accurate and quick to respond, so there's a great get-up-and-go feeling behind the wheel, although you really can't qualify it as sporty, since tires that equip the GL are under-sized.

+ HANDLING. It's come a long way compared to the early days, chiefly due to tire quality, but also due to the simple-design four-wheel independent suspension that does the trick and the stiffer, more solid structure.

+ FUEL EFFICIENCY. The Elantra's engine benefits from a favorable power to weight ratio for this category and fuel consumption is frugal at normal speeds.

+ RIDE COMFORT. Travel feel has improved with the more flexible suspension, more sculpted seats, lower noise level and fewer shakes and rattles.

+ STATION WAGON. Sales have stagnated, but it's a practical way of putting off buying a more expensive minivan for a few years.

+ EQUIPMENT. The more richly equipped GLS is a better buy and it's a handier car than the Spartan GL that's tougher to sell as a used car.

CONS

- SAFETY. The safety index for collision tests given by the NHTSA and the owner satisfaction rate are below average for the category.

- BRAKES. The standard braking system is mediocre, since it lacks bite and stability on emergency stops and the optional rear disc brakes with ABS are a must for safety reasons.

- ENGINE. It peaks at high r.p.m., it's noisy as heck and thirsty when pushed hard.

- SEAT UPHOLSTERY. Seat shape has improved, but cushions still aren't comfy enough to our taste, especially the rear seats that are flat and thinly upholstered.

- AUTOMATIC GEARBOX. It «pumps» lots of the available power and the shifter is very sluggish when downshifting, so you often have to work the gears.

- TRUNK. Volume is decent, but its narrow opening makes for awkward luggage handling.

- TO BE IMPROVED UPON: The quality of some finish details and some design touches that look pretty cheap.

CONCLUSION

The Elantra is winning over more and more potential buyers. From one generation to the next, it's travelled light years and will soon no longer be thought of as a Korean Corolla, but as a valid alternative to its famous rival.

RATING
HYUNDAI Elantra

CONCEPT : 59%
Technology	75
Safety :	60
Interior space :	45
Trunk volume:	45
Quality/fit/finish :	70

DRIVING: 60%
Cockpit :	70
Performance :	50
Handling :	60
Steering :	70
Braking :	50

ORIGINAL EQUIPMENT: 69%
Tires :	75
Headlights :	70
Wipers :	70
Rear defroster :	65
Radio :	65

COMFORT : 64%
Seats :	70
Suspension :	70
Sound level :	50
Conveniences :	60
Air conditioning :	70

BUDGET : 70%
Price :	65
Fuel economy :	75
Insurance :	75
Satisfaction :	70
Depreciation :	65

Overall rating: 64.4%

NEW FOR 1999

- Stylistic touches on the front and rear extremities.
- The 2.0L inherited from the Tiburon.
- New-design rims.
- Rotary control levers replacing the previous slide buttons.
- Redesigned steering wheel.

ENGINES · TRANSMISSIONS · PERFORMANCES

Model/ version	Type / timing valve / fuel system	Displacement cu in	Power bhp @ rpm	Torque lb-ft @ rpm	Compres. ratio	Driving wheels / transmission	Final ratio	Acceler. 0-60 mph s	Standing 1/4 & 5/8 mile s	Acceler. 50-75 mph s	Braking 60-0 mph f	Top speed mph	Lateral acceler. G	Noise level dBA	Fuel economy mpg City	Highway	Fuel type Octane
Base	L4 2.0 DOHC-16-MPFI	121	140 @ 6000	133 @ 4800	10.3 :1	front - M5	3.650	9.7	16.8 30.8	6.8	144	109	0.80	67	24	32	R 87
Option	L4 2.0 DOHC-16-MPFI	121	140 @ 6000	133 @ 4800	10.3 :1	front - A4	3.659	11.0	17.8 32.0	7.8	151	106	0.80	67	22	30	R 87

PRICE & EQUIPMENT

HYUNDAI Elantra	base	GLS
Retail price $:	11,499	12,549
Dealer invoice $:	10,541	11,245
Shipping & handling $:	435	435
Automatic transmission:	O	O
Cruise control:	O	O
Power steering:	S	S
Anti-lock brakes:	-	O
Traction control:	-	-
Air conditioning:	O	O
Leather:	-	-
AM/FM/radio-cassette:	S	S
Power door locks:	-	S
Power windows:	-	S
Tilt steering:	S	S
Dual adjustable mirrors:	SM	SE
Alloy wheels:	-	O
Anti-theft system:	-	-

Colors

Exterior: Green, Red, White, Black, Sandal, Blue, Gray.

Interior: Gray, Beige.

AT A GLANCE...

Category: front-wheel drive compact sedans & wagons. **Class :** 3

HISTORIC
Introduced in:	1991-1995
Made in:	Ulsan, South Korea

DEMOGRAPHICS
Model	Men./Wom.	Age	Married	College	Income
Elantra	62/38 %	43	64 %	33 %	$ 25 000

INDEX
Safety:	60 %	Satisfaction:	68 %
Depreciation:	50 %	Insurance:	$775
Cost per mile:	$ 0.42	Number of dealers:	500

SALES
Model	1996	1997	Result
Elantra	39 801	40 303	+ 3.8 %

MAIN COMPETITORS
CHEVROLET Cavalier, FORD Escort, HONDA Civic, MAZDA Protegé, NISSAN Sentra, PONTIAC Sunfire, SATURN SL1/SL2, SUBARU Impreza, TOYOTA Corolla, VW Golf, Jetta.

MAINTENANCE REQUIRED BY WARRANTY
First revision:	Frequency:	Diagnostic plug:
3 000 miles	3 mois/3 000 miles	No

SPECIFICATIONS

General warranty: 3 years / 36 000 miles; powertrain: 5 years / 60 000 miles; corrosion perforation: 5 years / 60 000 miles; antipollution: 5 years / 36 000 miles.

Model	Version Trim	Body/ Seats	Interior volume cu ft	Trunk volume cu ft	Cd	Wheel base in	Lght x Wdgth x Hght in x in x in	Curb weight lb	Susp. ft/rr	Brake ft/rr	Steering type	Turning diameter ft	Steer. turns nber.	Fuel tank gal	tire size	Standard tires make	model	Standard powertrain
HYUNDAI																		
Elantra	base	4dr.sdn.4/5	93.6	11.4	0.32	100.4	174.0x66.9x54.9	2522	ih/ih	dc/dr	pwr.r&p.	32.5	3.02	14.5	175/65R14	Michelin	XGT+4	L4/2.0/M5
Elantra	base	4dr.wgn.4/5	94.6	32.3	0.34	100.4	175.2x66.9x58.8	2619	ih/ih	dc/dr	pwr.r&p.	32.5	3.02	14.5	175/65R14	Michelin	XGT+4	L4/2.0/M5
Elantra	GLS	4dr.sdn.4/5	93.6	11.4	0.32	100.4	174.0x66.9x54.9	2586	ih/ih	dc/dr	pwr.r&p.	32.5	3.02	14.5	195/60R14	Michelin	XGT+4	L4/2.0/M5
Elantra	GLS	4dr.wgn.4/5	94.6	32.3	0.34	100.4	175.2x66.9x58.8	2685	ih/ih	dc/dr	pwr.r&p.	32.5	3.02	14.5	195/60R14	Michelin	XGT+4	L4/2.0/M5

HYUNDAI Sonata
On The Right Track...

The Sonata is an affordable car, but sales aren't mind-boggling. This situation could no doubt be turned around if the new model proves to be really comparable to cars produced by Japanese carmakers who have a monopoly on the mid-size automobile market segment. The Honda Accord and Toyota Camry are the biggest stars in that segment, so the Korean firm is going to have a tough time convincing customers that they've come up with a car that benefits from the same high tech features as those built by the two Japanese, since American carmakers are trying to copy same, but so far, such an endeavor has not been a piece of cake. Nevertheless, Hyundai has come up with a much-improved product, since the latest Sonata model is equipped with a brand new automatic transmission and two spanking new engines.

But it's the new Sonata's looks that first grab your attention. In fact, its design is quite different from that of models that have snubbed the rounded «bio» look and opted for a lean, sleek «Edge» silhouette reintroduced by Ford. The car has a nice, cohesive grace about it, but it's the rear end stylistics that add the most character with an attempt made to blend the various vehicle sections into a classic, but mod appearance. Front headlamp and grille details give a bit of an agressive look to car that the automaker qualifies as sporty, but at any rate it's dynamic. Even though Hyundai states that the Sonata has undergone umpteen wind tunnel tests to refine its aerodynamic finesse, there is no official figure disclosed that could prove the truth of this statement. Designers were guided by several criteria. They wanted to create a car that had luxury looks and exuded a

sensation of space, carefully crafted ergonomics and meticulous treatment when it came down to details. This approach is reflected in the large window surfaces that make the cabin look roomier. Inside the cabin, the instrument panel has been redesigned to be as rational and ergonomic as possible. The design is really neat-looking with its rounded shapes and clean layout and the buffed plastic looks attractive, even if the wood appliqués on the main section are a bit overdone. It's a shame Hyundai didn't see fit to equip all Sonata's with the pollen filter. Do only the wealthy suffer from allergies? At any rate, the over-all effect is less chintzy-looking than on the previous model and color shades and textures used add to this impression. On the technical level, the update consisted of redesigning the suspensions to improve handling and ride comfort and that's why all models now come

with gas-filled shocks. The engine design has progressed as well, since it's covered with a guard that accents the intake manifold, like you see on upper-crust cars. No doubt about it, Hyundai's good intentions will spark interest for the Sonata if product quality, and above all reliability, are on a par with attributes of Japanese rivals. In this very competitive, top of the heap market, you have to be serious and confident enough to establish long-term bonds with customers, so as to get the good news out and reinstate the vehicle's reputation.

You have to hand it to the Koreans. If there's one quality they have, it's being stubborn and never giving up. For more than fifteen years, the Hyundai firm has been having a hard time in North America, but now it's about to finally reach its objective, namely to become a respected automaker on an equal footing with the Japanese. The Hyundai Pony era is long gone. One look at the new Sonata will convince you. The Korean giant has gone from being an economy car producer to achieving rival status in comparison with the big Nipponese automakers, and in more ways than one. The new Sonata is proof of same, with its significantly improved finish job, original design and modern, winsome looks.

MODEL RANGE

The Sonata is an intermediate sedan offered in two trim levels: GL and GLS. The first receives a 2.4L DOHC 4-in-line engine (instead of the 2.0L on the previous Sonata) and the second gets a «small» 2.5L DOHC V6 (instead of a 3.0L). The only transmission available is a 4-speed automatic transmission with overdrive. The cabin can seat five adults. Original equipment is fairly extensive and includes, among other items, power steering, power windows, cruise control, intermittent-function wipers, climate control, height-adjustable driver's seat and a 60/40 split-folding rear seatbench. The GLS differs, apart from its engine, in respect to other items: more posh cabin and accessories like a pollen air filter, sound system with tape deck and CD player, alloy wheels, faux-bois trim, bucket seat with adjustable lumbar support for the driver and 15-inch Michelin tires. Leather-clad seats and sunroof are listed as extras.

TECHNICAL FEATURES

The Sonata's steel unibody is built on the same platform as the previous model. The wheelbase is the same length, but wheel tracks have been widened by 1 inch up front and 0.8 inch at the rear. The body has gained 0.4 inch lengthwise, almost 2 inches in height and 0.2 in width. Besides these modifications to the exterior dimensions, the cabin on the new model offers more head room up front (+ 0.7 inch), less shoulder (- 1.3 inch) and hip room (-2 inches), but more leg room. In the rear seats, there's less head room

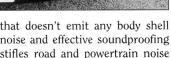

(-1.2 inch), less shoulder (-0.7 inch) and hip room (-2.7 inches) as well as less room to stretch your legs (-0.4 inch). There's a four-wheel independent suspension. Hyundai now uses a double wishbone set up at the front, rather than MacPherson struts. But at the rear, the multilink system on the previous model has been maintained and there are stabilizer bars both front and rear. The GL model has four oil dampers and those on the GLS are nitrogen-fed. A disc and drum duo takes care of braking on the GL, while the GLX benefits from four disc brakes. Antilock braking and traction control systems are sold as extras exclusively on the GLS. Safety-wise, Hyundai offers optional side-impact airbags for front seat passengers. On the other hand, standard equipment on both models includes a «passenger detector», a new device that deactivates the airbag on the front passenger side when no one is occupying this seat as well as pretension seatbelts up front.

PROS

+ SOUNDPROOFING. The new Sonata has a much more rigid chassis that doesn't emit any body shell noise and effective soundproofing stifles road and powertrain noise like a champion.

+ TRUNK. The 60/40 split-folding rear seatbench lets you extend the trunk and trunk access is great with the wide, nicely shaped lid.

+ V6 ENGINE. The new V6 delivers 21 more hp, is super smooth and achieves honorable performances, given the family orientation of this sedan.

+ AUTOMATIC GEARBOX. The transmission is very smooth, literally hiding gear shifts and it offers a bit of breaking effect when downshifting.

+ RIDE. The suspension takes care of road bumps and such and keeps vehicle sway pretty well under control.

+ BRAKES. The GLS' four disc brakes are reassuring and you can apply them nice and gradually, just as needed!

+ REAR SEATS. There may be a few inches less space, but rear seat adult passengers will have adequate room in all directions.

+ STYLE. The Sonata's new body design gives it a unique character, so you don't confuse it with rivals. The front end look is original, but the rear end is sensational. In fact, the trunk profile, contrary to the current trend, isn't too high and doesn't bulge at the top, so it doesn't obstruct rearward view.

CONS

- ACCESS. It's tricky boarding up front because doors don't open wide enough and the back cushions on the seats bulge out so much that you have trouble getting past or around them!

- A MISSING FEATURE. This car isn't equipped with an alarm chime to indicate that you've forgotten to turn off the headlights when you turn off the engine. This will no doubt cause many an accidental battery discharge in the wintertime...

- STEERING. It's light and vague at center when driving straight ahead and when making quick lane changes, due partly to over-assistance.

- TRANSMISSION. The kickdown isn't instantaneous. You have to allow for a time response delay when you want some braking effect or to accelerate so as to pass safely and quickly on the highway.

- TIRES. Compared to the 15-inch Michelin MXV4 tires that equip the GLS, the original Hankook and Kumho tires strip this car of some of its class.

- BRAKES. It's too bad you have to opt for the upper-end GLS to be able to benefit from antilock braking and traction control that aren't billed as extras, but come as standard equipment on this model!

- TO BE IMPROVED UPON: The trunk is skimpy height-wise, so you have to place some objects flat on their side and radio controls located underneath the climate control dials.

CONCLUSION

With its elegant and unusual body design, the latest Sonata stands out from the competition and will cause quite a stir in the streets. It has admirable attributes such as sturdy build, clean finish job and spiffy trimmings. Enough to get us comparing it to several Nipponese models, with its more competitive price in mind. ☺

RATING
HYUNDAI Sonata

CONCEPT :		70%
Technology	75	
Safety :	75	
Interior space :	70	
Trunk volume:	55	
Quality/fit/finish :	75	

DRIVING:		62%
Cockpit :	80	
Performance :	45	
Handling :	55	
Steering :	75	
Braking :	55	

ORIGINAL EQUIPMENT:		72%
Tires :	75	
Headlights :	75	
Wipers :	75	
Rear defroster :	65	
Radio :	70	

COMFORT :		68%
Seats :	75	
Suspension :	70	
Sound level:	50	
Conveniences :	70	
Air conditioning :	75	

BUDGET :		64%
Price :	50	
Fuel economy :	70	
Insurance :	75	
Satisfaction :	75	
Depreciation :	50	

Overall rating:		67.2%

NEW FOR 1999
- **Reworked model based on the previous model's platform.**
- **Two new engines: a 2.4L 4-cyliner and a 2.5L V6 paired up exclusively with a new four-speed automatic transmission.**
- **«Passenger detector» device that prevents the front passenger-side airbag from deploying if no one is occupying this seat.**
- **Pollen filter on the GLS.**

ENGINES / TRANSMISSIONS / PERFORMANCES

Model/ version	Type / timing valve / fuel system	Displacement cu in	Power bhp @ rpm	Torque lb-ft @ rpm	Compres. ratio	Driving wheels / transmission	Final ratio	Acceler. 0-60 mph s	Standing 1/4 & 5/8 mile s	Acceler. 50-75 mph s	Braking 60-0 mph f	Top speed mph	Lateral acceler. G	Noise level dBA	Fuel economy mpg City	Highway	Fuel type Octane
GL	L4 2.4 DOHC-16-MPFI	143	148 @ 5500	156 @ 3000	10.0 :1	front - A4	3.77	11.0	17.6	31.8	7.8	148	112	0.78	68	20	29	R 87
GLS	V6 2.5 DOHC-24-MPFI	152	163 @ 6000	167 @ 4000	10.0 :1	front - A4	3.77	10.0	17.3	30.8	6.9	144	124	0.78	67	20	29	R 87

PRICE & EQUIPMENT

HYUNDAI Sonata	GL	GLS
Retail price $:	15,500	19,500
Dealer invoice $:	-	-
Shipping & handling $:	435	435
Automatic transmission:	S	S
Cruise control:	S	S
Power steering:	S	S
Anti-lock brakes:	-	O
Traction control:	-	O
Air conditioning:	S	S
Leather:	-	O
AM/FM/radio-cassette:	S	SCD
Power door locks:	S	S
Power windows:	S	S
Tilt steering:	S	S
Dual adjustable mirrors:	SEH	SEH
Alloy wheels:	-	S
Anti-theft system:		

Colors
Exterior: Cherry, Black, Green, Silver, Gray, White.

Interior: Gray-brown.

AT A GLANCE...

Category: front-wheel drive mid-sise sedans.　Class : 5

HISTORIC
Introduced in: 1989-1994-1999
Made in: Ulsan, South Korea

DEMOGRAPHICS

Model	Men./Wom.	Age	Married	College	Income
Sonata	81/19 %	49	78 %	41 %	$ 30 000

INDEX

Safety:	80 %	Satisfaction:	73 %
Depreciation:	52 %	Insurance:	$ 785
Cost per mile:	$0.47	Number of dealers:	500

SALES

Model	1996	1997	Result
Sonata	14 616	22 128	+ 51.4 %

MAIN COMPETITORS
CHEVROLET Malibu, CHRYSLER Cirrus, DODGE Stratus, FORD Contour-Taurus, HONDA Accord, MAZDA 626, MERCURY Mystique-Sable, NISSAN Altima-Maxima, OLDSMOBILE Alero, PONTIAC Grand Am, SUBARU Legacy, TOYOTA Camry, VOLKSWAGEN Passat.

MAINTENANCE REQUIRED BY WARRANTY

First revision:	Frequency:	Diagnostic plug:
3 000 miles	3 mois/3 000 miles	No

SPECIFICATIONS

Model	Version Trim	Body/ Seats	Interior volume cu ft	Trunk volume cu ft	Cd	Wheel base in	Lght x Wdgth x Hght in x in x in	Curb weight lb	Susp. ft/rr	Brake ft/rr	Steering type	Turning diameter ft	Steer. turns nber.	Fuel tank gal	tire size	Standard tires make	model	Standard powertrain
HYUNDAI	General warranty: 3 years / 36 000 miles; powertrain: 5 years / 60 000 miles; corrosion perforation: 5 years / 60 000 miles; antipollution: 5 years / 36 000 miles.																	
Sonata	GL	4dr.sdn.5	-	13.2	-	106.3	185.4x71.6x55.5	3106	ih/ih	dc/dr	pwr.r&p.	34.5	2.92	17.2	195/70R14	Hankook	-	L4/2.4/A4
Sonata	GLS	4dr.sdn.5	-	13.2	-	106.3	185.4x71.6x55.5	3106	ih/ih	dc/dc	pwr.r&p.	34.5	2.92	17.2	205/60R15	Michelin	MXV4	V6/2.5/A4

Since its introduction two years ago, this little "shark" has had quite an appetite, since it's swallowed up several rivals in the entry-level sports coupe bracket. It's no surprise, really, because ever since Hyundai decided to use quality and daring as its strong suits, you can sense a generalized change of attitude towards this Korean firm. You must admit that the ritziest Tiburon model body design sure knocks your socks off and it's infinitely more affordable than other models, budget-wise.

MODEL RANGE
The Tiburon sports coupe is sold in two trim levels: a base model equipped with a 1.8L 4-cylinder engine or FX powered by a 2.0L engine. The base model's original equipment items include power steering, adjustable mirrors and steering wheel, power windows and a radio with tape deck. The FX gets added power locks, higher-caliber stereo sound system, light alloy wheels, rear spoiler (shark fin?) and rear wiper, rear-wheel disc brakes and fog lamps. Only the FX version can be equipped with the Touring options package, including four-channel ABS, variable assist steering and leather seats.

TECHNICAL FEATURES
The Tiburon is inspired by the Elantra platform. Its style derives from those exhibited based on the various designs for the HCD III concept car that Hyundai took on a world tour. The general public simply loved this car, so the automaker decided to build it. The steel monocoque body has sleek, flowing lines but it only has a fair to midling aerodynamic prowess with a drag coefficient of only 0.33. The four-wheel indepent suspension is made up of MacPherson struts up front and a dual-link setup at the rear along with gas-filled shocks. The base model is equipped with disc and drum brakes, wheras the FX benefits from four-wheel disc brakes, but the antilock braking system is sold as an extra. The 16-valve DOHC Beta engine was developed exclusively by Hyundai engineers. It's equipped with electronic fuel-injection, automatically adjusting hydraulic valve lifters, dual-port fuel injectors and an electronic distributorless ignition system. The 130-hp 1.8L and 140-hp 2.0L provide all the muscle and torque re-

Recognized...

quired. As for the automatic gearbox, it's equipped with a new technological feature called electronic control feedback to improve gear selection.

PROS
+ **STYLE.** It's nervous and very «muscular» with forms that seem to be sculpted by the very wind, an agressive-looking airscoop and rounded, aerodynamic lines that give it an unmistakable Tiburon appearance.

+ **DRIVING.** This car zips nimbly around, even with its front-wheel drive, and this is true for both versions. Engine and car response are lively and crisp, so you can take curves with ease and steering responds beautifully in this situation, so handling is taut and clean. The

outward view is generous with the thin roof supports, high windshield and frameless windows.

+ **PERFORMANCES.** The 2.0L is really the only engine that deserves to really be called sporty but with some reservations, since figures obtained for accelerations and pickup are comparable to those of the Elantra. But it provides enough torque to give you a thrill, even with the automatic.

+ **HANDLING.** It's competent because of the well-honed suspension developed in association with Porsche and good-quality original tires.

+ **RIDE COMFORT.** It's pretty amazing for a vehicle of this type. The cabin is roomy up front and front seats provide excellent lateral

support and noise interference is quite discreet at cruising speed.

+ **VALUE.** The price/equipment ratio is interesting, especially for the FX that's the faster car and easier to resell as a used car.

+ **CABIN DESIGN.** It's pretty trim and looks a bit like the first Eagle Talon interior with its asymmetrical instrument panel and the white-on-black analog instruments that are easy to read.

+ **CABIN SPACE.** It's average for the category thanks to the longer wheelbase and wide wheel tracks. Yet front seat passengers have more breathing room than the poor folks in the rear seats that should be used only in a pinch, as is always the case on this type of vehicle.

+ **CONVENIENCE FEATURES.** This isn't a usual feature for this type of car, but it hasn't been overlooked since there are lots of handy storage spots here and there throughout the cabin and the modular trunk can hold an adequate amount of luggage.

CONS
- **ERGONOMICS.** The instrument panel isn't too great in this regard, for the main section curves inward rather than outward, so you have to lean forward to reach some controls such as the radio and air conditioning dials, that are in reverse order.

- **REAR SEATS.** They're more suitable for small children than for adults, for leg and head room are too snug and getting aboard is rather dangerous.

- **PERFORMANCES.** There's nothing exotic about the base model's capabilities, so you'll have to use this engine with a manual gearbox, otherwise you'll be passed on the highway by drivers out for a 4X4 frolic...

- **GLARE.** The instrument panel reflecting up into the windshield and the reflecting glass on the instruments are distracting and tiring on really sunny days.

CONCLUSION
By electing the Tiburon by a large majority, the public has let Hyundai know that they're aware that progress has been made and that they want to encourage the carmaker to continue in the same direction, that sooner or later will lead to a major breakthrough. ☺

RATING
HYUNDAI Tiburon

CONCEPT : **64%**
Technology	80
Safety :	70
Interior space :	40
Trunk volume:	55
Quality/fit/finish :	75

DRIVING: **67%**
Cockpit :	80
Performance :	60
Handling :	60
Steering :	80
Braking :	55

ORIGINAL EQUIPMENT: **76%**
Tires :	80
Headlights :	75
Wipers :	75
Rear defroster :	70
Radio :	80

COMFORT : **73%**
Seats :	80
Suspension :	70
Sound level:	60
Conveniences :	80
Air conditioning :	75

BUDGET : **61%**
Price :	70
Fuel economy :	75
Insurance :	55
Satisfaction :	75
Depreciation :	30

Overall rating: **68.2%**

NEW FOR 1999

- **No major change.**

ENGINES

Model/ version	Type / timing valve / fuel system	Displacement cu in	Power bhp @ rpm	Torque lb-ft @ rpm
base	L4*1.8 DOHC-16-MPFI	110	130 @ 6000	122 @ 5000
FX	L4*2.0 DOHC-16-MPFI	121	140 @ 6000	133 @ 4800

TRANSMISSIONS

Compres. ratio	Driving wheels / transmission	Final ratio
10.0 :1	front - M5*	3.84
	front - A4	4.35
10.3 :1	front - M5*	3.84
	front - A4	4.35

PERFORMANCES

Acceler. 0-60 mph s	Standing 1/4 & 5/8 mile s	Acceler. 50-75 mph s	Braking 60-0 mph f	Top speed mph	Lateral acceler. G	Noise level dBA	Fuel economy mpg City	Highway	Fuel type Octane
9.2	16.5 30.4	6.5	144	109	0.80	66-70	22	31	R 87
NA									
8.7	16.0 29.5	6.3	138	115	0.80	66-70	21	31	R 87
9.5	16.7 30.6	6.7	144	112	0.80	66-70	20	30	R 87

PRICE & EQUIPMENT

HYUNDAI Tiburon	base	FX
Retail price $:	13,599	14,899
Dealer invoice $:	12,236	13,198
Shipping & handling $:	435	435
Automatic transmission:	O	O
Cruise control:	-	S
Power steering:	S	S
Anti-lock brakes:	-	O
Traction control:	-	-
Air conditioning:	O	O
Leather:	-	O
AM/FM/radio-cassette:	S	S
Power door locks:	-	S
Power windows:	S	S
Tilt steering:	S	S
Dual adjustable mirrors:	SM	SE
Alloy wheels:	O	S
Anti-theft system:	-	-

Colors

Exterior: Silver, Violet, Green, Red, White, Black.

Interior: Black.

AT A GLANCE...

Category: front-wheel drive sport coupes. **Class :** 3S

HISTORIC
Introduced in: 1997
Made in: Ulsan, South Korea

DEMOGRAPHICS
Model	Men./Wom.	Age	Married	College	Income
Tiburon	50/50 %	30	40 %	35 %	$ 22 000

INDEX
Safety:	70 %	Satisfaction:	77 %
Depreciation:	45 %	Insurance:	$ 950
Cost per mile:	$0.42	Number of dealers:	500

SALES
Model	1996	1997	Result
Tiburon	341	9 391	-

MAIN COMPETITORS
CHEVROLET Cavalier, DODGE-PLYMOUTH Neon, FORD ZX2, HONDA Civic, PONTIAC Sunfire, SATURN SC, TOYOTA Celica.

MAINTENANCE REQUIRED BY WARRANTY
First revision:	Frequency:	Diagnostic plug:
4 000 miles	3 months/4 000 miles	No

SPECIFICATIONS

General warranty: 3years / 36 000 miles; powertrain: 5 years / 60 000 miles; corrosion perforation: 5 years / 60 000 miles; antipollution: 5 years / 36 000 miles.

Model	Version Trim	Body/ Seats	Interior volume cu ft	Trunk volume cu ft	Cd	Wheel base in	Lght x Wdgth x Hght in x in x in	Curb weight lb	Susp. ft/rr	Brake ft/rr	Steering type	Turning diameter ft	Steer. turns nber.	Fuel tank gal	tire size	Standard tires make	model	Standard powertrain
HYUNDAI																		
Tiburon	base	2dr.cpe. 2+2	80.0	12.8	0.33	97.4	170.9x68.1x51.3	2549	ih/ih	dc/dr	pwr.r&p.	34.1	2.8	14.5	195/60R14	Michelin	XGTV4	L4/1.8/M5
Tiburon	FX	2dr.cpe. 2+2	80.0	12.8	0.33	97.4	170.9x68.1x51.3	2586	ih/ih	dc/dc	pwr.r&p.	34.1	2.8	14.5	195/55R15	Michelin	XGTV4	L4/2.0/M5

INFINITI G20
PeekaBoo It's Back...

The G20 is no stranger and by no means a newcomer. It seems that circumstances surrounding its return are fairly nebulous, if you listen to what the carmaker has to say. Imported between 1991 and 96, this car was the Infiniti entry model. Inspired by the Primera, a car developed for the European market, it's a sporty compact car that's quite richly equipped, a combination aimed to please customers looking for a BMW 3-Series, a Mercedes-Benz C-Class or a Volvo V70. Nothing less...

Potential buyers will be looking for a compact car animated by a 4-cylinder engine that has a unique sportscar behavior. On paper, the G20 has most of these attributes, but when you look it over it doesn't have one tenth the personality it would take to really compete with so-called rivals. The G20 is still a solidly furbished car. On the technical side, its compact body is super solid for starters. An elaborate suspension provides a good compromise between crisp handling and appreciable ride comfort. Lastly, its 2.0L engine is fairly responsive and revvy, so it feels like a high-performance powerplant. Safety-wise, this small car is equipped as well as bigger bodied cars, since it has standard side and front-impact airbags and pretension front seatbelts. The horn has been relocated, so it's handier in emergencies and an anti-theft alarm system comes standard on all models.

Nissan used the former G20 platform as a starting point, which explains why main mechanical organs and vehicle size are just about identical. But

side panels and window design have a brand-new look. The car's silhouette is more sleek, the grille is more elaborate and the rear extremity is more sculpted with its new taillights. Side panels sport skirts that really accentuate the overall look, front and rear bumpers are more massive, tires have gone from a 14 to 15 inch diameter, so the car now looks more muscular. The cabin design has been completely revamped with an eye to using all available space to best advantage and with a view to good ergonomics. New-design seats are fitted with adjustable headrests to soothe front and rear seat travellers. The instrument panel has a tidy business look, maybe a bit too much so, since the wood appliqués on the former model have been discontinued. Luckily a generous array of equipment compensates for a certain lack of glamor that's the norm for European cars wearing strong emblems ...

The G20 is unique in the Infiniti lineup and doesn't really have an equivalent at Lexus, BMW (the 4-cylinder model was withdrawn from the 3-Series) or Volvo. But they're out there; there's the Acura Integra, Mercedes-Benz C-Class, Honda Accord, Toyota Camry, Volkswagen Jetta GLX, but especially the Nissan Altima that's its most serious rival, one of the most popular compact cars in North America that's blessed with original looks, similar performance scores and equally sophisticated upper-crust equipment items and that costs less. We'd like to be wrong, but the general feeling is that nothing worthwhile will come of the G20 once again...

Nissan seems to be in search of its identity these last few years and they really seem to have botched things up. The number-2 Japanese automaker made a lot of wrong moves at the wrong time over quite a few years, but it's trying to patch things up by attempting to snatch sales in every single market segment with cars that already exist, that is without having to invest too much. The G20 is a perfect example of this strategy, since this model was withdrawn two years ago now, and voilà, it's back in the 1999 lineup.

MODEL RANGE

The Infiniti G20 is hard to classify, it's a compact car, it has sportscar attributes and it's a luxury car as well. This four-door sedan is sold in base model Luxury or «t» for Touring. The latter version benefits from a firmer suspension, rear spoiler, wheels and tires that smack of sportscar traits and demeanor. But both versions are equipped with the same engine, that is a 2.0L 4-cylinder model associated with a 5-speed manual gearbox that's standard on the «t» version as well as a viscous-coupled antilock braking system device. The 4-speed automatic transmission is an extra on the «t» version, but it comes standard on the Luxury, as do leather-clad seats. The G20 is furbished with posh equipment indeed, such as automatic climate control, main power accessories, sunroof, a Bose sound system, front heated seats, all of which bestows a luxury-class status on this car.

TECHNICAL FEATURES

The monocoque body is built of tempered steel called Durasteel and is assembled according to a typical Nissan I.B.A.S. approach («Intelligent Body Assembly System»), measuring 60 points on the body via a comparator according to a standard model. This stringent system allows for about 1mm tolerance, so assembly is super solid and precise, side panels being welded together in a single piece. Body stylistics are rather ho-hum, but the car benefits from good aerodynamics, namely a drag coefficient of 0.30. The independent suspension consists of a double wishbone arrangement up front and the famous MultiLink axle, made up of multiple control arms at the rear, with an

anti-roll bar for each axle. Disc brakes are aided by a four-wheel ABS device fitted with four sensors. The single engine model is a 2.0L DOHC 4-cylinder that develops 140 hp. The crankshaft is equipped with eight balancers to reduce vibration. The 5-speed manual transmission is standard, as is the viscous-coupled locking differential on the sporty «t» model, but the automatic transmission is available as an option in this case, but it comes standard on the Luxury version.

PROS

+ DRIVING PLEASURE. It's great, mainly due to right-on suspension, steering and engine response, so like European cars' demeanor. The driver is comfortably seated behind the wheel and enjoys superb visibility all-round. Handling on the «t» version is a cut above, for its refined suspension allows for more competent, level and precise handling of curves, no matter how wide or how tight.

+ EQUIPMENT. It's very rich, which explains partially why the price tag is steeper than for most

cars of this format.

+ RIDE COMFORT. Rear seat passengers enjoy a bit more space than those seated up front, but the rear seat still only accomodates two passengers. Seats provide good lumbar and lateral support and they're nice and cushy. The base model suspension is more flexible than that on the «t» model and soundproofing is better, so there's less road noise. But you do hear engine roar when gunning it.

+ CONVENIENCE FEATURES. Storage spots and other amenities are more generous up front and the trunk can be extended by lowering the rear seatbench back.

+ CLEAN OVERALL DESIGN. Assembly technique and compact size really exude a feeling of single-minded design and solidity. Models we tested didn't exhibit any squeaks and such, due to fine fit and finish.

+ THE «t» MODEL. It has more dashing, daring looks and is easy to identify with its rear spoiler.

+ SERVICE. Customers like how they're treated and fussed over by their dealer.

CONS

- LOOKS. The base model looks terribly ordinary, so the G20 breezes through traffic without getting so much as a second glance. It sure doesn't look like a luxury sports car.

-PERFORMANCES. They're rather midling, since accelerations and pickup are awfully average, so lots of current, less furbished cars can do better, and they cost less.

- FRONT SUSPENSION. Suspension travel is more limited up front than at the rear, so the car often goes into a nose-dive on poor roads when at full capacity, which really affects ride comfort.

-REAR SEATS. The car is bigger, but rear seats are somewhat cramped and rear storage spots are scarce. Only two passengers will be at ease on long trips.

- TOO BAD. The wood appliqués that graced former models are nowhere in sight, so the interior sorely lacks class and warmth.

-DEPRECIATION. Up until now, the G20 hasn't been the best investment, since poor retail sales cut down on resale value that's lower than for rivals.

- TO BE IMPROVED UPON. The poorly designed main armrest on the center console is a hassle. The horsewhip radio antenna is terribly out-of-date on a car in this price range. After all, lowly GM models are equipped with rear window built-in antennas. Are the Japanese still the gadget geniuses and electronic wizards they once were?

-SERVICE NETWORK. There aren't too many Infiniti dealerships out there, which doesn't help sales and can complicate vehicle maintenance.

CONCLUSION

It's hard to believe that the G20, a dismal failure in the past, can become by some stroke of luck, an overnight success, by just toting a few enhanced items. You have to be pretty optimistic or naïve to think that this car will at long last carve out a niche in a market crammed with more sophisticated and prestigious rivals that have a good hold on the sales scene. ☺

RATING
INFINITI G20

CONCEPT : **72%**
Technology	80
Safety :	90
Interior space :	50
Trunk volume:	60
Quality/fit/finish :	80

DRIVING: **69%**
Cockpit :	75
Performance :	60
Handling :	65
Steering :	80
Braking :	65

ORIGINAL EQUIPMENT: **79%**
Tires :	80
Headlights :	80
Wipers :	80
Rear defroster :	75
Radio :	80

COMFORT : **72%**
Seats :	80
Suspension :	80
Sound level :	50
Conveniences :	70
Air conditioning :	80

BUDGET : **64%**
Price :	35
Fuel economy :	80
Insurance :	45
Satisfaction :	90
Depreciation :	70

Overall rating: **71.2%**

NEW FOR 1999

- Renewed model inspired by the Nissan Primera that's sold in Europe.
- Extended wheelbase, overall length and height.
- Trunk connecting with the cabin.

ENGINES / TRANSMISSIONS / PERFORMANCES

Model/ version	Type / timing valve / fuel system	Displacement cu in	Power bhp @ rpm	Torque lb-ft @ rpm	Compres. ratio	Driving wheels / transmission	Final ratio	Acceler. 0-60 mph s	Standing 1/4 & 5/8 mile s	Acceler. 50-75 mph s	Braking 60-0 mph f	Top speed mph	Lateral acceler. G	Noise level dBA	Fuel economy mpg City	Highway	Fuel type Octane
G20	L4* 2.0 DOHC-16-MPSFI	122	140 @ 6400	132 @ 4800	9.5 :1	front - M5*	4.176	9.0	16.8 29.8	6.4	138	127	0.82	66-70	22	30	S 91
						front - A4	4.072	9.6	17.2 30.4	6.7	144	124	0.82	66-70	22	32	S 91

PRICE & EQUIPMENT

INFINITI G20	base	«t»	«t» leather
Retail price $:	20,995	22,495	24,095
Dealer invoice $:	-	-	-
Shipping & handling $:	-	-	-
Automatic transmission:	S	O	O
Cruise control:	S	S	S
Power steering:	S	S	S
Anti-lock brakes:	S	S	S
Traction control:	S	S	S
Air conditioning:	SA	SA	SA
Leather:	S	O	S
AM/FM/radio-cassette:	SCD	SCD	SCD
Power door locks:	S	S	S
Power windows:	S	S	S
Tilt steering:	S	S	S
Dual adjustable mirrors:	SEH	SEH	SEH
Alloy wheels:	S	S	S
Anti-theft system:	S	S	S

Colors
Exterior: White, Black, Red, Blue, Green, Beige, Bronze, Titanium.

Interior: Beige, Black.

AT A GLANCE...

Category:	front-wheel drive compact luxury sedans.	Class : 7

HISTORIC
Introduced in:	1991
Made in:	Tochigi, Japan.

DEMOGRAPHICS
Model	Men./Wom.	Age	Married	College	Income
G20	70/30%	48	72%	70%	$ 57 000

Safety:	90 %		**INDEX**	
Depreciation:	30 %	Satisfaction:		88 %
Cost per mile:	$0.55	Insurance:		$ 1 250
		Number of dealers:		150

SALES
Model	1996	1997	Result
G20	Not on the market at that time		

MAIN COMPETITORS
ACURA Integra, HONDA Accord, MAZDA 626, NISSAN Altima, TOYOTA Camry, VOLKSWAGEN Jetta GLX, VOLVO S70.

MAINTENANCE REQUIRED BY WARRANTY
First revision:	Frequency:	Diagnostic plug:
7 500 miles	6 months/7 500 miles	Yes

SPECIFICATIONS

Warranty: general 4 years / 60 000 miles; powertrain & antipollution: 6 years / 100 000 miles; corrosion perforation: 7 years / unlimited.

Model	Version Trim	Body/ Seats	Interior volume cu ft	Trunk volume cu ft	Cd	Wheel base in	Lght x Wdgth x Hght in x in x in	Curb weight lb	Susp. ft/rr	Brake ft/rr	Steering type	Turning diameter ft	Steer. turns nber.	Fuel tank gal	tire size	Standard tires make	model	Standard powertrain
INFINITI																		
G20	base	4dr.sdn. 4	90.3	14.2	0.30	102.4	177.5x66.7x55.1	2936	ih/ih	dc/ABS	pwr.r&p.	37.4	3.28	15.8	195/65HR15	Bridgestone Potenza	RE92	L4/2.0/M5
G20	"t"	4dr.sdn. 4	90.3	14.2	0.30	102.4	177.5x66.7x55.1	3002	ih/ih	dc/ABS	pwr.r&p.	37.4	3.28	15.8	195/65HR15	Bridgestone Potenza	RE92	L4/2.0/M5

Top luxury models have been a smashing hit these last few years and the trend doesn't seem to be letting up. Car sales at Volvo, BMW, Audi and Mercedes-Benz have dramatically increased and the Cadillac Catera, for one, has created quite a stir. Same-class Japanese products don't seem to be as popular since they bring up the rear as far as sales go. Such prestigious brand crests and ultra-conservative Japanese styling, bereft of the least glimmer of imagination, are the reason behind this phenomenon.

MODEL RANGE

The I30 is a 4-door sedan proposed in base or «t» for touring models. The latter has a firmer suspension, unique rim design and a spoiler that give it a distinct personality and look. Both versions are equipped with the same engine and powertrains, except for a shorter differential ratio on the high-performance «t» version. The 3.0L V6 engine is paired up to a 4-speed automatic transmission.

TECHNICAL FEATURES

The I30 has the same body design as the Maxima, but it has typical Infiniti stylistic touches at the front and rear extremities. The steel monocoque body is super rigid in regard to flexion and torsion resistance, but aerodynamic finesse is only average, as proven by the 0.32 drag coefficient. The front suspension, mounted to the chassis via an independent cradle, consists of MacPherson struts, whereas the rear rigid axle is fitted with what is known as a MultiLink setup derived from the Scott-Russell principle, that allows for constant wheel camber. Four-wheel disc brakes are assisted by a standard ABS system, as well as viscous-coupled locking differential that acts as traction control.

PROS

+ STYLE. This car is gorgeous thanks to a few added clever touches so that you don't feel like you're at the wheel of a creamy Maxima model car. But Infiniti didn't rack its brains to come up with a really unique-looking car as Lexus designers did to distinguish the ES 300 from the Camry.

+ RELIABILITY. It's remarkable, since 95% of owners are thrilled to bits with their vehicle and have had very few, if any, problems.

+ DRIVING FEEL. Keeping this

Too Flashy..?

car right on target is a breeze with such a robust build and competent suspensions. The engine, one of the most well-designed of its generation, lacks neither the power nor the torque needed to put out respectable performances. Yet accelerations and pickup are more vigorous on the «t» version that benefits from a shorter axle ratio.

+ HANDLING. It's very competent indeed mainly due to the rear suspension that keeps the car straight-ahead stable on curves, by reducing wheel camber variations while making quick lane changes as well as rear end lift on sudden stops. The I30 is neutral in most normal driving situations and is quite spritely on slalom runs.

+ ENGINE. The 3.0L V6 yields excellent gas mileage since this frugal high-performance engine rarely goes over 20 mpg.

+ RIDE COMFORT. The ride is simply regal on the highway. The suspension is nice and cushy, shocks are superb and there's sufficient wheel travel. Noise is kept at a fairly comfy, quiet level thanks to good soundproofing.

+ BRAKES. They do their stuff, emergency stops are achieved below 135 ft and they're amazingly balanced and lasting when put to the test.

+ STEERING. It's noteworthy, since it's so quick on the draw, right on target, nicely powered and benefits from a good reduction ratio at regular speeds, while the short steer angle diameter allows for slick moves.

+ CABIN DESIGN. The cabin and trunk can nicely accomodate four passengers and their effects. The car is quite compact, yet there's lots of room to breathe and stretch, especially height-wise.

+ CONVENIENCE AMENITIES. Storage compartments are more generous than is the case inside the Maxima, since cup-holders and coat hooks are included as original equipment, as are heated front seats, a feature that people in the Great White North sure do appreciate.

CONS

- SEATS. They're not comfy, since terribly flat and firmly upholstered. They don't offer much lateral or lumbar support, so long trips are tiring for rear seat travellers. As well, front seat adjustments are hard to reach with such skimpy space between the seat and door.

- INSTRUMENT PANEL. Its design isn't any better than on the Maxima, for the main section curves inward rather than out and controls are way out of the driver's reach.

- DESIGN. It's rather cluttered on the exterior, so some people say the car's a bit too dolled up with all that chrome...

- TRUNK. It's not as spacious as you'd expect, given vehicle size, nor can it be extended. It's only fitted with a ski-size slot.

- TO BE IMPROVED UPON: no indicator gauge for automatic shifter position, tiny-tot exterior mirrors, poor windshield wipers, washers and defroster. There aren't any air vents in the rear seat area, as is the case on other models in this category.

CONCLUSION

The Infiniti 30 doesn't enjoy the same sales as its rival ES 300, because the builder didn't go the extra mile to create a truly unique car and the brand isn't terribly popular. Nonetheless, being at the wheel of this car is very pleasurable, but we're wondering why pay more than for a Maxima, a car that's just as good, if not better, and can be acquired by handing over less hard-earned cash... ☺

RATING
INFINITI I30

CONCEPT : 78%
Technology   85
Safety :   90
Interior space :   70
Trunk volume: 60
Quality/fit/finish : 85

DRIVING: 66%
Cockpit :   75
Performance :   60
Handling :   60
Steering :   80
Braking :   55

ORIGINAL EQUIPMENT: 73%
Tires :   80
Headlights :   80
Wipers :   75
Rear defroster :   50
Radio :   80

COMFORT : 77%
Seats :   70
Suspension :   80
Sound level: 75
Conveniences :   80
Air conditioning : 80

BUDGET : 58%
Price :   15
Fuel economy :   75
Insurance :   45
Satisfaction :   90
Depreciation :   65

Overall rating: 70.4%

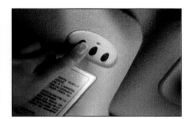

NEW FOR 1999

- Standard side-impact airbags for front seat passengers (offering head and chest protection).
- Standard traction control system.
- Cut-off switch hooked up to anti-theft system.
- Some sound system modifications.

ENGINES

Model/version	Type / timing valve / fuel system	Displacement cu in	Power bhp @ rpm	Torque lb-ft @ rpm
I30	V6* 3.0 DOHC-24-MPSFI	182	190 @ 5600	205 @ 4000
I30t	V6* 3.0 DOHC-24-MPSFI	182	190 @ 5600	205 @ 4000

TRANSMISSIONS

Compres. ratio	Driving wheels / transmission	Final ratio
10.0 :1	front - A4*	3.619
10.0 :1	front - A4*	3.823

PERFORMANCES

Acceler. 0-60 mph s	Standing 1/4 & 5/8 mile s	Acceler. 50-75 mph s	Braking 60-0 mph f	Top speed mph	Lateral acceler. G	Noise level dBA	Fuel economy mpg City	Fuel economy mpg Highway	Fuel type Octane
9.0	16.4 30.8	6.6	128	124	0.80	62-68	20	29	M 89
8.0	15.7 27.5	5.9	131	121	0.82	62-68	20	29	M 89

PRICE & EQUIPMENT

INFINITI I30	base	«t»
Retail price $:	28,900	31,500
Dealer invoice $:	25,935	27,947
Shipping & handling $:	495	495
Automatic transmission:	S	S
Cruise control:	S	S
Power steering:	S	S
Anti-lock brakes:	S	S
Traction control:	S	S
Air conditioning:	SA	SA
Leather:	S	S
AM/FM/radio-cassette:	SCD	SCD
Power door locks:	S	S
Power windows:	S	S
Tilt steering:	S	S
Dual adjustable mirrors:	SEH	SEH
Alloy wheels:	S	S
Anti-theft system:	S	S

Colors

Exterior: Beige, Olive green, White, Black, Chestnut, Blue, Aubergine, Crystal.

Interior: Sage, Beige, Black.

AT A GLANCE...

Category: front-wheel drive luxury sedans.　**Class :** 7

HISTORIC
Introduced in: 1995
Made in: Oppama, Japan.

DEMOGRAPHICS

Model	Men./Wom.	Age	Married	College	Income
I30	85/15 %	48	88 %	60 %	$ 84 000

INDEX
Safety: 90 %　Satisfaction: 92 %
Depreciation: 35 %　Insurance: $ 1 175
Cost per mile: $ 0.60　Number of dealers: 150

SALES

Model	1996	1997	Result
I30	27 057	31 303	+ 15.7 %

MAIN COMPETITORS
ACURA TL, AUDI A4, BMW 3-Series, LEXUS ES 300, MAZDA Millenia, NISSAN Maxima, SAAB 9³ & 9⁵, VOLVO S70.

MAINTENANCE REQUIRED BY WARRANTY
First revision: 7 500 miles　Frequency: 6 months/7 500 miles　Diagnostic plug: Yes

SPECIFICATIONS

Model	Version Trim	Body/Seats	Interior volume cu ft	Trunk volume cu ft	Cd	Wheel base in	Lght x Wdgth x Hght in x in x in	Curb weight lb	Susp. ft/rr	Brake ft/rr	Steering type	Turning diameter ft	Steer. turns nber.	Fuel tank gal	tire size	Standard tires make	model	Standard powertrain
INFINITI		Warranty: general 4 years / 60 000 miles; powertrain & antipollution: 6 years / 100 000 miles; corrosion perforation: 7 years / unlimited.																
I30	base	4dr.sdn. 5	99.6	14.1	0.32	106.3	189.6x69.7x55.7	3150	ih/ih	dc/ABS	pwr.r&p.	34.8	2.9	18.5	205/65R15	Bridgestone	Potenza RE92	V6/3.0/A4
I30	t	4dr.sdn. 5	99.6	14.1	0.32	106.3	189.6x69.7x55.7	3225	ih/ih	dc/ABS	pwr.r&p.	34.8	2.9	18.5	215/55R16	Toyo	Proxes Ao6	V6/3.0/A4

The QX4 was the first Infiniti vehicle to enjoy instant success. In fact, it was the best seller in the automaker's lineup in 1997. This record wasn't hard to beat, given that buyers aren't exactly rushing out to buy the I30 and Q45. The NDI stylists in San Diego get all the credit for this vehicle's popularity, since these bright lights changed the Pathfinder pumpkin into a luxury carriage called the QX4. Equipment items, price and Infiniti service did the rest.

MODEL RANGE

The QX4 is a 5-door deluxe SUV derived from the Nissan Pathfinder. It's equipped with the same engine and powertrain as its august ancestor, namely a 3.3L V6 linked to a 4-speed automatic transmission. But it benefits from a shorter axle ratio and has full-time all-wheel drive. Equipment is quite lavish, since the only extra available is the sunroof, which explains why it weighs 288 lb. more than the Pathfinder.

TECHNICAL FEATURES

The steel unibody integrates an H-frame into its structure, so the vehicle is robust and very resistant to flexion and torsion. The only standard protective plate is the one covering the gas tank. The front independent suspension consists of MacPherson struts and a rigid rear axle guided by five control arms with coil springs and stabilizer bar both front and rear. Disc and drum brakes benefit from standard ABS, traction control and automatic front-wheel lock. The QX4 is equipped with full-time all-wheel drive that's engaged by a switch mounted on the dashboard, at three various settings: automatic rear-wheel drive, four-wheel drive and all-wheel with locking differential on low gear. Nissan opted for the ATTESA device created for the Japanese Skyline GT-R sports coupe, because of its almost instantaneous response time and velvety smooth shifting from rear to all-wheel drive. When the transmission switch is on automatic mode, electromagnetic clutches gradually send torque to the front wheels. But this transfer is only activated when the computer detects rear

The 4x4 Cinderella...

wheel slippage and it increases bit by bit as the various clutch baskets catch.

PROS

+ STYLE. The front end design is different enough from that of the Pathfinder, so the QX4 has a distinctive look that's quite appealing. The bumper cover and headlamp design is so original that it's started a trend and most models have borrowed these elements ever since.

+ TRANSMISSION. It's highly sophisticated, so the QX4 benefits from competent sport car handling, whatever the wheel grip and you can switch smoothly and competently from rear to all-wheel drive.

+ PERFORMANCES. The shorter differential ratio and the V6 engine's bigger displacement yield super-smooth, car-like accelerations and pickup.

+ HANDLING. This vehicle is one of the most competent in its category due to a really rigid architecture that keeps powertrains right on track. Sway is well under control and the center of gravity isn't perched too high, so you can take curves with assurance and it's almost agile on slalom runs.

+ BRAKES. They're easy to gauge, provide straight as an arrow emergency stops in fairly short distances for a vehicle weighing more than 4,200 lbs. when at full load capacity.

+ RIDE COMFORT. Highway driving is very car-like with the cushy suspension, nice-design, well-upholstered seats and great noise dampening system.

+ STEERING. The rack-and-pinion steering is direct, quick, nicely assisted and procures adequate maneuveribility due to a relatively short steer angle diameter.

+ CABIN DESIGN. The cockpit is well organized, the driver is comfortably seated and enjoys good, all-round visibility, now that the spare tire is located under the rear floor of the vehicle. The instrument panel borrows heavily from the Pathfinder dashboard, it's uncomplicated, ergonomic and logical.

+ QUALITY. Construction, finish job and trim materials are meticulously rendered and equipment is generous and quite posh. Leather seats and wood appliqués look and feel lovely. This vehicle comes with a better warranty than does the Pathfinder.

CONS

- ENGINE. It's come a long way, but it still lacks power and torque when passing or taking jaunts on tough turf. Which explains why most of the competition is equipped with a bigger V8.

- GROUND CLEARANCE. Lower than before, it takes the fun out of those rambles in the rough. You sometimes bottom out of get stuck on rough terrain and it's good to know that only the gas tank has a protective plate, whereas transmission components are vulnerable.

- SPACE. Rear seats are plusher and thicker than on the Pathfinder, but you feel cramped when you want to stretch your legs and it's tough climbing in or out.

- FUEL CONSUMPTION. It's high due to hefty vehicle weight, sluggish torque that obliges the engine to rev higher, huge 16-inch tires and pretty clunky aerodynamics.

CONCLUSION

The QX4 is popular mostly because of handsome looks, sophisticated suspension, creamy equipment and fine finish job. But its car engine isn't really the best suited to its needs and having to deal with weak torque and power on low r.p.m. really spoils things... If Infiniti doesn't soon graft the Q45 V8 engine into this lovely carriage, it will no doubt turn into... ☺ a pumpkin.

RATING INFINITI QX4		
CONCEPT :		**76%**
Technology	80	
Safety :	80	
Interior space :	70	
Trunk volume:	70	
Quality/fit/finish :	80	
DRIVING:		**62%**
Cockpit :	75	
Performance :	40	
Handling :	45	
Steering :	80	
Braking :	70	
ORIGINAL EQUIPMENT:		**78%**
Tires :	80	
Headlights :	80	
Wipers :	75	
Rear defroster :	75	
Radio :	80	
COMFORT :		**73%**
Seats :	75	
Suspension :	70	
Sound level:	60	
Conveniences :	80	
Air conditioning :	80	
BUDGET :		**45%**
Price :	0	
Fuel economy :	40	
Insurance :	45	
Satisfaction :	85	
Depreciation :	55	
Overall rating:		**66.8%**

NEW FOR 1999

- **No major change.**

ENGINES / TRANSMISSIONS / PERFORMANCES

Model/ version	Type / timing valve / fuel system	Displacement cu in	Power bhp @ rpm	Torque lb-ft @ rpm	Compres. ratio	Driving wheels / transmission	Final ratio	Acceler. 0-60 mph s	Standing 1/4 & 5/8 mile s	Acceler. 50-75 mph s	Braking 60-0 mph f	Top speed mph	Lateral acceler. G	Noise level dBA	Fuel economy mpg City	Highway	Fuel type Octane
base	V6* 3.3 SOHC-12-MPSFI	200	168 @ 4800	196 @ 2800	8.9 :1	rear/4 - A4	4.636	11.2	18.4 32.8	8.9	138	109	0.73	64-70	14	19	R 87

PRICE & EQUIPMENT

INFINITI QX4	base
Retail price $:	35,550
Dealer invoice $:	31,976
Shipping & handling $:	495
Automatic transmission:	S
Cruise control:	S
Power steering:	S
Anti-lock brakes:	S
Traction control:	S
Air conditioning:	S
Leather:	S
AM/FM/radio-cassette:	SCD
Power door locks:	S
Power windows:	S
Tilt steering:	S
Dual adjustable mirrors:	SEH
Alloy wheels:	S
Anti-theft system:	S

Colors

Exterior: Blue, Black, Chestnut, Beige, Bronze, Sage, White.

Interior: Gray, Beige.

AT A GLANCE...

Category: rear-wheel drive &AWD sport-utility.   **Class :** utility

HISTORIC

Introduced in:	1997
Made in:	Kyushu, Japan.

DEMOGRAPHICS

Model	Men./Wom.	Age	Married	College	Income
QX4	76/24 %	39	68 %	57 %	$ 49 000

INDEX

Safety:	75 %	Satisfaction:	85 %
Depreciation:	45 %	Insurance:	$ 1 385
Cost per mile:	$ 0.58	Number of dealers:	150

SALES

Model	1996	1997	Result
QX4	1 983	18 793	-

MAIN COMPETITORS

CHEVROLET Blazer, FORD Explorer, GMC Envoy, ISUZU Rodeo & Trooper, JEEP Grand Cherokee, LEXUS RX 300, MERCEDES-BENZ ML 320, TOYOTA 4Runner.

MAINTENANCE REQUIRED BY WARRANTY

First revision:	Frequency:	Diagnostic plug:
7 500 miles	6 months/7 500 miles	Yes

SPECIFICATIONS

Model	Version Trim	Body/ Seats	Interior volume cu ft	Trunk volume cu ft	Cd	Wheel base in	Lght x Wdgth x Hght in x in x in	Curb weight lb	Susp. ft/rr	Brake ft/rr	Steering type	Turning diameter ft	Steer. turns nber.	Fuel tank gal	tire size	Standard tires make	model	Standard powertrain
INFINITI QX4	base	5dr.wgn.5	92.9	38.0	0.48	106.3	183.9x72.4x70.7	4274	ih/rhdc/dr/ABS	pwr.r&p.	37.4	3.1	21.1	245/70R16	Bridgestone	Dueler H/T	V6/3.3/A4

Warranty: general 4 years / 60 000 miles; powertrain & antipollution: 6 years / 100 000 miles; corrosion perforation: 7 years / unlimited.

In the past, the Q45 was never a true match for its direct rival, the Lexus LS 400. A botched launching campaign and rather dubious looks didn't give this car much of a chance. Reworked in 1997, the Q45 seems to have what it takes to be a serious contender and sales are definitely on the rise, since they represent 68% of Lexus sales. The body and cabin design have had a face-lift and are now more angular and more conservative.

MODEL RANGE

The Q45 is a four-door sedan offered in either base or «t» for touring models. The «t» model has a firmer suspension with bulkier anti-roll bar at the rear, rear spoiler and forged aluminum rims. Both versions are equipped with a 4.1L V8 linked to a 4-speed automatic gearbox. Equipment is very generous and includes all the amenities you'd look for in a car in this price range, such as front heated seats.

TECHNICAL FEATURES

The Q45 is derived from the Cima, a Nissan-built car sold in Japan, with new front and rear end stylistic accents, thanks to NDI, the Infiniti stylistics bureau located in California, so as to better tickle North American tastes. The body is more angular, but more lackluster than was the former Q45. There's no real hint as to where these design details come from, they're sort of generic and generally typical of what you see on cars in this category, such as the classic grille and chrome details. The steel monocoque body is fitted with four-wheel independent suspensions consisting of MacPherson struts up front and rear rigid axle with multiple control arms. The four-wheel disc brakes are linked to a standard ultra-modern ABS system. The aluminum 4.1L V8 engine is at the cutting edge of technology, delivering 266 hp, a very impressive amount of juice since it's in the same league as the GM Northstar or Ford Intech engines. The automatic transmission doesn't include a manual setting, but it's equipped with viscous-coupled locking differential and standard antilock braking system. The latter reduces engine power when it detects the first sign of wheel slippage.

PROS

+ DESIGN. First off, the Q45 makes a good impression. From the out-

Phantom of the Opera...

side, it looks lush and solid, yet has a discreet appearance. Inside, the cabin is more obviously luxurious with the posh leather-clad seats and faux-bois trim. The many chrome accents add a touch of class and the steering wheel is inviting with its attractive punched leather rim.

+ PRICE. Less expensive than last year's model, without any compromise as to quality, equipment or performances, the Q45 is a good buy.

+ RIDE COMFORT. The spacious cabin seats five passengers. Seats and suspension are as comfy as it gets, even on the «t» version equipped with a more flexible suspension than before and sound-proofing does the silence trick.

+ ENGINE. It's silky and powerful, delivering excellent performances thanks to a remarkable 14.5 lb/hp power to weight ratio. Accelerations and pickup are lively and the transmission is right on the ball. Gas mileage is a nice surprise, since the engine settles for 20 mpg on average for normal driving, which corresponds to the normal petrol appetite of a V6.

+ ROADHOLDING. It's generally neutral and very stable at high speeds. This car is amazingly agile on serpentine stretches, especially the «t» version that exhibits more crisp moves due to a less flexible suspension design.

+ BRAKES. Always easy to apply just as needed and brawny, providing straight stops in 130 ft, no mean feat considering the vehicle weight.

+ MANEUVERABILITY. It's better than before, due to a shorter steer angle diameter and variable assist steering, so parking is a breeze.

+ EQUIPMENT. It's lavish, including all the power and luxury accessories that come with luxury car territory and convenience features haven't been overlooked either, since there are many storage compartments scattered throughout the cabin.

+ QUALITY. It's evident everywhere you look. Assembly, fit and finish and trim materials are dramatically better than they once were. Dependability is a definite asset as well, since 95% of owners are very happy with their Q45 and are proud to own such a car.

CONS

- STYLE. You could never say that the Q45 is oozing with charm, since it was built for the Japanese market and acts as a sort of American surrogate...

- BUDGET. The Q45 sells for less this year, but not everyone can afford to buy one and upkeep and insurance premiums aren't cheap, yet resale value isn't at all a sure thing.

- TRUNK. It's fairly tiny for such a big car, since it can hold as much as a...Sentra! But it has a nice, regular shape and tapered lid, so it can be used to full advantage.

- CONTROLS. Radio and climate control dials are in reverse order, so you have to dodge the shifter if you want to change radio stations.

- TO BE IMPROVED UPON: no rear stabilizer bar on the base model, so there's a soft, squishy feel and wishy washy demeanor that will only thrill American car fanatics...

CONCLUSION

It's a well-kept secret. Under its mask, the Q45 hides a high-performance luxury car that's competent, solidly built and sold at a really reasonable going price. The only hitch: too few potential buyers aren't even aware that Infiniti makes good-quality automobiles, which unfortunately lowers its resale value and doesn't add much to its public image. ☺

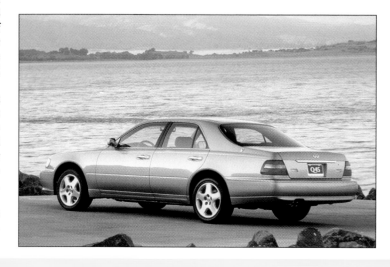

RATING
INFINITI Q45

CONCEPT :   74%
Technology   85
Safety :   90
Interior space :   70
Trunk volume: 40
Quality/fit/finish :   85

DRIVING: 72%
Cockpit :   85
Performance :   65
Handling :   70
Steering :   80
Braking :   60

ORIGINAL EQUIPMENT: 84%
Tires :   85
Headlights :   85
Wipers :   80
Rear defroster :   80
Radio :   90

COMFORT :   82%
Seats :   85
Suspension :   80
Sound level: 80
Conveniences :   80
Air conditioning :   85

BUDGET :   48%
Price :   0
Fuel economy :   60
Insurance :   40
Satisfaction :   90
Depreciation :   50

Overall rating: 72.0%

NEW FOR 1999

- New exterior design details, including grille, high-intensity headlamps and rear taillights.
- Clock on middle of dashboard, automatic touch-button sunroof control, new-design controls for electronically adjusted suspension, side-impact airbags and power rear window curtain.

ENGINES

Model/ version	Type / timing valve / fuel system	Displacement cu in	Power bhp @ rpm	Torque lb-ft @ rpm
base	V8* 4.1 DOHC-32-MPSFI	252	266 @ 5600	278 @ 4000

TRANSMISSIONS

Compres. ratio	Driving wheels / transmission	Final ratio
10.5 :1	rear - A4*	3.692

PERFORMANCES

Acceler. 0-60 mph s	Standing 1/4 & 5/8 mile s	Acceler. 50-75 mph s	Braking 60-0 mph f	Top speed mph	Lateral acceler. G	Noise level dBA	Fuel economy mpg City	Highway	Fuel type Octane
8.0	16.0 27.5	4.9	131	143	0.75	62-66	17	25	S 91

PRICE & EQUIPMENT

INFINITI Q45	base	«t»
Retail price $:	47,900	49,900
Dealer invoice $:	42,985	44,780
Shipping & handling $:	495	495
Automatic transmission:	S	S
Cruise control:	S	S
Power steering:	S	S
Anti-lock brakes:	S	S
Traction control:	S	S
Air conditioning:	S	S
Leather:	S	S
AM/FM/radio-cassette:	SCD	SCD
Power door locks:	S	S
Power windows:	S	S
Tilt steering:	S	S
Dual adjustable mirrors:	S	S
Alloy wheels:	S	S
Anti-theft system:	S	S

Colors
Exterior: Green, Black, Titanium, Pewter, White.
Interior: Beige, Pebble, Black.

AT A GLANCE...

Category: rear-wheel drive luxury sedans.   **Class :** 7

HISTORIC
Introduced in: 1990-1997
Made in: Tochigi, Japan.

DEMOGRAPHICS

Model	Men./Wom.	Age	Married	College	Income
Q45	97/3 %	49	90 %	60 %	$ 95 000

INDEX
Safety: 90 %   Satisfaction: 90 %
Depreciation: 55 %   Insurance: $ 1 880
Cost per mile: $ 0.97   Number of dealers: 150

SALES

Model	1996	1997	Result
Q45	5 896	10 443	+77.1 %

MAIN COMPETITORS
BMW 5-7 Series, CADILLAC DeVille & Seville, LEXUS GS-LS 400, LINCOLN Continental & Town Car, MERCEDES-BENZ E-S-Class.

MAINTENANCE REQUIRED BY WARRANTY
First revision: 7 500 miles
Frequency: 6 months/7 500 miles
Diagnostic plug: Yes

SPECIFICATIONS

Model	Version Trim	Body/ Seats	Interior volume cu ft	Trunk volume cu ft	Cd	Wheel base in	Lght x Wdgth x Hght in x in x in	Curb weight lb	Susp. ft/rr	Brake ft/rr	Steering type	Turning diameter ft	Steer. turns nber.	Fuel tank gal	tire size	Standard tires make	model	Standard powertrain
INFINITI Q45t	«t»	4dr.sdn. 5	97.4	12.6	0.32	111.4	199.2x71.7x56.9	3891	ih/ih	dc/ABS	pwr.r&p.	36.0	3.2	21.4	225/50VR17	Michelin Energy MXV4		V8/4.1/A4

Warranty: general 4 years / 60 000 miles; powertrain & antipollution: 6 years / 100 000 miles; corrosion perforation: 7 years / unlimited.

It's hard to know why the Rodeo isn't more popular, especially these days, when this type of vehicle is the rage. How can you explain why potential buyers ignore this handsome and pretty competent SUV? The answer no doubt lies in its steep price tag and poor sales network.

MODEL RANGE

The latest Rodeo is sold as a 4-door station wagon in S and LS trim levels. The base model sold in the United States is a rear-wheel drive vehicle animated by a 2.2L in-line 4 engine with 5-speed manual gearbox. Both models sold in Canada are all-wheel drive vehicles powered by a 3.2L V6 with standard 5-speed manual gearbox on the S version and standard 4-speed automatic on the LS. The S version has pretty basic equipment, but it does include a radio-cassette player, whereas the LS is more richly equipped, since the only major option available is leather seat trim.

TECHNICAL FEATURES

The Rodeo's basic structure consists of a 6-crossmember steel H-frame to which the body is affixed. The vehicle has been pared down, so it's shorter, wider and more lightweight. The front suspension is made up of double transverse Y-shaped trailing arms with torsion and anti-roll bars, while the rear rigid axle is supported by five longitudinal control arms and suspended on coil springs. Standard protective plates cover the radiator, gas tank, crankcase and transfer case. Four-wheel disc brakes are linked to four-wheel ABS on all models. Weight has been reduced by 285 lb. due to modifications to the chassis, rear suspension and aluminum main drive shaft and due to more compact engines made up of aluminum and magnesium components as is the ABS control unit containing hydraulic and electronic controls. The new V6 engine pumps out more power and torque than its predecessors, thanks to its four valves per cylinder and its variable intake system that optimizes engine power no matter what the r.p.m. All-wheel drive remains «on demand», but it's activated by a button rather than a shifter and a hydraulic pressure system makes such an operation smooth below 60 mph.

PROS

+ LOOKS. It looks more compact

Improving with Age...

and muscular than ever and exudes a solid, invincible feel that's the key to any SUV's success. The ribbed side stone deflectors and wider wheelhouses really suit the Rodeo's build.

+ CABIN SPACE. The cabin is a bit wider and accomodates four passengers who'll appreciate the nicely proportioned space.

+ ENGINE. The 3.2L V6 now finally has the wallop that was sorely lacking on the Rodeo. Accelerations and pickup are zippy on roads and on off-road maneuvers, more generous torque really helps you make tracks.

+ HANDLING. On good road surfaces, it benefits from the vehicle's structural rigidity and crisp steering.

+ COCKPIT. Driving is made easy due to the excellent driver's position who'll enjoy the nice blend created by the steering wheel, seat and pedals. And visibility all-round is super with the nice, big mirrors and instruments that are well-organized and easy to read.

+ OFF-THE-ROAD MANEUVERS. The Rodeo can really tackle rough terrain nicely due to its generous ground clearance, big entry and exit angles and its new rear suspension that keeps it more level and provides better grip on really rough turf.

+ NICE FEATURES. The more traditional rear HATCH design that facilitates baggage compartment access, rear windows that lower all the way down and standard steel

plates protecting powertrain components when driving on uneven terrain.

CONS

- PRICE. It's less competitive than before, since the LS version sells at prices comparable to top-of-the-line American rivals, once it gets all the trimmings, yet it doesn't fetch as good a resale price. Even the S version is stripped down to basics and is expensive considering what it has to offer.

-SUSPENSION. It's mushy and the vehicle slips at the least bump on the road, which really affects ride comfort and handling as soon as the going gets rough. It's the most controversial element on the Rodeo, for this wild and wooly suspension really jostles passengers and those big tires, soft shocks and wheelbase that's 4 inches shorter than on the Explorer don't help any either.

- STEERING. Assistance is more positive than before, but its high reduction ratio and wide steer angle cripple maneuverability.

- INSTRUMENT PANEL. Its design is pretty straightforward, yet some controls aren't located where you'd expect them to be, like the inverted radio and climate control dials and the switches located to the left of the steering wheel that are clean out of sight.

-ACCESS. Narrow doors don't open wide at all, so rear seat access is problematic with such skimpy space to wrestle into. Lastly, we'd like to see standard, conveniently located footrests and assist grips.

-THE S VERSION. Stingy equipment makes it hell to resell, especially since the better equipped LS doesn't cost much more.

- DISTRIBUTION. Dealerships are few and far between, which can complicate upkeep and needed repairs.

CONCLUSION

Let's hope that the latest Rodeo's attributes will attract former buyers who have wandered off in search of greener pastures since the automaker took its sweet time getting this vehicle back on track. If it weren't for the jittery suspension, it would have our blessing... ☺

RATING
ISUZU Rodeo

CONCEPT : 76%
Technology	80
Safety :	75
Interior space :	60
Trunk volume:	90
Quality/fit/finish :	75

DRIVING: 61%
Cockpit :	80
Performance :	55
Handling :	45
Steering :	70
Braking :	55

ORIGINAL EQUIPMENT: 76%
Tires :	80
Headlights :	75
Wipers :	75
Rear defroster :	75
Radio :	75

COMFORT : 64%
Seats :	75
Suspension :	65
Sound level :	40
Conveniences :	60
Air conditioning :	80

BUDGET : 55%
Price :	20
Fuel economy :	50
Insurance :	60
Satisfaction :	80
Depreciation :	65

Overall rating: 66.4%

NEW FOR 1999

- New LSE luxury model..

ENGINES / TRANSMISSIONS / PERFORMANCES

Model/ version	Type / timing valve / fuel system	Displacement cu in	Power bhp @ rpm	Torque lb-ft @ rpm	Compres. ratio	Driving wheels / transmission	Final ratio	Acceler. 0-60 mph s	Standing 1/4 & 5/8 mile s	Acceler. 50-75 mph s	Braking 60-0 mph f	Top speed mph	Lateral acceler. G	Noise level dBA	Fuel economy mpg City	Highway	Fuel type Octane
S	V6* 3.2 DOHC-24-MPFI	193	205 @ 5400	214 @ 3000	9.1 :1	rear/4 - M5*	4.3	9.0	16.8 30.4	6.6	148	106	0.72	68-70	16	21	R 87
LS/LSE	V6* 3.2 DOHC-24-MPFI	193	205 @ 5400	214 @ 3000	9.1 :1	rear/4 - A4	4.3	9.7	17.0 31.7	6.9	154	103	0.72	68-70	17	21	R 87

PRICE & EQUIPMENT

ISUZU Rodeo/Amigo	S	LS	LSE	S	V6 4WD
Retail price $:	17,995	26,390	-	14,995	19,350
Dealer invoice $:	16,916	23,488	-	14,095	17,802
Shipping & handling $:	445	445	-	445	445
Automatic transmission:	O	S	S		
Cruise control:	O	S	S		
Power steering:	S	S	S		
Anti-lock brakes:	S	S	S		
Traction control:	-	-	-		
Air conditioning:	O	S	S		
Leather:	-	O	S		
AM/FM/radio-cassette:	S	SCD	SCD		
Power door locks:	O	S	S		
Power windows:	O	S	S		
Tilt steering:	O	S	S		
Dual adjustable mirrors:	SM	SEH	SEH		
Alloy wheels:	O	S	S		
Anti-theft system:	O	S	S		

Colors
Exterior: Black, Silver, White, Green, Bordeaux.

Interior: Gray, Beige.

AT A GLANCE...

Category: 2WD & 4WD all-purpose vehicles. **Class :** utility

HISTORIC
Introduced in: 1991-1998
Made in: Lafayette, Indiana, USA.

DEMOGRAPHICS
Model	Men./Wom.	Age	Married	College	Income
Rodeo	75/25 %	46	74 %	50 %	$ 40 000

INDEX
Safety:	75 %	Satisfaction:	80 %
Depreciation:	28 % (1 year)	Insurance:	$ 850-975
Cost per mile:	$0.50	Number of dealers:	NA

SALES
Model	1996	1997	Result
Rodeo	61 071	63 627	+ 4.2 %

MAIN COMPETITORS
CHEVROLET Blazer, FORD Explorer, GMC Jimmy, JEEP Cherokee-Grand Cherokee, NISSAN Pathfinder, TOYOTA 4Runner.

MAINTENANCE REQUIRED BY WARRANTY
First revision:	Frequency:	Diagnostic plug:
3 000 miles	6 000 miles	No

SPECIFICATIONS

Warranty: 3 years / 36 000 miles; powertrain:5 years / 60 000 miles ; perforation 6 years / 100 000miles.

Model	Version Trim	Traction	Body/ Seats	Wheel base in	Lght x Wdgth x Hght in x in x in	Curb weight lb	Susp. ft/rr	Brake ft/rr	Steering type	Turning diameter ft	Steer. turns nber.	Fuel tank gal	tire size	Standard tires make	model	Standard powertrain
ISUZU																
Rodeo	S	4x4	4dr.wgn. 5	106.4	183.2x70.4x66.1	3853	ih/rh	dc/ABS	pwr.r&p.	38.4	3.64	21.1	235/75R15	Bridgestone	Dueller 684	V6/3.2/M5
Rodeo	LS/LSE	4x4	4dr.wgn. 5	106.4	183.2x70.4x66.4	3929	ih/rh	dc/ABS	pwr.r&p.	38.4	3.64	21.1	245/70R16	Bridgestone	Dueller 684	V6/3.2/A4
Amigo	S	4x2	2dr.wgn. 5	96.9	167.8x70.4x66.6	4450	ih/rh	dc/dr	pwr.r&p.	-	-	17.7	225/75R15	Bridgestone	Dueller 684	L4/2.2/M5
Amigo	S	4x4	2dr.wgn. 5	96.9	167.8x70.4x66.6	4650	ih/rh	dc/ABS	pwr.r&p.	-	-	17.7	225/75R15	Bridgestone	Dueller 684	V6/3.2/A4

Too Conservative

After all the snags encountered on last year's model, that some test pilots found had the annoying tendency of overturning during the moose test, well, we expected the replacement model to be a horse of a different color. This is not so and if you wanted to be picky about it, you could say that this vehicle is being advertised for what it isn't, since there are hardly any differences at all between both models. The Trooper isn't one of the sales leaders in its category, due in large part to a weak sales network and not too attractive price.

MODEL RANGE
This big multi-purpose all-terrain vehicle is offered in a 5-door station wagon model with all-wheel drive on demand, in S, LS and Limited trim. All models are equipped with a standard updated 3.5L V6 engine linked to a standard manual transmission for the L and LS and four-speed automatic for the Limited. The Limited is blessed with rather unlimited equipment, the LS is richly equipped, but the lower-end S model has been really spruced up, since it now has all the main power accessories, aluminum rims, cruise control and a theft-deterrent system, all of which really add to its value.

TECHNICAL FEATURES
The steel unibody is mounted on a 7-crossmember H-frame. Aerodynamics aren't too great, not with its squarish front end and hefty tires. Standard steel protective plates keep the radiator, gas tank, crankcase and transfer case out of harm's way. The independent front suspension consists of transverse A-arms with torsion and stabilizer bar, whereas the rear rigid axle is rigged up to four trailing arms, torque arm, stabilizer bar and coil springs. A four-link navigational system controls wheel camber when torque is applied on accelerations and wheel travel has been increased both front and rear to provide for a smoother ride. Four-wheel disc brakes are assisted by a standard all-wheel ABS device. The new larger-displacement engine benefits from a variable intake system so as to maximize power and torque. A new full-time all-wheel drive equips the S version only, while the other two versions are equipped with an on-demand system, a feature that's the cat's meow for buyers. It can be engaged via shift-on-the-fly at whatever speed; this T.O.D. system distributes torque equally to front and rear wheels, so handling is really neutral and there's no oversteer or understeer effect, since it reacts to the accelerator pedal position and to the clean emission system valves.

PROS
+ STYLE. It's bold and forever young, no matter what the trend. It especially appeals to buyers who are hankering for a Range Rover, but don't have half the cash needed to purchase one. But this vehicle's technical features and performances are a far cry from what you get on a Rover.

+ RIDE COMFORT. It's velvety on highways and you almost feel like you're travelling in a big sedan with such a smooth suspension and nice-design, cushy seats.

+ EQUIPMENT. Last year's base model was very stripped down to basics, but now the S version is almost on a par with the LS, except for a few luxury items that aren't too vital.

+ VERSATILITY. The spacious cabin is as roomy as a minivan and can accomodate five passengers. The luggage compartment is generous and easy to get to thanks to un-equal-width double swing doors.

+ COCKPIT. The driver sits nice and high, and can enjoy good straight-ahead and lateral view and the nicely organized dashboard has lots of instruments.

+ QUALITY. No doubt about it, this vehicle is well-built. Construction, finish details and trim components are spiffy, which can't be said about the rather bizarre overall design since some interior and exterior color shades may be splashy, but they aren't well-coordinated.

+ NICE FEATURES. The rear seatbench can be removed like a charm and front seat armrests are ajustable.

CONS
- SUSPENSION. It's far too flexible, so you have to really watch it, since it creates a lot of sway and wishy washy behavior in crosswinds or on gouged-out surfaces where the rear axle tends to bounce and rough up occupants and wheels go haywire. You get the same old nonsense as on the former model, which is a bit disappointing, since handling is uncertain in some situations.

- BRAKES. They were tough on our test vehicle, but lacked oomph and were unstable on sudden stops that were hard to control with such a soft pedal.

- BUDGET. The Trooper isn't cheap to buy or operate, since fuel consumption rarely goes over 14 mpg: a V8 wouldn't be any greedier and would put out more juice and torque.

- ACCESS. It's always awkward boarding with those narrow doors that don't open wide and the high as blazes ground clearance. A running board isn't even available as an extra.

- NOISE. The engine isn't a quiet, genteel sort and wind gusts around the cabin as you accelerate, a sure sign of poor aerodynamics.

- VISIBILITY. It's hampered towards the rear because of the thick roof supports and the spare tire installed on the rear door exterior.

- TO BE IMPROVED UPON: crummy-performance headlights, wipers and climate control and really skimpy storage compartments for rear seat travellers.

CONCLUSION
The Trooper is a big all-wheel drive station wagon that provides for cushy travel rather than adventurous roving. The driver has to be aware of its design limitations if he or she doesn't want to get in sticky or scary situations. 😐

RATING
ISUZU Trooper

CONCEPT : — 77%
Technology	80
Safety :	70
Interior space :	65
Trunk volume:	90
Quality/fit/finish :	80

DRIVING: — 59%
Cockpit :	80
Performance :	55
Handling :	45
Steering :	70
Braking :	45

ORIGINAL EQUIPMENT: — 76%
Tires :	75
Headlights :	80
Wipers :	80
Rear defroster :	70
Radio :	75

COMFORT : — 66%
Seats :	75
Suspension :	80
Sound level :	35
Conveniences :	65
Air conditioning :	75

BUDGET : — 41%
Price :	0
Fuel economy :	20
Insurance :	50
Satisfaction :	85
Depreciation :	50

Overall rating: — 63.8%

NEW FOR 1999

• No major change.

ENGINES / TRANSMISSIONS / PERFORMANCES

Model/ version	Type / timing valve / fuel system	Displacement cu in	Power bhp @ rpm	Torque lb-ft @ rpm	Compres. ratio	Driving wheels / transmission	Final ratio	Acceler. 0-60 mph s	Standing 1/4 & 5/8 mile s	Acceler. 50-75 mph s	Braking 60-0 mph f	Top speed mph	Lateral acceler. G	Noise level dBA	Fuel economy mpg City	Fuel economy mpg Highway	Fuel type Octane
base	V6* 3.5 DOHC-24-MPFI	213	215 @ 5400	230 @ 3000	9.1 :1	rear/4 - M5*	4.56	9.0	16.8 30.4	7.5	157	112	0.72	68-72	15	21	R 87
						rear/4 - A4	4.30	9.8	17.3 31.8	8.2	168	109	0.72	68-72	15	21	R 87

PRICE & EQUIPMENT

ISUZU Trooper	S	LS	Limited
Retail price $:	27,800	29,980	31,800
Dealer invoice $:	24,742	26,486	28,102
Shipping & handling $:	445	445	445
Automatic transmission:	O	O	S
Cruise control:	S	S	S
Power steering:	S	S	S
Anti-lock brakes:	S	S	S
Traction control:	S	S	S
Air conditioning:	S	S	S
Leather:	-	-	S
AM/FM/radio-cassette:	S	SCD	SCD
Power door locks:	S	S	S
Power windows:	S	S	S
Tilt steering:	S	S	S
Dual adjustable mirrors:	SEH	SEH	SEH
Alloy wheels:	S	S	S
Anti-theft system:	S	S	S

Colors

Exterior: White, Green, Silver, Red, Black, Blue.

Interior: Brown, Gray, Beige.

AT A GLANCE...

Category: 2WD & 4WD all-purpose vehicles.   **Class :** Utility

HISTORIC
Introduced in:	1981-1998.
Made in:	Fujisawa, Japon.

DEMOGRAPHICS
Model	Men./Wom.	Age	Married	College	Income
Trooper	55/45 %	50	94 %	45 %	$ 60 000

INDEX
Safety:	70 %	Satisfaction:	85 %
Depreciation:	48 %	Insurance:	$ 1050
Cost per mile:	$ 0.58	Number of dealers:	NA

SALES
Model	1996	1997	Result
Trooper	18 495	10 964	- 40.7 %

MAIN COMPETITORS
CADILLAC Escalade, CHEVROLET Blazer-Tahoe-Denali, FORD Explorer-Expedition, GMC Jimmy-Yukon-Envoy, INFINITI QX4, JEEP Grand Cherokee, LEXUS RX 300 & LX 470, LINCOLN Navigator.

MAINTENANCE REQUIRED BY WARRANTY
First revision:	Frequency:	Diagnostic plug:
3 000 miles	6 000 miles	Yes

SPECIFICATIONS

Model	Version Trim	Traction	Body/ Seats	Wheel base in	Lght x Wdgth x Hght in x in x in	Curb weight lb	Susp. ft/rr	Brake ft/rr	Steering type	Turning diameter ft	Steer. turns nber.	Fuel tank gal	tire size	Standard tires make	model	Standard powertrain
ISUZU		Warranty: 3 years / 36 000 miles; powertrain:5 years / 60 000 miles ; perforation 6 years / 100 000miles.														
Trooper	S	4x4	5dr.wgn.5	108.7	187.8x69.5x72.2	4389	it/rh	dc/ABS	pwr.ball	38.1	3.7	22.5	245/70R16	Bridgestone	Dueller 684	V6/3.5/M5
Trooper	LS	4x4	5dr.wgn.5	108.7	187.8x69.5x72.2	4398	it/rh	dc/ABS	pwr.ball	38.1	3.7	22.5	245/70R16	Bridgestone	Dueller 684	V6/3.5/M5
Trooper	Limited	4x4	5dr.wgn.5	108.7	187.8x69.5x72.2	4539	it/rh	dc/ABS	pwr.ball	38.1	3.7	22.5	245/70R16	Bridgestone	Dueller 684	V6/3.5/A4

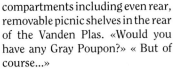
After all these years and umpteen face-lifts, the Jaguar has kept all its alluring charm. This beauty hasn't been scheduled for a complete make-over, but has undergone many minor changes, yet hasn't achieved the same technical prowess as her rivals that are, in this regard, light years ahead. She doesn't mind and pursues her own path, satisfied with her status as the perfect icon of what a thrilling car is meant to be. Actually, she doesn't have to worry one bit, she's one of a kind and mere mortals bestow Oscar status on this great lady.

MODEL RANGE

The XJ family consists of 4-door sedans called XJ8, XJ8 L, Vanden Plas and XJR. The 4.0L V8 engine is common to all models, but the first two are animated by a conventional engine, whereas the XJR is powered by a supercharged engine. Two new 5-speed transmissions equip these cars, a ZF with the conventional powerplant and a Mercedes-Benz with the supercharged model. These cars are lavishly equipped and some items only vary according to the degree of decadent luxury they provide.

TECHNICAL FEATURES

XJ sedans were reworked last year so as to integrate the V8 engine borrowed from the XK8 coupes and convertibles. This year, there's a cleaner burning engine offered to meet American emission standards. Their steel monocoque body includes two subframes on which are mounted the four-wheel independent suspensions consisting of double wishbones with anti-dive, anti-lift devices and stabilizer bars. Four-wheel disc brakes benefit from ABS linked to traction control. The V8 conventional engine develops 290 hp, while the model equipped with an Eaton supercharger pumps out 370 hp. Five-speed automatic transmissions provide very efficient dual-mode settings. Cars are equipped with more safety features, since dual side-impact airbags are located in the front doors and front seatbelts are fitted with heat-sensitive tensioners.

SIMPLY SUPER

++ STYLE. Always classy and elegant, with lovely, flowing lines and dressed up with chrome details that put it in a class apart.

++ DESIGN. The cabin interior reminds you of an English parlor

Venerable Mistress...

with its rich Connolly leather and simply exquisite walnut appliqués that have a lovely look and feel. Too bad the leather has lost its aura of perfume...

PROS

+ DRIVING FEEL. It's a treat beyond words, with the perfect osmosis between available power and a transmission blessed with the best sequential shifter on the market, responsive steering, strong brakes that are easy to apply and superb roadholding benefitting from the more robust body.

+ PERFORMANCES. They're remarkable. The engine can propulse these rather heavy vehicles and hit top speeds in no time flat. The 370-hp engine that motivates the XJR, the most savage of the lot, shouldn't be handed over to anyone but an

experienced driver who knows what he or she is doing.

+ RIDE COMFORT. The creamy suspension and ruthless sound-proofing that stifles most unwanted noise create a cozy, typically English ambience.

+ QUALITY. Craftsmanship, fit and finish details and trim components keep getting better and reliability is no problem for cars in this price range. Original items such as tires, headlamps and climate control are more effective than before.

+ INSTRUMENT PANEL. More logical and ergonomic than before and everything is where you'd expect it to be, typical to the brand dashboard design.

+ CONVENIENCE FEATURES. They haven't been disregarded, since there are numerous, roomy storage

compartments including even rear, removable picnic shelves in the rear of the Vanden Plas. «Would you have any Gray Poupon?» « But of course...»

+ VALUE. It increases according to quality and reliability, so these cars don't lose as much resale value as was once the case...

CONS

- BUDGET. These cars are demanding mistresses, for their upkeep is costly and they consume a lot: the XJR supercharged engine can easily go as low as 11 mpg. Luckily, the conventional engine is less greedy, at least for normal driving.

- TECHNOLOGY. The XJ versions are falling further and further behind with each passing year and their simple charm may have held them in good stead up until now, but it soon won't be enough to do the trick.

- HANDLING. These sedans are heavier and more plump, so they're considered to be rather sedate, that is they prefer gentlemen to wild sporty types.

- USEFUL SPACE. The XJ8 cabin isn't as roomy as you'd expect for such a big car and the extended Vanden Plas version is practical by comparison. The same applies to the trunk, for it's ridiculously small with the huge spare tire gobbling up all the available space.

- SEATS. They're weirdly shaped and do take some getting used to.

- MANEUVERABILITY. The Vanden Plas is handicapped by a wide steer angle diameter.

- TO BE IMPROVED UPON: some unusual controls, limited visibility at rear quarterback and some finish details such as the Taurus/Sable exterior door handles or the illegible instruments sunken into the massive dashboard. During our test run, hubcaps covering wheel bolts came off the rims with disarming ease.

CONCLUSION

Like an old, cherished mistress, the XJ lacks neither charm nor class. It may go through the motions with great flair and be quite appealing in this respect, but it's hard to maintain and some of its ploys are getting a bit hackneyed... Deliciously British... ☺

RATING
JAGUAR XJ8-XJR

CONCEPT :		75%
Technology	85	
Safety :	90	
Interior space :	70	
Trunk volume:	40	
Quality/fit/finish :	90	

DRIVING:		74%
Cockpit :	80	
Performance :	70	
Handling :	60	
Steering :	80	
Braking :	80	

ORIGINAL EQUIPMENT:		81%
Tires :	85	
Headlights :	80	
Wipers :	80	
Rear defroster :	75	
Radio :	85	

COMFORT :		80%
Seats :	80	
Suspension :	80	
Sound level:	80	
Conveniences :	80	
Air conditioning :	80	

BUDGET :		40%
Price :	0	
Fuel economy :	30	
Insurance :	40	
Satisfaction :	80	
Depreciation :	50	

| **Overall rating:** | | **70.0%** |

NEW FOR 1999

- Modified V8 engine to meet current clean emission standards.
- Two new body shades for the Vanden Plas: Olive Green and Dark Green.

ENGINES

Model/ version	Type / timing valve / fuel system	Displacement cu in	Power bhp @ rpm	Torque lb-ft @ rpm
XJ8	V8* 4.0 DOHC-32-MPSFI	244	290 @ 6100	290 @ 4250
XJ* L- VdP	V8* 4.0 DOHC-32-MPSFI	244	290 @ 6100	290 @ 4250
XJR	V8*C 4.0 DOHC 32-MPSFI	244	370 @ 6150	387 @ 3600

TRANSMISSIONS

Compres. ratio	Driving wheels / transmission	Final ratio
10.75 :1	rear-ZFA5*	3.06
10.75 :1	rear-ZFA5*	3.06
9.00 :1	rear-M-B A5*	3.06

PERFORMANCES

Acceler. 0-60 mph s	Standing 1/4 & 5/8 mile s	Acceler. 50-75 mph s	Braking 60-0 mph f	Top speed mph	Lateral acceler. G	Noise level dBA	Fuel economy mpg City	Fuel economy mpg Highway	Fuel type Octane
7.6	15.2 26.6	5.4	128	143	0.80	64-66	17	24	S 91
8.2	16.4 29.0	5.7	134	137	0.80	64-68	16	24	S 91
6.0	14.2 25.7	4.2	144	149	0.80	65-68	14	22	S 91

PRICE & EQUIPMENT

JAGUAR XJ8 JAGUAR XJR	XJ8	XJ8 L	Vanden Plas	base
Retail price $:	54,750	59,750	63,800	67,400
Dealer invoice $:	47,830	52,198	55,736	55,881
Shipping & handling $:	580	580	580	580
Automatic transmission:	S	S	S	S
Cruise control:	S	S	S	S
Power steering:	S	S	S	S
Anti-lock brakes:	S	S	S	S
Traction control:	S	S	S	S
Air conditioning:	SA	SA	SA	SA
Leather:	S	S	S	S
AM/FM/radio-cassette:	S	S	SCD	SCD
Power door locks:	S	S	S	S
Power windows:	S	S	S	S
Tilt steering:	S	S	S	S
Dual adjustable mirrors:	S	S	S	S
Alloy wheels:	S	S	S	S
Anti-theft system:	S	S	S	S

Colors

Exterior: Gray, White, Black, Mistral blue, Meteorite, Green, Topaz, Anthracite, Cabernet, Titanium, Turquoise, Amaranth & Madeira red , Sherwood.
Interior: Blue, Charcoal, Oatmeal, Coffee, Nimbus.

AT A GLANCE...

Category: rear-wheel drive grand luxury sedans.   **Class :** 7

HISTORIC
Introduced in: 1987
Made in: Browns Lane, Coventry, England.

DEMOGRAPHICS

Model	Men./Wom.	Age	Married	College	Income
XJ8	92/8 %	52	90 %	53 %	$130 000
XJR	98/2 %	48	90 %	57 %	$180 000

INDEX
Safety: 90 %   **Satisfaction:** 80 %
Depreciation: 48 %   **Insurance:** $1 950-2 150
Cost per mile: $ 1.00   **Number of dealers:** 130

SALES

Model	1996	1997	Result
XJ8-XJR	12 958	12 588	- 2.9 %

MAIN COMPETITORS
AUDI A8, BMW 4-7-Series, CADILLAC Seville, INFINITI Q45, LEXUS LS 400, MERCEDES-BENZ E-S-Class, OLDSMOBILE Aurora.

MAINTENANCE REQUIRED BY WARRANTY
First revision: 4 000 miles   **Frequency:** 6-10 000 miles   **Diagnostic plug:** Yes

SPECIFICATIONS

Model	Version Trim	Body/ Seats	Interior volume cu ft	Trunk volume cu ft	Cd	Wheel base in	Lght x Wdgth x Hght in x in x in	Curb weight lb	Susp. ft/rr	Brake ft/rr	Steering type	Turning diameter ft	Steer. turns nber.	Fuel tank gal	tire size	Standard tires make	model	Standard powertrain
JAGUAR							Warranty: 4 years / 50 000 miles; corrosion: 6 years / unlimited; antipollution : 4 years / 50 000 miles ; free maintenance: 2 years / 20 000 miles.											
XJ8		4dr.sdn.5	93.0	12.7	0.37	113.0	197.8x70.8x52.7	3997	ih/ih	dc/ABS	pwr.r&p.	42.0	2.8	21.4	225/60ZR16	Pirelli	P4000	V8/4.0/A5
XJ8	L	4dr.sdn.5	NA	12.7	0.37	117.9	202.7x70.8x53.2	4012	ih/ih	dc/ABS	pwr.r&p.	43.3	2.8	21.4	225/60ZR16	Pirelli	P4000	V8/4.0/A5
XJ8	Vanden Plas	4dr.sdn.5	NA	12.7	0.37	117.9	202.7x70.8x53.2	4048	ih/ih	dc/ABS	pwr.r&p.	43.3	2.8	21.4	225/60ZR16	Pirelli	P4000	V8/4.0/A5
XJR		4dr.sdn.5	93.0	12.7	0.39	113.0	197.8x70.8x52.7	4074	ih/ih	dc/ABS	pwr.r&p.	42.0	2.8	21.4	255/40ZR18	Pirelli	P Zero	V8C/4.0/A5

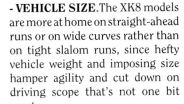

The XK8's were the first fresh signs of renewal at Jaguar, influenced by the American giant Ford that acquired the British firm eight years ago now. These cars replaced the XJS models, the only sports cars built by Jaguar for more than a dozen years. These new, exceptional cars are technically very modern, yet their body design is inspired by a tradition set by the famous XKE models of the sixties.

MODEL RANGE

The XK8's are offered as a 2-door, 2-passenger coupe and convertible in a single trim level, equipped with a 4L V8 engine associated with a five-speed automatic transmission with regular or sequential shifter. As to be expected for such expensive cars, equipment is very rich. It includes more particularly an antilock braking system and traction control.

TECHNICAL FEATURES

The steel monocoque body includes some galvanized panels. Aerodynamics are quite good, since the drag coefficient is 0.35 for the coupe and 0.36 for the convertible. The fully independent suspension consists of a double wishbone arrangement, mounted on an aluminum cradle and adjusted so as to offset front nosedive effect. The same system holds for the rear end, that controls rearing up on acceleration, and there's a stabilizer bar both front and rear. Disc brakes benefit from an ABS device and the P Zero tires were designed by Pirelli, specifically for these versions. The engine that motivates the XK8's is a V8, the first in the Coventry firm's history. This engine design isn't of Ford origin, but it still took advantage of project planning advice from the American giant. It's a 4.0L model that develops 290 hp and 290 lb.ft torque. The engine block and cylinder head are made of an aluminum alloy. The engine has DOHC distribution with four valves per cylinder. It's equipped with a device called «Variable Cam Phasing», that allows for varying camshaft timing, so as to obtain 80% maximum torque between 1,400 and 6,400 r.p.m. This mechanism, located at the camshafts' extremity, modifies when exactly the intake valves open, but not how long they remain so. The ZF 5-speed automatic transmission maximizes engine performances while maintaining low fuel consumption.

True To Tradition..

SIMPLY SUPER

++ SILHOUETTE. It's irresistibly like the legendary XK-E design. The car is a different size from the original, but the overall look is very zippy and stylistic touches are super sleek, maybe a bit too much so.

PROS

+ THE V8 ENGINE. It's the lion's heart of this model, it's responsive, zesty and creamy smooth, and yet it has a discreet and serene demeanor. It provides awesome performances, no mean feat since these vehicles aren't exactly featherweights, but the power to weight ratio is nice and comfortable.

+ DRIVING PLEASURE. It's terrific with such clean, right-on front and rear end directional flow due to the rigid structure, even on the con-

vertible. Accurate steering and brakes make the pilot look like a champion.

+ QUALITY. It's better than it was, since assembly is more meticulous and the fit and finish job is very fine, but it's still not on a par with what you get on German or Japanese rivals. Leather seats have a typical, velvety Connolly feel, but the lovely scent is gone forever, a real pity. The convertible soft top is of impeccable construction, for it's lined and can be raised or lowered automatically.

+ HANDLING. It's by far superior to that of former XJS versions, since behavior is stable and easy to control in all situations. This is due to the stiff build and sophisticated suspension components.

+ STEERING. It's smooth, direct and crisp, so you can control car path with remarkable ease on the highway and on city streets where maneuvers are reasonably good.

CONS

- VEHICLE SIZE. The XK8 models are more at home on straight-ahead runs or on wide curves rather than on tight slalom runs, since hefty vehicle weight and imposing size hamper agility and cut down on driving scope that's not one bit sporty.

- BODY. It's a bit too stripped down, since it isn't dressed up in the usual Jaguar chrome finery on rims, mirrors, taillights and bumpers... Jaguar should take care of this sad state of affairs pretty quick.

- COCKPIT. It's penalized by the seat design and somehow you don't feel that you're benefitting from much lateral or lumbar support. Toe and hip room are awfully snug and it's no fun getting aboard with the unusually wide door threshold.

- VISIBILITY. It's nowhere wonderful, due to the high frame belt, bulky windshield supports and the blind spot at rear quarterback caused by the convertible top, less obvious on the coupe, but both models are afflicted with a narrow, severely slanted rear window.

- INSTRUMENT PANEL. Like the exterior, it lacks stylistic accents with those thick, massive wood panels. Ergonomics aren't too great either, not with the inverted order climate control and sound system dials and the switches located at the right that are out of reach.

- REAR SEATS. They're totally useless due to terribly stingy head and leg room. It would have been clever to come up with a design that lets you store luggage by lowering the seatbench back to form a platform.

-TO BE IMPROVED UPON: no rear wiper on the coupe.

CONCLUSION

The XK8 models don't presume to be true blue sports cars. They're lovely to look at, luxury two-seaters that provide very good passenger protection, so that those who can afford these beauties will be out of harm's way and won't have to deal with other nonsense that's the lot of exotic car owners. In this regard, Jaguar has come up with a perfect concept of what luxury passenger cars should be in this day and age...

RATING JAGUAR XK8

CONCEPT: 68%
- Technology: 85
- Safety: 90
- Interior space: 40
- Trunk volume: 40
- Quality/fit/finish: 85

DRIVING: 77%
- Cockpit: 75
- Performance: 80
- Handling: 70
- Steering: 80
- Braking: 80

ORIGINAL EQUIPMENT: 80%
- Tires: 85
- Headlights: 80
- Wipers: 80
- Rear defroster: 75
- Radio: 80

COMFORT: 70%
- Seats: 80
- Suspension: 80
- Sound level: 50
- Conveniences: 60
- Air conditioning: 80

BUDGET: 45%
- Price: 0
- Fuel economy: 50
- Insurance: 30
- Satisfaction: 85
- Depreciation: 60

Overall rating: 68.0%

NEW FOR 1999
- Two new exterior shades: Phoenix red and Alpine olive green.
- The convertible top now available in a beige shade.

ENGINES / TRANSMISSIONS / PERFORMANCES

Model/version	Type/timing valve/fuel system	Displacement cu in	Power bhp @ rpm	Torque lb-ft @ rpm	Compres. ratio	Driving wheels/transmission	Final ratio	Acceler. 0-60 mph s	Standing 1/4 & 5/8 mile s	Acceler. 50-75 mph s	Braking 60-0 mph f	Top speed mph	Lateral acceler. G	Noise level dBA	Fuel economy mpg City	Highway	Fuel type Octane
XK8 cpe.	V8* 4.0 DOHC-32-EFI	244	290 @ 6100	290 @ 4250	10.75:1	rear - A5*	3.06	6.7	15.0	28.0	4.4	125	152	0.85	64-72	17	25	S 91
XK8 con.	V8* 4.0 DOHC-32-EFI	244	290 @ 6100	290 @ 4250	10.75:1	rear - A5*	3.06	7.0	15.2	28.4	4.6	131	149	0.85	64-72	17	25	S 91

PRICE & EQUIPMENT

JAGUAR XK8	coupe	convertible
Retail price $:	64,900	69,900
Dealer invoice $:	57,104	61,472
Shipping & handling $:	580	580
Automatic transmission:	S	S
Cruise control:	S	S
Power steering:	S	S
Anti-lock brakes:	S	S
Traction control:	S	S
Air conditioning:	S	S
Leather:	S	S
AM/FM/radio-cassette:	SCD	SCD
Power door locks:	S	S
Power windows:	S	S
Tilt steering:	S	S
Dual adjustable mirrors:	S	S
Alloy wheels:	S	S
Anti-theft system:		S

Colors
Exterior: Green, Black, Beige, White, Red, Blue.
Interior: Black, White, Tan, Blue.

AT A GLANCE...
Category: GT coupes & convertibles. Class: GT

HISTORIC
Introduced in: 1997
Made in: Browns Lane, Coventry, England.

DEMOGRAPHICS

Model	Men./Wom.	Age	Married	College	Income
XK8	83%/17%	49	78%	50%	$ 240 000

INDEX
Safety: 90 % Satisfaction: 87%
Depreciation: 40 % Insurance: $ 1975
Cost per mile: $ 1.10 Number of dealers: 130

SALES

Model	1996	1997	Result
XK8	4 920	6 915	+ 40.7 %

MAIN COMPETITORS
ACURA NSX-T, MERCEDES-BENZ SC-SL, PORSCHE Boxster-911, VOLVO C70.

MAINTENANCE REQUIRED BY WARRANTY
First revision: 4 000 miles Frequency: 6 000 miles Diagnostic plug: Yes

SPECIFICATIONS

Warranty: 4 years / 50 000 miles; corrosion: 6 years / unlimited; antipollution: 4 years / 50 000 miles ; free maintenance: 2 years / 20 000 miles.

Model	Version Trim	Body/Seats	Interior volume cu ft	Trunk volume cu ft	Cd	Wheel base in	Lght x Wdgth x Hght in x in x in	Curb weight lb	Susp. ft/rr	Brake ft/rr	Steering type	Turning diameter ft	Steer. turns nber.	Fuel tank gal	tire size	Standard tires make	model	Standard powertrain
JAGUAR XK8	coupe	2dr.cpe.2+2	NA	11.1	0.35	101.9	187.4x72.0x50.5	3673	i/i	d/dc/ABS	pwr.r&p.	40.7	2.8	20.0	245/50ZR17	Pirelli	P Zero	V8/4.0/A5
XK8	convertible	2dr.con.2+2	NA	9.5	0.36	101.9	187.4x72.0x51.0	3867	i/i	d/dc/ABS	pwr.r&p.	40.7	2.8	20.0	245/50ZR17	Pirelli	P Zero	V8/4.0/A5

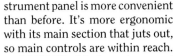

In spite of its age, the Cherokee is still impressive, thanks to its hard to beat value-price combination. It's the only compact all-terrain vehicle to offer a 190-hp 6-cylinder engine that allows for trailering capabilities up to 5,000 lb. Its classic body design is part of the daily landscape and you see it on a lot of roads. Last year's facelift gave a fresh spurt to its popularity, as was the case for the Sport, Classic and Limited models with super designs and equipped with pretty tantalizing equipment items.

MODEL RANGE

The Cherokee is available in 3 or 5-door models, with either RWD or AWD in SE, Sport, Classic and Limited versions, the two latter replacing the Country. The SE version is animated by a 2.5L 4-cylinder engine, but the Sport, Classic and Limited receive a 4.0L in-line 6 engine. The manual gearbox comes standard and the 3 or 4-speed automatic is sold as an extra. Dual airbags are part of the original equipment but four-wheel ABS is still only an option.

TECHNICAL FEATURES

The Cherokee consists of a steel structure made up of an H-frame built into a steel unibody. Vehicle design isn't too refined when it comes to aerodynamics, since the drag coefficient sits at about 0.50. The rigid axle suspensions are equipped with longitudinal control arms, anti-roll bar as well as coil springs up front and leaf springs at the rear. Vehicles are equipped with disc and drum brakes, but the ABS system is only available as an extra. The 4X4's benefit from on-demand «Select-Trac» all-wheel drive, standard on the SE version, but from a full-time «Command-Trac» system that's part of the original equipment on other versions. Both engines that are starting to show their age are linked up with a standard manual transmission and an optional 3-speed (2.5L) or 4-speed automatic, the latter being standard on the Classic and Limited versions.

PROS

+ STYLE. Handsome and familiar, it's a real classic and exudes a reassuring solid as a rock feeling.

+ SIZE. It's very compact, so you can go anywhere and this vehicle maneuvers beautifully. The 4.0L 6-cylinder engine gives it a unique

Lovely Remains...

top of the heap athletic status, so it makes light work of heavy loads.

+ OFF-ROAD CAPABILITIES. The Cherokee is a real acrobat. It can tackle off-road maneuvers with no trouble at all, due to wide entrance and exit angles, effective traction, reasonable weight and spare tire stored inside the cargo hold to optimize ground clearance.

+ SLICK MOVES. This vehicle is nice and compact, benefits from a short steer angle diameter and lively steering, though the latter suffers from a slightly poor reduction ratio, so it doesn't require much maneuvering space. Visibility is terrific in all directions due to large windows and relatively thin roof supports.

+ PERFORMANCES. They have more zip with the 6-cylinder engine since the power to weight ratio is more favorable than for the 4-cylinder.

+ MODEL CHOICE. The Cherokee is one of the few SUV's that comes in 2 body designs, 4 trim levels, equipped with RWD or AWD, 3 all-wheel drive transmission modes...

+ HANDLING. This vehicle has a high center of gravity, but it's amazingly confident for a vehicle of this type, sway is limited and the big tires let you take curves, even tighties, with a certain aplomb.

+ VALUE. The Cherokee is among the vehicles that have top resale value in the category, due to dependability and long-life components, at a more appealing price than for some of the competition.

+ CABIN LAYOUT. The new instrument panel is more convenient than before. It's more ergonomic with its main section that juts out, so main controls are within reach.

+ COCKPIT. It's been improved with the new steering column and the seat enfolds you more and is quite nicely upholstered.

+ QUALITY. It's been noticeably enhanced when it comes to finish job and trim materials and the vehicle looks generally less bare bone basic.

CONS

- DESIGN. It's starting to get terribly outdated with its narrow, low clearance cabin, and the luggage compartment isn't huge and it holds the spare tire.

- ACCESS. You have to go through a workout to board and unboard because of the narrow doors on the 4-door model and high ground clearance, so some folks will have to opt for the 2-door version that's equipped with add-on running boards.

- SAFETY FEATURES. They're penalized by missing standard rear seat headrests and chronically weak headlights.

-BRAKES. They're not too hot, emergency stops take longer than average to achieve and ABS isn't standard, so vehicle path is very unpredictable. The automatic transmission doesn't provide much braking effect.

- PERFORMANCES. The 2.5L engine is anemic, especially with the automatic gearbox when the air conditioner is on. With the manual, you have to often shift gears to maintain speeds.

-FUEL CONSUMPTION. It's poor with both engines that are God-awful old. They're very greedy, given the real power they can put out.

- RIDE COMFORT. It's far from perfect with those big tires and rigid axles that give occupants quite a shaking up and the seat and back cushions on the seatbench are too short. Wind whistling around the angular body and roaring engines create loud, pervasive noise.

- TO BE IMPROVED UPON: Missing storage spots on the door panels and no footrest for the driver.

CONCLUSION

The Cherokee keeps its well-earned popularity due to its compact size and big 4.0L powerplant that makes it one of the toughest 4X4's in its category at a price that's hard to beat, given the equipment... ☺

RATING
JEEP Cherokee

CONCEPT :		66%
Technology	75	
Safety :	70	
Interior space :	60	
Trunk volume:	50	
Quality/fit/finish :	75	

DRIVING:		54%
Cockpit :	75	
Performance :	35	
Handling :	40	
Steering :	70	
Braking :	50	

ORIGINAL EQUIPMENT:		77%
Tires :	80	
Headlights :	70	
Wipers :	80	
Rear defroster :	75	
Radio :	80	

COMFORT :		61%
Seats :	70	
Suspension :	60	
Sound level:	50	
Conveniences :	50	
Air conditioning :	75	

BUDGET :		57%
Price :	50	
Fuel economy :	55	
Insurance :	50	
Satisfaction :	80	
Depreciation :	50	

Overall rating:	63.0%

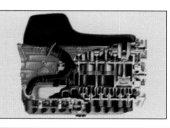

NEW FOR 1999
- The new 2.5L engine meeting TLEV clean emission standards.
- New exterior shades, Forest Green and Desert Sand as well as new Camel and Agate interior trim shades.
- Optional theft-deterrent system and front heated seats on the Limited.
- Climate control geared to optimum performance.
- Improved cabin design on the Sport version.

ENGINES

Model/ version	Type / timing valve / fuel system	Displacement cu in	Power bhp @ rpm	Torque lb-ft @ rpm
1)	L4* 2.5 OHV-8-MPSFI	150	125 @ 5400	150 @ 3250
2)	L6* 4.0 OHV-12-MPSFI	242	190 @ 4600	225 @ 3000

1) SE. 2) Sport, Classic, Limited, option SE.

TRANSMISSIONS

Compres. ratio	Driving wheels / transmission	Final ratio
9.2 :1	rear/4 - M5*	4.10
	rear/4 - A3	3.55
8.8 :1	rear/4 - M5*	3.07
	rear/4 - A4*	3.55

PERFORMANCES

Acceler. 0-60 mph s	Standing 1/4 & 5/8 mile s		Acceler. 50-75 mph s	Braking 60-0 mph f	Top speed mph	Lateral acceler. G	Noise level dBA	Fuel economy mpg City	Highway	Fuel type Octane
12.5	18.8	35.2	11.0	157	93	0.68	69	19	28	R 87
13.5	19.5	36.8	11.8	161	90	0.68	68	18	22	R 87
9.0	16.6	30.5	7.0	167	112	0.70	69	18	22	R 87
10.0	17.5	31.3	8.0	164	109	0.70	69	15	21	R 87

PRICE & EQUIPMENT

JEEP Cherokee	SE 3dr.wgn. 4x2	Sport 3dr.wgn. 4x4	Classic 4dr.wgn. 4x4	Limited 4dr.wgn. 4x4
Retail price $:	15,665	19,810	22,240	24,605
Dealer invoice $:	14,716	17,913	20,071	22,081
Shipping & handling $:	525	525	525	525
Automatic transmission:	O	O	S	S
Cruise control:	O	O	O	S
Power steering:	S	S	S	S
Anti-lock brakes:	O	O	O	O
Traction control:	O	O	O	O
Air conditioning:	O	O	O	O
Leather:	-	-	-	S
AM/FM/radio-cassette:	O	S	S	S
Power door locks:	-	O	O	S
Power windows:	-	O	O	S
Tilt steering:	O	O	O	S
Dual adjustable mirrors:	SM	SE	SE	SEC
Alloy wheels:	O	O	S	S
Anti-theft system:	O	O	O	O

Colors
Exterior: Red, Blue, Green, Gray, White, Black, Chili Pepper, Gold, Jade, Sand.

interior: Camel, Pebble.

AT A GLANCE...

Category:	2WD or 4WD sport-utility.	Class :	Utility

HISTORIC
Introduced in: 1984.
Made in: Toledo, Ohio, USA

DEMOGRAPHICS

Model	Men./Wom.	Age	Married	College	Income
Cherokee	68/32 %	42	64 %	53 %	$ 42 000

INDEX

Safety:	70 %	Satisfaction:	78 %
Depreciation:	48 %	Insurance:	$ 985
Cost per mile:	$ 0.53	Number of dealers:	1 029

SALES

Model	1996	1997	Result
Cherokee	148,544	130,041	- 12.5 %

MAIN COMPETITORS
CHEVROLET Blazer, DODGE Durango, FORD Explorer, ISUZU Rodeo, GMC Jimmy, NISSAN Pathfinder, SUZUKI Grand Vitara, TOYOTA 4Runner.

MAINTENANCE REQUIRED BY WARRANTY

First revision:	Frequency:	Diagnostic plug:
7 500 miles	6 months	Yes

SPECIFICATIONS

Model	Version Trim	Traction	Body/ Seats	Wheel base in	Lght x Wdgth x Hght in x in x in	Curb weight lb	Susp. ft/rr	Brake ft/rr	Steering type	Turning diameter ft	Steer. turns nber.	Fuel tank gal	tire size	Standard tires make	model	Standard powertrain
JEEP	General warranty: 3 years / 36 000 miles; surface rust 1 year / 12 000 miles; perforation 7 years / 100 000 miles; roadside assistance 3 years / 36 000 miles.															
Cherokee	SE	4X2	3dr.wgn.5	101.4	167.5x69.4x63.9	3018	rh/rl	dc/dr	pwr.ball	35.1	2.94	20.0	215/75R15	Goodyear	Wrangler AP	L4/2.5/M5
Cherokee	Sport	4X2	5dr.wgn.5	101.4	167.5x69.4x63.9	3154	rh/rl	dc/dr	pwr.ball	35.1	2.94	20.0	225/75R15	Goodyear	Wrangler RT/S	L6/4.0/M5
Cherokee	Classic/Limited	4X2	5dr.wgn.5	101.4	167.5x69.4x63.9	3194	rh/rl	dc/dr	pwr.ball	35.1	2.94	20.0	225/70R15	Goodyear	Wrangler RT/S	L6/4.0/A4
Cherokee	SE	4X4	3dr.wgn.5	101.4	167.5x69.4x64.0	3179	rh/rl	dc/dr	pwr.ball	35.1	2.94	20.0	215/75R15	Goodyear	Wrangler AP	L4/2.5/M5
Cherokee	Sport	4X4	5dr.wgn.5	101.4	167.5x69.4x64.0	3353	rh/rl	dc/dr	pwr.ball	35.1	2.94	20.0	225/75R15	Goodyear	Wrangler RT/S	L6/4.0/M5
Cherokee	Classic/Limited	4X4	5dr.wgn.5	101.4	167.5x69.4x64.0	3395	rh/rl	dc/dr	pwr.ball	35.1	2.94	20.0	225/70R15	Goodyear	Wrangler RT/S	L6/4.0/A4

JEEP Grand Cherokee
A Fine Vintage

The novello Grand Cherokee has arrived. After beating popularity and sales records just about everywhere on planet Earth, Jeep has decided that it was time to spruce up its standard bearer. So, five years after the very first model was introduced, a vehicle that was going to be nothing short of a phenomenon in its own right, the second generation is making its entrance with all the appropriate fuss and fanfare.

At first glance, the body design doesn't look much different than that of its predecessor, still sporting the grille design with the typical seven-"tooth" arrangement that's a brand name signature. Yet everything about the Grand Cherokee is new except for all the big screws and bolts, interior mirror and oil filter that hail from the former model. We can certainly understand why Jeep designers walked on eggs when it came to tampering with the vehicle's appearance. The body needed to have a face-lift to look more with it, but not look terribly different from the handsome bod that was so gosh darn popular with folks. It's often a lot easier to start from scratch rather than be limited by criteria that are too stringent. You could say that the latest Grand Cherokee possesses attributes that are characteristic of the Jeep brand and also recognizable traits of its illustrious predecessor. On the exterior, traditional size has been respected, the rocker panel guards constituting a sort of stylistic signature and scads of other details have been well blended in to procure a curious mix of lap of luxury looks and the rough and tough, functional side worthy of a genuine SUV. The same applies to the interior that's understated and yet very elegant-looking. Trim materials

were chosen with an eye to appearance and texture, yet they're not overly ritzy, but down to earth. Vehicle size hasn't been beefed up to excess. Some dimensions have been extended to provide more ride comfort, but not in an overboard fashion. The Grand Cherokee is still an intermediate vehicle, but designers were keeping an eye out for direct rivals like the Mercedes-Benz M-Class. To be a serious contender, this vehicle now offers more space in the rear seats and the rear seatbench can be folded down in a snap and the spare tire is finally stored under the floor to make more room for luggage, but without affecting the crucial exit angle.

It only took 20 months to come up with the final design for this vehicle that benefits from a dramatically different suspension that, as we'll see further on, is going to be this newcomer's ace in the hand. Engineers went at it with

no holds barred, to make sure the Grand Cherokee will keep its popular status. So the vehicle is equipped with an entirely new modular V8 engine derived from the Jeep V6, associated to a spanking new transmission and a new all-wheel drive transmission coined "Quadra-Drive".

In a market where sales have gone from 500,000 units sold in 1984 to 2.4 million last year and with a projected 3.3 million in the year 2003, you can't give one inch to the competition and you have to be always on top of things. Jeep is now organized to build 500,000 Grand Cherokee's per year and claims it's ready to equip other plants across the world if the demand is higher than production. Creating this new vehicle took a 2.6 billion dollars U.S. investment, of which 800 million went into developing the new engine and planning its production procedures.

Jeep didn't hold back a bit when it came to keeping the Grand Cherokee among the leaders of the pack in the most popular North American market segment, namely the all-wheel drive SUV. This vehicle's revision wasn't just a cosmetic job on body and cabin design, since it's built on a new platform and is equipped with new mechanical components that are on the cutting edge and are superbly honed, making the Grand Cherokee our best rookie for 1999.

MODEL RANGE

This SUV is sold as a four-door station wagon, with either RWD or AWD, in Laredo and Limited trim, equipped with the 4.0L in-line 6 that powered the former model as standard equipment or with the latest 4.7L V8 linked to a new 4-speed automatic gearbox. The 4X4 versions offer several all-wheel drive devices including the latest «Quadra-Drive». Base equipment is very lush, since the Laredo and Limited only differ in respect to leather-clad seats and theft-deterrent device, optional items on the Laredo and original assets on the Limited.

TECHNICAL FEATURES

The Grand Cherokee body is still a steel unibody, so overall height can be trimmed down, while maintaining generous ground clearance, which isn't the case for a body-on-frame formula. It's extremely rigid because it integrates a chassis frame to the lower body. Yet, even with its taut lines, aerodynamic yield isn't that of a car, but it's more efficient than on the former model. The vehicle has exactly the same wheelbase as before, but it's 4.4 inches longer, 1.6 inches wider and 1.5 inches taller. Wheel tracks have been widened out, but trunk volume has been pared down, yet it's not cluttered up with the full-size spare tire that's now stored under the cargo hold floor. The Grand Cherokee's road competence and ride comfort are the direct result of the sturdy multiple control arm links connecting the rigid axles to the body structure. Suspension components have been reorganized with a view to increasing suspension travel and providing better wheel adherence. The recirculating ball steering system was created to provide more right-on precision than is possible with a rack-and-pinion arrangement and four-wheel disc brakes benefit from a standard antilock braking system. The new V8 engine is modular, that is, the 3.5L V6 gets two more cylinders. This engine is more muscular than the 5.2L engine that animated the former ver-

sion, but torque isn't as gutsy, yet fuel consumption and pollutant emissions are lower. The new 4-speed automatic gearbox is quite unique since it applies overdrive as soon as you hit second gear and the «Quadra-Drive» full-time all-wheel drive benefits from viscous coupling power distribution and it comes as original equipment with the V8. Lastly, climate control uses an infrared sensor that adjusts cabin temperature to occupants' body temperature.

PROS

+ **STYLE.** The esthetic charm still works its magic, which is the secret behind this vehicle's appeal. The overall design is a dashing blend of refined luxury and rugged, make my day traits.

+ **SUSPENSION.** It's the latest Grand Cherokee's forte since it procures super-competent handling both on and off the road and offers ride comfort worthy of a regal, top of the heap sedan.

+ **VALUE.** Prices are pretty well what they were for the older models, yet original equipment is very extensive and incorporates a number of major, state-of-the-art technical features, so this vehicle is

a real bargain and it doesn't depreciate as much as most of the competition out there.

+ **RIDE COMFORT.** Jeep engineers have once again demonstrated their cunning way of taming rigid axle suspensions so as to procure ride comfort similar to that achieved by a MacPherson strut setup. There are neat-design, thickly cushioned seats both front and rear, soundproofing takes its task seriously and climate control provides nice, even temperatures.

+ **HANDLING.** This vehicle is extremely stable and neutral on all kinds of curves, with no center of gravity fallout and off-road capabilities are absolutely amazing.

+ **PERFORMANCES.** The new 4.7L V8 brings a whole new driving dimension to the latest Grand Cherokee. Power output, lively response and a clever transmission put it on a par with lots of cars when it comes to accelerations and pickup. Locomotion elements are responsive and quick on the draw and the turbine roars away at full tilt.

+ **BRAKES.** They grip like champions and are easy to apply, stops are achieved within short distances and with straight-ahead confidence and

they're tough as nails.

+ **THE «QUADRA-DRIVE».** This feature is a perfect example of top-notch Jeep know-how when it comes to all-wheel drive, for this device automatically transfers available torque to the wheel or wheels with the best grip on things.

+ **NICE FEATURES:** How easily the cargo hold can be transformed, the big rear hatch and door handles, the window that opens on the hatch door, the rear fender that serves as a running board, storage bins that make up for the slim, trim glove compartment.

CONS

- **CABIN SPACE.** The Grand Cherokee has a shorter wheelbase than rivals, which makes for slicker off-road maneuvers, but cabin space is pretty snug and there isn't enough leg room for either front or rear seat passengers and rear doors are still awfully narrow, so getting aboard is a bit of a chore. To make matters worse, the inner doors and center console take up a lot of room and cut down on essential breathing space, and only four passengers will really feel comfy inside.

- **NOISE.** The body is well insulated, but engine and wind keep humming the same monotonous tune that can be quite wearing.

- **SAFETY FEATURES.** Strange that this vehicle doesn't come equipped with side-impact airbags, a definite must on such a high tech vehicle...

- **STORAGE SPACE.** There aren't many spots to store stuff up front and compartments are teeny tiny, they don't even exist in the rear and backseat travellers have to settle for two seat pockets and cup-holders.

- **APPEARANCE.** The plastic parts that make up the dashboard look just about as cheap as those on the latest LH Chrysler products.

- **INSTRUMENT PANEL.** It's terribly plain and dull-looking, gauges and instruments are hard to read and there's no indicator for the shifter position, an item that you find on even the lowliest Honda Civic...

CONCLUSION

Jeep consulted Grand Cherokee customers to get an idea of what needed to be improved upon and so most snags have been taken care of, one after the other. The end result is a new model that is a top-performance vehicle that handles beautifully, is furbished with lots of luxury items and provides a cushy ride, without having to sell out on essentials that make it such a star seller... ☺

RATING
JEEP Grand Cherokee

CONCEPT : **78%**
Technology : 85
Safety : 90
Interior space : 70
Trunk volume : 65
Quality/fit/finish : 80

DRIVING: **70%**
Cockpit : 80
Performance : 60
Handling : 50
Steering : 80
Braking : 80

ORIGINAL EQUIPMENT: **79%**
Tires : 80
Headlights : 80
Wipers : 80
Rear defroster : 75
Radio : 80

COMFORT : **74%**
Seats : 80
Suspension : 80
Sound level : 60
Conveniences : 70
Air conditioning : 80

BUDGET : **39%**
Price : 10
Fuel economy : 30
Insurance : 45
Satisfaction : 85
Depreciation : 25

Overall rating: **68.0%**

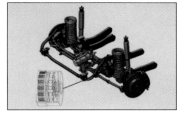

Anecdote

Launching new vehicles has become the ultimate showcase where everyone is trying to outdo the competition, in other words, the sky's the limit when it comes to impressing journalists, the main concern being to provide moments to remember. The latest Grand Cherokee unveiling took place in the Seattle area, on a peninsula that you could only get to by boat or seaplane. The night before, dinner was served at the glass-blower Sahuly's home, located right on the Seattle harbor and the place looked like a weird and wonderful gallery full of enormous, multicolored glass flowers.

ENGINES / TRANSMISSIONS / PERFORMANCES

Model/ version	Type / timing valve / fuel system	Displacement cu in	Power bhp @ rpm	Torque lb-ft @ rpm	Compres. ratio	Driving wheels / transmission	Final ratio	Acceler. 0-60 mph s	Standing 1/4 & 5/8 mile s	Acceler. 50-75 mph s	Braking 60-0 mph f	Top speed mph	Lateral acceler. G	Noise level dBA	Fuel economy mpg City Highway	Fuel type Octane
base	L6* 4.0 OHV-12-MPSFI	242	195 @ 4600	230 @ 3000	8.8 :1	rear/4 - A4*	3.73	9.5	17.0	30.4	6.9	131	118	0.75	66-72	15 22	R 87
option	V8 4.7 SOHC-16-MPSFI	288	235 @ 4800	295 @ 3200	9.3 :1	rear/4 - A4*	3.73	8.5	16.4	29.6	6.2	134	124	0.75	65-72	14 20	R 87

PRICE & EQUIPMENT

JEEP Grand Cherokee	Laredo 4x2	Limited 4x2	Laredo 4x4	Limited 4x4
Retail price $:	25,945	31,460	27,915	38,275
Dealer invoice $:	23,507	28,360	25,275	34,392
Shipping & handling $:	525	525	525	525
Automatic transmission:	S	S	S	S
Cruise control:	S	S	S	S
Power steering:	S	S	S	S
Anti-lock brakes:	S	S	S	S
Traction control:				
Air conditioning:	SM	SA	SM	SA
Leather:	O	S	O	S
AM/FM/radio-cassette:	S	SCD	S	SCD
Power door locks:	S	S	S	S
Power windows:	S	S	S	S
Tilt steering:	S	S	S	S
Dual adjustable mirrors:	SE	SEH	SE	SEH
Alloy wheels:	S	S	S	S
Anti-theft system:	O	S	O	S

Colors
Exterior: Black, Platinum, White, Champagne, Amethyst, Slate, Red, Blue, Sienna, Taupe.
Interior: Pebble, Camel, Taupe.

AT A GLANCE...

Category: 2WD or 4WD sport-utility. Class : utility

HISTORIC
Introduced in: 1993-1999
Made in: Jefferson North, Detroit, USA & Graz, Austria.

DEMOGRAPHICS

Model	Men./Wom.	Age	Married	College	Income
Grand Cherokee	70/30 %	46	80 %	51 %	$ 55 500

INDEX
Safety: 80 % | Satisfaction: 85 %
Depreciation: 25 % | Insurance: $ 975-1185
Cost per mile: $ 0.51 | Number of dealers: 1 029

SALES

Model	1996	1997	Result
Grand Cherokee	279 195	260 875	- 6.6 %

MAIN COMPETITORS
CHEVROLET Blazer, DODGE Durango, FORD Explorer, ISUZU Trooper, INFINITI QX4, GMC Jimmy-Envoy, LEXUS RX 300, MERCEDES-BENZ M-Class, NISSAN Pathfinder, TOYOTA 4Runner.

MAINTENANCE REQUIRED BY WARRANTY
First revision: 3 000 miles
Frequency: 6 months/6 000 miles
Diagnostic plug: Yes

SPECIFICATIONS

Model	Version Trim	Traction	Body/ Seats	Wheel base in	Lght x Wdgth x Hght in x in x in	Curb weight lb	Susp. ft/rr	Brake ft/rr	Steering type	Turning diameter ft	Steer. turns nber.	Fuel tank gal	tire size	Standard tires make	model	Standard powertrain
JEEP	General warranty: 3 years / 36 000 miles; surface rust 1 year / 12 000 miles; perforation 7 years / 100 000 miles; roadside assistance 3 years / 36 000 miles.															
Gd Cherokee	Laredo	4x2	4dr.wgn. 5	105.9	181.5x72.3x69.4	3739	rh/rh	dc/ABS	pwr.ball	36.4	2.94	20.6	225/75R16	Goodyear	Wrangler ST	L6/4.0/A4
Gd Cherokee	Limited	4x2	4dr.wgn. 5	105.9	181.5x72.3x69.4	3814	rh/rh	dc/ABS	pwr.ball	36.4	2.94	20.6	245/70R16	Goodyear	Eagle LS	L6/4.0/A4
Gd Cherokee	Laredo	4x4	4dr.wgn. 5	105.9	181.5x72.3x69.4	3915	rh/rh	dc/ABS	pwr.ball	36.4	2.94	20.6	225/75R16	Goodyear	Wrangler ST	L6/4.0/A4
Gd Cherokee	Limited	4x4	4dr.wgn. 5	105.9	181.5x72.3x69.4	4050	rh/rh	dc/ABS	pwr.ball	36.4	2.94	20.6	245/70R16	Goodyear	Eagle LS	L6/4.0/A4

With this vehicle a legend was born. First created for the United States Army during the Second World War as an all-purpose, all-terrain vehicle, the Jeep made an easy shift to civilian life once the war was over. This vehicle finally gave birth to a family of all-terrain vehicles that's at peak popularity at the present time. The fifth generation Jeep appeals to those who want to stand out from the crowd by driving a wild, renegade sort of vehicle...

MODEL RANGE

The Jeep Wrangler is sold in a soft top convertible SE model driven by a 2.5L 4-cylinder engine or Sport and Sahara powered by a 4.0L in-line 6 engine. The SE is rather poorly equipped, since it doesn't even receive power steering, radio or rear seatbench. All you get are dual airbags, a soft top and two half-doors with vinyl tops and a spare tire. You have to pick the Sport trim level to be equipped with power steering, AM/FM radio and rear seatbench, while the Sahara also gets radio and tape deck, adjustable steering column, intermittent wipers, more generous-size tires and gas tank as well as distinctive stylistic accents, including light alloy rims. In all cases, the automatic transmission, air conditioning, hard top, antilock braking system and cruise control are among items found on the long list of options.

TECHNICAL FEATURES

The Jeep Wrangler is made up of a steel body mounted on a steel frame that's been reworked so as to integrate the «Quadra Coil» coil spring suspension inherited from the former Grand Cherokee. Front and rear axles are still rigid, but they're maintained and directed by various longitudinal and transverse control arms and assisted by stabilizer bars. All models are equipped with disc and drum brakes and a rustic ABS system is available as an option only on versions equipped with a six-cylinder engine. The engines are the venerable 4-cylinder and in-line 6-cylinder models that can be linked to an antique 3-speed automatic transmission that's sold as an extra.

PROS

+ IN FASHION. The Jeep is still the preferred vehicle of those who like being different and living on the edge. They like to project the image of being wild and wooly adventurous sorts...

Still Temperamental...

+ STYLE. This vehicle's legendary look has not only been respected, but it's even sporting some items more akin to those on the original model.

+ HANDLING. Vehicle stability is more of a sure thing since it's been revised to receive Grand Cherokee suspension components.

+ CAPABILITIES. The Jeep shines on off-road maneuvers, since it can overcome all kinds of obstacles due to generous entrance and exit angles, very gutsy traction, high ground clearance and agility due to its trim size.

+ INSTRUMENT PANEL. It's straightforward and functional, well-suited to this type of vehicle, for gauges and controls are located according to good ergonomics.

+ CLIMATE CONTROL. It's finally works as it should, due to an efficient air vent system that nicely distributes warm or cool air throughout the cabin interior.

+ ACCESS. It's lots less of a chore getting to the rear seats because of the cleverly designed front passenger seat that frees up lots of boarding space. Too bad the driver's seat isn't equipped with the same device.

+ CONVENIENCE FEATURES. Storage space includes a genuine glove compartment, small door side-pockets, a tub located on the dashboard and a cup-holder on the center console.

CONS

- BRAKES. The ones equipping our various test vehicles were dangerous on sudden stops, for wheel lock set in early on and in a disshevelled, unpredictable way, throwing the vehicle off balance and so stopping distances really stretched out, with or without ABS.

- FUEL EFFICIENCY. Both engines are behind the times in this department. The 4-cylinder is rough, noisy as heck and lacks both power and torque, even with the manual gearbox. The 6-cylinder engine has more get up and go, but it guzzles a lot of gas.

- RIDE COMFORT. It's only manageable on silky California highways, elsewhere the suspension kicks up a fuss. Then there's the constant ruckus of wind, engine and road noise to add to the torture.

- STEERING. It's quick and makes for good moves, but it's over-assisted, so it's light as a feather and you really have to keep an eye on it, for it can throw the vehicle off-course.

- CABIN SPACE. It's cramped and terribly narrow. Front seat passengers get squished against the doors and the rear seatbench is, well, a seatbench.

- CONVERTIBLE SOFT TOP. It's nicely tailored, waterproof and less noisy than before, but it's a nightmare removing even the smallest section, so imagine what you have to deal with when you want to remove it completely...

- SUSPENSIONS. They're quite sophisticated (especially up front), so repairs would probably cost a fortune, even after a minor accident.

- CARGO HOLD. It's ridiculously skimpy and doesn't hold much at all and access is no picnic.

- TO BE IMPROVED UPON: insufficient road autonomy with the standard 15 gallon gas tank that the 6-cylinder engine drinks up in no time. It would make a heck of a lot more sense to equip all models with the 19 gallon tank that's sold as an extra...

CONCLUSION

The Jeep is getting on in years and the most recent model hasn't undergone enough modifications and updates to warrant our approval. Driving this vehicle should be a lot safer and there are still some handling and brake system problems that have to be attended to... ☹

RATING
JEEP Wrangler

CONCEPT :   54%
Technology	75
Safety :	80
Interior space :	40
Trunk volume:	0
Quality/fit/finish :	75

DRIVING: 45%
Cockpit :	75
Performance :	30
Handling :	45
Steering :	60
Braking :	15

ORIGINAL EQUIPMENT: 60%
Tires :	75
Headlights :	75
Wipers :	75
Rear defroster :	0
Radio :	75

COMFORT :   43%
Seats :	70
Suspension :	30
Sound level :	0
Conveniences :	40
Air conditioning :	75

BUDGET :   55%
Price :	50
Fuel economy :	40
Insurance :	50
Satisfaction :	80
Depreciation :	55

Overall rating: 51.4%

NEW FOR 1999

- Soft top and hard top available in dark Tan shade.
- Improved air conditioning with rotary controls.
- The 2.5L TLEV engine that meets clean emission standards.
- Dark green seat fabric for the Sahara trim level.
- New exterior shades: Blue, Sand, Green.
- New interior shades: Camel and Pebble.

ENGINES

Model/ version	Type / timing valve / fuel system	Displacement cu in	Power bhp @ rpm	Torque lb-ft @ rpm
1)	L4* 2.5 OHV-8-MPSFI	150	120 @ 5400	140 @ 3500
2)	L6* 4.0 OHV-12-MPSFI	242	185 @ 4600	222 @ 2800

1) SE.   2) Sport, Sahara, option SE.

TRANSMISSIONS

Compres. ratio	Driving wheels / transmission	Final ratio
9.2 :1	rear/4 - M5*	4.11
	rear/4 - A3	3.73
8.8 :1	rear/4 - M5*	3.07
	rear/4 - A3	3.07

PERFORMANCES

Acceler. 0-60 mph s	Standing 1/4 & 5/8 mile s		Acceler. 50-75 mph s	Braking 60-0 mph f	Top speed mph	Lateral acceler. G	Noise level dBA	Fuel economy mpg City	Highway	Fuel type Octane
13.5	18.6	36.5	10.8	197	87	0.75	68-76	18	20	R 87
14.8	20.0	37.2	11.5	190	81	0.75	68-76	16	19	R 87
10.5	17.3	32.5	8.1	157	103	0.75	68-78	16	22	R 87
11.2	18.8	34.0	9.9	167	100	0.75	68-78	15	20	R 87

PRICE & EQUIPMENT

JEEP Wrangler	SE	Sport	Sahara
Retail price $:	14,215	17,630	19,790
Dealer invoice $:	13,620	15,914	17,815
Shipping & handling $:	525	525	525
Automatic transmission:	O	O	O
Cruise control:	O	O	O
Power steering:	S	S	S
Anti-lock brakes:	-	O	O
Traction control:	-	-	-
Air conditioning:	O	O	O
Leather:	-	-	-
AM/FM/radio-cassette:	O	O	S
Power door locks:	-	-	-
Power windows:	-	-	-
Tilt steering:	O	O	S
Dual adjustable mirrors:	SM	SM	SM
Alloy wheels:	O	O	S
Anti-theft system:	O	O	O

Colors

Exterior: Chili Pepper, Amethyst, Gray, Blue, Green, Sand.

Interior: Blue, Tan, Gray.

AT A GLANCE...

Category: 2WD or 4WD sport-utility.   **Class :** utility

HISTORIC
Introduced in: 1987-1997.
Made in: Toledo, Ohio, USA.

DEMOGRAPHICS

Model	Men./Wom.	Age	Married	College	Income
Wrangler	67/33 %	34	39 %	44 %	$ 35 400

INDEX

Safety:	80 %	Satisfaction:	80%
Depreciation:	45 %	Insurance:	$ 950
Cost per mile:	$ 0.49	Number of dealers:	1 029

SALES

Model	1996	1997	Result
Wrangler	81 844	81 956	+0.6 %

MAIN COMPETITORS
CHEVROLET Tracker, HONDA CR-V, SUZUKI Vitara, TOYOTA RAV4.

MAINTENANCE REQUIRED BY WARRANTY

First revision:	Frequency:	Diagnostic plug:
3 000 miles	6 months /6 000 miles	Yes

SPECIFICATIONS

Model	Version Trim	Traction	Body/ Seats	Wheel base in	Lght x Wdgth x Hght in x in x in	Curb weight lb	Susp. ft/rr	Brake ft/rr	Steering type	Turning diameter ft	Steer. turns nber.	Fuel tank gal	tire size	Standard tires make	model	Standard powertrain
JEEP		General warranty: 3 years / 36 000 miles; surface rust 1 year / 12 000 miles; perforation 7 years / 100 000 miles; roadside assistance 3 years / 36 000 miles.														
Wrangler	SE	4x4	2dr.con.2	93.4	147.7x66.7x71.1	3318	rh/rh	dc/dr	pwr.ball	32.8	3.0	15.1	205/75R15	Goodyear	Wrangler RT/S	L4/2.5/M5
Wrangler	Sport	4x4	2dr.con.4	93.4	147.7x66.7x71.1	3437	rh/rh	dc/dr	pwr.ball	32.8	3.0	15.1	215/75R15	Goodyear	Wrangler RT/S	L6/4.0/M5
Wrangler	Sahara	4x4	2dr.con.4	93.4	147.7x66.7x71.1	3461	rh/rh	dc/dr	pwr.ball	32.8	3.0	19.0	225/75R15	Goodyear	Wrangler GS-A	L6/4.0/M5

The Diablo's are in their last production year, since in 1999 they'll be replaced by a new model called.......... Now that Lamborghini has been bought out by Volkswagen, we can expect the Santa Agata brand to get spruced up and become more competitive with its eternal rival, Ferrari. We'll at long last see a more compact model equipped with a V8 engine that resembles the prototype that's been around for about ten years now and that was never built, due to lack of funds. The firm's future now seems to be more solid, which is a reassuring thought.

MODEL RANGE

The Diablo is an exotic, high-performance vehicle with unique vertically raised doors that's available as a 2-door, 2-passenger coupe in a single rear-wheel drive trim level or VT with all-wheel drive, VT roadster and two lighter SV and SVR official racecar versions.

TECHNICAL FEATURES

The frame structure of the Diablo is very «low tech»; it's simply made of tubular steel and the body is made up of aluminum panels that are manually assembled and only the cabin floor, front and rear bumpers, hood and trunk lids and main tunnel are made of carbon fiber casting. The independent suspensions have anti-squat and anti-lift constructs now fitted with Koni electronically controlled shock absorbers varying with speed. Under 85 mph, the suspension is supple but it gets progressively firmer up to 150 mph and more. The 12-cylinder mid-engine and gearbox penetrate the cabin via the main tunnel, so front and rear weight is perfectly distributed in a 49/51 ratio. The V12 powerplant has undergone all kinds of updates and develops 492 hp on both versions and the ZF 5-speed manual gearbox is equipped with a racecar clutch and develops 532 hp on racecar models. Air-vented «competition» style brakes equip these babies, but no antilock braking system is available. On the all-wheel drive model, the main tunnel houses the drive shaft that powers the front wheels and that only delivers 0 to 25% of the available juice, so as to leave the Diablo's rear-wheel drive demeanor unscathed and so as not to affect the thrill of driving one of these beasts, even when road adherence is a bit iffy.

Hero or Monster ?

SIMPLY SUPER

++ LOOKS. The Diablo coupes and roadster, designed by Marcello Gandini, are some of the most notorious cars on the planet. Their design simply takes your breath away and is still right in style and all you have to do is observe the effect one of these cars has on passersby to be convinced of this fact.

++ PERFORMANCES. They're downright sensational. After all, with nearly 500 hp at your fingertips, the power to weight ratio hits a record 7.0 lb/hp. Accelerations and pickup are out of this world, at least when adherence is reasonable on the RWD model, which explains why the AWD model is a must in the lineup, even with those humungous tires. The transmission shifter is slow on the draw, but torque is so strong that you can accelerate at 40 mph while in 5th gear without the engine even noticing and so you can skip a few gear changes... As for the exhaust noise, it has a way of raising the adrenalin level not only of car occupants but of eager gawkers.

PROS

+ HANDLING. Driving one of these monster cars looks easy at first, but it does take some getting used to, for the Diablo is essentially a car that tends to go into understeer and when at full tilt, the rear end slips and sways brutally both on the VT and the regular model, so it takes lots of guts and pilot skills not to lose control of the vehicle. All-wheel drive doesn't help adherence on curves, since the viscous coupling is rather slow on slalom runs. On dry surfaces, the car holds its own with no help from the driver, on wide or tight curves, thanks to those wonderfully generous tires. But vehicle stability goes awry beyond 160 mph due to negative lift, so the optional rear spoiler is essential.

+ QUALITY. The Diablo's are handmade for the most part, which explains the exquisite craftsmanship of assembly and finish details, tasks confided to women, known to be more meticulous than their male counterparts...

+ STEERING. It's nicely powered, quick and direct, but handling is seriously affected by a very low ground clearance, wide steer angle diameter and generous vehicle size.

CONS

- RELIABILITY. Like Ferrari's, the Lamborghini's are fussy and fragile and it doesn't take much to upset them, which isn't normal for cars in this price range.

- RIDE COMFORT. It's very rudimentary, given the simplistic seat design and the fact that upholstery is thin and seats don't really recline. The suspension is stiff at all times, but less so on the VT that's equipped with adjustable shocks and as for the feline roar of the V12, well it wears you out in no time.

- CONVENIENCE FEATURES. They're merely symbolic, since the cabin doesn't offer any storage space worthy of the name and the trunk is skimpy indeed.

-COCKPIT. Visibility is very iffy at rear quarterback and getting into a comfortable position behind the wheel is no easy matter. The center console is more stylish than logical for several controls aren't within the driver's reach, so much so that he or she has to sit straight up from the seat to use them.

- BRAKES. They're super-effective, but they're hard to gauge just right due to the very stiff pedal. Sudden stops and accelerations suffer from the lack of an ABS/traction control system that would keep the vehicle on course in both cases, when travelling on slippery roads.

CONCLUSION

The Diablo's are amazing cars and car buffs the world over are in awe when they look at the sleek silhouette and when they catch sight of these legendary cars taking off like rockets. Only those who can afford them will have to keep their two feet firmly on the ground...

RATING
LAMBORGHINI Diablo

CONCEPT : 62%
Technology	100
Safety :	90
Interior space :	20
Trunk volume:	20
Quality/fit/finish :	80

DRIVING: 85%
Cockpit :	75
Performance :	100
Handling :	90
Steering :	80
Braking :	80

ORIGINAL EQUIPMENT: 83%
Tires :	90
Headlights :	90
Wipers :	80
Rear defroster :	70
Radio :	85

COMFORT : 38%
Seats :	60
Suspension :	50
Sound level:	0
Conveniences :	10
Air conditioning :	70

BUDGET : 30%
Price :	0
Fuel economy :	0
Insurance :	0
Satisfaction :	80
Depreciation :	70

Overall rating: 59.6%

NEW FOR 1999

- Model at career's end to be replaced during the course of 1999 by a new vehicle to be unveiled at the next Paris Auto Show.

ENGINES

Model/version	Type / timing valve / fuel system	Displacement cu in	Power bhp @ rpm	Torque lb-ft @ rpm
base	V12 5.7 DOHC-48-MPSFI	348	492 @ 6800	429 @ 5200
VT	V12 5.7 DOHC-48-MPSFI	348	492 @ 6800	429 @ 5200
SV	V12 5.7 DOHC-48-MPSFI	348	532 @ 7100	429 @ 5900
SVR	V12 5.7 DOHC-48-MPSFI	348	532 @ 7100	429 @ 5900

TRANSMISSIONS

Compres. ratio	Driving wheels / transmission	Final ratio
10.0:1	rear-M5	2.41
10.0:1	four-M5	2.41
10.0:1	rear-M5	2.529
10.0:1	rear-M5	2.529

PERFORMANCES

Acceler. 0-60 mph s	Standing 1/4 & 5/8 mile s	Acceler. 50-75 mph s	Braking 60-0 mph f	Top speed mph	Lateral acceler. G	Noise level dBA	Fuel economy mpg City	Fuel economy mpg Highway	Fuel type Octane
4.5	13.5 21.0	NA	131	202	0.90	70-79	7	15	S 91
4.7	13.8 21.5	NA	137	199	0.90	70-79	7	15	S 91
4.0	13.2 20.8	NA	125	205	0.95	72-80	7	15	S 91
NA									

PRICE & EQUIPMENT

LAMBORGHINI Diablo	base	VT	SV/SVR
Retail price $:	230,000	280,000	NA
Dealer invoice $:	-	-	-
Shipping & handling $:	-	-	-
Automatic transmission:	-	-	-
Cruise control:	-	-	-
Power steering:	S	S	S
Anti-lock brakes:	-	-	-
Traction control:		S	S
Air conditioning:	S	S	S
Leather:	S	S	S
AM/FM/radio-cassette:	S	S	S
Power door locks:	S	S	S
Power windows:	S	S	S
Tilt steering:	S	S	S
Dual adjustable mirrors:	S	S	S
Alloy wheels:	S	S	S
Anti-theft system:	S	S	S

Colors
Exterior: Red, Yellow, White, Black, Metallic gray, Blue.

Interior: Tan, White, Black.

AT A GLANCE...

Category: rear-wheel drive or 4WD GT coupes. **Class :** exotic

HISTORIC
Introduced in:	1990 : coupe; 1996:roadster & SV
Made in:	Santa Agata Bolognese, Bologna, Italy.

DEMOGRAPHICS
Model	Men./Wom.	Age	Married	College	Income
Diablo	98/2 %	58	78 %	38 %	$ 200 000

INDEX
Safety:	90 %	Satisfaction:	80 %
Depreciation:	47 %	Insurance:	$ 12 300
Cost per mile:	3,25 $	Number of dealers:	15

SALES
Model	1996	1997	Result
Diablo		NA	

MAIN COMPETITORS
FERRARI F550 Maranello.

MAINTENANCE REQUIRED BY WARRANTY
First revision:	Frequency:	Diagnostic plug:
1 500 miles	6 months/6 000 miles	Yes

SPECIFICATIONS

Model	Version Trim	Body/Seats	Interior volume cu ft	Trunk volume cu ft	Cd	Wheel base in	Lght x Wdgth x Hght in x in x in	Curb weight lb	Susp. ft/rr	Brake ft/rr	Steering type	Turning diameter ft	Steer. turns nber.	Fuel tank gal	tire size	Standard tires make	model	Standard powertrain
LAMBORGHINI Diablo		**Warranty: 2 years / 7 500 miles.**																
Diablo		2dr.cpe. 2	NA	4.9	0.30	104.7	175.6x80.3x43.5	3474	ih/ih	dc/dc	pwr.r&p.	41.2	3.2	26.4	fr.235/40ZR17 re.335/35ZR17	Pirelli	P Zero	V12/5.7/M5
Diablo	VT	2dr.cpe. 2	NA	4.9	0.30	104.7	175.6x80.3x43.5	3582	ih/ih	dc/dc	pwr.r&p.	41.2	3.2	26.4	fr.235/40ZR17 re.335/35ZR17	Pirelli	P Zero	V12/5.7/M5
Diablo	VT	2dr.cpe. 2	NA	4.9	0.30	104.7	176.0x80.3x43.9	3582	ih/ih	dc/dc	pwr.r&p.	41.2	3.2	26.4	fr.235/40ZR17 re.335/35ZR18	Pirelli	P Zero	V12/5.7/M5
Diablo	SV-SVR	2dr.cpe. 2	NA	4.9	0.30	104.7	176.0x80.3x43.9	3373	ih/ih	dc/dc	pwr.r&p.	41.2	3.2	26.4	fr.235/40ZR17 re.335/35ZR18	Pirelli	P Zero	V12/5.7/M5

In the affordable luxury car bracket, the Lexus ES 300 has become a sort of measuring stick that most rivals try to imitate, come hell or high water. So it's all the more curious that it isn't, and by far, the best seller in its category. This Camry offspring is the base model in the Lexus lineup and it's the most popular in terms of number of units sold. Rivals are especially envious of its assembly quality and finish job and they'd like to have the same pristine reputation when it comes to reliability...

MODEL RANGE

The Lexus ES 300 is sold in a single trim level 4-door sedan equipped with lush standard items including leather trim, traction control and antilock braking system, memory driver's seat and light alloy rims, not to mention climate control, cruise control, stereo sound system and all the usual power functions, to which can be added options or option packages...

TECHNICAL FEATURES

The ES 300 is derived from the Camry platform, so it's equipped with its mechanical features and bears traces of some similar body and window design details. During the last revision, it received a longer wheelbase and the car is now 2 in. longer from fender to fender. Its overall design borrows from the cab forward principle, inaugurated by Chrysler on its LH models, that expands cabin space and provides better visibility. Its very clean body design explains why the drag coefficient sits between 0.32 and 0.29. Most ot the steel unibody's panels are galvanized on both sides. The fully independent suspension uses MacPherson struts and stabilizer bars. The car can also be equipped with the optional Adaptive Variable Suspension (AVS) that constantly adjusts shock absorber pressure to road conditions and lets you select suspension travel in supple, normal or sport mode, according to 16 different combinations. The front and rear are mounted on independent cradles via rubber components that filter out noise and vibration. The 3.0L V6 engine is just like the one that powered the former model, but a dual exhaust system gives it another 2 hp. The adaptive transmission records the driver's style and anticipates his or her moves.

No Soul...

PROS

+ VALUE. The lower price and richer equipment make it a better buy than was the case for last year's model. By taking such an approach, Lexus is hoping to maintain sales volume in this market segment that's very competitive and almost totally dominated by European builders.

+ DESIGN. It's lovely both inside and out, graced with delicate, subtle touches. Body design is elegant and the cabin is meticulously rendered.

+ RIDE COMFORT. It's wonderful with the flexible suspension travel, nice cushy seats and very low noise level due to very effective soundproofing. The ride, more American than Japanese or European, which is the reason behind this model's success.

+PERFORMANCES. Accelerations and pickup are brisk due to a favorable power to weight ratio.

+ HANDLING. It's nice and stable in most circumstances, yet the car is quite agile on slalom runs due to reasonable vehicle size and weight (that has increased).

+ BRAKES. They're efficient, well-balanced and tough, but ABS sometimes causes snags as does the traction control that's linked to it.

+ DRIVING PLEASURE. It's the fine result of smooth controls, silky and discreet engine demeanor and the feeling of security when you know you have good control of the vehicle (while braking or accelerating) and you sure get used to all

those standard creature comforts in a hurry.

+ INSTRUMENT PANEL. It's slick and looks neat and uncluttered. It's nicely shaped and instrument gauges have cathode-ray tube lighting on which red LED-type needles move, adding a high tech touch to the ensemble.

+ QUALITY. It's obvious in every way: construction is well crafted, fit and finish are meticulously rendered and trim materials are treated to last. It all looks and feels lovely.

+ CONVENIENCE FEATURES. The trunk is very generous and easy to get to and there are more numerous and more convenient storage spots for front seat passengers.

CONS

- ADAPTIVE SUSPENSION. Even with the sophisticated AVS system, it isn't perfect for it doesn't really predict the driver's moves and exaggerates suspension response every which way.

- DRIVING. The ES 300 is capable of brilliant performances and is equipped with a high tech suspension, but it isn't really fun to drive, because it has no soul, so to speak. Everything is over-assisted and squeaky clean, like the steering and braking systems that are a bit wishy washy.

- USEFUL SPACE. There's slightly less of it and the cabin can really only comfortably accomodate four adults. The trunk is less roomy than on last year's model and it only connects with the cabin via a ski-sized pass-through. But the trunk door is lower to allow for handier luggage handling.

- ERGONOMICS. This aspect of the main section of the dashboard isn't too great, for it isn't angled toward the driver enough and switches located on the left are nearly clean out of sight.

- TO BE IMPROVED UPON: The rather useless front door side-pockets and lack of storage space for rear seat passengers, hard to adjust brakes and maneuverability that could be better.

CONCLUSION

The latest model Lexus ES 300 is too Americanized for our tastes, it's marvellously functional and exhibits high-level technical assets. But too much of a good thing isn't necessarily the best approach, so it's hard to fall in love with this car... ☺

RATING
LEXUS ES 300

CONCEPT :   75%
Technology   85
Safety :   90
Interior space :   60
Trunk volume :   55
Quality/fit/finish :   85

DRIVING: 72%
Cockpit :   80
Performance :   65
Handling :   60
Steering :   75
Braking :   80

ORIGINAL EQUIPMENT: 80%
Tires :   80
Headlights :   80
Wipers :   80
Rear defroster :   75
Radio :   85

COMFORT :   82%
Seats :   80
Suspension :   85
Sound level: 80
Conveniences :   80
Air conditioning :   85

BUDGET :   53%
Price :   10
Fuel economy :   65
Insurance :   45
Satisfaction :   90
Depreciation :   55

Overall rating: 72.4%

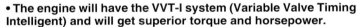

NEW FOR 1999

- **The engine will have the VVT-I system (Variable Valve Timing Intelligent) and will get superior torque and horsepower.**
- **An optional variable sway control (VSC) .**

ENGINES

Model/ version	Type / timing valve / fuel system	Displacement cu in	Power bhp @ rpm	Torque lb-ft @ rpm
ES 300	V6*3.0 DOHC-24-MPSFI	183	210 @ 5800	220 @ 4400

TRANSMISSIONS

Compres. ratio	Driving wheels / transmission	Final ratio
10.5:1	front - A4	3.72

PERFORMANCES

Acceler. 0-60 mph s	Standing 1/4 & 5/8 mile s	Acceler. 50-75 mph s	Braking 60-0 mph f	Top speed mph	Lateral acceler. G	Noise level dBA	Fuel economy mpg City	Highway	Fuel type Octane
8.3	16.3 29.3	5.8	134	140	0.80	64-68	18	27	R 87

PRICE & EQUIPMENT

LEXUS ES 300   base
Retail price $:   30,790
Dealer invoice $:   26,745
Shipping & handling $:   495
Automatic transmission: S
Cruise control: S
Power steering: S
Anti-lock brakes: S
Traction control: S
Air conditioning: S
Leather: S
AM/FM/radio-cassette: S
Power door locks: S
Power windows: S
Tilt steering: S
Dual adjustable mirrors: S
Alloy wheels: S
Anti-theft system: S

Colors
Exterior: White, Black, Silver, Ruby, Beige, Pink, Green, Blue.

Interior: Cloth: Black, Taupe. Leather: Black, Ivory, Taupe, Oak.

AT A GLANCE...

Category: front-wheel drive luxury sedans.   **Class :** 7

HISTORIC
Introduced in: 1992-1997
Made in: Tahara, Japan.

DEMOGRAPHICS

Model	Men./Wom.	Age	Married	College	Income
ES 300	85/15 %	46	89 %	61 %	$ 85 000

INDEX
Safety: 90 %   **Satisfaction:** 90 %
Depreciation: 44 %   **Insurance:** $ 1 250
Cost per mile: $ 0.66   **Number of dealers:** 167

SALES

Model	1996	1997	Result
ES 300	44 773	58 428	+ 30.5 %

MAIN COMPETITORS
ACURA TL, AUDI A4-A6, BMW 3-Series, INFINITI I30, MAZDA Millenia, NISSAN Maxima, SAAB 9³ & 9⁵, TOYOTA Camry V6 & Avalon, VOLVO S70.

MAINTENANCE REQUIRED BY WARRANTY
First revision: 4 000 miles   **Frequency:** 4 000 miles   **Diagnostic plug:** Yes

SPECIFICATIONS

Model	Version Trim	Body/ Seats	Interior volume cu ft	Trunk volume cu ft	Cd	Wheel base in	Lght x Wdgth x Hght in x in x in	Curb weight lb	Susp. ft/rr	Brake ft/rr	Steering type	Turning diameter ft	Steer. turns nber.	Fuel tank gal	tire size	Standard tires make	model	Standard powertrain
LEXUS ES 300	base	4dr.sdn.5	92.1	13.0	0.29	105.1	190.2x70.5x54.9	3378	ih/ih	dc/ABS	pwr.r&p.	36.7	3.0	18.5	205/65VR15	Dunlop Goodyear Bridgestone	SP Sport Eagle GA Potenza RE 88	V6/3.0/A4

General warranty: 4 years / 50 000 miles; **powertrain:** 6 years / 70 000 miles; **corrosion perforation:** 6 years / unlimited mileage & roadside assistance.

The GS is no longer the lowly toad it once was. It's miraculously turned into a thoroughbred, due to the magic rendered by the LS 400 V8 engine that Lexus bestowed on it last year and that really helped this model come into its own. The 300 version doesn't seem to have a future that's any more exciting than for last year's model, but the 400 version has promising prospects of competing with European luxury cars precisely on ground that is their preferred domain, namely, high performance. Yet even if these models rake in the big bucks, they don't sell in sufficient enough quantities to make much of a difference.

MODEL RANGE

Sitting between the ES 300 and the LS 400, the GS 300 and 400 now offer an added luxury and performance level to the Lexus model range. This 4-door sedan is available in the GS 300 version, animated by the same 3.0L in-line 6 engine as last year or in the GS 400 version powered by the 4.0L V8 borrowed from the LS 400. These cars are equipped with a 5-speed automatic transmission, but other items such as leather trim offered as an extra on the 300, vary according to model, so each has distinctive traits, while heated seats, sunroof, xenon headlamps, navigation system, CD changer, chrome wheels and bigger tires are available as options.

TECHNICAL FEATURES

The latest Lexus GS models have a completely new architecture and are built on a brand new platform. It's a steel moncoque structure with front-engine and rear-wheel drive. These cars' silhouette yields effective aerodynamics, since the drag coefficient sometimes drops to 0.30. The suspension, mounted on independent cradles isolating it from the body, is fully independent, consisting of a double wishbone design with stabilizer bar both front and rear. Cars are equipped with disc brakes, a standard ABS/traction control device as well as variable assist steering. Both versions benefit from a standard anti-skid system that helps the driver keep control of the vehicle in the event of skidding or slipping.

PROS

+ STYLE. The distinctively tight, taut stylistics add a lot more personality than before.

+ PERFORMANCES. The GS 400

Metamorphosis...

driven by the V8 puts out very zoomy accelerations and pickup, due to a favorable power to weight ratio. The GS 300 has more zip than before, but it doesn't hold a candle to the 400 that has a lot more panache.

+ HANDLING. It's very safe and competent, in spite of the pronounced roll and this is the case even on wet roads, since the ABS, traction control and anti-skid systems blend their magic potion to assure optimal stability and a nice neutral demeanor that's easy to maintain with the accelerator. But the anti-skid system doesn't always let the driver step on the gas at the right moment.

+ RIDE COMFORT. It's all-round cushy, since seats are nicely shaped and offer good support even for rear seat travellers, the well-honed suspension filters out road faults and superb sound dampening keeps the noise level nice and low.

+ PRICES. They're fairly reasonable, since the GS 400 price tag compares very favorably with that of the BMW 540i. Whether the tranquil Nipponese approach or Bavarian prestige comes out as number one in the race, remains to be seen...

+ QUALITY. Construction, finish details and trim materials are beyond reproach and the high customer satisfaction rate as well as one of the top standings in J.D. Power's hit parade confirm Lexus' enviable reputation. The leather seat covers are velvety smooth and the wood appliqués are elegant and very posh.

+ DRIVING PLEASURE. It's simply super due to compact size that makes it easy to maneuver these cars, also due to straight as an arrow steering that works wonders on really tight curves, but the GS 400 is more agile than the 300 in this case, and being at the wheel is a joy with such gutsy engines and competent roadholding.

+ NICE FEATURES: Efficient wipers that sweep 90% of the windshield, powerful xenon headlamps that unfortunately are billed as extras...

CONS

- SUSPENSION. As is the case for the ES 300, it isn't too versatile, even though it's pretty high tech. Its excessive flexibility provokes rear end slipping and sliding, so it's tough staying right on track at high speeds.

- CABIN SPACE. It only seats four passengers, even with the fifth rear seat headrest, since the cabin is quite narrow, especially towards the rear.

- SEQUENTIAL SHIFTER. It doesn't add much oomph to performances or overall competence, since the touch buttons installed on the steering wheel that control speed changes require a lot of tending to on snaky roads.

- INSTRUMENT PANEL. It's cluttered with all those deep honeycomb shapes and the lighting system is pervasive and distracting. Ergonomics aren't perfect either, since some controls are poorly located.

- VISIBILITY. The rearward view is far from perfect due to the narrow rear window, high-perched headrests and at rear quarterback the thick base C pillar gets in the way.

- TRUNK. It can't be used to maximum because it's weirdly shaped, the floor isn't perfectly flat and it doesn't hold enough because it's short and can't be extended towards the cabin. Rear seat passengers don't have much storage space because the main armrest only includes two cup-holders.

CONCLUSION

It'll take more than a V8 engine and provocative looks to put a dint in the dominance of German automakers who are among the top dogs in this sales category. Lexus' attempt is honorable, but it still has a ways to go... ☺

RATING
LEXUS GS 300-400

CONCEPT : **78%**
Technology	85
Safety :	90
Interior space :	70
Trunk volume:	60
Quality/fit/finish :	85

DRIVING: **73%**
Cockpit :	80
Performance :	75
Handling :	70
Steering :	80
Braking :	60

ORIGINAL EQUIPMENT: **82%**
Tires :	85
Headlights :	80
Wipers :	85
Rear defroster :	75
Radio :	85

COMFORT : **75%**
Seats :	80
Suspension :	70
Sound level :	70
Conveniences :	70
Air conditioning :	85

BUDGET : **50%**
Price :	0
Fuel economy :	60
Insurance :	45
Satisfaction :	90
Depreciation :	55

Overall rating: **71.6%**

NEW FOR 1999

- GS rear spoiler in now part of the option list.

ENGINES / TRANSMISSIONS / PERFORMANCES

Model/ version	Type / timing valve / fuel system	Displacement cu in	Power bhp @ rpm	Torque lb-ft @ rpm	Compres. ratio	Driving wheels / transmission	Final ratio	Acceler. 0-60 mph s	Standing 1/4 & 5/8 mile s	Acceler. 50-75 mph s	Braking 60-0 mph f	Top speed mph	Lateral acceler. G	Noise level dBA	Fuel economy mpg City	Highway	Fuel type Octane
GS 300	L6* 3.0 DOHC-24-EFI	183	225 @ 6000	220 @ 4000	10.5 :1	rear-A5	3.916	8.0	15.8 27.8	5.2	121	137	0.85	65-68	20	26	S 91
GS 400	V8* 4.0 DOHC-32-EFI	242	300 @ 6000	310 @ 4000	10.5 :1	rear-A5	3.266	6.8	14.6 26.5	4.2	125	149	0.85	64-68	17	25	S 91

PRICE & EQUIPMENT

LEXUS	GS 300	GS 400
Retail price $:	36,900	44,950
Dealer invoice $:	32,051	38,590
Shipping & handling $:	495	495
Automatic transmission:	S	S
Cruise control:	S	S
Power steering:	S	S
Anti-lock brakes:	S	S
Traction control:	S	S
Air conditioning:	SA	SA
Leather:	O	S
AM/FM/radio-cassette:	S	S
Power door locks:	S	S
Power windows:	S	S
Tilt steering:	S	S
Dual adjustable mirrors:	SE	SE
Alloy wheels:	S	S
Anti-theft system:	S	S

Colors
Exterior: White, Silver, Bronze, Black onyx , Gold, Ruby, Jade, Blue.

Interior: Cloth: Gray. Leather: Gray, Ivory, Spruce.

AT A GLANCE...

Category: rear-wheel drive luxury sedans. **Class :** 7

HISTORIC
Introduced in: 1993-1998
Made in: Tahara, Japan.

DEMOGRAPHICS
Model	Men./Wom.	Age	Married	College	Income
GS 300	83/17%	47	93%	61%	$ 82 500

INDEX
Safety:	90%	Satisfaction:	90%
Depreciation:	35%	Insurance:	$ 1575
Cost per mile:	$ 0.84	Number of dealers:	170

SALES
Model	1996	1997	Result
GS 300	2 044	3 823	+ 87.2 %
GS 400	-	3 890	

MAIN COMPETITORS
GS 300 : ACURA RL, BMW 528i, MERCEDES-BENZ E320, SAAB 9⁵, VOLVO S70.
GS 400 : CADILLAC Seville, BMW 540i, LINCOLN Continental, MERCEDES-BENZ E420.

MAINTENANCE REQUIRED BY WARRANTY
First revision:	Frequency:	Diagnostic plug:
4 000 miles	4 000 miles	Yes

SPECIFICATIONS

Model	Version Trim	Body/ Seats	Interior volume cu ft	Trunk volume cu ft	Cd	Wheel base in	Lght x Wdgth x Hght in x in x in	Curb weight lb	Susp. ft/rr	Brake ft/rr	Steering type	Turning diameter ft	Steer. turns nber.	Fuel tank gal	tire size	Standard tires make	model	Standard powertrain
LEXUS		General warranty: 4 years / 50 000 miles; powertrain: 6 years / 70 000 miles; corrosion perforation: 6 years / unlimited mileage & roadside assistance.																
GS	300	4dr.sdn. 4/5	100.0	14.8	0.29	110.2	189.0x70.9x56.7	3635	ih/ih	dc/ABS	pwr.r&p.	36.1	3.38	19.8	215/60VR16	Bridgestone	Turanza ER 30	L6/3.0/A5
GS	400	4dr.sdn. 4/5	100.0	14.8	0.29	110.2	189.0x70.9x56.7	3690	ih/ih	dc/ABS	pwr.r&p.	36.1	3.38	19.8	225/55VR16	Michelin	Pilot HX MXM	V8/4.0/A5
															235/45ZR17	Bridgestone	Potenza RE030	

These Lexus models can boast of only a fraction of the sales achieved by Mercedes-Benz rivals, but they're designed to be the Japanese counterparts of their illustrious arch-rivals. They use remarkable reliability and good resale value as weapons against traditional fame. On the technical level, they aren't as sophisticated as the European competition, but Lexus makes up for this lack by offering exceptionally attentive and courteous service that buyers across the street envy.

MODEL RANGE

The LS 400 is a 4-door sedan sold in a unique trim level to which can be added a few rare options, whereas the SC coupes are no longer sold in the United States under the same conditions. Coupes are motivated by a 3.0L in-line 6 (SC 300) and 4.0L V8 (SC 400) linked to a 5-speed automatic transmission, the latter equipping solely the LS 400 sedan. Original equipment is very rich and the only options available are sunroof, self-adjusting air suspension (LS 400), heated seats and chrome wheels.

TECHNICAL FEATURES

These cars don't seem to change much, but in fact they're constantly being revised and share the same, identical platform and main mechanical features. The steel monocoque body is galvanized on both sides and benefits from good aerodynamics, namely a drag coefficient of 0.28 for the sedan and 0.32 for the coupes. The four-wheel independent suspension consists of a double wishbone organization with stabilizer bar both front and rear. Vented disc brakes are linked to an ABS, traction control and anti-skid system (VSC), so vehicle behavior is well under control when adherence or car path go askew. The latest 4.0L V8 pumps out 30 more hp and 30 lb.ft. more torque than its predecessor, yet it has the same displacement and main characteristics.

PROS

+ QUALITY. It's spiffy all-round. Design, craftsmanship, fit and finish job and trim materials are exquisite. Toyota is a genius when it comes to inner door and dashboard design, they look simply superb and

LEXUS LS 400

Not as Appealing...

really add a touch of class.

+ RELIABILITY. You just have to look at the high owner satisfaction rate to know why Lexus has scored among the finest cars sold for some time now.

+ RIDE COMFORT. The sedan is more cushy with its spacious interior, supple suspension (especially the optional air suspension), nicely designed and cushioned seats and amazing sound dampening that provides impressive quiet at cruising speed.

+ THE V8 ENGINE. It really moves these big, heavy cars and is amazingly civilized, since it emits little or no noise or vibration. It provides the power and torque needed to achieve accelerations, pickup and

top speed comparable to those of zippy German rivals.

+ BRAKES. They aren't the best on the market, but they're quite competent given the weight of the cars they have to bring to a full halt.

+ FUEL ECONOMY. The V8 is quite fuel-efficient for an engine of this displacement that animates such a beastly bulk. It does around 18 miles per gallon.

+ HANDLING. The car is more neutral than before due to various driving aids such as an anti-skid system and traction control that make for more competent demeanor.

+ LOOKS. The elegant and discreet sedan borrows from the great classics in this category and has a definite similarity to the Mercedes sil-

houette and shape. The coupe has more character and its looks don't owe a thing to any other car out there.

+ INSTRUMENT PANEL. It's no doubt one of the most straightforward, rational and ergonomic designs on the market. Your hand reaches instinctively for the right controls, such as the most frequently needed big dials that control temperature or radio volume.

+ RESALE VALUE. It's quite good compared to that of other equally sophisticated cars.

+ A NICE FEATURE. The automatically sliding front seats that slide forward on the coupe, so as to facilitate rear seat access, always a bit of a snag on this type of car.

CONS

- PRICE. It's clearly less competitive than it used to be, so many potential buyers hesitate, since the brand logo on the hood becomes an important choice factor.

- DESIGN. It's still terribly hohum, both inside and out and owners sure won't have to deal with flashy stylistic nonsense. What's really strange is that most owners say that it's precisely the discreet design that appealed to them.

- SUSPENSION. The coupe's suspension is hard and so sensitive to road faults that it's unpleasant and it's funny that nobody at Lexus thought of offering an adjustable suspension.

- STEERING. It's over-assisted and suffers from a poor reduction ratio, so it's light, sensitive and offers no road feel, so driving is really quite dull.

- TRUNK. It's relatively small on the sedan given the vehicle size, but it's nice and square and has a low opening, so luggage handling is convenient. It's too bad the trunk on the coupe isn't convertible and can't be extended to hold more goods.

CONCLUSION

The Asian crisis should bring prices for these models to a more competitive level, otherwise sales will plummet even more in comparison with European products that are considered to be the cat's meow and are more technically sophisticated.

LEXUS SC 400

RATING
LEXUS LS 400

CONCEPT :   81%
Technology	90
Safety :	90
Interior space :	75
Trunk volume:	60
Quality/fit/finish :	90

DRIVING: 73%
Cockpit :	85
Performance :	75
Handling :	55
Steering :	80
Braking :	70

ORIGINAL EQUIPMENT: 80%
Tires :	80
Headlights :	80
Wipers :	80
Rear defroster :	75
Radio :	85

COMFORT :   80%
Seats :	80
Suspension :	80
Sound level:	80
Conveniences :	80
Air conditioning :	80

BUDGET :   51%
Price :	0
Fuel economy :	65
Insurance :	40
Satisfaction :	95
Depreciation :	55

Overall rating: 73.0%

NEW FOR 1999

- No major change.

ENGINES / TRANSMISSIONS / PERFORMANCES

Model/ version	Type / timing valve / fuel system	Displacement cu in	Power bhp @ rpm	Torque lb-ft @ rpm	Compres. ratio	Driving wheels / transmission	Final ratio	Acceler. 0-60 mph s	Standing 1/4 & 5/8 mile s	Acceler. 50-75 mph s	Braking 60-0 mph f	Top speed mph	Lateral acceler. G	Noise level dBA	Fuel economy mpg City	Highway	Fuel type Octane
LS 400	V8* 4.0 DOHC-32-MPSFI	242	290 @ 6000	300 @ 4000	10.5 :1	rear - A5	3.266	7.2	15.5 26.6	5.2	125	143	0.80	65-69	17	26	S 91
SC 300	L6* 3.0 DOHC-24-MPSFI	183	225 @ 6000	220 @ 4000	10.0 :1	rear - A4	4.272	8.6	16.3 29.5	6.2	131	137	0.85	66-69	18	26	S 91
SC 400	V8* 4.0 DOHC-32-MPSFI	242	290 @ 6000	300 @ 4000	10.5 :1	rear - A5	3.266	7.5	15.2 26.5	5.2	125	149	0.87	64-68	17	26	S 91

PRICE & EQUIPMENT

LEXUS	LS 400	SC300	SC400
Retail price $:	53,200	41,100	53,000
Dealer invoice $:	45,135	35,699	45,501
Shipping & handling $:	495	495	495
Automatic transmission:	S		
Cruise control:	S		
Power steering:	S		
Anti-lock brakes:	S		
Traction control:	S		
Air conditioning:	S		
Leather:	S		
AM/FM/radio-cassette:	S		
Power door locks:	S		
Power windows:	S		
Tilt steering:	S		
Dual adjustable mirrors:	S		
Alloy wheels:	S		
Anti-theft system:	S		

Colors

Exterior: White, Silver, Black, Red, Beige, Jade, Mica, Teal, Wildberry.

Interior: Ivory, Gray, Black, Pebble.

AT A GLANCE...

Category: rear-wheel drive luxury sedans & coupes.   **Class :** 7

HISTORIC

Introduced in:	1990
Made in:	Tahara, Japan.

DEMOGRAPHICS

Model	Men./Wom.	Age	Married	College	Income
LS 400	86/14 %	54	90 %	61 %	$ 172 000
SC 400	68/32%	49	82%	37%	$ 102 000

INDEX

Safety:	90 %	Satisfaction:	95 %
Depreciation:	46 %	Insurance:	$ 1 705
Cost per mile:	$ 0.95	Number of dealers:	170

SALES

Model	1996	1997	Result
LS 400	22 237	19 618	-11.8 %
SC 400	2 557	2 042	- 20.1 %
SC 300	2 390	2 999	+ 25.5 %

MAIN COMPETITORS

AUDI A8, BMW 740i, CADILLAC Seville, INFINITI Q45, JAGUAR XJ8, LINCOLN Continental, OLDSMOBILE Aurora.

MAINTENANCE REQUIRED BY WARRANTY

First revision:	Frequency:	Diagnostic plug:
4 000 miles	4 000 miles	Yes

SPECIFICATIONS

Model	Version Trim	Body/ Seats	Interior volume cu ft	Trunk volume cu ft	Cd	Wheel base in	Lght x Wdgth x Hght in x in x in	Curb weight lb	Susp. ft/rr	Brake ft/rr	Steering type	Turning diameter ft	Steer. turns nber.	Fuel tank gal	tire size	Standard tires make	model	Standard powertrain
LEXUS		General warranty: 4 years / 50 000 miles; powertrain: 6 years / 70 000 miles; corrosion perforation: 6 years / unlimited mileage & roadside assistance.																
LS	400	4dr.sdn.5	102.0	13.9	0.28	112.2	196.7x72.0x56.5	3891	ih/ih	dc/ABS	pwr.r&p.	34.8	3.46	22.5	225/60VR16	Bridgestone Goodyear	Turanza ER 33 Eagle GA	V8/4.0/A5
SC	300	2dr.cpe.2+2	75.4	9.3	0.32	105.9	192.5x70.9x53.2	3560	ih/ih	dc/ABS	pwr.r&p.	36.1	3.10	20.6	225/55VR16	Michelin Pilot HX MXM		L6/3.0/A4
SC	400	2dr.cpe.2+2	75.4	9.3	0.32	105.9	192.5x70.9x53.2	3655	ih/ih	dc/ABS	pwr.r&p.	36.1	3.10	20.6	225/55VR16	Michelin Pilot HX MXM		V8/4.0/A5

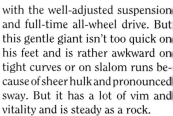

Lexus was the first non-domestic builder to jump into the big SUV race that was initiated by General Motors in 1995 when it first sold the Yukon-Tahoe models. Since then, Ford primed its Expedition and Navigator vehicles and Lexus replaced the dusty LX 450 with the LX 470 derived from the latest version of the impressive Toyota Land Cruiser. Of all vehicles sold in North America, the LX 470 has the best ammunition to compete with the famous Range Rover that blazed the trail 28 years ago...

MODEL RANGE

The LX 470 only comes in a big four-door station wagon version in a single trim that has traded the old 6-cylinder engine for a 4.7L V8 with four-speed automatic transmission, full-time all-wheel drive and an adjustable hydropneumatic suspension. Other equipment items are quite extensive, since the only factory option is the sunroof. This vehicle has some distinctive stylistic traits such as grille, side guards, bulging wheelhouses, running boards, light alloy rims and roof rack.

TECHNICAL FEATURES

Just like its predecessor the LX 450, the 470 is based on the Land Cruiser platform. It consists of a shell chassis integrated with the steel body. For a vehicle with such a wide front surface, big tires and orifices, aerodynamic yield is remarkable since the drag coefficient is 0.40. The front suspension is now independent and uses A-arms and torsion bars, whereas the rigid rear axle is supported by four trailing arms. A hydropneumatic device provides three different ground clearance settings: high, normal and low. But as soon as vehicle speed goes beyond 19 mph, the suspension shifts back automatically to the normal setting. Another system controls shock absorber response depending on road conditions. The engine is now a DOHC 32-valve 4.7L V8 that develops 230 hp, linked to a 4-speed automatic transmission. All-wheel drive is full-time, benefitting from a viscous-coupled main differential that can be locked on demand so as to distribute available power to both front and rear wheels and there's a limited-slip differential at the rear. Four-wheel disc brakes have a servomechanism that's hy-

Sumo wagon...

draulically activated and are associated with an ABS device. Lastly, a suprising feature on such a bulky vehicle, there's rack-and-pinion steering for clean, crisp precision.

PROS

+ PERFORMANCES. They literally blew us away, since this brute that weighs in at 5401 lbs. accelerates better than most lightweight, economy cars and passing on the highway is super-safe.

+ RIDE COMFORT. It's amazing and offers more of a lush limo feel rather than an SUV sensation, thanks to well-adjusted suspension travel that works like a charm over major off-road obstacles and is cool as a cucumber on the highway.

+ USEFUL SPACE. The cabin can accomodate 5 or even 8 passengers when the second optional seatbench is installed in the cargo hold. There's lots of stretching space, even in the rear seats that are roomier than was the case on the 450. The rear hatch isn't the handiest around, but the luggage compartment is really huge when the third seatbench isn't installed.

+ DRIVING PLEASURE. It's more fun than you'd expect it to be. The cockpit is comparable to the minivan arrangement, visibility is good and the dashboard layout is well-organized.

+ ACCESS. Boarding is more convenient with the running boards and nine cleverly located assist grips, but it's still a bit tough getting to the third seatbench.

+ HANDLING. It's pretty amazing

with the well-adjusted suspension and full-time all-wheel drive. But this gentle giant isn't too quick on his feet and is rather awkward on tight curves or on slalom runs because of sheer hulk and pronounced sway. But it has a lot of vim and vitality and is steady as a rock.

+ QUALITY. Every last detail on this vehicle has been carefully attended to, be it design, build and finish job and the LX 470 is much less of a sport-utility vehicle per se than its predecessor.

CONS

-BUDGET. The LX 470 has many assets but it's sold at an appalling price that's much higher than that of its closest rivals. You can almost purchase two Expedition's for the same price... Not to mention the insurance premium that isn't cheap and fuel consumption that varies between 12 and 14 mpg, depending on needed juice...

- VEHICLE SIZE. The LX 470 isn't an ideal format for either city driving or for rambles in the underbrush, for this vehicle gets around in a lumbering sort of way and you have to be prudent when attempting delicate maneuvers.

- BRAKES. They didn't really satisfy us, since stopping distances stretch out pretty far, the stiff pedal is hard to gauge just right and even with the ABS device, you had to have your wits about you to keep this vehicle on the road during our test runs.

- STEERING. It's nicely powered, but a poor reduction ratio (3.8 tr) and wide turn angle diameter convert each move into a real chore and quick lane changes are dicey when it comes to keeping vehicle balance.

- TO BE IMPROVED UPON: Dull headlights that jar with other items on this superb vehicle and the inconvenient rear hatch door that could lift all in one piece and be powered, given the going price...

CONCLUSION

The LX 470 is the most serious rival for the Range Rover, a more snobbish sort that isn't as dependable or generous. This vehicle impressed us in a number of ways, so much so that we were almost convinced it was worth every penny... ☺

RATING LEXUS LX 470		
CONCEPT :		**84%**
Technology	80	
Safety :	90	
Interior space :	90	
Trunk volume:	80	
Quality/fit/finish :	80	
DRIVING:		**56%**
Cockpit :	80	
Performance :	50	
Handling :	50	
Steering :	80	
Braking :	20	
ORIGINAL EQUIPMENT:		**76%**
Tires :	80	
Headlights :	70	
Wipers :	75	
Rear defroster :	75	
Radio :	80	
COMFORT :		**76%**
Seats :	80	
Suspension :	75	
Sound level:	70	
Conveniences :	75	
Air conditioning :	80	
BUDGET :		**43%**
Price :	0	
Fuel economy :	20	
Insurance :	35	
Satisfaction :	90	
Depreciation :	70	
Overall rating:		**67.0%**

NEW FOR 1999

• No major change.

ENGINES

Model/ version	Type / timing valve / fuel system	Displacement cu in	Power bhp @ rpm	Torque lb-ft @ rpm
LX 470	V8 4.7 DOHC-32-MPSFI	285	230 @ 4800	320 @ 3400

TRANSMISSIONS

Compres. ratio	Driving wheels / transmission	Final ratio
9.6 :1	all - A4	4.30

PERFORMANCES

Acceler. 0-60 mph s	Standing 1/4 & 5/8 mile s	Acceler. 50-75 mph s	Braking 60-0 mph f	Top speed mph	Lateral acceler. G	Noise level dBA	Fuel economy mpg City	Highway	Fuel type Octane
10.5	17.6 31.5	7.6	157	109	0.76	64-68	13	16	R 87

PRICE & EQUIPMENT

LEXUS	LX 470
Retail price $:	54,950
Dealer invoice $:	47,175
Shipping & handling $:	495
Automatic transmission:	S
Cruise control:	S
Power steering:	S
Anti-lock brakes:	S
Traction control:	-
Air conditioning:	S
Leather:	S
AM/FM/radio-cassette:	SCD
Power door locks:	S
Power windows:	S
Tilt steering:	S
Dual adjustable mirrors:	S
Alloy wheels:	S
Anti-theft system:	S

Colors

Exterior: White, Black, Gold, Emerald, Beige, Mica, Green.

Interior: Taupe, Medium gray.

AT A GLANCE...

Category: 4x4 luxury sport-utility. **Class :** utility

HISTORIC

Introduced in:	1998
Made in:	Hino, Japan.

DEMOGRAPHICS

Model	Men./Wom.	Age	Married	College	Income
LX 470	NA				

INDEX

Safety:	90 %	Satisfaction:	90 %
Depreciation:	30 %	Insurance:	$ 1 650
Cost per mile:	$ 1.05	Number of dealers:	170

SALES

Model	1996	1997	Result
LX 450	7 528	6 785	- 9.9 %

MAIN COMPETITORS

CADILLAC Escalade, CHEVROLET Tahoe-Suburban, FORD Expedition, GMC Denali-Suburban, JEEP Grand Cherokee, LINCOLN Navigator.

MAINTENANCE REQUIRED BY WARRANTY

First revision:	Frequency:	Diagnostic plug:
4 000 miles	4 000 miles	Yes

SPECIFICATIONS

Model	Version Trim	Traction	Body/ Seats	Wheel base in	Lght x Wdgth x Hght in x in x in	Curb weight lb	Susp. ft/rr	Brake ft/rr	Steering type	Turning diameter ft	Steer. turns nber.	Fuel tank gal	tire size	Standard tires make	model	Standard powertrain
LEXUS LX 470	base	4X4	4 dr .8	112.2	192.5x76.4x72.8	5401	it/rh	dc/ABS	pwr.r&p.	42.0	3.8	25.4	275/70R16	Michelin	LTX M/S	V8/4.7/A4

General warranty: 4 years / 50 000 miles; powertrain: 6 years / 70 000 miles; corrosion perforation: 6 years / unlimited mileage & roadside assistance.

The sports utility vehicle market includes a phenomenal range of very diverse products and now it's engendered a new hybrid that's an all-terrain vehicle, car and minivan. According to the engineers, the Lexus RX 300 can even be categorized as a sports car because of its zip and zoom! Yet this type of vehicle is more like the Volvo V70XC and Subaru Outback than the Mercedes Benz M-Class, Infiniti QX-4 or Range Rover Discovery.

MODEL RANGE

The RX 300 is a luxury all-purpose vehicle offered in a unique version powered by a single 3.0L multivalve V6 that develops 220 hp, linked to an electronically controlled four-speed automatic transmission. The U.S. model is sold with front-wheel or all-wheel drive. As is the case for all Lexus vehicles, original equipment is very rich, but this model can also be equipped with a rear spoiler, category II trailer hookup and roof rack with several adapters.

TECHNICAL FEATURES

The RX 300 is closely inspired by the ES 300 sedan and shares its platform consisting of a steel unitized body equipped with front and rear independent cradles supporting the drive shaft as well as transmission and suspension elements. The structure is super solid with a special view to achieving optimum handling and good resistance in the event of a collision. Exterior dimensions are a tad bigger than those of the Grand Cherokee and like the Mercedes-Benz M-Class, this vehicle is equipped with four airbags protecting front seat passengers, namely two frontal and two side-impact devices. The streamlined shape has good aerodynamic yield, since the drag coefficient is recorded at 0.36, better than that of the Mercedes with only a 0.39 Cx. Front and rear suspensions are made up of specially designed MacPherson struts. The vehicle is equipped with four-wheel disc brakes assisted by a standard antilock braking device. The V6 is derived from the Lexus ES 300 engine. It hits 80% of its torque at 1,600 r.p.m., thanks to variable valve timing called VVTi. The all-wheel drive system is borrowed from the Celica All-Trac model that's sold in Asia and Europe. In normal situations, power is distributed 50/50 between front and rear wheels. A

A New Hybrid...

viscous-coupled main differential and a rear limited-slip Torsen differential redistribute juice to wheels benefitting from the best grip, when there's wheel slip.

PROS

+ **PRICE.** It's pretty down-to-earth, so it can compete with that of the Mercedes ML 320, its main rival.

+ **STYLE.** Its elegance makes you clean forget that the RX 300 is a 4X4, since its silhouette is more refined than that of an SUV, as is often the case on such a vehicle.

+ **PERFORMANCES.** It only takes about 9 seconds to accelerate from 0 to 60 mph and pickup is just as peppy due to a favorable power to weight ratio, which explains why fuel consumption is so efficient.

+ **RIDE COMFORT.** There's a pretty high ground clearance, but it's still no problem getting inside the front seats and no need to put your back out in the process. In the rear seat area, the seatbench is mounted on tracks, so it can be pushed forward and its back cushion can recline, so together with those on the front seats, behold, you have a bed...

+ **CONVENIENCE FEATURES.** The cargo hold is nice and convenient and the seatbench can be folded down to obtain a perfectly flat floor. The console between the front seats holds all kinds of clever storage compartments. The 6-CD changer is housed inside the dashboard and the ventilation system is fitted with a particulate air filter that you only need to change ever three years,

simply by hand and without any tool required, via the glove compartment.

+ **QUALITY.** It's simply great all-round, since assembly, finish job and choice of trim components are impeccable. But the leather seating and wood appliqués aren't exactly posh...

+ **A NICE FEATURE:** Amazingly bright headlamps.

CONS

- **SUSPENSION.** Insufficient travel and too much flexibility cripples off-road maneuvers, so the RX 300 is mostly an on-road or smooth terrain vehicle. On the road, the suspension causes lots of sway so, along with the hard, crummy-quality tires, you're in for some pretty awful surprises.

- **BRAKES.** We weren't convinced that they were effective, not with those ever so long stops, touchy application and we had to readjust vehicle path even with ABS.

- **MANEUVERABILITY.** Steering is quick and accurate, but it's over-assisted and suffers from too wide a steer angle diameter and poor visibility due to thick C and D pillars.

- **NOISE LEVEL.** There's more racket than you'd ever expect on a vehicle in this snobby class.

- **ACCESS.** It's awkward with those narrow doors and really slanting C pillar in the rear seat area.

- **INSTRUMENT PANEL.** Such an overdone, style-is-all design is out of date as soon as the vehicle comes off the assembly line. When it's not showing data from the GPS navigation system, the liquid crystal screen is indicating air ventilation and stereo settings, but readings are hard to see. Lastly, some touch screen controls are highly unusual.

- **TO BE IMPROVED UPON:** The low-slung seatbench, poorly located cup-holders for rear seat passengers (on the center console) and the sluggish sweep of wipers that often slip off the windshield surface.

CONCLUSION

The RX 300 comes with exactly what customers who like this ilk of SUV are looking for: forgiving all-wheel drive, distinctive looks and the ability to get around on tough roads without being a genuine 4X4. Last of all, it will thrill those who like its body design, luxury attributes and especially its reliability. ☺

RATING
LEXUS RX 300

CONCEPT :		80%
Technology	85	
Safety :	90	
Interior space :	80	
Trunk volume:	60	
Quality/fit/finish :	85	

DRIVING:		59%
Cockpit :	70	
Performance :	50	
Handling :	40	
Steering :	70	
Braking :	65	

ORIGINAL EQUIPMENT:		77%
Tires :	70	
Headlights :	85	
Wipers :	75	
Rear defroster :	75	
Radio :	80	

COMFORT :		71%
Seats :	75	
Suspension :	75	
Sound level:	45	
Conveniences :	80	
Air conditioning :	80	

BUDGET :		45%
Price :	10	
Fuel economy :	60	
Insurance :	40	
Satisfaction :	90	
Depreciation :	25	

Overall rating:	66.4%

NEW FOR 1999

• No major change.

ENGINES

Model/version	Type / timing valve / fuel system	Displacement cu in	Power bhp @ rpm	Torque lb-ft @ rpm
RX 300	V6* 3.0 DOHC-24-MPSFI	183	220 @ 5800	222 @ 4400
RX 300	V6* 3.0 DOHC-24-MPSFI	183	220 @ 5800	222 @ 4400

TRANSMISSIONS

Compres. ratio	Driving wheels / transmission	Final ratio
10.5 :1	front - A4*	3.080
10.5 :1	all - A4*	3.291

PERFORMANCES

Acceler. 0-60 mph s	Standing 1/4 & 5/8 mile s	Acceler. 50-75 mph s	Braking 60-0 mph f	Top speed mph	Lateral acceler. G	Noise level dBA	Fuel economy mpg City	Highway	Fuel type Octane
9.5	16.6 30.2	6.5	131	112	0.71	66-72	18	21	R 87
10.4	17.2 29.9	6.7	144	112	0.71	66-72	17	20	R 87

PRICE & EQUIPMENT

LEXUS RX 300	2WD	AWD
Retail price $:	31,550	32,950
Dealer invoice $:	27,404	28,620
Shipping & handling $:	495	495
Automatic transmission:		S
Cruise control:		S
Power steering:		S
Anti-lock brakes:		S
Traction control:		S
Air conditioning:		SA
Leather:		O
AM/FM/radio-cassette:		S
Power door locks:		S
Power windows:		SA
Tilt steering:		S
Dual adjustable mirrors:		SEH
Alloy wheels:		S
Anti-theft system:		S

Colors

Exterior: Gold, Silver, Black, Red, Blue, Brown, Bronze.

Interior: Cloth: Ivory. Leather: Black, Ivory.

AT A GLANCE...

Category: 2WD & 4WD all purpose vehicles.   **Class :** utility

HISTORIC

Introduced in: 1999
Made in: -

DEMOGRAPHICS

Model	Men./Wom.	Age	Married	College	Income
RX 300	60/40 %	46	82 %	50%	$ 68 000

INDEX

Safety:	90 %	Satisfaction:	92 %
Depreciation:	47 %	Insurance:	$ 1 550
Cost per mile:	$ 0.58	Number of dealers:	170

SALES

Model	1996	1997	Result
RX 300	Not on the market at that time.		

MAIN COMPETITORS

CHEVROLET Blazer, DODGE Durango, FORD Explorer, ISUZU Trooper, JEEP Grand Cherokee, GMC Envoy, INFINITI QX4, MERCEDES-BENZ M-Class, TOYOTA 4Runner.

MAINTENANCE REQUIRED BY WARRANTY

First revision:	Frequency:	Diagnostic plug:
4 000 miles	4 000 miles	Yes

SPECIFICATIONS

Model	Version Trim	Traction	Body/Seats	Wheel base in	Lght x Wdgth x Hght in x in x in	Curb weight lb	Susp. ft/rr	Brake ft/rr	Steering type	Turning diameter ft	Steer. turns nber.	Fuel tank gal	tire size	Standard tires make	model	Standard powertrain
LEXUS					General warranty: 4 years / 50 000 miles; powertrain: 6 years / 70 000 miles; corrosion perforation: 6 years / unlimited mileage & roadside assistance.											
RX 300	base	4x2	4dr.wgn. 5	103.0	180.1x71.5x65.7	3900	ih/ih	dc/ABS	pwr.r&p.	41.3	2.6	17.2	225/70R16	Goodyear	Eagle LS	V6/3.0/A4
RX 300	base	4x4	4dr.wgn. 5	103.0	180.1x71.5x65.7	3693	ih/ih	dc/ABS	pwr.r&p.	41.3	2.6	17.2	225/70R16	Bridgestone	Dueler HT	V6/3.0/A4

The Continental's last face-lift got so much flak that Lincoln had to bring major modifications to this model in the third production year. These changes gave the Continental a whole new character, something it never had much of, and created a Jaguar air and feel (a company affiliated with Ford) that's quite charming. It's too soon to know if these improvements will have any impact on sales, but at least the car is now significantly different from its Cadillac rivals.

MODEL RANGE

This big four-door, front-wheel drive sedan is sold in a single trim model driven by the 4.6L V6 «Intech» engine developing 260 hp, coupled to a 4-speed automatic transmission. Its already extensive equipment no longer includes the custom driver style system that lets you drive «à la carte», the most unique feature on the original model. The idea was no doubt too advanced for potential buyers and for the rest of the industry...

TECHNICAL FEATURES

The Continental is the only front-wheel drive Lincoln. Its steel monocoque architecture offers average aerodynamic finesse with a drag coefficient of 0.32. The fully independent suspension is based on the MacPherson strut principle up front and a multi-link system at the rear with a stabilizer bar both front and rear. Air springs keep the rear extremity on an even keel and shock absorbers are hydraulic. Four-wheel disc brakes benefit from an antilock braking device linked to standard traction control. Rack-and-pinion steering is variable assist and can also be adjusted according to 3 settings. All the electronic data is controlled by a Multiplex communication system. The Continental's V8 is exactly the same as equips the Town Car. This «Intech» engine is now on a par with the Cadillac Northstar engine , but when it comes to prestige, it doesn't hold a candle to its rival the Cadillac Seville, a car with much more international ambitions.

PROS

+ STYLE. The body exterior and cabin design have a neat, new look that reflects the fact that Ford now also owns Jaguar. This trait is more

American Jaguar..?

noticeable towards the rear, due to taillights that look a lot like those on the XJ8 and that God-awful chrome bar is gone forever.

+ PERFORMANCES. They're quite remarkable, since this very heavy car achieves accelerations and pickup nowhere near being laughable. The «Intech» engine really does its stuff and is very efficient as well, a pleasant surprise, since fuel consumption is very low when travelling on the highway at cruising speed, so much so that it's comparable to a V6's yield...

+ HANDLING. It's generally neutral for normal driving, but goes into understeer when on sports mode due to the overly elastic suspension that isn't adjustable, not

even as an option. At any rate, traction control and ABS provide nice, straight directional flow in all kinds of weather.

+ RIDE COMFORT. Travelling in a Continental is literally like being on cloud nine. The cushy suspension takes care of road nonsense, seats are thick and plush and soundproofing takes the starch out of engine and road noise. The body doesn't generate much wind whistle either.

+ TRUNK. It can hold lots of luggage, even when the (optional) storage box, that can be removed and slides in like a drawer, is installed. This accessory is such a clever concept that GM borrowed the idea and equipped the Seville and Bravada

with it. This storage box is really handy, since it's divided into sections, so small objects don't roll around or get knocked over. When loading larger pieces of luggage, it slides to the back or can be removed.

CONS

- PRICE. Now that high tech items are listed among the options, it should drop significantly. The Continental doesn't have the prestige that is the Seville's lucky lot, even though its engine is now just as impressive as the shining Northstar...

-MANEUVERABILITY. It's hampered by the big bod and wide turning radius.

- DRIVING. The «à la carte» driving feature is now sold as an extra because it's so darn costly. It lets you adjust suspension and steering firmness as well as the seat, mirror and radio station position memory according to three different drivers. One day, all cars will be equipped with this feature that lets you tailor the same model to satisfy umpteen pilots' wishes.

-CABIN SPACE. It isn't anywhere near what it should be for such a generous-size car and it's downright nasty even thinking of seating a fifth passenger in the middle of the rear seatbench, even for a five-minute errand.

-SEATS. They look super plush but they aren't too comfy. They're well upholstered but the seat cushion is short and the back is flat, so they don't offer good hip and shoulder support.

- STORAGE COMPARTMENTS. They're few and far between inside the cabin and the glove compartment and door side-pockets are stingy as heck. The center console is stuffed with the CD changer or the cellular phone. Rear seat passengers only have access to seat pockets and stylists didn't even think of adding a compartment and cup holders in the center armrest, as is more and more the custom...

CONCLUSION

Time will tell if modifications undergone by the Continental satisfy the usual customers or if other new buyers will bite. At any rate, sales results will tell all. ☺

RATING
LINCOLN Continental

CONCEPT :		82%
Technology	90	
Safety :	90	
Interior space :	70	
Trunk volume:	80	
Quality/fit/finish :	80	

DRIVING:		72%
Cockpit :	80	
Performance :	65	
Handling :	65	
Steering :	80	
Braking :	70	

ORIGINAL EQUIPMENT:		79%
Tires :	80	
Headlights :	80	
Wipers :	80	
Rear defroster :	75	
Radio :	80	

COMFORT :		73%
Seats :	70	
Suspension :	80	
Sound level :	70	
Conveniences :	60	
Air conditioning :	85	

BUDGET :		43%
Price :	0	
Fuel economy :	50	
Insurance :	40	
Satisfaction :	85	
Depreciation :	40	

Overall rating: 69.8%

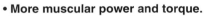

NEW FOR 1999

- More muscular power and torque.
- Ten-spoke chrome wheels.
- Standard side-impact airbags.
- Four-way adjustable headrests.
- Long-life coolant.

ENGINES

Model/ version	Type / timing valve / fuel system	Displacement cu in	Power bhp @ rpm	Torque lb-ft @ rpm
base	V8 4.6 DOHC-32-MPSFI	281	275 @ 5750	275 @ 4750

TRANSMISSIONS

Compres. ratio	Driving wheels / transmission	Final ratio
9.85 :1	front - A4*	3.56

PERFORMANCES

Acceler. 0-60 mph s	Standing 1/4 & 5/8 mile s	Acceler. 50-75 mph s	Braking 60-0 mph f	Top speed mph	Lateral acceler. G	Noise level dBA	Fuel economy mpg City	Fuel economy mpg Highway	Fuel type Octane
8.3	15.9 28.6	5.7	138	124	0.82	66	16	24	S 91

PRICE & EQUIPMENT

LINCOLN	Continental
Retail price $:	37,930
Dealer invoice $:	34,613
Shipping & handling $:	670
Automatic transmission:	S
Cruise control:	S
Power steering:	S
Anti-lock brakes:	S
Traction control:	S
Air conditioning:	SA
Leather:	S
AM/FM/radio-cassette:	S
Power door locks:	S
Power windows:	S
Tilt steering:	S
Dual adjustable mirrors:	SEH
Alloy wheels:	S
Anti-theft system:	S

Colors

Exterior: Gold, Ivory, Red, Blue, Green, Gray, Silver, Black, White.

Interior: Parchment

AT A GLANCE...

Category: front-wheel drive luxury sedans. **Class :** 7

HISTORIC
Introduced in: 1988 et 1995.
Made in: Wixom, MI, USA.

DEMOGRAPHICS

Model	Men./Wom.	Age	Married	College	Income
Continental	83/17 %	66	87 %	29 %	$ 60 000

INDEX
Safety:	90 %	Satisfaction:	87 %
Depreciation:	58 %	Insurance:	$ 1 450
Cost per mile:	$ 0.68	Number of dealers:	5 200

SALES

Model	1996	1997	Result
Continental	32 019	31 220	- 2.5 %

MAIN COMPETITORS
BMW 540i, CADILLAC DeVille & Seville, INFINITI Q45, JAGUAR XJ8, LEXUS GS & LS 400, LINCOLN Town Car.

MAINTENANCE REQUIRED BY WARRANTY

First revision:	Frequency:	Diagnostic plug:
5 000 miles	6 months/ 6 000 miles	Yes

SPECIFICATIONS

Model	Version Trim	Body/ Seats	Interior volume cu ft	Trunk volume cu ft	Cd	Wheel base in	Lght x Wdgth x Hght in x in x in	Curb weight lb	Susp. ft/rr	Brake ft/rr	Steering type	Turning diameter ft	Steer. turns nber.	Fuel tank gal	tire size	Standard tires make	model	Standard powertrain
LINCOLN Continental																		

LINCOLN Continental — Warranty: 4 years / 50 000 miles; corrosion perforation antipollution: 4 years / 50 000 miles.

Model	Version Trim	Body/ Seats	Interior vol.	Trunk vol.	Cd	Wheel base	Lght x Wdgth x Hght	Curb weight	Susp.	Brake	Steering	Turning diameter	Steer. turns	Fuel tank	tire size	make	model	powertrain
	4dr.sdn.5		102.0	18.4	0.32	109.0	208.5x73.6x56.0	3869	ih/ih	dc/ABS	pwr.r&p.	41.1	2.86	20.0	225/60R16	Michelin	MXV4 ZP	V8/4.6/A4

General Motors may have initiated the big deluxe all-terrain vehicle market when it launched the Tahoe and Yukon in 1995, both derived from the illustrious Suburban, but it's Ford who takes the credit for having caused the absolute sales frenzy that has taken off and gone to the moon. The Expedition and Navigator started a trend that even GM can't keep up with, as proven by the rush to get the GMC Denali and Cadillac Escalade, of dinosaur ancestry, on the market...

MODEL RANGE

The Navigator is a luxury SUV with RWD or AWD that comes in a generous 4-door station wagon equipped with a lifting rear hatch with window that opens, in a single trim level. It's animated by a 5.4L Triton V8 linked to a 4-speed automatic transmission. Equipment is lush and includes neat rear seating, namely two bucket seats like those up front, separated by an enormous center console that could hold a refrigerator...

TECHNICAL FEATURES

The Navigator owes almost all its attributes to the Expedition that's a spin-off of the F-150 pickup. It consists of a rugged H-frame on which the body is mounted via rubber insulators that take care of ruckus and shakes. The independent front suspension uses unequal-length control arms and the rear rigid axle is guided by five control arms and supported by load-levelling air springs. The 4X4 versions are also equipped with similar-design air springs up front, so the vehicle is kept on an even keel in both directions, allowing for variable ground clearance. Four-wheel disc brakes benefit from all-wheel ABS. You can change the all-wheel drive operating mode by touching a button on the dashboard, according to 4X2, 4X4 H, 4X4 L and Auto settings, the latter only engaging front wheels when things get slick and slippery.

PROS

+ CABIN SPACE. This spacious vehicle can't accomodate any more passengers than the competiton, but there's all kinds of room, so you feel like you're travelling first class in an airplane.

+ STYLE. It's gorgeous with the high-perched front grille, muscular silhouette and solid, built-in running boards.

+ PRICE. It's pretty stiff, but it's a

First Class Seats...

really good buy compared to the Lexus LX 470 or the Expedition Eddie Bauer that aren't as well equipped or so terribly one-of-a-kind handsome.

+ LUXURY. The interior is quite spiffy with bucket seats dressed in leather finery, elegant wood trim and spacious center consoles.

+ RIDE COMFORT. The ride is amazing for a vehicle in this category. The suspension is silky smooth, even on the 4X4 model. Thick, cushy seats offer good support even if the seat cushion is a bit short and soundproofing takes care of most of the unwanted noise.

+ MANEUVERABILITY. It's awesome for such a hulk on wheels since the turn angle diameter is short, so you can make slick moves

without blinking an eye, even in really tight spots.

+ STEERING. Quick, right-on steering benefits from a good reduction ratio, which, along with the new, highly sophisticated front suspension, keeps the car right on course.

+ CONVENIENCE FEATURES. The convenient rear hatch is equipped with a window that opens, so you have access to the big cargo hold without having to open the hatch door itself. Inside the cabin, there are loads of generous-size storage spots, including a roomy glove compartment, door side-pockets and those great center consoles that hold all kinds of stuff and serve as writing tablets.

+ PERFORMANCES. They're very

zippy, given this mammoth's weight, with accelerations from 0 to 60 mph achieved in 11 seconds or less.

+ DRIVING PLEASURE. It's super with such limo-like response and you sure don't feel like you're at the wheel of an SUV. Controls are creamy and the vehicle is willing and able, the ambience is quiet and soothing and handling is a piece of cake, so you're right at ease, even in such a huge vehicle with its inherent limitations.

+ QUALITY. The Navigator is a neat blend of rugged Ford traits and lush Lincoln luxury. Finish details and trim components are superbly crafted, so this vehicle is on a posh par with the Continental and Town Car models.

+ NICE FEATURES: The easy to use "Control-Trac" function that has an automatic 4X4 mode, illuminated running boards for safer boarding and rear seat controls for the sound system and climate control.

CONS

- FUEL CONSUMPTION. It's pretty average for such a heavy vehicle that can haul up to 8,000 lb. but it'll horrify folks who don't like wasting Mother Earth's fossil fuels...

-BRAKES. They're easy to apply as needed and really hold up to roughing up, but they're not as effective as they should be, since you need quite a stretch to come to a sudden stop.

-VEHICLE SIZE. It sure doesn't help when it comes to parking in those tight spots in the city.

- PICKUP. Pickup response is less brisk than for accelerations and you have to be careful when passing since you need lots of space to do so.

-RUNNING BOARDS. They should be modified for they're narrow and slippery when wet.

- THE THIRD SEATBENCH. It's flat, so it offers only fair to midling comfort and it's hell getting to it.

CONCLUSION

The Navigator is a perfect specimen of a product that blends everything it takes to make its mark in an expanding market segment. It's versatile, solidly built and brawny, yet it's luxurious and lovely to look at, all this at a decent price, so how could it not be the smashing success it was and is, more so than anyone's wildest dreams. ☺

RATING
LINCOLN Navigator

CONCEPT : 86%
Technology	80
Safety :	80
Interior space :	100
Trunk volume:	90
Quality/fit/finish :	80

DRIVING: 48%
Cockpit :	80
Performance :	40
Handling :	35
Steering :	75
Braking :	10

ORIGINAL EQUIPMENT: 80%
Tires :	85
Headlights :	70
Wipers :	80
Rear defroster :	80
Radio :	85

COMFORT : 75%
Seats :	75
Suspension :	75
Sound level:	60
Conveniences :	80
Air conditioning :	85

BUDGET : 44%
Price :	0
Fuel economy :	20
Insurance :	45
Satisfaction :	80
Depreciation :	75

Overall rating: 66.6%

NEW FOR 1999

- Power-adjusting pedal assembly.
- Wheels added to the third seatbench.
- The 5.4L DOHC replaces the 5.4L SOHC.

ENGINES

Model/version	Type / timing valve / fuel system	Displacement cu in	Power bhp @ rpm	Torque lb-ft @ rpm
base	V8 5.4 DOHC-32-MPSFI	330	300 @ 5000	335 @ 2750

TRANSMISSIONS

Compres. ratio	Driving wheels / transmission	Final ratio
9.5 :1	rear - A4	3.31
	rear/4 - A4	3.73

PERFORMANCES

Acceler. 0-60 mph s	Standing 1/4 & 5/8 mile s	Acceler. 50-75 mph s	Braking 60-0 mph f	Top speed mph	Lateral acceler. G	Noise level dBA	Fuel economy mpg City	Fuel economy mpg Highway	Fuel type Octane
9.8	16.8 30.8	7.0	157	112	0.62	68	12	17	R 87
10.5	17.6 31.5	7.8	177	109	0.62	68	11	17	R 87

PRICE & EQUIPMENT

LINCOLN	Navigator 2WD	4WD
Retail price $:	39,310	42,960
Dealer invoice $:	34,333	37,436
Shipping & handling $:	640	640
Automatic transmission:	S	
Cruise control:	S	
Power steering:	S	
Anti-lock brakes:	S	
Traction control:	-	
Air conditioning:	SA	
Leather:	S	
AM/FM/radio-cassette:	S	
Power door locks:	S	
Power windows:	S	
Tilt steering:	S	
Dual adjustable mirrors:	SEH	
Alloy wheels:	S	
Anti-theft system:	S	

Colors

Exterior: Gold, Red, Green, Blue, Black, Silver, White.

Interior: Graphite, Brown.

AT A GLANCE...

Category:	2WD & 4WD all purpose vehicles. **Class :** utility

HISTORIC

Introduced in:	1998
Made in:	Wayne, Michigan, USA.

DEMOGRAPHICS

Model	Men./Wom.	Age	Married	College	Income
Navigator	ND				

INDEX

Safety:	75 %	**Satisfaction:**	82
Depreciation:	27 %	**Insurance:**	$ 1 395
Cost per mile:	$ 0.90	**Number of dealers:**	5 200

SALES

Model	1996	1997	Result
Navigator	-	26 231	

MAIN COMPETITORS

CADILLAC Escalade, CHEVROLET Tahoe-Suburban, FORD Expedition, GMC Denali-Suburban, JEEP Grand Cherokee, Range ROVER, LEXUS LX 470.

MAINTENANCE REQUIRED BY WARRANTY

First revision:	Frequency:	Diagnostic plug:
5 000 miles	6 months/ 6 000 miles	Yes

SPECIFICATIONS

Model	Version Trim	Traction	Body/ Seats	Wheel base in	Lght x Wdgth x Hght in x in x in	Curb weight lb	Susp. ft/rr	Brake ft/rr	Steering type	Turning diameter ft	Steer. turns nber.	Fuel tank gal	tire size	Standard tires make	model	Standard powertrain
LINCOLN	Warranty: 4 years / 50 000 miles; corrosion perforation antipollution: 4 years / 50 000 miles.															
Navigator	base	4x2	4dr.wgn.7/8	119.0	204.8x79.9x75.2	NA	ih/ra	dc/ABS	pwr.ball	40.4	3.3	30.0	245/75R16	Continental	Contitrac AT	V8/5.4/A4
Navigator	base	4X4	4dr.wgn.7/8	119.0	204.8x79.9x76.7	5392	ih/ra	dc/ABS	pwr.ball	40.5	3.3	30.0	245/75R16	Continental	Contitrac AT	V8/5.4/A4

It's a well known fact, you can get used to anything, even if it isn't perfect. Yet, for most people, it's hard to understand the rationale behind the stylistic approach at Ford ever since Claude Lobo took over as head of this department. In the long run, the #2 American automaker may be able to come up with a unique, distinctive design, but in the meantime, it will lose customers and there'll be a certain mistrust in regard to models that were among the most popular of the lot. In this respect, the Town Car's fate is similar to that of the Taurus-Sable models...

MODEL RANGE

Like the model it replaces, the Lincoln Town Car is a 4-door sedan available in 4 different versions: Executive, Signature, Signature TS and Cartier. All versions are equipped with the same mechanical features, namely a V8 "Intech" engine coupled with a 4-speed automatic transmission. An antilock braking system is part of the original equipment on all models, along with traction control.

TECHNICAL FEATURES

The Town Car consists of a surrounding chassis made of steel on which is mounted the monocoque body that's made up of mostly galvanized panels. Aerodynamics aren't too hot since the unofficial drag coefficient is 0.34. The front suspension still uses unequal-length control arms with coil springs and stabilizer bar, while the rear suspension consists of a Watt setup with air springs, gas-filled shocks and stabilizer bar with an automatic load-levelling device. Electronic sway and swerve control no longer equips this car, but roadholding is now achieved by the Watt suspension geometry. Disc brakes are beefier up front and the ABS-traction control system comes as original equipment. Steering is still a recirculating ball system but it's no longer variable assist on demand as was once the case. The 4.6L V8 has undergone major modifications in regard to cylinder head and pistons and it's protected from seizure in the event of a coolant leak. Radiator vents are electric and the coil ignition system now includes one coil per ignition plug, thus eliminating wiring between plugs and the center-load coil and loss of power in damp weather.

Too Adventurous?

PROS

+ DRIVING PLEASURE. It feels less like a "boat" than before thanks to the more elaborate rear axle design (that could still have benefitted from an independent suspension setup), more accurate steering, more competent suspensions and a stronger structure that has greater torsion and flexion resistance.

+ RIDE COMFORT. It's pretty impressive with such a generous cabin that comfortably seats five (but head room is a bit snug in the rear seats), cool and collected suspension (even with the rigid rear axle) and plush seats that could, however, offer more lateral support. Noise is kept to a civilized minimum.

+ HANDLING. The body exhibits more solid, structural integrity so there's less rattling and much less pronounced roll and rear end directional flow is cleaner, which all amounts to a longer neutrality on curves and a less noticeable oversteer effect.

+ ENGINE. It's quite competent for this car category, more geared to comfort than to breaking records, since accelerations and pickup are quick and allow for safe passing on the highway. And not to mention that it's pretty efficient since gas consumption sits at around 19 mpg at normal speeds.

+ NICE FEATURES: Some handy items like the rear seat adjustable air vents, and the sound system and climate control remote power switches located on the steering wheel spokes.

- STYLE. It'll take a while for this model to be accepted because it borrows too heavily from well known models such as the Chrysler LHS (rear window design) or the Jaguar (trunk extremity look) to have a clean, single-minded style. The Town Car traded in its official status tuxedo for a spectacular "patchwork" look that's far from being classic.

- REAR AXLE. Depending on road quality, handling and ride comfort are very up and down. A cheap solution that's unworthy of such an upper-crust car.

- TRUNK. It has a funny shape, so it's hard to use it to full advantage, even if theoretically it's supposed to hold a lot, and the spare tire thrown smack in the middle doesn't help one iota. A problem Lincoln will have to take a serious look at.

- CONVENIENCE FEATURES. They're awfully stingy, since there isn't even a door side-pocket for the front passenger and rear seat passengers have a center armrest, but it doesn't contain any storage space. Front seat passengers don't have a real center storage console either.

- INSTRUMENT PANEL. Its plain Jane instruments and design jar with the Cartier clock and climate control dials are too low to be really within reach.

- VISIBILITY. It's obstructed by the thick roof supports, especially at rear quarterback and the narrow rear window doesn't help.

- TO BE IMPROVED UPON: Poor-quality headlamps that are out of keeping with such lap of luxury equipment, the texture and look of some plastic components that really jar with the Jag leather and wood trim. The Anglo-American blend could have been smoother. There is no footrest for the driver and rear headrests are pretty simplistic since they aren't even adjustable.

CONCLUSION

The latest Town Car is disappointing. Creamy criteria that were its trademark and guaranteed its status have been discarded. Beyond esthetics, which are a matter of personal taste, this car looks like a pretty chintzy luxury product and some of its essential traits, dear to traditional customers, have been brushed away without a second thought by the builder. ☺

RATING
LINCOLN Town Car

CONCEPT : 86%
Technology — 80
Safety : — 90
Interior space : — 90
Trunk volume: — 90
Quality/fit/finish : — 80

DRIVING: 62%
Cockpit — 70
Performance : — 50
Handling : — 60
Steering : — 80
Braking : — 50

ORIGINAL EQUIPMENT: 77%
Tires : — 80
Headlights : — 70
Wipers : — 80
Rear defroster : — 75
Radio : — 80

COMFORT : 73%
Seats : — 75
Suspension : — 80
Sound level : — 70
Conveniences : — 50
Air conditioning : — 90

BUDGET : 45%
Price : — 0
Fuel economy : — 50
Insurance : — 45
Satisfaction : — 85
Depreciation : — 45

Overall rating: 68.6%

NEW FOR 1999
- The 4.6L engine's improved power and torque output.
- Side-impact airbags for front seat passengers.
- Five new exterior shades.
- JBL sound system replaces the Alpine model.
- Center fold-up armrest containing two cup-holders.

ENGINES / TRANSMISSIONS / PERFORMANCES

Model/ version	Type / timing valve / fuel system	Displacement cu in	Power bhp @ rpm	Torque lb-ft @ rpm	Compres. ratio	Driving wheels / transmission	Final ratio	Acceler. 0-60 mph s	Standing 1/4 & 5/8 mile s	Acceler. 50-75 mph s	Braking 60-0 mph f	Top speed mph	Lateral acceler. G	Noise level dBA	Fuel economy mpg City	Highway	Fuel type Octane
1)	V8* 4.6-SOHC-16-MPSFI	281	205 @ 4250	280 @ 3000	9.0 :1	rear - A4*	3.08	10.0	18.0	32.0	7.7	148	109	0.78	65-70	16	26	R 87
2)	V8* 4.6-SOHC-16-MPSFI	281	220 @ 4500	290 @ 3500	9.0 :1	rear - A4*	3.08	9.5	17.6	31.4	7.2	154	112	0.78	65-70	16	26	R 87

1) Executive & Signature   2) SignatureTouring Sedan & Cartier

PRICE & EQUIPMENT

LINCOLN Town Car	Executive	Signature/TS	Cartier
Retail price $:	38,030	41,830	42,830
Dealer invoice $:	34,702	38,804	38,974
Shipping & handling $:	670	670	670
Automatic transmission:	S	S	S
Cruise control:	S	S	S
Power steering:	S	S	S
Anti-lock brakes:	S	S	S
Traction control:	S	S	S
Air conditioning:	SA	SA	SA
Leather:	S	S	S
AM/FM/radio-cassette:	S	S	S
Power door locks:	S	S	S
Power windows:	S	S	S
Tilt steering:	S	S	S
Dual adjustable mirrors:	SEH	SEH	SEH
Alloy wheels:	S	S	S
Anti-theft system:	S	S	S

Colors
Exterior: Parchment, Gold, Red, Cordouan, Blue, Green, Gray, Silver, Black, White.

Interior: Graphite, Parchment, Blue, Black, White.

AT A GLANCE...

Category: rear-wheel drive luxury limousine. **Class :** 7

HISTORIC
Introduced in: 1980
Made in: Wixon, MI, USA.

DEMOGRAPHICS
Model	Men./Wom.	Age	Married	College	Income
Town Car	89/11 %	67	91 %	29 %	$ 53 000

INDEX
Safety:	90 %	Satisfaction:	87 %
Depreciation:	55 %	Insurance:	$1 425
Cost per mile:	$ 0.95	Number of dealers:	5 200

SALES
Model	1996	1997	Result
Town Car	93 598	92 297	-1.4 %

MAIN COMPETITORS
BMW 740i, CADILLAC DeVille & Seville, INFINITI Q45, JAGUAR XJ8, LEXUS LS 400.

MAINTENANCE REQUIRED BY WARRANTY
First revision:	Frequency:	Diagnostic plug:
5 000 miles	6 months	Yes

SPECIFICATIONS

Model	Version Trim	Body/ Seats	Interior volume cu ft	Trunk volume cu ft	Cd	Wheel base in	Lght x Wdgth x Hght in x in x in	Curb weight lb	Susp. ft/rr	Brake ft/rr	Steering type	Turning diameter ft	Steer. turns nber.	Fuel tank gal	tire size	Standard tires make	model	Standard powertrain
LINCOLN	Warranty: 4 years / 50 000 miles; corrosion perforation antipollution: 4 years / 50 000 miles.																	
Town Car Executive	4dr.sdn. 6		112.3	20.6	0.37	117.7	215.3x78.2x58.0	3979	ih/rh	dc/ABS	pwr.ball	42.2	3.4	19.0	225/60R16	Michelin	MXV4	V8/4.6/A4
Town Car Signature	4dr.sdn. 6		112.3	20.6	0.37	117.7	215.3x78.2x58.0	4015	ih/rh	dc/ABS	pwr.ball	42.2	3.4	19.0	225/60R16	Michelin	MXV4	V8/4.6/A4
Town Car Cartier	4dr.sdn. 6		112.3	20.6	0.37	117.7	215.3x78.2x58.0	4045	ih/rh	dc/ABS	pwr.ball	42.2	3.4	19.0	235/60R16	Michelin	Symetry	V8/4.6/A4

When you find out what the official sales figures are for Mazda pickups, you realize that maybe cloning the Ranger wasn't the best approach, even if it did save megabucks. The Ranger has many attributes, but it doesn't possess all the assets that made models designed and built by Mazda so darn popular with customers. There's always an identitiy issue related to a product and to its builder in the conglomerate that's the result of company fusions, regrouping and hasty streamlining.

MODEL RANGE

The B-series pickup is sold with rear or all-wheel drive, with regular or extended box, regular or extended cabin in B2500, B3000 and B4000 versions in either SX or SE trim. This year the extended cabin models benefit from the many doors offered on the Ranger. This year again, due to some disgruntled buyers, the model range has been streamlined for practical reasons. The base engine that equips the B2500 4X2's is a 2.5L 4-cylinder, the B3000 4X4's get a 3.0L V6 and the 4.0L V6 is available as an extra for the B4000's. The 5-speed manual transmission comes standard and the 4-speed automatic is offered as an option, as is the 5-speed automatic paired up with the 4.0L V6.

TECHNICAL FEATURES

These sports-utility vehicles are built on a steel H-frame made up of seven crossmembers (six on the 4X4) on which the body is mounted via rubber insulation components. The B-series pickups differ from their Ford homologues in regard to esthetic touches on the front grille and box shape and silhouette. The front suspension, identical for the 4X2's and 4X4's, is independent and consists of unequal-length control arms, while the rear rigid axle is suspended by leaf springs. The antilock braking system is only linked to the rear wheels on the rear-wheel drive models but to all four wheels on AWD models. All-wheel drive is activated by a simple electric switch located on the dashboard. This partial system isn't equipped with a main differential and can only be used on slippery surfaces and at moderate speeds. The 5-speed automatic gearbox is in fact a 4-speed to which Ford added a fifth gear between 1st and 2nd gear, by a technique called «Swap-Shift».

PROS

+ **REPUTATION.** Solid build and

Less Prized...

dependability are confirmed by the high owner satisfaction rate and validate Ford's predilection for simple, durable technical solutions rather than fly-by-night revolutionary wonders.

+ **HANDLING.** It's improved with the new front suspension that provides crisper vehicle control and doesn't jump as much with an empty box and on less than perfect roads

+ **STEERING.** The rack-and-pinion steering system that now equips these models has really improved the driving experience, since it springs back to center nicely and is well assisted. Turn angle diameter measurements aren't available, but it seems that maneuverability is a cut above as a result of this important modification.

+ **ENGINE.** The 2.5L 4-cylinder

engine is more gutsy and has more vim and vigor than before. Yet it's still load-sensitive and loses some juice when the air conditioning is on, so accelerations, pickup and fuel consumption are adversely affected.

+ **SHIFTER.** The manual gearbox is more fun to use with such a right-on and quick on the draw shifter, but clutch pedal effort and travel are average.

+ **LOAD CAPACITY.** Engines procure particularly interesting hauling and trailering capabilities.

+ **REGULAR CABIN.** It's now much more serviceable since it's 3 inches longer, so a small suitcase or other small items can be stored behind the seats.

+ **NICE FEATURES.** The wipers that are brisk enough and sweep enough of the window to assure

good visibility, even in driving rain, and the comfortable bucket seats and 60/40 split-folding seatbench that offer good support.

CONS

- **THE V6 ENGINES.** In our opinion, they aren't the best suited to these sports utility vehicles, for they're wimpy at low r.p.m. and rough around the edges and drink up so much gas that you hanker for a more muscular V8.

- **SPARTAN SIMPLE.** The base model that's been bereft of goodies so as to be able to be sold at the lowest price possible...

- **RIDE COMFORT.** Even the RWD models don't provide anywhere near car-like comfort, since the suspension is always jumping about, making the least trip exhausting.

- **BRAKES.** They're awfully iffy on the RWD models equipped with only rear-wheel ABS and that aren't always dependable, especially with a full load.

- **HANDLING.** Being at the wheel of the base model on slippery roads is nerve-wracking due to the overly soft suspension and undersize tires. The same applies for the AWD models, but for the opposite reasons, since the suspension is too hard and the huge tires bounce up a storm.

- **THE 4X4 SYSTEM.** It's a pretty basic system, use is limited since you can only have recourse to it in slippery conditions and at moderate speeds, otherwise you could damage it. There should be an automatic mode like the one that equips the F-series and the Expedition.

- **FUEL CONSUMPTION.** The V6's gas intake is never cheap, especially for rough, all-terrain use.

- **THE V8 ENGINE.** Not offering this engine option deprives these pickups of versatility and hauling and trailering capabilities that are the pride and joy of their rival the Dodge Dakota. What a shame!

- **POOR FEATURE:** The base model seatbench that doesn't provide enough lateral and lumbar support.

CONCLUSION

Mazda pickups are benefitting from the rapid technical developments reflected in the Ford Ranger, but they've lost the unique identity and format that appealed to buyers in the past. Rationalizing has its price, but it certainly isn't up to the customer to pay for the consequences...

RATING MAZDA-B

CONCEPT :		**60%**
Technology	80	
Safety :	70	
Interior space :	40	
Trunk volume:	35	
Quality/fit/finish :	75	
DRIVING:		**51%**
Cockpit :	70	
Performance :	30	
Handling :	40	
Steering :	75	
Braking :	40	
ORIGINAL EQUIPMENT:		**54%**
Tires :	70	
Headlights :	80	
Wipers :	70	
Rear defroster :	0	
Radio :	50	
COMFORT :		**56%**
Seats :	65	
Suspension :	50	
Sound level:	50	
Conveniences :	40	
Air conditioning :	75	
BUDGET :		**62%**
Price :	60	
Fuel economy :	60	
Insurance :	65	
Satisfaction :	75	
Depreciation :	50	
Overall rating:		**56.6%**

NEW FOR 1999
- Streamlined model range.
- Bigger, new-design rims.
- Lock for spare tire on the SE models.
- Decorative strips no longer available on the SX and SE versions.
- Two new exterior shades: Amazon Green and Harvest Gold.

ENGINES

Model/ version	Type / timing valve / fuel system	Displacement cu in	Power bhp @ rpm	Torque lb-ft @ rpm
4x2	L4* 2.5 SOHC-8-MPSFI	153	119 @ 5000	146 @ 3000
4x4	V6* 3.0 OHV-12-MPSFI	182	150 @ 5000	185 @ 3750
option	V6 4.0 OHV-12-MPSFI	245	160 @ 4250	225 @ 3000

TRANSMISSIONS

Compres. ratio	Driving wheels / transmission	Final ratio
9.4 :1	rear - M5*	3.73
	rear - A4	4.10
9.1 :1	rear/4- M5*	3.73
	rear/4 - A4	3.73
9.0 :1	rear/4- M5	3.55
	rear/4- A5	3.73

PERFORMANCES

Acceler. 0-60 mph s	Standing 1/4 & 5/8 mile s		Acceler. 50-75 mph s	Braking 60-0 mph f	Top speed mph	Lateral acceler. G	Noise level dBA	Fuel economy mpg City	Highway	Fuel type Octane
12.0	18.7	33.8	9.8	138	97	0.69	70	21	28	R 87
12.8	18.8	34.2	10.5	148	93	0.69	69	20	26	R 87
11.0	18.3	32.2	8.7	151	100	0.71	68	16	24	R 87
12.2	18.8	33.8	9.8	157	97	0.71	68	16	24	R 87
9.5	17.2	31.4	7.5	157	106	0.73	68	18	22	R 87
10.8	17.7	32.0	8.0	164	103	0.73	68	16	22	R 87

PRICE & EQUIPMENT

MAZDA B-Series	SX 2500 4x2 short	SE 2500 4x2 CP	SX 3000 4x4 short	SE 4000 4x4 CP
Retail price $:	11,485	15,445	15,415	18,430
Dealer invoice $:	10,624	13,804	14,397	16,464
Shipping & handling $:	510	510	510	510
Automatic transmission:	O	O	O	O
Cruise control:	O	O	O	O
Power steering:	S	S	S	S
Anti-lock brakes:	Sre.	Sre.	Sre.	Sre.
Traction control:	-	-	-	-
Air conditioning:	O	O	O	O
Leather:	-	-	-	-
AM/FM/radio-cassette:	O	O	S	S
Power door locks:	-	O	O	O
Power windows:	-	O	O	O
Tilt steering:	-	O	O	O
Dual adjustable mirrors:	SM	SM	SM	SE
Alloy wheels:	-	S	-	S
Anti-theft system:	-	-	-	-

Colors
Exterior: Black, White, Red, Scarlet, Platinum, Green, Gold.

Interior: Medium graphite , Brown.

AT A GLANCE...

Category:	4x2 & 4x4 compact pickups.
Class :	utility

HISTORIC
Introduced in:	1983
Made in:	Edison, New Jersey, USA.

DEMOGRAPHICS
Model	Men./Wom.	Age	Married	College	Income
B-Series 4x2	91/9 %	41	68 %	32 %	$ 29 000
B-Series 4x4	88/12%	40	70 %	36 %	$ 31 000

INDEX
Safety:	75 %	Satisfaction:	75 %
Depreciation:	47 %	Insurance:	$ 835-950
Cost per mile:	$ 0.43	Number of dealers:	875

SALES
Model	1996	1997	Result
B-Series	42 815	37 697	- 12.0 %

MAIN COMPETITORS
DODGE Dakota, CHEVROLET S-10, FORD Ranger, GMC Sonoma, ISUZU, NISSAN Frontier, TOYOTA Tacoma.

MAINTENANCE REQUIRED BY WARRANTY
First revision:	Frequency:	Diagnostic plug:
5 000 miles	6 months/ 5 000 miles	Yes

SPECIFICATIONS

Total warranty, antipollution & battery: 3 years /36 000 miles; corrosion perforation: 5 years / unlimited.

Model	Version Trim	Traction	Body/ Seats	Wheel base in	Lght x Wdgth x Hght in x in x in	Curb weight lb	Susp. ft/rr	Brake ft/rr	Steering type	Turning diameter ft	Steer. turns nber.	Fuel tank gal	tire size	Standard tires make	model	Standard powertrain
MAZDA																
B-Series	short SX	4x2	2dr.p-u.2	111.6	187.5x69.4x64.9	3024	ih/rl	dc/dr/ABS*	pwr.r&p.	36.4	3.5	16.4	205/70R14	Firestone	Wilderness	L4/2.5/M5
	CabPlus SE	4x2	2dr.p-u.2+2	125.7	202.9x69.4x64.9	3205	ih/rl	dc/dr/ABS*	pwr.r&p.	41.3	3.5	19.5	225/70R15	Firestone	Wilderness	V6/3.0/M5
	short SX	4x4	2dr.p-u.2	111.6	187.7x70.3x64.7	3441	it/rl	dc/dr/ABS*	pwr.r&p.	37.4	3.5	16.4	215/75R15	Firestone	Wilderness	V6/3.0/M5
	CabPlus SE	4x4	2dr.p-u.2+2	125.9	201.7x70.3x64.7	3602	it/rl	dc/dr/ABS*	pwr.r&p.	41.3	3.5	19.5	235/75R15	Firestone	Wilderness	V6/3.0/M5

* on rear wheels.

MAZDA Miata
I'm Worth It...

The Miata roadster is one of the finest-built cars in current automobile history. In just a few years, this neat little car has carved an impregnable niche the world over and is the true forerunner of the small sports car renaissance that paved the way for the BMW Z3, Mercedes-Benz SLK and Porsche Boxster. The Miata is the ideal leisure car, a car you purchase not for any down-to-earth, logical reason, but to be able to express just who you are: a free spirit, someone who knows what you want to get out of life and who has an irrepressible zest for life. The Miata is the perfect symbol of a holiday mood, a fun-loving attitude and carefree joie de vivre, since you can really only drive this car for part of the year, as is more or less the case for a motorcycle.

The Miata owes its ancestry and soul to the British roadsters that took the world by storm in the fifties and it did wonders when it came to bringing a dependable and durable, never-say-die character to the sports car, qualities that were in the past totally foreign to this vehicle species. As well, the Miata played a dramatic role in improving safety features that weren't exactly the forte of these daredevil cars and that, in their time, cost a lot of lives. Today we can say that it's stringent Japanese design and construction standards that finally guaranteed its survival as a species. Lastly, looking back, what Mazda can be proud of is having kept the Miata's winsome character, since even if it's a more and more expensive car, it's still reasonably affordable for those whose state of mind dictates its therapeutic thrills.

That's why doing a face-lift on a car that's become an institution and that's hardly been changed since it was first introduced ten years ago, representented a delicate operation in more ways than one. So engineers and designers decided to give the Miata a few new touches without turning its vital assets topsy-turvey. The overall structure has the very same dimensions, but the body is sturdier and it's modified towards the rear to provide more trunk space, the suspension has been reworked, the engine is brawnier, the link between the engine and differential, a kind of backbone to the vehicle, is more dynamic, there's a new-design instrument panel and the soft top is equipped with a glass window and electric defogger. In short, lots of in-depth changes were made to improve the original design. Yet, it's the car's looks than seem more dramatically different.

The first Miata exuded a rather bulky and tame temperament at the front end, but its heir has more fluid lines. It no longer has pop-up headlights, the side panels, front and rear extremities are more streamlined giving the Miata zippy traits that are more in keeping with its character. The latest model is actually a bit shorter and higher, but it looks lower-slung and longer that its predecessor. A neat touch: the Ferrari-inspired door handles on which ladies often broke their nails have been reworked and are now safer to manipulate. Even though the Miata appeals to young people in Japan, Mazda doesn't expect a customer shift in North America, since 35% of customers are in the 35 to 44 year-old age bracket and 27% of them are between 45 and 54 years of age.

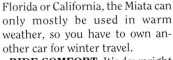

The new Miata roadster was unveiled at the most recent Tokyo Auto Show. This was a long-awaited event and everyone was on pins and needles and could hardly wait to see how the Japanese builder had rejuvenated the most well-loved convertible in the world without altering its signature traits that were the key to its success. Lastly, purists and «Miata maniacs» were relieved when they discovered that Tom Matano, head of the design department in California, had, as usual, accomplished his mission with real flair.

MODEL RANGE

The Miata is a small two-seater roadster motivated by a 1.8L 4-cylinder engine linked to a standard 5-speed manual gearbox or optional 4-speed automatic. Original equipment items include power steering, aluminum rims and a radio receiver and CD player. The «Leather» options package adds power windows and locks, cruise control, Torsen differential, antilock braking device as well as a more sophisticated Bose sound system.

TECHNICAL FEATURES

The steel unibody has been reinforced so it's even sturdier than before. It includes a fully independent suspension, based on the MacPherson strut setup both front and rear, with gas-filled shocks and stabilizer bar for both axles. Mazda has also improved the dual aluminum rail organization, a sort of subframe linking front and rear power trains, that was used so brilliantly on the original model. The car is equipped with disc brakes, but an antilock braking device is still only available as an extra. The 1.8L DOHC 4-cylinder engine now develops 140 hp, giving an added edge to the power to weight ratio.

SIMPLY SUPER

++ BUDGET. It's very reasonable, given the fact that you can get zoomy sports car kicks without having to lose your shirt or break a single law of the land...

++ STYLE. Such a classic bod appeals to most people, but, like its predecessor, it lacks a certain make my day flavor. The first version was inspired by the Lotus Elan, but the second looks a lot like the Triumph Spitfire of the seventies.

++ DRIVING PLEASURE. The feeling is out of this world with such a lively, frisky engine, transmission,

steering and suspension. You feel like you're melded to the machine. Controls are right where you want them and average-height drivers will find the cockpit made-to-measure.

PROS

+ PERFORMANCES. Accelerations and pickup are noticeably more powerful so you can really let loose with this brawnier engine. Yet it's a pity that a more exotic engine such as the 1.8L V6 that powered the former MX-3 coupe isn't offered with the Leather option package.

+ ROADHOLDING. It's still very competent thanks to a perfect weight distribution (50/50). The Miata takes even tight curves with perfect aplomb, it literally sticks to the road and wheel function is amazingly assured. Yet it's more genteel than it was, due to suspension modifications that makes for smoother travel, but of course, car path remains highly dependable.

+ CONTROLS. The gearbox is a real joy to use; gears are nicely calibrated and changing gears is quick and very precise and the small shifter that you control with a flick of the

wrist is downright fun. The same goes for steering that now sports a tidy Momo steering wheel that's really neat. The nifty-design pedal lets you do the famous heel and toe of yore and the logical, ergonomic dashboard is an added plus.

+ CONVERTIBLE TOPS. They're really neat, waterproof and a breeze to install. The soft top can be folded down with one hand and the hard top lets you drive this beauty even in the winter, with the right tires. The hard top is also equipped with an electric defroster and good news for owners, the hard top on the former model fits perfectly on the new model...

+ BRAKES. They're easy to gauge, dig in when needed and are tough soldiers, achieving trim, stable stops, thanks to effective ABS.

+ NICE FEATURES: The nicer convertible top that now includes a glass window and electric defroster, the wind deflector that does its stuff when the top is down and effective wipers and washers.

CONS

- LIMITED USE. Unless you live in

Florida or California, the Miata can only mostly be used in warm weather, so you have to own another car for winter travel.

- RIDE COMFORT. It's downright Spartan with such a gritty suspension, firm seats and high noise level attributed mostly to poor soundproofing, since wind noise stays at a reasonable level.

- CONVENIENCE FEATURES. They're noticeably a cut above when it comes to trunk space, since the spare tire and battery are now lodged inside the trunk floor, but storage spots inside the snug cabin are stingy indeed.

- FUEL CONSUMPTION. It would be more economical if the car weighed more (more than a ton) and if it were possible to drive the Miata in a cool, collected manner...

- SAFETY FEATURES. Mazda would have demonstrated a greater sense of responsibility if it had installed a roll bar, even as an extra, integrated into the body design.

- VISIBILITY. It's poor at rear quarterback with both convertible tops, since there are big lateral blind spots and exterior mirrors are too small and set too far back.

- DESIGN DETAILS. The interior is terribly basic and dreary with all that black and trim materials aren't too spiffy, such as the plastic stuff on the door trim that's very chintzy-looking. A bit of imagination wouldn't hurt, would it?

- ACCESSORIES. Mazda doesn't go out of its way to offer standard accessories that would give the Miata a unique character; there are no roll bars, fender skirts or original rims, which is too bad, really. If owners felt like they belonged to an exclusive «club», sales would be all the more brisk...

- POOR FEATURES: Weak headlights, ho-hum exhaust noise and poorly located cup-holders.

CONCLUSION

More than ever, the Miata is a coveted car for fun driving in the warm season and for remembering the good old days of sports car soar...

RATING
MAZDA Miata

CONCEPT :		52%
Technology	80	
Safety :	70	
Interior space :	20	
Trunk volume:	10	
Quality/fit/finish :	80	

DRIVING:		71%
Cockpit :	80	
Performance :	60	
Handling :	75	
Steering :	80	
Braking :	60	

ORIGINAL EQUIPMENT:		78%
Tires :	80	
Headlights :	75	
Wipers :	80	
Rear defroster :	80	
Radio :	75	

COMFORT :		53%
Seats :	70	
Suspension :	60	
Sound level :	20	
Conveniences :	40	
Air conditioning :	75	

BUDGET :		62%
Price :	50	
Fuel economy :	75	
Insurance :	45	
Satisfaction :	85	
Depreciation :	55	

Overall rating:		**63.2%**

Anecdote
Mazda is known to make quite a splash when introducing new models. These events are carefully orchestrated and are a lot of fun for car experts on the guest list. But the Japanese automaker didn't have too much luck with the latest convertible launch. Who could have predicted that it would rain buckets in Santa Barbara, California in early summer? El Niño, no doubt...

ENGINES / TRANSMISSIONS / PERFORMANCES

Model/ version	Type / timing valve / fuel system	Displacement cu in	Power bhp @ rpm	Torque lb-ft @ rpm	Compres. ratio	Driving wheels / transmission	Final ratio	Acceler. 0-60 mph s	Standing 1/4 & 5/8 mile s	Acceler. 50-75 mph s	Braking 60-0 mph f	Top speed mph	Lateral acceler. G	Noise level dBA	Fuel economy mpg City	Highway	Fuel type Octane
Miata 1998 L4* 1.8 DOHC-16-EFI		112	133 @ 6500	114 @ 5000	9.0 :1	rear - M5*	4.10	9.0	16.8 30.4	6.5	131	119	0.85	72-78	21	29	R 87
						rear - A4	3.91	10.4	17.8 31.7	6.9	137	112	0.85	72-78	21	29	R 87
Miata 1999 L4* 1.8 DOHC-16-IEPM		112	140 @ 6500	119 @ 5000	9.5 :1	rear - M5*	4.30	8.2	16.1 28.4	5.8	144	124	0.88	72-78	20	31	R 87
						rear - A4	4.10	9.5	17.2 30.7	6.5	151	115	0.88	72-78	21	31	R 87

PRICE & EQUIPMENT

MAZDA Miata	base
Retail price $:	19,770
Dealer invoice $:	18,115
Shipping & handling $:	450
Automatic transmission:	O
Cruise control:	O
Power steering:	S
Anti-lock brakes:	O
Traction control:	O
Air conditioning:	O
Leather:	O
AM/FM/radio-cassette:	SDc
Power door locks:	O
Power windows:	O
Tilt steering:	O
Dual adjustable mirrors:	SM
Alloy wheels:	S
Anti-theft system:	-
Colors	

Exterior: White, Black, Red, Blue, Silver, Green.

Interior: Cloth: Black. Leather: Tan.

AT A GLANCE...

Category: rear-wheel drive sport convertibles. **Class :** 3S

HISTORIC
Introduced in: 1989.
Made in: Hofu, Japan.

DEMOGRAPHICS
Model	Men./Wom.	Age	Married	College	Income
Miata	63/37 %	40	60 %	60 %	$ 45 000

INDEX
Safety:	65 %	Satisfaction:	85 %
Depreciation:	40 %	Insurance:	$1 155
Cost per mile:	$ 0.46	Number of dealers:	871

SALES
Model	1996	1997	Result
Miata	18 408	17 218	- 6.5 %

MAIN COMPETITORS
CHEVROLET Cavalier convertible, PONTIAC Sunfire convertible.

MAINTENANCE REQUIRED BY WARRANTY
First revision:	Frequency:	Diagnostic plug:
5 000 miles	5 000 miles	Yes

SPECIFICATIONS

Model	Version Trim	Body/ Seats	Interior volume cu ft	Trunk volume cu ft	Cd	Wheel base in	Lght x Wdgth x Hght in x in x in	Curb weight lb	Susp. ft/rr	Brake ft/rr	Steering type	Turning diameter ft	Steer. turns nber.	Fuel tank gal	tire size	Standard tires make	model	Standard powertrain
MAZDA		General warranty: 3 years / 50 000 miles; powertrain: 5 years / 100 000 miles; corrosion: 5 years / unlimited.																
Miata 1998	base	2dr.con.2	NA	4.4	0.39	89.2	155.1x66.0x48.2	2293	ih/ih	dc/dc	pwr.r&p.	31.8	2.8	12.7	185/60R14	Toyo	R22	L4/1.8/M5
Miata 1998	leather	2dr.con.2	NA	4.4	0.39	89.2	155.1x66.0x48.2	2304	ih/ih	dc/dc	pwr.r&p.	31.8	2.8	12.7	195/50R15	Michelin	Pilot SX	L4/1.8/M5
Miata 1999	base	2dr.con.2	NA	144	0.37	89.2	155.3x66.0x48.4	2275	ih/ih	dc/dc	pwr.r&p.	30.2	2.7	12.7	185/60R14	Toyo	R22	L4/1.8/M5
Miata 1999	leather	2dr.con.2	NA	144	0.37	89.2	155.3x66.0x48.4	2282	ih/ihd	dc/dc	pwr.r&p.	30.2	2.7	12.7	195/50R15	Michelin	Pilot SX	L4/1.8/M5

The Millenia is the only indication that Mazda is trying to seriously compete with Toyota, Nissan and Honda in the luxury car arena. This car was actually designed to be part of the Amati lineup that, in the long run, never saw the light of day. Sold elsewhere in the world as the Xedos, it was a last-ditch effort to replace the snubbed 929. It's equipped with admirable and original high tech features typical of Mazda marvels, but Millenia sales bring up the rear in the category.

MODEL RANGE

The Millenia is a four-door front-wheel drive sedan. The base model, called the «Millenia Leather» is powered by the 2.5L V6 that equipped the 626, whereas the S version receives a 3.2L V6 that benefits from the Miller cycle. Both models are richly equipped and items include leather-clad seats, front heated seats, traction control associated with an antilock braking device, as well as all the plush power functions that go with this luxury category.

TECHNICAL FEATURES

The Millenia has a steel monocoque body blessed with lovely, flowing lines and the 0.29 drag coefficient, proof that aerodynamics are simply great. The fully independent suspension uses shock struts and transverse A-arms with stabilizer bars. Cars are equipped with variable assist steering and disc brakes linked to a standard ABS-traction control system. The S version engine benefits from the Miller cycle which allows for a high expansion rate with a low compression ratio, thanks to well-tailored valve settings and a Lysholm supercharger. Compression time is pared down to create a fifth stroke cycle that optimizes cylinder feed and generates a stronger explosion with equal displacement, the end result being 1.5 more torque and juice, yet fuel consumption is cut down by 10 to 15%.

PROS

+ PRICE. By lowering the sales price of 99 models, Mazda will make undecided customers think twice and so it'll attract new buyers until the next model hits the market.

+ SILHOUETTE. It's aristocratic elegance has a certain charm, but it doesn't exactly grab your attention.

+ RIDE COMFORT. The base model had a more cushy suspen-

Lack of Charisma...

sion than the S model, the latter being rather stiff. Seats provide good lateral and lumbar support and low noise interference is the direct result of effective soundproofing.

+ PERFORMANCES. The Miller engine's output on the S version derives from the sports car kind of power to weight ratio, even with the hefty weight and smaller displacement than average for this category.

+ HANDLING. It's super, since well-controlled sway lets you negotiate curves with assurance. Responsive steering benefits from a good reduction ratio so directional flow is accurate and the car is agile on snaky runs.

+ EQUIPMENT. Both versions are richly equipped and only differ in regard to engine model. For once,

front heated seats come standard, a feature that will be appreciated by folks living in northern climes.

+ QUALITY. Assembly has a solid, rugged feel, finish job is clean and trim materials have a nice look and texture.

+ TRUNK. It's unusually deep, so it holds loads of luggage, but it isn't convertible since the rear seatbench is fixed and the CD player cuts down on height.

CONS

-DEPRECIATION. It's dramatic for these models don't have the reputation of the well-loved ES 300 or the panache of the zoomy Nissan Maxima.

- PERFORMANCES. The base engine's ouput is rather blah for the 626 V6 can't cope too well with the

added 238 lb. So it isn't surprising that accelerations and pickup are lethargic, and torque is weak at low r.p.m.

-AUTOMATIC. It won't turn all sportsy drivers' crank, for it's slow as molasses when upshifting and downshifting and in some cases, you have to force the downshift.

-FUEL CONSUMPTION. The Miller engine isn't as efficient as Mazda states it is, for fuel consumption varies between 17 and 19 mpg.

- BRAKES. They aren't the best match for the S version's zippy style, since stopping distances are quite long in emergency situations. But the antilock braking system works beautifully, so stops are straight and brakes hold up well when put through the works.

-SUSPENSION. The S version's suspension is stiff both at the front that's overloaded and at the rear where wheel travel is limited.

- INSTRUMENT PANEL. Its stylistic appeal isn't at all like that of the body design and the shape of gauges and layout are distracting, for some controls are a bit weird.

- CABIN SPACE. It's limited for rear seat passengers who have to put up with cramped toe and head room, so much so that a third passenger won't persevere too long. Lastly, the rounded arch design and short rear doors obstruct easy access.

- CONVENIENCE FEATURES. Storage space goes lacking, since the glove compartment has been replaced by the airbag housing and the compartment in the center console, though fairly roomy, can't really replace it.

- FRONT-WHEEL DRIVE. It doesn't do justice to the capabilities of the Miller engine that would be better suited to a rear-wheel car.

CONCLUSION

Until it's replaced by a new model, the Millenia is doing its darndest to attract buyers thanks to its more competitive price tag and brilliant Miller engine. Will it be enough to forget the anonymous character of the design and the bizarre instrument panel? ☺

RATING
MAZDA Millenia

CONCEPT : 75%
Technology	80
Safety :	100
Interior space :	60
Trunk volume:	55
Quality/fit/finish :	80

DRIVING: 66%
Cockpit :	70
Performance :	60
Handling :	60
Steering :	80
Braking :	60

ORIGINAL EQUIPMENT: 77%
Tires :	80
Headlights :	80
Wipers :	80
Rear defroster :	70
Radio :	75

COMFORT : 72%
Seats :	80
Suspension :	80
Sound level :	70
Conveniences :	50
Air conditioning :	80

BUDGET : 52%
Price :	20
Fuel economy :	65
Insurance :	45
Satisfaction :	85
Depreciation :	45

Overall rating: 68.4%

NEW FOR 1999
- Stylistic touches on the front end (grille, headlamps, etc.)
- Several exterior/interior design features.
- Standard 16-inch aluminum rims with the Leather option package.
- 17-inch aluminum rims and new tires on the S version.
- Two control units for the remote control doors locks.

ENGINES / TRANSMISSIONS / PERFORMANCES

Model/ version	Type / timing valve / fuel system	Displacement cu in	Power bhp @ rpm	Torque lb-ft @ rpm	Compres. ratio	Driving wheels / transmission	Final ratio	Acceler. 0-60 mph s	Standing 1/4 & 5/8 mile s	Acceler. 50-75 mph s	Braking 60-0 mph f	Top speed mph	Lateral acceler. G	Noise level dBA	Fuel economy mpg City	Fuel economy mpg Highway	Fuel type Octane
Leather	V6*2.5 DOHC-24-MPFI	152	170 @ 5800	160 @ 4800	9.2:1	front - A4	4.375	10.2	17.7	31.5	7.1	148	124	0.80	65	18	27	S 91
S	V6C*2.3 DOHC-24-MPFI	138	210 @ 5300	210 @ 3500	10.0:1	front - A4	3.805	8.2	16.4	29.1	6.5	144	137	0.80	67	18	27	S 91

PRICE & EQUIPMENT

MAZDA Millenia	Leather	S
Retail price $:	28,995	36,595
Dealer invoice $:	25,562	31,514
Shipping & handling $:	450	450
Automatic transmission:	S	S
Cruise control:	S	S
Power steering:	S	S
Anti-lock brakes:	S	S
Traction control:	S	S
Air conditioning:	SA	SA
Leather:	SC	SC
AM/FM/radio-cassette:	SCD	SCD
Power door locks:	S	S
Power windows:	S	S
Tilt steering:	S	S
Dual adjustable mirrors:	SEH	SEH
Alloy wheels:	S	S
Anti-theft system:	S	S

Colors

Exterior: Sand, Black, Red, Blue, White, Green, Champagne, Silver.

Interior: Beige, Grey.

AT A GLANCE...

Category: rear-wheel drive luxury sedans. **Class :** 7

HISTORIC
Introduced in: 1994
Made in: Hofu, Japon.

DEMOGRAPHICS
Model	Men./Wom.	Age	Married	College	Income
Millenia	80/20 %	48	73 %	71 %	$ 55 000

INDEX
Safety:	100 %	Satisfaction:	85 %
Depreciation:	53 %	Insurance:	$ 1 150-1 275
Cost per mile:	$ 0.67	Number of dealers:	871

SALES
Model	1996	1997	Result
Millenia	13 019	18 020	+ 38.4 %

MAIN COMPETITORS
ACURA TL , AUDI A4, CADILLAC DeVille, INFINITI I30, LEXUS ES 300, LINCOLN Continental, OLDSMOBILE Aurora, SAAB 9³, TOYOTA Avalon, VOLVO S70.

MAINTENANCE REQUIRED BY WARRANTY
First revision:	Frequency:	Diagnostic plug:
5 000 miles	5 000 miles	Yes

SPECIFICATIONS

Model	Version Trim	Body/ Seats	Interior volume cu ft	Trunk volume cu ft	Cd	Wheel base in	Lght x Wdgth x Hght in x in x in	Curb weight lb	Susp. ft/rr	Brake ft/rr	Steering type	Turning diameter ft	Steer. turns nber.	Fuel tank gal	tire size	Standard tires make	model	Standard powertrain
MAZDA	General warranty: 3 years / 50 000 miles; powertrain: 5 years / 100 000 miles; corrosion: 5 years / unlimited.																	
Millenia	Leather	4dr.sdn. 5	94.0	13.0	0.29	108.3	189.7x69.7x54.9	3240	ih/ih	dc/ABS	pwr.r&p.	37.4	2.9	18.0	215/55VR16	Michelin	XGTV4	V6/2.5/A4
Millenia	S	4dr.sdn. 5	94.0	13.0	0.29	108.3	189.7x69.7x54.9	3355	ih/ih	dc/ABS	pwr.r&p.	37.4	2.9	18.0	215/50VR17	Dunlop	SP Sport 4000	V6C/2.3/A4

Mazda just couldn't convince buyers that its MPV minivan was a viable concept, either in rear-wheel or all-wheel drive, since the sportsy character associated with these two different modes isn't as yet common currency in North America. Poor fuel efficiency didn't help either. In the spring of 1999, Mazda will introduce a completely new model more in keeping with current trends, namely a front-wheel drive vehicle equipped with two sliding doors and about the same size as Caravan-Voyager models.

MODEL RANGE

The MPV is a minivan with short wheelbase, available in either RWD or AWD with four swing doors and that can seat 7 or 8 passengers. The 4X2 model is available in L or LX versions and the 4X4 is sold only in LX , that can receive a set of optional equipment called «All Sport». The MPV is equipped with standard automatic transmission, power steering, ABS-traction control, power windows, locks and mirrors, as well as radio and CD player and adjustable steering wheel. The middle seatbench can be replaced by two captain's chairs and the third seatbench can be removed to free up more luggage space.

TECHNICAL FEATURES.

The MPV's steel unitized body is very robust since it includes an auxiliary frame welded to the platform. The body design is about ten years old, but its drag coefficient is comparable to that of some more recent models. The suspension consists of MacPherson struts up front and rear rigid axle that's held in place by longitudinal control arms and Panhard rod. Disc brakes are associated with four-wheel ABS. The MPV is animated by a 3.0L V6 coupled to a 4-speed automatic transmission. The «on demand» all-wheel drive is activated when the main differential is locked by a simple touch of a switch.

PROS

+ STYLE. It's still quite mod thanks to some esthetic touches added two years ago. With its 4 swing doors, the MPV is more like a station wagon than an SUV.

+ SAFETY FEATURES. Passive security is a cut above that of some rivals, due to the really rigid build of the reinforced body that earns this vehicle top marks in collision tests, but also explains its very hefty

Throwing the Towel...

weight, especially the AWD version that easily weighs more than two tons at full load capacity.

+ ROADABILITY. It's characterized by an effective shock absorber system and guidance components so handling is very car-like. Even in spite of its height (especially the 4X4), it takes curves with aplomb and its typical understeer is easily adjusted.

+ COCKPIT. The instrument panel is rational and ergonomic, the driver is comfortably seated and generous windows offer good visibility all-round.

+ RIDE COMFORT. It's nifty with such a competent suspension that's never brutal and takes the starch out of road faults and due to good-quality soundproofing.

+ QUALITY. The build is down-to-earth and robust, the finish job is neat as a pin and trim materials look and feel better than in the past.

+ ACCESS. The wide swing doors help when climbing aboard and they're sturdier than some of the sliding doors that equip rivals.

+ NICE FEATURES. The rear door side-pockets and windows that lower all the way as well as the interesting hauling capabilities with the optional equipment sold by the carmaker.

CONS

-REAR-WHEEL DRIVE. This feature is more suited to sports cars and pickup trucks than to minivans and it complicates winter driving in snowbelt regions, so you have to opt for all-wheel drive if you want to

travel safely during the icy season.

-USEFUL SPACE. It's limited, especially in the rear section of the cabin since leg room between the seatbenches is very tight.

- BRAKES. They're not the greatest due to heavy vehicle weight, so sudden stopping distances are very long, linings have only average lasting power and they wear out in a hurry. We also observed that, depending on load and the state of the road, the antilock braking system didn't always do its stuff as it should.

- PERFORMANCES. Here again, hefty vehicle weight siphons off acceleration and pickup power, since the V6 huffs and puffs and really lacks torque at low r.p.m.

- STEERING. It's well-powered, but is afflicted by a poor reduction ratio (3.6 and 3.8 turns), so it's vague at the center and even with the relatively short sheelbase, its wide steer angle diameter complicates some moves.

- FUEL CONSUMPTION. The 4X4 version literally gobbles gas since it can go as low 11 mpg with a full load or when pulling a trailer...

-DEPENDABILITY. It's improved over time, but some parts are hard to find and they cost a bundle.

-SEATS. The really firm upholstery wears you out, since cushions give you a sore backside on long trips...

- CARGO HOLD. It doesn't hold much at all with full passenger capacity, but as of quite recently, you can remove the rear seatbench to store more luggage.

- TO BE IMPROVED UPON: The middle seatbench can't be moved and both seatbenches weigh a ton and are hard to manipulate and loud wind and road noise are unpleasant.

CONCLUSION

It'll take a little more time to see if this minivan-all-terrain vehicle will win out. Mazda was a bit too quick on the draw and potential buyers weren't really ready to purchase such a vehicle. Yet this fusion of advantages typical of both types of super-popular vehicles will no doubt be more common in the near future.

RATING
MAZDA MPV

CONCEPT :   73%
Technology	75
Safety :	90
Interior space :	80
Trunk volume:	40
Quality/fit/finish :	80

DRIVING: 51%
Cockpit :	80
Performance :	35
Handling :	40
Steering :	60
Braking :	40

ORIGINAL EQUIPMENT: 73%
Tires :	80
Headlights :	75
Wipers :	80
Rear defroster :	70
Radio :	60

COMFORT :   70%
Seats :	70
Suspension :	70
Sound level :	70
Conveniences :	70
Air conditioning :	70

BUDGET :   49%
Price :	40
Fuel economy :	30
Insurance :	50
Satisfaction :	80
Depreciation :	45

Overall rating: 63.2%

NEW FOR 1999

- No change for the current model that will be sold until next spring, when it will be replaced by a new front-wheel drive version equipped with two sliding doors.

ENGINES
Model/ version	Type / timing valve / fuel system	Displacement cu in	Power bhp @ rpm	Torque lb-ft @ rpm
MPV 4x2	V6* 3.0 SOHC-18-MPFI	180	155 @ 5000	169 @ 4000
MPV 4x4	V6* 3.0 SOHC-18-MPFI	180	155 @ 5000	169 @ 4000

TRANSMISSIONS
Compres. ratio	Driving wheels / transmission	Final ratio
8.5 :1	rear-A4*	3.909
8.5 :1	rear/4-A4*	4.300

PERFORMANCES
Acceler. 0-60 mph s	Standing 1/4 & 5/8 mile s	Acceler. 50-75 mph s	Braking 60-0 mph f	Top speed mph	Lateral acceler. G	Noise level dBA	Fuel economy mpg City	Fuel economy mpg Highway	Fuel type Octane
11.0	18.0	32.8	8.0	151	106	0.70	66	15 21	R 87
11.8	18.4	34.5	9.5	157	103	0.70	66	14 18	R 87

PRICE & EQUIPMENT

MAZDA MPV	4x2 LX	4x2 LX	4x4 ES
Retail price $:	23,095	26,895	28,895
Dealer invoice $:	20,834	24,258	26,060
Shipping & handling $:	480	480	480
Automatic transmission:	S	S	S
Cruise control:	S	S	S
Power steering:	S	S	S
Anti-lock brakes:	S	S	S
Traction control:	-	S	-
Air conditioning:	O	O	S
Leather:	O	O	S
AM/FM/radio-cassette:	S	S	S
Power door locks:	S	S	S
Power windows:	S	S	S
Tilt steering:	S	S	S
Dual adjustable mirrors:	SE	SE	SE
Alloy wheels:	S	S	S
Anti-theft system:	O	O	O

Colors
Exterior: White, Green, Silver, Sand, White/Silver, Green/Silver, Blue/Silver, Black/Silver.
Interior: Grey, Taupe.

AT A GLANCE...

Category:	rear-wheel drive or 4WD compact vans.	Class :	utility

HISTORIC
Introduced in:	1988
Made in:	Hiroshima, Japan.

DEMOGRAPHICS
Model	Men./Wom.	Age	Married	College	Income
MPV	75/25 %	43	74 %	51.5 %	$35 000

INDEX
Safety:	90 %	Satisfaction:	80 %
Depreciation:	55 %	Insurance:	$ 975
Cost per mile:	$ 0.53	Number of dealers:	871

SALES
Model	1996	1997	Result
MPV	14 427	15 599	+8.1%

MAIN COMPETITORS
CHEVROLET Astro & Venture, DODGE-PLYMOUTH Caravan-Voyager, FORD Aerostar & Windstar, HONDA Odyssey, MERCURY Villager, NISSAN Quest, PONTIAC Trans Sport, TOYOTA Sienna, VW EuroVan.

MAINTENANCE REQUIRED BY WARRANTY
First revision:	Frequency:	Diagnostic plug:
5 000 miles	5 000 miles	Yes

SPECIFICATIONS

General warranty: 3 years / 50 000 miles; powertrain: 5 years / 100 000 miles; corrosion: 5 years / unlimited.

Model	Version Trim	Traction	Body/ Seats	Wheel base in	Lght x Wdgth x Hght in x in x in	Curb weight lb	Susp. ft/rr	Brake ft/rr	Steering type	Turning diameter ft	Steer. turns nber.	Fuel tank gal	tire size	Standard tires make	model	Standard powertrain
MAZDA																
MPV	LX	4x2	5dr.van8	110.4	183.5x71.9x68.9	3730	ih/rh	dc/ABS	pwr.r&p.	33.1	3.8	19.5	195/75R15	-	-	V6/3.0/A4
MPV	LX	4x2	5dr.van8/7	110.4	183.5x71.9x68.9	3790	ih/rh	dc/ABS	pwr.r&p.	33.1	3.8	19.5	215/65R15	-	-	V6/3.0/A4
MPV	ES	4x4	5dr.van8/7	110.4	183.5x71.9x71,5	4061	ih/rh	dc/ABS	pwr.r&p.	39.7	3.6	19.8	225/70R15	-	-	V6/3.0/A4

MAZDA Protegé
Changing of the Guard

At Mazda the Protegé has become a sort of institution. It hasn't always been called Protegé, but the GLC and 323 that preceded it didn't go unnoticed in their time. The saga began in 1977 with the GLC up until 1986, when the 323 took over up until 1990, when the name Protegé was used for the first time. In 1995, the 323 was quickly taken off the North American market soon after its unveiling, giving full rein to the Protegé that since then has been the lower end base model of the Hiroshima carmaker. The choice and exact meaning of this name made up of French phonetics are a bit nebulous, since in Japan they often use foreign words because of their musical or exotic flavor.

The Protegé's main rivals are, in order of popularity, the Toyota Corolla, Honda Civic and Nissan Sentra. When you compare the main dimensions of these models with those of new and former Protegé models, you realize that the latest small Mazda has been pared down a bit, but cabin size is bigger, such as overall width in both front and rear seats and it offers more space than its main rivals. This increase in interior volume, compared to a slight trimming down of exterior dimensions, enhances car competence since it can do more while expending less energy since vehicle weight has been cut down. Mazda engineers took advantage of this revision by improving loads of details, such as the higher seat position for clearer visibility. The interior design has been spruced up right down to the finest details so as to

make it more welcoming and convenient. For example, the well-thought out ergonomics and the convenient storage spaces that are standard on all models. Ride comfort is the direct result of greater structural rigidity due to a clean, cohesive design so there's less noise and vibration from the axles and power trains. So the platform, lateral supports and roof pillars create a solid cage that provides good resistance in the event of a collision. Some hollow structural units have been filled with urethane foam to reinforce and soundproof the body even more and the body paint is one of the most resistant ever used by Mazda. In order to protect the car (no pun intended) from stone chips and peeling, the most exposed sections have been coated with a thick polyvinyl layer to offset the effects of ambient acids (rain,

insects, bird excrements and tree resins).

With a view to minimize environmental impact, the most recent Protegé is 90% recyclable since it doesn't contain any harmful substances like asbestos in the seals or brake linings or any lead. Its 1.6L engine has received the California ULEV (Ultra Low Emission Vehicle) certificate and the 1.8L engine has a LEV standing. Thus equipped, the Protegé is better prepared to compete with rivals and to have a really good chance of gaining market shares in a very competitive segment.

The Protégé is by far the best sold Mazda in North America but also in the world, for it's sold in 120 countries in all. This type of vehicle is always reworked with utmost caution, when one realizes the impact of potential buyers' acceptance or dislike. So no wonder the latest Protégé hasn't undergone any earth-shattering modifications, in regard to style or technical features, but that it's been chiefly refined when it comes to minute touches and details.

MODEL RANGE

The Protégé is still offered as a 4-door sedan that comes in DX and SE versions with a 1.6L engine delivering 105 hp and in LX with a DOHC 1.8L engine that develops 122 hp. The standard transmission is a 5-speed manual but a 4-speed automatic is available as an extra. Original equipment on the DX includes power steering and power windows while the SE also receives radio and CD player. The LX gets added cruise control, power locks and mirrors and adjustable steering wheel. This year all three versions are equipped with 14-inch wheels and tires and an ABS device is optional on the SE and LX only.

TECHNICAL FEATURES

The Protégé's monocoque body is made of steel of which 90% of the panels are galvanized. It's more rigid to resist impact from every angle. A rare feature, this new model is a bit smaller than its predecessor, since dimensions are slightly less than those of the former model, which doesn't affect the fact that it offers more generous cabin space.

The silhouette is more angular, but aerodynamics are just as good, since the drag coefficient sits at 0.32. Suspensions are independent, made up of Macpherson struts and double trapezoidal control arms with stabilizer bar both front and rear on all versions that are equipped with disc and drum brakes and standard power steering. The new 1.6L engine is an extrapolation of the former 1.5 that's been modernized and reinforced. The gearbox is new too and contains 26% fewer parts and weighs 8 lb. less than the former model.

PROS

+ STYLE. It's simple and nicely balanced, so it pleases the ladies who represent more than half of this model's buyers. It doesn't have

any trait that's out of the ordinary but it's lovely, for it's polished and well-proportioned.

+ FORMAT. Neither too big nor too small, the Protégé sits between two categories. Subcompact due to its engines, but it's almost a class 3 compact due to its cabin that can accomodate five passengers quite nicely. Interior space is generous and the trunk is convenient with its good-size opening that lowers to bumper level. The trunk can also be extended by lowering the seatbench back.

+ HANDLING. The Protégé has always exhibited good road adherence due to its elaborate suspension. With a suspension including dual anti-roll bars, more precise steering and good-size tires, the most recent Protégé is even easier to control and it behaves in a crisp, predictable way even on poor roads.

+ FUEL EFFICIENCY. Both engines meet anti-pollution ULEV (1.6) and LEV (1.8) standards and are super fuel-efficient even with the automatic, since consumption varies between 26 to 28 mpg

+ PERFORMANCES. The 1.8L engine is smooth and chomping at the bit, so it's fun to drive and you can achieve almost racy moves. The 1.6L isn't as colorful, but it performs better when linked to the manual gearbox.

+ RIDE COMFORT. It's surprisingly cushy for a car in this category, the shock sytem is effective and seats are nicely shaped, more so in the front seats, and cushion upholstery seems less firm than it once was.

+ CABIN DESIGN. The cabin interior seems less blah than before and the main trim components have a nice feel. Plastic components look more spiffy and their simili-perforated design on the dashboard is original.

+ QUALITY. Construction, finish details and trim components are typical of Japanese products and give the Protégé its very cohesive character.

+ CONFIDENCE. The Protégé has always had a great reputation when it comes to dependablity since again last year, 80% of owners were very satisfied.

+ WARRANTY. It's more advantageous at Mazda than for some of the competition.

+ PRICES. Compared to some rivals, the Protégé prices seem pretty reasonable, but equipment is quite rudimentary, expect on the LX version.

+ CONVENIENCE FEATURES. The Protégé is an economy car, but it still has enough storage compartments in the cabin, especially for front seat passengers, the glove compartment is generous, as are door side-pockets and storage shelves on the center console that also contains two cup-holders.

CONS

- STEERING. It's gained in precision, but it's over-assisted, so it's light, which takes some getting used to.

- BRAKES. All models are equipped with disc and drum brakes, so braking is only fairly effective. Stops take long stretches to achieve in emergency situations, since wheels lock without ABS, so the car tends to swerve. Even with the rather simplistic ABS, some wheel lock still occurs, but it's more of a hassle than a real hazard.

- THE 1.6L ENGINE. It's tougher than its predecessor, but accelerations and pickup are laborious with the automatic transmission, especially if the vehicle is loaded or equipped with air conditioning. In these conditions, passing should be done with caution.

- TRUNK. The trunk is slightly smaller and it isn't quite proportional to cabin space, but it can be extended by lowering the rear seatbench, which makes up for this aspect.

- NOISE. The small Mazda's have always been noisier than average and the most recent Protégé is no exception. The noisy engines and weak soundproofing are the cause.

CONCLUSION

The Protégé's stylistics, performance and convenience features have been freshened up enough to give sales a new boost. It's a neat-looking little car that's practical and economical, not revolutionary by any means, but carefully enough crafted to compete with its numerous rivals.

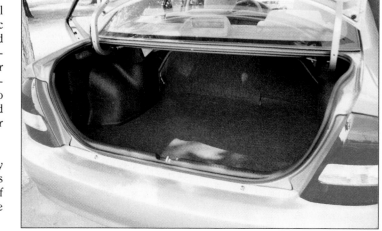

RATING
MAZDA Protegé

CONCEPT : **72%**
Technology	80
Safety :	80
Interior space :	65
Trunk volume:	55
Quality/fit/finish :	80

DRIVING: **60%**
Cockpit	80
Performance :	40
Handling :	55
Steering :	70
Braking :	55

ORIGINAL EQUIPMENT: **75%**
Tires :	75
Headlights :	80
Wipers :	75
Rear defroster :	70
Radio :	75

COMFORT : **67%**
Seats :	70
Suspension :	70
Sound level :	50
Conveniences :	70
Air conditioning :	75

BUDGET : **70%**
Price :	80
Fuel economy :	70
Insurance :	70
Satisfaction :	80
Depreciation :	50

Overall rating: **68.8%**

NEW FOR 1999

- Completely revamped body design.
- Improved suspension with 14-in. wheels on all models.
- New automatic transmission.
- The 1.6L engine on DX and SE versions.

ENGINES / TRANSMISSIONS / PERFORMANCES

Model/ version	Type / timing valve / fuel system	Displacement cu in	Power bhp @ rpm	Torque lb-ft @ rpm	Compres. ratio	Driving wheels / transmission	Final ratio	Acceler. 0-60 mph s	Standing 1/4 & 5/8 mile s	Acceler. 50-75 mph s	Braking 60-0 mph f	Top speed mph	Lateral acceler. G	Noise level dBA	Fuel economy mpg City	Fuel economy mpg Highway	Fuel type Octane
DX & SE	L4* 1.6 DOHC-16-EFI	98	105 @ 5500	107 @ 4000	9.0 :1	front-M5*	3.850	11.6	18.4	32.7	8.3	144	109	0.78	68-72	27	34	R 87
						front-A4	3.904	13.5	19.3	33.4	8.9	148	103	0.78	68-72	24	34	R 87
LX	L4* 1.8 DOHC-16-EFI	112	122 @ 6000	120 @ 4000	9.1 :1	front-M5*	4.105	10.5	17.5	31.6	7.1	141	119	0.80	67-72	25	34	R 87
						front-A4	3.904	12.6	18.7	32.2	7.9	144	109	0.80	67-72	23	32	R 87

PRICE & EQUIPMENT

MAZDA Protegé	DX	LX	ES
Retail price $:	12,145	13,545	15,295
Dealer invoice $:	11,455	12,498	13,956
Shipping & handling $:	450	450	450
Automatic transmission:	O	O	O
Cruise control:	-	S	S
Power steering:	S	S	S
Anti-lock brakes:	-	O	O
Traction control:	-	-	-
Air conditioning:	O	O	S
Leather:	-	-	-
AM/FM/radio-cassette:	O	SCD	SCD
Power door locks:	-	S	S
Power windows:	S	S	S
Tilt steering:	-	-	S
Dual adjustable mirrors:	SM	SM	SE
Alloy wheels:	-	-	O
Anti-theft system:	-	-	-

Colors
Exterior: White, Sand, Green, Black, Cranberry, Red, Sandalwood, Blue.

Interior: Grey, Beige.

AT A GLANCE...

Category: front-wheel drive compact sedans. **Class : 3**

HISTORIC
Introduced in:	1977 -1995
Made in:	Hiroshima, Japan.

DEMOGRAPHICS
Model	Men./Wom.	Age	Married	College	Income
Protegé	44/56 %	36	61 %	67 %	$ 34 000

INDEX
Safety:	80 %	Satisfaction:	82 %
Depreciation:	50 %	Insurance:	$ 765-835
Cost per mile:	$ 0.39	Number of dealers:	871

SALES
Model	1996	1997	Result
Protegé	59 644	53 930	- 9.6%

MAIN COMPETITORS
CHEVROLET Cavalier, DODGE-PLYMOUTH Neon, FORD Escort, HONDA Civic 4dr, HYUNDAI Elantra, MERCURY Tracer, PONTIAC Sunfire, SATURN SL1, TOYOTA Corolla, VW Jetta.

MAINTENANCE REQUIRED BY WARRANTY
First revision:	Frequency:	Diagnostic plug:
5 000 miles	5 000 miles	Yes

SPECIFICATIONS

Model	Version Trim	Body/ Seats	Interior volume cu ft	Trunk volume cu ft	Cd	Wheel base in	Lght x Wdgth x Hght in x in x in	Curb weight lb	Susp. ft/rr	Brake ft/rr	Steering type	Turning diameter ft	Steer. turns nber.	Fuel tank gal	tire size	Standard tires make	model	Standard powertrain
MAZDA		General warranty: 3 years / 50 000 miles; powertrain: 5 years / 100 000 miles; corrosion: 5 years / unlimited.																
Protegé	DX	4dr.sdn.5	92.6	12.9	0.32	102.8	174.8x67.3x55.9	2436	ih/ih	dc/dr	pwr.r&p.	34.1	2.7	13.2	185/65R14	-	-	L4/1.6/M5
Protegé	LX	4dr.sdn.5	92.6	12.9	0.32	102.8	174.8x67.3x55.9	2436	ih/ih	dc/dr	pwr.r&p.	34.1	2.7	13.2	185/65R14	Brisgestone	Potenza RE92	L4/1.6/M5
Protegé	ES	4dr.sdn.5	92.6	12.9	0.32	102.8	174.8x67.3x55.9	2518	ih/ih	dc/dr	pwr.r&p.	34.1	2.7	13.2	185/65R14	Brisgestone	Potenza RE92	L4/1.8/M5

The Mazda 626 underwent a revision last year and was actually overhauled to have more of a chance of competing in the compact car category, the most popular market segment on the North American continent , after mid-size cars like the Honda Accord and Toyota Camry. Once again, Mazda has demonstrated lots of conservatism, giving the 626 a very conventional body design that really ended up looking rather humdrum and easy to confuse with others in the category.

MODEL RANGE
This 626 was tailored to the North American market and it's built by Auto Alliance, an associate of Ford and Mazda located at Flat Rock, Michigan. The 626 is a 4-door front-wheel drive sedan available in DX and LX versions equipped with a 2.0L 4-cylinder engine and in LX-V6 and ES animated by a 2.5L V6. The original transmission is a 5-speed manual, whereas the 4-speed automatic is sold as an extra, but antilock braking and traction control are only standard on the upper end ES version.

TECHNICAL FEATURES
During its last make-over, the 626's structure was reinforced. The steel unibody includes two cradles supporting the suspension and power trains, so most of the wheel and power train noise and vibration are eliminated. The MacPherson strut suspension is fully independent and is completed by two trapezoidal control arms at the rear axle and an anti-roll bar both front and rear. The DX is equipped with disc and drum brakes, the LX-V6 and ES benefit from disc brakes, whereas ABS is standard on the ES, optional on the LX-V6 and not proposed on the other models. Engines and transmissions are those that equipped the former model.

PROS
+ BODY DESIGN. It's very simple and straightforward, but it's quite harmonious and resembles the Millenia. It doesn't have much personality, but at least it has the advantage of being discreet, so it won't go out of style too quickly.

+ SIZE. The 626 has a spacious interior given its reasonable size and weight, for the cabin and trunk can accomodate four adults and their effects.

+ PERFORMANCES. The V6 is perky, either with the automatic

Somewhat Colorless..

transmission or the manual that procures a more sporty demeanor and that emits very thrilling revs and exhaust noise.

+ HANDLING. It's neutral most of the time, but does tend to go into understeer when pushed to the edge and even with the flexible suspension that equips it, the 626 is ready and able to take on a whole series of curves.

+ RIDE COMFORT. It derives from the roomy interior, supple suspension, neat-design seats that support well and soundproofing that keeps the noise level down to a whisper at cruising speed, even with the 4-cylinder engine.

+ STEERING. It's silky and accurate and assistance is better than in the past. It benefits from a good

reduction ratio and steer angle, so it's easy to maneuver and torque wallop that was typical of its predecessor on hard accelerations is almost unnoticeable, at least on dry surfaces.

+ BRAKES. Disc brakes are more effective and easier to apply smoothly than the disc and drum duo that equips the DX and LX, for sudden stopping distances are normal, but it's too bad ABS isn't offered as an option on the DX and LX.

+ QUALITY. Assembly and finish details are nicer than in the past, components have a tighter, cleaner fit and materials used are more pleasing to the eye, such as the leather trim on the ES versions that looks quite elegant.

+ NICE FEATURES: The air vents

that pivot automatically and serve as a fan, that Mazda had the ingenuity of adding to the current models. Passengers who find the pivoting movement annoying can turn off this function. Storage compartments are generous up front, since the glove compartment and door side-pockets are nice and roomy.

CONS
- LOOKS. It's awfully anonymous and looks too much like its predecessor or like the many rivals that are look-alike identical twins...

-CABIN DESIGN. The humdrum is lord and master inside the 626 models. These cars are affordable but also terribly run of the mill. Designers could have put a little more effort into livening up the cabin that is bereft of even an ounce of imagination. At least for once, the interior and exterior are a good match...

- PERFORMANCES. The gutsier 4-cylinder engine and the automatic transmission don't have much vitality when the vehicle is at full load capacity, accelerations and pickup take forever and the transmission is constantly trying to make up its mind which gear to use.

- UPHOLSTERY. Seats are terribly firm, especially the thinly clad seatbench and it doesn't have a center console as is the the case on some models.

- BASE MODEL. It isn't the best buy in spite of its attractive price, for equipment is church mouse poor and disc and drum brakes without ABS aren't too dependable.

- STORAGE COMPARTMENTS. There aren't any in the rear seat area and door side-pockets and cupholders are nowhere in sight.

- VISIBILITY. It would be better if the visor on the instrument panel were lower, if the side mirrors were higher and the C pillar less thick at its base.

-DEPRECIATION. It's higher than for most rivals and the V6 model sells more briskly than the 4-cylinder model.

CONCLUSION
The Mazda 626 is a neat car that's pleasant to drive when equipped with the V6 that makes it a family car with an adventurous side. Unfortunately, it isn't exactly a looker and the interior design is too blah to really make buyers fall in love with it at first sight... ☺

RATING MAZDA 626

CONCEPT : **75%**
Technology — 80
Safety : — 90
Interior space : — 65
Trunk volume: — 60
Quality/fit/finish : — 80

DRIVING: **65%**
Cockpit : — 80
Performance : — 50
Handling : — 60
Steering : — 80
Braking : — 55

ORIGINAL EQUIPMENT: **75%**
Tires : — 80
Headlights : — 80
Wipers : — 70
Rear defroster : — 70
Radio : — 75

COMFORT : **71%**
Seats : — 80
Suspension : — 70
Sound level: — 65
Conveniences : — 60
Air conditioning : — 80

BUDGET : **61%**
Price : — 50
Fuel economy : — 75
Insurance : — 50
Satisfaction : — 80
Depreciation : — 50

Overall rating: **69.4%**

NEW FOR 1999

- DX models get standard: remote trunk door opener and vanity mirrors on driver and passenger sides.
- LX models get standard: power antenna, illuminated vanity mirrors on driver and passenger sides.
- Standard adjustable intermittent wipers (LX, LX-V6 and ES).

ENGINES / TRANSMISSIONS / PERFORMANCES

Model/ version	Type / timing valve / fuel system	Displacement cu in	Power bhp @ rpm	Torque lb-ft @ rpm	Compres. ratio	Driving wheels / transmission	Final ratio	Acceler. 0-60 mph s	Standing 1/4 & 5/8 mile s	Acceler. 50-75 mph s	Braking 60-0 mph f	Top speed mph	Lateral acceler. G	Noise level dBA	Fuel economy mpg City	Highway	Fuel type Octane
DX, LX	L4*2.0 DOHC-16-MPSFI	121	125 @ 5500	127 @ 3000	9.0 :1	front - M5*	4.105	10.0	17.2 31.0	7.0	134	112	0.78	67	25	34	R 87
						front - A4	4.230	12.2	18.4 33.2	9.5	144	109	0.78	67	22	30	R 87
LX-V6, ES	V6*2.5 DOHC-24-MPSFI	152	170 @ 6000	163 @ 5000	9.5 :1	front - M5*	4.105	8.0	15.8 28.2	5.7	125	131	0.80	66	16	26	S 91
						front - A4	4.157	10.4	17.6 31.5	7.2	137	124	0.80	66	118	26	S 91

PRICE & EQUIPMENT

MAZDA 626:	DX	LX	LX-V6	ES
Retail price $:	15,550	17,650	20,665	23,240
Dealer invoice $:	14,021	15,909	18,619	20,933
Shipping & handling $:	450	450	450	450
Automatic transmission:	O	O	O	O
Cruise control:	-	S	S	S
Power steering:	S	S	S	S
Anti-lock brakes:	-	-	O	S
Traction control:	-	-	-	S
Air conditioning:	O	SM	SM	SM
Leather:	-	-	-	S
AM/FM/radio-cassette:	SCD	SCD	SCD	SCD
Power door locks:	-	S	S	S
Power windows:	-	S	S	S
Tilt steering:	S	S	S	S
Dual adjustable mirrors:	SE	SE	SE	SE
Alloy wheels:	-	-	S	S
Anti-theft system:	-	-	-	-

Colors

Exterior: White, Black, Green, Red, Blue, Beige, Driftwood.

Interior: Grey, Beige.

AT A GLANCE...

Category: front-wheel compact sedans. **Class :** 4

HISTORIC
Introduced in: 1979-1998
Made in: Flat Rock, Michigan, USA.

DEMOGRAPHICS

Model	Men./Wom.	Age	Married	College	Income
626	65/35 %	42	75 %	62 %	$ 45 000

INDEX
Safety: 90 % **Satisfaction:** 85 %
Depreciation: 48 % **Insurance:** $ 965-1 065
Cost per mile: $ 0.46 **Number of dealers:** 871

SALES

Model	1996	1997	Result
626	79 354	75 800	- 4.5 %

MAIN COMPETITORS
CHEVROLET Malibu, CHRYSLER Cirrus, DODGE Stratus, FORD Contour, NISSAN Altima, MERCURY Mystique, OLDSMOBILE Alero, PONTIAC Grand Am, SUBARU Legacy, VOLKSWAGEN Jetta.

MAINTENANCE REQUIRED BY WARRANTY
First revision: 5 000 miles **Frequency:** 5 000 miles **Diagnostic plug:** Yes

SPECIFICATIONS

General warranty: 3 years / 50 000 miles; powertrain: 5 years / 100 000 miles; corrosion: 5 years / unlimited.

Model	Version Trim	Body/ Seats	Interior volume cu ft	Trunk volume cu ft	Cd	Wheel base in	Lght x Wdgth x Hght in x in x in	Curb weight lb	Susp. ft/rr	Brake ft/rr	Steering type	Turning diameter ft	Steer. turns nber.	Fuel tank gal	tire size	Standard tires make	model	Standard powertrain
MAZDA																		
626	DX	4dr.sdn.5	97.1	14.2	0.33	105.1	186.8x69.3x55.1	2798	ih/ih	dc/dr	pwr.r&p.	36.1	2.9	16.9	185/70R14	Bridgestone	SF408	L4/2.0/M5
626	LX	4dr.sdn.5	97.1	14.2	0.33	105.1	186.8x69.3x55.1	2798	ih/ih	dc/dr	pwr.r&p.	36.1	2.9	16.9	185/70R14	Bridgestone	SF408	L4/2.0/M5
626	LX-V6	4dr.sdn.5	97.1	14.2	0.33	105.1	186.8x69.3x55.1	2994	ih/ih	dc/dc	pwr.r&p.	36.1	2.9	16.9	205/60R15	Bridgestone	Potenza RE92	V6/2.5/M5
626	ES	4dr.sdn.5	97.1	14.2	0.33	105.1	186.8x69.3x55.1	2994	ih/ih	dc/ABS	pwr.r&p.	36.1	2.9	16.9	205/60R15	Bridgestone	Potenza RE92	V6/2.5/M5

BMW's dynamic approach that's reflected in the recent renewal of the 3-Series, now offered in several versions, forced its direct rival to spruce up its C-Class a bit, a lineup that seemed stuck in a sort of staid immobility. The base engine has been replaced by a supercharged model and the arrival of the high-performance C43 is going to add zest to the face-off between the two German giants. Especially since the small Mercedes is the second biggest seller of the Stuttgart automaker, behind the sublime E-Class.

MODEL RANGE

The mini-Mercedes is a 4-door sedan offered in three different versions: the C230K animated by a 2.3L 4-cylinder engine this year zoomed up by a supercharger, the C280 with 2.8L V6 and the C43, the sportiest of the bunch, that comes equipped with a 4.3L V8 like the one on the CLK's, the E-Class and M-Class. Each of these versions receives a 5-speed automatic transmission including a «Winter» mode that achieves a standing start in 2nd gear and changes speed at low r.p.m. to facilitate certain maneuvers. The antilock braking-traction control combination are standard on all models, while the ASR anti-skid system is standard on the C280 and C43. But the latter also benefits from standard ESP (Electronic Stability Program). Apart from these features, general equipment is lavish, including climate control, cruise control, leather trim and a new Audio 30 sound system with eight speakers.

TECHNICAL FEATURES

The steel monocoque body includes fully galvanized panels but only yields average aerodynamics, since the drag coefficient is a mere 0.32. The structure is very rigid and includes some unusual passenger protection features for the category. The fully independent suspension consists of MacPherson struts and lower A-arms with an anti-dive device and negative roll camber. At the rear, Mercedes has once again refined its famous «multi-link» system, including anti-lift and anti-dive devices with hydropneumatic shocks. Cars are equipped with disc brakes assisted by a standard ABS device.

PROS

+ SAFETY FEATURES. These cars are super-solid and offer optimum resistance in all kinds of collisions

Stimulus...

and are equipped with all the usual passenger protection devices, even if all these high tech elements aren't reflected in the score given by the N.H.T.S.A.

+ QUALITY. A Mercedes worth its salt is sturdily built, benefits from a meticulous finish job and is furbished with top-notch trim materials, elements that give an exceptional cohesiveness to these vehicles.

+ STYLE. It's more flowing and balanced than before. Over the years, the C-Class has had a lot of face-lifts and they now look less staid and bulky.

+ ROADHOLDING. It's very reassuring with the superb rear suspension that ensures perfect directional flow and the more competent adherence with the sophisticated and

effective traction control. These well-honed systems are amazing since the C-Class now benefits from technical features designed for the E and S-Class.

+ PERFORMANCES. The various engines tested achieved accelerations and pickup, each in their own way, that were truly worthy of sports cars. The supercharger on the 4-cylinder brings a welcome boost, even if this approach doesn't seem to make the most sense.

+ BRAKES. They're very effective since they bring things to a halt in a hurry and car path is straight as an arrow in all situations and brakes can really take a beating.

+ STEERING. It's smooth, crisp and nicely powered and benefits from a better reduction ratio than was once the case, but the steering

wheel diameter is still wider than average.

+ CABIN SPACE. It finally accomodates four adults comfortably and the trunk is a good size, it's convenient and can be lengthened by folding down the rear split-fold seatbench.

+ NICE FEATURES: The cruise control that's regulated by a control that's well in sight and within easy reach.

CONS

- CABIN DESIGN. The interior is rather plain for such a pricey car.

- VISIBILITY: Rear view at quarterback is obstructed by the thick C pillar, so some parking maneuvers are a bit tricky.

- RIDE COMFORT. It's never been super-cushy for the suspension and seat upholstery are firm and some power train, road and wind noise reach occupants' ears inside the model equipped with the 4-cylinder model.

- SHIFTER. The automatic transmission is afflicted with one of the most annoying shifters around, it zigzags this way and that so you have to keep looking down to check your moves.

- ACCESS. Tall passengers still have a tough time climbing into the rear seats, since the doors are narrow and ceiling clearance is rather snug.

- DRIVING. On really slick and slippery roads, you have to keep your wits about you, even with all the electronic devices such as the ABS, traction control and anti-skid system, for when adherence gets iffy, the rear end swings and swerves abruptly, not giving the driver much latitude, since he or she can't always accelerate as needed to get things under control.

- TO BE IMPROVED UPON: Certain accessories (windshield wipers, climate control, radio) or controls (headlights, parking brake) aren't in keeping with current world standards and you need a serious briefing or practice session to learn to use them adequately.

CONCLUSION

Stimulated by the competition, Mercedes is making some pretty slick moves on the market checkerboard so as not to be left behind and the use of the V8 in this category gives this car a real advantage over its main BMW rival that isn't quite in the same ballpark yet. ☺

RATING
MERCEDES-BENZ Class C

CONCEPT : 74%
Technology	90
Safety :	90
Interior space :	45
Trunk volume:	55
Quality/fit/finish :	90

DRIVING: 70%
Cockpit	80
Performance :	60
Handling :	60
Steering :	80
Braking :	70

ORIGINAL EQUIPMENT: 79%
Tires :	80
Headlights :	80
Wipers :	75
Rear defroster :	80
Radio :	80

COMFORT : 74%
Seats :	75
Suspension :	75
Sound level:	70
Conveniences :	70
Air conditioning :	80

BUDGET : 53%
Price :	0
Fuel economy :	75
Insurance :	45
Satisfaction :	85
Depreciation :	60

Overall rating: 70.0%

NEW FOR 1999

- The C230 Kompressor Classique, Elegance, Elegance-Sport equipped with a 2.3L supercharged engine and C43 equipped with a 4.3L V8.
- Audio 30 radio-tape deck and CD player with eight speakers.
- Non-glare driver's side and rear mirrors.

ENGINES / TRANSMISSIONS / PERFORMANCES

Model/version	Type / timing valve / fuel system	Displacement cu in	Power bhp @ rpm	Torque lb-ft @ rpm	Compres. ratio	Driving wheels / transmission	Final ratio	Acceler. 0-60 mph s	Standing 1/4 & 5/8 mile s	Acceler. 50-75 mph s	Braking 60-0 mph f	Top speed mph	Lateral acceler. G	Noise level dBA	Fuel economy mpg City	Highway	Fuel type Octane
C230K	L4C 2.3 DOHC-16-SFI	140	185 @ 5300	200 @ 2500	8.8 :1	rear - A5	3.27	NA									
C280	V6 2.8 SOHC-18-SFI	171	194 @ 5800	195 @ 3000	10.0 :1	rear - A5	3.07	8.2	16.1 28.4	5.8	131	131	0.80	66	19	28	S 92
C43	V8 4.3 SOHC-24-SFI	260	302 @ 5850	302 @ 3250	10.0 :1	rear - A5	3.07	NA									

PRICE & EQUIPMENT

MERCEDES-BENZ	C230K	C280	C43
Retail price $:	30,450	35,400	52,750
Dealer invoice $:	26,490	30,800	45,890
Shipping & handling $:	595	595	595
Automatic transmission:	S	S	S
Cruise control:	S	S	S
Power steering:	S	S	S
Anti-lock brakes:	S	S	S
Traction control:	S	S	S
Air conditioning:	SM	SA	SA
Leather:	O	S	S
AM/FM/radio-cassette:	S	S	S
Power door locks:	S	S	S
Power windows:	S	S	S
Tilt steering:	S	S	S
Dual adjustable mirrors:	SE	SE	SE
Alloy wheels:	S	S	S
Anti-theft system:	S	S	S

Colors

Exterior: Black, Red, Ivory, Blue, White, Grey, Green, Silver, Taupe.

Interior: Black, Blue, Burgundy, Beige, Grey, Green.

AT A GLANCE...

Category: rear-wheel drive luxury sedans. **Class :** 7

HISTORIC
Introduced in: 1993 (C)
Made in: Sindelfingen & Brement, Germany.

DEMOGRAPHICS
Model	Men./Wom.	Age	Married	College	Income
C-Class	73/27 %	48	80%	61%	$ 60 000

INDEX
Safety:	90 %	Satisfaction:	85%
Depreciation:	40 %	Insurance:	$1725
Cost per mile:	$ 0.68	Number of dealers:	380

SALES
Model	1996	1997	Result
C-Class	28 715	32 543	+ 13.3 %

MAIN COMPETITORS
ACURA TL, AUDI A4, BMW 3-series, Infiniti I30, LEXUS ES 300, MAZDA Millenia, MITSUBISHI Diamante, SAAB 9³, VOLVO S70.

MAINTENANCE REQUIRED BY WARRANTY
First revision:	Frequency:	Diagnostic plug:
3 000 miles	7 500 miles	Yes

SPECIFICATIONS

Model	Version Trim	Body/ Seats	Interior volume cu ft	Trunk volume cu ft	Cd	Wheel base in	Lght x Wdgth x Hght in x in x in	Curb weight lb	Susp. ft/rr	Brake ft/rr	Steering type	Turning diameter ft	Steer. turns nber.	Fuel tank gal	tire size	Standard tires make	model	Standard powertrain
MERCEDES-BENZ		Total warranty: 4 years / 50 000 miles with road assistance.																
C230	K	4dr.sdn.5	88.0	12.9	0.32	105.9	177.4x67.7x56.1	3250	ih/ihdc/ABS		pwr.ball	35.1	3.1	16.4	205/60R15	Michelin	Energy MXV4	L4C/2.3/A5
C280		4dr.sdn.5	88.0	12.9	0.32	105.9	177.4x67.7x56.1	3316	ih/ih	dc/ABS	pwr.ball.	35.1	3.2	16.4	205/60R15	Michelin	Energy MXV4	V6/2.8/A5
C43		4dr.sdn.5	88.0	12.9	0.33	105.9	177.4x67.7x56.1	3448	ih/ih	dc/ABS	pwr.ball.	35.1	3.1	16.4	fr.225/45ZR17 re.245/40ZR17	Michelin	Pilot SX	V8/4.3/A5

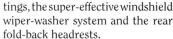

The Stuttgart carmaker has finally decided to develop original-design coupes and convertible on the C-Class platform rather than try to transform the body design on these cars as was the case in the past. This approach has the advantage of giving the impression of offering a whole range of models, when in actual fact, all cars share the same mechanical features.

MODEL RANGE

The CLK family includes a two-door coupe and a convertible offered in a base model equipped with a 3.2L V6 paired up with a 5-speed automatic transmission. This year, a new sportier coupe is being introduced bearing the name 430, which indicates that it's animated by a 4.3L V8 that it shares with the C43, E430 and ML 430. This distinctive model looks a lot more bold and brassy.

TECHNICAL FEATURES

Built on the C-Class platform, the CLK coupes and convertible have a unique body design. This neat, streamlined car has good aerodynamics, yielding a 0.31 drag coefficient. The headlamp design, similar to that of the E-Class, adds a special flavor to the ensemble and it really blends in nicely with the traditional grille, bringing a fresh new look to these models.

The steel unitized body is incredibly rugged, especially that of the convertible to which Mercedes brought some ingenious applications so that the body could adequately withstand torsion and flexion. The front suspension is make up of a double wishbone arrangement with geometry designed to improve stability, reduce rolling resistance and give longer life to tires as well as offset rear end lift and nosedive.

On the rear, there's the famous multi-link trailing arm setup that's one of the finest and most lightweight systems in the world. Disc brakes are associated with a device that adapts response to driver style so as to offer optimum efficiency. The antilock braking system and traction control use the same electronic components to ensure vital vehicle stability that also benefits from an optional anti-skid system (ESP) that keeps the car on an even keel during extreme maneuvers like taking a curve or skidding on a slippery surface.

Refuge...

PROS

+ LOOKS. These vehicles are quite compact, but they're lovely, more at 3/4 front and in profile than at 3/4 rear where they look quite narrow.

+ PRICE. Considering their gorgeous looks, state-of-the-art technical assets, rich equipment and exquisite craftsmanship, the price for these two models seems very competitive.

+ SAFETY FEATURES. This car is equipped with four airbags, so it's ahead of other rival models when it comes to passive or active safety devices. Mercedes-Benz was the first carmaker to take this route even before such matters fell under government jurisdiction.

+ PERFORMANCES. They were pretty zippy with the 3.2L V6, but they've become out of this world exotic with the 4.3L V8 that brings a whole new driving sensation to this car category.

+ DRIVING PLEASURE. These well-thought out cars are very competent and they're reassuring to drive. They're solid and cohesive, so they can be driven in a relaxed and layed-back manner and suddenly be unleashed in a whole series of curves where the driver will wonder if he or she has lost the magic touch...

+ TRUNK. It's really generous for this type of vehicle, especially since it can be extended by lowering the rear seatbench that's also fitted with a ski-size pass-through.

+ NICE FEATURES: The high tech climate control that has several set-

tings, the super-effective windshield wiper-washer system and the rear fold-back headrests.

+ VERY CLEVER: «High tech» cupholders and the rain-sensitive sensor that adapts wiper speed to rain intensity.

CONS

- NOISE. It's strange that on such a technically sophisticated car, road noise should be so pervasive and the engine should let you know it's there whenever your toe touches the accelerator. It seems that German carmakers don't consider low noise level as being a comfort factor.

- STEERING. It suffers from a poor reduction ratio, so it adversely affects the spontaneous soar of sporty driving, and agility and precision aren't what they should be on slalom runs.

- REAR SEATS. They've undergone a lot of modifications but they're still only useful in a pinch, for space is snug and upholstery is terribly hard on the backside.

- CONTROLS. Those located on the center console aren't too handy and the zigzag shifter can really get to you, especially since there's no shifter position indicator on the instrument panel.

- STABILITY. Several times during our road test, the CLK exhibited sensitivity to crosswinds and to road surface quality. In the latter case, it should be pointed out that it was equipped with good-quality snow tires, which can't really be considered to be a factor causing such uncivilized behavior.

- STORAGE COMPARTMENTS. The door side-pockets are neat, but the glove compartment and center console compartment are terribly tiny.

- UPKEEP. The purchase price and fuel consumption are relatively understandable, but upkeep bills seem a bit much at times, even if you can afford to dish out the cash.

- TO BE IMPROVED UPON: Power windows that are annoyingly slow and headlamps that aren't too impressive on low beam.

CONCLUSION

In a market where sports-utility vehicles are at the top of the heap, there are niches where coupes and convertibles are still the all-time favorites for some folks. The midsize CLK's have the advantage of offering sophisticated technical features in a practical format and at a price, all things considered, that's reasonable. ☺

RATING
MERCEDES-BENZ CLK320

CONCEPT : 69%
Technology	90
Safety :	90
Interior space :	35
Trunk volume:	40
Quality/fit/finish :	90

DRIVING: 74%
Cockpit :	80
Performance :	80
Handling :	70
Steering :	80
Braking :	60

ORIGINAL EQUIPMENT: 84%
Tires :	80
Headlights :	80
Wipers :	90
Rear defroster :	85
Radio :	85

COMFORT : 69%
Seats :	80
Suspension :	80
Sound level :	40
Conveniences :	65
Air conditioning :	80

BUDGET : 51%
Price :	0
Fuel economy :	55
Insurance :	35
Satisfaction :	90
Depreciation :	75

Overall rating: 69.4%

NEW FOR 1999

- The CLK320 convertible.
- The 4.3L V8 on the CLK430 coupe.
- Standard ASR system on all models.
- Standard electronic stability system (ESP) on the CLK430 coupe and optional on the CLK320 models.
- Audio 30 radio-tape deck with CD player.

ENGINES / TRANSMISSIONS / PERFORMANCES

Model/ version	Type / timing valve / fuel system	Displacement cu in	Power bhp @ rpm	Torque lb-ft @ rpm	Compres. ratio	Driving wheels / transmission	Final ratio	Acceler. 0-60 mph s	Standing 1/4 & 5/8 mile s	Acceler. 50-75 mph s	Braking 60-0 mph f	Top speed mph	Lateral acceler. G	Noise level dBA	Fuel economy mpg City	Highway	Fuel type Octane
320	V6 3.2 SOHC-18-SFI	195	215 @ 5700	229 @ 3000	10.0 :1	rear - A5	3.07	7.3	15.5 26.4	5.2	125	131	0.83	66	20	30	S 91
430	V8 4.3 SOHC-24-SFI	260	275 @ 5750	295 @ 3000	10.0 :1	rear - A5	2.87	NA									

PRICE & EQUIPMENT

MERCEDES-BENZ CLK	coupe	convertible
Retail price $:	39,850	NA
Dealer invoice $:	34,670	-
Shipping & handling $:	595	-
Automatic transmission:	S	S
Cruise control:	S	S
Power steering:	S	S
Anti-lock brakes:	S	S
Traction control:	S	S
Air conditioning:	SA	SA
Leather:	S	S
AM/FM/radio-cassette:	SCD	SCD
Power door locks:	S	S
Power windows:	S	S
Tilt steering:	S	S
Dual adjustable mirrors:	SEH	SEH
Alloy wheels:	S	S
Anti-theft system:	S	S

Colors

Exterior: Black, White, Blue, Bordeaux, Red, Silver, Green.

Interior: Convertible : Black, Blue, Green.   Coupe : Black, Oyster, Ash.

AT A GLANCE...

Category: rear-wheel drive luxury coupes.   **Class :** 7

HISTORIC
Introduced in: coupe : 1998 convertible: 1999.
Made in: Sindelfingen, Germany.

DEMOGRAPHICS
Model	Men./Wom.	Age	Married	College	Income
CLK	NA				

INDEX
Safety:	90 %	Satisfaction:	88 %
Depreciation:	25 %	Insurance:	$1850-2250
Cost per mile:	$ 0.95-1.05	Number of dealers:	380

SALES
Model	1996	1997	Result
CLK	Not on the market at that time.		

MAIN COMPETITORS
JAGUAR XK8

MAINTENANCE REQUIRED BY WARRANTY
First revision:	Frequency:	Diagnostic plug:
3 000 km	10 000 miles	Yes

SPECIFICATIONS

Model	Version Trim	Body/ Seats	Interior volume cu ft	Trunk volume cu ft	Cd	Wheel base in	Lght x Wdgth x Hght in x in x in	Curb weight lb	Susp. ft/rr	Brake ft/rr	Steering type	Turning diameter ft	Steer. turns nber.	Fuel tank gal	tire size	Standard tires make	model	Standard powertrain
MERCEDES-BENZ	General warranty: 4 years / 50 000 miles; corrosion perforation; 5 years / unlimited																	
CLK	320	2dr.cpe.5	80.7	11.0	0.31	105.9	180.2x68.7x53.0	3240	ih/ih	dc/ABS	pwr.ball	35.1	3.2	16.4	205/55R16	Michelin Energy MXV4		V6/3.2/A5
CLK	320	2dr.con.4	75.7	9.6	0.32	105.9	180.2x68.7x54.3	NA	ih/ih	dc/ABS	pwr.ball	35.1	3.2	16.4	205/55R16	Michelin Energy MXV4		V6/3.2/A5
CLK	430	2dr.cpe.5	80.7	11.0	0.31	105.9	180.2x68.7x54.0	3362	ih/ih	dc/ABS	pwr.ball	35.1	3.2	16.4	fr.225/45ZR17	Michelin	Pilot SX	V8/4.3/A5
															re.245/40ZR17	Michelin	Pilot SX	

The E-Class is without doubt the model that best represents Mercedes-Benz. It's by far the best sold model throughout the world, a status that used to belong to the C-Class. Its design that constituted an intermediate stage in Mercedes-Benz styling is already quite distinctive from that of the most recent S-Class models, which doesn't mean it isn't at the cutting edge of the very latest technical advances.

MODEL RANGE
The E-Class includes a 4-door sedan, the E300 that's equipped with a 3.0L Turbo Diesel 6-cylinder, a E320 sedan and station wagon equipped with the new 3.2L V6 and that can receive all-wheel drive and lastly the 430 that's powered by a 4.3L V8. All models benefit from a 5-speed automatic transmission, antilock braking (ABS) and traction control (ASR) to which can be added the ESP anti-skid system. Equipment is lush and includes all the amenities that are typical of this car category.

TECHNICAL FEATURES
The E-Class models have a steel monocoque body that's been rigidified, but that's also been pared down weight-wise. It benefits from good aerodynamics since the drag coefficient is 0.29. The front suspension consists of a double wishbone setup, while at the rear, the «five-lever» assembly is now more lightweight. Cars are equipped with power rack-and-pinion steering and four disc brakes with ABS linked to an ASR 5 traction control system on the E300-320's, to which can be added an anti-skid system on the E430 (optional on the E320). This system, called ESP, detects the least instability, lateral slippage, oversteer, skidding or swerve and uses the ABS and ASR to control car path and keep the car level. Passive safety devices include two front-impact airbags, but Mercedes has also installed side-impact airbags located in the doors that are activated by separate sensors that kick in when there's more than 3 pounds pressure. Front seat belts are fitted with electronic tension retractors and emergency-locking retractors designed to reduce chest injuries. Nice features: the intermittent wiper speed controlled by diodes that measure rain intensity on the windshield and rear bumper radar

Perfect Balance...

that detects if children or objects are in the way when parking.

SIMPLY SUPER
++ CLEAN DESIGN. It's superb, for this model exudes an unusual solid and safe character.

++ FUEL EFFICIENCY. All engines that equip the E-Class are very zoomy and perform like race car counterparts, yet do so with a reasonable fuel consumption.

PROS
+ STYLE. It's less angular than it once was and yields better aerodynamics and those oval headlamps really add class and panache.

+ QUALITY. It's absolutely exquisite right down to the finest details, when it comes to engineering, construction, finish job, materials and equipment.

+ SAFETY FEATURES. Passive safety benefits from the latest advances in architectural solidity since this car is highly resistant to all kinds of collisions and active devices include front and side-impact airbags and air curtains protecting passengers from head and chest injuries.

+ HANDLING. It's much better in regard to precision, agility and safety thanks to all the neat driving aids (ABS-ASR-ESP) that let the driver regain control of the vehicle after skidding. Class-E models are the summum of competence and they stay superbly neutral in winter driving situations.

+ PERFORMANCES. The gas engines put out racecar-caliber performances, especially the ones that

equip the E430 that looks like any other car, but can sure zoom along like some so-called exotic models.

+ RIDE COMFORT. It's remarkable for the cabin is roomy enough to seat five passengers more than comfortably. The tough suspension takes care of major road flaws, yet it's civilized and the seats, though still awfully firm, are shaped better, so they're cushier than they once were.

+ MANEUVERABILITY. It's super for a car of this format, due to a reasonable steer angle, which no doubt explains why in Europe, it's the choice of many cab drivers.

+ CONVENIENCE FEATURES. Increased North American sales have encouraged Mercedes to pay more attention to details such as storage spots, cup-holders and coat hangers, items considered useless at one time.

CONS
- DIESEL ENGINE. North American buyers will be really frustrated by this engine, since they're more used to creamy conventional V8's and frugal fuel consumption isn't enough of an incentive to have to put up with more sluggish output, noise, vibration and undesirable smoke.

- HEADLAMPS. The xenon headlights work wonderfully well at night, yet they don't blind oncoming drivers. It's really too bad that they aren't included as standard items for this vehicle, because they'd sure make for safer driving.

- VISIBILITY. It's obstructed at rear quarterback by the thick, slanting B pillars and when it rains, the one and only wiper isn't brisk enoug to handle hard rain.

- TO BE IMPROVED UPON: The trunk size that's out of whack with the generous cabin space, cumbersome knee bolsters, especially on the driver's side and the annoying shifter travel.

CONCLUSION
You really can't go too wrong by opting for one of these cars, since they're a perfect blend of what an average-size sedan should be by current standards, namely safe, competent and pleasant to drive, yet offering adequate comfort and luxury. ☺

RATING
MERCEDES-BENZ E Class

CONCEPT — 83%
Technology	90
Safety :	100
Interior space :	65
Trunk volume:	70
Quality/fit/finish :	90

DRIVING: — 71%
Cockpit :	80
Performance :	70
Handling :	65
Steering :	80
Braking :	60

ORIGINAL EQUIPMENT: — 78%
Tires :	80
Headlights :	80
Wipers :	75
Rear defroster :	75
Radio :	80

COMFORT : — 75%
Seats :	80
Suspension :	80
Sound level :	70
Conveniences :	65
Air conditioning :	80

BUDGET : — 51%
Price :	0
Fuel economy :	70
Insurance :	40
Satisfaction :	90
Depreciation :	55

Overall rating: 71.6%

NEW FOR 1999
- The 4.3L V8 replaces the 4.2L on the E430.
- Standard electronic stability system (ESP) on the E430, optional on the other models.
- Standard air curtains that offset head injuries on the sedans.
- Original leather trim on the E300 Diesel and Wagon.
- Audio 30 radio-tape deck with CD player.
- Walnut appliqué around the speed shifter.

ENGINES / TRANSMISSIONS / PERFORMANCES

Model/ version	Type / timing valve / fuel system	Displacement cu in	Power bhp @ rpm	Torque lb-ft @ rpm	Compres. ratio	Driving wheels / transmission	Final ratio	Acceler. 0-60 mph s	Standing 1/4 & 5/8 mile s	Acceler. 50-75 mph s	Braking 60-0 mph f	Top speed mph	Lateral acceler. G	Noise level dBA	Fuel economy mpg City	Fuel economy mpg Highway	Fuel type Octane
E300	L6TD* 3.0 DOHC-24-PI	191	174 @ 5000	244 @ 1600	22.0 :1	rear - A5*	3.46	9.0	16.9	30.3	6.8	131	131	0.82	67	25	35	D
E320	V6* 3.2 SOHC-18-SFI	195	221 @ 5600	232 @ 3000	10.0 :1	rear - A5*	3.07	7.5	15.6	26.8	5.4	128	131	0.82	65	20	30	S 91
E320 AWD	V6* 3.2 SOHC-18-SFI	195	221 @ 5600	232 @ 3000	10.0 :1	rear/4 - A5*	3.07	7.8	16.0	27.0	5.7	128	131	0.82	65	19	29	S 91
E430	V8*4.3 DOHC-24-MFI	260	275 @ 5750	295 @ 3000	10.0 :1	rear - A5*	2.87	6.5	14.5	26.0	4.5	134	131	0.82	65	15	23	S 91

PRICE & EQUIPMENT

MERCEDES-BENZ	E300TD	E320	E430
Retail price $:	41,800	45,500	50,600
Dealer invoice $:	36,370	39,580	44,020
Shipping & handling $:	595	595	595
Automatic transmission:	S	S	S
Cruise control:	S	S	S
Power steering:	S	S	S
Anti-lock brakes:	S	S	S
Traction control:	S	S	S
Air conditioning:	SA	SA	SA
Leather:	O	S	S
AM/FM/radio-cassette:	SCD	SCD	SCD
Power door locks:	S	S	S
Power windows:	S	S	S
Tilt steering:	S	S	S
Dual adjustable mirrors:	SEH	SEH	SEH
Alloy wheels:	S	S	S
Anti-theft system:	S	S	S

Colors
Exterior: Black, White, Turquoise, Indigo, Blue, Bordeaux, Silver, Green.

Interior: Black, Blue, Gray, Parchment.

AT A GLANCE...

Category: rear-wheel drive and AWD luxury cars.   **Class :** 7

HISTORIC
Introduced in:	1996.
Made in:	Sindelfingen, (Stuttgart) Germany.

DEMOGRAPHICS
Model	Men./Wom.	Age	Married	College	Income
E-Class	81/19%	50	82%	62%	$ 85 000

INDEX
Safety:	100 %	Satisfaction:	92 %
Depreciation:	40 %	Insurance:	$ 1 700 à 2 200
Cost per mile:	$ 0.85 -1.05	Number of dealers:	380

SALES
Model	1996	1997	Result
E-Class	37 956	42 883	+ 13.0 %

MAIN COMPETITORS
ACURA RL, AUDI A6, BMW 5-Series, INFINITI Q45, LEXUS GS 300-400, SAAB 9⁵, VOLVO S80.

MAINTENANCE REQUIRED BY WARRANTY
First revision:	Frequency:	Diagnostic plug:
3 000 km	10 000 miles	Yes

SPECIFICATIONS

MERCEDES-BENZ — General warranty: 4 years / 50 000 miles; corrosion perforation; 5 years / unlimited

Model	Version Trim	Body/ Seats	Interior volume cu ft	Trunk volume cu ft	Cd	Wheel base in	Lght x Wdgth x Hght in x in x in	Curb weight lb	Susp. ft/rr	Brake ft/rr	Steering type	Turning diameter ft	Steer. turns nber.	Fuel tank gal	tire size	Standard tires make	model	Standard powertrain
E300	Diesel	4dr.sdn.5	95.0	15.3	0.29	111.5	189.4x70.8x56.7	3638	ih/ih	dc/ABS	pwr.r&p.	37.2	3.3	21.1	215/55HR16	Continental	Eco Plus	L6D/3.0/A5
E320	Gasoline	4dr.sdn.5	95.0	15.3	0.29	111.5	189.4x70.8x56.7	3461	ih/ih	dc/ABS	pwr.r&p.	37.2	3.3	21.1	215/55HR16	Continental	Eco Plus	V6/3.2/A5
E320 AWD	Gasoline	4dr.wgn.7	97.7	43.8	0.34	111.5	190.0x70.8x59.3	3869	ih/ih	dc/ABS	pwr.r&p.	37.2	3.3	18.5	215/55HR16	Continental	Eco Plus	V6/3.2/A5
E430	Gasoline	4dr.sdn.5	95.0	15.3	0.29	111.5	189.4x70.8x56.7	3781	ih/ih	dc/ABS	pwr.r&p.	37.2	3.3	21.1	215/55HR16	Continental	Eco Plus	V8/4.3/A5

Mercedes sure knew what it was doing when it designed and built a sports-utility vehicle for the North American market. The ML320 is so much the rage that there's a one-year waiting list and you can't even get your hands on a used model, for they're selling as fast as the new ones right off the assembly line. This year, the V8 version won't do much to calm things down, but will rather have the opposite effect. The strategy is working like a charm, for all these new clients represent an undreamed of sales potential when it comes to other models built by this German automaker.

MODEL RANGE

The M-Class is a lineup of intermediate SUV's of the same format as the currently most popular models. This vehicle is available as a four-door station wagon with lifting rear hatch in Classique or Elegance trim, as a ML320 model equipped with a V6 or a V8-animated ML430. The Classique version is really loaded with nice items, including most of the usual comfort and luxury features. The Elegance model and the 430 also receive leather-trim seats and eight-way adjustable power front seats that are heated as well, a power sunroof, wood appliqués and Bose high-fidelity sound system. All 1999 models are equipped with a brake-assisted system and an ESP anti-skid device.

TECHNICAL FEATURES

When Mercedes was working on its star North American-bound product design, the carmaker adopted tried and true solutions. The M-Class is more like the Ford Explorer than the Grand Cherokee, build-wise, with its body mounted on a separate chassis, procuring maximum strength and stifling as much noise, vibration and shakes from the axles and powertrains as possible. The chassis is built of rust-proof steel and is equipped with a fully independent suspension, based on unequal-length control arms, torsion bars and anti-roll bars. Rack-and-pinion steering is variable assist and four-wheel disc brakes are linked to a four-channel antilock braking system. The all-wheel drive system is neat, since it doesn't use locking differentials to maintain continuous wheel function. It takes up the 4ETS system already used on Mercedes all-wheel drive models,

Selling Like Hot Cakes..

including an electronic system that controls individual wheel rotation via the ABS sensors and that distributes power depending on the best adherence by activating the differentials. On off-road maneuvers, you get a shorter axle ratio by touching a button located on the dashboard. When it comes to safety, Mercedes is way ahead of most of the competition, since it uses a safety cage around the cabin, front and side-impact airbags as well as tensioner front seat belts.

PROS

+ PRESTIGE. Why deprive yourself of showing off a Mercedes in your driveway for a price not terribly higher than what you'd have to dish out for an Explorer Limited?

+ PRICE. The Classique version is almost affordable and is comparable to the upper-crust «Limited» versions of American rivals, given the really rich array of equipment.

+ SAFETY. It's the best around both for passive protection with its four airbags and safety anti-roll cage and for active protection, with such competent demeanor due to all those nice driving aids such as anti-skid control, ABS and traction control that put it in a class all its own.

+ DRIVING PLEASURE. All the driving enhancements put the M-Class way above the horde of rivals, for engine and transmission oomph and ease procure topnotch performances and pleasure. Such car-like traits are dramatically different from those of rivals of pickup ancestry.

+ STYLE. It's created a trend that

Lexus cloned in no time flat, but its soft lines aren't any more efficient when it comes to aerodynamics since the drag coefficient is only 0.39.

+ SIZE. This intermediate vehicle is well suited to scads of North American buyers' needs. It's quite trim yet it offers lots of cabin and luggage storage space and the cargo hold is bigger than is the case for most of the competition.

+ RIDE COMFORT. It's simply remarkable, the suspension is a silky sophisticate, seats are super-comfy and noise is kept to a decent minimum at cruising speed.

+ NICE FEATURES: The bright headlights for safer travel, enough storage spots and the handy luggage cover.

CONS

- QUALITY. Some finish details don't jive with the German carmaker's reputation and plastic components are pretty run of the mill. Our test vehicle squeaked and rattled quite a bit.

- STEERING. It suffers from a poor reduction ratio, so you have to reel it in on off-road rambles and when trying to park.

- REAR SEATBENCH. Hard to get to with those narrow doors and it isn't too useful with its really snug three-passenger capacity. To make matters worse, the seat removal device is so bloody complicated that even an engineer won't make it work at the first attempt.

- TO BE IMPROVED UPON: The weird control for cruise control, the awkward power window control that's located on the center console, the far from precise gas gauge, the CD player that's located in the cargo hold and that you can't get to when the hold is full of luggage. And we're still complaining because there's no shifter position indicator and no assist grips to help out when boarding.

CONCLUSION

This sport-utility vehicle is causing quite a stir and it'll gobble up other pieces of the market pie if the competition doesn't get its act together in a hurry. At any rate, a vehicle sporting the Mercedes star, sold at an affordable price, will have less trouble finding takers than the carmaker will have trying to supply enough vehicles to meet the demand... ☺

RATING
MERCEDES-BENZ M Class

CONCEPT : 78%
Technology	85
Safety :	90
Interior space :	65
Trunk volume:	70
Quality/fit/finish :	80

DRIVING: 69%
Cockpit :	80
Performance :	60
Handling :	50
Steering :	80
Braking :	75

ORIGINAL EQUIPMENT: 79%
Tires :	80
Headlights :	80
Wipers :	75
Rear defroster :	80
Radio :	80

COMFORT : 75%
Seats :	80
Suspension :	75
Sound level :	60
Conveniences :	80
Air conditioning :	80

BUDGET : 49%
Price :	10
Fuel economy :	50
Insurance :	35
Satisfaction :	80
Depreciation :	70

Overall rating: 70.0%

NEW FOR 1999

- New ML430 model equipped with a 4.3L V8.
- Built-in garage door opener.
- Brake-assisted and ESP systems standard on both models.
- Color-coordinated bumpers.

ENGINES

Model/ version	Type / timing valve / fuel system	Displacement cu in	Power bhp @ rpm	Torque lb-ft @ rpm
ML320	V6 3.2 SOHC-18-SFI	195	215 @ 5500	233 @ 3000
ML430	V8 4.3 SOHC-24-SFI	260	268 @ 5500	288 @ 3000

TRANSMISSIONS

Compres. ratio	Driving wheels / transmission	Final ratio
10.0 :1	all- A5	3.69
10.0 :1	all- A5	3.46

PERFORMANCES

Acceler. 0-60 mph s	Standing 1/4 & 5/8 mile s		Acceler. 50-75 mph s	Braking 60-0 mph f	Top speed mph	Lateral acceler. G	Noise level dBA	Fuel economy mpg City	Highway	Fuel type Octane
9.0	17.0	30.5	7.2	134	112	0.75	65-70	16	22	S 91
NA										

PRICE & EQUIPMENT

MERCEDES-BENZ	ML320 Classic	ML320 Elegance	ML430
Retail price $:	33,950	36,900	NA
Dealer invoice $:	29,540	32,100	-
Shipping & handling $:	595	595	-
Automatic transmission:	S	S	S
Cruise control:	S	S	S
Power steering:	S	S	S
Anti-lock brakes:	S	S	S
Traction control:	S	S	S
Air conditioning:	SM	SA	SA
Leather:	-	S	S
AM/FM/radio-cassette:	SCD	SCD	SCD
Power door locks:	S	S	S
Power windows:	S	S	S
Tilt steering:	S	S	S
Dual adjustable mirrors:	SEH	SEH	SEH
Alloy wheels:	S	S	S
Anti-theft system:	S	S	S

Colors
Exterior: Silver, Black, White, Ruby, Green, Emerald.

Interior: Cloth : Gray. Leather: Sand, Gray.

AT A GLANCE...

Category: 4WD all terrain sport-utility.　　**Class :** utility

HISTORIC
Introduced in: 1998
Made in: Tuscaloosa, Alabama, USA.

DEMOGRAPHICS
Model	Men./Wom.	Age	Married	College	Income
ML320	65/35%	45	80%	52%	$ 60 000

INDEX
Safety:	90%	Satisfaction:	82 %
Depreciation:	30%	Insurance:	$1675
Cost per mile:	$ 0.55	Number of dealers:	380

SALES
Model	1996	1997	Result
ML320	-	14 569	-

MAIN COMPETITORS
CHEVROLET Blazer, DODGE Durango, FORD Explorer, ISUZU Trooper, JEEP Grand Cherokee, GMC Jimmy, LAND ROVER Range & Discovery, LEXUS RX 300, MITSUBISHI Montero, NISSAN Pathfinder, TOYOTA 4Runner & Land Cruiser.

MAINTENANCE REQUIRED BY WARRANTY
First revision:	Frequency:	Diagnostic plug:
3 000 km	10 000 miles	Yes

SPECIFICATIONS

Model	Version Trim	Traction	Body/ Seats	Wheel base in	Lght x Wdgth x Hght in x in x in	Curb weight lb	Susp. ft/rr	Brake ft/rr	Steering type	Turning diameter ft	Steer. turns nber.	Fuel tank gal	tire size	Standard tires make	model	Standard powertrain
MERCEDES-BENZ			General warranty: 4 years / 50 000 miles with 24 hours road assistance.													
ML320	Classic	4x4	4dr.wgn. 5/7	111.0	180.6x72.2x69.9	4200	ih/ih	dc/ABS	pwr.r&p.	37.1	3.62	18.5	255/65R16	General	Grabberst	V6/3.2/A5
ML320	Elegance	4x4	4dr.wgn. 5/7	111.0	180.6x72.2x69.9	4237	ih/ih	dc/ABS	pwr.r&p.	37.1	3.62	18.5	255/65R16	General	Grabberst	V6/3.2/A5
ML430		4x4	4dr.wgn. 5/7	111.0	180.6x72.2x69.9	4431	ih/ih	dc/ABS	pwr.r&p.	37.1	3.62	18.5	275/55R17	General	Grabberst	V8/4.3/A5

The S-Class has always been the Stuttgart carmaker's most prestigious technological showcase. Yet because Mercedes was bent on building yet bigger, more sophisticated and more expensive cars, it met some customer resistance in regard to the current model that's been controversial ever since its last face-lift. To calm the critics, it was decided to renew this lineup earlier than planned and replace it with trimmer, more graceful-looking cars, but furbished with even more ultra-modern features. (See p. 64)

MODEL RANGE

The S-Class is made up of four-door sedans sold in two different wheelbase models, namely, the S320 short-wheelbse model and the longer S420, S500 and S600 versions, two-door coupes called CL500 and CL600 and two convertibles, the SL500 and SL600. The S320 is the only model powered by a 3.2L 6-cylinder engine, while the 420's share a 4.2L V8, the 500's are equipped with a 5.0L V8 and the 600's with a 6.0L V12. The 5-speed automatic transmission comes standard on all models. When you're in this creamy price range, equipment is very lavish and high tech, including from four to six airbags, dual-zone climate control fitted with a smoke detector that activates the internal ventilation system when carbon monoxyde levels warrant it, as well as highly unusual, one-of-a-kind driving features. The S-Class was the first car to offer double side windows so as to better stifle exterior noise.

TECHNICAL FEATURES

The S-Class lineup is made up of vehicles that are loaded with the world's best technical innovations and unprecedented, posh luxury items. The steel monocoque body of these vehicles gets special rustproofing and is designed to hide their sheer bulk and they're more graceful with their pure, flowing lines for better aerodynamics, and the drag coefficient is about 0.32. The fully independent suspension consists of a double wishbone setup up front and a multi-link arrangement at the rear. It's adjustable on the 600 models that also benefit from anti-skid control and a rear axle load-levelling system, an optional feature elsewhere. Cars are equipped with recirculating ball steering and four-wheel disc brakes with standard ABS and traction control on all models.

Farewell For Now...

PROS

+ OVERALL DESIGN. It's exceptional for all these cars are simply loaded with high tech attributes that provide topnotch active and passive passenger protection, especially in regard to wheel adherence thanks to a whole array of complex electronic devices, activated by an army of sensors.

+ SAFETY. It's one of the safest cars in the world due to extreme structural rigidity that provides a built-in safety cage on both sedans and coupes and a folding anti-roll bar on the convertibles, front and side-impact airbags and automatic tensioner seatbelts that it would be best to buckle up, as proven by Lady Diana's fatal car accident.

+ PERFORMANCES. They're very gutsy with all engine models, given the impressive vehicle weight and hulk. Even the in-line 6-cylinder engine has lots of vim and doesn't burn too much gas, a rare feat in this glamorous guzzler lineup...

+ HANDLING. It's superb with the clever, concerted efforts of the suspension, steering, brakes, wheel function and adherence that only vehicle weight can sometimes alter on slippery roads.

+ QUALITY. It's obvious in every respect: build craftsmanship, finish details and trim components. It's among the creamiest of mass-produced cars, due to consistent, strict standards and execution.

+ RIDE COMFORT. It's regal with such a spacious cabin on all models, more comfy, better-design seats, well-honed suspension, superb sound dampening with the double-pane windows and an impressive amount of insulating materials.

+ EQUIPMENT. You can't get much more than this on the current market and it includes all sorts of modern wizardry, accessories, gadgets or refined, luxury amenities, so these cars enjoy one of the best resale value ratings.

CONS

- COCOON EFFECT. It's hazardous, so you have to stay alert to analyze and really master the driving aids, especially in slippery conditions, since you're only aware of slippage and skidding at the very last moment, which in extreme cases, can be a problem.

- BUDGET. Purchase price, insurance premium, gas and repair bills for such upper-crust cars aren't within everyone's budget and the regular guy or gal won't have to deal with such nonsense...

- SIZE. Vehicle weight and size make some maneuvers awkward and don't help those slick moves and you have to be wary of what you're not «feeling» inside one of these beauties and of course, parking in the city is no joy.

- DESIGN DETAILS. These terribly expensive cars look pretty plain, really, both inside and out and some components are far from ritzy-looking. There isn't much chrome and those rather plebeian plastic bumper covers tarnish the overall look. The cabin interior is far from cozy, in spite of the leather and wood trim.

- DRIVING. The sluggish sedans aren't much fun to drive and all the power functions are one jump ahead of driver response, and these cars are awfully big and don't have much personality. The coupes and convertibles are more lush than lively, given the top performances they're capable of, for the very same reasons.

CONCLUSION

A new cohort of S-Class sedans will be displayed at the 1999 Geneva Auto Show. Then will come the new CL coupes to be exhibited in Frankfurt in the fall of 1999, to end up with the convertibles that will be ready to strut their stuff in the year 2000. Until their arrival, there's still the car that best symbolizes 20th century social status and affluence.

RATING
MERCEDES-BENZ S Class

CONCEPT : **92%**
Technology	100
Safety :	100
Interior space :	90
Trunk volume:	80
Quality/fit/finish :	90

DRIVING: **72%**
Cockpit :	80
Performance :	75
Handling :	65
Steering :	80
Braking :	60

ORIGINAL EQUIPMENT: **82%**
Tires :	85
Headlights :	80
Wipers :	80
Rear defroster :	80
Radio :	85

COMFORT : **84%**
Seats :	80
Suspension :	80
Sound level :	90
Conveniences :	80
Air conditioning :	90

BUDGET : **37%**
Price :	0
Fuel economy :	20
Insurance :	20
Satisfaction :	90
Depreciation :	55

Overall rating: **73.4%**

NEW FOR 1999

• No major change, the new S-Class models will be presented at the next Geneva Auto Show.

ENGINES

Model/ version	Type / timing valve / fuel system	Displacement cu in	Power bhp @ rpm	Torque lb-ft @ rpm
S320	L6* 3.2 DOHC-24-MPSFI	195	228 @ 5600	232 @ 3750
S420	V8* 4.2 DOHC-32-MPSFI	256	275 @ 5700	295 @ 3900
S500	V8* 5.0 DOHC-32-MPSFI	303	315 @ 5600	347 @ 3900
S600	V12* 6.0 DOHC-48-MPSFI	365	389 @ 5200	420 @ 3800

TRANSMISSIONS

Compres. ratio	Driving wheels / transmission	Final ratio
10.0 :1	rear - A5*	3.45
11.0 :1	rear - A5*	2.82
11.0 :1	rear - A5*	2.65
10.0 :1	rear - A5*	2.65

PERFORMANCES

Acceler. 0-60 mph s	Standing 1/4 & 5/8 mile s		Acceler. 50-75 mph s	Braking 60-0 mph f	Top speed mph	Lateral acceler. G	Noise level dBA	Fuel economy mpg City	Highway	Fuel type Octane
9.3	16.6	30.5	6.6	138	131	0.72	67	18	26	S 91
8.5	16.4	29.6	6.0	141	131	0.78	67	15	23	S 91
7.8	15.8	26.8	5.6	144	131	0.79	66	14	22	S 91
7.0	14.6	26.0	4.8	144	149	0.76	64	12	20	S 91

PRICE & EQUIPMENT

MERCEDES-BENZ	S320 SWB	S420	S500	S600	SL500	SL600
Retail price $:	64,750	73,900	87,500	134,250	79,900	125,000
Dealer invoice $:	56,330	64,290	76,120	116,800	69,510	108,750
Shipping & handling $:	595	595	595	595	595	595
Automatic transmission:	S	S	S	S	S	S
Cruise control:	S	S	S	S	S	S
Power steering:	S	S	S	S	S	S
Anti-lock brakes:	S	S	S	S	S	S
Traction control:	S	S	S	S	S	S
Air conditioning:	SA	SA	SA	SA	SA	SA
Leather:	S	S	S	S	S	S
AM/FM/radio-cassette:	SCD	SCD	SCD	SCD	SCD	SCD
Power door locks:	S	S	S	S	S	S
Power windows:	S	S	S	S	S	S
Tilt steering:	S	S	S	S	S	S
Dual adjustable mirrors:	SEH	SEH	SEH	SEH	SEH	SEH
Alloy wheels:	S	S	S	S	S	S
Anti-theft system:	S	S	S	S	S	S

Colors

Exterior: Black, White, Red, Blue, Silver, Indigo. SL: Turquoise, Red, Green.

Interior: Black, Blue, Parchment, Gray. SL: Ash, Java, Shell.

AT A GLANCE...

Category: rear-wheel drive grand luxury cars. **Class :** 7

HISTORIC
Introduced in: 1992 berline.
Made in: Sindelfingen, (Stuttgart) Germany.

DEMOGRAPHICS
Model	Men./Wom.	Age	Married	College	Income
S	90/10%	48	91 %	51 %	$ 120 000
SL	93/7 %	43	48 %	58 %	$ 180 000

INDEX
Safety:	100 %	Satisfaction:	87 %
Depreciation:	45 %	Insurance:	$ 2 750-8 950
Cost per mile:	$ 1.10 - 1.55	Number of dealers:	380

SALES
Model	1996	1997	Result
S	17 317	16 119	- 6.9 %
SL/CL	6 856	8 025	+ 17.1 %

MAIN COMPETITORS
S: BMW 7-Series, INFINITI Q45, JAGUAR XJ8, LEXUS LS 400.
SL-CL: ASTON MARTIN DB7, JAGUAR XK8.

MAINTENANCE REQUIRED BY WARRANTY
First revision:	Frequency:	Diagnostic plug:
3 000 km	10 000 miles	Yes

SPECIFICATIONS

Model	Version Trim	Body/ Seats	Interior volume cu ft	Trunk volume cu ft	Cd	Wheel base in	Lght x Wdgth x Hght in x in x in	Curb weight lb	Susp. ft/rr	Brake ft/rr	Steering type	Turning diameter ft	Steer. turns nber.	Fuel tank gal	tire size	Standard tires make	model	Standard powertrain
MERCEDES-BENZ		General warranty: 4 years / 50 000 miles; corrosion perforation; 5 years / unlimited																
SL500	2dr.con.2	50.4	7.9	0.32	99.0	177.1x71.3x51.3	4165	ih/ih	vd/ABS	pwr.ball	35.4	3.0	21.1	245/45ZR17	Michelin Energy MXV4		V8/5.0/A5
SL600	2dr.con.2	50.4	7.9	0.32	99.0	177.1x71.3x51.3	4455	ih/ih	vd/ABS	pwr.ball	35.4	3.0	21.1	245/40ZR18	-	-	V12/6.0/A5
CL500	2dr.cpe.5	92.7	14.2	0.30	115.9	199.4x75.3x56.9	4695	ih/ih	vd/ABS	pwr.ball	28.4	3.2	26.4	235/60R16	Michelin Energy MXV4		V8/5.0/A5
CL600	2dr.cpe.5	92.7	14.2	0.30	115.9	199.4x75.3x56.9	4960	ih/ih	vd/ABS	pwr.ball	38.4	3.2	26.4	235/60R16	-	-	V12/6.0/A5
S320	4dr.sdn.5	108.1	15.6	0.32	119.7	201.3x74.3x58.5	4500	ih/ih	vd/ABS	pwr.ball	39.9	3.2	26.4	225/60R16	Michelin Energy MXV4		L6/3.2/A5
S420	4dr.sdn.5	112.4	15.6	0.32	123.6	205.2x74.3x58.5	4650	ih/ih	vd/ABS	pwr.ball	41.0	3.2	26.4	235/60R16	Michelin Energy MXV4		V8/4.2/A5
S500	4dr.sdn.5	112.4	15.6	0.32	123.6	205.2x74.3x58.5	4700	ih/ih	vd/ABS	pwr.ball	41.0	3.2	26.4	235/60R16	Michelin Energy MXV4		V8/5.0/A5
S600	4dr.sdn.5	112.4	15.6	0.32	123.6	205.2x74.3x58.5	4960	ih/ih	vd/ABS	pwr.ball	41.0	3.2	26.4	235/60R16	-	-	V12/6.0/A5

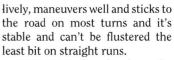

In a sense, BMW forced Mercedes to tread on ground that the carmaker would have perhaps not explored otherwise. The convertible market niche has been livened up by the Mazda Miata, so the Z3 was launched, then the Boxster, two cars that are waging a war of equals to grab sales from other more conventional products. As to be expected, Mercedes couldn't create just any old car to get in on the race, so we now have a spunky convertible coupe equipped with a unique folding hardtop, a feature that really adds pizzazz and is an ace in the hand when it comes to sales.

MODEL RANGE

The SLK is a compact roadster whose folding hardtop automatically drops above the trunk on sunny days and lifts back into place if poor weather sets in. It's sold in a single model equipped with a 2.3L supercharged 4-cylinder engine associated with a 5-speed automatic or manual transmission. Original equipment is very extensive, which explains in part the stiff price. The SLK benefits from air conditioning, antilock braking system, leather seats, light alloy wheels, Bose high fidelity sound system, oodles of power accessories, theft-deterrent system and the only options are metallic exterior body paint, heated seats, CD player and cellular phone.

TECHNICAL FEATURES

The SLK convertible coupe is a from-scratch original, since it isn't inspired by any model already existing in the Mercedes lineup. Its steel monocoque build has remarkable aerodynamics for this type of vehicle, since it has an average 0.35 drag coefficient . To cut down on weight, a cast-magnesium partition separates the gas tank from the trunk. The fully independent suspension consists of a double wishbone arrangement up front including anti-dive geometry and a multilink setup at the rear with anti-lift geomety and stabilizer bar on both axles. The car is equipped with power rack-and-pinion steering and disc brakes paired up with a standard ABS device. The 185-hp engine is borrowed from the C-Class and gets a boost from the Roots supercharger equipped with an intercooler.

PROS

+ VERSATILITY. You can buy this handsome roadster at a pretty reasonable price and enjoy the benefits

Over The Top...

of both a zippy coupe and a convertible. The biggest bonus this combination has to offer is the hardtop, a solid, insulated and soundproofed design as well as windows that will dissuade thieves or vandals. Visibility is enhanced by the generous windows, even in the winter since the rear window is equipped with an electric defroster.

+ STYLE. This tiny car is elegant and has lots of panache. It has a nicely balanced shape and is stuffed with highly polished features. The cabin is lovely as well and has a neat retro look, just enough to set a warm, classic atmosphere.

+ HARDTOP. It folds down automatically and is an incredibly clever piece of engineering know-how and daring as eager onlookers will agree

when they watch the roof being raised or lowered in the twinkle of an eye. It's waterproof and insulated so the car can be used year round. The top is activated automatically via a hydraulic pump that does its magic trick in a mere 25 seconds.

+ EFFECTIVE. Steering is clean and nicely assisted but it could be a bit more direct. Brakes procure smooth, level stops and they're easy to apply.

+ PERFORMANCES. They're wonderful with such vigorous accelerations and pickup, in spite of sluggish supercharger response time, since its effects are only perceived at 3,000 rpm.

+ ROADHOLDING. The SLK stays really cool and level-headed. It's

lively, maneuvers well and sticks to the road on most turns and it's stable and can't be flustered the least bit on straight runs.

+ SAFETY. It benefits from the robust car build that incorporates a folding roll bar, four airbags and 3-point pretensioner seatbelts.

+ QUALITY. This vehicle can boast of a super-neat design and enviable craftsmanship, perfectly in keeping with Mercedes standards. Its structure is quite rigid and is solidly put together, finish details are meticulously rendered and materials used are attractive and chosen to last.

+ NICE FEATURES: Nifty, efficient original accessories such as headlights, wipers, tires, air conditioning and defroster that equips the rear window.

CONS

- DRIVING. It's hard getting comfy behind the wheel because the steering column doesn't tilt. The engine is a poor match for this car and it needs the supercharger to really zoom. The 2.3L engine shakes and rattles like a regular, run of the mill model and unpleasant exhaust noise is a real disappointment. In this regard, the SLK is a total fiasco, for a small 6-cylinder engine would give it a lot more character and provide more torque and more impressive roar.

- TRUNK. It's small and hard to get to when the top is stored inside and there isn't a sliver of space behind the seats to store anything at all.

- VISIBILITY. It isn't perfect towards the rear since the headrests and wind deflector block the view in the main mirror and exterior mirrors are terribly smallish.

- CONVERTIBLE TOP. The complex power mechanism tends to break down and often needs to be adjusted.

- TO BE IMPROVED UPON: Some items like the tiny sun visors that are pretty useless and could fold up in half.

CONCLUSION

Mercedes succeeded in designing a trim little car that's fun to drive all year round and it achieves pretty interesting performances even if the engine isn't the one we'd like to see under the hood. Financially speaking, the SLK is a good investment since it doesn't lose much value on the used car market and buyers rush to buy one... ☺

RATING
MERCEDES-BENZ SLK

CONCEPT :   56%
Technology	85
Safety :	80
Interior space :	20
Trunk volume :	15
Quality/fit/finish :	80

DRIVING: 74%
Cockpit :	80
Performance :	70
Handling :	80
Steering :	80
Braking :	60

ORIGINAL EQUIPMENT: 80%
Tires :	80
Headlights :	80
Wipers :	80
Rear defroster :	80
Radio :	80

COMFORT :   69%
Seats :	80
Suspension :	70
Sound level:	40
Conveniences :	75
Air conditioning :	80

BUDGET :   49%
Price :	0
Fuel economy :	70
Insurance :	45
Satisfaction :	80
Depreciation :	50

Overall rating: 65.6%

NEW FOR 1999

• Optional 5-speed manual gearbox.

ENGINES
Model/ version	Type / timing valve / fuel system	Displacement cu in	Power bhp @ rpm	Torque lb-ft @ rpm
SLK	L4*C2.3 DOHC 16 SFI	140	185 @ 5300	200 @ 2500

TRANSMISSIONS
Compres. ratio	Driving wheels / transmission	Final ratio
8.8 :1	rear - A5	3.27
	rear - M5	3.46

PERFORMANCES
Acceler. 0-60 mph s	Standing 1/4 & 5/8 mile s	Acceler. 50-75 mph s	Braking 60-0 mph f	Top speed mph	Lateral acceler. G	Noise level dBA	Fuel economy City mpg	Highway	Fuel type Octane
7.8 NA	15.8	28.2	5.5	134	143	0.88	70	21	32

Fuel type: S 91

PRICE & EQUIPMENT
MERCEDES-BENZ	SLK
Retail price $:	39,700
Dealer invoice $:	34,540
Shipping & handling $:	595
Automatic transmission:	S
Cruise control:	S
Power steering:	S
Anti-lock brakes:	S
Traction control:	S
Air conditioning:	SA
Leather:	S
AM/FM/radio-cassette:	SCD
Power door locks:	S
Power windows:	S
Tilt steering:	S
Dual adjustable mirrors:	SEH
Alloy wheels:	S
Anti-theft system:	S

Colors
Exterior: Black, White, Blue, Red, Yellow, Silver.
Interior: Black, Blue, Oyster, Salsa.

AT A GLANCE...
Category: rear-wheel drive sports coupes.   **Class :** GT
HISTORIC
Introduced in: 1997
Made in: Sindelfingen, Germany.
DEMOGRAPHICS
Model	Men./Wom.	Age	Married	College	Income
SLK	NA				

INDEX
Safety:	80 %	Satisfaction:	85 %
Depreciation:	75 %	Insurance:	$1 500
Cost per mile:	$0.69	Number of dealers:	380

SALES
Model	1996	1997	Result
SLK	-	6 890	-

MAIN COMPETITORS
CHEVROLET Corvette, BMW Z3, PORSCHE Boxster, PLYMOUTH Prowler.

MAINTENANCE REQUIRED BY WARRANTY
First revision:	Frequency:	Diagnostic plug:
3 000 km	10 000 miles	Yes

SPECIFICATIONS
Model	Version Trim	Body/ Seats	Interior volume cu ft	Trunk volume cu ft	Cd	Wheel base in	Lght x Wdgth x Hght in x in x in	Curb weight lb	Susp. ft/rr	Brake ft/rr	Steering type	Turning diameter ft	Steer. turns nber.	Fuel tank gal	tire size	Standard tires make	model	Standard powertrain
MERCEDES-BENZ																		
SLK	Kompressor	2dr.cpe. 2	-	3.6-9.5	0.35	94.5	157.3x67.5x50.7	3036	ih/ih	vd/ABS	pwr.ball	34.7	3.1	14.0	fr.205/55R16	Dunlop	SP8080	L4C/2.3/A5
															re.225/50R16	Dunlop	SP8080	

General warranty: 4 years / 50 000 miles; corrosion perforation; 5 years / unlimited

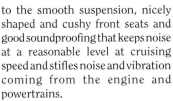

The Nissan Altima is a winner and year after year, sales prove it. It was reworked last year but it's still popular at the dealers, since buyers really like its neat looks, attractive price and the attractive model range is out to please just about everyone. The single 4-cylinder engine choice doesn't seem to affect its appeal too much, since it came in fifth place behind the American products in its category. At any rate, the Altima is a better buy than its cousin the Infiniti G20 that just came back on stage after two years' absence.

MODEL RANGE

This compact 4-door sedan comes in XE, GXE, SE and GLE trim, all equipped with the same mechanical features consisting of a 2.4L 4-cylinder engine and standard manual transmission or an optional automatic on the XE, GXE and SE, but the automatic is included in the original equipment on the richer GLE version. These cars are pretty much the same, essentially, except for a few variant design details, whereas equipment items for all models include: power steering, tilt steering wheel, adjustable exterior mirrors and intermittent wiper function. The SE also gets light alloy wheels and the luxo-sedan GLE receives leather seat trim. In all cases, the antilock braking system and sunroof are billed as extra items.

TECHNICAL FEATURES

The Altima architecture and shape got a complete make-over, with the former model's platform as a starting point. The steel monocoque body is sleeker and has gained in aerodynamic finesse since its drag coefficient went from 0.35 to 0.32. The four-wheel independent suspension is based on the MacPherson strut principle and includes a stabilizer bar for each axle. Disc and drum brakes equip the XE/GXE/GLE and the sportiest SE benefits from standard four-wheel disc brakes with a variable grip system for the rear axle, that sure improves road adherence. The engine under the hood is the same as for the 1998 model, it has lighter-weight pistons and more generous air filter and it's more lightweight. Displacement is a bit bigger than average and it develops 150 hp yielding an adequate power to weight ratio. In fact, this engine's displacement is equivalent to that of the V6 that animates some rivals, so Nissan was

Definite Asset..

able to avoid offering a second engine model, yet the Altima still takes a bite out of Maxima sales, both models now being on a par in this department.

PROS

+ LOOKS. It's cool and sensible-looking, less curved and more refined, in keeping with the current «Edge Design». It isn't terribly original, but it does get admiring glances, especially the SE and GLE that have luxury car touches comparable to what you get on much more expensive cars.

+ PRICE. It's more affordable than for some of the competition, given that the only engine available is a 4-cylinder.

+ CABIN SPACE. It's roomier with the added length and width that has

freed up more elbow and leg room, but ceiling height is the same. Four adults will enjoy comfortable seating and even a fifth, for short trips.

+ DRIVING PLEASURE. The 2.4L engine has enough juice to muster good accelerations and pickup thanks to wider band torque at low r.p.m. Steering is responsive and brakes are easy to gauge in normal situations.

+ HANDLING. It derives from the more rigid structure and supple suspension that generates just a bit of sway and doesn't bottom out as it once did on major road faults. The SE is more at ease taking one curve after another because it's equipped with firmer springs and shocks so it stays nice and level on curves.

+ RIDE COMFORT. It's super due

to the smooth suspension, nicely shaped and cushy front seats and good soundproofing that keeps noise at a reasonable level at cruising speed and stifles noise and vibration coming from the engine and powertrains.

+ CABIN DESIGN. It provides a pleasant driving environment, for the instrument panel is attractive and logical, now free of that rather flashy imitation wood trim.

CONS

- VEHICLE WEIGHT. It's still quite high even with the trimming down. This is due to the beefier, more rigid body, but it still adversely affects performances that are quite ordinary and fuel consumption climbs at higher speeds, especially with the automatic gearbox.

- MANUAL GEARBOX. It's not at all as smooth or logical as the automatic, since shifting gears is a bit tricky and gears are poorly spaced. There's a terrible gap between first and second gear and the top gear is too long.

- TRUNK. It's stingy compared to the generous cabin size and given the Altima's dimensions, since it isn't too high at all and the opening is narrow. It now connects with the cabin, but you can't get much stuff through the tiny slot provided.

- BRAKES. Brakes are normally quite effective when first applied and car path is predictable on stops, even without ABS, but linings fade with intensive use.

- SEATS. Leather-clad seats aren't as well-contoured as fabric-covered seats and their upholstery is more firm. And rear seat travellers on the more richly equipped models don't have headrests.

-ACCESS. It's tricky climbing aboard into the rear seats with the arched door design and you have to duck, otherwise you could knock your head against the roof.

- TO BE IMPROVED UPON: Climate control dials where sound system dials should be and vice versa, located back there behind the speed shifter...

CONCLUSION

The Altima is one of the best Nissan products at the present time. It's not too pricey, yet it has a distinguished appearance, provides good performances and adequate travel comfort. In fact, it's the 4-cylinder counterpart of its sister the Maxima. ☺

RATING
NISSAN Altima

CONCEPT : — **75%**
Technology	75
Safety :	80
Interior space :	80
Trunk volume:	60
Quality/fit/finish :	80

DRIVING: — **72%**
Cockpit :	80
Performance :	60
Handling :	60
Steering :	80
Braking :	80

ORIGINAL EQUIPMENT: — **77%**
Tires :	75
Headlights :	80
Wipers :	75
Rear defroster :	75
Radio :	80

COMFORT : — **75%**
Seats :	75
Suspension :	75
Sound level:	75
Conveniences :	70
Air conditioning :	80

BUDGET : — **66%**
Price :	50
Fuel economy :	75
Insurance :	70
Satisfaction :	85
Depreciation :	50

Overall rating: **73.0%**

NEW FOR 1999

- Standard variable intermittent wipers on the SE and GXE.
- New exterior shades.
- Standard power adjustable driver's seat on the SE.

ENGINES

Model/ version	Type / timing valve / fuel system	Displacement cu in	Power bhp @ rpm	Torque lb-ft @ rpm
1)	L4* 2.4 DOHC-16-SFI	145	150 @ 5600	154 @ 4400
2)	L4* 2.4 DOHC-16-SFI	145	150 @ 5600	154 @ 4400

1) XE, GXE, SE. 2) GLE, option XE, GXE, SE.

TRANSMISSIONS

Compres. ratio	Driving wheels / transmission	Final ratio
9.2 :1	front - M5*	3.650
9.2 :1	front - A4*	3.619

PERFORMANCES

Acceler. 0-60 mph s	Standing 1/4 & 5/8 mile s	Acceler. 50-75 mph s	Braking 60-0 mph f	Top speed mph	Lateral acceler. G	Noise level dBA	Fuel economy mpg City	Fuel economy mpg Highway	Fuel type Octane
9.0	16.6 30.1	6.6	125	118	0.80	65	23	32	R 87
10.2	17.3 31.2	7.0	131	112	0.80	65	22	32	R 87

PRICE & EQUIPMENT

NISSAN Altima	XE	GXE	SE	GLE
Retail price $:	14,990	17,190	18,490	19,890
Dealer invoice $:	14,265	15,646	16,638	17,897
Shipping & handling $:	420	420	420	420
Automatic transmission:	O	O	O	S
Cruise control:	S	S	S	S
Power steering:	S	S	S	S
Anti-lock brakes:	-	O	S	S
Traction control:	-	-	-	-
Air conditioning:	-	SM	SM	SM
Leather:	-	-	O	S
AM/FM/radio-cassette:	S	S	SCD	SCD
Power door locks:	-	S	S	S
Power windows:	S	S	S	S
Tilt steering:	S	S	S	S
Dual adjustable mirrors:	SE	SE	SE	SE
Alloy wheels:	-	-	S	S
Anti-theft system:	-	O	S	S

Colors

Exterior: Wildberry, Blue, Green, Ebony, Platinum, Gray, White, Pewter, Champagne.

Interior: Dawn, Blonde, Olive.

AT A GLANCE...

Category: front-wheel compact sedans **Class :** 4

HISTORIC
Introduced in:	1993-1998
Made in:	Smyrna, TE, USA.

DEMOGRAPHICS
Model	Men./Wom.	Age	Married	College	Income
Altima	67/33 %	44	79 %	47 %	$ 39 000

INDEX
Safety:	80 %	Satisfaction:	88 %
Depreciation:	48 %	Insurance:	$ 800
Cost per mile:	$0.44	Number of dealers:	1 100

SALES
Model	1996	1997	Result
Altima	147 910	144 483	- 2.3 %

MAIN COMPETITORS
CHEVROLET Cavalier, CHRYSLER Cirrus L4, DODGE Stratus L4, FORD Contour L4, HONDA Civic 4dr & Accord L4, MAZDA 626 L4, MERCURY Mystique L4, OLDSMOBILE Alero L4, PLYMOUTH Breeze, PONTIAC Grand Am L4, SUBARU Legacy, TOYOTA Camry L4, VOLKSWAGEN Passat L4.

MAINTENANCE REQUIRED BY WARRANTY
First revision:	Frequency:	Diagnostic plug:
7 500 miles	7 500 miles	Yes

SPECIFICATIONS

General warranty: 3 years / 50 000 miles; powertrain: 6 years / 60 000 miles; perforation corrosion & antipollution: 6 years / unlimited.

Model	Version Trim	Body/ Seats	Interior volume cu ft	Trunk volume cu ft	Cd	Wheel base in	Lght x Wdgth x Hght in x in x in	Curb weight lb	Susp. ft/rr	Brake ft/rr	Steering type	Turning diameter ft	Steer. turns nber.	Fuel tank gal	tire size	Standard tires make	model	Standard powertrain
NISSAN																		
Altima	XE	4dr.sdn.5	94.0	13.8	0.32	103.1	183.1x69.1x55.9	2875	ih/ih	dc/dr	pwr.r&p.	37.4	2.9	15.9	195/65R15	General	XP2000	L4/2.4/M5
Altima	GXE	4dr.sdn.5	94.0	13.8	0.32	103.1	183.1x69.1x55.9	2919	ih/ih	dc/dr	pwr.r&p.	37.4	2.9	15.9	195/65R15	General	XP2000	L4/2.4/M5
Altima	SE	4dr.sdn.5	94.0	13.8	0.32	103.1	183.1x69.1x55.9	2921	ih/ih	dc/dc	pwr.r&p.	37.4	2.9	15.9	205/60R15	Firestone	Affinity	L4/2.4/M5
Altima	GLE	4dr.sdn.5	94.0	13.8	0.32	103.1	183.1x69.1x55.9	2943	ih/ih	dc/dr	pwr.r&p.	37.4	2.9	15.9	195/65R15	General	XP2000	L4/2.4/A4

Over the years, Nissan has lost the edge that the original extended cabin design once gave it in the past. After lots of humming and hawing (typical Nissan behavior) and a few unexpected delays, last year the 4-cylinder Frontier pickup finally replaced the Hardbody. This year, the 3.3L V6 borrowed from the Pathfinder can now equip the 4X4 King Cab, providing performances more worthy of the name. Everybody's talking and speculating about the 4-door pickup that Nissan will soon be selling at a dealership near you.

MODEL RANGE

Frontier pickups are available in regular or extended frame, regular cabin or King Cab, with rear or all-wheel drive, in XE and SE trim levels. The single engine model offered is the 2.4L 4-cylinder paired up with a 5-speed manual gearbox or an optional 4-speed automatic. In 1999, the King Cab all-wheel drive will be equipped with a 3.3L V6 developing 170 hp and 200 lb.ft of torque. Engine, transmission and gas tank on the 4X4 versions are protected by standard metallic plates.

TECHNICAL FEATURES

This compact Nissan pickup consists of a steel unibody and double-sided frame are mounted on an H-frame made up of five crossmembers. The independent front suspension consists of torsion and stabilizer bar on both the 4X2 and 4X4 versions, and the rear rigid axle is supported by conventional leaf springs. Disc and drum brakes are linked to rear-wheel ABS on the 4X2 models and all-wheel ABS on the 4X4 models, with front wheels that engage automatically.000 (It's been refined, it's more muscular and benefits from more torque, and it's more efficient as well, with reduced internal friction and thus, less noise, shakes and rattles.) All-wheel drive is on demand but it can be engaged when driving at less than 25 mph, providing equal wheel function on both axles and it only comes with a manual gearbox. The V6 engine with bigger 3.3L displacement, that only represents 18% of sales is once again available, but not on all models, which is a bit of a bugbear, for the 4-cylinder engines are real wimps on the 4X4's and they consume a lot of fuel.

One Step At The Time...

PROS

+ MODEL CHOICE. The Frontier now offers a wider model range now that the V6 engine has been added to the lineup.

+ RIDE COMFORT. It's pretty cushy since this vehicle feels more like a car than an SUV, due to the really competent front suspension that takes care of those mean streaks on the road and the rear axle doesn't bounce you to kingdom come with an empty box. The split seatbench and bucket seats are reasonably comfy and they're not too firm. Noise is kept within a comfortable range as well.

+ PERFORMANCES. The 4-cylinder engine finally has some get up and go and provides good torque at low r.p.m. for better fuel economy.

But it's better suited to a RWD transmission and it's equally competent with either the manual or the automatic. The V6 offers more energy ooze, so it's more fun to put through its paces, at least on good-quality roads.

+ HANDLING. It's stable even on the base versions, but it would be a good idea to weigh down the rear end a bit when driving with an empty box in slippery conditions.

+ KING CAB. It's a definite ace in the hand for Nissan, since it's bigger than its Toyota counterpart. Two children can be seated behind the seat when needed or you can stash stuff back there.

+ COCKPIT. It's straightforward, but nicely set up, so the driver sits more comfortably inside the King

Cab equipped with its individual seats that are more like the seating you get in a car. Outward view is super in all directions and the short, competent shifter on the manual gearbox is neat, as is the shifter for the automatic, located under the steering wheel.

+ CONVENIENCE FEATURES. This aspect is more obvious now that there are long, divided door side-pockets, a good-size glove compartment and notches in the box that let you divide it into sections with wooden boards or panels and it's roomy since you can transport 4X8-ft. sheets of material.

+ QUALITY. Build is tough, the finish job is neat and tight and materials used are spiffy, as is the cabin itself, much more so than in the past.

CONS

- 4-CYLINDER ENGINE. It just doesn't have what it takes to really move the King Cab 4X4 over rough terrain, for torque output is too limited and gas consumption soars sky-high.

- BRAKES. They could be be brawnier and tougher, since stops are long and resistance to overheating is mediocre. But the antilock braking system keeps the vehicle straight on course.

- MANEUVERABILITY. The King Cab 4X4's agility is really crippled by the big steer angle diameter.

- SENSITIVITY. Crosswinds really affect demeanor for all models, but especially the King Cab 4X4.

- SEATBENCH. The original one on the base models is awfully uncomfortable, since it offers no lateral or lumbar support whatsoever.

-TO BE IMPROVED UPON: Poor-quality tires, paint and fabrics and owners complain about how hard it is to find some replacement parts and how expensive they are.

CONCLUSION

Nissan isn't going overboard when it comes to power or vehicle size, which is a good move. The automaker is concentrating on customers who are looking for a small sport-utility vehicle able to handle light loads or as a second family vehicle. The Frontier is just the right choice for such needs and its current limitations in regard to engine choice shouldn't be a major obstacle. ☹

RATING
NISSAN Frontier

CONCEPT : 59%
Technology	75
Safety :	70
Interior space :	50
Trunk volume:	25
Quality/fit/finish :	75

DRIVING: 54%
Cockpit :	75
Performance :	35
Handling :	40
Steering :	75
Braking :	45

ORIGINAL EQUIPMENT: 56%
Tires :	70
Headlights :	70
Wipers :	70
Rear defroster :	0
Radio :	70

COMFORT : 67%
Seats :	70
Suspension :	70
Sound level:	60
Conveniences :	60
Air conditioning :	75

BUDGET : 66%
Price :	60
Fuel economy :	75
Insurance :	60
Satisfaction :	85
Depreciation :	50

Overall rating: 60.4%

NEW FOR 1999

- Standard 3.3L V6 for the King Cab, XE & SE 4X4.
- Standard viscous-coupled locking differential and automatic locking front hubs on the V6 4X4.
- Bucket seats offered as an extra on the regular cab.
- Color-coordinated fender skirts and body mouldings.

ENGINES
Model/version	Type / timing valve / fuel system	Displacement cu in	Power bhp @ rpm	Torque lb-ft @ rpm
4x2	L4*2.4 SOHC-16-MPSFI	145	143 @ 5200	154 @ 4000
4x4 XE	L4*2.4 SOHC-16-MPSFI	145	143 @ 5200	154 @ 4000
4x4 KC	V6 3.3 SOHC-12-MPSFI	200	170 @ 4800	200 @ 2800

TRANSMISSIONS
Compres. ratio	Driving wheels / transmission	Final ratio
9.2 :1	rear - M5*	3.54
	rear - A4	3.70
9.2 :1	rear/all-M5*	3.88
8.9 :1	rear/all-M5	4.37
	rear/all-A4	4.37

PERFORMANCES
Acceler. 0-60 mph s	Standing 1/4 & 5/8 mile s	Acceler. 50-75 mph s	Braking 60-0 mph f	Top speed mph	Lateral acceler. G	Noise level dBA	Fuel economy mpg City	Highway	Fuel type Octane
12.5	18.8 35.5	9.5	164	97	NA	68	21	27	R 87
13.8	19.5 37.0	11.0	167	100	NA	68	18	25	R 87
NA									
NA									

PRICE & EQUIPMENT
NISSAN Frontier Cabine	XE std. 4x2	XE std. 4x4	XE K.Cab 4x2	SE K.Cab 4x4
Retail price $:	13,190	16,990	14,640	20,990
Dealer invoice $:	11,541	15,650	13,486	18,900
Shipping & handling $:	490	490	490	490
Automatic transmission:	O	O	O	O
Cruise control:	O	O	O	S
Power steering:	Sre.	S	Sre.	S
Anti-lock brakes:	S	S	S	S
Traction control:	-	O	-	S
Air conditioning:	-	O	O	S
Leather:	-	-	-	-
AM/FM/radio-cassette:	O	O	O	SCD
Power door locks:	-	-	-	S
Power windows:	-	-	-	S
Tilt steering:	O	O	O	S
Dual adjustable mirrors:	SM	SM	SM	SE
Alloy wheels:	O	O	S	S
Anti-theft system:	-	-	-	S

Colors

Exterior: Red, Bronze, Blue, Green, Ebony, White, Beige, Sandstone.

Interior: Gray, Beige.

AT A GLANCE...
Category: 4x2 or 4x4 compact pickups. **Class :** utility

HISTORIC
Introduced in: 1965-1998
Made in: Smyrna, Tennessee, USA.

DEMOGRAPHICS
Model	Men./Wom.	Age	Married	College	Income
Frontier-Costaud	88/12%	43	69%	33%	$ 36 000

INDEX
Safety:	75 %	Satisfaction:	85 %
Depreciation:	50 %	Insurance:	$ 825-1 150
Cost per mile:	$0.41	Number of dealers:	1 100

SALES
Model	1996	1997	Result
Frontier	127 081	121 861	- 4.1 %

MAIN COMPETITORS
DODGE Dakota, FORD Ranger, CHEVROLET S-10, GMC Sonoma, MAZDA B-Series, TOYOTA Tacoma.

MAINTENANCE REQUIRED BY WARRANTY
First revision:	Frequency:	Diagnostic plug:
7 500 miles	7 500 miles	No

SPECIFICATIONS
Model	Version Trim	Traction	Body/ Seats	Wheel base in	Lght x Wdgth x Hght in x in x in	Curb weight lb	Susp. ft/rr	Brake ft/rr	Steering type	Turning diameter ft	Steer. turns nber.	Fuel tank gal	tire size	Standard tires make	model	Standard powertrain
NISSAN	General warranty: 3 years / 50 000 miles; powertrain: 6 years / 60 000 miles; perforation corrosion & antipollution: 6 years / unlimited.															
Frontier	XE	4x2	2dr.p-u.2	104.3	184.3x66.5x62.8	3031	ih/rl	dc/dr/ABSre.pwr.ball		33.5	3.8	15.9	215/65R15	Firestone	Wilderness	L4/2.4/M5
Frontier	XE KC	4x2	2dr.p-u.2+2	116.1	196.1x66.5x62.6	3172	ih/rl	dc/dr/ABSre.pwr.ball		36.7	3.8	15.9	215/65R15	Firestone	Wilderness	L4/2.4/M5
Frontier	SE KC	4x2	2dr.p-u.2+2	104.3	184.3x66.5x62.6	3238	ih/rl	dc/dr/ABSre.pwr.ball		36.7	3.8	15.9	215/65R15	BF Goodrich	-	L4/2.4/M5
Frontier	XE	4x4	2dr.p-u.2	104.3	184.3x66.5x66.1	3554	ih/rl	dc/dr/ABS	pwr.ball	35.4	3.8	15.9	235/75R15	Firestone	Wilderness	L4/2.4/M5
Frontier	XE-V6 KC	4x4	2dr.p-u.2+2	116.1	196.1x66.5x65.9	3700	ih/rl	dc/dr/ABS	pwr.ball	NA	3.8	19.3	235/75R15	Firestone	Wilderness	V6/3.3/M5
Frontier	SE-V6 KC	4x4	2dr.p-u.2+2	116.1	196.1x66.5x65.9	3726	ih/rl	dc/dr/ABS	pwr.ball	NA	3.8	19.3	265/70R15	BF Goodrich	-	V6/3.3/M5

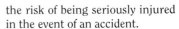

Slowly but surely, in its own quiet way, the Maxima is gaining respectable sales for Nissan in the unique market segment that sits between mid-size and entry-level luxury cars. Whether it be in GLX or GLE versions, this car is competing with the Altima that's more expensive and the Infiniti I30. Customer loyalty is truly amazing and some owners have purchased at least three of these cars, and this isn't an exception... You have to admit that, in spite of some disappointing aspects, the Maxima is equipped with an engine and a rear suspension that have no equal in this category.

MODEL RANGE

The Maxima is an intermediate four-door sedan offered in base GXE, sport SE and luxury ES or GLE that only differ depending on equipment level and design details, for their engine and mechanical components are absolutely identical. All benefit from the fine standard 3.0L V6 linked to a manual or automatic transmission depending on trim level. The base model is quite well-equipped for starters, since equipment includes standard climate control, cruise control, most of the vital power accessories, radio and tape deck and tilt steering wheel.

TECHNICAL FEATURES

Its steel unibody has an average aerodynamic efficiency, with a drag coefficient of 0.32. Since it was reworked, build is even sturdier, and it was already one of the most robust before. The front suspension consists of a MacPherson strut design and the rear rigid axle is equipped with the Nissan version of the Scott-Russell multi-link system that allows for constant camber. Cars are equipped with disc brakes, but the antilock braking system is only offered as an option and no traction control system is available. The latter consists of a viscous-coupled locking differential. The 3.0L DOHC V6 develops 190 hp and is assisted by a 5-speed manual transmission on the GXE and SE and a 4-speed automatic on the GLE.

SIMPLY SUPER

++ V6 ENGINE. It's one of a kind, for it responds to the slightest request to rev and procures zoomy accelerations and pickup and you're in for lots of driving spontaneity thanks to both nicely adjusted transmissions. Fuel consumption is very normal since the V6 is good for a solid 22 mpg.

Brilliant...

PROS

+ PRICE. It's competitive enough for all versions that can be compared to a whole flock of other models, going from the Honda Accord to the Lexus ES300, and stepping on a few toes in Infinit I30 territory.

+ ROADABILITY. It's pretty impressive thanks to the super rear suspension with differential that keeps these cars solid either on straight stretches or on winding curves. Camber is less obvious on quick lane changes so there's less rear end lift when making emergency stops.

+ RIDE COMFORT. The Maxima ride is super smooth. The suspension keeps things in line, shock absorbers are ruthless, wheel travel is nice and generous and the noise is kept fairly low.

+ STEERING. It's a bit over-assisted, so it gets light in some situations, but it's quick on the ball, accurate and benefits from a good reduction ratio. The short steer angle sure helps make all the moves you have in mind.

+ CABIN SPACE. It's adequate for four adults who'll have generous leg, elbow and head room, but a fifth passenger would only be comfy on short trips.

+ TRUNK. Its volume is in sync with cabin space, but it's only connected to same via a ski slot.

CONS

-SAFETY. The Maxima didn't earn too good a mark from the American highway bureau in collision tests, an indication that passengers run the risk of being seriously injured in the event of an accident.

- BRAKES. They could be better, as those relatively long stops indicate and without an antilock braking system, the car tends to swerve on sudden stops, so things get pretty hairy. The soft pedal is a hassle as well, since it doesn't help you brake as needed.

-COMPROMISES. The Maxima receives some rather unusual accessories, since some normally standard items for this class don't equip this car and are billed as extras, which, in a sense, explains the GXE's bargain sticker price.

- DESIGN DETAILS. The GXE is a real disgrace to Nissan. Trim details both on the exterior and inside the cabin are pretty awful, such as the frumpy seat fabric and the plastic stuff, items unworthy of a car in this price range.

- MANUAL GEARBOX. The shifter is stiff initially and vague at all times, which takes all the pleasure out of driving the SE, which, if it weren't for this crummy feature, would be a truly topnotch, zippy sport model.

- SEATS. The seats inside the GXE are horriblel, upholstery is a poor excuse for same and the caved-in seat cushions and backs don't offer enough hip or lumbar support.

-ERGONOMICS. The instrument panel is disappointing, since the center console curves inward rather than outward, so controls are way out of the driver's reach.

- COMMODIITES. They're rare as hen's teeth on the GXE, door side-pockets are narrow and there aren't even any good old coat hooks in the rear seat area.

- TO BE IMPROVED UPON: Inefficient heating system to tackle really cold weather conditions, the missing shifter indicator among the instrument gauges on the dashboard (unforgivable), the windshield wiper-washer ensemble that never clears the window surface in the wintertime and the rear defroster that takes forever to do its stuff.

CONCLUSION

As long as you avoid the GXE that's there to catch eager bargain-hunters hook, line and sinker, the other Maxima versions are still good investments. You can pick between the zippy SE or the more luscious ES and GLE models that are equipped with different transmissions and kind of equipment. ☺

RATING
NISSAN Maxima

CONCEPT : — 75%
Technology	85
Safety :	80
Interior space :	70
Trunk volume:	60
Quality/fit/finish :	80

DRIVING: — 70%
Cockpit :	75
Performance :	70
Handling :	60
Steering :	80
Braking :	65

ORIGINAL EQUIPMENT: — 71%
Tires :	75
Headlights :	75
Wipers :	65
Rear defroster :	65
Radio :	75

COMFORT : — 69%
Seats :	70
Suspension :	80
Sound level :	60
Conveniences :	55
Air conditioning :	80

BUDGET : — 63%
Price :	40
Fuel economy :	75
Insurance :	50
Satisfaction :	95
Depreciation :	55

Overall rating: — 69.6%

NEW FOR 1999

- The anti-theft system hooked up with the cut-off switch.
- Standard traction control with the automatic gearbox and ABS.
- Five new exterior shades.
- Different-design wood trim.

ENGINES / TRANSMISSIONS / PERFORMANCES

Model/ version	Type / timing valve / fuel system	Displacement cu in	Power bhp @ rpm	Torque lb-ft @ rpm	Compres. ratio	Driving wheels / transmission	Final ratio	Acceler. 0-60 mph s	Standing 1/4 & 5/8 mile s	Acceler. 50-75 mph s	Braking 60-0 mph f	Top speed mph	Lateral acceler. G	Noise level dBA	Fuel economy mpg City	Highway	Fuel type Octane
GXE,SE	V6* 3.0 DOHC-24-MPSFI	182	190 @ 5600	205 @ 4000	10.0 :1	front - M5*	3.823	8.0	15.7 27.9	5.5	138	137	0.80	66-70	21	27	S 91
GLE	V6* 3.0 DOHC-24-MPSFI	182	190 @ 5600	205 @ 4000	10.0 :1	front - A4*	3.619	8.5	16.3 29.2	6.0	147	130	0.80	66-70	20	29	S 91

PRICE & EQUIPMENT

NISSAN Maxima	GXE	SE	GLE
Retail price $:	21,499	23,499	26,899
Dealer invoice $:	19,470	20,916	23,943
Shipping & handling $:	490	490	490
Automatic transmission:	O	O	S
Cruise control:	S	S	S
Power steering:	S	S	S
Anti-lock brakes:	-	S	S
Traction control:	-	O	S
Air conditioning:	SM	SA	SA
Leather:	-	SC	SC
AM/FM/radio-cassette:	S	SCD	SCD
Power door locks:	S	S	S
Power windows:	S	S	S
Tilt steering:	S	S	S
Dual adjustable mirrors:	SEH	SEH	SEH
Alloy wheels:	-	S	S
Anti-theft system:	-	-	S

Colors
Exterior: Mahogany, Green Olive, Sand, Ebony, White, Blue, Silver.

Interior: Cloth & Leather: Gray-Green, Charcoal, Beige.

AT A GLANCE...

Category: front-wheel drive luxury sedans. — **Class :** 7

HISTORIC
Introduced in:	1981-1995
Made in:	Oppama & Tochigi, Japan.

DEMOGRAPHICS
Model	Men./Wom.	Age	Married	College	Income
Maxima	83/17 %	48	85 %	55 %	$ 53 000

INDEX
Safety:	80 %	Satisfaction:	93 %
Depreciation:	47 %	Insurance:	$ 1 150
Cost per mile:	$ 0.47	Number of dealers:	1 100

SALES
Model	1996	1997	Result
Maxima	128 395	123 215	- 4.0 %

MAIN COMPETITORS
ACURA TL, AUDI A4, BMW 3-Series, HONDA Accord V6, LEXUS ES 300, MAZDA Millenia, SAAB 9⁵, TOYOTA Camry V6, VOLVO S70.

MAINTENANCE REQUIRED BY WARRANTY
First revision:	Frequency:	Diagnostic plug:
7 500 miles	7 500 miles	Yes

SPECIFICATIONS

General warranty: 3 years / 50 000 miles; powertrain: 6 years / 60 000 miles; perforation corrosion & antipollution: 6 years / unlimited.

Model	Version Trim	Body/ Seats	Interior volume cu ft	Trunk volume cu ft	Cd	Wheel base in	Lght x Wdgth x Hght in x in x in	Curb weight lb	Susp. ft/rr	Brake ft/rr	Steering type	Turning diameter ft	Steer. turns nber.	Fuel tank gal	tire size	Standard tires make	model	Standard powertrain
NISSAN Maxima	GXE	4dr.sdn.5	99.6	14.5	0.32	106.3	189.4x69.7x55.7	3018	ih/ih	dc/dc	pwr.r&p.	34.8	2.9	18.5	205/65R15	Goodyear	Eagle GA	V6/3.0/M5
Maxima	SE	4dr.sdn.5	99.6	14.5	0.32	106.3	189.4x69.7x55.7	3078	ih/ih	dc/ABS	pwr.r&p.	34.8	2.9	18.5	215/55R16	Goodyear	Eagle GA	V6/3.0/M5
Maxima	GLE	4dr.sdn.5	99.6	14.5	0.32	106.3	189.4x69.7x55.7	3084	ih/ih	dc/ABS	pwr.r&p.	34.8	2.9	18.5	205/65R15	Goodyear	Eagle GA	V6/3.0/A4

Since its last revision, the Pathfinder has gradually undergone other modifications. It's no longer the true grit all-terrain vehicle of the first generation, the one that took all kinds of turf - and the world - by storm. The customer is always right, as they say, so this vehicle has evolved into a polished, super-civilized, middle class, boring sort. Which explains why it no longer has its original rugged look, but has a more graceful and genteel appearance. Pathfinder sales are among the top five, behind, of course, the top guns in this category. In other words, this vehicle is still well-liked even after twelve years. It inspired the Infiniti QX4, an impressive success in the luxury sport-utility vehicle segment.

MODEL RANGE
The Pathfinder is a 4-door SUV with rear or all-wheel drive sold in XE and LE rear-wheel drive versions and XE, SE and LE all-wheel drive versions. All models are animated by the same 3.3L V6 engine paired up with a standard manual gearbox on the XE and SE and with a standard automatic on LE models. The base model XE is equipped with power steering, antilock braking, manual air conditioning, radio and tape deck and tilt steering column. The LE is loaded with all the posh amenities you could dream of enjoying on an upper-crust vehicle, all but the sunroof.

TECHNICAL FEATURES
The Pathfinder has a steel unibody integrating an H-frame (monoframe), so as to achieve rock of Gibraltar flexion and torsion resistance. The only standard protective plate on these vehicles covers the gas tank. The fully independent suspension is made up of MacPherson struts up front and of a rigid axle guided by five control arms with coil springs and stabilizer bar at the rear extremity. Disc and drum brakes are hooked up to standard ABS on all versions. Vehicles are equipped with rack-and-pinion steering and a 3.3L V6 that delivers 168 hp. The all-wheel drive is «on demand». It includes two conventional differentials on front and rear axles, but the latter can be replaced by another viscous-coupled limited-slip differential. The transfer case can be engaged via shift-on-the-fly at speeds up to 50 mph and front hub lock is automatic.

PROS
+ OVERALL DESIGN. The Pathfinder has inherited some family traits from its predecessor, but it's now more like a car than a true blue utility vehicle.

Nice, But...

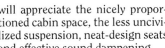

+ SIZE. The Pathfinder is a super-hancy vehicle that takes full advantage of its overall size to provide really roomy cabin space. Leg room is quite generous in the rear seat section and the luggage compartment is absolutely humungous, modular and easily accessible via the clever-design rear hatch. Climbing on board is a breeze with the comfortable ground clearance and several convenient assist grips.

+ HANDLING. The structure is much more rigid and this pays off when it comes to competent, crisp vehicle control. There isn't as much sway thanks to better calibrated springs and shocks. So this vehicle takes curves with aplomb, especially since the center of gravity isn't perched quite as high as in the past.

+ RIDE COMFORT. Passengers will appreciate the nicely proportioned cabin space, the less uncivilized suspension, neat-design seats and effective sound dampening.

+ STEERING. The rack-and-pinion system is direct, willing and easy to adjust, which yields good maneuverability, since the steer angle diameter is relatively short.

+ COCKPIT. Nothing fancy, but it has a good layout and the driver, sitting nice and high, enjoys good peripheral vision all round, now that the spare tire is stashed under the cargo hold floor. The dashboard is no-frills plain, which is an understatement, but at least it's more ergonomic than on the previous model.

+ QUALITY. Assembly is solid, finish touches are neat and materials are spiffy. Equipment is fairly extensive, even on the base model.

CONS
- SAFETY. The American highway bureau (NHTSA) didn't give a high score to this vehicle, given the serious passenger injuries that could occur in the event of a collision. But the sturdier frame has improved handling and ride comfort and brakes do benefit from a standard antilock braking device.

- ENGINE. The Pathfinder's V6 has never for one minute been the best choice for this type of vehicle, since torque is only fair to midling. Accelerations and pickup are far from brilliant with an engine that's always straining and catching its breath.

- BRAKES. They're smooth and easy to apply and achieve straight-on stops in emergency situations, even though there's a bit of wheel lock. But stopping distances are far too long, which could lead to a sad state of affairs.

- TIRES. The Dunlop's installed on some of the models are the culprits behind the awful directional instability and so you're in for white-knuckle driving. These tires are very slippery, yes, even on dry as desert roads.

- FUEL CONSUMPTION. It's far from efficient since fuel bills are always high, and let's face it, performances are rather blah. This engine would be better suited to a car than an SUV.

- TRANSMISSION. Gears are poorly spaced on both the manual and the automatic, so you can't really get the energy ooze out of the high-end torque characteristic of this engine.

- GROUND CLEARANCE. It's lower than before, which cripples some maneuvers on rough terrain and the vehicle has a tendency to bottom out with those 15-inch wheels. We regret that there are still no standard protective plates keeping the engine and transmission components out of harm's way.

- TO BE IMPROVED UPON: Seat upholstery that's terribly firm, poorly designed left footrest for the driver and some inconveniently located controls, such as those for the rear wiper.

CONCLUSION
The Pathfinder has its attributes, but it would be more worth its salt if it could count on an engine that could match its potential.

RATING
NISSAN Pathfinder

CONCEPT :		72%
Technology	80	
Safety :	60	
Interior space :	70	
Trunk volume:	70	
Quality/fit/finish :	80	

DRIVING:		57%
Cockpit :	75	
Performance :	35	
Handling :	35	
Steering :	80	
Braking :	60	

ORIGINAL EQUIPMENT:		75%
Tires :	75	
Headlights :	75	
Wipers :	75	
Rear defroster :	75	
Radio :	75	

COMFORT :		70%
Seats :	75	
Suspension :	60	
Sound level:	70	
Conveniences :	70	
Air conditioning :	75	

BUDGET :		52%
Price :	35	
Fuel economy :	40	
Insurance :	45	
Satisfaction :	90	
Depreciation :	50	

Overall rating:		**65.2%**

NEW FOR 1999

• LE model equipped with color-coordinated fender skirts, alloy wheels and running boards like those on the SE.

ENGINES / TRANSMISSIONS / PERFORMANCES

Model/ version	Type / timing valve / fuel system	Displacement cu in	Power bhp @ rpm	Torque lb-ft @ rpm	Compres. ratio	Driving wheels / transmission	Final ratio	Acceler. 0-60 mph s	Standing 1/4 & 5/8 mile s	Acceler. 50-75 mph s	Braking 60-0 mph f	Top speed mph	Lateral acceler. G	Noise level dBA	Fuel economy mpg City	Highway	Fuel type Octane
base	V6* 3.3 SOHC-12-MPSFI	200	168 @ 4800	196 @ 2800	8.9 :1	rear/4 - M5*	4.636	10.3	17.3 31.4	7.0	154	103	0.68	64-70	15	19	R 87
						rear/4 - A4	4.636	11.6	18.4 33.7	9.0	148	100	0.68	65-70	14	19	R 87

PRICE & EQUIPMENT

NISSAN Pathfinder	XE	SE	LE
Retail price $:	25,999	29,099	32,849
Dealer invoice $:	23,410	26,202	29,580
Shipping & handling $:	490	490	490
Automatic transmission:	O	O	S
Cruise control:	-	S	S
Power steering:	S	S	S
Anti-lock brakes:	S	S	S
Traction control:	-	-	-
Air conditioning:	SM	SA	SA
Leather:	-	O	SC
AM/FM/radio-cassette:	SCD	SCD	SCD
Power door locks:	-	S	S
Power windows:	-	S	S
Tilt steering:	S	S	S
Dual adjustable mirrors:	SM	SEH	SEH
Alloy wheels:	O	S	S
Anti-theft system:	-	S	S

Colors
Exterior: Red, Blue, Chestnut, Beige, Green, Ebony, Gray, White.

Interior: Gray, Beige.

AT A GLANCE...

Category: rear-wheel drive or AWD sport-utility **Class :** utility

HISTORIC
Introduced in: 1986-1996
Made in: Kyushu, Japan.

DEMOGRAPHICS

Model	Men./Wom.	Age	Married	College	Income
Pathfinder	76/24 %	39	68 %	57 %	$ 49 000

INDEX
Safety:	60 %	Satisfaction:		92 %
Depreciation:	50 %	Insurance:		$ 1065 -1 155
Cost per mile:	$ 0.51	Number of dealers:		1 100

SALES
Model	1996	1997	Result
Pathfinder	73 686	73 365	- 0.4 %

MAIN COMPETITORS
CHEVROLET Blazer, FORD Explorer, GMC Jimmy, ISUZU Rodeo & Trooper, JEEP Cherokee & Grand Cherokee, SUZUKI Sidekick, TOYOTA 4Runner.

MAINTENANCE REQUIRED BY WARRANTY
First revision:	Frequency:	Diagnostic plug:
7 500 miles	7 500 miles	No

SPECIFICATIONS

Model	Version Trim	Traction	Body/ Seats	Wheel base in	Lght x Wdgth x Hght in x in x in	Curb weight lb	Susp. ft/rr	Brake ft/rr	Steering type	Turning diameter ft	Steer. turns nber.	Fuel tank gal	tire size	Standard tires make	model	Standard powertrain
NISSAN	General warranty: 3 years / 50 000 miles; powertrain: 6 years / 60 000 miles; perforation corrosion & antipollution: 6 years / unlimited.															
Pathfinder	XE	4x4	4dr.wgn.5	106.3	178.3x68.7x67.1	3975	ih/rh	dc/dr/ABS	pwr.r&p.	42.0	3.2	21.1	265/70R15 Bridgestone	Dueller HT	V6/3.3/M5
Pathfinder	SE	4x4	4dr.wgn.5	106.3	178.3x68.7x67.1	4065	ih/rh	dc/dr/ABS	pwr.r&p.	42.0	3.2	21.1	265/70R15 Bridgestone	Dueller HT	V6/3.3/M5
Pathfinder	LE	4x4	4dr.wgn.5	106.3	178.3x68.7x67.1	4034	ih/rh	dc/dr/ABS	pwr.r&p.	42.0	3.2	21.1	265/70R15 Bridgestone	Dueller HT	V6/3.3/A4

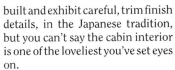

It's no secret, the Sentra isn't a big seller. Since the latest generation Sentra was equipped with an enhanced rear suspension and new body design, sales have stagnated at a very low level for a model that has such a wide sales distribution. In the subcompact category, only the Suzuki Esteem is in even more dire straits, which isn't a good measuring stick, really... The small base engine does its darndest, but it does have its limitations and maybe the 2.0L engine borrowed from the defunct 200SX will be enough to light the fire once more? God only knows, we haven't a clue.

MODEL RANGE
The Sentra is sold in Canada in four versions: base, XE, GXE and SE to which the United States market adds the GLE. They're equipped with a standard 1.6L engine or 2.0L (SE) linked to a 5-speed manual transmission. The base model gets only the most rock-bottom, essential equipment, but the other models are more richly equipped, although antilock braking, automatic transmission and sunroof (SE) are sold as extras for each and every model.

TECHNICAL FEATURES
The Sentra has a steel monocoque body that's now more resistant to torsion due to added reinforcements aimed at providing better passenger protection in the event of a collision. The resonance frequency of the chassis sits at 26 Hertz and stifles noise and vibration so that it doesn't assail passengers inside the cabin and the structure has a drag coeffient of 0.33. The front suspension is a MacPherson strut setup and the rear suspension consists of a Scott-Russell multilink design that frees up more cabin and trunk space, while ensuring better than average demeanor and ride comfort. All models are equipped with standard disc and drum brakes, except the SE, and GXE models can receive optional rear-wheel disc brakes and antilock braking system. All versions benefit from power rack-and-pinion steering except the base model that also only has a single exterior mirror.

PROS
+ STYLE. The Sentra's trim, prim and uncluttered body design makes it look bigger than it actually is, so much so that some people think it's a compact.

+ CABIN SPACE. It's less stingy than for some of its rivals in the subcompact category, so much so that a fifth passenger can even be

Snuffed Flame...

seated in the middle of the rear seatbench, when really necessary.

+ HANDLING. The famous «multilink» rear axle is the secret ingredient that yields such yummy road holding. This straightforward, simple design ensures more precise vehicle control, so the car is nice and stable on curves and is much more competent than some of the rivals in this department. Tire quality on the various models is also a major factor and the end result varies a lot between the base model's roadability and that of the SE model.

+ PERFORMANCES. They're sprightly even with the base engine since accelerations and pickup are right in keeping with this brave little engine's roar and you feel like you're travelling faster than is actually the case.

+ FUEL ECONOMY. The 1.6L engine is one of the most fuel-efficient in its category since it settles for 28 mpg.

+ STEERING. The power steering system is neat, since it's accurate and benefits from a good reduction ratio, so this little car zips around wherever it pleases in the city.

+ RIDE COMFORT. It's really something for a subcompact car, the suspension is very silky and the nice-design seats procure good hip and shoulder support that isn't spoiled by the rather firm upholstery.

+ PERFORMANCES. The 2.0L engine behavior makes you realize how very weak the lowly 1.6L is, especially with the automatic gearbox.

+ QUALITY. These cars are well-built and exhibit careful, trim finish details, in the Japanese tradition, but you can't say the cabin interior is one of the loveliest you've set eyes on.

+ CONVENIENCE FEATURES. Just great with all those roomy storage areas. The trunk is a fairly good size and connects with the cabin via a slot located behind the rear seatbench.

+ ERGONOMICS. The dashboard is handy and logical and the main section curves outwards, so controls are within easy reach. Too bad the radio and climate control dials are reversed.

CONS
- BRAKES. The base, XE and GXE aren't equipped with a really good braking system, not with those incredibly long stops in emergency situations, quite unusual for such a lightweight car. The pedal is a bit spongy so brakes are hard to apply as needed. One good thing: even without ABS, car path stays on the straight and narrow.

-SWAY. It's generated by the overly soft suspension that equips all three models, and it provokes understeer effect that's really more of a bother than a real concern.

- STEERING. It's over-assisted, so it's light and frothy, which complicates things in strong crosswinds.

- TIRES. Those installed on the base model are too small and of mediocre quality. They must be replaced when winter is on its way, no if's, and's or but's, since they're hazardous.

- NOISE LEVEL. It stays at top volume all the livelong day, since the engine roars when coaxed to perform and the body is poorly insulated, so road noise is very pervasive.

- CABIN DESIGN. It's very dreary and seat fabrics and plastic trim components sure don't help liven things up and a bit of color would dress the cabin up a bit...

- EQUIPMENT. The base model is so poorly equipped that it's a real disgrace for Nissan that dares to put such a lowly car on the market, so as to offer the best bargain around...

CONCLUSION
The Sentra is an urban sort that's lost its appeal because of Nissan's ultra-conservatism due to restructuring, after having experienced serious financial problems. ☺

RATING
NISSAN Sentra

CONCEPT: 63%
Technology	75
Safety :	75
Interior space :	50
Trunk volume:	40
Quality/fit/finish :	75

DRIVING: 59%
Cockpit :	75
Performance :	50
Handling :	55
Steering :	75
Braking :	40

ORIGINAL EQUIPMENT: 73%
Tires :	70
Headlights :	75
Wipers :	75
Rear defroster :	70
Radio :	75

COMFORT : 69%
Seats :	70
Suspension :	70
Sound level:	50
Conveniences :	80
Air conditioning :	75

BUDGET : 80%
Price :	75
Fuel economy :	85
Insurance :	90
Satisfaction :	80
Depreciation :	70

Overall rating: 68.8%

NEW FOR 1999

• The 1.6L version still available equipped with: power locks and mirrors and color-coordinated exterior door handles.
• The new 140-hp 2.0L version equipped with climate control, antilock braking, bucket seats, 15-in. alloy wheels, rear spoiler and fog lamps.

ENGINES / TRANSMISSIONS / PERFORMANCES

Model/version	Type / timing valve / fuel system	Displacement cu in	Power bhp @ rpm	Torque lb-ft @ rpm	Compres. ratio	Driving wheels / transmission	Final ratio	Acceler. 0-60 mph s	Standing 1/4 & 5/8 mile s	Acceler. 50-75 mph s	Braking 60-0 mph f	Top speed mph	Lateral acceler. G	Noise level dBA	Fuel economy City	mpg Highway	Fuel type Octane
Sentra	L4* 1.6 DOHC-16-MPSFI	97	115 @ 6000	108 @ 4000	9.9 :1	front - M5*	3.789	10.3	17.4 31.6	7.0	157	103	0.78	69	28	41	R 87
						front - A4	3.827	11.5	18.3 32.7	8.1	170	100	0.78	69	26	38	R 87
SE	L4* 2.0 DOHC-16-MPSFI	122	140 @ 6400	132 @ 4800	9.5 :1	front - M5*	4.176	9.0	16.6 30.5	6.5	157	112	0.80	70	25	6.9	R 87
						front - A4	3.827	NA									

PRICE & EQUIPMENT

NISSAN Sentra	base	XE	GXE	SE
Retail price $:	11,499	13,699	14,899	16,749
Dealer invoice $:	10,950	12,761	13,494	15,168
Shipping & handling $:	490	490	490	490
Automatic transmission:	-	O	O	O
Cruise control:	-	-	S	S
Power steering:	-	S	S	S
Anti-lock brakes:	-	-	O	S
Traction control:	-	-	-	-
Air conditioning:	-	O	S	S
Leather:	-	-	-	-
AM/FM/radio-cassette:	-	O	S	SDc
Power door locks:	-	-	S	S
Power windows:	-	-	S	S
Tilt steering:	S	S	S	S
Dual adjustable mirrors:	-	-	SE	SE
Alloy wheels:	-	-	-	S
Anti-theft system:	-	-	-	S

Colors
Exterior: Bronze, Blue, Ebony, Charcoal, Sandstone, White, Green, Beige.
Interior: Gray, Brown, Charcoal.

AT A GLANCE...

Category: front-wheel drive sub-compact sedans. **Class :** 3

HISTORIC
Introduced in: 1981-1995.
Made in: Aguascalientes, Mexico & Smyrna TE, USA.

DEMOGRAPHICS
Model	Men./Wom.	Age	Married	College	Income
Sentra	54/46 %	44	71 %	61 %	$ 31 000

INDEX
Safety:	75 %	Satisfaction:	80 %
Depreciation:	47 %	Insurance:	$ 835
Cost per mile:	$ 0.35	Number of dealers:	1 100

SALES
Model	1996	1997	Result
Sentra	129 592	122 468	- 5.5 %

MAIN COMPETITORS
HONDA Civic sedan, HYUNDAI Accent, MAZDA Protegé, TOYOTA Tercel, VOLKSWAGEN Golf.

MAINTENANCE REQUIRED BY WARRANTY
First revision:	Frequency:	Diagnostic plug:
500 miles	7 500 miles	Yes

SPECIFICATIONS

Model	Version Trim	Body/ Seats	Interior volume cu ft	Trunk volume cu ft	Cd	Wheel base in	Lght x Wdgth x Hght in x in x in	Curb weight lb	Susp. ft/rr	Brake ft/rr	Steering type	Turning diameter ft	Steer. turns nber.	Fuel tank gal	tire size	Standard tires make	model	Standard powertrain
NISSAN		General warranty: 3 years / 50 000 miles; powertrain: 6 years / 60 000 miles; perforation corrosion & antipollution: 6 years / unlimited.																
Sentra	base	4dr.sdn.5	87.2	10.7	0.33	99.8	171.1x66.6x54.5	2315	ih/sih	dc/dr	r&p.	34.1	3.01	13.2	155/80R13	Dunlop	-	L4/1.6/M5
Sentra	XE	4dr.sdn.5	87.2	10.7	0.33	99.8	171.1x66.6x54.5	2381	ih/sih	dc/dr	pwr.r&p.	34.1	3.01	13.2	175/70R13	General	Ameri 45	L4/1.6/M5
Sentra	GXE	4dr.sdn.5	87.2	10.7	0.33	99.8	171.1x66.6x54.5	2429	ih/sih	dc/dr	pwr.r&p.	34.1	3.01	13.2	175/65R14	General	Ameri 45	L4/1.6/M5
Sentra	SE	4dr.sdn.5	87.2	10.7	0.33	99.8	171.1x66.6x54.5	2619	ih/sih	dc/dcABS	pwr.r&p.	34.1	3.01	13.2	195/55R15	General	Ameri 45	L4/2.0/M5

OLDSMOBILE Alero
A Little Luck For a Daring Move..

Aurora came along and took everyone by surprise, including the people at Oldsmobile themselves. **John Rock, the top dog at the time, had the foresight to understand that the only way his brand could make it was by opting for autonomy from the rest of the GM conglomerate. Working in association, yes, no getting around it, since the underlying principle at the number-1 world carmaker is to share production and development costs among all brands, but working independently, like Cadillac.**

The Intrigue, unveiled last year, followed the same course, even though it's more like the Buick Century-Regal models than the Aurora was in regard to Cadillac models. The Intrigue launched unique family traits so lacking

to Oldsmobile models in the past. The Aurora's full curves spawned simple, wavy lines that are lovely and nicely proportioned, with a touch of pounce. After having developed two Auto Show prototypes to test public feeling, Oldsmobile set about reworking the Achieva in partnership with Pontiac that was also in the process of rejuvenating the Grand Am. It'll be interesting to watch sales for these two models in the upcoming months and we'll see which combination will win out, the Alero's graceful beauty or the Grand Am's psychedelic dream...

Apart from style, it's the technological investment reflected in the latest Oldsmobile model that is the most striking, since its renewal is much more than the usual skin-deep face-lift. The new platform has a longer wheelbase

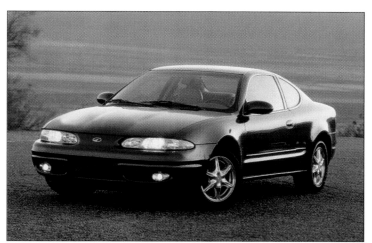

and wider wheel tracks than the previous model, so as to increase the car's size and give it a more solid, square on its feet, base.

If you look underneath the car, you're amazed by the neat subframe layout that looks as solid as a rock. The front suspension control arms are made of aluminum, the front powertrain cradle is hydroformed and two longitudinal rails solidify the front section. You can observe the same simple, clean design at the rear, since the crossmember holding the suspension components can be removed for repairs and adjustments and the overall arrangement is ultra-modern and super-efficient. The exhaust system is made of stainless steel and the car is equipped with disc brakes and original ABS-traction control. Not bad for a mass-produced car. Safety-wise, the frame forms a robust cage that vibrates at a 25 Hz frequency and the rear end has been dramatically reinforced, to offset structural weaknesses caused by the wide trunk opening and the slot connecting it to the cabin. Wheelhouses are built of thicker steel and stamped in a single piece. The powertrain is mounted on the front cradle with supports that are resistant to torque and that stifle mechanical vibration. By «pushing the Alero's envelope» to the very edge of the Environment Protection Agency (EPA)'s American classification, GM wanted to compete directly with the extremely popular Accord coupes and sedans that are the Alero's number-1 target and explain its body design, technical features and price. Time will tell if this daring move will pay off...

Oldsmobile was the sacrifice division of General Motors for many a year, and now, contrary to all expectations, it's becoming one of the most dynamic and successful assets to the conglomerate. Of course, it must be said that John Rock had understood before anyone else that the future of GM depended on a greater autonomy for its divisions and that sharing common elements had its limitations. Once again, the Aurora adventure is an example of same, since this model maybe won't go down in automobile history, other than as a catalyst that proved that success is achieved by those who dare to be different.

MODEL RANGE

The Alero shares its platform and a number of mechanical features and finish details with the Pontiac Grand Am. It's offered as a 2-door coupe or 4-door sedan in GX, GL or GLS versions equipped with an original 2.4L Twin Cam 4-cylinder engine on the GX and GL or the new 3400 overhead valve V6 on the GLS. Strangely enough, no manual gearbox will be available for some time, so the 4-speed automatic is currently the only choice available. The Alero comes equipped with a very extensive list of standard items, even on the least expensive model. Besides ABS-traction control, there's climate control, power door locks, tilt steering wheel, theft-deterrent system and a tire pressure control device.

TECHNICAL FEATURES

Like its sister the Pontiac Grand Am, the Alero is a brand new car. First, size-wise. Compared to the former Achieva, its body is slightly shorter, but it's wider and higher so as to offer more generous cabin space. But it's the trunk that's gained proportionally more volume. The steel unibody has an average aero-dynamic efficiency, a tad better than that of the Achieva, with a drag coefficient of 0.32. But its resistance to impact during collision tests has improved since it earned top marks from the NHTSA. It includes an independent cradle up front that supports the powertrain and suspension elements and at the rear end, these elements are mounted on a bolted crossmember. The suspension is now fully independent. There's a MacPherson strut design up front and the rear suspension is

new and highly sophisticated, since axles are supported by a three-link arrangement on each side. There are anti-roll bars both front and rear. All three versions share the same springs and shocks, with both engines. Only the GLS can receive the optional FE3 sporty suspension. Cars are equipped with standard disc brakes paired up with the now inseparable duo: ABS-traction control. Steering is variable assist.

PROS

+ STYLE. This newcomer's a real winner and its body design is sensational, blotting out any memory of the lackluster Achieva. It's inspired by the Aurora's curves, but it's different from the Intrigue and so the Alero has a winsome and solid as a rock character. Inside, there are lots of those GM round shapes, but after all, you do inherit some family traits, and everything exhibits a neat «soft touch» approach.

+ ENGINEERING. For once GM pulled out all the stops and spent the cash needed to build this worthy Alero model. The body, suspension, brake system and V6 engine

attest to this determination to do things right, which in in the long run, does beef up the price that may be higher than for previous models, but at any rate, they didn't sell.

+ HANDLING. What strikes you right off once you're behind the wheel is the one-of-a-piece Alero design, a real first, like the feeling you got on the hot-off-the-press Aurora and Intrigue. Roadability is clean and competent and depending on the tires used, there's a nice cohesive directional flow and the car takes really tight curves with amazing assurance. Compared to the previous generation's wishy washy demeanor, this type of crisp handling is a really pleasant surprise. Quality pays.

+ PERFORMANCES. Result stats indicate that they're quite acceptable, especially with the more torquy V6. Accelerations are sprightly and pickup is peppy, so passing on the highway is very safe.

+ DRIVING. It's great with the relatively comfy cockpit and adequate visibility (more so on the sedan than the coupe) but the simple, straight-

forward dashboard layout is a real treat, and the steering wheel and speed shifter are just where you want them. The driver even has a footrest on the left...

+ NICE FEATURES: Handy storage compartments throughout the cabin, more nicely contoured seats and speed shifter position indicator on the instrument panel.

CONS

- TORQUE. We shouldn't have to mention this phenomenon on such a recent car, but it's due to the unequal-length drive shafts. But it's only a problem on really slick roads.

- ENGINES. They're fairly new, but they're far from being as smooth and refined as their Japanese homologues that equip the Accord and Camry-Solara. The 4-cylinder is really rough around the edges and you'd think it had farm tractor genes in its blood and the V6 isn't as silky as its rivals.

- CABIN SPACE. Rear seats are wider and higher, but there isn't much leg room if the front seats are pushed back too far.

- MANUAL GEARBOX. The automatic's okay for the sedan, but the coupe should be able to be equipped with an optional manual gearbox with both engines, since statistically the latter doesn't sell as well. This will be the case next year for the 4-cylinder, but not for the V6.

- PRICE. Quality pays, but you have to pay for quality. The Alero is a better car than the Achieva, but it also costs more and its price is dangerously close to that of the Intrigue that offers more generous space and performances, for just a few extra dollars. This same phenomenon is affecting the Cirrus-Stratus-Breeze compared with the Concorde-Intrepid. Sales will be shared depending on age bracket and market segment.

CONCLUSION

The Alero is amazingly solid and competent, the telltale attributes of a well-built car, but it also reflects a serious technological development that GM decided to invest in to the detriment of the almighty production cost, and in this case the customer cashes in on all the benefits. ☺

RATING
OLDSMOBILE Alero

CONCEPT :		**75%**
Technology	80	
Safety :	90	
Interior space :	60	
Trunk volume :	70	
Quality/fit/finish :	75	
DRIVING:		**68%**
Cockpit :	80	
Performance :	55	
Handling :	65	
Steering :	80	
Braking :	60	
ORIGINAL EQUIPMENT:		**76%**
Tires :	75	
Headlights :	80	
Wipers :	75	
Rear defroster :	75	
Radio :	75	
COMFORT :		**73%**
Seats :	75	
Suspension :	75	
Sound level:	60	
Conveniences :	75	
Air conditioning :	80	
BUDGET :		**58%**
Price :	60	
Fuel economy :	75	
Insurance :	55	
Satisfaction :	75	
Depreciation :	25	
Overall rating:		**70.0%**

NEW FOR 1999

- Completely revamped model replacing the Achieva, available as coupes and sedans equipped with either a 2.4L 4-cylinder engine or a 3.4L V6.

ENGINES / TRANSMISSIONS / PERFORMANCES

Model/ version	Type / timing valve / fuel system	Displacement cu in	Power bhp @ rpm	Torque lb-ft @ rpm	Compres. ratio	Driving wheels / transmission	Final ratio	Acceler. 0-60 mph s	Standing 1/4 & 5/8 mile s	Acceler. 50-75 mph s	Braking 60-0 mph f	Top speed mph	Lateral acceler. G	Noise level dBA	Fuel economy mpg City	Fuel economy mpg Highway	Fuel type Octane
1)	L4 2.4 DOHC-16-MPSFI	146	150 @ 5600	155 @ 4400	9.5 :1	front - A4	3.42	10.0	17.0	30.4	6.8	144	103	0.82	68	21	32	R 87
2)	V6 3.4 OHV-12-MPSFI	204	170 @ 4800	200 @ 4000	9.5 :1	front - A4	3.05	8.7	16.5	29.7	6.2	148	106	0.82	67	20	28	R 87

1) Std GX, GL. 2) std GLS, opt. GL.

PRICE & EQUIPMENT

OLDSMOBILE Alero	GX	GL	GLS
Retail price $:	16,325	18,220	20,875
Dealer invoice $:	15,264	16,671	18,892
Shipping & handling $:	525	525	525
Automatic transmission:	S	S	S
Cruise control:	O	S	S
Power steering:	S	S	S
Anti-lock brakes:	S	S	S
Traction control:	S	S	S
Air conditioning:	S	O	S
Leather:	-	O	S
AM/FM/radio-cassette:	O	S	SCD
Power door locks:	S	S	S
Power windows:	-	S	S
Tilt steering:	S	S	S
Dual adjustable mirrors:	SM	SE	SE
Alloy wheels:	-	S	S
Anti-theft system:	S	S	S

Colors
Exterior: Silver, White, Blue, Black, Green, Red, Gray, Jade, Sand, Orchid.

Interior: Gray, Beige, Red, Blue, Taupe, Lime, Graphite, Jade.

AT A GLANCE...

Category: front-wheel drive compact coupes & sedans. **Class :** 4

HISTORIC
Introduced in: 1999
Made in: Lansing, Michigan, USA.

DEMOGRAPHICS
Model	Men./Wom.	Age	Married	College	Income
Achieva	72/28 %	52	72 %	31 %	$ 29 000

INDEX
Safety:	90 %	Satisfaction:	73 %
Depreciation:	28 %	Insurance:	$ 836
Cost per mile:	$ 0.44	Number of dealers:	3 100

SALES
Model	1996	1997	Result
Achieva	40 344	63 196	+ 56.6 %

MAIN COMPETITORS
coupe: CHRYSLER Sebring, DODGE Avenger, HONDA Accord, MITSUBISHI Eclipse.
sedan : CHRYSLER Cirrus, DODGE Stratus, FORD Contour, MAZDA 626, MERCURY Mystique, NISSAN Altima, PLYMOUTH Breeze, PONTIAC Grand Am, SUBARU Legacy.

MAINTENANCE REQUIRED BY WARRANTY
First revision:	Frequency:	Diagnostic plug:
3 000 miles	6 000 miles	Yes

SPECIFICATIONS

Model	Version Trim	Body/ Seats	Interior volume cu ft	Trunk volume cu ft	Cd	Wheel base in	Lght x Wdgth x Hght in x in x in	Curb weight lb	Susp. ft/rr	Brake ft/rr	Steering type	Turning diameter ft	Steer. turns nber.	Fuel tank gal	tire size	Standard tires make	model	Standard powertrain
OLDSMOBILE		General warranty: 3 years / 36 000 miles; antipollution: 5 years / 50 000 miles; perforation corrosion: 6 years / 100 000 miles. Roadside assistance.																
Achieva	1998	4dr.sdn.5	89.8	14.0	0.33	103.4	187.9x68.1x53.5	2917	ih/sih	dc/dr/ABS	pwr.r&p.	35.3	2.3	15.2	195/65R15	-	-	L4/2.4/A4
Alero GX	1999	2dr.cpe.5	92.6	15.3	0.32	107.0	186.7x70.1x54.5	3024	ih/ih	dc/ABS	pwr.r&p.	35.1	2.6	15.0	215/60R15	BFGoodrich	Touring T/A	L4/2.4/A4
Alero GLS	1999	4dr.sdn.5	91.0	15.3	0.32	107.0	186.7x70.1x54.5	3077	ih/ih	dc/ABS	pwr.r&p.	35.2	2.6	15.0	225/50R16	Goodyear	Eagle LS	V6/3.4/A4

Catalyst For Change

When the Aurora was unveiled in 1995, no one really thought much of it, so much so that Oldsmobile couldn't make up its mind about a name for this creation...At that time, this brand was on the brink of disappearing altogether, but the executives at General Motors gave it the okay, so it was able to celebrate its centenary to which the Aurora added quite a bit of flair. The success of this car paved the way for a whole generation of new models, all bearing a strange resemblance to this star, that will ensure a rosy future for Oldsmobile that just couldn't get its act together for the longest time.

MODEL RANGE

Oldsmobile offers only a single version of the Aurora. This classy four-door sedan benefits from a 4.0L DOHC V8, a spin-off from the Cadillac Northstar. It's paired up with a 4-speed automatic transmission. This car is literally loaded with goodies and the only options available in the catalogue are the Autobahn package (V-rated tires and axle ratio of 3.71), chrome rims, an Acoustimass sound system with seven speakers, a 12-CD changer in the trunk, sunroof, 45/45 bucket seats and gold-plated insignia!

TECHNICAL FEATURES

The Aurora is the upshot of the work of engineers at Cadillac who designed it based on the Riviera platform. The steel body is a unitized structure and in spite of its bold shape, the drag coefficient sits at only an average 0.32. In order to keep vehicle weight down, lightweight materials were used: for example, aluminum for the hood and nylon for the gas tank. A tubular cage provides passenger protection and the chassis has a natural frequency of 25 Hz. The 4.0L V8 engine on this front-wheel drive car was developed precisely for this model; in fact, 14 patents were registered in the process. This transversely mounted V8 pumps out 250 hp. The fully independent suspension uses MacPherson struts up front and semi-trailing arms with lateral joints at the rear with stabilizer bar at both ends. The disc brakes benefit from standard ABS-traction control.

PROS

+ CONCEPT. The Aurora is a beauty, but her appeal is more than skin-deep. The Aurora concept aims at producing a modern, topnotch product at an affordable price. This new approach represents a something of a dramatic change at General Motors who don't usually have this attitude.

+ VALUE. Compared to rivals, the Aurora is a darn good buy with its sophisticated V8 and lush equipment, offered at a price equivalent to that of V6-animated rivals.

+ ESTHETICS. The body design isn't revolutionary, but it's unique and is easily recognizable. Owners like its avant-garde style and the way the cabin interior is rendered.

+ QUALITY. Assembly is robust, finish job is more meticulous than usual at GM and most trim materials look spiffy.

+ CABIN DESIGN. Inside there's a superb instrument panel with main section curved toward the driver.

+ HANDLING. The Aurora is anything but nimble on its feet, for its plump weight is a real handicap. Generally speaking, it stays neutral.

+ RIDE COMFORT. The smooth suspension, nicely contoured seats and powerful sound dampening really add to comfort. The cabin is really lovely too and is equipped with details like the rear center armrest that holds a storage compartment and two cup-holders, and the multi-panel sunvisors.

+ QUALITY. For a U.S.-built car, overall craftsmanship is outstanding. Tolerance points are tight and clean, trim materials are lovely and the finish job is more nicely executed than usual.

+ INSTRUMENT PANEL. The dashboard design is neat and original, including the outcurving center section that offers nicely clustered controls within easy reach.

+ STORAGE SPACE. For once, no one can complain that storage spots aren't handy or original!

CONS

- SAFETY. The Aurora only earned poor scores in NHTSA tests. This suggests that passengers enjoy only limited protection in the event of an accident, a chronic problem for several GM products, like the Venture, Trans Sport and Silhouette minivans.

- BRAKES. Linings lose their oomph in a hurry when put to the never-say-die test.

- PERFORMANCES. Even with the V8 engine, The Aurora's performances aren't startling. Some of the rivals out there do a lot better and they benefit from an equivalent power to weight ratio.

- FUEL CONSUMPTION. Hefty weight disadvantages the Aurora when compared to less heavy rivals.

- STEERING. The Magnasteer is too light. To make matters worse, the Aurora isn't too competent when faced with maneuvers in the city, due to wide steer angle and poor reduction ratio. At least, steering is more precise on straight runs than it was in 1995.

- VISIBILITY. The body belt is very high and seats are too low-slung, so occupants will feel claustrophobic and won't have a clear view of the outside world.

- CABIN SPACE. Rear seats aren't too wonderfully welcoming: ceiling clearance is limited and the rear section of the cabin is too narrow to accomodate three passengers really comfortably.

- TRUNK. It's fairly roomy, but its tapered opening and high threshold make for awkward luggage handling. At least there's a ski slot connecting to the cabin.

- TO BE IMPROVED UPON: This fancy car should be equipped with a shifter position indicator behind the steering wheel. Besides, the front shoulder belts aren't height-adjustable and belt buckles are annoying to use.

CONCLUSION

The Aurora isn't perfect and it's starting to show its age, but in spite of all the compromises regarding safety features and engine power, this car is a sign that things are changing at GM. ☺

RATING
OLDSMOBILE Aurora

CONCEPT : 74%
Technology 80
Safety : 60
Interior space : 80
Trunk volume: 70
Quality/fit/finish : 80

DRIVING: 68%
Cockpit : 80
Performance : 60
Handling : 60
Steering : 80
Braking : 60

ORIGINAL EQUIPMENT: 76%
Tires : 75
Headlights : 75
Wipers : 75
Rear defroster : 75
Radio : 80

COMFORT : 78%
Seats : 75
Suspension : 75
Sound level: 70
Conveniences : 80
Air conditioning : 90

BUDGET : 49%
Price : 0
Fuel economy : 50
Insurance : 45
Satisfaction : 90
Depreciation : 55

Overall rating: 68.4%

NEW FOR 1999

• The number of hydraulic engine supports: formerly one, now there are three.
• New exterior shades.

ENGINES / TRANSMISSIONS / PERFORMANCES

Model/version	Type / timing valve / fuel system	Displacement cu in	Power bhp @ rpm	Torque lb-ft @ rpm	Compres. ratio	Driving wheels / transmission	Final ratio	Acceler. 0-60 mph s	Standing 1/4 & 5/8 mile s	Acceler. 50-75 mph s	Braking 60-0 mph f	Top speed mph	Lateral acceler. G	Noise level dBA	Fuel economy mpg City	Highway	Fuel type Octane
Aurora	V8* 4.0 DOHC-32-SFI	244	250 @ 5600	260 @ 4400	10.3 :1	front - A4	3.48	9.0	16.7 30.4	6.5	134	134	0.80	66	17	25	S 92

PRICE & EQUIPMENT

OLDSMOBILE Aurora	base
Retail price $:	36,160
Dealer invoice $:	32,724
Shipping & handling $:	665
Automatic transmission:	S
Cruise control:	S
Power steering:	S
Anti-lock brakes:	S
Traction control:	S
Air conditioning:	S
Leather:	S
AM/FM/radio-cassette:	SDc
Power door locks:	S
Power windows:	S
Tilt steering:	S
Dual adjustable mirrors:	S
Alloy wheels:	S
Anti-theft system:	S

Colors
Exterior: Gray, White, Green, Silver, Blue, Black, Red, Cherry, Champagne, Gold, Bronze, Copper
Interior: Graphite, Blue, Tan.

AT A GLANCE...

Category: front-wheel drive luxury sedans. **Class :** 7

HISTORIC
Introduced in: 1995
Made in: Lake Orion, Michigan, USA.

DEMOGRAPHICS
Model	Men./Wom.	Age	Married	College	Income
Aurora	89/11%	59	85%	35%	$ 63 000

INDEX
Safety: 60 % Satisfaction: 90 %
Depreciation: 45 % Insurance: $ 1 390
Cost per mile: $ 0.65 Number of dealers: 3 100

SALES
Model	1996	1997	Result
Aurora	23 717	25 404	+ 7.1 %

MAIN COMPETITORS
AUDI A6, BMW 540i, CADILLAC Seville, CHRYSLER LHS, INFINITI Q45, LEXUS GS & LS 400, LINCOLN Continental, MERCEDES-BENZ E420.

MAINTENANCE REQUIRED BY WARRANTY
First revision: 3 000 miles **Frequency:** 6 000 miles **Diagnostic plug:** Yes

SPECIFICATIONS

Model	Version Trim	Body/Seats	Interior volume cu ft	Trunk volume cu ft	Cd	Wheel base in	Lght x Wdgth x Hght in x in x in	Curb weight lb	Susp. ft/rr	Brake ft/rr	Steering type	Turning diameter ft	Steer. turns nber.	Fuel tank gal	tire size	Standard tires make	model	Standard powertrain
OLDSMOBILE Aurora	base	4dr.sdn. 5	100.5	19.8	0.31	113.8	205.4x74.4x55.4	3967	ih/ih	dc/ABS	pwr.r&p.	41.9	2.5	20	235/60R16	Michelin	MXV4	V8/4.0/A4

General warranty: 3 years / 36 000 miles; antipollution: 5 years / 50 000 miles; perforation corrosion: 6 years / 100 000 miles. Roadside assistance.

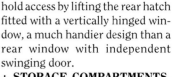

Out Of Context...

Oldsmobile was the first brand in the GM group to offer an all-wheel drive sport-utiliity vehicle with luxury pretentions. A sign of the times, other divisions of the number-1 automaker have followed suit. The Bravada is equipped with a super-cushy, posh interior, so obviously, this vehicle is geared to buyers who are ready to cough up more cash for a 4X4, that is, those who buy the Jeep Grand Cherokee Limited, Ford Explorer Limited and Mercury Mountaineer. This Oldsmobile vehicle isn't sold on the Canadian market, but its clone is: the new GMC Envoy.

MODEL RANGE

The Bravada is offered solely as a 4-door station wagon. Like the Aurora, it only comes in a single version, equipped with all-wheel drive. This year, another equipment item is added to the impressive list of goodies: a less bulky steering wheel. New sets of options are also available, such as heated seats and electrochromic mirrors.

TECHNICAL FEATURES

The Bravada is a close variant of the 4X4 Blazer and Jimmy SUV's. It has a distinctive front grille design, side guards and cabin details. Its body is made up of steel panels that are galvanized on both sides (except the roof), mounted on an H-frame. The all-wheel drive «Smart Trak» system is completely automatic and requires no driver intervention whatsoever. It uses an electronically controlled transfer case that redistributes power from the rear to the front axle, as needed, in less than 250 milliseconds. The front suspension consists of transverse control arms and A-arms, whereas at the rear, the rigid axle is supported by leaf springs. Both axles benefit from a stabilizer bar. The suspension offers three shock absorber settings: «Premium» that's geared to ride comfort; the middle setting, that's firmer and useful when hauling average loads; the third setting is very stiff and is suitable when pulling heavy loads. Standard disc brakes are linked to an antilock braking system. When it comes to power, the Vortec V6 has to bow to the Explorer's DOHC V6 and no V8 engine is available.

PROS

+ **PERFORMANCES.** The V6 has lots of vim and vigor. With RWD, the Bravada achieves accelerations and pickup akin to those of a regular passenger sedan.

+ **RIDE COMFORT.** Highway travel is silky smooth, except maybe with the reinforced suspension that keeps a stiff upper lip. The suspension and big tires know what to do when faced with bumps and potholes.

+ **BRAKES.** The added rear-wheel disc brakes make a difference when it comes to bringing this vehicle to a halt: emergency stops are shorter and ABS helps keep the vehicle on an even keel. But the pedal is still spongy and hard to gauge. Luckily, brakes hold on like weasels when the going gets rough.

+ **QUALITY.** Assembly exudes an impression of solid build and finish details look carefully executed. Materials are so attractive they even look posh!

+ **SMARTTRAK.** It only takes a quarter of a second for the SmartTrak system to convert from RWD to AWD, with not the least jolt or vibration. This «invisible», no-seam system will appeal to drivers who are purchasing their first 4X4.

+ **CABIN SPACE.** It looks great and trim details are neat and spiffy. The layout is super, since most controls and accessories are within easy reach.

+ **SEATS.** The new 1998 design is more comfy. Seats are nicely shaped, so they offer lots of lateral and lumbar support. The driver is comfy in a flash. The rear seatbench is less flat and more cushy.

+ **REAR HATCH.** You have cargo hold access by lifting the rear hatch fitted with a vertically hinged window, a much handier design than a rear window with independent swinging door.

+ **STORAGE COMPARTMENTS.** Big door side-pockets both front and rear make up for the stingy-size glove compartment.

CONS

- **FUEL CONSUMPTION.** The greedy V6 and heavy vehicle weight (4,045 lb.) penalize fuel efficiency, especially when the Bravada is roaming on rough turf or pulling a heavy load.

- **STRUCTURAL RIGIDITY.** The body squeaks and groans on rough terrain, a sign that maybe it could be beefed up even more.

- **QUALITY.** The overall design is quite attractive, yet some details indicate that the finish job could be better executed, for some assembly tolerances are irregular and some components aren't aligned properly inside the cabin and the plastic trim isn't too ritzy-looking.

- **CABIN SPACE.** The Bravada has a bulky build, so you'd expect the cabin to be airy and spacious. But only four adults will really be comfy inside, and a fifth passenger could cause cramped conditions on long trips.

- **NOISE LEVEL.** The engine, transmission and axle noise are telltale signs that soundproofing isn't up to par.

- **ACCESS.** Rear seat access is obstructed by the narrow doors and high threshold. Built-in running boards would be a real bonus and door handles should be better located.

- **TO BE IMPROVED UPON:** The ridiculously complicated shifter to the left of the steering wheel that controls turn signal lights and heaps of other functions, and why doesn't a luxury vehicle such as this not come equipped with rear seat headrests?

CONCLUSION

The Bravada doesn't quite fit in with the Oldsmobile lineup; on the other hand, the Envoy, its clone, blends in perfectly with the GMC model range. This is probably a significant factor when it comes to sales. Oldsmobile has never succeeded in getting more than 6% of Blazer sales and only 3.7% of Explorer sales!

RATING
OLDSMOBILE Bravada

CONCEPT :		73%
Technology	75	
Safety :	75	
Interior space :	65	
Trunk volume:	75	
Quality/fit/finish :	75	

DRIVING:		57%
Cockpit :	75	
Performance :	55	
Handling :	45	
Steering :	70	
Braking :	40	

ORIGINAL EQUIPMENT:		74%
Tires :	80	
Headlights :	80	
Wipers :	70	
Rear defroster :	60	
Radio :	80	

COMFORT :		67%
Seats :	75	
Suspension :	70	
Sound level :	50	
Conveniences :	60	
Air conditioning :	80	

BUDGET :		52%
Price :	45	
Fuel economy :	40	
Insurance :	50	
Satisfaction :	75	
Depreciation :	50	

Overall rating: 64.6%

NEW FOR 1999
- Steering wheel equipped with a mini-module airbag.
- Power driver's seat adjustments with memory.
- External electrochromic mirrors.
- Warning light for open rear hatch.
- Bose sound system.
- 6-CD changer and theft-deterrent system.
- Radio controls on the steering wheel.

ENGINES

Model/ version	Type / timing valve / fuel system	Displacement cu in	Power bhp @ rpm	Torque lb-ft @ rpm
4x4	V6 4.3 OHV-12-SFI	262	190 @ 4400	250 @ 2800

TRANSMISSIONS

Compres. ratio	Driving wheels / transmission	Final ratio
9.2 :1	rear/four-A4	3.70

PERFORMANCES

Acceler. 0-60 mph s	Standing 1/4 & 5/8 mile s	Acceler. 50-75 mph s	Braking 60-0 mph f	Top speed mph	Lateral acceler. G	Noise level dBA	Fuel economy mpg City	Highway	Fuel type Octane
10.7	17.8 30.6	7.7	154	112	0.72	69	15	19	R 87

PRICE & EQUIPMENT

OLDSMOBILE	Bravada
Retail price $:	30,715
Dealer invoice $:	27,797
Shipping & handling $:	515
Automatic transmission:	S
Cruise control:	S
Power steering:	S
Anti-lock brakes:	S
Traction control:	-
Air conditioning:	SA
Leather:	S
AM/FM/radio-cassette:	SCD
Power door locks:	S
Power windows:	S
Tilt steering:	S
Dual adjustable mirrors:	S
Alloy wheels:	S
Anti-theft system:	S

Colors
Exterior: White, Black Blue, Green, Red, Copper, Beige, Silver.
Interior: Gray, Marine, Graphite, Beige.

AT A GLANCE...

Category:	AWD sport-utility		Class :	utility

HISTORIC

Introduced in:	1991-1996
Made in:	Moraine, OH, É-U.

DEMOGRAPHICS

Model	Men./Wom.	Age	Married	College	Income
Bravada	75/25 %	56	80 %	35 %	$ 60 000

INDEX

Safety:	75 %	Satisfaction:	75 %
Depreciation:	50 %	Insurance:	NA
Cost per mile:	$ 0.45	Number of dealers:	3 100

SALES

Model	1996	1997	Result
Bravada	15 471	28 481	+ 84.1 %

MAIN COMPETITORS
CHEVROLET-GMC Blazer-Jimmy, FORD Explorer, ISUZU Rodeo & Trooper, JEEP Cherokee & Grand Cherokee, LEXUS RX 300, MERCEDES-BENZ M-Class, NISSAN Pathfinder, TOYOTA 4Runner.

MAINTENANCE REQUIRED BY WARRANTY

First revision:	Frequency:	Diagnostic plug:
3 000 miles	6 months/6 000 miles	Yes

SPECIFICATIONS

Model	Version Trim	Traction	Body/ Seats	Wheel base in	Lght x Wdgth x Hght in x in x in	Curb weight lb	Susp. ft/rr	Brake ft/rr	Steering type	Turning diameter ft	Steer. turns nber.	Fuel tank gal	tire size	Standard tires make	model	Standard powertrain
OLDSMOBILE Bravada base		4x4	t.t. 5 p.5	107.0	183.7x67.8x63.2	4050	it/rl	dc/ABS	pwr.ball.	39.5	2.97	18.6	235/70R15	Uniroyal		V6/4.3/A4

General warranty: 3 years / 36 000 miles; antipollution: 5 years / 50 000 miles; perforation corrosion: 6 years / 100 000 miles. Roadside assistance.

The Intrigue is a brisk seller, as is the case for the Oldsmobile brand itself. So much so that the carmaker now exhibits its name on the Intrigue's exterior! This car's mission is to blot out all memories of the Cutlass Supreme and its unimaginative design, for it's more like the popular Japanese midsize models. Of course, it does share the Buick Century-Regal and Pontiac Grand Prix platform, but it offers a more refined silhouette generally inspired by the Aurora.

MODEL RANGE

The Oldsmobile Intrigue is a 4-door sedan that's available in three trim levels: GX, the base model, equipped with disc brakes, ABS, climate control and alloy rims; the GL, the mid-range model that has added driver's bucket seat that's power-adjustable, 60/40 split-folding rear seatbench, fog lamps and heated exterior mirrors; and finally, the GLS, that has leather seat coverings, a passenger's bucket seat that's power -adjustable, faux-bois trim, sound system including tape deck and CD player and an electrochromic interior rearview mirror. This year, all three versions can be equipped with the «Autobahn» options package that includes H-rated tires and higher performance brakes (12-inch discs up front and a different power braking system).

TECHNICAL FEATURES

Two different engines will be available for part of the year. The GX and GL will be equipped with the 3.8L 3800 Series V6, whereas the GLX will be animated by the new 3.5L DOHC V6. But the latter will replace the 3800 Series V6 during the course of the year. The Intrigue has a steel body mounted on a monocoque chassis. All panels are galvanized on both sides, except the roof. With a drag coefficient of 0.32, aerodynamics are in the average range. The four-wheel independent suspension consists of MacPherson struts up front and a three-link setup at the rear. There are coil springs and an anti-roll bar at each extremity. Disc brakes, an antilock braking system and traction control are standard features, as is the latest Magnasteer II that's a progressive, variable assist system.

PROS

+ **STYLE.** Inspired as well by the Aurora, the Intrigue is elegant and its distinctive looks attract

A Nice Formula...

passersby, especially when clad in dark shades that really add class. This simple design will look lovely for many a moon.

+ **EQUIPMENT.** Compared to the Cutlass Supreme, the Intrigue offers a lush interior and scads of luxury items. Not at all like traditional American cars sold at tempting prices, but really low on the totem pole when it came to equipment, unless, of course you added on lots of options... which had a way of becoming awfully expensive!

+ **PERFORMANCES.** The new 3.5L DOHC V6 bestows on the Intrigue a trait that was really lacking: an engine worthy of its chassis and sophisticated suspensions. With 215 hp, accelerations and pickup are akin to those of the Regal supercharged model. The newcomer lets

you really let loose at the wheel, without adversely affecting fuel economy, since fuel consumption sat at around 19 mpg during our road test.

+ **RIDE COMFORT.** On the highway the Intrigue behaves like an import. The suspension is perfectly adjusted and disguises road faults like magic. And the thickly upholstered seats provide lots of support, which adds to travel pleasure.

+ **HANDLING.** The Intrigue takes curves with superb assurance, thanks to the effective suspension and tires that have excellent grip on wet or dry surfaces.

+ **QUALITY.** With this vehicle, Oldsmobile is exhibiting a very high level of craftsmanship. Assembly and fit and finish are superb. Every-

thing is uniform and fits perfectly together, with not the slightest gap or such. The same goes for the equipment on this car that's above average when it comes to caliber (tires, headlamps, wipers, etc.)

+ **NICE FEATURES:** We really liked the two neat levers on the steering column that control headlamps, turn signal lights and wipers, as well as the great visibility all-round, due partly to the generous-size exterior mirrors.

CONS

- **TRANSMISSION.** The shifter has gears set too far apart; and you have to know how to adjust the accelerator pedal pressure in just the «right» way to shift into overdrive or to downshift at the right moment. And there isn't much braking effect in 3rd gear.

- **PERFORMANCES.** The 3800 Series V6 achieves average accelerations and pickup, when compared to the Intrigue's rivals, but they're quite acceptable. You often get the impression you're driving faster than you really are. The new DOHC V6 should add a bit of pizzazz!

- **STEERING.** It's precise and very direct, with only 2.5 turns lock-to-lock. Yet the Magnasteer system is crippled by over-assistance, so it gets light and sensitive in strong winds or when driving over poor pavement.

- **MATERIALS.** Some of the plastic used inside the cabin affects the look of other items (especially the leather trim) , because of its lackluster shade (gray) and shiny texture.

- **COCKPIT SETUP.** The center console is too low, more so than on the Buick Century-Regal and Pontiac Grand Prix. And the shifter is smack in front of the climate control dials.

- **NOISE.** It's strange that such a sleek bod generates so much wind noise, unless its stay in the wind tunnel was a bit too short for its own good...

CONCLUSION

The Oldsmobile Intrigue demonstrates, as did the Buick Regal and Chevrolet Malibu, that General Motors is once again able to build current-standard vehicles able to compete with Japanese products. ☺

RATING
OLDSMOBILE Intrigue

CONCEPT : 78%
Technology	80
Safety :	80
Interior space :	75
Trunk volume:	75
Quality/fit/finish :	80

DRIVING: 64%
Cockpit :	80
Performance :	60
Handling :	60
Steering :	75
Braking :	45

ORIGINAL EQUIPMENT: 84%
Tires :	85
Headlights :	85
Wipers :	85
Rear defroster :	80
Radio :	85

COMFORT : 73%
Seats :	80
Suspension :	75
Sound level :	60
Conveniences :	70
Air conditioning :	80

BUDGET : 62%
Price :	40
Fuel economy :	65
Insurance :	60
Satisfaction :	75
Depreciation :	70

Overall rating: 72.2%

NEW FOR 1999
- Standard 3.5L DOHC V6 for the GLS, optional for the GX and GL, it will eventually replace the 3.8L 3800 Series V6.
- Traction control and Magnasteer system with the 3.5L V6.
- New name «GX» for the base model.
- «Autobahn» options package now available for all 3 versions.
- Reworked automatic transmission.
- Radio antenna built into the rear window.

ENGINES / TRANSMISSIONS / PERFORMANCES

Model/version	Type / timing valve / fuel system	Displacement cu in	Power bhp @ rpm	Torque lb-ft @ rpm	Compres. ratio	Driving wheels / transmission	Final ratio	Acceler. 0-60 mph s	Standing 1/4 & 5/8 mile s	Acceler. 50-75 mph s	Braking 60-0 mph f	Top speed mph	Lateral acceler. G	Noise level dBA	Fuel economy City	Highway	Fuel type Octane
Intrigue	V6* 3.8 OHV-12-SFI	231	195 @ 5200	220 @ 4000	9.4 :1	front - A4*	3.05	9.0	16.5	30.0	6.3	154	115	0.80	67	18	30	R 87
GLS	V6* 3.5 DOHC-24-SFI	212	215 @ 5600	230 @ 4400	9.3 :1	front - A4*	3.29	NA								18	29	R 87

PRICE & EQUIPMENT

OLDSMOBILE Intrigue	GX	GL	GLS
Retail price $:	20,890	22,290	24,110
Dealer invoice $:	19,114	20,395	22,061
Shipping & handling $:	550	550	550
Automatic transmission:	S	S	S
Cruise control:	S	S	S
Power steering:	S	S	S
Anti-lock brakes:	S	S	S
Traction control:	S	S	S
Air conditioning:	SM	SA	SA
Leather:	-	O	S
AM/FM/radio-cassette:	S	S	SCD
Power door locks:	O	S	S
Power windows:	S	S	S
Tilt steering:	S	S	S
Dual adjustable mirrors:	S	S	S
Alloy wheels:	S	S	S
Anti-theft system:	S	S	S

Colors
Exterior: White, Silver, Blue, Green, Black, Gray, Red, Gold, Plum.
Interior: Cloth : Gray, Beige. Leather : Gray, Beige, Oak.

AT A GLANCE...
Category: front-wheel drive mid-size sedans. **Class :** 5
HISTORIC
Introduced in: 1998
Made in: Fairfax, Kansas, USA.
DEMOGRAPHICS
Model	Men./Wom.	Age	Married	College	Income
Intrigue	75/25%	56	76%	26%	$ 38 000

INDEX
Safety:	80 %	Satisfaction:	78 %
Depreciation:	28 %	Insurance:	$ 800
Cost per mile:	$ 0.45	Number of dealers:	3 100

SALES
Model	1996	1997	Result
Intrigue	-	23 460	-	-

MAIN COMPETITORS
BUICK Century-Regal, CHEVROLET Lumina, CHRYSLER Concorde-Intrepid, FORD Taurus, HONDA Accord V6, HYUNDAI Sonata V6, MAZDA 626 V6, MERCURY Sable, NISSAN Maxima, PONTIAC Grand Prix, TOYOTA Camry, VW Passat.

MAINTENANCE REQUIRED BY WARRANTY
First revision:	Frequency:	Diagnostic plug:
000 miles	6 000 miles	Yes

SPECIFICATIONS

Model	Version Trim	Body/Seats	Interior volume cu ft	Trunk volume cu ft	Cd	Wheel base in	Lght x Wdgth x Hght in x in x in	Curb weight lb	Susp. ft/rr	Brake ft/rr	Steering type	Turning diameter ft	Steer. turns nber.	Fuel tank gal	tire size	Standard tires make	model	Standard powertrain
OLDSMOBILE	General warranty: 3 years / 36 000 miles; antipollution: 5 years / 50 000 miles; perforation corrosion: 6 years / 100 000 miles. Roadside assistance.																	
Intrigue	GX	4dr.sdn. 5	102.2	16.3	0.32	109.0	195.9x73.6x56.6	3428	ih/ih	dc/ABS	pwr.r&p.	36.6	2.50	18.0	225/60SR16	Goodyear	Eagle LS	V6/3.8/A4
Intrigue	GL	4dr.sdn. 5	102.2	16.3	0.32	109.0	195.9x73.6x56.6	3455	ih/ih	dc/ABS	pwr.r&p.	36.6	2.50	18.0	225/60SR16	Goodyear	Eagle LS	V6/3.8/A4
Intrigue	GLS	4dr.sdn. 5	102.2	16.3	-	109.0	195.9x73.6x56.6	-	ih/ih	dc/ABS	pwr.r&p.	36.6	2.50	18.0	225/60SR16	Goodyear	Eagle LS	V6/3.5/A4

Originally the Silhouette was designed for the American market where it would enter the fray against the Chrysler Town & Country. It's more richly endowed than GM minivans, at least not until Cadillac comes up with a model called Escapade, perhaps? This vehicle was around before the current tendency to doll up SUV's with frills so as to grab sales from prestigious luxury cars. It still comes with the on-board entertainment center that keeps young and old occupied throughout the trip.

MODEL RANGE

The Silhouette is similar to the Venture and Trans Sport, except for a few cosmetic touches and equipment items. It's sold in regular length (GS) or extended (GL and GLS), all equipped with a standard second sliding door on the driver's side. Original equipment includes automatic gearbox, manual air conditioning, power steering and antilock braking system. Among the options we noted traction control and a living room ensemble including a tape recorder and several monitors.

TECHNICAL FEATURES

The Silhouette has a steel unibody with panels that are galvanized on both sides, except for the roof. It also integrates an H-frame for maximum structural robustness. The front suspension is independent and based on the MacPherson strut design and it's mounted, along with the power train, on an independent cradle affixed to the body via rubber insulating components. At the rear, the semi-independent suspension is made up of a torsion axle suspended on coil springs. The vehicle is equipped with disc brakes up front and drum brakes at the rear, controlled by a four-wheel ABS system and benefits from power rack-and-pinion steering. The only engine available isn't new, it's the 3.4L V6 that animates other vehicles built by GM. It develops 180 hp and 205 lb.ft. torque, so it's currently the gutsiest original engine in this market segment. It's associated with an electronically controlled four-speed automatic transmission. On the practical side, there's a remote power door-opener for the passenger-side sliding door.

PROS

+ MODULARITY. The rear end can

Right At Home...

be organized according to three different configurations, thanks to the individual seats inherited from previous models, or the full or split-folding seatbenches. The vehicle has a 7-passenger capacity for starters, but some versions include three seats in the middle, so 8 passengers can be accomodated. Each seat weighs 37 lb., so they're easy to manipulate.

+ RIDE COMFORT. It's great on the highway with the velvety suspension, nicely shaped and cushy front seats and effective soundproofing, since the loudest noise you hear are the tires when driving over road faults.

+ 3.4L ENGINE. It's quite energetic, since the Silhouette has enough acceleration and pickup

power to provide safe passing on the highway, at least with half a load, for above that, a 3.8L engine would be more suitable and fuel consumption wouldn't be that much higher.

+ TRANSMISSION. It's super-effective since the shifter is smooth as silk and you can slow down nicely by downshifting in 3rd or 2nd gear.

+ HANDLING. It's competent is most situations, thanks to good vehicle balance so you can take even tight curves with assurance.

+ NICE FEATURES: the power door opener for the passenger-side sliding door (optional), the standard sliding door on the driver's side, useful storage spots, rear bumper serving as a running board, effective wipers that quickly clear most of the windshield.

- SEATS. They're awfully low-slung, due to the low ceiling clearance and you simply can't get comfy in them. Besides, rear seats are flat and hard on the backside and the headrests are almost useless.

- ENGINEERING. It's deficient since lots of details look poorly done. Wires and ducts were hanging loosely under the test vehicles, because the fixtures had given out, and the electrical wiring located in the engine compartment was in the same sad state. Wipers and climate control air vents located at the base of the windshield under the hood are forever icing up in the winter, so they don't work as they should. The body on the extended model lacks rigidity and squeaks and groans quite a bit on poor roads.

- QUALITY. It's rather poor when it comes to construction and finish details, since lots of squeaks and such are heard even at low mileage and some plastic components don't look too nice.

- BRAKES. They're rather iffy since stops are long as heck to achieve and pedal pressure is hard to adjust as needed.

- SHIFTER. The one and only shifter that controls turn signal lights, wipers, washers, cruise control and dimming of headlights can be a real conundrum.

- SUSPENSION. It's rather rustic, so it bounces on poor road surfaces and the front axle bottoms out in no time, due to poor suspension travel and the overloaded front end.

- ACCESS. It's tricky when it comes to mechanical repairs since the engine is just as inconveniently located as before, namely under the windshield and dashboard.

- CABIN DESIGN. It's blah and lackluster and those cheap-looking plastic components sure don't help.

CONCLUSION

The Silhouette has prim, sprightly looks, but it doesn't have the same attributes as the Town & Country. It doesn't have the same posh ambience inside the cabin, all-wheel drive, nowhere near its smooth ride comfort and quiet atmosphere typical of this Chrysler product. Too bad these GM minivans didn't benefit from upgrading that's presently in progress in the rest of the industry... ☺

RATING
OLDSMOBILE Silhouette

CONCEPT :   71%
Technology	75
Safety :	60
Interior space :	80
Trunk volume:	70
Quality/fit/finish :	70

DRIVING: 52%
Cockpit :	75
Performance :	35
Handling :	45
Steering :	70
Braking :	35

ORIGINAL EQUIPMENT: 81%
Tires :	70
Headlights :	80
Wipers :	90
Rear defroster :	85
Radio :	80

COMFORT :   70%
Seats :	70
Suspension :	75
Sound level :	50
Conveniences :	75
Air conditioning :	80

BUDGET :   66%
Price :	50
Fuel economy :	65
Insurance :	70
Satisfaction :	80
Depreciation :	65

Overall rating: 68.0%

NEW FOR 1999

- Standard heated exterior mirrors and theft-deterrent system.
- Video Edition package offered as an option.
- Optional «Gold» decoration.
- Four new exterior shades.
- OnStar stystem sold as an extra.

ENGINES / TRANSMISSIONS / PERFORMANCES

Model/ version	Type / timing valve / fuel system	Displacement cu in	Power bhp @ rpm	Torque lb-ft @ rpm	Compres. ratio	Driving wheels / transmission	Final ratio	Acceler. 0-60 mph s	Standing 1/4 & 5/8 mile s	Acceler. 50-75 mph s	Braking 60-0 mph f	Top speed mph	Lateral acceler. G	Noise level dBA	Fuel economy mpg City	Highway	Fuel type Octane
regular	V6* 3.4 OHV-12-SFI	204	185 @ 5200	210 @ 4000	9.5 :1	front-A4	3.29	11.0	17.7 32.2	8.6	148	106	0.72	67	18	24	R 87
long	V6* 3.4 OHV-12-SFI	204	185 @ 5200	210 @ 4000	9.5 :1	front-A4	3.29	11.7	18.0 33.0	9.2	174	103	0.71	68	18	24	R 87

PRICE & EQUIPMENT

OLDSMOBILE Silhouette	GL long	GS SWB	GLS long
Retail price $:	24,065	24,430	27,320
Dealer invoice $:	21,779	22,109	24,725
Shipping & handling $:	570	570	570
Automatic transmission:	S	S	S
Cruise control:	S	S	S
Power steering:	S	S	S
Anti-lock brakes:	S	S	S
Traction control:	O	O	S
Air conditioning:	SM	SM	SM
Leather:	O	O	S
AM/FM/radio-cassette:	S	S	S
Power door locks:	S	S	S
Power windows:	S	S	S
Tilt steering:	S	S	S
Dual adjustable mirrors:	SEH	SEH	SEH
Alloy wheels:	O	O	S
Anti-theft system:	S	S	S

Colors

Exterior: Brown, White, Green, Red, Malachite, Silver, Sand, Granite.

Interior: Gray, Beige, Brown.

AT A GLANCE...

Category:	front-wheel drive minivans.
Class :	utility

HISTORIC
Introduced in:	1997
Made in:	Doraville, Georgia, USA.

DEMOGRAPHICS
Model	Men./Wom.	Age	Married	College	Income
Silhouette	76%/24%	45	88 %	35 %	$ 40 000

INDEX
Safety:	60 %	Satisfaction:	85 %
Depreciation:	35 %	Insurance:	$ 835
Cost per mile:	$ 0.51	Number of dealers:	3 100

SALES
Model	1996	1997	Result
Silhouette	9 330	24 615	+163.8 %

MAIN COMPETITORS
CHEVROLET Venture, CHRYSLER Town & Country, DODGE Caravan, Gd Caravan, FORD Windstar, HONDA Odyssey, MAZDA MPV, MERCURY Villager, NISSAN Quest, PONTIAC Montana, PLYMOUTH Voyager, Gd Voyager, TOYOTA Sienna, VW EuroVan.

MAINTENANCE REQUIRED BY WARRANTY
First revision:	Frequency:	Diagnostic plug:
3 000 miles	6 months/6 000 miles	Yes

SPECIFICATIONS

Model Version Trim	Body/ Seats	Interior volume cu ft	Trunk volume cu ft	Cd	Wheel base in	Lght x Wdgth x Hght in x in x in	Curb weight lb	Susp. ft/rr	Brake ft/rr	Steering type	Turning diameter ft	Steer. turns nber.	Fuel tank gal	tire size	Standard tires make	model	Standard powertrain
OLDSMOBILE	General warranty: 3 years / 36 000 miles; antipollution: 5 years / 50 000 miles; perforation corrosion: 6 years / 100 000 miles. Roadside assistance.																
Silhouette SWB GL	4dr.wgn.7/8	-	133	0.35	112.0	187.4x72.2x67.4	3746	ih/rh	dc/dr/ABS	pwr.r&p.	37.4	3.05	20.0	205/70R15	BFGoodrich	Touring	V6/3.4/A4
Silhouette extended GLS	4dr.wgn.7/8	-	156	0.35	120.0	201.4x72.2x68.1	3942	ih/rh	dc/dr/ABS	pwr.r&p.	39.7	3.05	25.0	215/70R15	BFGoodrich	Touring	V6/3.4/A4

The Oldsmobile 88 sedan looks a bit dusty beside modern cars like the Alero, Intrigue and Aurora. It's based on the old H platform that the Buick LeSabre and Pontiac Bonneville share. In spite of a «face-lift» undergone three years ago, it can't hide its wrinkles, since after all, this body design was first introduced in 1992. So the 88 is a relic from the past, the ghost of former stylistics and technological trends, that are diametrically opposed to those that constitute the basis of modern Oldsmobile cars. Nevertheless, it valiantly pursues its career, appealing to a more conservative customer segment.

MODEL RANGE

The 88 is a big four-door sedan that's offered in two versions: LS and LSS. The latter is no longer called «88», by the way. In both cases the 3800 Series II V6 comes as the standard engine. It delivers 205 hp. A supercharged version of this 3.8L engine is offered as an extra on the LSS. This boost helps it achieve 240 hp. We classify these cars as true luxury cars because their equipment is as creamy as it gets.

TECHNICAL FEATURES

The 88 shares the H platform, so it has components, some body stylistics and attributes of the LeSabre and Bonneville. The 88 has a steel body mounted on a monoframe. Body panels (except the roof) and fenders are galvanized on both sides. The last reworking of this model yielded a more impact-resistant cabin in the event of a collision, especially in regard to side-impact mishaps. Yet the cosmetic modifications made in 1996, even though the car has a neat, sleek look, have not blessed this car with particularly efficient aerodynamics.

The car is equipped with a four-wheel independent suspension. Up front, it's inspired by the MacPherson strut principle and Chapman struts at the rear. Both suspensions also benefit from coil springs and stabilizer bars. There's a disc and drum duo that takes care of braking and antilock braking is a standard feature. It's a pity the LSS isn't equipped

Keeping Traditions...

with rear-wheel disc brakes and that traction control is still only sold as an extra...

PROS

+ CABIN SPACE. Thanks to its spacious interior that can seat up to six passengers, and its roomy trunk, this front-wheel sedan has replaced the Caprice and Roadmaster for some drivers, even if exterior car dimensions are much more imposing.

+ ESTHETICS. The clean, classic body design exudes quiet elegance.

+ ENGINE. The 3800 Series II V6 puts out good performances. Accelerations and pickup are astounding and you can pass on the highway with assurance, thanks to the smooth transmission with nicely spaced gears, that's willing and able and doesn't jolt in the slightest.

+ RIDE COMFORT. The supple suspension and effective cabin soundproofing, at cruising speed, add to ride comfort. The LSS version has a firmer suspension, that keeps the vehicle right on keel.

+ FUEL EFFICIENCY. The 88 yields good mileage per gallon, given the large engine displacement and what this engine is capable of.

+ INSTRUMENT PANEL. The 88 has a very extensive and impressive array of standard equipment items. Yet the wipers could be more efficient at handling heavy rain.

+ TRACTION CONTROL. It has a pretty down-home basic design, yet it provides more reassuring and safer driving in winter conditions and it's too bad this feature is optional, both for the LS and the LSS.

CONS

- HANDLING. On poor pavement, the 88 LS suspension generates a lot of swish and sway. The suspension is too flexible and wheel travel isn't too generous, so handling and travel comfort are affected.

- VISIBILITY. High body belt, really wide roof supports, stingy-size exterior mirrors and low seating, well, this all amounts to pretty obstructed visibility.

- SUSPENSION. The one that equips the LSS is stiff as it gets and faithfully sends every single road fault to the wheels.

- QUALITY. It isn't terrific. Here's the list: poor finish job, imprecise component fit and some rather poor-quality items like the imitation wood and plastic stuff on the dashboard.

-TO BE IMPROVED UPON: Storage areas are scarce and the ones you get are impractical and poorly located. The speed shifter located on the floor is awful. Last of all, some controls should get a design workover, such as the multiple shifter to the left of the steering wheel that controls lights, wipers and cruise control that's just too darned complicated to use.

CONCLUSION

You can understand why some people like this car: it's a classic, discreet model that you can really depend on, that isn't expensive to operate and that's furbished with many amenities. This big classic sedan represents a traditional purchase for some social strata ☺

RATING
OLDSMOBILE 88

CONCEPT : **80%**
Technology	80
Safety :	80
Interior space :	80
Trunk volume:	80
Quality/fit/finish :	80

DRIVING: **66%**
Cockpit :	80
Performance :	65
Handling :	55
Steering :	75
Braking :	55

ORIGINAL EQUIPMENT: **75%**
Tires :	75
Headlights :	80
Wipers :	60
Rear defroster :	80
Radio :	80

COMFORT : **71%**
Seats :	75
Suspension :	70
Sound level:	70
Conveniences :	60
Air conditioning :	80

BUDGET : **56%**
Price :	35
Fuel economy :	60
Insurance :	50
Satisfaction :	80
Depreciation :	55

Overall rating: **69.6%**

NEW FOR 1999

- Two exterior shades.
- 16-inch white wall tires offered on the 88 LS.
- Standard sound system on the LSS that now includes a tape deck and CD player.
- 50th anniversary edition.

ENGINES / TRANSMISSIONS / PERFORMANCES

Model/ version	Type / timing valve / fuel system	Displacement cu in	Power bhp @ rpm	Torque lb-ft @ rpm	Compres. ratio	Driving wheels / transmission	Final ratio	Acceler. 0-60 mph s	Standing 1/4 & 5/8 mile s	Acceler. 50-75 mph s	Braking 60-0 mph f	Top speed mph	Lateral acceler. G	Noise level dBA	Fuel economy mpg City	Highway	Fuel type Octane
1)	V6* 3.8 OHV-12-SFI	231	205 @ 5200	230 @ 4000	9.4 :1	front - A4	3.05	8.6	16.3	29.8	6.1	144	115	0.78	66	18	30	R 87
2)	V6C 3.8 OHV-12-SFI	231	240 @ 5200	280 @ 3600	8.5 :1	front - A4	2.93	7.7	15.7	28.4	5.2	138	124	0.80	66	17	27	S 92

1) Base 88, LS, LSS.   2) Option LSS.

PRICE & EQUIPMENT

OLDSMOBILE 88	Base	LS	LSS
Retail price $:	22,795	24,195	28,095
Dealer invoice $:	20,587	22,138	25,706
Shipping & handling $:	605	605	605
Automatic transmission:	S	S	S
Cruise control:	S	S	S
Power steering:	S	S	S
Anti-lock brakes:	S	S	S
Traction control:	S	S	S
Air conditioning:	SM	SA	SA
Leather:	O	S	S
AM/FM/radio-cassette:	S	S	SCD
Power door locks:	S	S	S
Power windows:	S	S	S
Tilt steering:	S	S	S
Dual adjustable mirrors:	SM	SE	SE
Alloy wheels:	S	S	S
Anti-theft system:	S	S	S

Colors
Exterior: Gray, Beige, Green, Blue, Bordeaux, Black, White, Silver, Lime, Champagne.
Interior: Taupe, Bordeaux, Blue, Gray.

AT A GLANCE...

Category: front-wheel drive full-size sedans.   **Class :** 6

HISTORIC
Introduced in: 1996
Made in: Lake Orion, Michigan, USA.

DEMOGRAPHICS
Model	Men./Wom.	Age	Married	College	Income
88	82/18 %	66	82 %	36 %	$ 40 000

INDEX
Safety:	80 %	Satisfaction:	78 %
Depreciation:	48 %	Insurance:	$975
Cost per mile:	$ 0.58	Number of dealers:	3 100

SALES
Model	1996	1997	Result
88	58 525	67 190	+14.8 %

MAIN COMPETITORS
BUICK LeSabre, CHRYSLER Concorde, Intrepid, LHS, FORD Crown Victoria, MERCURY Grand Marquis, NISSAN Maxima, PONTIAC Bonneville, TOYOTA Avalon.

MAINTENANCE REQUIRED BY WARRANTY
First revision:	Frequency:	Diagnostic plug:
3 000 miles	6 months/6 000 miles	Yes

SPECIFICATIONS

Model	Version Trim	Body/ Seats	Interior volume cu ft	Trunk volume cu ft	Cd	Wheel base in	Lght x Wdgth x Hght in x in x in	Curb weight lb	Susp. ft/rr	Brake ft/rr	Steering type	Turning diameter ft	Steer. turns nber.	Fuel tank gal	tire size	Standard tires make	model	Standard powertrain
OLDSMOBILE	General warranty: 3 years / 36 000 miles; antipollution: 5 years / 50 000 miles; perforation corrosion: 6 years / 100 000 miles. Roadside assistance.																	
88	Base	4dr.sdn.5/6	106.2	18.0	0.31	110.8	200.4x74.1x55.7	3455	ih/ih	dc/dr/ABS	pwr.r&p.	40.7	2.97	18.0	205/70R15	-	-	V6/3.8/A4
88	LS	4dr.sdn.5/6	106.2	18.0	0.31	110.8	200.4x74.1x55.7	3459	ih/ih	dc/dr/ABS	pwr.r&p.	40.7	2.97	18.0	215/65R15	-	-	V6/3.8/A4
88	LSS	4dr.sdn.5	106.2	18.0	0.31	110.8	200.4x74.1x55.7	3547	ih/ih	dc/dr/ABS	pwr.r&p.	40.7	2.97	18.0	225/60R16	Goodyear	Eagle RS-A	V6/3.8/A4

At Pontiac, the Bonneville is a top-of-the-line model seasoned with a pinch of performance. After all, it's the usual approach for this brand. Besides, who could ever imagine that the Bonneville shares the same platform as the Buick LeSabre and Oldsmobile 88? And of the bunch, isn't it the car that has the most personality and pizzazz? It's an integral part of American legend, even if today its prestige isn't what it was in the sixties.

MODEL RANGE

The Bonneville is a 4-door sedan that's sold in two versions: SE and SSE. Two other names, the SLE and SSEi identify sets of options: the first, strictly stylistic, is offered for the SE, whereas the second that's available for the SSE adds performance-oriented accessories. The original engine is the 3.8L 3800 V6 that develops 205 hp. A supercharged version developing 240 hp equips the SSEi. Equipment on each version varies with its status on the totem pole.

TECHNICAL FEATURES

The Bonneville body structure is made of steel that's galvanized on both sides (except the roof panel). It's monocoque and shares some mechanical features with the Buick LeSabre and Oldsmobile 88 models, as well as some exterior touches and window design details. The super sleek silhouette is deceiving, since the drag coefficient is only very fair to midling. The fully independent suspension consists of MacPherson struts up front and Chapman struts at the rear, supported by coil springs and an anti-roll bar at each extremity. All versions have front disc brakes and rear drum brakes, linked to a Bosch antilock braking system. The car is equipped with Magnasteer, just like the Aurora. Lastly, besides the cosmetic touches and supercharged engine, the SSEi also benefits from an axle ratio of 2.93.

PROS

+ SILHOUETTE. The Bonneville still catches people's attention. With its muscular traits and pointed «nose» up front, it's hard to miss. Either you like it or you don't. The interior design also has a sensational design approach, including, among other items, a steering wheel loaded with switches.

+ PERFORMANCES. Beneath the

An Athlete Heart..

hood, the venerable 3800 V6 demonstrates that it's still able to do its stuff. Accelerations and pickup on the conventional gas engine are actually very close to those of the supercharged version!

+ CABIN SPACE. The cabin and trunk are roomy enough to accomodate five passengers and all their luggage.

+ RIDE COMFORT. The SE is a really comfy car, thanks to the velvety suspension and well-insulated mechanical components. The suspension on the SSE and SSEi is a bit stiffer and the exhaust noise on these models is less tame, but it's not overly unpleasant. An adjustable suspension is listed among the options for both models.

+ ENGINE. The V6 atmospheric engine is quite efficient, given its displacement and pretty zippy performances, for at normal speeds, it remains pretty fuel-frugal.

+ TRACTION CONTROL. This system is rather simplistic in design, but it helps keep the car steady on slippery surfaces, in regions where there's heavy snowfall.

+ CONTROLS. The steering wheel on the luxury versions is loaded with lots of handy controls, which you do finally figure out how to use.

+ EQUIPMENT. The Bonneville is richly equipped when it comes to original items, especially the SE that's the best buy of the lot. The Head-Up display system that indicates vehicle speed on the windshield is one of the best on the current market.

-HANDLING. The Bonneville SE exhibits really vague road behavior, generated by the soft suspension. This makes for a lot of wide swishing and swaying.

- STEERING. It's over-assisted and doesn't give you any road feel and it's terribly sensitive.

- BRAKES. For a car with a sporty temperament, they could be a heck of a lot more effective. Stops are long and linings don't hold up well to intensive use. Pedal effort is hard to gauge and the pedal stiffens up on emergency stops and ABS doesn't iron out all the wheel lock.

- SEATS. The Bonneville SE doesn't provide seating that's as comfy or elegant as inside the SSE. On the base model, seats are flatter and are thinly upholstered.

- CONTROLS. The steering wheel on the SSE is covered with scads of switches, so the driver has to get a full briefing on how to use them, which isn't always enough to master all the functions!

-STYLE. Some stylistic details on the SSEi exterior are rather overdone and a bit gawdy. It's definitely a car that wants to show off.

- FINISH DETAILS. The fit and finish job inside the cabin isn't flawless: the imitation wood appliqués aren't perfectly aligned and some plastic used on the instrument panel looks pretty cheap.

- TRANSMISSION. The automatic transmission provides very little braking power when downshifting manually. And the shifter mounted on the steering wheel (except on the SSEi) is too short, so it's hard to adjust properly.

- TO BE IMPROVED UPON: The size and location of some storage compartments and the transmission shifter on the floor of the SSEi that's no picnic to use. Finally, some controls are poorly located.

CONCLUSION

In the big family sedan category, the Bonneville SE is a good buy, compared to its Buick and Oldsmobile counterparts. It appeals to people who know how to enjoy life and who aren't afraid to show it. The SSE and its high-performance homologue, the SSEi, combine style, performance and competence in one single package. ☺

RATING
PONTIAC Bonneville

CONCEPT :		78%
Technology	75	
Safety :	75	
Interior space :	85	
Trunk volume:	80	
Quality/fit/finish :	75	

DRIVING:		66%
Cockpit :	75	
Performance :	65	
Handling :	60	
Steering :	75	
Braking :	55	

ORIGINAL EQUIPMENT:		76%
Tires :	75	
Headlights :	80	
Wipers :	65	
Rear defroster :	80	
Radio :	80	

COMFORT :		71%
Seats :	75	
Suspension :	70	
Sound level :	70	
Conveniences :	60	
Air conditioning :	80	

BUDGET :		54%
Price :	35	
Fuel economy :	55	
Insurance :	50	
Satisfaction :	80	
Depreciation :	45	

Overall rating:	68.8%

NEW FOR 1999

- OnStar system available as an extra.
- Three new exterior shades.

ENGINES / TRANSMISSIONS / PERFORMANCES

Model/ version	Type / timing valve / fuel system	Displacement cu in	Power bhp @ rpm	Torque lb-ft @ rpm	Compres. ratio	Driving wheels / transmission	Final ratio	Acceler. 0-60 mph s	Standing 1/4 & 5/8 mile s	Acceler. 50-75 mph s	Braking 60-0 mph f	Top speed mph	Lateral acceler. G	Noise level dBA	Fuel economy mpg City	Highway	Fuel type Octane
1)	V6* 3.8 OHV-12-SFI	231	205 @ 5200	230 @ 4000	9.4 :1	front - A4	2.84	9.6	16.9	30.8	6.8	144	185	0.78	66	18	30	R 87
2)	V6C*3.8 OHV-12-SFI	231	240 @ 5200	280 @ 3200	9.0 :1	front - A4	2.93	8.3	16.2	29.4	6.0	138	200	0.80	66	17	27	S 92

1) base SE & SSE. 2) standard SSEi, option SSE & SLE.

PRICE & EQUIPMENT

PONTIAC Bonneville	SE	SSE
Retail price $:	22,545	29,545
Dealer invoice $:	20,629	27,034
Shipping & handling $:	605	605
Automatic transmission:	S	S
Cruise control:	S	S
Power steering:	S	S
Anti-lock brakes:	O	S
Traction control:	SM	SA
Air conditioning:	O	S
Leather:	S	SCD
AM/FM/radio-cassette:	S	S
Power door locks:	S	S
Power windows:	S	S
Tilt steering:	SM	SEH
Dual adjustable mirrors:	O	S
Alloy wheels:	S	S
Anti-theft system:		

Colors

Exterior: Gray, Beige, Green, Blue, Bordeaux, Black, White, Silver, Lime, Topaz, Emerald.
Interior: Taupe, Bordeaux, Blue, Gray, Tan.

AT A GLANCE...

Category: front-wheel drive full-size sedans. **Class :** 6

HISTORIC
Introduced in: 1992
Made in: Buick City, Flint, Michigan, USA.

DEMOGRAPHICS

Model	Men./Wom.	Age	Married	College	Income
Bonneville	86/14 %	66	86 %	28 %	$ 35 000

INDEX

Safety:	75 %	Satisfaction:	82 %
Depreciation:	52 %	Insurance:	$935-1133
Cost per mile:	$0.58	Number of dealers:	2 953

SALES

Model	1996	1997	Result
Bonneville	73 849	75 882	+2.8 %

MAIN COMPETITORS
BUICK LeSabre, CHRYSLER Concorde, Intrepid et LHS, FORD Crown Victoria, MAZDA Millenia, MERCURY Grand Marquis, NISSAN Maxima, OLDSMOBILE 88, TOYOTA Avalon.

MAINTENANCE REQUIRED BY WARRANTY

First revision:	Frequency:	Diagnostic plug:
3 000 miles	6 000 miles	Yes

SPECIFICATIONS

Model	Version Trim	Body/ Seats	Interior volume cu ft	Trunk volume cu ft	Cd	Wheel base in	Lght x Wdgth x Hght in x in x in	Curb weight lb	Susp. ft/rr	Brake ft/rr	Steering type	Turning diameter ft	Steer. turns nber.	Fuel tank gal	tire size	Standard tires make	model	Standard powertrain
PONTIAC	General warranty: 3 years / 36 000 miles; antipollution: 5 years / 50 000 miles; perforation corrosion: 6 years / 100 000 miles. Roadside assistance.																	
Bonneville	SE	4dr.sdn.6	108.8	18.0	NA	110.8	202.1x74.5x55.7	3446	ih/ih	dc/dr/ABS	pwr.r&p.	40.5	2.79	18.0	215/65R15	-	-	V6/3.8/A4
Bonneville	SSE	4dr.sdn.5	108.8	18.0	NA	110.8	202.1x74.5x55.7	3587	ih/ih	dc/dr/ABS	pwr.r&p.	40.5	2.86	18.0	225/60R16	Goodyear	Eagle RS-A	V6/3.8/A4

The Firebird has taken the path less travelled, directly opposite to current market trends, so much so that today it sits at the very bottom of the sales heap. In an age that's into all-wheel drive sports-utility vehicles, this big sports car is an anachronism, it's impractical and awkward all-round. Besides, it costs big bucks, drinks lots of gas and costs a fortune to insure. Those who love this car are nostalgic sorts who hanker for the days of yore, since today the Firebird sits at the crossroads: do it right or die.

MODEL RANGE
The Firebird is identical to the Camaro, but for a few minor details. It shares the same platform, several body design touches and is equipped with the same engine. The Firebird rear hatch coupe is sold in base, Formula and Trans Am versions and the convertible is offered in base and Trans Am. Base model cars are equipped with a 3.8L 3800 Series II V6, paired up with a 5-speed manual transmission or an optional 4-speed automatic. The Formula and Trans Am coupes as well as the Trans Am convertible are animated by a 5.7L LS1 V8 engine that develops 305 hp, or 320 hp with the optional Ram Air intake system. On these models, the 4-speed automatic shifter is part of the original equipment and the 6-speed manual is sold as an extra.

TECHNICAL FEATURES
The unitized body is made up of polymer panels (front fenders, roof, doors, hatch door and front and rear sections) and galvanized steel (hood and rear side panels). The body is quite aerodynamic, since the drag coefficient is 0.32 for the coupe and 0.36 for the convertible. During its redesign in 1993, the chassis was beefed up by adding numerous reinforcements, including tubes inserted into the hollow sections of the side rocker panels. The front suspension consists of unequal-length transversal control arms and the rear rigid axle is supported by a Salisbury-type multi-link arrangement and Panhard rod. There are also front and rear anti-roll bars of various diameters, depending on the version. Disc brakes benefit from a Bosch antilock braking system. Power rack-and-pinion steering is adjusted to the performance level of the various models;

Muscle Car of A Gone By Era...

the reduction ratio is shorter for the Formula and Trans Am.

PROS
+ LOOKS. The front end body design sports a new look for 1999, so this racecar has an even more spectacular appearance. Even after 30 years, the Firebird still turns heads, especially the Trans Am Ram Air.

+ PERFORMANCES. The LS1 engine, derived from the Corvette's V8, pumps out enough power to literally rip up the road! Enough to compete with the Corvette itself!

+ DRIVING PLEASURE. The brawny, brutish power that the Trans Am puts at your fingertips is definitely a thrill. This car just zooms along, but it also lets out a fine feline roar on accelerations, so the adrenalin count goes off the charts!

+ VALUE. Given the price, equipment and performances that this racecar offers, it's really a great buy for American-style speedster fanatics.

+ ROADHOLDING. Handling is satisfactory on roads that are in good condition. The rigid chassis on the coupes keeps the car on the straight and narrow and controls sway, so you can hit awesome lateral speeds, but lower than those of the Corvette that benefits from a lower center of gravity, tougher tires and a more sophisticated suspension than that of the Trans Am.

+ INSTRUMENT PANEL. Redesigned in 1997, it's ergonomic and looks really neat. Plastic components no longer have a «Rubbermaid» look!

+ CONVERTIBLE. The rooftop folds down by activating an effective mechanism. It has a good lining, glass rear windows and electric defroster.

CONS
- VISIBILITY. The field of vision is obstructed, especially on the convertible. The cockpit is low, the body belt is high, the B pillar is bulky and the instrument panel blocks frontward view. The rear window is tiny and really slanted on the convertible.

- NOSTALGIA. The Firebird belongs to days gone by. It's huge, heavy and is equipped with technical features that are definitely passé.

- V6 ENGINE. The one that equips the base model puts out adequate performances for a quiet Sunday drive, but it doesn't really jive with the mental image of what a sports car is like. Its power to weight ratio isn't as favorable as that of the V8.

- RIDE COMFORT. The Trans Am isn't exactly super comfy. The gutsy engine lets loose whenever you gun it and the suspension bounces the rear end on poor pavement.

- RIGIDITY. The convertibles are clearly less sturdy than the coupes, which generates imprecise moves, something that can get scary at high speeds.

- CABIN DESIGN. These big bod cars don't offer too many amenities, in fact, the bigger the car, the fewer conveniences. Getting aboard is tricky, even with the big doors; rear seats are pretty useless; storage spots are almost non-existent; finally, the trunk is weirdly shaped and is teeny tiny.

- TO BE IMPROVED UPON: The catalytic converter is awkward, since it protrudes into the floor, crowding the front passenger's legs. The Firebird has a wide steer angle diameter, so it's tough to maneuver. The manual shifter often grinds when you're changing gears. Last of all, the convertible top is a real pain to use.

CONCLUSION
The Firebird has sassy, spectacular looks and puts out thrilling performances, thanks to the V8 engine, but it's really almost out-of-date. Maybe all it would take would be to put this name on a 4X4, so that this model would be a smashing success! Who knows?

RATING
PONTIAC Firebird

CONCEPT : — **62%**
Technology	75
Safety :	90
Interior space :	35
Trunk volume:	40
Quality/fit/finish :	70

DRIVING: — **69%**
Cockpit :	75
Performance :	70
Handling :	70
Steering :	70
Braking :	60

ORIGINAL EQUIPMENT: — **77%**
Tires :	80
Headlights :	75
Wipers :	80
Rear defroster :	70
Radio :	80

COMFORT : — **58%**
Seats :	60
Suspension :	60
Sound level :	40
Conveniences :	50
Air conditioning :	80

BUDGET : — **48%**
Price :	45
Fuel economy :	40
Insurance :	40
Satisfaction :	75
Depreciation :	40

Overall rating: **62.8%**

NEW FOR 1999

- Zexel Torsen differential for all no-slip differentials.
- Indicator for engine oil service life.
- Standard Monsoon sound system on the convertible.
- Traction control now available on the V6 models.
- Plastic gas tank with 63.6-liter capacity.
- Two new exterior shades.

ENGINES / TRANSMISSIONS / PERFORMANCES

Model/ version	Type / timing valve / fuel system	Displacement cu in	Power bhp @ rpm	Torque lb-ft @ rpm	Compres. ratio	Driving wheels / transmission	Final ratio	Acceler. 0-60 mph s	Standing 1/4 & 5/8 mile s	Acceler. 50-75 mph s	Braking 60-0 mph f	Top speed mph	Lateral acceler. G	Noise level dBA	Fuel economy mpg City	Fuel economy mpg Highway	Fuel type Octane
1)	V6* 3.8 OHV-12-SFI	231	200 @ 5200	225 @ 4000	9.4 :1	rear - M5*	3.23	9.0	15.8 29.7	6.2	131	115	0.85	68	18	31	R 87
						rear - A4	3.08	9.8	17.0 30.8	6.7	138	112	0.85	68	18	29	R 87
2)	V8* 5.7 OHV-16-SFI	350	305 @ 5200	335 @ 4000	10.1 :1	rear - M6	3.42	5.5	14.0 25.4	3.8	125	149	0.87	72	15	27	S 91
						rear - A4*	2.73	6.0	14.5 26.0	4.0	131	137	0.87	72	16	25	S 91
3)	V8 5.7 OHV-16-SFI	350	320 @ 5200	345 @ 4400	10.1 :1	rear -M6	3.42	5.3	13.8 25.2	3.6	125	143	0.88	72	15	25	S 91

1) base 2) standard, Formula & Trans Am 3) option, WS6 Ram Air, Formula & Trans Am

PRICE & EQUIPMENT

PONTIAC Firebird	base cpe	base con.	Formula cpe	Trans Am cpe	con.
Retail price $:	18,015	24,305	22,865	25,975	29,715
Dealer invoice $:	16,484	22,239	20,921	23,767	27,189
Shipping & handling $:	525	525	525	525	525
Automatic transmission:	O	O	O	S	S
Cruise control:	S	S	S	S	S
Power steering:	S	S	S	S	S
Anti-lock brakes:	O	O	O	O	O
Traction control:	SM	SM	SM	SM	SM
Air conditioning:	SM	SM	SM	SM	SM
Leather:	O	O	O	S	S
AM/FM/radio-cassette:	SCD	SCD	SCD	SCD	SCD
Power door locks:	O	O	S	S	S
Power windows:	O	O	S	S	S
Tilt steering:	S	S	S	S	S
Dual adjustable mirrors:	SM	SE	SE	SE	SE
Alloy wheels:	S	S	S	S	S
Anti-theft system:	S	S	S	S	S

Colors
Exterior: Crimson, White, Cayenne, Silver, Lime, Green, Red, Black, Blue.

Interior: Neutral, Graphite, Medium gray, Red, Taupe.

AT A GLANCE...

Category: rear-wheel drive sports coupes. **Class :** S

HISTORIC
Introduced in: 1993
Made in: Ste-Thérèse, Boisbriand, Québec, Canada.

DEMOGRAPHICS
Model	Men./Wom.	Age	Married	College	Income
Firebird	72/28 %	39	52 %	40 %	$ 41 000

INDEX
Safety:	95 %	Satisfaction:	75 %
Depreciation:	49 %	Insurance:	$ 1 385-1 475
Cost per mile:	$ 0.57	Number of dealers:	2 953

SALES
Model	1996	1997	Result
Firebird	32 622	32 524	- 0.3 %

MAIN COMPETITORS
ACURA Integra, CHRYSLER Sebring, DODGE Avenger, FORD Mustang, HONDA Prelude, NISSAN 240SX, TOYOTA Supra.

MAINTENANCE REQUIRED BY WARRANTY
First revision:	Frequency:	Diagnostic plug:
3 000 miles	6 000 miles	Yes

SPECIFICATIONS

Model	Version Trim	Body/ Seats	Interior volume cu ft	Trunk volume cu ft	Cd	Wheel base in	Lght x Wdgth x Hght in x in x in	Curb weight lb	Susp. ft/rr	Brake ft/rr	Steering type	Turning diameter ft	Steer. turns nber.	Fuel tank gal	tire size	Standard tires make	model	Standard powertrain
PONTIAC		General warranty: 3 years / 36 000 miles; antipollution: 5 years / 50 000 miles; perforation corrosion: 6 years / 100 000 miles. Roadside assistance.																
Firebird	base	2dr.cpe. 2+2	84.0	12.9	0.32	101.1	193.3x74.4x51.1	3322	ih/rh	dc/ABS	pwr.r&p.	L 37.9	2.67	16.8	215/60R16	BFGoodrich	Comp T/A	V6/3.8/M5
Firebird	base	2dr.con. 2+2	80.6	7.6	0.36	101.1	193.3x74.4x51.8	3402	ih/rh	dc/ABS	pwr.r&p.	R 40.6	2.67	16.8	215/60R16	BFGoodrich	Comp T/A	V6/3.8/M5
Firebird	Formula	2dr.cpe. 2+2	84.0	12.9	0.32	101.1	193.3x74.4x51.1	3340	ih/rh	dc/ABS	pwr.r&p.	L 37.8	2.28	16.8	245/50ZR16	Goodyear	Eagle GS-D	V8/5.7/A4
Firebird	Trans Am	2dr.cpe. 2+2	84.0	12.9	0.32	101.1	193.3x74.4x51.8	3397	ih/rh	dc/ABS	pwr.r&p.	-	2.28	16.8	245/50ZR16	Goodyear	Eagle GS-D	V8/5.7/A4
Firebird	Trans Am	2dr.con. 2+2	80.6	7.6	0.36	101.1	193.3x74.4x51.8	3514	ih/rh	dc/ABS	pwr.r&p.	R 40.1	2.28	16.8	245/50ZR16	Goodyear	Eagle GS-D	V8/5.7/A4

The Grand Am is the most popular model in the Pontiac lineup. It's built on the new P90 platform that it shares with the Chevrolet Malibu, Oldsmobile Cutlass and Alero, so its renewal represents a major event for this GM division. In order to really ensure this newcomer's success, this model's most striking trait has remained intact, namely its exuberant style both inside and out. In general, it's obvious that technically speaking, it's really a cut above, thanks to sophisticated solutions applied on this new model.

MODEL RANGE
Just as before, the Pontiac Grand Am comes in a 4-door sedan and 2-door coupe in SE and GT trim. The SE is equipped with the same 2.4L 4-cylinder engine that powered the previous Grand Am, but a new 3.4L overhead valve V6 now equips the GT version. Each model can receive the other engine, on request. The only transmission offered is a 4-speed automatic, with a higher axle ratio for the GT. Original items include air conditioning, automatic transmission, power steering, traction control and antilock braking, remote control trunk release and lock as well as intermittent wipers.

TECHNICAL FEATURES
The unibody is 32% more rigid than on the previous model. It's made up of galvanized (on both sides) steel panels and yields a drag coefficient of 0.34, which is simply out to lunch for a 1999 car. Wheelbase and wheel tracks have been widened by 3,3 inches, cabin and trunk space are 20% more generous and a hydroformed cradle supports the front powertrain and suspension. The Grand Am now benefits from a fully independent suspension, with MacPherson struts and aluminum lower control arms up front and a three-link arrangement at the rear. There's an anti-roll bar at both extremities. The SE models are equipped with disc and drum brakes and GT models benefit from disc brakes. But ABS and traction control are original equipment items for both versions. Cars animated by a V6 are equipped with variable assist power rack-and-pinion steering.

PROS
+ STYLE. This new design still smacks of the exuberant and showy looks typical of the Grand Am,

Psychadelic!

thanks to various stylistic accents, including, among other things, those humungous fog floodlights set on the base of the front bumper.

+ GT VERSION. It's a good bargain. For a reasonable sum, you get a zippy V6 powerplant, silky automatic transmission and traction control, features not all rivals come equipped with.

+ V6 ENGINE. Compared to the 3.1L V6 that motivated the former Grand Am, the new V6 has a lot more vim and vitality. It puts the 4-cylinder in its lowly place, with its high torque achieved at lower r.p.m. The 2.4L is less willing when car is at full load capacity or going uphill and it roars and shakes a heck of a lot.

+ HANDLING. The GT exhibits better road adherence thanks to the firmer suspension and wider, more ruthless tires.

+ CABIN SPACE. The coupe is just as roomy as the sedan, but it's easier to board the sedan, with those nice and wide rear doors.

+ SEATS. Bucket seats are quite comfy with their wrap-around design and they have higher seat backs.

+ TRUNK. It's fairly roomy, but on the GT versions, the split-folding rear seat (optional on the SE versions) makes it modular, but the opening is really tapered and it has a high threshold.

+ INSTRUMENT PANEL. Its daring style is a real hommage to Dolly Parton's feminine attributes.

+ STEERING. It's accurate and

responsive, so it makes for relaxed driving, especially the vari-rate power steering on the V6-powered models.

+ DEPENDABILITY. The previous model boasted of 80% reliability, so this should help sales for the new model that looks really well-built.

CONS
- HANDLING. The SE models suffer from quite a bit of sway due to their overly soft suspension. The new 15-inch tires help offset this tendency, along with the more robust frame. But the GT versions are generally more stable.

- PERFORMANCES. The 4-cylinder is pretty competent, but it's still noisy and shakes, rattles and rolls on accelerations.

- NOISE LEVEL. Compared to the previous model, soundproofing has improved, but there's still wind interference and the GT's exhaust roars away, so it wears you down after a while.

- FIT AND FINISH. It's better than it was, but there's still room for improvement because some components still look pretty chintzy.

- BRAKES. They're still not a match for the performances these models can muster. It takes forever to come to a full stop and the spongy pedal makes it hard to apply brakes as required. And ABS doesn't always help keep the car right on track.

- ACCESS. Even with the new body, it's still tough getting to the rear seats, especially on the coupes.

- STORAGE SPOTS. They're somewhat skimpy. Door side-pockets are small but the glove compartment is a bit roomier.

- TO BE IMPROVED UPON: The parking brake lever is in a strange place. And there's still no indicator for the shifter position up on the instrument panel.

CONCLUSION
The Grand Am appeals to young people and family types. Equipment meets the needs of this customer bracket, as does its new extraverted style that you can't really ignore. This formula has worked up until now and we don't see why this trend should come to an end at the present time. ☺

RATING
PONTIAC Grand Am

CONCEPT :		69%
Technology :	75	
Safety :	95	
Interior space :	50	
Trunk volume:	50	
Quality/fit/finish :	75	

DRIVING:		62%
Cockpit :	75	
Performance :	50	
Handling :	55	
Steering :	75	
Braking :	55	

ORIGINAL EQUIPMENT:		73%
Tires :	75	
Headlights :	75	
Wipers :	75	
Rear defroster :	70	
Radio :	75	

COMFORT :		65%
Seats :	75	
Suspension :	70	
Sound level :	50	
Conveniences :	50	
Air conditioning :	80	

BUDGET :		63%
Price :	60	
Fuel economy :	70	
Insurance :	55	
Satisfaction :	80	
Depreciation :	50	

Overall rating: 66.4%

NEW FOR 1999

• Completely redesigned model with longer wheelbase, wider wheel tracks and fully independent suspension.
• Four new exterior shades.
• 3.4L V6 that develops 170 hp, automatic transmission, independent rear suspension.
• Low tire pressure and oil change warning lamps.

ENGINES / TRANSMISSIONS / PERFORMANCES

Model/version	Type / timing valve / fuel system	Displacement cu in	Power bhp @ rpm	Torque lb-ft @ rpm	Compres. ratio	Driving wheels / transmission	Final ratio	Acceler. 0-60 mph s	Standing 1/4 & 5/8 mile s	Acceler. 50-75 mph s	Braking 60-0 mph f	Top speed mph	Lateral acceler. G	Noise level dBA	Fuel economy mpg City	Fuel economy mpg Highway	Fuel type Octane
base	L4* 2.4 DOHC-16-ISP	146	150 @ 5600	155 @ 4400	9.5 :1	front - A4*	3.42	10.0	17.2 30.8	6.9	144	109	0.75	68	21	32	R 87
option	V6 3.4 OHV -12-ISP	204	170 @ 5200	195 @ 4000	9.5 :1	front - A4*	3.05	8.5	16,4 29.5	6.2	131	112	0.76	67	18	27	R 87
GT	V6 3.4 OHV -12-ISP	204	175 @ 5200	205 @ 4000	9.5 :1	front - A4*	3.29	NA							18	27	R 87

PRICE & EQUIPMENT

PONTIAC Grand Am	SE	GT
Retail price $:	15,870	19,070
Dealer invoice $:	14,521	17,449
Shipping & handling $:	525	525
Automatic transmission:	S	S
Cruise control:	O	S
Power steering:	S	S
Anti-lock brakes:	S	S
Traction control:	S	S
Air conditioning:	SM	SM
Leather:	-	O
AM/FM/radio-cassette:	S	SCD
Power door locks:	S	S
Power windows:	S	S
Tilt steering:	S	S
Dual adjustable mirrors:	SM	SE
Alloy wheels:	O	S
Anti-theft system:	S	S

Colors
Exterior: White, Blue, Black, Green, Red, Gray, Jade, Sand, Orchid.
Interior: Gray, Beige, Red, Blue, Taupe, Lime, Graphite, Jade.

AT A GLANCE...

Category: front-wheel drive compact coupes & sedans. **Class : 4**

HISTORIC
Introduced in: 1994
Made in: Lansing, Michigan, USA

DEMOGRAPHICS

Model	Men./Wom.	Age	Married	College	Income
Grand Am	64/36 %	47	70 %	43 %	$ 35 000

INDEX

Safety:	95 %	Satisfaction:	83 %
Depreciation:	51 %	Insurance:	$ 965
Cost per mile:	$ 0.43	Number of dealers:	2 953

SALES

Model	1996	1997	Result
Grand Am	222 477	204 078	- 8.3 %

MAIN COMPETITORS
sedans: BUICK Century, CHRYSLER Cirrus, DODGE Stratus, FORD Contour, HONDA Accord, HYUNDAI Sonata, MAZDA 626, MERCURY Mystique, NISSAN Altima, OLDS-MOBILE Alero, SUBARU Legacy, TOYOTA Camry, VOLKSWAGEN Passat.
coupe: ACURA Integra, CHRYSLER Sebring, DODGE Avenger, HONDA Accord, Prelude, NISSAN 240SX,TOYOTA Celica.

MAINTENANCE REQUIRED BY WARRANTY

First revision:	Frequency:	Diagnostic plug:
3 000 miles	6 000 miles	Yes

SPECIFICATIONS

Model	Version Trim	Body/ Seats	Interior volume cu ft	Trunk volume cu ft	Cd	Wheel base in	Lght x Wdgth x Hght in x in x in	Curb weight lb	Susp. ft/rr	Brake ft/rr	Steering type	Turning diameter ft	Steer. turns nber.	Fuel tank gal	tire size	Standard tires make	model	Standard powertrain
PONTIAC	General warranty: 3 years / 36 000 miles; antipollution: 5 years / 50 000 miles; perforation corrosion: 6 years / 100 000 miles. Roadside assistance.																	
Grand Am SE		2dr.cpe.5	107.3	14.3	0.32	107.0	186.3x70.4x55.	3066	ih/ih	dc/dr/ABS	pwr.r&p.	37.7	2.5	15.2	215/60R15	-	-	L4/2.4/A4
Grand Am SE		4dr.sdn.5	105.4	14.3	0.32	107.0	186.3x70.4x55.	3115	ih/ih	dc/dr/ABS	pwr.r&p.	37.7	2.5	15.2	215/60R15	-	-	L4/2.4/A4
Grand Am GT		2dr.cpe.5	107.3	14.3	0.32	107.0	186.3x70.4x55.	3090	ih/ih	dc/dr/ABS	pwr.r&p.	37.7	2.5	15.2	225/50R16	Goodyear	Eagle RS-A	V6/3.4/A4
Grand Am GT		4dr.sdn.5	105.4	14.3	0.32	107.0	186.3x70.4x55.	3168	ih/ih	dc/dr/ABS	pwr.r&p.	37.7	2.5	15.2	225/50R16	Goodyear	Eagle RS-A	V6/3.4/A4

The Grand Prix is the perfect specimen of what the Pontiac philosophy is all about. More than the Grand Am, it takes its brawny physique in its stride and is the boldest and brassiest brat around in the GTP version that's quite a show-off. But to each his or her own and sales figures indicate that lots of folks really like this car...

The Grand Prix was restyled in 1997 and now has a wider platform. Unlike the Buick Century-Regal and Oldsmobile Intrigue that belong to the W family, the Grand Prix is the only car in this lineup that's available as a coupe.

MODEL RANGE

The Pontiac Grand Prix is available as a 4-door sedan and 2-door coupe. The sedan is offered in three trim levels: SE, GT and GTP, whereas the coupe is sold in two trim levels: GT and GTP. The SE sedan receives the 3.1L 3100 V6, the GT versions are animated by the 3.8L 3800 Series II V6 and the GTP's are powered by a 3800 SC Series V6, a supercharged version of the same engine. Standard equipment on these cars is quite generous, since it includes an automatic transmission, traction control and antilock braking, main power accessories, manual climate control and theft-deterrent system.

TECHNICAL FEATURES

The Grand Prix's W platform has a long wheelbase and very wide wheel tracks. The main structure is of monocoque design with steel panels that are galvanized on both sides (except the roof panel). The body yields average aerodynamics, with a 0.32 drag coefficient for the sedan and 0.34 for the coupe. An underframe supports the powertrain and the suspension is fully independent, based on MacPherson struts up front and a three-link system at the rear. Front and rear are equipped with coil springs and an anti-roll bar. Four-wheel disc brakes are associated with a Bosch antilock braking system and traction control, both hooked up to the same sensors. The SE version is equipped with conventional power rack-and-pinion steering, but the GT and GTP versions receive a variable assist MagnaSteer system developed for Cadillac.

SIMPLY SUPER

++ ESTHETICS. The Grand Prix has a beauteous bod. Its nicely curved form exudes feline pounce

Bold Styling..

power. And the GT and GTP, with their bright-colored exterior, always catch people's attention. Such bold and brassy traits inspire a sense of pride for the lucky guy or gal at the wheel, who tends to make the exhaust system roar like blazes!

PROS

+ **CABIN DESIGN.** The GT is blessed with a neat interior design. This model is a good buy with its rich equipment, loaded instrument panel and very elaborate seats.

+ **HANDLING.** The new Grand Prix is much more road-competent. The really wide wheel tracks sure help keep things on an even keel.

+ **SEATS.** The bucket seats are the cat's meow. They follow the contours of your body and provide lots of hip and lower back support, even

though upholstery is a bit thin and quite firm.

+ **DRIVING PLEASURE.** The GT is more fun to zip around in. Steering is quick on the draw and accurate and the suspension is simply super, providing good vehicle control. Sportscar fans will love it!

+ **PERFORMANCES.** The 200-hp 3.8L V6 is a gutsy engine and the Roots supercharger enhances output by letting another 40 hp loose to do their stuff. Accelerations and pickup are amost akin to those achieved by an exotic car!

+ **INSTRUMENT PANEL.** It's loaded with controls and gauges that are legible and within easy reach. There are several controls on the steering wheel as well, which does take some getting used to.

+ **NICE FEATURES:** Assist grips and Head-Up display system that lets you keep track of what's happening by checking the reading on the inner windshield, without having to look down at the instrument panel.

CONS

- **SUSPENSION.** The suspension on the GT is brutal and really shakes up occupants to its cruel heart's content on rough road surfaces. And the exhaust racket gets on your nerves pretty quick.

- **VISIBILITY.** The restyled body cuts down on lateral visibility and the view at rear quarterback. The body belt is high, roof supports are wide and the rear window is really slanted, so all these factors add up to poor visibility all-round.

- **FIT AND FINISH.** Some materials don't look too spiffy and there isn't the same craftsmanship as you get on an Oldsmobile Intrigue, for example.

- **STRUCTURAL RIGIDITY.** The structure on our test vehicle wasn't super-solid, since we heard lots of interference on rough surfaces and the suspension often bottomed out.

- **ACCESS.** Getting into the rear seats is a chore, both on the sedan and the coupe, due to the really strongly arched roof design.

- **TIRES.** The SE and GT models are equipped with undersized tires and only the GTP's tires are well suited to the car's capabilities.

- **PRICE.** The GTP price tag looks pretty steep compared to that of the GT that can brag about pretty good performances!

- **CONVENIENCE FEATURES.** Car dimensions are quite generous, but this aspect seems to have been overlooked. There aren't too many storage spots and the ones you have at your disposal don't hold too much. The trunk isn't high enough, it isn't modular and luggage handling is no picnic with the narrow opening and high trunk threshold.

- **TO BE IMPROVED UPON:** Front armrest that's too wide and you have to fold it up to drive comfortably.

CONCLUSION

The Grand Prix is a good ambassador for GM «performance» products and it has a bold style like no other. At least now it can boast of performances in keeping with its image. ☺

RATING
PONTIAC Grand Prix

CONCEPT :	**77%**
Technology	80
Safety :	90
Interior space :	70
Trunk volume :	70
Quality/fit/finish :	75
DRIVING:	**67%**
Cockpit :	80
Performance :	65
Handling :	55
Steering :	80
Braking :	55
ORIGINAL EQUIPMENT:	**79%**
Tires :	75
Headlights :	80
Wipers :	75
Rear defroster :	80
Radio :	85
COMFORT :	**68%**
Seats :	75
Suspension :	65
Sound level:	50
Conveniences :	70
Air conditioning :	80
BUDGET :	**59%**
Price :	50
Fuel economy :	70
Insurance :	50
Satisfaction :	75
Depreciation :	50
Overall rating:	**70.0%**

NEW FOR 1999

- Courtesy lights on front doors.
- Theft-deterrent system hooked up to Keyless entry system.
- New aluminum 16-inch wheels.
- Two new exterior shades.
- 3.8L base engine now developing 5 more hp.

ENGINES

Model/ version	Type / timing valve / fuel system	Displacement cu in	Power bhp @ rpm	Torque lb-ft @ rpm
1)	V6* 3.1 OHV-12-SFI	191	160 @ 5200	185 @ 4000
2)	V6* 3.8 OHV-12-SFI	231	200 @ 5200	225 @ 4000
3)	V6C 3.8 OHV-12-SFI	231	240 @ 5200	280 @ 3200

1) base SE sedan 2) base GT, option SE 3) base GTP, option GT

TRANSMISSIONS

Compres. ratio	Driving wheels / transmission	Final ratio
9.6 :1	front - A4*	3.29
9.4 :1	front - A4*	3.29
8.5 :1	front - A4*	2.93

PERFORMANCES

Acceler. 0-60 mph s	Standing 1/4 & 5/8 mile s		Acceler. 50-75 mph s	Braking 60-0 mph f	Top speed mph	Lateral acceler. G	Noise level dBA	Fuel economy mpg		Fuel type Octane
								City	Highway	
10.0	17.2	31.0	6.8	138	109	0.78	67	19	28	R 87
8.5	16.5	29.7	6.4	134	115	0.78	67	18	29	R 87
7.2	15.3	28.5	4.6	134	124	0.78	68	17	27	S 92

PRICE & EQUIPMENT

PONTIAC Grand Prix	SE	GT
Retail price $:	18,795	20,415
Dealer invoice $:	17,197	18,680
Shipping & handling $:	550	550
Automatic transmission:	S	S
Cruise control:	O	S
Power steering:	S	S
Anti-lock brakes:	S	S
Traction control:	S	S
Air conditioning:	SM	SM
Leather:	O	O
AM/FM/radio-cassette:	O	S
Power door locks:	S	S
Power windows:	S	S
Tilt steering:	S	S
Dual adjustable mirrors:	SE	SE
Alloy wheels:	O	S
Anti-theft system:	S	S

Colors

Exterior: White, Blue, Black, Green, Red, Bronze.

Interior: Blue, Gray, Taupe, Black.

AT A GLANCE...

Category: front-wheel drive mid-size coupes & sedans. **Class :** 5

HISTORIC
Introduced in: 1997
Made in: Fairfax-Kansas City, Kansas, USA.

DEMOGRAPHICS

Model	Men./Wom.	Age	Married	College	Income
Grand Prix sdn.	67/33 %	51	78 %	29 %	$ 34 000
Grand Prix cpe.	74/26 %	43	54 %	42 %	$ 30 000

INDEX
Safety:	90 %	Satisfaction:	75 %
Depreciation:	52 %	Insurance:	$ 1045-1135
Cost per mile:	$ 0.47	Number of dealers:	2 953

SALES
Model	1996	1997	Result
Grand Prix	104 979	142 018	+ 35.3 %

MAIN COMPETITORS
sedans: DODGE Intrepid, FORD Taurus, MERCURY Sable, NISSAN Maxima, TOYOTA Camry.
coupe: CHEVROLET Monte Carlo Z34, CHRYSLER Sebring, DODGE Avenger, HONDA Accord V6, Prelude.

MAINTENANCE REQUIRED BY WARRANTY
First revision:	Frequency:	Diagnostic plug:
3 000 miles	6 000 miles	Yes

SPECIFICATIONS

PONTIAC General warranty: 3 years / 36 000 miles; antipollution: 5 years / 50 000 miles; perforation corrosion: 6 years / 100 000 miles. Roadside assistance.

Model	Version Trim	Body/ Seats	Interior volume cu ft	Trunk volume cu ft	Cd	Wheel base in	Lght x Wdgth x Hght in x in x in	Curb weight lb	Susp. ft/rr	Brake ft/rr	Steering type	Turning diameter ft	Steer. turns nber.	Fuel tank gal	tire size	Standard tires make	model	Standard powertrain
Grand Prix	sedan SE	4dr.sdn.5	99.0	16.0	-	110.5	196.5x72.7x54.7	3415	ih/ih	dc/ABS	pwr.r&p.	36.9	2.26	18.0	205/70R15	Goodyear	Eagle LS	V6/3.1/A4
Grand Prix	coupe GT	2dr.cpe.5	99.0	16.0	-	110.5	196.5x72.7x54.7	3396	ih/ih	dc/ABS	pwr.r&p.	36.9	2.26	18.0	225/60R16	Goodyear	Eagle RS-A	V6/3.8/A4
Grand Prix	sedan GT	4dr.sdn.5	99.0	16.0	-	110.5	196.5x72.7x54.7	3415	ih/ih	dc/ABS	pwr.r&p.	36.9	2.26	18.0	225/60R16	Goodyear	Eagle RS-A	V6/3.8/A4

Just before printing, we found out that Pontiac had decided to rename the Trans Sport the Montana, after the special trim level that was available up until now. This minivan will now constitute, along with its twins, the Chevrolet Venture and Oldsmobile Silhouette, a serious rival against Chrysler products and the Ford Windstar. These new vehicles are definitely more practical and competent than the models with a polymer body that they replaced in 1998.

MODEL RANGE

The Montana is different from the Venture and Silhouette in regard to a few items such as seating configurations and stylistic details. It's offered in short and extended body and now only the short version can be ordered without a sliding door on the driver's side. There's only a single trim level sold and a stylistic options package that was called «Montana» up until now. Standard equipment includes manual climate control, power steering, intermittent wipers and a cabin arrangement that can accomodate seven passengers. Powered opening function for the sliding door on the passenger's side is listed among options, along with traction control.

TECHNICAL FEATURES

The Montana has a body consisting of steel panels that are galvanized on both sides (except the roof panel), mounted on a monoframe with H-subframe. The engine hood is made of aluminum. The front independent suspension uses MacPherson struts and like the powertrain, it's mounted on a subframe via rubber elements. The rear semi-independent suspension consists of a torsion axle suspended by coil springs. There's a stabilizer bar both front and rear. At the rear, self-levelling shocks are included in the «Sport» option package. A disc and drum duo take care of braking, assisted by a Delco Moraine antilock braking system. The vehicle is equipped with power rack-and-pinion steering. Lastly, the only engine available is the 3.4L 3400 V6 that equips many other GM vehicles. For 1999, it gains 5 more hp and 5 more lb.ft. torque, so it now develops 185 hp and 210 lb.ft. torque. This powerplant is the most brawny standard engine in this segment and it's paired up with an electronically controlled 4-speed automatic transmission.

Quest For Quality...

PROS

+ VERSATILITY. This minivan's best feature is its multi-purpose cabin. The rear section can be arranged in umpteen ways, depending on whether you opt for 50/50 split-folding seatbenches, captain's chairs or the super-light bucket seats (only 37 lbs.) inherited from the former polymer-clad minivans. You can also obtain an eight-passenger seating setup as an extra.

+ RIDE COMFORT. Highway travel is adequate when it comes to comfort. The suspension tackles road irregularities with aplomb; front seats are nicely shaped and upholstered; soundproofing is effective, since the most noticeable noise comes from the tires.

+ PERFORMANCES. Accelerations and pickup are more than satisfactory, which warrants safe passing on the highway, at least up to a half-load capacity. Beyond that, a greater displacement engine would sure be appreciated.

+ AUTOMATIC GEARBOX. It's silky smooth and provides enough braking effect in 3rd or 2nd gear, so you don't have to brake to slow down.

+ HANDLING. This vehicle has a reassuring and even-keel demeanor, since there isn't much sway, so you can take the tightest curves without blinking an eye.

+ NICE FEATURES: The power mechanism that opens the sliding door on the passenger side, all the many handy storage spots, rear bumper that serves as a running

board and effective wipers that quickly clear a large section of the windshield.

- SEATS. They're really low-slung due to low ceiling clearance. It's hard to get comfy, especially tall folks who'll experience trip fatigue in no time. Rear seatbenches are flat and hard and headrests are practically useless.

- CONCEPT. Our test vehicles demonstrated a pretty botched up engineering job. Wires and ducts were visible inside the cabin, since they had come loose. Under the hood, same story: electric wiring hanging loose. In the winter, the wipers and air vents located at the base of the windshield often ice up, so they don't function normally. Lastly, the extended model body squeaks and groans on poor roads, a telltale sign that the structure isn't rigid enough.

- QUALITY. Assembly and fit and finish job could be better. You hear squeaks and such at even low mileage and some plastic trim components are far from ritzy-looking.

- BRAKES. They're quite poor: stopping distances stretch out and the soft as molasses pedal is hard to gauge just right.

- CONTROLS. The one and only lever that controls turn signal lights, wipers, window washers, cruise control and headlights is unnecessarily complicated and can be confusing to use.

- SUSPENSION. It's pretty rustic, so it acts up on poor roads. The overloaded front end tends to bottom out due to poor wheel travel.

- ACCESS. Getting to the engine for repairs and maintenance purposes is awkward as heck, just like it was on the former Trans Sport, since the engine is located mostly way under the windshield and dashboard.

- FINISH DETAILS. Some plastic trim inside the cabin really makes for a lackluster travel environment. Too bad...

CONCLUSION

The Montana is now more competitive, but over-all quality must be seriously looked at if the carmaker wants it to be on a par with its Chrysler and Ford rivals that, in this regard, are superior vehicles.

RATING
PONTIAC Montana

CONCEPT : **71%**
Technology	75
Safety :	60
Interior space :	80
Trunk volume:	70
Quality/fit/finish :	70

DRIVING: **52%**
Cockpit :	75
Performance :	35
Handling :	45
Steering :	70
Braking :	35

ORIGINAL EQUIPMENT: **79%**
Tires :	70
Headlights :	80
Wipers :	80
Rear defroster :	85
Radio :	80

COMFORT : **70%**
Seats :	70
Suspension :	75
Sound level:	50
Conveniences :	75
Air conditioning :	80

BUDGET : **64%**
Price :	50
Fuel economy :	65
Insurance :	70
Satisfaction :	80
Depreciation :	55

Overall rating: **67.2%**

NEW FOR 1999

- 3.4L V6 that develops more horsepower and torque.
- New name: no longer Trans Sport, but Montana.
- Second-generation sliding doors.
- Four new exterior shades.
- Tires with white lettering.

ENGINES / TRANSMISSIONS / PERFORMANCES

Model/ version	Type / timing valve / fuel system	Displacement cu in	Power bhp @ rpm	Torque lb-ft @ rpm	Compres. ratio	Driving wheels / transmission	Final ratio	Acceler. 0-60 mph s	Standing 1/4 & 5/8 mile s	Acceler. 50-75 mph s	Braking 60-0 mph f	Top speed mph	Lateral acceler. G	Noise level dBA	Fuel economy mpg City	Fuel economy Highway	Fuel type Octane
court	V6* 3.4 OHV-12-SFI	204	185 @ 5200	210 @ 3200	9.5 :1	front-A4	3.29	11.0	17.7 32.2	8.6	148	106	0.72	67	18	24	R 87
long	V6* 3.4 OHV-12-SFI	204	185 @ 5200	210 @ 3200	9.5 :1	front-A4	3.29	11.7	18.0 33.0	9.2	174	103	0.71	68	18	24	R 87

PRICE & EQUIPMENT

PONTIAC Montana	base
Retail price $:	22,065
Dealer invoice $:	19,950
Shipping & handling $:	570
Automatic transmission:	S
Cruise control:	O
Power steering:	S
Anti-lock brakes:	S
Traction control:	O
Air conditioning:	SM
Leather:	O
AM/FM/radio-cassette:	O
Power door locks:	S
Power windows:	O
Tilt steering:	S
Dual adjustable mirrors:	SEH
Alloy wheels:	O
Anti-theft system:	S

Colors

Exterior: brown, White, Green, Red, Malachite, Silver, Sand, Granite.

Interior: Gray, Beige, Brown.

AT A GLANCE...

Category:	front-wheel drive minivan.		Class :	utility

HISTORIC

Introduced in:	1997
Made in:	Doraville, Georgia, USA.

DEMOGRAPHICS

Model	Men./Wom.	Age	Married	College	Income
Trans Sport	76%/24%	45	88 %	35 %	$ 40 000

INDEX

Safety:	60 %	Satisfaction:	85 %
Depreciation:	43 %	Insurance:	$ 800
Cost per mile:	$0.51	Number of dealers:	2 953

SALES

Model	1996	1997	Result
Trans Sport	21 397	51 961	+ 142.8 %

MAIN COMPETITORS

CHEVROLET Venture, CHRYSLER Town & Country, DODGE Caravan, Gd Caravan, FORD Windstar, HONDA Odyssey, MAZDA MPV, MERCURY Villager, NISSAN Quest, OLDSMOBILE Silhouette, PLYMOUTH Voyager, Gd Voyager, TOYOTA Sienna, VW EuroVan.

MAINTENANCE REQUIRED BY WARRANTY

First revision:	Frequency:	Diagnostic plug:
3 000 miles	6 months/6 000 miles	Yes

SPECIFICATIONS

Model	Version Trim	Body/ Seats	Interior volume cu ft	Trunk volume cu ft	Cd	Wheel base in	Lght x Wdgth x Hght in x in x in	Curb weight lb	Susp. ft/rr	Brake ft/rr	Steering type	Turning diameter ft	Steer. turns nber.	Fuel tank gal	tire size	Standard tires make	model	Standard powertrain
PONTIAC	General warranty: 3 years / 36 000 miles; antipollution: 5 years / 50 000 miles; perforation corrosion: 6 years / 100 000 miles. Roadside assistance.																	
Montana	SWB	4dr.van.7/8	126.6	NA	NA	112.0	187.3x7.7x67.4	3730	ih/rh	dc/dr/ABS	pwr.r&p.	37.4	3.05	20.0	215/70R15	General	XP2000GT	V6/3.4/A4
Montana	Extd	4dr.van.7/8	156.0	NA	NA	120.0	201.3x72.7x68.1	3942	ih/rh	dc/dr/ABS	pwr.r&p.	39.7	3.05	25.0	215/70R15	General	XP2000GT	V6/3.4/A4

The Sunfire is the Chevrolet Cavalier's sister, but it has a uniquely distinctive, typically Pontiac appearance. In other words, this car's looks are just what Pontiac fanatics are looking for in a car that will be an extension and expression of their personality. Like the Cavalier, the Sunfire is a really popular car. It's a looker and it's affordable, so it appeals especially to young people who are living on a tight budget. Not surprising that with this duo, GM was able to come in third place in North American car sales in 1997, behind the Toyota Camry and Ford Taurus.

MODEL RANGE
The Pontiac Sunfire is sold as an SE coupe and sedan as well as a GT coupe and convertible. The 2.2L 4-cylinder engine equips the SE models, while the GT's are animated by a 2.4L DOHC 4-cylinder. This engine can also equip the SE sedan. The 5-speed manual gearbox comes standard and a 4-speed automatic is sold as an extra. The SE 2.2L models can receive a 3-speed automatic at a lower price.

TECHNICAL FEATURES
The Sunfire's steel monocoque body is made up of steel panels that are galvanized on both sides. The athletic-looking body disguises poor aerodynamic yield, since the drag coefficient is a whopping 0.38! The independent front suspension consists of MacPherson struts and the rear suspension is made up a simple semi-rigid axle. Cars are equipped with front disc and rear drum brakes linked to standard ABS. Traction control is available with the 4-speed automatic transmission. Engines aren't new, in fact, they've been around for a while and are really rough around the edges. Compared to their polite and poised Japanese homologues, these engines are ruffians.

PROS
+ VALUE. Folks buy the Sunfire because it's a good buy. It's a good-size car, so it doesn't look like a tiny compact, it has a pretty good range of equipment and it's sold at an affordable price.

+ LOOKS. The Sunfire is a crowd pleaser with its bold body design and nearly half of the owners are women.

+ RIDE COMFORT. The sedan cabin is quite nice, both up front

Fired Up Youth...

and in the rear seat area. Travel is quite comfy due to sturdy shocks and nicely shaped front seats.

+ CONVENIENCE FEATURE. These compact cars offer good cabin space, given their dimensions. Inside the cabin, you'll find lots of good-size, conveniently located storage spots. Finally, the trunk is nice and roomy and it's modular since you can lower the rear seatbench back to extend its volume.

+ SAFETY. The Sunfire provides a respectable level of passenger protection, thanks to its rigid structure, two front airbags (standard) and adjustable shoulder belts up front.

+ CABIN DESIGN. The interior is

quite neat and spiffy-looking, trim fabrics are sprightly and materials seem to be better-quality than they once were.

+ HANDLING. It's more competent now that the sway that afflicted former models is under control. Only the undersized tires on the SE model are inefficient and should be replaced.

+ PERFORMANCES. The 2.4L engine has a lot of zip. Accelerations and pickup are vigorous, but this engine isn't as smooth or versatile as the V6 that used to equip the previous Sunfire models.

+ BODY DESIGN. Compared to the Cavalier shape, the Sunfire bod looks better crafted and more polished, right down to the smallest

details, so it's more appealing than that of the Cavalier.

CONS
- SAFETY. This car received average scores (75%) for passive passenger protection and owner satisfaction rate. It's not as safe as you might think. The same goes for dependability and assembly quality.

- PERFORMANCES. The 2.2L engine has only fair to midling zing, it strains, especially with the 3-speed automatic that doesn't have overdrive, so it's pretty darn noisy.

- TIRES. The 14-inch tires on the SE are downright awful. They have little or no grip on damp roads and they sure make quite a ruckus.

- STEERING. It benefits from a good reduction ratio but it's overassisted, so it's light and sometimes wanders. The Sunfire is sluggish to respond on some moves and maneuverability is only average.

- BRAKES. They're hard to apply just right and they don't like getting roughed up. Stops are long to achieve and the simplistic ABS kicks in too quickly and sometimes doesn't control all wheel lock!

- ACCELERATOR. It's hard to gauge because pedal travel is too short, which makes travel in slick conditions a bit tricky and jerky.

- NOISE LEVEL. Both 4-cylinder engines are rather rustic and generate a lot of racket and vibration.

- CABIN SPACE. The coupe offers only skimpy space in the rear seat area, seats are small and head room is cramped due to the arched roof design.

- FUEL CONSUMPTION. The 3-speed automatic gearbox generates high r.p.m., which has a direct effect on gas consumption.

- TRUNK. The lid doesn't lift high enough. Besides, the tiny opening and high threshold sure don't make for handy luggage handling.

- CONTROLS. At night, the instrumentation lighting reflects into the windshield and the orange glow makes gauges hard to read.

CONCLUSION
Far from being the prototype of the ideal vehicle, the Sunfire is neverthelsess quite a good vehicle, especially considering its price and the equipment it offers. The convertible model is the only one in its category that offers seating for four passengers and costs less than $25,000. ☺

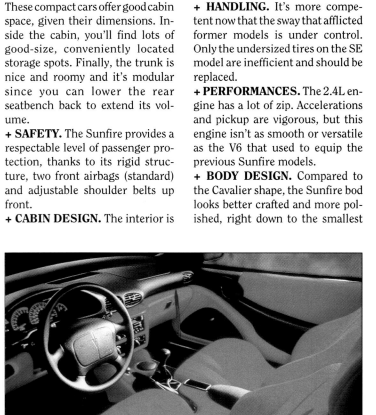

RATING
PONTIAC Sunfire

CONCEPT :   64%
Technology	75
Safety :	75
Interior space :	50
Trunk volume :	50
Quality/fit/finish :	70

DRIVING: 58%
Cockpit :	75
Performance :	50
Handling :	55
Steering :	70
Braking :	40

ORIGINAL EQUIPMENT: 72%
Tires :	60
Headlights :	80
Wipers :	80
Rear defroster :	70
Radio :	70

COMFORT :   68%
Seats :	70
Suspension :	70
Sound level :	50
Conveniences :	70
Air conditioning :	80

BUDGET :   66%
Price :	70
Fuel economy :	70
Insurance :	60
Satisfaction :	75
Depreciation :	55

Overall rating: 65.6%

NEW FOR 1999

- New exterior shade.
- 2.4L engine with new components.
- New rear spoiler on the sedan.

ENGINES

Model/ version	Type / timing valve / fuel system	Displacement cu in	Power bhp @ rpm	Torque lb-ft @ rpm
1)	L4* 2.2 SOHC-8-SFI	134	115 @ 5000	135 @ 3600
2)	L4* 2.4 DOHC-16-SFI	146	150 @ 5600	155 @ 4400

1) base SE   2) base GT coupe & convertible, option on all SE models.

TRANSMISSIONS

Compres. ratio	Driving wheels / transmission	Final ratio
9.0 :1	front - M5*	3.58
	front - A3-A4	3.91
9.5 :1	front - M5*	3.94
	front - A4	3.91

PERFORMANCES

Acceler. 0-60 mph s	Standing 1/4 & 5/8 mile s	Acceler. 50-75 mph s	Braking 60-0 mph f	Top speed mph	Lateral acceler. G	Noise level dBA	Fuel economy mpg City	Highway	Fuel type Octane
10.0	17.2 31.0	6.9	154	103	0.76	68	23	34	R 87
11.2	17.4 31.2	7.0	157	100	0.76	68	23	30	R 87
9.0	16.8 30.5	6.6	148	112	0.78	70	19	28	R 87
9.8	17.4 30.8	6.4	154	109	0.78	70	22	32	R 87

PRICE & EQUIPMENT

PONTIAC Sunfire	SE cpe	SE sdn.	GT cpe	SE con.
Retail price $:	12,495	12,495	15,495	19,495
Dealer invoice $:	11,558	11,558	14,332	18,033
Shipping & handling $:	645	645	645	645
Automatic transmission:	O	O	O	S
Cruise control:	O	O	O	S
Power steering:	S	S	S	S
Anti-lock brakes:	S	S	S	S
Traction control:	O	O	O	S
Air conditioning:	O	O	S	S
Leather:	-	-	-	-
AM/FM/radio-cassette:	O	O	SCD	SCD
Power door locks:	O	O	O	O
Power windows:	O	O	O	O
Tilt steering:	O	O	S	S
Dual adjustable mirrors:	SM	SM	SM	SM
Alloy wheels:	O	O	S	O
Anti-theft system:	S	S	S	S

Colors

Exterior: White, Red, Black, Green, Crimson, Orchid, Cayenne, Blue, Sand, Aqua, Violet.
Interior: Blue Aqua, Red, Neutral, Graphite, White, Gray.

AT A GLANCE...

Category: front-wheel drive compacts.   **Class :** 3

HISTORIC
Introduced in: 1995
Made in: Ramos Arizpe, Mexico Lordstown, Ohio, Lansing, Michigan, USA.

DEMOGRAPHICS

Model	Men./Wom.	Age	Married	College	Income
coupe	45/55 %	38	50 %	44 %	$ 30 000
Sedan	53/47 %	40	68 %	41 %	$ 29 000

INDEX
Safety:	75 %	Satisfaction:	73 %
Depreciation:	48 %	Insurance:	$ 775 - 1085
Cost per mile:	$ 0.35	Number of dealers:	2 953

SALES

Model	1996	1997	Result
Sunfire	95 783	102 160	+ 6.7 %

MAIN COMPETITORS
DODGE-PLYMOUTH Neon, FORD Escort, ZX2, HONDA Civic, HYUNDAI Elantra, MAZDA Protegé, NISSAN 200SX, Sentra, SATURN, SUBARU Impreza, TOYOTA Corolla, Paseo, VOLKSWAGEN Golf, Jetta. CONVERTIBLE: CHRYSLER Sebring, FORD Mustang.

MAINTENANCE REQUIRED BY WARRANTY
First revision:	Frequency:	Diagnostic plug:
3 000 miles	6 000 miles	Yes

SPECIFICATIONS

Model	Version Trim	Body/ Seats	Interior volume cu ft	Trunk volume cu ft	Cd	Wheel base in	Lght x Wdgth x Hght in x in x in	Curb weight lb	Susp. ft/rr	Brake ft/rr	Steering type	Turning diameter ft	Steer. turns nber.	Fuel tank gal	tire size	Standard tires make	model	Standard powertrain
PONTIAC	General warranty: 3 years / 36 000 miles; antipollution: 5 years / 50 000 miles; perforation corrosion: 6 years / 100 000 miles. Roadside assistance.																	
Sunfire	SE	2dr.cpe.4	87.2	12.4	0.39	104.1	181.9x67.4x53.0	2630	ih/sih	dc/dr/ABS	pwr.r&p.	35.6	2.66	15.0	195/70R14	Goodyear	Conquest	L4/2.2/M5
Sunfire	SE	4dr.sdn.5	91.6	13.1	0.38	104.1	181.9x67.3x54.7	2670	ih/sih	dc/dr/ABS	pwr.r&p.	35.6	2.66	15.0	195/70R14	Goodyear	Conquest	L4/2.2/M5
Sunfire	GT	2dr.cpe.4	87.2	12.4	0.39	104.1	181.9x67.4x53.0	2822	ih/sih	dc/dr/ABS	pwr.r&p.	35.6	2.83	15.0	205/55R16	BFGoodrich	Touring T/A	L4/2.4/M5
Sunfire	GT	2dr.con.4	91.6	9.9	0.42	104.1	181.9x67.4x54.1	2999	ih/sih	dc/dr/ABS	pwr.r&p.	35.6	2.66	15.0	195/65R15	BFGoodrich	Touring T/A	L4/2.4/A4

The 911 was developed after the Boxster that, in a sense, played the role of a mentor. These two vehicles now share many common features. This was the upshot of the firm's restructuring and streamlining that occured due to serious financial problems. But are current Porshe models in the process of becoming what they were never meant to be? In other words, industrial products that have become humdrum due to super-efficient production methods and that are built for profit rather than for quality or character. One thing is certain, the price of these toys is just as high as their performance level...

MODEL RANGE

The Boxster is offered in a single version equipped with a 2.5L flat-6 and the most recent 911 is sold as a rear-wheel drive coupe or convertible driven by a 3.4L engine linked to a 6-speed manual transmission or 5-speed «Tiptronic» automatic. Equipment is very lap-of-luxury rich.

TECHNICAL FEATURES

After a fifty-year tradition of a rear-engine setup, Porsche has introduced the platform shared by the Boxster and the 911 model, that includes a mid-engine arrangement. Aerodynamics are excellent, since the drag coefficient is 0.30. The steel monocoque body is galvanized on both sides and is mounted on a subframe for greater structural rigidity. Front and rear suspensions consist of a MacPherson design, namely struts with transversal and longitudinal control arms, supported by coil springs and anti-roll bar at both ends. Disc brakes are equipped with single-piece calipers fitted with four pistons, like those used on Formula 1 racecars, linked to a fifth-generation antilock braking system. Cars benefit from power rack-and-pinion steering.

The engines that equip these cars were developed specifically for them. It's a 6-cylinder with cylinders set in opposed rows to form a Vee shape, tailored to meet the needs of the respective models. They're crammed with high tech features such as transversal flow water-cooling that maintains the temperature constant around the cylinders and separate cooling for the cylinder head. Actuators located in the camshaft chains of command (a system patented by Porsche called Variocam) allow for variable intake valve opening time. The Tiptronic automatic transmission includes an electronic traction control device and a limited slip differential that stabilizes accelerations on slippery roads.

On Your Marks...

SIMPLY SUPER

++ STYLE. You have to admit that Porsche's are gorgeous cars with their smooth, polished lines. The 911 was redesigned but didn't lose an ounce of the charisma that buyers have loved over the years, while the Boxster roadster, derived from the same source, adds a touch of mischievous non-conformity.

PROS

+ PERFORMANCES. The 911 powerplant transport speed fanatics to a nirvana never-never land, since Porsche is the only carmaker in the world who doesn't like to put limits on its fast cars: 170 mph top speed and it takes less than 6 seconds to go from 0 to 60 mph.

+ BRAKES. They're brawny, balanced, easy to apply and tough as nails, so they provide optimal safety.

+ HANDLING. It's in keeping with this carmaker's reputation. These cars handle beautifully, due to the mid-engine setup, excellent tire quality and highly honed suspensions.

+ SAFETY. Passenger protection is assured due to the generous collapsible section at the front end (which explains the big overhang), magnesium roll bars, reinforced windshield frame and the two front-impact and two side-impact airbags.

+ RIDE COMFORT. It's quite good, in spite of the snug cockpit that seats two comfortably and all the luxury accessories add to travel pleasure.

+ CONVERTIBLE TOP. Its power mechanism works like a charm and it's super rigid and waterproof. But the wind deflector is a must for travelling with the top down...

CONS

- PERFORMANCES. The Boxster's output is disappointing, especially with the Tiptronic transmission, for performances aren't at all exotic, since staid sedans (Regal or Intrigue) achieve the same acceleration and pickup figures, in spite of their more lowly origins...

- TRANSMISSION. The Tiptronic formula doesn't seem as solid as when it was first introduced, compared to others offered on the market. Dials located on the steering wheel are only useful for some Jacques Villeneuve role-playing, for speeds shift on their own when the needle hits the red zone. Trying to change speeds on curve could lead to serious thumb sprains...

- QUALITY. The cabin design on these recent cars isn't exactly a showcase for pristine quality, not compared to the polished touches and impeccable trim materials you were spoiled with inside previous models.

-CONVENIENCE FEATURES. As was to be expected, such an elitist car doesn't offer too many down-to-earth amenities. Door side-pockets replace the glove compartment and both trunks contain precious little.

- NOISE LEVEL. It's high at all times and gets tiring after a while. It's mostly made up of wind and exhaust noise.

- AUTONOMY. Depending on driving style, it will be limited by the restricted gas tank capacity and fuel consumption is pretty high with lows at around 16 miles per gallon.

VERY POOR FEATURES

-- PRICE. Like all luxury products, Porsche cars don't go for a song, but as long as their are fools rushing in to buy one...

-- WARRANTY. It's one of the most restrictive in the industry, a lovely gesture that says reams about the carmaker's confidence in his product...

CONCLUSION

The latest Porsche models are lovely to look at and they demonstrate a lot of superb engineering, but we aren't impressed by the inevitable «economic» compromises and short cuts taken to provide a good profit margin. As if even a soul had its price... ☺

RATING
PORSCHE 911-Boxster

CONCEPT :   **62%**
Technology	90
Safety :	90
Interior space :	20
Trunk volume:	30
Quality/fit/finish :	80

DRIVING: **83%**
Cockpit :	80
Performance :	85
Handling :	80
Steering :	80
Braking :	90

ORIGINAL EQUIPMENT: **81%**
Tires :	90
Headlights :	80
Wipers :	80
Rear defroster :	75
Radio :	80

COMFORT :   **60%**
Seats :	80
Suspension :	70
Sound level:	10
Conveniences :	60
Air conditioning :	80

BUDGET :   **53%**
Price :	0
Fuel economy :	65
Insurance :	35
Satisfaction :	85
Depreciation :	80

Overall rating: **67.8%**

NEW FOR 1999

• No information available when book was ready for publication.

ENGINES / TRANSMISSIONS / PERFORMANCES

Model/ version	Type / timing valve / fuel system	Displacement cu in	Power bhp @ rpm	Torque lb-ft @ rpm	Compres. ratio	Driving wheels / transmission	Final ratio	Acceler. 0-60 mph s	Standing 1/4 & 5/8 mile s	Acceler. 50-75 mph s	Braking 60-0 mph f	Top speed mph	Lateral acceler. G	Noise level dBA	Fuel economy mpg City	Highway	Fuel type Octane
Boxster	H6* 2.5 DOHC- 24-SFI	151	201 @ 6000	181 @ 4500	11.0 :1	rear - M5	3.89	7.0	14.8 27.7	4.8	115	146	0.91	70-75	18	27	S 92
						rear - A5	4.21	7.8	15.2 28.4	5.1	118	143	0.91	70-75	16	25	S 92
911	H6* 3.4 DOHC-24-DEI	207	296 @ 6800	258 @ 4600	11.3 :1	rear - M6	3.44	5.4	13.6 25.8	4.3	121	170	0.91	68-74	18	30	S 92
						rear - A5	3.45	6.2	14.2 26.2	4.5	125	167	0.91	68-74	18	30	S 92

PRICE & EQUIPMENT

PORSCHE	Boxster cabrio	911 coupe	911 cabrio
Retail price $:	41,000	65,030	74,460
Dealer invoice $:	35,895	54,621	64,523
Shipping & handling $:	765	765	765
Automatic transmission:	O	O	O
Cruise control:	S	S	S
Power steering:	S	S	S
Anti-lock brakes:	S	S	S
Traction control:	S	S	S
Air conditioning:	SA	SA	SA
Leather:	S	S	S
AM/FM/radio-cassette:	S	S	S
Power door locks:	S	S	S
Power windows:	S	S	S
Tilt steering:	S	S	S
Dual adjustable mirrors:	SEH	SEH	SEH
Alloy wheels:	S	S	S
Anti-theft system:	S	S	S

Colors

Exterior: Gray, White, Red, Black, Blue, Yellow.

Interior: Gray, Black, Red, Green.

AT A GLANCE...

Category: rear-wheel drive GT coupes & convertibles.   **Class :** GT

HISTORIC
Introduced in: 1997: Boxster; 1999: 911.
Made in: Zuffenhausen, Stuttgart, Germany.

DEMOGRAPHICS
Model	Men./Wom.	Age	Married	College	Income
911-Boxster	100/0 %	38	80 %	40 %	$ 85 000

INDEX
Safety:	90 %	Satisfaction:	87 %
Depreciation:	22 %	Insurance:	$ 1 685
Cost per mile:	$ 0.77-1.05	Number of dealers:	210

SALES
Model	1996	1997	Result
Boxster	-	6 996	
911	7 150	5 980	- 16.4 %

MAIN COMPETITORS
AUDI TT, BMW Z3, MERCEDES-BENZ SLK.

MAINTENANCE REQUIRED BY WARRANTY
First revision:	Frequency:	Diagnostic plug:
15 000 miles	15 000 miles	Yes

SPECIFICATIONS

Model	Version Trim	Body/ Seats	Interior volume cu ft	Trunk volume cu ft	Cd	Wheel base in	Lght x Wdgth x Hght in x in x in	Curb weight lb	Susp. ft/rr	Brake ft/rr	Steering type	Turning diameter ft	Steer. turns nber.	Fuel tank gal	tire size	Standard tires make	model	Standard powertrain
PORSCHE	General warranty : 2 years / unlimited; antipollution : 2 years / 25 000 miles; surface rust-perforration 3 years-10 years / unlimited.																	
911 Carrera Coupe	2dr.cpe.2+2	NA	4.6	0.30	92.6	174.5X65.5X51.8	2910	ih/ih	vd/ABS	pwr.r&p.	34.8	2.98	16.9	fr.205/50ZR17	Bridgestone	S-02	H6/3.4/M6
911 Carrera Cabriolet	2dr.con.2+2	NA	4.6	0.32	92.6	174.5X65.5X51.4	3075	ih/ih	vd/ABS	pwr.r&p.	34.8	2.98	16.9	re.255/40ZR17	Bridgestone	S-02	H6/3.4/A5
Boxster	base	2dr.con. 2	NA	9.2	0.31	95.2	171.0X70.1X50.8	2822	ih/ih	dc/ABS	pwr.r&p.	35.8	2.98	15.3	fr.205/55ZR16	Bridgestone	S-02	H6/2.5/M5
Boxster	Triptronic	2dr.con. 2	NA	9.2	0.31	95.2	171.0X70.1X50.8	2954	ih/ih	dc/ABS	pwr.r&p.	35.8	2.98	15.3	re.225/50ZR16	Bridgestone	S-02	H6/2.5/A5

Needed: One Great Idea

Saab is always hoping to improve its sales performances in North America, but in spite of all its efforts, sales stagnate at a level much lower than those achieved by its direct rivals. The renewal of the 900 Series, recently renamed the 9-3, and sprucing up the 9-5 are bringing more than a glimmer of hope to this company's top brass, who'd like nothing more than to turn things around for this firm. This carmaker builds rather anonymous cars, yet it has come up with some special features, such as the turbocharged engine, that has become a handicap on markets where V6 and V8 engines rule as lords and masters...

MODEL RANGE

The Saab 9-3 comes in a 5-door sedan, a 3-door coupe or a 2-door convertilbe offered in base or SE trim. The only engines now available are 2.0L 4-cylinder conventional gas engines on the base models and a turbocharged version on the SE models. The 5-speed manual transmission is standard and a 4-speed automatic is sold as an extra. Standard equipment on the 9-3 models is very rich, since it includes luxury items such as heated seats and climate control and the only options for the base model are the automatic transmission, leather-trim seats and sunroof.

TECHNICAL FEATURES

The 9-3's steel unibody was derived from the Opel Vectra platform. But it still has the main stylistic attributes that characterized previous models. All the elements are there, car dimensions and shape and the over-all look that make it unmistakably a Saab. The car body is much more robust, especially that of the convertible, that's equipped with a roof, designed and built by ASC, and that's lined and has a power mechanism. Aerodynamics are great, since the drag coefficient is 0.30 for the sedan and 0.36 for the convertible with the roof on. The transversal engines have allowed engineers to trim down the front overhang and improve weight distribution in a 60/40% ratio. The independent front suspension is a MacPherson design with A-arms and struts, while at the rear, there's the semi-independent self-steering axle There's an anti-roll bar at both extremities. Cars are equipped with four-wheel disc brakes linked to a standard ABS system. The auto-

matic transmission (Aisin-Warner) functions according to three settings: normal, sport or winter, the latter allowing the driver to accelerate in 3rd gear at speeds up to 80 km/hr, for better road adherence. Surprising that traction control isn't included on a car that hails from Sweden...

PROS

+ LOOKS. The 9-3 has a conservative, classic body design that is in keeping with the carmaker's traditions and was a real asset on previous models.

+ SAFETY FEATURES. This meticulously designed, robust car protects occupants in the event of a collision and is equipped with side-impact airbags, still a rather rare feature in this category.

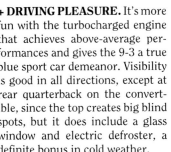

+ DRIVING PLEASURE. It's more fun with the turbocharged engine that achieves above-average performances and gives the 9-3 a true blue sport car demeanor. Visibility is good in all directions, except at rear quarterback on the convertible, since the top creates big blind spots, but it does include a glass window and electric defroster, a definite bonus in cold weather.

+ QUALITY. These cars are solidly built, finish job is clean and tight and trim materials look very sophisticated and creamy, like the superb leather seat coverings.

+ PRICE. The 9-3's aren't too expensive when you consider their luxury and sporty attributes as well as their extensive equipment.

+ BRAKES. They're gutsy, easy to

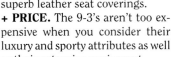

apply and balanced in all circumstances and lining endurance is better than what it's been up until now.

+ INSTRUMENT PANEL. The layout is neat and logical, but it's nothing like an airplane cockpit, as Saab marketing experts purport it to be.

+ CONVENIENCE FEATURES. The trunk is very spacious and modular and there are numerous storage areas throughout the cabin.

+ EQUIPMENT. It's very rich and extensive, bestowing a luxury status to even the base model, thus justifying its price and putting in a favorable, albeit theoretical, position when compared with rivals.

+ INSTRUMENTS. An original feature: you can turn off the instrumentation lighting for night driving, leaving only the speedometer illuminated, to improve concentration. In the event of an emergency, the lighting turns on automatically.

CONS

- DEPRECIATION. It's the biggest handicap so these cars aren't a really wise investment.

-V6 ENGINE. Its absence puts the Saab 9-3 in a disadvantageous position compared to most rivals.

- RIDE COMFORT. The suspension isn't the most velvety around and limited suspension travel makes the front end bottom out fairly quickly. On the SE versions, the small tires don't do anyone a favor and noise is always annoyingly loud due to the uncivilized engines and pervasive road noise.

-TORQUE. It really affects models equipped with the turbocharged engine since there's a lot of wheel slippage on quick accelerations and car path all over the map.

- CONTROLS. They're too unusual and take some getting used to, like the ignition key on the main tunnel or the window or interior lighting switches, always hard to find, since they're located in weird places.

- TO BE IMPROVED UPON: narrow cabin space, only average-efficient climate control and limited sales network.

CONCLUSION

Saab needs to come up with a great idea to sell its products that in a sense are no more unique than other cars on the current market. A 4X4 Outback model advertised by Indiana Jones driving across New Zealand, rather than a Top Gun publicity campaign for models that really can't get off the ground... ☺

RATING SAAB 9³		
CONCEPT :		74%
Technology	80	
Safety :	90	
Interior space :	50	
Trunk volume:	70	
Quality/fit/finish :	80	
DRIVING:		68%
Cockpit :	80	
Performance :	60	
Handling :	60	
Steering :	80	
Braking :	60	
ORIGINAL EQUIPMENT:		78%
Tires :	80	
Headlights :	80	
Wipers :	75	
Rear defroster :	80	
Radio :	75	
COMFORT :		70%
Seats :	80	
Suspension :	70	
Sound level :	50	
Conveniences :	70	
Air conditioning :	80	
BUDGET :		50%
Price :	25	
Fuel economy :	60	
Insurance :	45	
Satisfaction :	80	
Depreciation :	40	
Overall rating:		**68.0%**

NEW FOR 1999

- 2.0L turbocharged engine delivering 200 hp.
- Reworked gear ratios on the manual gearbox.
- 16-inch, 5-spoke aluminum wheels on the SE.
- Built-in armrest and pivoting cup-holder.
- Roof trim.
- Metallic exterior shade: Frost Grey.

ENGINES / TRANSMISSIONS / PERFORMANCES

Model/ version	Type / timing valve / fuel system	Displacement cu in	Power bhp @ rpm	Torque lb-ft @ rpm	Compres. ratio	Driving wheels / transmission	Final ratio	Acceler. 0-60 mph s	Standing 1/4 & 5/8 mile s	Acceler. 50-75 mph s	Braking 60-0 mph f	Top speed mph	Lateral acceler. G	Noise level dBA	Fuel economy mpg City Highway	Fuel type Octane
base, 1)	L4T 2.0 DOHC-16-EFI	121	185 @ 5500	194 @ 2100	9.2: 1	front - M5*	3.82	10.2	17.4	31.3	7.0	131	127	0.80	68	19 30	S 91
			185 @ 5750	170 @ 2000	9.2: 1	front - A4	2.86	11.0	18.0	31.9	7.6	128	124	0.80	68	18 29	S 91
SE	L4T 2.0 DOHC-16-EFI	121	200 @ 5500	209 @ 2300	10.5 :1	front - M5*	3.82	7.5	15.6	27.6	5.5	125	137	0.80	68	18 29	S 91
						front - A4	2.86	8.3	16.4	28.3	6.0	134	127	0.80	68	17 26	S 91

1) and automatic SE

PRICE & EQUIPMENT

SAAB 9³	Coupe	Sedan	Conv	SE sdn.	SE con.
Retail price $:	25,500	26,000	36,500	31,500	41,500
Dealer invoice $:	24,126	24,230	34,895	29,795	39.845
Shipping & handling $:	550	550	550	550	550
Automatic transmission:	O	O	O	O	O
Cruise control:	S	S	S	S	S
Power steering:	S	S	S	S	S
Anti-lock brakes:	S	S	S	S	S
Traction control:	-	-	-	-	-
Air conditioning:	SM	SM	SM	SA	SA
Leather:	OH	OH	SH	SH	SH
AM/FM/radio-cassette:	S	S	S	S	S
Power door locks:	S	S	S	S	S
Power windows:	S	S	S	S	S
Tilt steering:	S	S	S	S	S
Dual adjustable mirrors:	SEH	SEH	SEH	SEH	SEH
Alloy wheels:	S	S	S	S	S
Anti-theft system:	S	S	S	S	S

Colors

Exterior: White, Black, Blue, Red, Grey, Green, Silver, Violet.

Interior: Gray, Beige, Black, Tan.

AT A GLANCE...

Category: front-wheel drive luxury coupes, conv. & sedans   **Class :** 7

HISTORIC

Introduced in:	1969-1993
Made in:	Trollhattan, Sweden & Nystad, Finland (convertible).

DEMOGRAPHICS

Model	Men./Wom.	Age	Married	College	Income
9³	85/15 %	47	83 %	85 %	$ 80 000

INDEX

Safety:	90 %	Satisfaction:	80 %
Depreciation:	60 %	Insurance:	$ 1 250-1 475
Cost per mile:	$ 0.62	Number of dealers:	365

SALES

Model	1996	1997	Result
9³	22 288	22 949	+ 3.0 %

MAIN COMPETITORS

ACURA TL , AUDI A4, BMW 3-Series, INFINITI I30, LEXUS ES 300, MAZDA Millenia, NISSAN Maxima, VOLVO 70.

MAINTENANCE REQUIRED BY WARRANTY

First revision:	Frequency:	Diagnostic plug:
3 000 miles	6 000 miles	Yes

SPECIFICATIONS

Model	Version Trim	Body/ Seats	Interior volume cu ft	Trunk volume cu ft	Cd	Wheel base in	Lght x Wdgth x Hght in x in x in	Curb weight lb	Susp. ft/rr	Brake ft/rr	Steering type	Turning diameter ft	Steer. turns nber.	Fuel tank gal	tire size	Standard tires make	model	Standard powertrain
SAAB		Warranty: 4 years / 50 000 miles; corrosion, perforation: 6 years / 100 000 miles.																
9³	S	2dr.con.4	80.0	12.5	0.34	102.6	182.2x67.4x56.0	3197	ih/sih	dc/ABS	pwr.r&p.	34.4	3.0	18.0	195/60VR15	Michelin	-	L4T/2.0/M5
9³	S	3dr.cpe.5	89.6	21.7	0.30	102.6	182.2x67.4x56.2	2987	ih/sih	dc/ABS	pwr.r&p.	34.4	3.0	18.0	205/50ZR16	Michelin	-	L4T/2.0/M5
9³	S	5dr.sdn.5	89.6	21.7	0.30	102.6	182.2x67.4x56.2	3031	ih/sih	dc/ABS	pwr.r&p.	34.4	3.0	18.0	195/60VR15	Michelin	-	L4T/2.0/M5
9³	SE	2dr.con.4	80.0	12.5	0.34	102.6	182.2x67.4x56.0	3196	ih/sih	dc/ABS	pwr.r&p.	34.4	3.0	18.0	205/50ZR16	Michelin	Pilot	L4T/2.0/M5
9³	SE	5dr.sdn.5	89.6	21.7	0.30	102.6	182.2x67.4x56.2	3031	ih/sih	dc/ABS	pwr.r&p.	34.4	3.0	18.0	205/50ZR16	Michelin	Pilot	L4T/2.0/M5

After fourteen years of good and loyal service, the 9000 has finally been replaced by a newcomer that resembles it quite a bit, at least physically, because on the technical level, the 9-5 has come a long way. Yet when you say it's progressed, it has done so in a very conservative way. The build is more robust and the rear suspension is now independent, but the engines are the same as before. All other modifications are geared to enhance ride comfort and esthetics.

MODEL RANGE

The 9-5 comes as a four-door sedan in base or SE, animated by a standard 2.3L turbocharged 4-cylinder engine developing 170 hp or equipped with an optional 3.0L turbocharged V6 that develops 200 hp. A 5-speed manual transmission is standard with the 2.3L, but the V6 is only available with an automatic. Original equipment items are very extensive and luxurious since they include such things as climate control, heated seats, antilock braking system, traction control and radio-tape deck and CD player. The most important options are still the automatic transmission, leather seats and sunroof.

TECHNICAL FEATURES

The 9000's successor is inspired by the Opel Vectra platform, a GM product designed and built in Europe. The galvanized steel unibody benefits from super-efficient aerodynamics since the drag coefficient is only 0.29. It's extremely robust so as to provide maximum passenger protection in the event of a collision. The front suspension is independent and consists of a MacPherson strut design, whereas at the rear, the axle is supported by several control arms and both suspensions include an anti-roll bar. The disc brake system is paired up with an antilock braking device that shares its sensors with the traction control system, both being standard items. The 2.3L 4-cylinder engine, equipped with two balancing arbors to reduce friction, is highly efficient, thanks to the 16-valve DOHC distribution and a Saab-designed distributionless ignition system. The V6 develops 200 hp with the help of a Garrett T3 compressor with air interchanger that reduces pollutant emissions, but doesn't produce sheer, brute power that's rather average for an engine of this displacement.

In Progress..?

PROS

+ **PERFORMANCES.** The V6 engine is more muscular than the 4-cylinder, since it benefits from a better power to weight ratio on accelerations and pickup, that are average in this category and aren't really noteworthy.

+ **SAFETY.** The 9-5's body has been beefed up to effectively protect occupants in the event of an accident. So much so that at Auto Shows, Saab exhibits a model that's undergone a collision test and has come out unscathed.

+ **SILHOUETTE.** The 9-5 is a gorgeous car. Its clean, discreet design has an unmistakable resemblance to the previous model, preserving typical Saab traits.

+ **DRIVING PLEASURE.** The cockpit is super, visibility is only slightly obstructed at rear quarterback, the neatly organized instrument panel is loaded with gauges and such.

+ **RIDE COMFORT.** Things have really improved in this department, since the rear axle profits from more generous suspension travel and both suspensions are smoother and handle road faults like champions. Seats are just as comfy as before, providing effective lateral and lumbar support.

+ **USEFUL SPACE.** The 9-5's cabin is even more spacious than on the 9000. Five passengers will be right at home and the trunk gobbles up all their luggage with no problem at all. It's also convertible, so you can store heaps of stuff when the seatbench is folded down.

+ **QUALITY.** This car has a very robust feel, the finish job is beautifully executed and trim materials are of superb qualtiy and of course, there are all kinds of amenities.

+ **NEAT FEATURE:** The convex exterior mirror on the driver's side that eliminates the lateral blind spot.

CONS

- **PERFORMANCES.** The 4-cylinder engine isn't up to much and only musters run-of-the-mill accelerations and pickup and lots of less expensive cars do a heck of a lot better. The turbocharged engine's response time is rather slow and you have to get used to this gap, otherwise you'll be forever frustrated.

- **HANDLING.** It's fine at normal speeds, but you have to remember that the 9-5 doesn't have the same spontaneous sports car capabilities as its predecessor. The soft suspension generates lots of sway and car demeanor is sensitive to the state the road's in. It's tough keeping this car on the straight and narrow in crosswinds and the steering is over-assisted so it's a bit light and you have to keep compensating for this tendency to wander off.

- **TRANSMISSION.** The manual isn't too zippy and quick on the draw for gears are slow to kick in. You often get the impression that the engine's stalling n first gear, due to very sluggish turbocharger response time.

- **BRAKES.** They weren't great on our test car (that was in super shape). Sudden stops were achieved at an average 165 ft. Brakes are nice and gradual, but ABS doesn't get rid of all wheel lock, so car path isn't a sure, straight-ahead thing.

- **BUDGET.** Saab's aren't great buys. They're fun to drive, but they're pricey and upkeep is costly and then there's the poor resale value to consider. Such an expensive venture is ridiculous, unless of course, you're a dyed-in-the-wool car buff.

- **STORAGE SPACE.** The glove compartment is a reasonable size, but other storage spots are skimpy, such as the slim door side-pockets. Cup-holders aren't terribly convenient.

- **TO BE IMPROVED UPON:** The flat pancake spare tire that doesn't jive with such and expensive car.

CONCLUSION

The 9-5 has become a safer, more comfy car, but it doesn't have true sports car attributes, with all the pros and cons that this entails. Which, in our opinion, won't attract too many new customers☺

RATING SAAB 9⁵		
CONCEPT :		**86%**
Technology	80	
Safety :	100	
Interior space :	80	
Trunk volume:	90	
Quality/fit/finish :	80	
DRIVING:		**62%**
Cockpit :	80	
Performance :	50	
Handling :	60	
Steering :	75	
Braking :	45	
ORIGINAL EQUIPMENT:		**78%**
Tires :	80	
Headlights :	80	
Wipers :	75	
Rear defroster :	75	
Radio :	80	
COMFORT :		**69%**
Seats :	80	
Suspension :	75	
Sound level :	50	
Conveniences :	60	
Air conditioning :	80	
BUDGET :		**44%**
Price :	0	
Fuel economy :	65	
Insurance :	30	
Satisfaction :	80	
Depreciation :	45	
Overall rating:		**67.8%**

NEW FOR 1999

- Dual-section side-impact airbags.
- New-design safety belts.
- Metallic exterior shade: Frost Grey.
- SE option package that includes: leather seat coverings, memory mirrors and seats, five-spoke rims, sunroof and Harman/Kardon sound system.

ENGINES

Model/ version	Type / timing valve / fuel system	Displacement cu in	Power bhp @ rpm	Torque lb-ft @ rpm
base/SE	L4T* 2.3 DOHC-16-EFI	140	170 @ 5500	206 @ 1800
option	V6T 3.0 DOHC-24-EFI	181	200 @ 5000	229 @ 2100

TRANSMISSIONS

Compres. ratio	Driving wheels / transmission	Final ratio
9.3 :1	front - M5*	4.05
	front - A4	2.55
9.5 :1	front - A4*	2.55

PERFORMANCES

Acceler. 0-60 mph s	Standing 1/4 & 5/8 mile s	Acceler. 50-75 mph s	Braking 60-0 mph f	Top speed mph	Lateral acceler. G	Noise level dBA	Fuel economy mpg City	Highway	Fuel type Octane
10.6	17.2 29.5	6.4	157	137	0.80	65-72	19	32	S 91
11.7	17.7 31.2	7.5	167	130	0.80	65-72	17	27	S 91
NA									S 91

PRICE & EQUIPMENT

SAAB 9⁵	base	SE
Retail price $:	29,995	36,800
Dealer invoice $:	27,895	34,574
Shipping & handling $:	550	550
Automatic transmission:	O	O
Cruise control:	S	S
Power steering:	S	S
Anti-lock brakes:	S	S
Traction control:	S	S
Air conditioning:	SA	SA
Leather:	OH	SH
AM/FM/radio-cassette:	SCD	SCD
Power door locks:	S	S
Power windows:	S	S
Tilt steering:	S	S
Dual adjustable mirrors:	SEH	SEH
Alloy wheels:	S	S
Anti-theft system:	S	S

Colors

Exterior: White, Black, Blue, Red, Gray, Silver, Night blue.

Interior: Gray, Beige, Black, Tan.

AT A GLANCE...

Category: front-wheel drive luxury sport sedans.   **Class :** 7

HISTORIC

Introduced in:	1984-1999
Made in:	Trollhattan, Sweden

DEMOGRAPHICS

Model	Men./Wom.	Age	Married	College	Income
9⁵	68/32 %	49	100 %	100 %	$ 80 000

INDEX

Safety:	100 %	Satisfaction:	85 %
Depreciation:	40 %	Insurance:	$1 525
Cost per mile:	$ 0.67	Number of dealers:	365

SALES

Model	1996	1997	Result	
9000	5 167	4 692	- 9.2 %	1.8 %

MAIN COMPETITORS

ACURA 3.5 RL, AUDI A6, BMW 5-Series, VOLVO 90.

MAINTENANCE REQUIRED BY WARRANTY

First revision:	Frequency:	Diagnostic plug:
3 000 miles	6 000 miles	Yes

SPECIFICATIONS

Model Version Trim	Body/ Seats	Interior volume cu ft	Trunk volume cu ft	Cd	Wheel base in	Lght x Wdgth x Hght in x in x in	Curb weight lb	Susp. ft/rr	Brake ft/rr	Steering type	Turning diameter ft	Steer. turns nber.	Fuel tank gal	tire size	Standard tires make	model	Standard powertrain
SAAB		Warranty: 4 years / 50 000 miles; corrosion, perforation: 6 years / 100 000 miles.															
9⁵ base	4dr.sdn5	99.0	15.9	0.29	106.4	189.2x70.5x57.0	3285	ih/lh	dc/ABS	pwr.r&p.	35.4	2.9	19.8	215/55R16	-		- L4T/2.3/M5
9⁵ SE	4dr.sdn5	99.0	15.9	0.29	106.4	189.2x70.5x57.0	3560	ih/lh	dc/ABS	pwr.r&p.	35.4	2.9	19.8	215/55R16	-		- L4T/2.3/M5

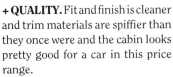
The more time passes, the more the real truth about Saturn is brought to light. At first, these cars were unusual, because they were different, and they were built by a carmaker with a different approach, so we thought we were witnessing a special event in the automobile industry. A few years later, we realize that no real progress has been made since, quite the opposite, the product has regressed and no new model has come along to beef up this fragile lineup. It's easier to organize reunions and customers' birthdays rather than bring real reform to an administration that has to bow to the folks at General Motors headquarters.

MODEL RANGE

The Saturn family is available in three different body designs: a 2-door coupe in SC1 and SC2 trim levels, a four-door sedan in SL, SL1 and SL2 trim and a four-door station wagon in SW1 and SW2 versions. Cars are equipped with a standard 5-speed manual transmission or a 4-speed automatic that's available as an extra. The 100-hp SOHC 1.9L engine equips the 1 versions and its 124-hp DOHC counterpart animates the 2 versions. Original equipment varies, from Spartan simple on the SL sedan to the chromed-up, fancy-looking 2 versions and the option list is as long as your arm.

TECHNICAL FEATURES

All Saturn's have the same structural design, consisting of a metallic cage mounted on a steel platform (that includes some galvanized panels), on which rests the body that includes steel horizontal panels (engine hood, trunk lid and roof) and thermoformed polymer for vertical panels (fenders, doors and rear hatch on the station wagon). The suspension is fully independent and disc and drum brakes can benefit from optional ABS on all models, including the 2 versions.

PROS

+ STYLE. It's rather lovely, but it isn't terribly original, really. Yet this kind of quiet elegance will virtually always be in style and the car has a distinctive look that's easily identified.

+ DESIGN CONCEPT. It's quite unique on the North American

Average...

market since the demise of General Motors minivans based on the same technology. The polymer-clad steel structure is rust-resistant as well as ding-and dent-resistant and Saturn is the only carmaker in the world to still use this technique that isn't cheap by any means.

+ CABIN SPACE. There's higher ceiling clearance, but otherwise it has the same dimensions. Two adults and two children will be comfortably seated aboard, even in the rear seats of the most recent coupe and there's quite a bit of room to breathe even with the low ceiling.

+ RIDE COMFORT. It's improved since the front seats were redesigned and they now provide adequate lateral and lumbar support. And more

generous suspension travel handles road bumps with more aplomb and the car doesn't bottom out as much.

+ HANDLING. It's a definite asset on these cars that tend to go into understeer, but they stay nice and neutral, so the average driver isn't in for any unpleasant surprises.

+ BRAKES. They're efficient and the average-length sudden stopping distances prove it. The car stays nice and straight with the optional ABS and linings are pretty tough.

+ PERFORMANCES. They're adequate for both engines, but these brutes are rough and rambunctious.

+ VISIBILITY. It's super on all models with the generous window surfaces and reasonably slim roof supports.

+ QUALITY. Fit and finish is cleaner and trim materials are spiffier than they once were and the cabin looks pretty good for a car in this price range.

CONS

- PRICE. It goes up and up, as soon as you start checking out all the options, so you end up paying a lot more than the advertised price.

- NOISE LEVEL. It's pervasive and doesn't let up and it comes at you from everywhere. From the rough and ready engines and the thumping tires that telegraph every bloody bump on the road, so much so that you're in for a drum concert that blots out all other noise.

- STEERING. The manual on the SL is an insult to the intelligence. It's imprecise, suffers from a poor reduction ratio and turns every parking maneuver into a nightmare.

-BRAKES. Without ABS, emergency stops can be pretty awful due to front wheel lock that engenders dangerous swerving that's hard to control when you're caught off guard. The antilock braking system and traction control aren't worth their salt, since accelerations and braking can be pretty rough

-TRANSMISSION. The automatic shifter is jerky and, like the manual, it provides little braking effect, so you often have to brake to slow down.

- CONVENIENCE FEATURES. Storage spots are skimpy when it comes to size and the cargo hold may be modular, but it isn't too deep or wide due to the big wheel housings.

- REAR SEATS. It isn't easy climbing aboard with those slim doors and the curved roof design. Once you're seated, you aren't too comfy either, because the seat cushion is short and the back is hard and flat.

-TO BE IMPROVED UPON: Power window controls poorly located on the center console and poor-quality original tires.

CONCLUSION

The Saturn's aren't as up-to-date as they were when they were first sold. The best asset remains the friendly service you get at the dealers': you get the red carpet treatment, so much so that at Saturn you can find anything, even a friend.. ☺

RATING
SATURN SC-SL-SW

CONCEPT :		73%
Technology	80	
Safety :	100	
Interior space :	60	
Trunk volume:	50	
Quality/fit/finish :	75	

DRIVING:		63%
Cockpit :	80	
Performance :	50	
Handling :	60	
Steering :	75	
Braking :	50	

ORIGINAL EQUIPMENT:		68%
Tires :	75	
Headlights :	70	
Wipers :	70	
Rear defroster :	60	
Radio :	65	

COMFORT :		72%
Seats :	75	
Suspension :	75	
Sound level :	60	
Conveniences :	70	
Air conditioning :	80	

BUDGET :		71%
Price :	70	
Fuel economy :	80	
Insurance :	70	
Satisfaction :	85	
Depreciation :	50	

| **Overall rating:** | | **69.4%** |

NEW FOR 1999
- Improved engine components for both models, better fuel efficiency and less noise and vibration.
- Rear drum brakes for the whole lineup.
- Better height adjustment on seat belts.
- New-design rims on the SC2.
- Bigger-capacity windshield washer reservoir.

ENGINES

Model/ version	Type / timing valve / fuel system	Displacement cu in	Power bhp @ rpm	Torque lb-ft @ rpm	Compres. ratio
1)	L4* 1.9 SOHC-8-MPSFI	116	100 @ 5000	114 @ 2400	9.3 :1
2)	L4* 1.9 DOHC-16-MPSFI	116	124 @ 5600	122 @ 4800	9.5 :1

1) SL,SL1,SC1.   2) SC2, SL2.

TRANSMISSIONS

Driving wheels / transmission	Final ratio
front - M5*	4.06
front - A4	4.06
front - M5*	4.06
front - A4	4.06

PERFORMANCES

Acceler. 0-60 mph s	Standing 1/4 & 5/8 mile s		Acceler. 50-75 mph s	Braking 60-0 mph f	Top speed mph	Lateral acceler. G	Noise level dBA	Fuel economy mpg City	Highway	Fuel type Octane
11.0	18.0	32.4	7.8	134	103	0.75	70	28	38	R 87
12.2	18.5	33.2	10.0	144	100	0.75	70	27	35	R 87
8.7	16.5	29.7	6.3	138	115	0.78	70	27	36	R 87
9.8	16.7	30.7	6.8	144	112	0.78	70	23	34	R 87

PRICE & EQUIPMENT

SATURN	SL	SC1-SL1-SW1	SC2-SL2-SW2
Retail price $:	10,595	11,295	12,755
Dealer invoice $:	9,535	10,166	11,480
Shipping & handling $:	440	440	440
Automatic transmission:	O	O	O
Cruise control:	-	O	O
Power steering:		S	S
Anti-lock brakes:	O	O	OCD
Traction control:	O	O	O
Air conditioning:	O	O	S
Leather:	-	-	O
AM/FM/radio-cassette:	O	O	O
Power door locks:	-	O	O
Power windows:	-	O	O
Tilt steering:	S	S	S
Dual adjustable mirrors:	O	SM	SM
Alloy wheels:	-	-	O
Anti-theft system:	O	O	O

Colors

Exterior: White, Navy blue, Wildberry, Silver, Plum, Green, Black, Red, Gold.

Interior: Tan, Gray, Black.

AT A GLANCE...

Category: front-wheel drive compact coupes, sdn & wgn.   **Class :** 3

HISTORIC
Introduced in: 1990-1996-97
Made in: Spring Hill, Tennessee, USA.

DEMOGRAPHICS
Model	Men./Wom.	Age	Married	College	Income
Coupe	30/70 %	36	36 %	53 %	$ 52 000
Sedan, Wagon	57/43 %	40	67 %	56 %	$ 48 000

INDEX
Safety:	100 %	Satisfaction:	90 %
Depreciation:	52 %	Insurance:	$ 775 -835
Cost per mile:	$ 0.35	Number of dealers:	300

SALES
Model	1996	1997	Result
Saturn	278 574	251 099	- 9.9 %

MAIN COMPETITORS
Saturn SL/SW: ACURA Integra, CHEVROLET Cavalier, DODGE-PLYMOUTH Neon, FORD Escort, HONDA Civic, HYUNDAI Elantra, MAZDA Protegé, NISSAN Sentra, PONTIAC Sunfire, SUBARU Impreza, TOYOTA Corolla, VW Jetta.
Saturn SC: EAGLE Talon, HYUNDAI Tiburon, NISSAN 200SX, TOYOTA Paseo, VOLKSWAGEN New Beetle.

MAINTENANCE REQUIRED BY WARRANTY
First revision:	Frequency:	Diagnostic plug:
3 000 miles	6 000 miles	Yes

SPECIFICATIONS

Model Version Trim	Body/ Seats	Interior volume cu ft	Trunk volume cu ft	Cd	Wheel base in	Lght x Wdgth x Hght in x in x in	Curb weight lb	Susp. ft/rr	Brake ft/rr	Steering type	Turning diameter ft	Steer. turns nber.	Fuel tank gal	tire size	Standard tires make	model	Standard powertrain
SATURN	General warranty: 3 years / 36 000 miles; antipollution: 5 years / 50 000 miles; perforation corrosion: 6 years / 100 000 miles. Roadside assistance.																
SC1	3dr.cpe. 4	84.1	11.4	0.33	102.4	180.0x67.3x53.0	2309	ih/ih	dc/dr	pwr.r&p.	37.1	3.00	12.1	175/70R14	-	-	L4/1.9/M5
SC2	3dr.cpe. 4	84.1	11.4	0.33	102.4	180.0x67.3x53.0	2380	ih/ih	dc/dr	pwr.r&p.	37.1	2.67	12.1	195/60R15	Firestone	GTA	L4/1.9/M5
SL	4dr.sdn 5	91.0	12.1	0.31	102.4	176.9x66.7x55.0	2326	ih/ih	dc/dr	r&p.	37.1	4.00	12.1	175/70R14	-	-	L4/1.9/M5
SL1	4dr.sdn 5	91.0	12.1	0.31	102.4	176.9x66.7x55.0	2326	ih/ih	dc/dr	pwr.r&p.	37.1	3.00	12.1	175/70R14	-	-	L4/1.9/M5
SL2	4dr.sdn 5	91.0	12.1	0.31	102.4	176.9x66.7x55.0	2392	ih/ih	dc/dr	pwr.r&p.	37.1	2.67	12.1	185/65R15	-	-	L4/1.9/M5
SW1	4dr.wgn. 5	91.8	24.9	0.36	102.4	176.9x66.7x55.6	2392	ih/ih	dc/dr	pwr.r&p.	37.1	3.00	12.1	175/70R14	-	-	L4/1.9/M5
SW2	4dr.wgn. 5	91.8	24.9	0.36	102.4	176.9x66.7x55.6	2454	ih/ih	dc/dr	pwr.r&p.	37.1	2.67	12.1	185/65R15	-	-	L4/1.9/M5

The Subaru Forester hit the market right in the midst of the Outback frenzy that created a renewed interest in Subaru's four-wheel drive vehicles, so it gained instant success. Since then, the 4X4 fever has subsided, since people realized that the first buyers, like some automobile journalists, had maybe got carried away and that this kind of enthusiasm was a bit premature. The fact is, in no time flat, the compact SUV market segment got literally crowded with super-competitive models out to be at the top of the heap.

MODEL RANGE

The Forester is a compact all-wheel drive sport-utility vehicle offered in a single 4-door station wagon model. It's driven by a 2.5L H4 engine attached to an original manual transmission or an optional automatic, sold in L and S trim levels. The first model is fairly well equipped since the second model only benefits from added cruise control and light alloy rims.

TECHNICAL FEATURES

The Forester was designed on the Impreza platform so it borrows its main mechanical components. The monocoque body is made of rust-resistant steel. Its bulky, boxy SUV build explains why aerodynamic efficiency is far from perfect, since it yields a coefficient more akin to that of trucks than cars. Both suspensions are independent and consist of MacPherson struts and stabilizer bar. The L model is equipped with standard disc and drum brakes, but the S version benefits from disc brakes linked to an antilock braking system. Both cars are equipped with power rack-and-pinion steering.

PROS

+ CONCEPT. The idea of building a vehicle that's half-car, half-SUV is pretty neat, similar to the concept behind the CR-V design at Honda and the RAV4 at Toyota. This blend ensures competent handling and yet offers the possibility of off-road maneuvers, albeit where the terrain isn't too rough.

+ SAFETY. Automatic all-wheel drive lets you make tracks with assurance in northerly regions where you're in for slippery conditions part of the year, not to mention the fun of being able to take a trek on roads ... in the forest.

+ HANDLING. The Forester is solid on its feet even with the generous ground clearance that raises the

Not Foolproof...

center of gravity so that it's higher than on a car. The Forester takes curves nicely and it stays neutral at normal speeds thanks to all-wheel drive.

+ DRIVING PLEASURE. You can make some pretty slick moves with this compact vehicle, due to the reasonable steer angle, even though steering does suffer from a reduction ratio that can cramp your style a bit (3.4 turns).

+ CONVENIENCE FEATURES. The baggage compartment is modular and it holds heaps of stuff for it's nice and high and access is super with the rear hatch that opens wide and that lowers to trunk level.

+ RIDE COMFORT. The suspension is fairly civilized when tackling road faults, the front seats are nicely shaped and noise interference is

reasonably low, so you can make long trips without tiring too much.

+ NICE FEATURES: Storage spots up front that include a good-sized glove compartment, door side-pockets that are small but can be closed, shelves on the dashboard and a center compartment divided into two sections. You can hide what's stored in the cargo hold with a luggage cover, a feature you don't get on rival vehicles. The cargo hold floor is well organized and there are scads of other convenience items that are really handy.

CONS

-CAPABILITIES. Off-road rambles are awkward, proof positive that you're inside a vehicle that's more like a high-perched car than a genuine 4X4 and those who'd like to wander off too far in the wild should

remember that the main mechanical components aren't covered with protective plates.

-PERFORMANCES. They're fair to midling, especially with the automatic gearbox. Pickup is far from peppy at full load capacity, something to consider if you want to pull a small trailer weighing up to 1,985 lb. It's hard to believe you have 165 hp under the hood when you compare this engine with the Jeep Cherokee powerplant that, with a mere 25 more hp, makes you feel like you could pull even a house hooked up to the rear...

- TRANSMISSION. The manual makes for more spontaneous driving, but it's tough getting it going, the shifter grinds and it isn't foolproof, if you look at the maintenance bulletins.

- ENGINE. It's noisy and gets the shakes just like the one on the first Beetle, its ancestor after all, and all the upgrading that Subaru has done hasn't corrected this congenital flaw. This engine is a bit of a wimp and doesn't generate much torque, given the displacement.

- CABIN SPACE. It's rather snug in the rear seats, since there isn't too much elbow or toe room, so more than two adults won't be too comfy back there and they'll have a tough time boarding, depending on their build, due to the narrow doors.

- SEATS. Upholstery is very firm especially on the seatbench that's flat as a duneless beach and doesn't offer much lateral or lumbar support and besides seat cushions are terribly short.

- QUALITY. Some of the plastic dashboard trim don't look too nice and jars with the neat, over-all look.

- TIRES. They're poorly suited to this vehicle and are equally awful on asphalt or on off the beaten track treks and the buyer should have at least two types of tires to choose from, depending on how he or she is going to use the vehicle.

- TO BE IMPROVED UPON: Not enough storage compartments in the rear seat area, really poor-quality radio and with dials located way down low.

CONCLUSION

The Forester doesn't do too badly when it comes to sales figures in this category, for it does have several definite assets in its favor. But its neat design hides its real size, since it's more like a station wagon than an all-terrain SUV. ☺

RATING
SUBARU Forester

CONCEPT : **69%**
Technology	75
Safety :	75
Interior space :	60
Trunk volume:	60
Quality/fit/finish :	75

DRIVING: **62%**
Cockpit :	75
Performance :	50
Handling :	50
Steering :	80
Braking :	55

ORIGINAL EQUIPMENT: **77%**
Tires :	75
Headlights :	80
Wipers :	80
Rear defroster :	75
Radio :	75

COMFORT : **66%**
Seats :	65
Suspension :	70
Sound level:	50
Conveniences :	70
Air conditioning :	75

BUDGET : **66%**
Price :	50
Fuel economy :	75
Insurance :	55
Satisfaction :	80
Depreciation :	70

Overall rating: **68.0%**

NEW FOR 1999

- **No major change.**

ENGINES

Model/ version	Type / timing valve / fuel system	Displacement cu in	Power bhp @ rpm	Torque lb-ft @ rpm
L, S.	H4* 2.5 DOHC-16-MPSFI	150	165 @ 5600	162 @ 4000

TRANSMISSIONS

Compres. ratio	Driving wheels / transmission	Final ratio
9.7 :1	four - M5*	4.11
	four - A4	4.44

PERFORMANCES

Acceler. 0-60 mph s	Standing 1/4 & 5/8 mile s	Acceler. 50-75 mph s	Braking 60-0 mph f	Top speed mph	Lateral acceler. G	Noise level dBA	Fuel economy mpg City	Fuel economy mpg Highway	Fuel type Octane
9.2	16.7 30.1	6.7	138	103	0.76	68	19	27	R 87
10.4	17.6 31.5	7.2	141	100	0.76	68	19	25	R 87

PRICE & EQUIPMENT

SUBARU Forester

	L	S
Retail price $:	19,995	22,195
Dealer invoice $:	18,034	19,295
Shipping & handling $:	495	495
Automatic transmission:	O	O
Cruise control:	O	S
Power steering:	S	S
Anti-lock brakes:	S	S
Traction control:	S	S
Air conditioning:	S	S
Leather:	-	-
AM/FM/radio-cassette:	S	S
Power door locks:	S	S
Power windows:	S	S
Tilt steering:	S	S
Dual adjustable mirrors:	SM	SE
Alloy wheels:	O	S
Anti-theft system:	-	-

Colors

Exterior: White, Black, Red, Green.

Interior: Beige,

AT A GLANCE...

Category:	4WD all-purpose vehicles
Class :	utility

HISTORIC
Introduced in:	1998
Made in:	Gunma, Japan.

DEMOGRAPHICS
Model	Men./Wom.	Age	Married	College	Income
Forester	NA				

INDEX
Safety:	75 %	Satisfaction:	78 %
Depreciation:	28 %	Insurance:	$ 965
Cost per mile:	$ 0.47	Number of dealers:	727

SALES
Model	1996	1997	Result
Forester	-	15 988	

MAIN COMPETITORS
CHEVROLET Tracker, HONDA CR-V, SUZUKI Sidekick, TOYOTA RAV4.

MAINTENANCE REQUIRED BY WARRANTY
First revision:	Frequency:	Diagnostic plug:
3 000 miles	7 500 miles	Yes

SPECIFICATIONS

Model	Version Trim	Body/ Seats	Interior volume cu ft	Trunk volume cu ft	Cd	Wheel base in	Lght x Wdgth x Hght in x in x in	Curb weight lb	Susp. ft/rr	Brake ft/rr	Steering type	Turning diameter ft	Steer. turns nber.	Fuel tank gal	tire size	Standard tires make	model	Standard powertrain
SUBARU	General warranty: 3 years / 36 000 miles; powertrain: 5 years / 60 000 miles; corrosion & antipollution: 5 years / unlimited.																	
Forester	L	4dr.wgn. 5	95.1	33.2	0.39	99.4	175.2x68.3x65.0	3040	ih/ih	dc/dr/ABS	pwr.r&p.	38.4	3.4	15.9	205/70R15	Bridgestone	Dueler	H4/2.5/M5
Forester	S	4dr.wgn. 5	95.1	33.2	0.39	99.4	175.2x68.3x65.0	3040	ih/ih	dc/dc/ABS	pwr.r&p.	38.4	3.4	15.9	215/60R16	Bridgestone	Dueler	H4/2.5/M5

In Europe, Subaru is selling lots and lots of these sports models in the Impreza lineup and wins all kinds of awards at international and local car rallies thanks to these all-wheel drive rockets that outclass the most prestigious cars on the planet. In North America, people are looking more for a versatile and safe means of travel that benefits from all-wheel drive. The Impreza is the most affordable car to be able to enjoy this feature, but sales figures indicate that it isn't the top seller in the Subaru lineup.

MODEL RANGE

The Impreza lineup now only includes three all-wheel drive models: a 2.5RS 2-door coupe, a base model four-door sedan and a four-door Outback Sport station wagon. The coupe is powered by a 2.5L engine associated with a 5-speed manual transmission and the two other models are equipped with a 2.2L engine hooked up to a standard manual gearbox or an optional automatic.

TECHNICAL FEATURES

The Impreza has a steel unibody derived from the Legacy platform, but with a shorter wheelbase. In spite of its graceful curves, it only benefits from midling aerodynamic efficiency since its drag coefficient sits at around 0.38. The fully independent suspension is made up of MacPherson struts. The sedan in equipped with disc and drum brakes linked to standard ABS and the Outback benefits from four-wheel disc brakes with ABS. All-wheel drive isn't full-time, so it can only be used on slippery roads when it's snowing or raining, otherwise you could damage it if you engage it. The RS model has full-time all-wheel drive made up of viscous-coupled main and rear differentials that really solidify the rear end, as well as the wheel that's lost its grip. Both 4-cylinder engines are horizontal engines, one of the most original features on these cars, along with all-wheel drive that is recognizable due to its characteristic sound.

PROS

+ LOOKS. This design is one-of-a-kind, especially the Outback station wagon that exudes a get up and go enthusiasm, a design that was inspired by the ingenious Subaru advertising campaign that put this carmaker on the map and in the leading cohort of all-wheel drive automobile engineers. Drivers who like zooming around in rocket-like noise will opt for the sassier-looking coupe.

+ PERFORMANCES. The 2.5 RS coupe isn't as impressive as its coun-

Forgotten..?

terpart sold in Europe that's equipped with a zoomy 280-hp engine, but let's just say that this car's performances are zippy enough to have a bit of fun at the wheel, without having to risk loss of life or limb, thanks to full-time all-wheel drive.

+ DRIVING PLEASURE. It's great with the 2.2L's impressive torque, nicely set shifter gears and of course, all-wheel drive that's a real bonus for winter wonderland driving.

+ BUILD. The Impreza is solidly built and finish job is meticulous, but the cabin looks very ordinary and it's a crying shame on the lush Outback model, since its plain Jane appearance doesn't really go with the gorgeous exterior design.

+ STEERING. It's smooth and gradual and benefits from a good reduction ratio, so you have right-

on vehicle control. The steer angle diameter is fairly reasonable, but some maneuvers are a bit awkward.

+ RIDE COMFORT. It's pretty impressive, thanks to the effective suspension that does its stuff without ever being rude and neatly designed seats that provide good support. Seat upholstery is firm, but nice and thick.

+ BRAKES. They're effective and well-balanced, even without ABS, since they're easy to apply so as not to hit wheel lock threshold on sudden stops, a rare feat that deserves mention.

+ EQUIPMENT. Even the ordinary sedan provides comfy travel with all the niceties like tilt steering wheel and adjustable mirrors and there are even more goodies on the other models, since the opulent Outback can only receive an optional sunroof

and automatic transmission.

+ TRANSMISSION. The automatic shifter is much better than the manual on the sedan or the station wagon, since it grinds when engaged, especially first off. The 2.5 RS coupe's manual transmission didn't exhibit this annoying tendency and so much the better, since it's the only one it can be equipped with.

CONS

- PERFORMANCES. The 2.2L engine isn't eager and willing, given its displacement. Heavy vehicle weight is at the root of this problem, so it has to puff and strain to maintain speeds , which results in gas bills that take a bite out of your wallet.

- CABIN SPACE. It's snugger in the rear seats that are hard to get into as well, which doesn' t really jive with the vehicle dimensions and leg room is really cramped in the two-door model, because the front seat doesn't free up enough space.

- PRICE. The Impreza's are no bargain at a price comparable to that of new sport-utility vehicles that are a lot more versatile and more technically with it and that benefit from full-time all-wheel drive, a feature that isn't available on the sedan or the Outback.

- TRUNK. The one on the sedan and the cargo hold on the station wagon are much smaller than average for the category. This aspect was sacrificed for rear end design purposes that's quite dashing, you have to admit, resembling that of the venerable AMC Pacer...

- NOISE. The Impreza doesn't provide for restful travel, since engine and tire noise are very pervasive every inch of the way.

-ERGONOMICS. The center section on the instrument panel isn't too ergonomic, since the driver has to sit straight up to reach some inconveniently located controls.

- CABIN LOOK. Trim components look very synthetic and some color schemes are quite, well, unusual, which is an understatement.

CONCLUSION

People aren't rushing to their Subaru dealer to buy this car, not with the Forester's sales feast that has meant famine for the Impreza. This compact car should sell like hot cakes in regions afflicted with unfavorable weather conditions, but this ain't so because it's too expensive for its own good and isn't too practical either, since useful space has been traded off for sheer style. ☺

RATING
SUBARU Impreza

CONCEPT :		70%
Technology	75	
Safety :	90	
Interior space :	50	
Trunk volume:	60	
Quality/fit/finish :	75	

DRIVING:		57%
Cockpit :	60	
Performance :	35	
Handling :	60	
Steering :	75	
Braking :	55	

ORIGINAL EQUIPMENT:		74%
Tires :	75	
Headlights :	80	
Wipers :	70	
Rear defroster :	70	
Radio :	75	

COMFORT :		67%
Seats :	70	
Suspension :	70	
Sound level:	45	
Conveniences :	75	
Air conditioning :	75	

BUDGET :		64%
Price :	60	
Fuel economy :	75	
Insurance :	60	
Satisfaction :	85	
Depreciation :	45	

Overall rating: 66.6%

NEW FOR 1999

• No major change.

ENGINES / TRANSMISSIONS / PERFORMANCES

Model/ version	Type / timing valve / fuel system	Displacement cu in	Power bhp @ rpm	Torque lb-ft @ rpm	Compres. ratio	Driving wheels / transmission	Final ratio	Acceler. 0-60 mph s	Standing 1/4 & 5/8 mile s	Acceler. 50-75 mph s	Braking 60-0 mph f	Top speed mph	Lateral acceler. G	Noise level dBA	Fuel economy mpg City	Highway	Fuel type Octane
1)	H4* 2.2 SOHC-16-MPSFI	135	137 @ 5400	145 @ 4000	9.7 :1	four - M5*	4.11	10.0	17.5 32.6	-	148	106	0.79	68	22	30	R 87
						four - A4	4.11	11.4	18.7 33.2	-	154	100	0.79	68	21	28	R 87
2)	H4* 2.5 DOHC-16-MPSFI	150	165 @ 5600	162 @ 4000	9.7 :1	four - M5*	4.11	NA									
						four - A4	4.44	NA									

1) base, Outback Sport.   2) 2.5 RS.

PRICE & EQUIPMENT

SUBARU Impreza	Sedan	Outback	2.5 RS
Retail price $:	15,895	17,995	19,195
Dealer invoice $:	14,445	16,321	17,404
Shipping & handling $:	495	495	495
Automatic transmission:	O	O	O
Cruise control:	O	O	O
Power steering:	S	S	S
Anti-lock brakes:	-	S	S
Traction control:	-	-	-
Air conditioning:	S	S	S
Leather:	-	-	S
AM/FM/radio-cassette:	S	S	S
Power door locks:	S	S	S
Power windows:	S	S	S
Tilt steering:	S	S	S
Dual adjustable mirrors:	SE	SE	SE
Alloy wheels:	O	S	S
Anti-theft system:	-	-	-

Colors
Exterior: White, Black, Red, Green, Blue.

Interior: Beige, Gray.

AT A GLANCE...

Category: AWD compact coupes, sedans & wagons.   **Class :** 3

HISTORIC
Introduced in: 1993
Made in: Gunma & Yajima, Japan.

DEMOGRAPHICS
Model	Men./Wom.	Age	Married	College	Income
Impreza	46/54 %	38	60 %	47 %	$ 35 000

INDEX
Safety:	90 %	Satisfaction:	83 %
Depreciation:	55 %	Insurance:	$ 855
Cost per mile:	$ 0.43	Number of dealers:	727

SALES
Model	1996	1997	Result
Impreza	24 687	24 242	- 1.8 %

MAIN COMPETITORS
CHEVROLET Cavalier, DODGE-PLYMOUTH Neon, FORD Escort-Contour, HONDA Civic, HYUNDAI Elantra, MAZDA Protegé, MERCURY Mystique, PONTIAC Sunfire, SATURN, TOYOTA Corolla, VOLKSWAGEN Golf-Jetta.

MAINTENANCE REQUIRED BY WARRANTY
First revision:	Frequency:	Diagnostic plug:
3 000 miles	7 500 miles	No

SPECIFICATIONS

Model	Version Trim	Body/ Seats	Interior volume cu ft	Trunk volume cu ft	Cd	Wheel base in	Lght x Wdgth x Hght in x in x in	Curb weight lb	Susp. ft/rr	Brake ft/rr	Steering type	Turning diameter ft	Steer. turns nber.	Fuel tank gal	tire size	Standard tires make	model	Standard powertrain
SUBARU	General warranty: 3 years / 36 000 miles; powertrain: 5 years / 60 000 miles; corrosion & antipollution: 5 years / unlimited.																	
Impreza	4x4 sedan	4dr.sdn4	84.4	11.1	0.32	99.2	172.2x67.1x55.5	2690	ih/ih	dc/dr	pwr.r&p.	33.5	3.2	13.2	195/60R15	Bridgestone	-	H4/2.2/M5
Impreza	4x4 Outback	4dr.wgn.5	85.1	25.5	0.36	2520	172.2x67.1x60.0	2835	ih/ih	dc/dr/ABS	pwr.r&p.	33.5	3.2	13.2	205/60R15	BFGoodrich	T/A	H4/2.2/M5
Impreza	4x4 2.5 RS	2dr.cpe.4	84.4	11.1	0.32	99.2	172.2x67.1x55.5	2824	ih/ih	dc/dc/ABS	pwr.r&p.	33.5	3.2	13.2	205/55R16	Michelin	-	H4/2.5/M5

The Legacy is by far the best seller at Subaru, at least on the North American continent. This is why there's such an extensive model range offered by the carmaker who wants to be sure to cover all the bases on his exclusive territory that belongs to the all-wheel drive car, that's, well let's say, almost affordable... No doubt about it, the Outback phenomenon thrust the Legacy to the covetted top car sales bracket, but we'd like to bet that keeping this status won't be a piece of cake, since this sales spurt may already be almost over. A new Legacy model will be introduced soon that'll have a more agressive, provocative personality than the current model.

MODEL RANGE
The Legacy is sold in an all-wheel drive station wagon model in Brighton, L, GT, Outback and Outback Limited trim and as a sedan that's available in L and GT trim. The Brighton and L versions are motivated by a 2.2L flat-4 engine and the other versions are equipped with a 2.5L engine. The manual transmission comes standard and the automatic is available as an option. Cars are generally well-equipped, which explains why they cost more than usual, which isn't the case for the Brighton that's the Orphan Annie of the bunch.

TECHNICAL FEATURES
Current Legacy models inherit the previous model's platform, with some modifications and extended vehicle dimensions. The Legacy's body is a steel moncocoque design, but aerodynamics can't be too great, since the drag coefficient is unpublished. The fully independent suspension consists of the sacrosanct MacPherson strut design both front and rear, along with A-arms and anti-roll bars. It's been reworked to provide more generous wheel travel which adds a lot to ride comfort and handling. The Brighton is equipped with disc and drum brakes and the other models benefit from four-wheel disc brakes assisted by ABS. The engine is still the traditional «boxer» design, the only horizontally opposed 4-cylinder in the world. The 2.2L engine is a 16-valve SOHC and the 2.5L has DOHC distribution. Full-time all-wheel drive comes with the manual gearbox and part-time with the automatic that automatically distributes torque via electronic sensors linked to the antilock braking system and in the long run, acts as traction control.

Remodeling Time...

PROS
+ EXCLUSIVE DESIGN. Legacy vehicles have practically no direct rivals, other than the Honda CR-V, Toyota RAV4, the Tracker/Vitara and Forester, all four-door vehicles, but that are more SUV's than cars.

+ ALL-WHEEL DRIVE. This feature really appeals to folks looking for hassle-free, relaxed, all-season driving. But tires have to be good quality if you want all-wheel drive to work as it should. The Legacy's aren't all-terrain vehicles, for they couldn't wander off too far with their limited ground clearance.

+ STEERING. It's crisp and nicely powered, but maneuverability is only fair to midling due to above-average reduction ratio and steer angle diameter.

+ HANDLING. The vehicle stays neutral most of the time thanks to the firm suspension that reduces roll and body waver on tight curves. The all-wheel drive provides super road adherence when things get slick and taking curves is no problem at reasonable speeds.

+ QUALITY. The Legacy is a robust, rigid car. Fit and finish are more attentively rendered than in the past and reliability is back to normal.

+ ORIGINAL FEATURE: The «hill holder» feature allows you to let go of the clutch when idling, so you can accelerate on an incline, a neat feature that inexperienced drivers will sure appreciate.

+ BRAKES. They've become brawnier over the years, since stopping distances are shorter than they used to be, but applying them just right is still a bit tricky with the spongy pedal.

CONS
- ENGINES. They're real ruffians, but worse still they don't have the juice or torque needed to handle the complex all-wheel drive system. At full load capacity, passing on the highway is a worry, engine noise is deafening and these beasts are real gas guzzlers.

- DRIVING. It would be a heck of a lot more enjoyable if the driver weren't sitting so low and if the driver's seat were less flat and firmly cushioned.

- CABIN SPACE. This is the most disappointing feature on these vehicles, for only four adults can really be comfortably accomodated, contrary to what the generous vehicle dimensions might lead to believe.

- SUSPENSION. It's stiff and jostles occupants as soon as the road is less than perfect and here again, the type of tires you use and their quality can make all the difference.

-WEIGHT. These cars aren't featherweights and so the 4-cylinder engine has a time of it, it's rough and lacks power and torque at some r.p.m., even with all the modifications and improvements on the part of Subaru engine manufacturers.

- CABIN DESIGN. The Legacy interior is terribly lackluster, which doesn't make much sense inside a vehicle that's supposed to be an adventurous sort, according to Subaru. In fact the only spark of imagination about this vehicle comes from the people who created the ad campaign.

- FUEL EFFICIENCY. It's not the greatest since fuel consumption really increases with the automatic gearbox and all-wheel drive.

- NOISE LEVEL. It's horrendous and much higher than usual. Engine and tire noise keep up their raucous ranting, so much so that you aren't sure if you really heard wind whistling around the windshield...

CONCLUSION
The next-generation Legacy should survive the Outback rage by offering a more clean and clearly thought out design and especially a more imaginative one. We hope that Subaru has finally decided to opt for another type of engine, but that may be a pipe dream... ☺

RATING
SUBARU Legacy

CONCEPT :   71%
Technology	75
Safety :	90
Interior space :	60
Trunk volume:	55
Quality/fit/finish :	75

DRIVING: 55%
Cockpit :	70
Performance :	30
Handling :	50
Steering :	75
Braking :	50

ORIGINAL EQUIPMENT: 73%
Tires :	75
Headlights :	80
Wipers :	75
Rear defroster :	70
Radio :	65

COMFORT :   70%
Seats :	70
Suspension :	70
Sound level:	60
Conveniences :	75
Air conditioning :	75

BUDGET :   63%
Price :	40
Fuel economy :	75
Insurance :	60
Satisfaction :	90
Depreciation :	50

Overall rating: **66.4%**

NEW FOR 1999

- This model will be completely revamped in early 1999.

ENGINES / TRANSMISSIONS / PERFORMANCES

Model/ version	Type / timing valve / fuel system	Displacement cu in	Power bhp @ rpm	Torque lb-ft @ rpm	Compres. ratio	Driving wheels / transmission	Final ratio	Acceler. 0-60 mph s	Standing 1/4 & 5/8 mile s	Acceler. 50-75 mph s	Braking 60-0 mph f	Top speed mph	Lateral acceler. G	Noise level dBA	Fuel economy mpg City	Highway	Fuel type Octane
base	H4* 2.2 SOHC-16-MPSFI	135	137 @ 5400	145 @ 4000	9.7 :1	four - M5*	3.90	11.0	18.0 33.3	7.8	138	112	0.78	68	22	30	R 87
						four - A4	4.11	12.2	18.7 34.8	10.5	144	109	0.78	68	22	30	R 87
GT/Outbk	H4* 2.5 DOHC-16-MPSFI	150	165 @ 5600	162 @ 4000	9.7 :1	four - M5*	4.11	10.0	17.5 31.8	7.0	148	118	0.78	67	19	28	R 87
1) standard GT Ltd.						1) four - A4	4.44	NA									

PRICE & EQUIPMENT

SUBARU Legacy	Brighton	S-L	S-GT	SUS	W-Otb	W-Ok/Ltd
Retail price $:	16,895	19,195	26,595	23,395	22,495	26,595
Dealer invoice $:	15,788	17,278	23,822	20,990	20,183	23,822
Shipping & handling $:	495	495	495	495	495	495
Automatic transmission:	O	O	O	O	O	S
Cruise control:	-	S	S	S	S	S
Power steering:	S	S	S	S	S	S
Anti-lock brakes:	-	S	S	S	S	S
Traction control:	S	S	S	S	S	S
Air conditioning:	-	S	S	S	S	S
Leather:	-	-	-	O	O	S
AM/FM/radio-cassette:	S	S	S	S	S	SCD
Power door locks:	-	O	O	O	S	S
Power windows:	-	S	S	S	S	S
Tilt steering:	S	S	S	S	S	S
Dual adjustable mirrors:	SE	SE	SE	SE	SE	SE
Alloy wheels:	-	O	S	S	S	S
Anti-theft system:	-	-	-	-	-	-

Colors
Exterior: Black, White, Silver, Ruby, Green, Sapphire, Red, Blue.

Interior: Gray, Beige.

AT A GLANCE...

Category:	AWD compact wagons & sedans.		Class : 4

HISTORIC
Introduced in:	1989-1995
Made in:	Gunma, Japan.

DEMOGRAPHICS
Model	Men./Wom.	Age	Married	College	Income
Legacy	73/27 %	47	78 %	35 %	$ 41 000

INDEX
Safety:	90 %	Satisfaction:	90 %
Depreciation:	50 %	Insurance:	$ 835-1 075
Cost per mile:	$ 0.47	Number of dealers:	727

SALES
Model	1996	1997	Result
Legacy	94 950	92 913	- 2.1 %

MAIN COMPETITORS
CHEVROLET Tracker 4dr, HONDA CR-V, TOYOTA RAV4, SUZUKI Sidekick 4dr., SUBARU Forester.

MAINTENANCE REQUIRED BY WARRANTY
First revision:	Frequency:	Diagnostic plug:
3 000 miles	7 500 miles	Yes

SPECIFICATIONS

Model	Version Trim	Body/ Seats	Interior volume cu ft	Trunk volume cu ft	Cd	Wheel base in	Lght x Wdgth x Hght in x in x in	Curb weight lb	Susp. ft/rr	Brake ft/rr	Steering type	Turning diameter ft	Steer. turns nber.	Fuel tank gal	tire size	Standard tires make	model	Standard powertrain
SUBARU		General warranty: 3 years / 36 000 miles; powertrain: 5 years / 60 000 miles; corrosion & antipollution: 5 years / unlimited.																
Legacy	Brighton	4dr.wgn.4/5	95.5	36.1	0.37	103.5	184.5x67.5x57.1	2906	ih/ih	dc/dr	pwr.r&p.	34.8	3.2	15.9	185/70HR1	Bridgestone	-	H4/2.2/M5
Legacy	L	4dr.sdn4/5	92.1	12.6	0.32	103.5	184.5x67.5x55.3	2886	ih/ih	dc/ABS	pwr.r&p.	34.8	3.2	15.9	185/70HR14	-	-	H4/2.2/M5
Legacy	L	4dr.wgn.4/5	95.2	36.1	0.37	103.5	184.5x67.5x55.5	2906	ih/ih	dc/ABS	pwr.r&p.	34.8	3.2	15.9	185/70HR14	-	-	H4/2.2/M5
Legacy	GT	4dr.sdn4/5	92.1	12.6	0.34	103.5	184.5x67.5x55.7	3091	ih/ih	dc/ABS	pwr.r&p.	34.8	3.2	15.9	205/55HR16	-	-	H4/2.5/M5
Legacy	GT	4dr.wgn.4/5	95.2	36.1	0.30	103.5	184.5x67.5x60.3	3179	ih/ih	dc/ABS	pwr.r&p.	34.8	3.2	15.9	205/55HR16	-	-	H4/2.5/M5
Legacy	Outback	4dr.wgn.4/5	96.8	36.5	0.40	103.5	184.5x67.5x63.0	3155	ih/ih	dc/ABS	pwr.r&p.	36.7	3.4	15.9	205/70SR15	Michelin	XW4	H4/2.5/M5
Legacy	Outback Ltd	4dr.wgn.4/5	96.8	36.5	0.41	103.5	184.5x67.5x63.0	3230	ih/ih	dc/ABS	pwr.r&p.	36.7	3.4	15.9	205/70SR15	Michelin	XW4	H4/2.5/A4

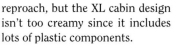

More American Than Japanese...

The Avalon was the Japanese carmaker's first serious incursion into American car producers' territory. Built on the Camry platform, Toyota literally copied an Oldsmobile 88 or a Buick LeSabre. The end result was pretty sensational, since Avalon sales are pretty brisk, at least in the United States and in Western Canada where folks appreciate its size and dependability that's a much surer thing than for American products.

MODEL RANGE

The Avalon is a five-passenger four-door sedan that's available in base XL or luxury XLS trim. Both cars are equipped with the same engine, namely a 3.0L V6 linked to a four-speed automatic transmission. Original equipment on the base model includes cruise control, antilock braking system, radio-tape deck sound system, climate control and power windows, locks and exterior mirrors. Light alloy wheels and sunroof are available as extras on this model. The XLS is equipped with standard automatic climate control, light alloy wheels and theft-deterrent system and can receive traction control, heated seats, leather seat covers and sunroof.

TECHNICAL FEATURES

The Avalon is built on the former Camry platform and inherits its main mechanical components. So as to provide for more generous cabin space, the wheelbase was extended by 3,9 in. and over-all vehicle length is 2.4 inches longer. The unibody is built of steel and the most exposed panels are galvanized. The front and rear powertrains are mounted on independent cradles, so as to insulate the body from wheel noise and vibration. The fully independent suspension is made up of MacPherson struts and a double wishbone arrangement up front and of a dual-link setup at the rear. The engine is also borrowed from the Camry, namely a 200-hp 3.0L V6 mated to a 4-speed automatic transmission and four-wheel disc brakes are teamed up with standard ABS, but only the XLS has disc brakes associated with a traction control device.

PROS

+ PERFORMANCES. They're pretty good for this type of engine, since it achieves energetic enough accelerations and pickup to provide for safe travel, thanks to a very comfortable reserve of power to be able to deal with any situation, especially with the transmission that has nicely spaced gears and that is willing and able and downshifts without having to be coaxed...

+ HANDLING. It's super-effective for a car that was designed with North American customers in mind. The Avalon suffers from a bit of sway, but it takes even tight curves with ease, so much so that you tend to accelerate and drive in a more inspired, carefree fashion.

+ CABIN SPACE. It's remarkable, given the tidy vehicle size that's a bit bigger than the current Camry dimensions. There's lots of head, elbow and leg room both front and rear and the big doors open nice and wide for easy boarding.

+ BRAKES. They're gutsy, nicely balanced and tough. They're easy to apply just right, even if the pedal isn't as sensitive as it could be.

+ RIDE COMFORT. It's the happy result of the flexible suspension, thickly cushioned seats that offer good support and soundproofing that would make some upper-crust models blush with shame...

+ QUALITY. It does credit to the carmaker's reputation in this department. Assembly is meticulous, finish details are flawless and most ot the trim materials are beyond reproach, but the XL cabin design isn't too creamy since it includes lots of plastic components.

+ COCKPIT. It's remarkably well organized. The driver has all the main functions and controls within easy reach and they're straightforward and easy to read and outward view is great in all directions. But the radio dials are complex, so best to look carefully at how they work before taking a trip.

+ CONVENIENCE FEATURES. It adds to the luxury experience, along with the spacious feel of the cabin. Storage compartments are within easy reach and there are enough of them, even if there are more up front than in the rear seat area. The trunk is deep and wide and luggage handling is great with its low threshold and lowering the rear seatbench towards the cabin doubles trunk size

CONS

- PRICE. It's steep for a model that isn't classified as a luxury car, so it's out of line. Even the XLS is still a Toyota and can't pretend to be a Lexus.

- STYLE. It's pretty much a carbon copy of a particular model at General Motors. It's hard to see real beauty in its design, no matter from which angle you contemplate it, for Toyota stylists are experts at creating lackluster products that haven't a hint of flavor.

- STEERING. It lacks definition and sometimes gets vague and you have to keep an eye on it in crosswinds. And the wide steer angle really cripples maneuverability.

- NOISE LEVEL. Strangely enough, it's a bit higher than on other equal-status vehicles, due to stereophonic tire thumping, a sure sign that sound dampening isn't what it should be. Wind whistle suggests that aerodynamics weren't a major issue for the carmaker.

CONCLUSION

The Avalon is geared to a very particular market segment and it reached its goal: to sell a car to conservative Americans who had sworn they'd never buy a Japanese model. The subterfuge worked perfectly, to the great satisfaction of those concerned... ☺

RATING
TOYOTA Avalon

CONCEPT :		84%
Technology	90	
Safety :	100	
Interior space :	80	
Trunk volume :	70	
Quality/fit/finish :	80	

DRIVING:		69%
Cockpit :	80	
Performance :	65	
Handling :	60	
Steering :	70	
Braking :	70	

ORIGINAL EQUIPMENT:		77%
Tires :	75	
Headlights :	80	
Wipers :	70	
Rear defroster :	80	
Radio :	80	

COMFORT :		78%
Seats :	80	
Suspension :	80	
Sound level:	80	
Conveniences :	70	
Air conditioning :	80	

BUDGET :		64%
Price :	30	
Fuel economy :	70	
Insurance :	70	
Satisfaction :	90	
Depreciation :	60	

Overall rating:	74.4%

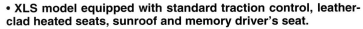

NEW FOR 1999

- XLS model equipped with standard traction control, leather-clad heated seats, sunroof and memory driver's seat.
- New exterior shade: Titanium.
- New leather shade: Black.

ENGINES

Model/ version	Type / timing valve / fuel system	Displacement cu in	Power bhp @ rpm	Torque lb-ft @ rpm
Avalon	V6 3.0 DOHC-24-MPSFI	183	200 @ 5200	214 @ 4400

TRANSMISSIONS

Compres. ratio	Driving wheels / transmission	Final ratio
10.5 :1	front - A4	3.625

PERFORMANCES

Acceler. 0-60 mph s	Standing 1/4 & 5/8 mile s	Acceler. 50-75 mph s	Braking 60-0 mph f	Top speed mph	Lateral acceler. G	Noise level dBA	Fuel economy mpg City	Fuel economy mpg Highway	Fuel type Octane
8.5	16.4	29.0	6.1	125	124	0.80	64	20	32	R 87

PRICE & EQUIPMENT

TOYOTA Avalon	XL	XLS
Retail price $:	25,248	28,288
Dealer invoice $:	22,104	24,474
Shipping & handling $:	420	420
Automatic transmission:	S	S
Cruise control:	S	S
Power steering:	S	S
Anti-lock brakes:	S	S
Traction control:	-	S
Air conditioning:	-	SA
Leather:	-	SC
AM/FM/radio-cassette:	S	SCD
Power door locks:	S	S
Power windows:	S	S
Tilt steering:	S	S
Dual adjustable mirrors:	S	S
Alloy wheels:	O	S
Anti-theft system:	O	S

Colors

Exterior: White, Black, Pink, Titanium, Sand, Spruce.

Interior: Black, Ivory, Quartz.

AT A GLANCE...

Category: front-wheel drive full-size sedans.   **Class :**

HISTORIC
Introduced in: 1995
Made in: Georgetown, Kentucky, USA.

DEMOGRAPHICS

Model	Men./Wom.	Age	Married	College	Income
Avalon	83/17 %	59	87 %	42 %	$ 52 000

INDEX

Safety:	100 %	Satisfaction:	92 %
Depreciation:	42 %	Insurance:	$ 825
Cost per mile:	$ 0.58	Number of dealers:	1 233

SALES

Model	1996	1997	Result
Avalon	73 308	71 309	- 2.7 %

MAIN COMPETITORS
ACURA RL, CHRYSLER LH & LHS, FORD Taurus & Crown Victoria, GM H-Series, MAZDA Millenia, NISSAN Maxima.

MAINTENANCE REQUIRED BY WARRANTY

First revision:	Frequency:	Diagnostic plug:
3 000 miles	3 000 miles	Yes

SPECIFICATIONS

Model	Version Trim	Body/ Seats	Interior volume cu ft	Trunk volume cu ft	Cd	Wheel base in	Lght x Wdgth x Hght in x in x in	Curb weight lb	Susp. ft/rr	Brake ft/rr	Steering type	Turning diameter ft	Steer. turns nber.	Fuel tank gal	tire size	Standard tires make	model	Standard powertrain
TOYOTA							General warranty: 3 years / 36 000 miles; powertrain 5 years / 60 000 miles; corrosion, perforation: 5 years / unlimited.										
Avalon	XL	4dr.sdn. 5	105.5	15.4	0.31	107.1	191.9x70.5x56.7	3340	ih/ih	d/dc/ABS	pwr.r&p.	37.6	2.7	18.5	205/65R15	Bridgestone	Potenza RE92	V6/3.0/A4
Avalon	XLS	4dr.sdn. 5	105.5	15.4	0.31	107.1	191.9x70.5x56.7	3340	ih/ih	d/dc/ABS	pwr.r&p.	37.6	2.7	18.5	205/65R15	Bridgestone	Potenza RE92	V6/3.0/A4

Toyota has come a long way and has finally fulfilled its ambition to put one of its models in the upper echelon of top North American car sales. The failure of the latest Taurus-Sable models as well as other American homologues no doubt helped the Japanese carmaker's task. Yet, apart from these factors, over the years the Camry has become a sort of world standard when it comes to car format and quality, a standard that automakers tend to compare their products with. It's the case for Honda who didn't think twice about extending the Accord's body dimensions so it would be classified as a mid-size car and, let's face it, be able to really compete with the Camry on an even footing.

MODEL RANGE

The Camry was renewed two years ago and is sold as a 4-door sedan in CE, CE V6, LE and XLE V6 trim. The CE and LE models are equipped with a 2.2L 4-cylinder engine that develops 133 hp, but the other versions receive a 3.0L V6 that develops 194 hp. The 5-speed manual transmission is part of the original equipment with the 4-cylinder, as is the 4-speed automatic with the V6. Standard equipment on the base model only includes power steering, two airbags, tilt steering wheel and intermittent wipers.

TECHNICAL FEATURES

The Camry's steel monocoque body was really beefed up and reinforced during the last redesign, including items such as floor, steering column, doors and front and rear extremities to absorb impact in the event of a collision. Its aerodynamic finesse was improved without spending megabucks, lowering the drag coefficient from 0.33 to 0.30 so as to reduce wind noise and improve fuel efficiency. The car's wheelbase is 2 inches longer and the vehicle has stretched by .5 inch, but cabin and trunk space are the same as on the former model. The car is also 10 mm wider and 7 mm higher, but there wasn't any significant weight gain. The independent suspensions still consist of MacPherson struts, yet they're more sophisticated to provide more accurate steering and crisper wheeltrain precision. Brakes are disc and drum on the 4-cylinder models, while the V6-powered models are equipped with four-wheel disc

Hail To The Queen...

brakes. ABS is standard on all models except the base CE. The XLE V6 is the only model that can be equipped with traction control. This system can be deactivated by flicking a switch on the instrument panel.

PROS

+ APPEARANCE. The latest remodelled version is more mod-looking and more refined, so the Camry looks like it's smaller than it actually is, and it does bear a resemblance to the Honda Accord, which says reams about Toyota's intentions.

+ DRIVING PLEASURE. It's due to the smooth blend of various controls: sprightly steering, accurate brakes, performance output for both model engines and especially those

of the V6 that can be super silky at cruising speed, but a raging bull on accelerations or pickup.

+ RIDE COMFORT. The cabin space has a lot to do with it, since four or five passengers can be more than comfortably accomodated, without feeling cramped. Ride comfort derives from the neat-design, thickly upholstered seats, more velvety suspension with the more generous wheel travel, that really takes care of road faults. Noise level has been turned down so low that wind and road noise seems louder than it really is.

+ ROADHOLDING. The car stays neutral forever, in spite of moderate sway generated by the flexible suspension and car path is predictable in most situations at regular

speeds.

+ DEPENDABILITY. It's the number one asset of this Japanese brand that has developed a quality control approach over the years that sparked people's imagination. Being equipped with such durable components earns the Camry high owner satisfaction rates.

+ CONVENIENCE FEATURES. This aspect is obvious with all the storage spots scattered throughout the cabin and the roomy trunk that connects with the cabin by lowering the split-folding rear seatbench.

CONS

- DESIGN. It's pretty plain both inside and out. Some instrument panel components don't seem to have as tight a fit as before and some plastic trim of the same shade is slightly different in color on some models, confirming that the Camry isn't a luxury car, in spite of its price tag. This sort of universal, generic style doesn't generate any emotion, but it will stay in style for years.

- STEERING. It's over-assisted, so it's light and sensitive to the slightest breeze, which can be a worry on slippery surfaces or when you're swerving to avoid a mishap.

-TIRES. The original tires are very slippery on damp roads and it would be a darn good idea to exchange them for better-quality tires the first chance you get.

-SUSPENSION. It goes haywire even on the tiniest bump, so the front end often takes a nosedive and wheels really lose their adherence.

- TO BE IMPROVED UPON: No adjustable air vents for rear seat passengers as is the case on several counterpart models and full-size spare tire that's hard to get to since the rug and cover aren't easy to remove. We'd also like to see a better-quality sound system more in keeping with the retail price.

CONCLUSION

The Camry has become one of the most solid American icons thanks to its mid-size format and reputation for reliability due to superb build quality. But it pays for its ability to please just about everyone, since it has a rather plain, anonymous design and after all, there are a lot of these cars on the road, so how can you be proud to own one?... ☺

RATING
TOYOTA Camry

CONCEPT : **75%**
Technology 80
Safety : 80
Interior space : 70
Trunk volume: 65
Quality/fit/finish : 80

DRIVING: **68%**
Cockpit : 80
Performance : 60
Handling : 60
Steering : 80
Braking : 60

ORIGINAL EQUIPMENT: **79%**
Tires : 80
Headlights : 80
Wipers : 80
Rear defroster : 80
Radio : 75

COMFORT : **78%**
Seats : 80
Suspension : 80
Sound level : 70
Conveniences : 80
Air conditioning : 80

BUDGET : **67%**
Price : 50
Fuel economy : 70
Insurance : 70
Satisfaction : 90
Depreciation : 55

Overall rating: **73.4%**

NEW FOR 1999
- Three new exterior shades.
- Control system for lighting.
- Streamlined sets of options.

ENGINES
Model/ version	Type / timing valve / fuel system	Displacement cu in	Power bhp @ rpm	Torque lb-ft @ rpm
CE	L4* 2.2 DOHC-16-MPSFI	132	139 @ 5200	147 @ 4400
CE, LE				
CE V6,XLE V6*	3.0 DOHC-24-MPSFI	183	194 @ 5200	209 @ 4400

TRANSMISSIONS
Compres. ratio	Driving wheels / transmission	Final ratio
9.5 :1	front - M5	3.944
	front - A4	3.944
10.5 :1	front - A4	3.933

PERFORMANCES
Acceler. 0-60 mph s	Standing 1/4 & 5/8 mile s	Acceler. 50-75 mph s	Braking 60-0 mph f	Top speed mph	Lateral acceler. G	Noise level dBA	Fuel economy mpg City	Highway	Fuel type Octane
10.5	17.7 31.4	7.2	131	112	0.80	67	22	33	R 87
11.8	18.6 32.8	8.6	131	109	0.78	67	21	31	R 87
8.7	16.5 29.6	6.2	125	131	0.78	66	18	28	R 87

PRICE & EQUIPMENT
TOYOTA Camry berline	CE	CE V6	LE	XLE V6
Retail price $:	16,938	19,828	20,218	24,868
Dealer invoice $:	15,003	17,563	17,699	21,771
Shipping & handling $:	420	420	420	420
Automatic transmission:	O/S	S	S	S
Cruise control:	S	S	S	S
Power steering:	S	S	S	S
Anti-lock brakes:	-	S	S	S
Traction control:	-	-	-	O
Air conditioning:	S	S	S	S
Leather:	-	-	-	S
AM/FM/radio-cassette:	S	S	S	S
Power door locks:	S	S	S	S
Power windows:	S	S	S	S
Tilt steering:	S	S	S	S
Dual adjustable mirrors:	SE	SE	SE	SE
Alloy wheels:	O	-	S	S
Anti-theft system:	-	-	-	O

Colors
Exterior: White, Sage, Black, Wood, Champagne, Red, Sand.
Interior: Gray, Oak, Sage.

AT A GLANCE...
Category: front-wheel drive mid-size sedans. **Class :** 5
HISTORIC
Introduced in: 1983-1997
Made in: Georgetown, Kentucky, USA.
DEMOGRAPHICS
Model	Men./Wom.	Age	Married	College	Income
Camry	70/30 %	54	79 %	47 %	$ 39 000

INDEX
Safety: 80 % **Satisfaction:** 95 %
Depreciation: 45 % **Insurance:** $ 835-985
Cost per mile: $ 0.44 **Number of dealers:** 1 233
SALES
Model	1996	1997	Result
Camry	359 433	397 756	+ 9.7 %

MAIN COMPETITORS
BUICK Century-Regal, CHEVROLET Malibu-Lumina, CHRYSLER Cirrus-Stratus-LH, FORD Contour-Taurus, HONDA Accord, HYUNDAI Sonata, MAZDA 626, NISSAN Altima-Maxima, OLDSMOBILE Alero-Intrigue, PONTIAC Grand Am-Grand Prix, SUBARU Legacy, VOLKSWAGEN Passat.
MAINTENANCE REQUIRED BY WARRANTY
First revision: 3 000 miles **Frequency:** 3 000 miles **Diagnostic plug:** Yes

SPECIFICATIONS
General warranty: 3 years / 36 000 miles; powertrain 5 years / 60 000 miles; corrosion, perforation: 5 years / unlimited.

Model	Version Trim	Body/ Seats	Interior volume cu ft	Trunk volume cu ft	Cd	Wheel base in	Lght x Wdgth x Hght in x in x in	Curb weight lb	Susp. ft/rr	Brake ft/rr	Steering type	Turning diameter ft	Steer. turns nber.	Fuel tank gal	tire size	Standard tires make	model	Standard powertrain
TOYOTA Camry	CE	4dr.sdn.5	96.9	14.1	0.30	105.2	188.5x70.1x55.7	2998	ih/ih	dc/dr	pwr.r&p.	35.4	3.06	18.5	195/70R14	Michelin	MX4	-L4/2.2/M5
Camry	CE V6	4dr.sdn.5	96.9	14.1	0.30	105.2	188.5x70.1x55.9	3120	ih/ih	dc/dc/ABS	pwr.r&p.	36.7	3.06	18.5	205/65R15	Dunlop	Sport 4000	V6/3.0/A4
Camry	LE	4dr.sdn.5	96.9	14.1	0.30	105.2	188.5x70.1x55.7	3120	ih/ih	dc/dr/ABS	pwr.r&p.	35.4	3.06	18.5	195/70R14	Michelin	MX4	L4/2.2/A4
Camry	XLE V6	4dr.sdn.5	96.9	14.1	0.30	105.2	188.5x70.1x55.9	3252	ih/ih	dc/dc/ABS	pwr.r&p.	36.7	3.06	18.5	205/65R15	Dunlop	Sport 4000	V6/3.0/A4

Sales for the small RAV4 are now higher than for the once-loved Celica coupe, a car that would never have dreamed, even in its brightest moments, ever being as popular as the small SUV is nowadays. This is a clear indication of how tastes and attitudes have really changed due to the all-terrain vehicle tidal wave that has struck this continent, at least in regard to all-wheel drive models. Yet in spite of unpublished sales results, the Celica will only be replaced next year by its successor. Nothing lasts under the sun and the wave that washed this car away into near-oblivion, will one day bring a new surge of popularity for this same car...

MODEL RANGE

The Celica coupe is still sold in a single Liftback GT version, driven by a 2.2L 4-cylinder engine linked to a standard manual transmission or an optional automatic. Standard equipment doesn't make much sense, really, since it includes leather-trim seats, radio and tape deck, power windows and exterior mirrors and tilt steering wheel, but, get this, the automatic transmission, cruise control, antilock braking system, airbags, climate control, power locks, light alloy wheels, sunroof and theft-deterrent system are all sold as extras.

TECHNICAL FEATURES

The Celica coupe has a steel unibody that's quite robust and offers good torsion and flexion resistance. The front and rear axles are mounted on two subframes added onto the body so as to better insulate it from unwanted wheel and engine noise and vibration. The suspension is fully independent and consists of a MacPherson strut design up front, whereas the rear axle is supported by trailing arms. A rotating valve mounted on the power steering circuitry improves steering crispness and response time. The car is equipped with four-wheel disc brakes, but ABS is only sold as an extra. The 130 hp 16-valve 2.2L DOHC 4-cylinder engine is equipped with an oil cooler and it doesn't look too modern with its cast-steel block topped with an aluminum cylinder head.

PROS

+ STYLE. The current model Celica's design is one of the best in its career, for it expresses the true, bold and brassy character of this

Forerunner Left Behind...

car. The silhouette is dynamic and has heart and soul and it's absolutely sensational in some shades.

+ DRIVING PLEASURE. It's great due to the quick response and well-powered steering that lets you put this car exactly where you want it and steering gives you pretty good road feel. The clutch pedal is nice and light and the speed shifter is very accurate.

+ ROADHOLDING. This car stays neutral and stable for a long time before understeer starts to set in, when accelerating a bit too much on tight curves. Even with its front-wheel drive, the Celica is a real treat and the driver who knows it well can pull out all the stops on slalom runs.

+ BRAKES. They're easy to apply as

needed and are really balanced, even without antilock braking. But stopping distances could be shorter for a so-called sports car since some family sedans do better in this department.

+ COCKPIT. The driver is comfy and enjoys satisfactory visibility and the instrument panel is functional and ergonomic with a design like that on the Supra (only better!).

+ FUEL EFFICIENCY. The 2.2L engine is remarkably fuel-efficient since at regular speeds it can cover 435 miles on a tank of gas, a rare accomplishment that deserves mention.

+ RIDE COMFORT. It's pretty impressive for this type of vehicle. The suspension makes light work of road bumps and such without really

bouncing hard. Seats are nicely shaped and firmly upholstered and offer adequate support and the noise level is fairly discreet at cruising speed. Engine noise sets in mostly on revving, which is completely normal and really not unpleasant in this case, since the exhaust system has that sports car roar.

+ CONVENIENCE FEATURES. This sports coupe is fairly practical with its convertible trunk that can be extended by lowering the 50/50 split-folding seatbench and there are pretty good-sized compartments located in convenient spots inside the cabin.

CONS

- PRICE. It's the main reason why the Celica hasn't sold too well over the last few years. You have to admit that its weird array of equipment condemns it to a marginal role in a market segment that's already come to a standstill.

- PERFORMANCES. They're disappointing in that the 2.2L engine delivers its power at high r.p.m., that is at illegal speeds. This is due to the transmission gears that are really spaced out to cut down on gas consumption, rather than pump out the juice needed for accelerations and pickup. A shorter differential ratio would provide more lively performances and would at least make you feel like you're at the wheel of a real, zippy sports coupe...

- CABIN SPACE. It's more restricted than it should be, since it's less generous than inside a Honda Civic hatchback and doesn't allow for much rear seating space, so those rear seats are practically useless and can only accomodate very small children, when they're asleep.

- NOISE LEVEL. The snorting, roaring engine makes a heck of a lot of racket and the body resonates due to poor soundproofing, especially in the wheel housings.

- TORQUE. It occurs as soon as you gun it and it really affects steering and vehicle path.

- ROADHOLDING. The Celica is sensitive to cross-winds and road faults, so you have to really keep a close eye on things, as well as a good grip on the wheel.

CONCLUSION

We'd better wait and see what the Celica's successor will be like. The current model is the end result of too many questionable compromises to spark true love. ☺

Celica   TOYOTA

RATING
TOYOTA Celica

CONCEPT :   **62%**
Technology   80
Safety :   80
Interior space :   30
Trunk volume: 40
Quality/fit/finish :   80

DRIVING: **68%**
Cockpit :   80
Performance :   55
Handling :   65
Steering :   80
Braking :   60

ORIGINAL EQUIPMENT: **77%**
Tires :   80
Headlights :   80
Wipers :   75
Rear defroster :   75
Radio :   75

COMFORT :   **67%**
Seats :   75
Suspension :   60
Sound level :   50
Conveniences :   70
Air conditioning :   80

BUDGET :   **61%**
Price :   40
Fuel economy :   75
Insurance :   50
Satisfaction :   90
Depreciation :   50

Overall rating: **67.0%**

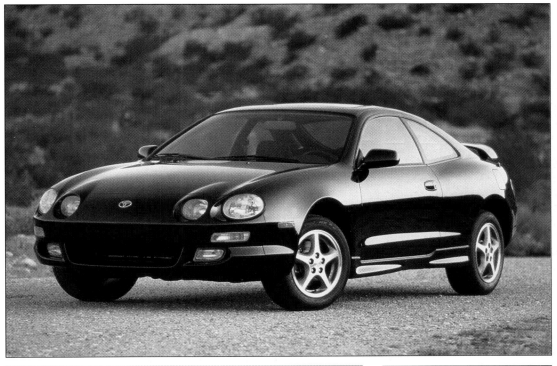

NEW FOR 1999

• Specifications identical to those of the 1998 model with the exception of two exterior shades removed from the catalogue: Black and Turquoise Green.

ENGINES / TRANSMISSIONS / PERFORMANCES

Model/version	Type / timing valve / fuel system	Displacement cu in	Power bhp @ rpm	Torque lb-ft @ rpm	Compres. ratio	Driving wheels / transmission	Final ratio	Acceler. 0-60 mph s	Standing 1/4 & 5/8 mile s	Acceler. 50-75 mph s	Braking 60-0 mph f	Top speed mph	Lateral acceler. G	Noise level dBA	Fuel economy mpg City	Highway	Fuel type Octane
GT-S	L4* 2.2-DOHC-16-MPSFI	132	130 @ 5400	145 @ 4400	9.5 :1	front - M5*	3.94	9.0	16.5	30.5	6.4	125	125	0.87	68	21	30	R 87
						front - A4	4.18	10.2	17.3	31.2	7.0	131	118	0.87	68	21	30	R 87

PRICE & EQUIPMENT

TOYOTA Celica	GT-S
Retail price $:	NA
Dealer invoice $:	NA
Shipping & handling $:	-
Automatic transmission:	O
Cruise control:	S
Power steering:	S
Anti-lock brakes:	S
Traction control:	-
Air conditioning:	S
Leather:	-
AM/FM/radio-cassette:	SCD
Power door locks:	S
Power windows:	S
Tilt steering:	S
Dual adjustable mirrors:	SE
Alloy wheels:	S
Anti-theft system:	O

Colors

Exterior: Iris, Red, Silver, White.

Interior: White, Ivory.

AT A GLANCE...

Category: front-wheel drive sports coupes.   **Class :** 3S

HISTORIC
Introduced in: 1971-1994.
Made in: Tahara, Japan.

DEMOGRAPHICS
Model	Men./Wom.	Age	Married	College	Income
Celica	59/41 %	41	54 %	48 %	$ 73 000

INDEX
Safety: 80 %   **Satisfaction:** 88 %
Depreciation: 50 %   **Insurance:** $ 1045
Cost per mile: $ 0.45   **Number of dealers:** 1 233

SALES
Model	1996	1997	Result
Celica	14 343	9 021	- 37.1 %

MAIN COMPETITORS
ACURA Integra, CHEVROLET Camaro, FORD Mustang, HONDA Prelude, HYUNDAI Tiburon, NISSAN 240SX, PONTIAC Firebird.

MAINTENANCE REQUIRED BY WARRANTY
First revision: 3 000 miles   **Frequency:** 3 000 miles   **Diagnostic plug:** Yes

SPECIFICATIONS

Model	Version Trim	Body/ Seats	Interior volume cu ft	Trunk volume cu ft	Cd	Wheel base in	Lght x Wdgth x Hght in x in x in	Curb weight lb	Susp. ft/rr	Brake ft/rr	Steering type	Turning diameter ft	Steer. turns nber.	Fuel tank gal	tire size	Standard tires make	model	Standard powertrain
TOYOTA	General warranty: 3 years / 36 000 miles; powertrain 5 years / 60 000 miles; corrosion, perforation: 5 years / unlimited.																	
Celica GT-S	3dr.cpe.2+2	77.2	16.2	0.32	99.9	174.2x68.9x50.8	2579	ih/ih	dc/dc/ABS	pwr.r&p.	36.7	2.9	15.9	205/55R15	Michelin	XGT4	L4/2.2/M5
Celica GT-S	2dr.con.2+2	-	-	0.32	99.9	177.0x68.9x51.0	2755	ih/ih	dc/dc/ABS	pwr.r&p.	36.7	2.9	15.9	205/55R15	Michelin	XGT4	L4/2.2/M5

The Corolla is the only car that truly deserves the term world car, since it's the only car that's sold in such great volume and built in the most countries on the face of the earth, which implies that the Corolla's model range is the most extensive of any car built. When you consider more closely this car's main asset, it's that it's an average car in every respect: size-wise, engine displacement, fuel consumption and price. The Corolla is the champion when it comes to the middle range.

MODEL RANGE

The Corolla is a 4-door sedan that's sold in VE, CE and LE models, powered by a 1.8L DOHC 4-cylinder engine delivering 120 hp. The 5-speed manual transmission is standard equipment on the VE and CE and the 4-speed automatic transmission comes as an extra. The latter is an original equipment item on the LE. The base model VE is equipped with dual airbags, power steering, radio and intermittent wipers. The CE also receives a manually adjusted steering wheel and side mirrors, while the LE is equipped with an automatic transmission, cruise control, power windows and locks. The antilock braking system, radio and tape deck and sunroof are optional items on the LE. Air conditioning is standard on the LE, but optional on the VE and CE.

TECHNICAL FEATURES

Since the 1998 redesign, the Corolla's steel monocoque body benefits from improved aerodynamic yield, since the drag coefficient has gone from 0.33 to 0.31. Its primary structure is really much more robust. It forms a sort of high-resistance steel cage around the cabin so as to provide passenger protection in the event of a collision and to resist to torsion and flexion on impact. The four-wheel independent suspension is still based on the MacPherson strut design, but now both powertrains are equipped with a stabilizer bar.

At the rear, the parallel control arm assembly enhances vehicle stability and provides a more neutral demeanor on curves. Power steering and disc and drum brakes are standard on all models, and only the LE version can receive an antilock braking system as an extra. There are some unique technical features, such as the valve in the main exhaust converter that allows for a short cycle at low r.p.m. and a long cycle at high r.p.m., which

World Stallion...

reduces pressure and allows for greater fuel circulation.

PROS

+ VALUE. The Corolla maintains an excellent resale value due to its reputation for reliability and never-say-die durability. So used models are rare and cost a pretty bundle. If the car doesn't sell, the car stays in the family, that is, parents pass it on to their children and so on.

+ SAFETY. It's a cut above now that the body is stiffer and now that cars are equipped with airbags. The Corolla has never been as solidly built and you feel really secure inside one.

+ STYLE. It's very conservative, but it has a certain appeal and has become a sort of classic, since it has a harmonious, well-balanced design, without any frills that won't

go out of style for many a moon.

+ CABIN SPACE. Four adults can be comfortably seated inside and, a rare occurrence, rear seat access is great with the good-sized doors that open wide.

+ DRIVING PLEASURE. Just great with the smooth, velvety controls, neat cockpit, satisfactory all-round visibility and rational dashboard setup.

+ PERFORMANCES. The latest 1.8L engine is pretty lively even with the automatic transmission and accelerations and pickup are very respectable given the efficient fuel yield, since fuel consumption is one of the most frugal around.

+ ROADABILITY. It stays neutral and level in most situations, so anyone can get behind the wheel and drive with assurance, if the car is

equipped with good-quality tires, that is.

+ RIDE COMFORT. It's super for a car of this format. The suspension is flexible, but not too much so, soundproofing does its stuff, but the front seats are more nicely contoured and cushioned than the rather flat rear seatbench.

+ CONVENIENCE FEATURES. Storage spots include a generous glove compartment, trim door side-pockets, a compartment located under the air conditioning controls and two storage bins on the center console. The trunk is easy to get to and its size is proportional to that of the cabin and it can be extended by lowering the rear seatbench back.

CONS

- QUALITY. It doesn't seem to be as obvious a trait as was the case on the previous model and the people at Toyota no longer talk about the «hidden quality» concept, that was the in-phrase for so long. Most trim materials are very plain and basic, even on the more well-equipped model.

- PRICE. It's too steep for a small North American-built car and with the «necessary» options that you have to add on, it isn't unusual to pay as much as for a higher-class car...

- PICKUP. They aren't wonderful as soon as the car is loaded at full capacity and in this case, the manual gearbox is more of a boon than the automatic that keeps looking for the best gear.

- TIRES. The Goodyear Integrity tires installed on our test model didn't have the best grab, even on dry pavement and they're noisy and slippery and the base model seems to be equipped with bicycle tires...

- STEERING. It's too light and at times a bit vague due to over-assistance, so you have to keep an eye on it.

- REAR SEATS. The rear seat area isn't as roomy as is the case up front and it's impossible to seat three passengers back there, as Toyota purports, for the seatbench isn't too wide, it doesn't offer much lateral support and upholstery is rather hard.

CONCLUSION

The Corolla will continue to provide average families with a simple, dependable and affordable means of transportation as well as a very adequate comfort level and a style that looks good in any neighborhood... ☺

RATING
TOYOTA Corolla

CONCEPT :   72%
Technology	80
Safety :	90
Interior space :	60
Trunk volume:	50
Quality/fit/finish :	80

DRIVING: 64%
Cockpit :	80
Performance :	50
Handling :	60
Steering :	75
Braking :	55

ORIGINAL EQUIPMENT: 75%
Tires :	75
Headlights :	80
Wipers :	75
Rear defroster :	75
Radio :	70

COMFORT :   72%
Seats :	75
Suspension :	70
Sound level :	70
Conveniences :	70
Air conditioning :	75

BUDGET :   76%
Price :	70
Fuel economy :	85
Insurance :	70
Satisfaction :	90
Depreciation :	65

Overall rating: **71.8%**

NEW FOR 1999

- **Three-speed automatic transmission is no longer available.**
- **Standard air conditioning on the LE model.**
- **Manually adjustable exterior mirrors on the VE model.**
- **Three exterior shades discarded and three new shades.**

ENGINES / TRANSMISSIONS / PERFORMANCES

Model/ version	Type / timing valve / fuel system	Displacement cu in	Power bhp @ rpm	Torque lb-ft @ rpm	Compres. ratio	Driving wheels / transmission	Final ratio	Acceler. 0-60 mph s	Standing 1/4 & 5/8 mile s	Acceler. 50-75 mph s	Braking 60-0 mph f	Top speed mph	Lateral acceler. G	Noise level dBA	Fuel economy mpg City	Highway	Fuel type Octane
1)	L4* 1.8 DOHC-16-MPSFI	109	120 @ 5600	122 @ 4400	10.5 :1	front - M5*	3.722	9.5	16.6	30.8	6.9	134	115	0.76	65	30	38	R 87
2)						front - A4*	2.655	11.2	17.8	32.2	7.8	137	112	0.78	67	27	37	R 87

1) base   2) standard LE, option VE, CE.

PRICE & EQUIPMENT

TOYOTA Corolla sedan	VE	CE	LE
Retail price $:	11,908	13,788	14,798
Dealer invoice $:	10,854	12,568	13,107
Shipping & handling $:	420	420	420
Automatic transmission:	O	O	S
Cruise control:	-	O	S
Power steering:	S	S	S
Anti-lock brakes:	-	-	O
Traction control:	-	-	-
Air conditioning:	O	O	S
Leather:	-	-	-
AM/FM/radio-cassette:	S	S	S
Power door locks:	-	-	S
Power windows:	-	-	S
Tilt steering:	O	S	S
Dual adjustable mirrors:	SM	SM	SE
Alloy wheels:	-	-	-
Anti-theft system:	-	-	-

Colors

Exterior: White, Black, Iris, Sand, Teal, Emerald.

Interior: Beige, Gray.

AT A GLANCE...

Category: front-wheel drive compact sedans.   **Class :** 3

HISTORIC
Introduced in:	1966-1998
Made in:	Cambridge, Ontario, Canada & Fremont, California, USA.

DEMOGRAPHICS
Model	Men./Wom.	Age	Married	College	Income
Corolla	50/50 %	43	70 %	50 %	$ 32 000

INDEX
Safety:	90 %	Satisfaction:	90 %
Depreciation:	35 %	Insurance:	$ 775
Cost per mile:	$ 0.43	Number of dealers:	1 233

SALES
Model	1996	1997	Result
Corolla	209 048	218 461	+ 4.6 %

MAIN COMPETITORS
CHEVROLET Cavalier, DODGE-PLYMOUTH Neon, FORD Escort, HONDA Civic, HYUNDAI Elantra, MAZDA Protegé, NISSAN Sentra, PONTIAC Sunfire, SATURN SL1 & SL2, SUBARU Impreza, SUZUKI Esteem, VOLKSWAGEN Jetta.

MAINTENANCE REQUIRED BY WARRANTY
First revision:	Frequency:	Diagnostic plug:
3 000 miles	3 000 miles	Yes

SPECIFICATIONS

Model	Version Trim	Body/ Seats	Interior volume cu ft	Trunk volume cu ft	Cd	Wheel base in	Lght x Wdgth x Hght in x in x in	Curb weight lb	Susp. ft/rr	Brake ft/rr	Steering type	Turning diameter ft	Steer. turns nber.	Fuel tank gal	tire size	Standard tires make	model	Standard powertrain
TOYOTA	General warranty: 3 years / 36 000 miles; powertrain 5 years / 60 000 miles; corrosion, perforation: 5 years / unlimited.																	
Corolla	VE	4dr.sdn.4/5	92.1	12.1	0.31	97.0	174.0x66.7x54.5	2414	ih/ih	dc/dr	pwr.r&p.	32.1	3.2	13.2	175/65R14	Michelin	MX4	L4/1.8/M5
Corolla	CE	4dr.sdn.4/5	92.1	12.1	0.31	97.0	174.0x66.7x54.5	2447	ih/ih	dc/dr	pwr.r&p.	32.1	3.2	13.2	175/65R14	Michelin	MX4	L4/1.8/M5
Corolla	LE	4dr.sdn.4/5	92.1	12.1	0.31	97.0	174.0x66.7x54.5	2524	ih/ih	dc/dr	pwr.r&p.	32.1	3.2	13.2	185/65R14	Michelin	MX4	L4/1.8/A4

Compact SUV's have made quite a breakthrough, since there are now five models in this category. Honda and Toyota got in on the action two years ago in this category that Suzuki created more than ten years ago with the Jimmy, Samurai and Sidekick. What's interesting in this case is that vehicles competing against one another aren't almost identical as for other market segments, but are, each and every one, quite unique. The RAV4 is more of a toy-vehicle, since it doesn't really have true blue SUV capabilities.

MODEL RANGE

The RAV4 is sold in a short-wheelbase two-door model or a longer four-door version both equipped with all-wheel drive. Both models share the same engine, namely a 2.0L 16-valve DOHC 4-cylinder paired up with a standard 5-speed manual transmission or an optional 4-speed automatic. The two-door model comes with fairly slim trimmings, since it only benefits from power steering, cruise control, radio and tape deck, manually adjusted exterior mirrors and light alloy rims. The 4-door is more lush, since it's equipped with added features such as antilock braking system, air conditioning, main power accessories and a theft-deterrent system.

TECHNICAL FEATURES

The RAV4's steel unibody includes some panels that are rustproofed and it gets special treatment since it's lighter-weight than a body mounted on a conventional frame and because it's fitted with appropriate reinforcements, so it's sufficiently rigid. The four-wheel independent suspension consists of MacPherson struts up front and the rear axle is supported by lower L-arms that act as a torsion bar. Vehicles are equipped with power rack and pinion steering and disc and drum brakes with standard ABS on the 4-door. The full-time all-wheel drive benefits from a main viscous-coupled non-slip differential that works automatically via a hydraulic system with the automatic gearbox and by pushing on a button located on the dashboard with the manual. The first gear ratio is fairly short on both gearboxes, eliminating the need for a high and low gear transfer case. The engine is a robust 4-valve per cylinder 2.0L DOHC with good muscle and torque.

Fun, But Within Reason...

PROS

+ PRICE. It seems more reasonable than when the vehicle was first introduced and considering the array of standard equipment, the RAV4 is a good buy, especially with its steady resale value...

+ PERFORMANCES. They're very much like those you get on a car thanks to the reasonable power to weight ratio, clever gear ratios on the transmission and the smooth, versatile engine that puts out good pickup power at low r.p.m., even with the automatic.

+ DESIGN. It looks full of vigor with its mischievous body stylistics and multicolored seat fabric that's a nice change from the run-of-the-mill gray you see on so many vehicles.

+ DRIVING PLEASURE. The driver benefits from nice and high seating, good straight-ahead and lateral visibility, logical instrument panel with easy to reach dials and controls.

+ HANDLING. It's reassuring, even on the short wheelbase model that behaves like a small car, but you have to take its high center of gravity into account when negotiating tight curves at high speeds. The RAV4 is nimble on slalom runs and it handles like a charm in the city.

+ RIDE COMFORT. The 4-door model is more comfy, since it benefits from a longer wheelbase and it's less jittery than the tiny 2-door model that plays leapfrog on poor roads.

+ QUALITY. It's totally in keeping with the top of the heap Toyota

philosophy. Assembly is super solid, finish job and trim materials are topnotch and not at all cheap-looking.

+ CONVENIENCE FEATURES. In this regard, the RAV4 is a real charmer, for there are lots of storage spots for travellers. The glove compartment is really big, door side-pockets are a generous size and there are storage shelves on the main section of the instrument panel. The trunk is versatile and is really handy with the big swing rear hatch door and you have loads of luggage space as required, even on the two-door version, but of course, it isn't as roomy when the rear seatbench is occupied.

CONS

- LIMITED PERFORMANCES. The RAV4 isn't a genuine all-terrain cowboy, for it isn't equipped with studded tires and a true grit transfer case is sorely missed when tackling tough terrain that's full of major obstacles or when adherence is really iffy. Before trailing behind other 4X4's, you have to be aware of its limitations and you should bring along a winch fitted with a long cable.

- CABIN SPACE. The vehicle is narrow and you feel like you're crammed alongside your travelling companions for the body design is slimmer towards the top.

- RIDE COMFORT. This tiny Toyota isn't great for long trips, since the seats don't offer much support and suspension jitters get more on your nerves than for short runs or when you're driving to work. The 2-door model short wheelbase generates a rocking chair effect that's far from soothing on rough road surfaces.

- VISIBILITY. It's rather poor towards the rear due to the spare tire and headrests that get in the way.

- TO BE IMPROVED UPON: The rear hatch that opens the wrong way from the sidewalk, because in Japan, people drive on the left side of the road...

CONCLUSION

The RAV4 is a fun vehicle that's safe if you don't stray off the beaten path. It's more at home in the city or in the suburbs than in the great outdoors that's dangerous ground if you don't keep the vehicle's limitations in mind... 😊

RATING
TOYOTA RAV4

CONCEPT :		70%
Technology	80	
Safety :	70	
Interior space :	50	
Trunk volume:	70	
Quality/fit/finish :	80	

DRIVING:		58%
Cockpit :	75	
Performance :	45	
Handling :	40	
Steering :	80	
Braking :	50	

ORIGINAL EQUIPMENT:		77%
Tires :	85	
Headlights :	75	
Wipers :	75	
Rear defroster :	70	
Radio :	80	

COMFORT :		71%
Seats :	80	
Suspension :	70	
Sound level:	50	
Conveniences :	80	
Air conditioning :	75	

BUDGET :		70%
Price :	55	
Fuel economy :	75	
Insurance :	55	
Satisfaction :	90	
Depreciation :	75	

Overall rating: 69.2%

NEW FOR 1999

- Rear-wheel drive models no longer available.
- Standard alloy wheels on the 2-door model.
- Standard manually adjustable exterior mirrors and cruise control on the 2-door model.
- Original power locks on the 4-door model.
- Three new exterior shades.

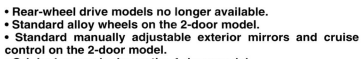

ENGINES / TRANSMISSIONS / PERFORMANCES

Model/ version	Type / timing valve / fuel system	Displacement cu in	Power bhp @ rpm	Torque lb-ft @ rpm	Compres. ratio	Driving wheels / transmission	Final ratio	Acceler. 0-60 mph s	Standing 1/4 & 5/8 mile s	Acceler. 50-75 mph s	Braking 60-0 mph f	Top speed mph	Lateral acceler. G	Noise level dBA	Fuel economy mpg City	Highway	Fuel type Octane
RAV4	L4* 2.0 DOHC-16-MPSFI	122	127 @ 5400	132 @ 4600	9.5 :1	all - M5*	4.933	11.5	18.2	32.7	9.5	141	103	0.70	68	22	26	R 87
						all - A4	4.404	13.0	18.5	34.2	12.1	147	100	0.70	68	22	26	R 87

PRICE & EQUIPMENT

TOYOTA RAV4 (4x4)	2 dr.	4 dr.
Retail price $:	16,848	17,708
Dealer invoice $:	15,097	15,868
Shipping & handling $:	420	420
Automatic transmission:	O	O
Cruise control:	S	S
Power steering:	S	S
Anti-lock brakes:	O	S
Traction control:	-	-
Air conditioning:	O	S
Leather:	-	-
AM/FM/radio-cassette:	S	SCD
Power door locks:	O	S
Power windows:	O	S
Tilt steering:	O	S
Dual adjustable mirrors:	SM	SE
Alloy wheels:	S	S
Anti-theft system:	O	S

Colors
Exterior: Violet, Red, White, Sequoia, Black, Green, Saphire, Silver.

Interior: Gray.

AT A GLANCE...

Category: 2WD or 4WD compact sport-utility. **Class :** utility

HISTORIC
Introduced in: 1997
Made in: Toyota City, Japan.

DEMOGRAPHICS
Model	Men./Wom.	Age	Married	College	Income
RAV4	NA				

INDEX
Safety:	70 %	Satisfaction:	87 %
Depreciation:	25 %	Insurance:	$ 955
Cost per mile:	$ 0.45	Number of dealers:	1 233

SALES
Model	1996	1997	Result
RAV4	56 709	67 489	+ 19.0 %

MAIN COMPETITORS
CHEVROLET Tracker, HONDA CR-V, JEEP TJ, SUBARU Forester, SUZUKI Sidekick.

MAINTENANCE REQUIRED BY WARRANTY
First revision: Frequency: Diagnostic plug:

SPECIFICATIONS

Model	Version Trim	Body/ Seats	Interior volume cu ft	Trunk volume cu ft	Cd	Wheel base in	Lght x Wdgth x Hght in x in x in	Curb weight lb	Susp. ft/rr	Brake ft/rr	Steering type	Turning diameter ft	Steer. turns nber.	Fuel tank gal	tire size	Standard tires make	model	Standard powertrain
TOYOTA		General warranty: 3 years / 36 000 miles; powertrain 5 years / 60 000 miles; corrosion, perforation: 5 years / unlimited.																
RAV4	4WD	2dr.wgn.4/5	-	9.6	-	86.6	147.6x66.7x64.8	2700	ih/ih	dc/dr	pwr.r&p.	33.5	2.7	15.3	235/60R16	Bridgestone Dueler H/T		L4/2.0/M5
RAV4	4WD	4dr.wgn. 4	-	31.4	-	94.9	163.8x66.7x65.0	2844	ih/ih	dc/dr/ABS	pwr.r&p.	36.1	2.7	15.3	235/60R16	Bridgestone Dueler H/T		L4/2.0/M5

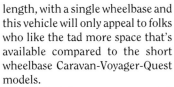

Last year Toyota launched the Sienna and thus really took its place in the North American minivan market. In the past, the Previa only turned true Toyota fans' crank, since it was a rear-wheel drive vehicle that made for treacherous winter travel and even equipped with all-wheel drive, its price was out of sight. Besides, the bizarre engine location under the front seats was derived from its conventional Tacoma pickup setup when it came to mechanical components... A real hybrid...

MODEL RANGE
The Sienna is a 3 or 4-door compact minivan that seats 7. Size-wise, it sits between the Caravan and the Windstar. It's sold in CE, LE and XLE versions, the latter being an options package. Original equipment includes the automatic transmission, two airbags, manual air conditioning, four-wheel antilock braking, radio and tape deck, tilt steering wheel and intermittent-function wipers. The LE also receives power locks, windows and mirrors and cruise control. Other items are available as extras on the LE, such as leather trim seats, light alloy wheels, sunroof and theft-deterrent system.

TECHNICAL FEATURES
The Sienna is built on the Camry platform with some modifications to suit its design. Compared to the Previa that it replaced, its engine location is much more contemporary, since the V6 is set transversely between the front wheels. The steel unitized body with some galvanized panels includes two independent cradles that support the suspensions, of MacPherson strut design up front and torsion bars at the rear. Vehicles are equipped with disc and drum brakes and standard power rack-and-pinion steering as well as a tire pressure surveillance system. The 3.0L 24-valve DOHC V6 engine is the most muscular of this displacement, since it develops 194 hp, almost as much as the 3.8L on the Windstar...

PROS
+ RIDE COMFORT. It's due to the nicely adjusted suspensions that are neither too soft nor too stiff and the robust frame that's well sound-proofed.

+ PERFORMANCES. Benefitting from a very favorable power to

Commonplace...

weight ratio, the Sienna achieves accelerations and pickup comparable to those of a passenger car and performance figures prove it.

+ VALUE. For a reasonable price, the Sienna comes with a good array of equipment, even the entry-level CE that comes with a perfectly decent number of items.

+ CABIN SPACE. This aspect was well thought out, since there's more room for seven occupants in the Sienna than in the Villager, Caravan or Venture with short wheelbase, without having to deal with rigidity problems that afflict extended wheelbase models.

+ ROADABILITY. It's competent and balanced, demonstrating sure moves on straight roads and a reassuring, level demeanor on wide

curves and turns, even when going at a good clip.

+ STEERING. It's quick, accurate and nicely powered, so it doesn't suffer from torque fallout on hard accelerations.

CONS
- STYLE. This vehicle design created by Toyota is very blah and looks too much like the Villager-Quest with a bigger rear overhang due to more generous cabin space. But we notice that the slide-rail for the sliding doors isn't as neatly integrated into the over-all design, as is the case on Chrysler or GM rivals. The Sienna doesn't have the unique traits that were the major asset of the Previa.

- CHOICE. You don't have much, since the Sienna comes in a single

length, with a single wheelbase and this vehicle will only appeal to folks who like the tad more space that's available compared to the short wheelbase Caravan-Voyager-Quest models.

- SEATS. They're pretty awful. They're flat, so offer no hip or shoulder support and upholstery is pretty thin. Also, the rear seatbench is tough to get to and its dual-section design isn't as handy when you want to remove it, not like the former design on the defunct Previa.

- PARKING BRAKE. The foot pedal is one of the most awkward on the market and Toyota could have come up with something more innovative.

- VISIBILITY. It's truncated at rear quarterback due to the bulky C pillar and the narrow rear window, not to mention the rear seat headrests.

- SWISH & SWAY. On snaky roads, the overly flexible suspension generates so much sway that you have to slow down and the front end tends to nosedive on less than perfect road surfaces.

- MANEUVERABILITY. The steer angle diameter doesn't jive with the long wheelbase body design, so parking maneuvers are no joy.

- BRAKES. Those on the first models we tested were real wimps and simulated emergency stopping distances stretched out pretty far. But standard ABS helps keep vehicle path perfectly straight.

- TIRES. The Goodyear Affinity tires of our test vehicle didn't impress us too much, not with the poor gripping power they exhibited on dry roads and they groan at the least turning maneuver.

- CABIN DESIGN. The interior is very economy-line with the shiny finish on some plastic components that really looks cheap.

- TO BE IMPROVED UPON: Poor ergonomics on the instrument panel with the really low center console and some poorly located accessories, insufficient storage spots since only the front door side-pockets are of a suitable size.

CONCLUSION
Toyota made too many compromises when it designed this mid-size minivan that only meets some of the needs of the current market. On the other hand, Honda has opted for a single more spacious model, an approach borrowed a long time ago by Ford for its Windstar. ☺

RATING
TOYOTA Sienna

CONCEPT :   **75%**
Technology   80
Safety :   70
Interior space :   80
Trunk volume: 65
Quality/fit/finish : 80

DRIVING: **59%**
Cockpit :   75
Performance :   45
Handling :   50
Steering :   80
Braking :   45

ORIGINAL EQUIPMENT: **76%**
Tires :   70
Headlights :   80
Wipers :   80
Rear defroster :   75
Radio :   75

COMFORT :   **72%**
Seats :   70
Suspension :   80
Sound level: 50
Conveniences :   80
Air conditioning :   80

BUDGET :   **64%**
Price :   40
Fuel economy :   60
Insurance :   70
Satisfaction :   85
Depreciation :   65

Overall rating: **69.2%**

NEW FOR 1999

- Three-door LE model no longer available.
- Standard roof rack on the LE model.
- Engine cut-off system and power sliding door on the XLE.
- Sound system controls on the steering wheel.

ENGINES / TRANSMISSIONS / PERFORMANCES

Model/ version	Type / timing valve / fuel system	Displacement cu in	Power bhp @ rpm	Torque lb-ft @ rpm	Compres. ratio	Driving wheels / transmission	Final ratio	Acceler. 0-60 mph s	Standing 1/4 & 5/8 mile s	Acceler. 50-75 mph s	Braking 60-0 mph f	Top speed mph	Lateral acceler. G	Noise level dBA	Fuel economy mpg City	Highway	Fuel type Octane
CE, LE	V6* 3.0 DOHC-24-MPSFI	183	194 @ 5200	209 @ 4400	10.5 :1	front - A4	3.625	10.5	17.5	31.5	6.7	141	112	0.76	68	18	26	S91

PRICE & EQUIPMENT

TOYOTA Sienna	CE	LE 4dr	XLE
Retail price $:	21,255	24,105	27,230
Dealer invoice $:	18,826	21,102	23,626
Shipping & handling $:	420	420	420
Automatic transmission:	S	S	S
Cruise control:	O	S	S
Power steering:	S	S	S
Anti-lock brakes:	S	S	S
Traction control:	S	S	S
Air conditioning:	S	S	S
Leather:	-	O	O
AM/FM/radio-cassette:	S	S	SCD
Power door locks:	O	S	S
Power windows:	O	S	S
Tilt steering:	S	S	S
Dual adjustable mirrors:	S	SEH	SEH
Alloy wheels:	-	O	S
Anti-theft system:	O	O	S

Colors

Exterior: Black, Burgundy, Sable, Spruce, Green, Blue, Iris.

Interior: Gray, Oak.

AT A GLANCE...

Category: front-wheel drive minivan.   **Class :** utility.

HISTORIC
Introduced in: 1998: Sienna.
Made in: Georgetown, Kentucky, USA.

DEMOGRAPHICS

Model	Men./Wom.	Age	Married	College	Income
Sienna	75/25 %	45	90 %	58 %	$ 50 000

INDEX
Safety: 70 %   **Satisfaction:**   87 %
Depreciation: 35 %   **Insurance:** $ 845
Cost per mile: $ 0.51   **Number of dealers:**   1 233

SALES

Model	1996	1997	Result
Sienna	-	15 180	-

MAIN COMPETITORS
CHEVROLET Venture, FORD Windstar, HONDA Odyssey, MAZDA MPV, MERCURY Villager, NISSAN Quest, OLDSMOBILE Silhouette, PONTIAC Montana, VW EuroVan.

MAINTENANCE REQUIRED BY WARRANTY
First revision: **Frequency:**   **Diagnostic plug:**
3 000 miles   3 000 miles   Yes

SPECIFICATIONS

Model	Version Trim	Body/ Seats	Interior volume cu ft	Trunk volume cu ft	Cd	Wheel base in	Lght x Wdgth x Hght in x in x in	Curb weight lb	Susp. ft/rr	Brake ft/rr	Steering type	Turning diameter ft	Steer. turns nber.	Fuel tank gal	tire size	Standard tires make	model	Standard powertrain
TOYOTA	General warranty: 3 years / 36 000 miles; powertrain 5 years / 60 000 miles; corrosion, perforation: 5 years / unlimited.																	
Sienna	CE	3/4dr.van p.7-	17.9	-		114.2	193.5x73.4x67.3	3759	ih/sih	dc/dr/ABS	pwr.r&p.	40.0	2.88	20.9	205/70R15	Dunlop	SP 40	V6/3.0/A4
Sienna	LE	4dr.van p.7 -	17.9	-		114.2	193.5x73.4x67.3	3891	ih/sih	dc/dr/ABS	pwr.r&p.	40.0	2.88	20.9	205/70R15	Dunlop	SP 40	V6/3.0/A4
Sienna	XLE	4dr.van p.7 -	17.9	-		114.2	193.5x73.4x67.3	-	ih/sih	dc/dr/ABS	pwr.r&p.	40.0	2.88	20.9	205/70R15	Dunlop	SP 40	V6/3.0/A4

TOYOTA Solara
Visionary...

The top brass at Toyota think that coupes are going to come back in style. This phenomenon is cyclic, so they're already getting ready for the period after the "sport-utility" rage by launching a coupe inspired by the Camry, called Solara. This vehicle is built in Canada in Cambridge, Ontario on the same assembly line as the Corolla, in a ratio of one Solara for ten Corolla's. Most of the target customers for this new model are between 40 and 49 years of age. They're couples with grown-up children who no longer live at home and they're at the pre-retirement stage or already retired and they're busy starting a new life. These potential customers currently drive intermediate-size cars (25%), all-terrain vehicles (20%), luxury model cars (16%) and minivans.

The reasons why these folks will be interesting in checking out the Solara are product quality, Toyota's reputation for reliability and the Solara style that will act as a catalyst. If you look back in the past, you realize that car producers don't invest billions of dollars on mere impressions, feelings or projections. When the Avalon was introduced in 1994, not one journalist present would have bet on the future of this model that everyone found lackluster and destined to failure due to lack of interest.

Five years later, sales for this model have beat records, going beyond the most optimistic projections. But such an undertaking is not without its risks, for often projected events don't always happen within the presumed time frame. That's why ad campaigns exist to offset this problem; they create and precede the phenomenon that sponsors want to happen.

The Solara is the sixth vehicle to be built by Toyota in North America. The production capacity is 50,000 units per year, besides the 150,000 Corolla's that could be built here, providing employment for 2,700 people. The Solara was designed in California at Calty Design at Newport Beach who started to work on the project in 1994 under the code name 700T. The main idea was to build a coupe derived from the Camry, while giving it a totally different body design. This product had to belong not to a particular market niche but be a popular, mass-produced vehicle. It had to be a true blue coupe, without giving the impression of being a 2+2. Starting with sleek, flowing lines, designers had to come up with a car that had lots of character by creating distinctive front and rear end stylistics in which exterior lighting and grille would play a dominant role.

The Solara won't be sold anywhere else in the world, that is, only in North America. To give it a unique touch, the instrument panel and inner doors would have the quality and appearance of Lexus products and faux-bois appliqués would be an accent included in the trim design. A multitude of small convenience items were built into the design to add to the car's practical side and equipment on the various versions would be the richest possible so as to appeal to a very specific class of people. Toyota is expecting to sell 90% of the Solara's with V6 engines that will come from Japan and the plant in Georgetown producing at full capacity to supply parts.

The Solara isn't necessarily a forerunner of the coupe renaissance, but maybe Toyota and Honda have simply decided to share the small market that's left.

In order to come up with a match to the coupe derived from the Honda Accord that was launched last year, Toyota introduced its own direct rival, the Solara derived from the Camry. It's strange to observe that these two cars are competing in an arena where the only thing that's missing at the present time are buyers. After all, as everyone knows, they're busy elsewhere buying the Lincoln Navigator, Lexus RX 300 and other urban tanks. It could be one of two things. Either Honda and Toyota are visionaries who are reading in their crystal balls or else they're taking a chance and seeing whether a new market segment will develop.

MODEL RANGE
The Solara is a two-door, four-passenger coupe sold in SE trim, equipped with a 2.2L 4-cylinder engine, as well as an SE V6 and SLE versions equipped with a 3.0L engine. All three models will receive a 5-speed manual transmission or a 4-speed automatic and a set of options called SLE tops of the lineup. The base model SE is equipped with a standard 4-cylinder engine linked to an automatic transmission, cruise control, antilock braking, manual air conditioning, tilt steering wheel, radio and tape deck and power windows, locks and mirrors. The SE V6 also receives the same engine with a manual transmission, CD player and light alloy wheels. The SLE benefits from automatic air conditioning. In all cases, the theft-deterrent system is available as an extra as well as leather seat covers and traction control (SLE).

TECHNICAL FEATURES
The Solara is built directly on the Camry platform and inherits its main mechanical components. Its steel monocoque body is fitted with some galvanized panels. Aerodynamics are relatively good, yielding a drag coeffient of 0.32. The body is built so as to form a sort of tubular cage with elements carefully calculated to absorb and resist in a very precise and measured way the impact caused in the event of a collision so as to protect the cabin and its occupants. The four-wheel independent suspension consists of MacPherson struts, but they've been reworked to offer improved steering and better wheel control. Models animated by the 4-cylinder engine are equipped with disc and drum brakes, whereas versions powered by the V6 benefit from four-wheel disc brakes. Antilock braking is standard equipment on all models. Traction control is optional only on the SLE version and it can be

deactivated by flicking a switch located on the dashboard.

PROS
+ STYLE. It's quite gorgeous with the curved lines and front and rear extremities perfectly blended into the flow and feel of the vehicle, so there's a single-minded blend of various elements resulting in an unusual elegance. Proportions are perfect, various car sections are well-balanced and the exterior lighting components really blend in with the over-all look. The front grille is a final touch with its sharp little point at the bottom that looks like a beak to remind you that this lovely bird can wreak havoc. It's surprising that even with a certain similarity between the front end design and that of the Camry, the Solara really doesn't betray its origins and the rear end design is totally unique and different.

+ QUALITY. It exudes from every single pore of the Solara. Assembly is tight, over-all design and finish details are flawless and trim materials such as the plastic components and faux-bois accents are attractive.

+ SINGLE DESIGN. It's more obvious on the SE V6 version that's a single-piece design and components seem to fit perfectly into one other to form a single, seamless thing of beauty. The structure looks solid, engines have what it takes, the same applies to steering and brakes. What a winner!

+ DRIVING PLEASURE. The V6 engine linked to the automatic transmission is the best combination, since the engine is smooth and discreet and it can become agressive and zoom it up when coaxed. Vehicle flow is clean and a sure thing, as is the case for the Camry. The driver is comfy in no time and visibility is super and controls are organized in an ergonomic manner.

+ RIDE COMFORT. It's practically perfect with the flexible and well-honed suspension, thickly upholstered seats, but they don't offer quite enough lateral support, both up front and in the rear.

+ CONVENIENCE ITEMS. Nothing has been overlooked and the Solara offers lots of convenience items that make for comfy travel. The huge trunk can be extended by lowering the rear seatbench. But to preserve structural integrity, the orifice is relatively small.

CONS
- 4-CYLINDER ENGINE. It's hard to understand why Toyota complicates things unnecessarily by developing a model equipped with a 4-cylinder engine when the company knows that it only represents, at best, 10% of sales. This engine is all right theoretically speaking, but the V6 is so much more pleasant and gratifying to use that the smaller engine doesn't hold up well to the comparison.

- MANUAL GEARBOX. Synchronization is sluggish and even if it gives the V6 a certain temperament, it doesn't seem to be the kind of option that the targeted clientele will choose. The Solara is remarkably efficient and is a machine with a single soul when this engine is paired up with the automatic transmission, so why complicate things unnecessarily? Besides, gears are spaced too far apart, the clutch control is sometimes brutal and pedal travel is too short.

- SIDE-IMPACT AIRBAGS. It's strange that the Solara isn't equipped with side-impact airbags, since after all, it's a brand new product. No official reason was volunteered by the carmaker who even seemed embarrassed to have been asked such a question.

- BRAKES. They're effective and well-balanced, but they're hard to apply as needed since the stiff pedal doesn't allow for variations in pressure.

- STORAGE SPOTS. They're rare in the rear seat area since there are only seat pockets and two cup-holders on the center console. Toyota should have been able to include a fold-up armrest, as so many other carmakers do these days.

- NOISE. The engine is so polite and there's next to no road noise thanks to good soundproofing, so in this quiet ambience you're very aware of wind noise around the windshield and windows.

- TO BE IMPROVED UPON: Windshield wipers that are a bit sluggish.

CONCLUSION
The Solara has all the qualities needed to convert the most hardened truck driver into lettting him or herself go and enjoy smoother and more refined driving. For a reasonable price, this car offers the exclusive character of a classy car and the indispensable useful items needed for daily use. ☺

RATING
TOYOTA Solara

CONCEPT :		75%
Technology	85	
Safety :	90	
Interior space :	60	
Trunk volume:	55	
Quality/fit/finish :	85	

DRIVING:		69%
Cockpit :	85	
Performance :	55	
Handling :	60	
Steering :	75	
Braking :	70	

ORIGINAL EQUIPMENT:		79%
Tires :	80	
Headlights :	80	
Wipers :	75	
Rear defroster :	80	
Radio :	80	

COMFORT :		74%
Seats :	80	
Suspension :	80	
Sound level:	60	
Conveniences :	70	
Air conditioning :	80	

BUDGET :		55%
Price :	45	
Fuel economy :	80	
Insurance :	50	
Satisfaction :	50	
Depreciation :	50	

Overall rating:		**70.4%**

NEW FOR 1999

• New coupe derived from the Camry, equipped with the same mechanical components.

ENGINES / TRANSMISSIONS / PERFORMANCES

Model/version	Type / timing valve / fuel system	Displacement cu in	Power bhp @ rpm	Torque lb-ft @ rpm	Compres. ratio	Driving wheels / transmission	Final ratio	Acceler. 0-60 mph s	Standing 1/4 & 5/8 mile s	Acceler. 50-75 mph s	Braking 60-0 mph f	Top speed mph	Lateral acceler. G	Noise level dBA	Fuel economy mpg City	Fuel economy mpg Highway	Fuel type Octane
SE	L4 2.2 DOHC-16-MPSFI	132	135 @ 5200	147 @ 4400	9.5:1	front-A4	3.944	11.5	18.2 32.7	8.0	138	112	0.80	65-71	22	32	S 91
SE V6	V6 3.0 DOHC-24-MPSFI	183	200 @ 5200	214 @ 4400	10.5:1	front-M5	3.933	7.8	15.6 26.8	5.7	141	131	0.80	64-70	20	30	S 91
					1)	front-A4	3.944	8.4	16.3 28.0	6.0	144	124	0.80	64-70	19	29	S 91

1) SLE

PRICE & EQUIPMENT

TOYOTA Solara	SE	SE V6
Retail price $:	18,000	21,500
Dealer invoice $:	-	-
Shipping & handling $:	420	420
Automatic transmission:	S	O
Cruise control:	S	S
Power steering:	S	S
Anti-lock brakes:	S	S
Traction control:	-	O -> SLE
Air conditioning:	S	S/SA on SLE
Leather:	-	O
AM/FM/radio-cassette:	S	SCD
Power door locks:	S	S
Power windows:	S	S
Tilt steering:	S	S
Dual adjustable mirrors:	SEH	SEH
Alloy wheels:	-	S
Anti-theft system:	O	O

Colors

Exterior: White, Opal-Iris, Black, Sand, Red, Green, Blue.

Interior: Gray, Ivory.

AT A GLANCE...

Category: front-wheel drive compact coupes.   Class : 4

HISTORIC

Introduced in: 1999
Made in: Cambridge, Ontario, Canada.

DEMOGRAPHICS

Model	Men./Wom.	Age	Married	College	Income
Solara	ND				

INDEX

Safety:	90 %	Satisfaction:	ND %
Depreciation:	ND %	Insurance:	$ 955
Cost per mile:	$ 0.45	Number of dealers:	1 233

SALES

Model	1996	1997	Result
Solara	not on the market at that time.		

MAIN COMPETITORS

ACURA CL, HONDA Accord.

MAINTENANCE REQUIRED BY WARRANTY

First revision:	Frequency:	Diagnostic plug:
3 000 miles	3 000 miles	No

SPECIFICATIONS

Model	Version Trim	Body/Seats	Interior volume cu ft	Trunk volume cu ft	Cd	Wheel base in	Lght x Wdgth x Hght in x in x in	Curb weight lb	Susp. ft/rr	Brake ft/rr	Steering type	Turning diameter ft	Steer. turns nber.	Fuel tank gal	tire size	Standard tires make	model	Standard powertrain
TOYOTA																		
Solara	SE	2dr.cpe. 5	-	13.8	0.32	105.1	190.0x71.1x55.1	3175	ih/ih	dc/dr/ABS	pwr.r&p.	38.1	2.88	18.5	205/65R15	Bridgestone	Potenza RE92	L4/2.2/A4
Solara	SE V6	2dr.cpe. 5	-	13.8	0.32	105.1	190.0x71.1x55.1	3230	ih/ih	dc/ABS	pwr.r&p.	38.1	2.88	18.5	205/60R16	Michelin	XW4	V6/3.0/M5

General warranty: 3 years / 36 000 miles; powertrain 5 years / 60 000 miles; corrosion, perforation: 5 years / unlimited.

In spite of their good reputation, Toyota pickup trucks aren't the most popular around, since sales figures represent only a tiny fraction of the prima donna's sales performance in this category. Owners complain about missing features such as rear doors on the extended cabin model Xtracab, an innovative item that equips other current, more up-to-date models. The T100 pickup will be replaced next year by a model called Tundra that will be equipped with a V8 derived from the engine that powers Lexus model cars. So this lineup will no doubt soon have a top-of-the-line pickup truck to brag about, right?...

MODEL RANGE

The Tacoma pickup is sold in RWD or AWD models equipped with 4 or 6-cylinder engines linked to a standard manual gearbox or an optional automatic. They're available in base, Xtracab or SR5 trim levels. Body styles include regular cabin or extended (Xtracab) with regular, extended or cabin chassis. The base model Tacoma is equipped with power steering and dual airbags. The Xtracab gets added tilt steering wheel and intermittent wipers and the SR5 benefits from cruise control, antilock braking, radio and tape deck and light alloy wheels. All other items are included on the list of options.

TECHNICAL FEATURES

This pickup truck is built on a steel five-crossmember H-frame on which the cabin is mounted. The front suspension consists of a double wishbone setup and stabilizer bar and steering is rack-and-pinion. The rigid rear axle is supported by two leaf springs. Trucks are equipped with disc and drum brakes but four-wheel ABS is available as an extra for all models. ABS works differently on the all-wheel drive vehicles, since it's regulated by a deceleration detector. The engine, transfer case and gas tank on the 4X4's are covered with standard metallic protective plates. The Tacoma is powered by either a 142-hp 2.4L or 150 hp 4-cylinder engine or a 3.4L V6 that delivers 190 hp. All-wheel drive models are equipped with a system that allows you to shift from RWD to AWD via shift-on-the-fly at any speed, by simply pushing a button located on the transfer case lever. Safety-wise, the

Incognito...

frame and cabin have been reinforced to guarantee better structural integrity, doors are fitted with side-impact beams and vehicles are equipped with dual airbags, height-adjustable shoulder belts up front and the windshield washer reservoir can hold 4.5 liters of cleaner fluid. The more spacious extended cabin is equipped with auxiliary seats facing frontwards that can be folded down flat to free up the cargo area. A fold-up shelf with two cup-holders allows for enough room to install a child's seat and is a unique asset in this category.

PROS

+ REPUTATION. Toyota pickup trucks are known for their reliability and impressive durability, which explains in part their hefty price,

but these vehicles also fetch a higher than average resale price and recent models are as rare as hen's teeth on the used vehicle market.

+ QUALITY. This aspect is at the very foundation of Toyota's reputation. These trucks are robust and exhibit fine fit and finish details. The over-all effect and trim materials used are topnotch.

+ PERFORMANCES. The 2.7L 4-cylinder and 3.4L V6 pump out the power and have a nice and safe level of energy on reserve if needed and accelerations and pickup are brisk.

+ HANDLING. Some RWD models behave like cars as long as the box has a bit of ballast to assure good rear wheel function.

+ CAPABILITIES. Off-road prowess on the AWD models is a cut

above what the competition can muster, thanks to generous ground clearance and wide, fine-tuned entrance and exit angles.

+ FUEL EFFICIENCY. The 2.4L 4-cylinder engine is very frugal, but it's more suited to light tasks.

+ RIDE COMFORT. The Xtracab cabin is quite roomy and passengers will be more comfy in the individual seats that are nicely contoured and offer good lateral and lumbar support. But the original seatbench is another kettle of fish.

CONS

- SAFETY. The NHSTA gave low marks to these vehicles on collision tests, so occupants may be vulnerable to serious injury in the event of an accident.

- PRICE. Typical of Toyota products, Tacoma's are often more pricey than rivals with an equivalent equipment level. Luckily, their low depreciation compensates for this snag.

- TORQUE. It's lacking at low r.p.m., as is the case with all V6 engines that also get awfully thirsty when tackling heavy jobs or travelling over rough turf.

- BRAKES. They're not up to snuff and stopping distances in emergency situations are long and vehicle path is pretty iffy without ABS.

- CHOICE. It's more restricted than for American carmakers in regard to body style, engines and model range.

- REAR SEATS. Access is acrobatic on the Xtracab and these seats aren't too useful because they face frontwards and so there's precious little toe room.

- ROADHOLDING. The 4X4's aren't too competent on curves, due to the high-perched center of gravity and the Xtracab's are clumsy because of the wide steer angle diameter.

CONCLUSION

Toyota isn't agressive enough on the sports-utility vehicle market, so its main rivals are way ahead of the game. You'd think that SUV sales weren't of much interest to the numer one Japanese carmaker that, in other market segments, is an undisputed leader. Could it be the result of secret arrangements made with North American car producers in exchange for a few favors? ☺

RATING
TOYOTA Tacoma

CONCEPT :		60%
Technology	80	
Safety :	50	
Interior space :	30	
Trunk volume:	60	
Quality/fit/finish :	80	

DRIVING:		56%
Cockpit :	80	
Performance :	50	
Handling :	30	
Steering :	70	
Braking :	50	

ORIGINAL EQUIPMENT:		61%
Tires :	75	
Headlights :	80	
Wipers :	80	
Rear defroster :	0	
Radio :	70	

COMFORT :		60%
Seats :	70	
Suspension :	60	
Sound level :	50	
Conveniences :	40	
Air conditioning :	80	

BUDGET :		63%
Price :	60	
Fuel economy :	65	
Insurance :	50	
Satisfaction :	85	
Depreciation :	55	

Overall rating:		60.0%

NEW FOR 1999

- Four new exterior shades.
- Standard console on the Xtracab V6.
- More richly equipped SR5 V6 model.

ENGINES / TRANSMISSIONS / PERFORMANCES

Model/ version	Type / timing valve / fuel system	Displacement cu in	Power bhp @ rpm	Torque lb-ft @ rpm	Compres. ratio	Driving wheels / transmission	Final ratio	Acceler. 0-60 mph s	Standing 1/4 & 5/8 mile s	Acceler. 50-75 mph s	Braking 60-0 mph f	Top speed mph	Lateral acceler. G	Noise level dBA	Fuel economy mpg City	Highway	Fuel type Octane
1)	L4* 2.4 DOHC-16-MPSFI	149	142 @ 5000	160 @ 4000	9.5 :1	rear - M5*	3.416	NA							22	28	R 87
						rear - A4	3.583	NA							21	26	R 87
2)	L4* 2.7 DOHC-16-MPSFI	164	150 @ 4800	177 @ 4000	9.5 :1	rear/4 - M5*	3.615	12.5	19.0	36.5	10.8	151	100	0.75	68	17	23	R 87
3)	V6* 3.4 DOHC-24-MPSFI	206	190 @ 4800	220 @ 3600	9.6 :1	rear/4 - M5*	3.909	11.8	18.5	34.7	8.8	151	106	0.75	68	16	20	R 87
						rear/4 - A4	4.100	13.0	19.5	35.8	10,0	157	103	0.75	68	16	20	R 87

1) Tacoma 4X2. 2) Tacoma 4x4 Xtracab. 3) Tacoma V6

PRICE & EQUIPMENT

TOYOTA Tacoma Roues motrices:	Reg 2WD	Xtra 2WD	Xtra V6 4WD	Ltd V6 4WD
Retail price $:	12,538	14,708	19,968	24,028
Dealer invoice $:	11,493	13,330	17,892	21,531
Shipping & handling $:	420	420	420	420
Automatic transmission:	O	O	O	O
Cruise control:	-	O	O	S
Power steering:	S	S	S	S
Anti-lock brakes:	-	O	O	S
Traction control:	-	-	-	-
Air conditioning:	O	O	O	S
Leather:	-	-	-	-
AM/FM/radio-cassette:	O	SCD	SCD	SCD
Power door locks:	-	-	-	S
Power windows:	-	-	-	S
Tilt steering:	O	O	S	S
Dual adjustable mirrors:	-	-	-	SE
Alloy wheels:	-	O	O	S
Anti-theft system:	-	-	-	S

Colors
Exterior: White, Black, Red, Jade, Seaweed, Blue, Crimson.

Interior: Gray, Oak.

AT A GLANCE...

Category: 2WD or 4WD compact pickups. **Class :** utility

HISTORIC
Introduced in: 1995
Made in: Tahara+Hino, Japan; Fremont-California, Georgetown-Kentucky, USA.

DEMOGRAPHICS
Model	Men./Wom.	Age	Married	College	Income
Tacoma	89/11 %	35	69 %	42 %	$ 38 000

INDEX
Safety:	50 %	Satisfaction:	83 %
Depreciation:	46 %	Insurance:	$ 965
Cost per mile:	$ 0.47	Number of dealers:	1 233

SALES
Model	1996	1997	Result
Tacoma	142 281	145 870	+ 2.5 %

MAIN COMPETITORS
DODGE Dakota, FORD Ranger, CHEVROLET S-10, GMC Sonoma, MAZDA B, NISSAN Frontier.

MAINTENANCE REQUIRED BY WARRANTY
First revision:	Frequency:	Diagnostic plug:
3 000 miles	3 000 miles	No

SPECIFICATIONS

Model Trim	Version	Body/ Seats	Wheel base in	Lght x Wdgth x Hght in x in x in	Curb weight lb	Susp. ft/rr	Brake ft/rr	Steering type	Turning diameter ft	Steer. turns nber.	Fuel tank gal	Standard tires tire size	make	model	Standard powertrain
TOYOTA		General warranty: 3 years / 36 000 miles; powertrain 5 years / 60 000 miles; corrosion; perforation: 5 years / unlimited.													
Tacoma	4x2 Reg	2dr.p-u.3	103.3	184.5x66.5x61.8	2579	ih/rl	dc/dr	pwr.r&p.	35.4	3.7	15.1	195/75R14	Dunlop		L4/2.4/M5
Tacoma	4x2 Xtra	2dr.p-u.5	121.9	203.1x66.5x62.2	2760	ih/rl	dc/dr	pwr.r&p.	41.3	3.4	15.1	215/70R14	Firestone		L4/2.4/M5
Tacoma	4x4 Xtra	2dr.p-u.5	121.9	203.1x66.5x67.7	3360	ih/rl	dc/dr	pwr.r&p.	40.0	3.5	18.0	225/75R15	Dunlop	r	L4/2.7/M5
Tacoma	4x4 SR5 V6	2dr.p-u.4	121.9	203.1x66.5x68.8	3430	ih/rl	dc/drABS	pwr.r&p.	40.0	3.5	18.0	31x10.5R15	Goodyear Wrangler GSA		V6/3.4/M5

It looks like Toyota changed its mind about discarding the Tercel, the entry-level model in its North American model range and the Paseo coupe as well, since it's a derivation. At a time when consumers are forever buying more comfortable, bigger and less economical cars, keeping these "econo-cars" on the roster seems less rational than for other parts of the world. The problem is that these versions continue to sell, less than others, of course, but on a regular basis, so there's a clientele out there who's looking for just such cars.

MODEL RANGE

The 1999 Tercel is only available as a 4-door sedan in CE trim level and the Paseo is only offered as a 2-door coupe in a single version as well. Both are animated by the same engine, namely a 1.5L 4-cylinder engine associated with a standard 5-speed manual gearbox or a 4-speed automatic sold as an extra. The Tercel is equipped with standard airbags and power steering, the latter already equipping the Paseo. The only options available are the automatic transmission, air conditioning, antilock braking system and radio with tape deck.

The Paseo doesn't have much more equipment. Besides airbags, standard items include power windows, adjustable exterior mirrors and power steering. Optional equipment is similar to that on the Tercel, but it can also receive alloy rims, sunroof and intermittent-mode wipers.

TECHNICAL FEATURES

Both these vehicles have a steel monocoque body with some galvanized panels. The front suspension is made up of MacPherson struts with a torsion axle at the rear integrating an anti-roll bar. Cars are equipped with recirculating ball steering and standard disc and drum brakes, but the antilock braking system is only sold as an extra. Their simple body design yields good aerodynamic finesse since the drag coefficient is 0.32 for the Tercel and 0.31 for the Paseo.

PROS

+ **RELIABILITY.** The Tercel-Paseo's can be really proud of this attribute, since the owner satisfaction rate is still higher than 92%.

+ **SAFETY.** Passenger protection is more a sure thing now that the frame is more rigid and with the

Bare Minimum...

standard airbags, retracting seatbelts and side-impact beams installed in the doors to better withstand lateral impact.

+ **CABIN SPACE.** The most recent model is roomier thanks to the added length and height, especially in the rear seats where occupants will feel less cramped.

+ **FUEL CONSUMPTION.** It's very economical especially with the manual gearbox, performances are adequate, given the type of vehicle.

+ **HANDLING.** Cars stay level and car path is predictable, as is usually the case for small front-wheel drive cars, but tire size and quality are of primary importance.

+ **QUALITY.** These cars are entry-level models, but assembly and finish job are nicely executed. Trim

materials inside the cabin are very attractive, so you don't mind paying the rather high going price for these models, but you could almost buy a base model Corolla for just a bit more...

+ **DRIVING.** It's far from unpleasant, considering the stripped down to basics character of these vehicles. Engines are lively and the Tercel and Paseo are easy to drive with their precise, smooth controls.

+ **CONVENIENCE FEATURES.** The trunk can't always be extended but it holds enough luggage in a pinch and storage spots inside the cabin are trim, but they're welcome companions.

+ **RIDE COMFORT.** Contrary to the reputation of compact cars, these two models benefit from a

good suspension and seats provide satisfactory support, even if upholstery is a bit on the thin side.

CONS

- **SAFETY.** The Tercel received rather poor marks in NHTSA collision tests, which indicates that front seat passengers are at risk in the event of an accident.

- **PRICE.** It's higher than that of the competition and is justified by such factors as quality, reliability, more favorable resale value and also the fact that these cars are built in Japan.

- **RIDE COMFORT.** Trips can be tiring with all the noise, the unpleasant result of poor soundproofing and the rear cabin section on the Paseo is pretty snug, so only small children can be comfy seated back there.

- **BRAKES.** They're better than they were, but without ABS, front wheels tend to lock in no time in emergency situations, which translates into long stopping distances and rather uncertain car path.

- **EQUIPMENT.** It's at a strict minimum, so you have to add options if you want these cars to be decently equipped. Luckily, the resale value lets you recoup part of your investment.

- **TIRES.** The original tires on the Tercel are terribly small, unworthy of a well-respected brand like Toyota, for they constitute, along with the brakes, the number one active safety feature.

- **CONVERTIBLE.** Sold only in the United States, this model lacks structural rigidity, as is indicated by the unusually shaky doors and windshield when driving over poor roads.

- **ACCESS.** The rear seat area is pretty cramped and two passengers will be comfy, as long as they're slim and nimble...

CONCLUSION

The Tercel and Paseo are entry-level vehicles that do have their good points, since they weren't treated badly by the automaker. They provide a simple, effective but above all, inexpensive means of transportation. The Paseo is the only compact coupe still offered on the market that has a certain elegance, even though it's equipped with a strict minimum. ☺

RATING
TOYOTA Tercel-Paseo

CONCEPT :		61%
Technology	80	
Safety :	75	
Interior space :	35	
Trunk volume:	35	
Quality/fit/finish :	80	

DRIVING:		56%
Cockpit :	75	
Performance :	30	
Handling :	50	
Steering :	70	
Braking :	55	

ORIGINAL EQUIPMENT:		72%
Tires :	60	
Headlights :	75	
Wipers :	80	
Rear defroster :	75	
Radio :	70	

COMFORT :		65%
Seats :	70	
Suspension :	70	
Sound level:	50	
Conveniences :	60	
Air conditioning :	75	

BUDGET :		79%
Price :	80	
Fuel economy :	90	
Insurance :	80	
Satisfaction :	90	
Depreciation :	55	

| **Overall rating:** | | **66.6%** |

NEW FOR 1999

- The 2-door Tercel CE discarded.
- Two new exterior shades for the Tercel and one for the Paseo.

ENGINES / TRANSMISSIONS / PERFORMANCES

Model/ version	Type / timing valve / fuel system	Displacement cu in	Power bhp @ rpm	Torque lb-ft @ rpm	Compres. ratio	Driving wheels / transmission	Final ratio	Acceler. 0-60 mph s	Standing 1/4 & 5/8 mile s	Acceler. 50-75 mph s	Braking 60-0 mph f	Top speed mph	Lateral acceler. G	Noise level dBA	Fuel economy mpg City Highway	Fuel type Octane
Tercel	L4* 1.5 DOHC-16-MPSFI	91	93 @ 5400	100 @ 4400	9.4 :1	front - M5*	3.72	11.0	18.0 33.7	7.8	144	103	0.75	68	31 41	R 87
						front - A4	2.82	13.5	19.5 36.5	9.0	148	100	0.75	68	27 38	R 87
Paseo	L4* 1.5 DOHC-16-MPSFI	91	93 @ 5400	100 @ 4400	9.4 :1	front - M5*	3.94	10.5	17.3 32.5	7.2	144	106	0.77	68	30 38	R 87
						front - A4	3.27	11.8	17.9 33.5	8.0	151	103	0.77	68	26 34	R 87

PRICE & EQUIPMENT

TOYOTA	Tercel	Paseo
Retail price $:	10,698	-
Dealer invoice $:	10,080	-
Shipping & handling $:	420	420
Automatic transmission:	O	O
Cruise control:	-	-
Power steering:	S	S
Anti-lock brakes:	-	-
Traction control:	-	-
Air conditioning:	O	O
Leather:	-	-
AM/FM/radio-cassette:	O	SCD
Power door locks:	-	-
Power windows:	-	-
Tilt steering:	-	-
Dual adjustable mirrors:	O	SM
Alloy wheels:	-	-
Anti-theft system:	-	-

Colors

Exterior: White, Red, Silver, Black, Blue.

Interior: Black, Gray, Oak.

AT A GLANCE...

Category: front-wheel drive sub-compact coupes & sedans. **Class :** 3

HISTORIC
Introduced in: 1978-1995:Tercel; 1996:Paseo.
Made in: Takaoka-Toyota City, Japan.

DEMOGRAPHICS

Model	Men./Wom.	Age	Married	College	Income
Tercel	43/57 %	42	57 %	53 %	$ 25 000
Paseo	ND				

INDEX
Safety:	T-65% P-85 %	Satisfaction:	92 %
Depreciation:	45 %	Insurance:	$ 725
Cost per mile:	$ 0.35	Number of dealers:	1 233

SALES

Model	1996	1997	Result	
Tercel	14 343	9 021	- 37.1 %	13.1 %
Paseo	6 069	2 786	- 54.1 %	-

MAIN COMPETITORS
Tercel: HONDA Civic, CHEVROLET Metro (4 dr.) HYUNDAI Accent, NISSAN Sentra.
Paseo: HONDA Civic Si, SATURN SC1.

MAINTENANCE REQUIRED BY WARRANTY
First revision:	Frequency:	Diagnostic plug:
3 000 miles	3 000 miles	No

SPECIFICATIONS

Model	Version Trim	Body/ Seats	Interior volume cu ft	Trunk volume cu ft	Cd	Wheel base in	Lght x Wdgth x Hght in x in x in	Curb weight lb	Susp. ft/rr	Brake ft/rr	Steering type	Turning diameter ft	Steer. turns nber.	Fuel tank gal	tire size	Standard tires make	model	Standard powertrain
TOYOTA		General warranty: 3 years / 36 000 miles; powertrain 5 years / 60 000 miles; corrosion, perforation: 5 years / unlimited.																
Tercel	CE	4dr.sdn.4/5	81.0	9.3	0.32	93.7	161.8x64.8x53.2	2112	ih/sih	dc/dr	pwr.r&p.	32.8	3.8	11.9	155/80R13	Michelin	MX4	L4/1.5/M5
Paseo	man.	2dr.cpe.2+2	77.2	7.5	0.31	93.7	163.5x65.3x51.0	2075	ih/sih	dc/dr	pwr.r&p.	33.5	2.7	11.9	185/60R14	Goodyear		L4/1.5/M5
Paseo	autom.	2dr.cpe.2+2	77.2	212	0.31	93.7	163.5x65.3x51.0	2174	ih/sih	dc/dr	pwr.r&p.	33.5	2.7	11.9	185/60R14	Goodyear		L4/1.5/A4

Since its redesign, the 4Runner has seen its sales increase dramatically. It's caught up with the times so as to compete on an equal footing with the star performers in the category, namely the Explorer and Grand Cherokee. The previous vehicle was a rugged, down home sort, but now, behold, it's dressed up like a luxury limo. In the process, it also got a vitamin boost to make up for a few innate weaknesses, so as to be able to face the music and now both its engines are more muscular, each in its own way.

MODEL RANGE

The 4Runner is only available in a single 4-door body style, in SR5, SR5 V6 and Limited trim. The base engine is a 2.7L 4-cylinder linked to a 5-speed manual gearbox and as an extra, you can get a 3.4L V6 with 5-speed manual gearbox or 4-speed automatic, the latter being standard on the Limited version. All-wheel drive is on demand, otherwise the 4Runner is a rear-wheel drive vehicle. The SR5 version is equipped with power steering, radio and tape deck, tilt steering wheel, manually adjustable mirrors and intermittent wipers. You have to go to the SR5 V6 if you want a standard V6. This model also receives cruise control, antilock braking, power locks and windows, heated exterior mirrors, air conditioning, light alloy wheels and CD player. The Limited version is equipped with all of the above, as well as an automatic transmission, leather-clad seats, theft-deterrent system and sunroof.

TECHNICAL FEATURES

The 4Runner isn't just a simple inheritor of the Tacoma pickup's genes, since it now only borrows its chassis, main suspension components and engines. It has its own unique body that's built of steel and mounted on an H-frame. The front suspension is a double wishbone setup and the rigid rear axle is suspended on coil springs and held in place by four longitudinal control arms. All models are equipped with disc and drum brakes and the SR5 V6 and Limited benefit from four-wheel antilock braking. On the Limited, you can go from RWD to AWD via shift-on-the-fly by simply pressing a button located on the dashboard.

PROS

+ **STYLE.** During the last face-lift,

Professional

body stylistics got beefed up and the vehicle now has a more bulky, massive look and it also seems lower-slung on its wheels than before (optical illusion created by the running boards). This year again, its silhouette got a touch-up so it has an even more distinctive appearance.

+ **CABIN SPACE.** It's more generous with the longer wheelbase, so occupants can enjoy more leg room and access is easier with the lower floor threshold.

+ **COCKPIT.** The driver is comfy and benefits from better visibility than before.

+ **REAR HATCH.** It's definitely more convenient than the previous design, allowing easy access to the cargo hold that sits quite high off

the ground.

+ **FUEL EFFICIENCY.** Both engines are more powerful, but the 4-cylinder still strains a tad when it comes to moving this big hulk (3,745 lb.) on off-road maneuvers, even though its power to weight ratio is more favorable than on the previous model.

+ **QUALITY.** Toyota's signature is written all over this vehicle. Construction craftsmanship is superb, fit and finish are super-tight and trim materials are lovelier in spite of a total lack of imagination when it comes to the over-all look.

+ **OFF-ROAD MANEUVERS.** Capabilities are excellent thanks to generous ground clearance and wide cornering and exit angles, even if the running boards sometimes get

in the way when you're driving over really big mounds.

+ **RIDE COMFORT.** Front seats are now nicely shaped and cushion upholstery is plusher. Soundproofing is as effective as that of a car.

+ **SATISFACTION.** The high owner satisfaction rate indicates just how reliable this vehicle is and it keeps an excellent resale value, a rare fact on the used vehicle market.

CONS

- **PRICE.** It's steep, and it is a 4Runner after all, so we find the price unjustified for a vehicle that's more multi-purpose than a real SUV.

- **HANDLING.** Depending on the type of tire, it's not always a sure thing, due to the high center of gravity, flexible suspension that causes major wavering motion and big tires that sometimes bounce hard when you're not expecting it.

- **FUEL CONSUMPTION.** Such hefty vehicle weight translates into heavy fuel consumption comparable to that of rivals.

- **STEERING.** It's overly light due to over-assistance, which is an advantage on rough terrain since it reacts quickly, but it's a disadvantage on the road because it isn't always easy to keep the vehicle on course in slippery conditions or in crosswinds.

- **PERFORMANCES.** The rather timid 4-cylinder engine is only appropriate on the RWD version that weighs less.

- **MANUAL GEARBOX.** It isn't a joy to use, since it doesn't jive with engine capabilities and clutch pedal travel is too long.

- **RIDE COMFORT.** It's never perfect with this type of vehicle that's jumpy and jittery due to the humongous tires that faithfully render road faults every mile of the way. Road and wind noise are constant and undesirable companions.

- **ACCESS.** Tall or bulky folks will have a tough time climbing up into the rear seats. Even with the lower floor threshold, the doors are narrow and the step is high.

CONCLUSION

The 4Runner may not be the number one seller on the charts, but it's the most professional when it comes to sports-utility vehicles, so this partly justifies its higher price. ☺

RATING
TOYOTA 4Runner

CONCEPT : **71%**
Technology	80
Safety :	60
Interior space :	65
Trunk volume:	70
Quality/fit/finish :	80

DRIVING: **58%**
Cockpit :	80
Performance :	35
Handling :	50
Steering :	75
Braking :	50

ORIGINAL EQUIPMENT: **78%**
Tires :	75
Headlights :	80
Wipers :	80
Rear defroster :	75
Radio :	80

COMFORT : **70%**
Seats :	80
Suspension :	65
Sound level :	50
Conveniences :	75
Air conditioning :	80

BUDGET : **52%**
Price :	30
Fuel economy :	45
Insurance :	40
Satisfaction :	85
Depreciation :	60

Overall rating: **65.8%**

NEW FOR 1999

- Numerous changes, additions, improvements and relocation of interior and exterior components.
- The SR5 V6 version equipped with standard air conditioning.
- CD player, power windows, heated mirrors and light alloy rims.
- Standard theft-deterrent system and fog lamps on the Limited.

ENGINES

Model/ version	Type / timing valve / fuel system	Displacement cu in	Power bhp @ rpm	Torque lb-ft @ rpm
SR5	L4* 2.7 DOHC-16-MPSFI	164	150 @ 4800	177 @ 4000
SR5 V6	V6* 3.4 DOHC-24-MPSFI	206	183 @ 4800	217 @ 3600
Limited	V6* 3.4 DOHC-24-MPSFI	206	183 @ 4800	217 @ 3600

TRANSMISSIONS

Compres. ratio	Driving wheels / transmission	Final ratio
9.5 :1	rear/4 - M5*	4.10
	rear/4 - A4	4.10
9.6 :1	rear/4 - M5*	3.91
9.6 :1	rear/4 - A4*	3.91

PERFORMANCES

Acceler. 0-60 mph s	Standing 1/4 & 5/8 mile s	Acceler. 50-75 mph s	Braking 60-0 mph f	Top speed mph	Lateral acceler. G	Noise level dBA	Fuel economy mpg City	Highway	Fuel type Octane
NA							19	24	R 87
NA							20	24	R 87
10.0	17.2	31.1	7.0	43	165	0.75	68	16	19	R 87
11.5	18.3	32.8	8.2	45	160	0.75	68	17	20	R 87

PRICE & EQUIPMENT

TOYOTA 4RUNNER	SR5	SR5 V6	LIMITED
Retail price $:	25,248	26,398	34,718
Dealer invoice $:	22,104	23,110	30,395
Shipping & handling $:	420	420	420
Automatic transmission:	O	O	S
Cruise control:	O	S	S
Power steering:	S	S	S
Anti-lock brakes:	O	S	S
Traction control:	-	-	-
Air conditioning:	O	S	S
Leather:	O	O	S
AM/FM/radio-cassette:	S	SCD	SCD
Power door locks:	O	S	S
Power windows:	O	S	S
Tilt steering:	S	S	S
Dual adjustable mirrors:	SM	SEH	SEH
Alloy wheels:	-	S	S
Anti-theft system:	-	-	S

Colors
Exterior: White, Gray, Black, Teal, Blue, Blue steel, Silver, Jade.

Interior: Cloth: Gray, Oak. Leather: Oak.

AT A GLANCE...

Category: all-purpose 4WD vehicles. **Class :** utility

HISTORIC
Introduced in: 1985-1996
Made in: Tahara, Japan.

DEMOGRAPHICS
Model	Men./Wom.	Age	Married	College	Income
4Runner	81/19 %	42	66 %	51 %	$ 40 000

INDEX
Safety:	60 %	Satisfaction:	85 %
Depreciation:	38 %	Insurance:	$1 285
Cost per mile:	$ 0.51	Number of dealers:	1 233

SALES
Model	1996	1997	Result
4Runner	99 597	128,496	+ 29.0 %

MAIN COMPETITORS
CHEVROLET Blazer, FORD Explorer, ISUZU Rodeo & Trooper, GMC Jimmy, JEEP Cherokee-Grand Cherokee, LEXUS RX 300, MERCEDES-BENZ ML320, NISSAN Pathfinder.

MAINTENANCE REQUIRED BY WARRANTY
First revision:	Frequency:	Diagnostic plug:
3 000 miles	3 000 miles	No

SPECIFICATIONS

Model	Version Trim	Body/ Seats	Wheel base in	Lght x Wdgth x Hght in x in x in	Curb weight lb	Susp. ft/rr	Brake ft/rr	Steering type	Turning diameter ft	Steer. turns nber.	Fuel tank gal	tire size	Standard tires make	model	Standard powertrain
TOYOTA	General warranty: 3 years / 36 000 miles; powertrain 5 years / 60 000 miles; corrosion, perforation: 5 years / unlimited.														
4Runner 4x4	SR5	4dr.wgn. 5	105.3	178.7x66.5x67.5	3725	ih/rh	dc/dr	pwr.r&p.	37.4	3.5	18.5	225/75R15	Bridgestone	Dueler H/T	L4/2.7/M5
4Runner 4x4	SR5 V6	4dr.wgn. 5	105.3	178.7x68.1x69.3	3884	ih/rhdc/dr/ABS		pwr.r&p.	37.4	3.5	18.5	265/70R16	Bridgestone	Dueler H/T	V6/3.4/M5
4Runner 4x4	Limited	4dr.wgn. 5	105.3	178.7x70.9x69.3	3975	ih/rhdc/dr/ABS		pwr.r&p.	37.4	3.5	18.5	265/70R16	Bridgestone	Dueler H/T	V6/3.4/A4

Nothing is ever really and truly dead at Volkswagen. Distribution of the EuroVan was halted in 1998 and only the in-stock 1997 models were available. We've just learned that a new 1999 EuroVan will be with us soon. This is the much anticipated V6 that was only available last year to buyers of the Camper model. Last year's updated model from Europe will be imported to North America.

MODEL RANGE

For 1999, this minivan will be available in the GLS trim with 5 or 7 seats, the MV trim for MultiVan, and the Camper will be outfitted by Winnebago in the US. All models will be powered by a standard V6 140-bhp engine with a 4-speed automatic. Standard equipment on the GLS has been upgraded to include power steering, cruise control, stereo cassette, power windows, locks, and mirrors (heated), automatic air conditioning, anti-lock brakes with traction control, leather seats and alloy rims. The MultiVan's equipment will be the same, except for the leather seats.

TECHNICAL FEATURES

Certain aesthetic touchups improves the utilitarian look of the old EuroVan. The steel unibody's aerodynamics have improved, now with a drag coefficient of 0.35.

The engine is transverse mounted between the drive wheels in order to free up as much space as possible inside and improve handling with better weight balance.

The four-wheel independent suspension is based on a double arm system connected to front longitudinal torsion bars. Standard brakes are mixed, but all-disc ABS brakes are available as an option.

The VR6 engine is identical to those on the Golf GTI and Jetta and Passat GLXs. Horsepower has been cut back to 140, but torque is unchanged. The EuroVan can carry a load of 1,000 lbs. with a towing capacity of 4,400 lbs.

Newly Rich...

SIMPLY SUPER

++INTERIOR SPACE is incredible. There's plenty of room for up to seven people who can easily move between seats, and the easily accessible trunk can hold a mountain of luggage.

PROS

+THE V6 ENGINE was long in coming. It gives the EuroVan the performance that was always lacking in the past, and interestingly, without much change to fuel consumption which was pretty high for an anemic 5-cylinder.

+QUALITY. Fit and finish are up to par for Volkswagen Germany, where they're built. Materials are durable and with a good overall appearance that isn't as utilitarian.

+HANDLING is among the best in its class, in spite of the tall body. Roll and sway are well-handled by effective shock absorbers. On slippery roads, the EuroVan holds the road surprisingly well.

+EQUIPMENT has been seriously upgraded, along with the price. It now comes with leather upholstery, alloy wheels, automatic air conditioning. Not a bad idea perhaps since the luxury minivan market is beginning to heat up.

+THE DRIVING POSITION is high and straight, similar to a bus driver's position. The seat isn't uncomfortable on long hauls and visibility is superb with the large side mirrors.

+HEADRESTS abound. They are safe and the side openings provide excellent ventilation.

+THE CAMPER is multifunctional. It can be used as a mini-motorhome during the summer months and as a good, economical family car for the rest of the year.

+SEATS are comfortable, in spite of the firm padding. They offer good support and the foldable armrests are the only ones that are height-adjustable.

CONS

-THE PRICE has become astronomical for all Camper versions that now cost about as much as a limousine. We can only hope that the resale value will stay as high.

-BRAKES still require a certain getting used to because of the spongy pedal. The standard brakes are less efficient than the optional four-disc anti-lock system. Emergency stopping is long and uneven.

-STEERING is light and doesn't return to center, requiring constant attention in crosswinds, still a problem for the tall EuroVan.

-DASHBOARD. The ergonomics are poor and still look too utilitarian with confusing controls. Buttons in the middle of the dash are out of the driver's reach.

-SEATS. The benches are hard to get in and out, especially the back one.

CONCLUSION

In changing the EuroVan from a utility vehicle to a luxury minivan, Volkswagen is trying to seduce buyers who at the moment have only limited choices. They are definitely going to be interested in the quality of this German import.

RATING
VOLKSWAGEN EuroVan

CONCEPT :		87%
Technology	80	
Safety :	75	
Interior space :	100	
Trunk volume:	100	
Quality/fit/finish :	80	
DRIVING:		**53%**
Cockpit :	70	
Performance :	40	
Handling :	45	
Steering :	70	
Braking :	40	
ORIGINAL EQUIPMENT:		**76%**
Tires :	75	
Headlights :	80	
Wipers :	80	
Rear defroster :	75	
Radio :	70	
COMFORT :		**71%**
Seats :	75	
Suspension :	75	
Sound level:	50	
Conveniences :	80	
Air conditioning :	75	
BUDGET :		**51%**
Price :	10	
Fuel economy :	50	
Insurance :	50	
Satisfaction :	85	
Depreciation :	60	

Overall rating: 67.6%

NEW FOR 1999

• An updated model with a VR6 engine and A4 transmission, with a towing capacity of 4,400 lbs, greater safety and better equipment, available in GLX, MultiVan and Camper trims.

ENGINES / TRANSMISSIONS / PERFORMANCES

Model/ version	Type / timing valve / fuel system	Displacement cu in	Power bhp @ rpm	Torque lb-ft @ rpm	Compres. ratio	Driving wheels / transmission	Final ratio	Acceler. 0-60 mph s	Standing 1/4 & 5/8 mile s	Acceler. 50-75 mph s	Braking 60-0 mph f	Top speed mph	Lateral acceler. G	Noise level dBA	Fuel economy mpg City	Highway	Fuel type Octane
VR6	V6* 2.8 DOHC-12-MPSFI	170	140 @ 4500	177 @ 3200	10.0 :1	front - A4	4.91	NA							14	20	R 87

PRICE & EQUIPMENT

VOLKSWAGEN EuroVan	GLS	MV	Camper
Retail price $:	27,000	-	-
Dealer invoice $:	-	-	-
Shipping & handling $:	500	500	-
Automatic transmission:	S	S	S
Cruise control:	S	S	S
Power steering:	S	S	S
Anti-lock brakes:	S	S	S
Traction control:	S	S	S
Air conditioning:	SA	SA	SM
Leather:	S	-	-
AM/FM/radio-cassette:	S	-	-
Power door locks:	S	S	S
Power windows:	S	S	S
Tilt steering:	S	S	S
Dual adjustable mirrors:	SEH	SEH	SEH
Alloy wheels:	S	S	
Anti-theft system:			

Colors
Exterior: White, Blue, Gray, Red, Green, Brown, Bordeaux, Beige, Silver.

Interior: Gray, Blue, Beige.

AT A GLANCE...

Category: front-wheel drive vans.   Class : utility

HISTORIC
Introduced in: 1990-1999
Made in: Hanover, Germany.

DEMOGRAPHICS

Model	Men./Wom.	Age	Married	College	Income
EuroVan	87/13 %	50	73 %	37 %	$ 40 000

INDEX
Safety: 70 %   Satisfaction: 85 %
Depreciation: 36 %   Insurance: $ 1 125
Cost per mile: $ 0.55   Number of dealers: 650

SALES

Model	1996	1997	Result
EuroVan	995	1 792	+ 80.1 %

MAIN COMPETITORS
CHEVROLET Venture, CHEVROLET Astro, CHRYSLER Town & Country, DODGE Caravan, FORD Windstar, MAZDA MPV, MERCURY Villager, NISSAN Quest, PLYMOUTH Voyager, PONTIAC Montana, TOYOTA Sienna.

MAINTENANCE REQUIRED BY WARRANTY
First revision: 3 000 miles
Frequency: 3 000 miles
Diagnostic plug: No

SPECIFICATIONS

Model	Version Trim	Body/ Seats	Interior volume cu ft	Trunk volume cu ft	Cd	Wheel base in	Lght x Wdgth x Hght in x in x in	Curb weight lb	Susp. ft/rr	Brake ft/rr	Steering type	Turning diameter ft	Steer. turns nber.	Fuel tank gal	tire size	Standard tires make	model	Standard powertrain
VOLKSWAGEN	General warranty: 2 years / 25 000 miles; powertrain: 5 years / 50 000 miles; antipollution: 6 years/ 50 000 miles; corrosion perforation: 6 years.																	
EuroVan	GLS	4dr.van.7	150.0	-	0.36	115.0	188.5x72.4x76.4	4220	ih/ih	dc/ABS	pwr.r&p.	38.4	3.5	21.1	205/65R15	-	-	V6/2.8/A4
EuroVan	MultiVan	4dr.van.7	150.0	-	0.36	115.0	188.5x72.4x76.4	4347	ih/ih	dc/ABS	pwr.r&p.	38.4	3.5	21.1	205/65R15	-	-	V6/2.8/A4
EuroVan	Camper	4dr.van.6	-	-	0.36	130.7	204.3x72.4x80.0	5235	ih/ih	dc/ABS	pwr.r&p.	38.4	3.5	21.1	205/65R15	-	-	V6/2.8/A4

VOLKSWAGEN
Golf-Jetta
Late...

For many years, the German manufacturers have always been the last to announce or present their latest models. On September 15, they don't have a clue what their dealers are going to be selling two weeks later. And Volkswagen is the best at this little game. This is why, in spite of the best efforts by their North American reps, we weren't able to examine the true 1999 models before going to press. It's too bad since the new Golf has been available in Europe for the last two years. The all-new Jetta will be the first to land at our shores. But we'll still review all the features of these cars that will be available late this fall and early next spring.

Let's start with the Jetta, which will arrive first. The platform is totally new, entirely unrelated to the Golf. It's based on the Bora, falling somewhere between the Golf and the Passat. The GL and GLS trims will be powered by the 2.0-liter 4-cylinder on the present model, and the GLX will receive the VR6. The entire body will be galvanized with a 12-year rust-proof guarantee from Volkswagen, rigidity will be stronger than any model in this class, and the body will be precisely welded, using a new laser technique. These models come equipped with side airbags, a high quality stereo, antilock brakes, a fully adjustable steering column and heated exterior mirrors. The fourth-generation Golf has a more rounded body, improving the drag

coefficient to 0.31. The base version will be outfitted with a new 2.0-liter, 115 bhp engine or a 1.9-liter Turbo Direct diesel. Standard equipment still includes an antitheft alarm, high quality stereo, power locks, folding rear seats with three headrests, as well as a new pollen and odor filter for the ventilation system. Options include leather upholstery with heated front seats, alloy rims, a sunroof and express power windows that guard against any pinched fingers. Is there no end to progress? The Golf GTI will be available in the new body style with either a 115 bhp, 2.0-liter engine, or a 172 bhp on the VR-6. Following this is the Cabriolet, also with the new body and definitely improved rigidity. Interior styling has been freshened up and

the new grouping of headlights, fog lights and turn signals clearly sets it apart. The Cabriolet will also come with the 115 bhp, 2.0-liter in two trims: the reasonably-priced GL and the GLX with standard leather seats, power windows and automatic top. Obviously, there aren't any great changes to the present model range except that the body and main features are entirely new, dimensions are a little bigger, and the rigidity has been improved.

When this goes to press, we won't have had the chance to try out the new Jetta set to arrive soon on the North American continent, while the Golf isn't expected until the spring of 1999. All of the following remarks are based on the present models, but the specs have some information on the new Jetta. You will find the analysis of these two popular cars in the next edition of Road Report.

MODEL RANGE

The Golf comes as a 3- or 5-door hatchback or as a 2-door convertible, in four trims: CL, GL, GTI, and convertible. The Jetta, a 4-door sedan, is also available in four trims: GL, GLS, GT and GLX. The CL is equipped with the 1.8-liter engine, the GL, GLS, GT, Cabriolet, and GTI with the 2.0-liter, the GTI with the VR6, and the GLX with the 2.8-liter V6. The Turbo Diesel on the TDI models is the last of its kind. VW is the only manufacturer still selling this engine in North America in this category.

Features vary considerably, depending on the model. At the bottom end of the scale, the Golf CL includes two airbags, power steering, power doors connected to an antitheft system, adjustable outside mirrors and intermittent wipers. At the top, the GTI/GLX with the VR6 engine adds cruise control, antilock brakes, air conditioning, power windows and mirrors, alloy wheels and a sunroof. Automatic transmission and leather seats are optional.

TECHNICAL FEATURES

The drag coefficient of the steel unibody is acceptable at 0.32. The independent front suspension with MacPherson struts also includes anti-dive geometry. The rear torsion bar automatically adjusts any understeer. Brakes are mixed on the CL/GL and TDI, all-disc on the GLS, GT and GTI, with traction control added on the GTI and GLX VR6. Take note of the low consumption of the Turbo Diesel.

PROS

+BODY RIGIDITY has been seriously upgraded, improving handling, comfort and security, and gives it a solid feel.

+PERFORMANCE of the VR6 engine in the GTI VR6 and GLX is invigorating with quick acceleration and passing, causing disdain for the weak 2.0-liter in the fake GTI.

+HANDLING is very stable and constant, thanks to an efficient, sophisticated suspension that makes steering more exact. Even with the understeer, these cars are easy to control, and love sporty driving.

+STEERING is quick and precise, well-assisted, and its responsiveness is marvelous on winding two-lanes.

+COMFORT. Greater shock absorption and generous wheel travel have improved driving comfort, and seats aren't as hard as they once were.

+FUEL ECONOMY. The Diesel engine is more economical (but less powerful) than its gas counterparts.

+STYLING is not as harsh since colors are no longer simply gray and black, and plastics and fabrics don't look as cheap.

+ANTITHEFT SYSTEM. These cars are so popular among car thieves the world over that VW intelligently decided to factory install one in every model.

+THE CABRIOLET has caused a stir since it is the only convertible with room for four. The rear window defroster makes it usable year-round.

CONS

-RELIABILITY. Since manufacturing began in Mexico, several problems have annoyed owners to the point that they've deserted VW. Note that most of these hassles are caused by VW dealers rather than Volkswagen itself, who claim that the same quality controls are applied in both Puebla and Wolfsburg.

-INTERIOR SPACE hasn't improved over the years. Room in front is relatively generous, but there is a chronic lack of legroom in the back.

-PRICE. Golfs and Jettas are expensive compared to their less problematic Japanese competitors. This is surprising since these models are built in North America. This is especially true of the dull-looking Golf GTI and Jetta GLX which aren't worth the asking price, and aren't worthy of a respectable manufacturer. On other models, the soft suspension causes an understeer-inducing roll.

-PERFORMANCE on the 4-cylinder engine is mediocre, with slow acceleration and passing, especially on the 2.0-liter that is not even as responsive as the base 1.8-liter.

-ROAD NOISE. Travelling in these cars isn't at all relaxing because of a great amount of noise and vibration.

-GEAR SHIFTING. Surprisingly, the manual gearbox grinds when cold and the clutch is quickly imprecise once you reach a certain speed.

-HANDLING on the Golf GTI and Jetta GLX isn't reassuring and isn't for everyone, because the torque effect causes uncertain steering, inconsistent suspension and unstable handling. The body and suspension haven't been sufficiently strengthened for the overpowering V6 engine. Extreme caution is required on slippery roads since jerkiness and instability make for precarious steering.

CONCLUSION

Golfs and Jettas still have a number of faithful followers who enjoy their European feel, sportiness and responsiveness, even in the less inspiring versions. Until the 1999 models arrive, the previous ones will continue to sell.

RATING
VOLKSWAGEN Golf-Jetta

CONCEPT :		69%
Technology	80	
Safety :	60	
Interior space :	50	
Trunk volume:	80	
Quality/fit/finish :	75	

DRIVING:		67%
Cockpit :	80	
Performance :	50	
Handling :	60	
Steering :	80	
Braking :	65	

ORIGINAL EQUIPMENT:		76%
Tires :	75	
Headlights :	80	
Wipers :	80	
Rear defroster :	75	
Radio :	70	

COMFORT :		71%
Seats :	80	
Suspension :	70	
Sound level:	50	
Conveniences :	80	
Air conditioning :	75	

BUDGET :		57%
Price :	50	
Fuel economy :	70	
Insurance :	45	
Satisfaction :	70	
Depreciation :	50	

Overall rating: 68.0%

NEW FOR 1999

• The redesigned Jetta base on the Audi will come to market at the end of 1998 and the Golf (sedan and convertible) now being sold in Europe will arrive in spring 1999

ENGINES / TRANSMISSIONS / PERFORMANCES

Model/ version	Type / timing valve / fuel system	Displacement cu in	Power bhp @ rpm	Torque lb-ft @ rpm	Compres. ratio	Driving wheels / transmission	Final ratio	Acceler. 0-60 mph s	Standing 1/4 & 5/8 mile s		Acceler. 50-75 mph s	Braking 60-0 mph f	Top speed mph	Lateral acceler. G	Noise level dBA	Fuel economy mpg City Highway		Fuel type Octane
1)	L4* 1.8 SOHC-8-EFI	109	90 @ 5250	107 @ 2500	10.0 :1	front - M5*	3.67	11.8	18.5	33.0	8.8	128	109	0.80	67	24	34	R 87
2)	L4* 2.0 SOHC-8-MPSFI	121	115 @ 5200	122 @ 2600	10.0 :1	front - M5*	4.24	10.5	17.2	31.5	6.9	121	118	0.80	67	22	33	R 87
						front - A4	4.88	12.0	18.6	33.6	9.0	134	115	0.80	67	19	28	R 87
3)	V6* 2.8 DOHC-12-MPSFI	170	172 @ 5800	181 @ 3200	10.0 :1	front - M5*	3.39	8.0	15.8	27.0	5.6	125	137	0.81	69	18	27	R 87
						front - A4	4.27	NA										
4)	L4* 1.9 SOHC-8-DI	116	90 @ 3750	155 @ 1900	19.5 :1	front - M5*	3.39	NA										D

1) CL 2) GL,GT, GLS, GTI, Cabrio 3) GLX, GTI VR6, option GLS 4) TDI

PRICE & EQUIPMENT

VOLKSWAGEN Golf	CL	GL	Wolfsburg	TDI	Conv.GLS
VOLKSWAGEN Jetta		GL	GLS/GLX	TDI	
Retail price $:	-	13,495	16,945	-	22,290
Dealer invoice $:	-	12,455	15,341	-	20,240
Shipping & handling $:	-	500	500	500	500
Automatic transmission:	O	O	O	-	O
Cruise control:	O	O	S	O	O
Power steering:	S	S	S	S	S
Anti-lock brakes:	-	-/S	S	O	O
Traction control:	-	-	-/S	-	-
Air conditioning:	O	O	S/SA	O	O
Leather:	-	-	O/S	-	-
AM/FM/radio-cassette:	O	S	S	S	S
Power door locks:	S	S	S	S	S
Power windows:	O	O	S	O	S
Tilt steering:	-	O/S	S	O	S
Dual adjustable mirrors:	S	S/SEH	S/SEH	S	S
Alloy wheels:	-	-	O/S	O	S
Anti-theft system:	S	S	S	S	S

Colors
Exterior: White, Gray, Blue, Red, Silver, Black, Green, Suede, Violet, Wildberry, Yellow.

Interior: Gray, Black, Beige.

AT A GLANCE...

Category:	front-wheel drive sub-compact & compact cars.	**Class :**	3S & 3

HISTORIC
Introduced in:	1985-1993. Jetta: 1999.
Made in:	Mexico:Golf/Jetta;convertible: Osnabrück, Germany.

DEMOGRAPHICS
Model	Men./Wom.	Age	Married	College	Income
Golf	57/43 %	32	46 %	62 %	$ 35 000
Jetta	76/24 %	44	70 %	55 %	$ 40 000

INDEX
Safety:	50 %	Satisfaction:	75 %
Depreciation:	37 %	Insurance:	$ 935-1 150
Cost per mile:	$ 0.32-0.40	Number of dealers:	650

SALES
Model	1996	1997	Result
Golf	24 210	20 703	- 14.5 %
Jetta	85 025	90 984	+ 7.0 %

MAIN COMPETITORS
Golf: HONDA Civic, NISSAN Sentra, TOYOTA Tercel. **Jetta:** ACURA 1.6 EL, CHEVROLET Cavalier, DODGE Stratus-Neon, FORD Escort-Contour, HONDA Civic, HYUNDAI Elantra, MAZDA Protegé, MERCURY Mystique, PLYMOUTH Breeze-Neon, PONTIAC Sunfire, SATURN SL1 & SL2, SUBARU Impreza, TOYOTA Corolla.

MAINTENANCE REQUIRED BY WARRANTY
First revision:	Frequency:	Diagnostic plug:
3 000 miles	6 months/6 000miles	Yes

SPECIFICATIONS

Model	Version Trim	Body/ Seats	Interior volume cu ft	Trunk volume cu ft	Cd	Wheel base in	Lght x Wdgth x Hght in x in x in	Curb weight lb	Susp. ft/rr	Brake ft/rr	Steering type	Turning diameter ft	Steer. turns nber.	Fuel tank gal	tire size	Standard tires make	model	Standard powertrain
VOLKSWAGEN	General warranty: 2 years / 25 000 miles; powertrain: 5 years / 50 000 miles; antipollution: 6 years/ 50 000 miles; corrosion perforation: 6 years.																	
Golf	CL	3dr.sdn.5	88.0	17.5	0.32	97.4	160.4x66.7x56.2	2462	ih/sih	dc/dr	pwr.r&p.	35.1	3.2	14.5	195/60R14	Goodyear	Invicta	L4/1.8/M5
Golf	GL	5dr.sdn.5	88.0	17.5	0.32	97.4	160.4x66.7x56.2	2586	ih/sih	dc/dr	pwr.r&p.	35.1	3.2	14.5	195/60R14	Goodyear	Eagle GA	L4/2.0/M5
Golf	Convertible	2dr.con.5	75.6	9.5	0.38	97.4	160.4x66.7x56.0	2700	ih/sih	dc/dr	pwr.r&p.	35.1	3.2	14.5	195/60HR14	Goodyear	Eagle GA	L4/2.0/M5
Golf	GTI VR6	3dr.sdn.5	88.0	17.5	0.34	97.4	160.4x66.7x56.2	2760	ih/sih	dc/dc/ABS	pwr.r&p.	35.1	3.2	14.5	205/50HR15	Goodyear	Eagle GA	V6/2.8/M5
Jetta	GL	4dr.sdn.5	88.0	13.0	0.32	98.9	172.3x68.3x56.9	2819	ih/sih	dc/dc/ABS	pwr.r&p.	35.7	3.2	14.5	195/65R15	Goodyear	Invicta	L4/2.0/M5
Jetta	GLS	4dr.sdn.5	88.0	13.0	0.32	98.9	172.3x68.3x56.9	2828	ih/sih	dc/dc/ABS	pwr.r&p.	35.7	3.2	14.5	195/65R15	Goodyear	Eagle GA	L4/2.0/M5
Jetta	GLX VR6	4dr.sdn.5	84.7	13.2	0.34	98.9	172.3x68.3x56.9	3018	ih/sih	dc/dc/ABS	pwr.r&p.	35.7	3.2	14.5	195/65R15	Goodyear	Eagle GA	V6/2.8/M5

VOLKSWAGEN
New Beetle
Memories Of esteryears...

The return of the New Beetle was truly a stroke of marketing genius. At the beginning, the Concept 1 prototype unveiled at the Detroit Autoshow in 1994 was well-received and reminiscent of the old Beetle. It's not surprising that the response of the American public, fondly remembering the car of their youth, was so overwhelming, that it led Volkswagen directors to conclude that it might be a good idea to put it into production and market it like Chrysler did with its Viper and Prowler, causing such a stir that people were practically running to the dealerships. Dealers have been asking for something like this for ages.

And that's how the second legend was born. You don't have to be psychic to predict that if it isn't mass produced, the New Beetle will spoil all those who want to stand out from the crowd of run-of-the-mill cars. Having sold over 21 million Beetles around the world, 5 million in North America, there's a lot of nostalgia surrounding this little car. Even if only those who were still alive wanted to relive the experience, production at the Puebla factory in Mexico could rise to 100,000 cars per year and continue at the pace for the foreseeable future. What is especially touching with the latest New Beetle is its ability to evoke memories. Each person has their little stories, often describing how they were disappointed or let down by the

original's charming simplicity. But when you tell all these good people that the New Beetle has fixed the old problems, many get a dreamy look on their face and seem ready for another ride. Imagine then that the new model is based on the Golf. No more thumping lawn-mower engine in the back. Sure it would never die, but it was so noisy and slow! When they find out that the New Beetle is front-wheel drive, they recall the 360s they used to do on snowy roads, not to mention the missing heater. The new model not only includes a heater, but also air conditioning, automatic transmission and a trunk in the back. Imagine that. It seems almost too good to be true, or else too expensive. How much? Well, it does cost as much as a fully loaded Jetta,

but consider the style! It looks like a big toy, and will definitely turn some heads. It's more than just a car. We discovered that the New Beetle has more to offer than just an original means of transportation: it's an effective and peaceful way to communicate. Many conversations begin around the open front hood, and friendships and romances are made, just like before. The New Beetle is by no means perfect or practical in the logical way that we usually evaluate cars. But this Beetle is higher than logic, and its rebirth shows that its influence isn't limited by time, like all things that touch people. We would have liked to have had instruments to measure people's desire to own one right away, and their fond memories and affection for this timeless object, in order to discover its secret.

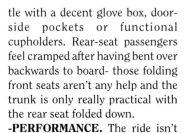

It's been a long time since a car attracted so much interest from both the media and the public (who absolutely loved it). The legend lives on, so there should be hordes of potential buyers taking the showrooms by storm. Its design and modern mechanical features have created something of a sensation and will no doubt inspire other carmakers. The New Beetle is a smashingly successful marketing campaign, thanks to its one-of-a-kind design and superb craftsmanship. After a well-organized ad campaign and sudden delivery of thousands of multicolor insects, it's here!

MODEL RANGE

For now, the Beetle is sold in a single 2-door trim equipped with a 2.0-liter 4-cylinder gas engine, a 1.9-liter turbodiesel engine or a 1.8-liter 4-cylinder turbo, all with a standard 5-speed manual transmission, or optional 4-speed automatic. Standard equipment includes four airbags (two front-impact and two side-impact), an air conditioner fitted with a pollen and odor filter, a six-speaker stereo with cassette, anti-theft alarm system, and remote-control door locks.

TECHNICAL FEATURES

The New Beetle is built on the newest Golf/Jetta platform (models to be introduced in the fall of 1998). It is no longer rear-wheel drive like its predecessor. Rather, it is front-wheel drive featuring water-cooled in-line 4-cylinder engines. The chassis structure is designed to offer maximum stiffness on impact. Aerodynamics aren't too hot, since the drag coefficient is crippled by all those stylistic curves. Fenders are bolted onto the fully galvanized steel unibody, so the car is built to last, and the 12-year/unlimited-mileage warranty against corrosion proves it. The fully independent suspension includes MacPherson struts up front and a torsion axle at the rear, with anti-roll bars on both ends. The car comes equipped with 4-wheel disc brakes, vented up front, but ABS is only available as an option. Lastly, the car is fitted with 16-inch tires and the teeny, pancake-size spare tire is stored under the trunk floor. Its semicircular roofline and flattened extremities make it simply irresistible and those bright body shades make heads turn.

PROS

+STYLING. Its semicircular roofline and flattened extremities make it simply irresistible and those bright body shades make heads turn.

+ENGINEERING is very modern, including safety and comfort features that were absent on the original Beetle. The heating and air conditioning systems are efficient in any kind of weather and four airbags protect passengers from road hazards.

+DRIVING. Safety-wise, it's light years ahead compared with the old model (that's still being assembled in Mexico, by the way). The New Beetle handles well. There isn't much swish and sway, and steering is nice and gradual, which makes for easy control. Brakes are trustworthy in most circumstances and both transmissions are slick and smooth.

+COMFORT is obviously better up front with easy access, and more than enough room. Seats are well-shaped and padded. The suspension is firm while not being harsh, typically German.

+THE LOOK is great. All materials (aluminum, plastics and fabrics) are good quality. The finish and construction are finely detailed.

+THE REAR HATCH is perfectly integrated, and well-crafted. You can tell by the lock hidden under the brand crest. A real work of art!

+DRIVING. In spite of weak performance, driving is pleasant. The car adequately maneuverable in the city because of precise steering and a reasonable turning radius.

+TRANSMISSION. The manual gearbox works like a charm. Shifting is precise and smooth, like a true VW.

+WELL DONE: instruments all combined into a single module with a mini tachometer and digital screen.

CONS

-IMPRACTICAL. This car may be fun, but it's none too practical. With such a typically rounded roofline, there isn't much cabin or trunk space, at least not according to present-day standards. Car designers didn't even bestow the New Bee-

tle with a decent glove box, door-side pockets or functional cupholders. Rear-seat passengers feel cramped after having bent over backwards to board- those folding front seats aren't any help and the trunk is only really practical with the rear seat folded down.

-PERFORMANCE. The ride isn't that great with either the 2.0-liter gas engine or the 1.9-liter diesel engine on our test models. The Beetle is heavy and feels a bit lethargic with either the manual or the automatic gearbox. Here's hoping things will improve with the 1.8-liter turbo.

-VISIBILITY. Visibility isn't any better than it was on the original Beetle, not with such a high body belt that sure cuts down on window size. The bulky roof pillars and tiny, high-perched exterior mirrors and slim interior mirrors don't help either. The digital data screen in amongst the other instruments is unreadable by day. Also the right side mirror is ridiculously small, similar to other Volkswagens.

-NOISE LEVELS. Volkswagens aren't world famous for their quiet ride and the New Beetle is no exception to the rule. The engine emits a loud sound and it shakes a lot. The rearview mirrors hum away at 50 mph and tires are far from unobtrusive.

-DRIVING POSITION. A good position is hard to find, and the windshield (and the outside world) seems far away.

-INSTRUMENT PANEL. The instrument panel is absolutely huge for what it holds, so the interior looks skimpier than it actually is.

-TO BE REVIEWED. A rear wiper would be nice to clear off the water that collects there in poor weather; rear windows can't be opened so you feel claustrophobic; sun visors are too small; headlights aren't bright enough; the clock is inconveniently located on the ceiling; and the cup-holders are hardly practical.

CONCLUSION

The latest Beetle is above all a marketing success. Its practicality for regular daily usage could be better, and driving enjoyment may wane because of mediocre performance. Nostalgia nuts who don't want to go unnoticed will love this car. ☺

RATING
VW New Beetle

CONCEPT :   **71%**
Technology	85
Safety :	100
Interior space :	40
Trunk volume:	50
Quality/fit/finish :	80

DRIVING: **60%**
Cockpit :	75
Performance :	40
Handling :	55
Steering :	80
Braking :	50

ORIGINAL EQUIPMENT: **78%**
Tires :	80
Headlights :	75
Wipers :	80
Rear defroster :	75
Radio :	80

COMFORT :   **61%**
Seats :	75
Suspension :	80
Sound level:	30
Conveniences :	40
Air conditioning :	80

BUDGET :   **68%**
Price :	50
Fuel economy :	80
Insurance :	50
Satisfaction :	80
Depreciation :	80

Overall rating: **67.6%**

NEW FOR 1999

- A 1.8-liter, 150-bhp turbo engine in the GLX trim that will also include ABS brakes, power windows, cruise control leather upholstery and alloy rims.

ENGINES

Model/version	Type / timing valve / fuel system	Displacement cu in	Power bhp @ rpm	Torque lb-ft @ rpm
base	L4* 2.0 SOHC-8-MPSFI	121	115 @ 5200	122 @ 2600
TDI	L4T* 1.9 SOHC-8-DI	116	90 @ 4000	149 @ 1900
GLX	L4T* 1.8 DOHC-20-EFI	109	150 @ 5700	155 @ 1750

TRANSMISSIONS

Compres. ratio	Driving wheels / transmission	Final ratio
10.0 :1	front- M5*	4.24
	front- A4	4.53
19.5 :1	front- M5*	3.39
	front- A4	3.71
9.5 :1	front- M5* A5	NA

PERFORMANCES

Acceler. 0-60 mph s		Standing 1/4 & 5/8 mile s		Acceler. 50-75 mph s	Braking 60-0 mph f	Top speed mph	Lateral acceler. G	Noise level dBA	Fuel economy mpg City	Highway	Fuel type Octane
11.5	17.5	31.8		7.3	39	180	0.80	68-72	23	29	R 87
12.0	18.0	33.3		9.0	44	180	0.80	68-72	22	27	R 87
NA									41	48	D
NA									34	44	D
NA											R 87

PRICE & EQUIPMENT

VOLKSWAGEN New Beetle	base	TDI	GLX
Retail price $:	15,200	16,475	-
Dealer invoice $:	14,336	15,527	-
Shipping & handling $:	500	500	-
Automatic transmission:	O	O	O
Cruise control:	O	O	S
Power steering:	S	S	S
Anti-lock brakes:	O	O	S
Traction control:	-	-	-
Air conditioning:	S	S	S
Leather:	O	O	S
AM/FM/radio-cassette:	S	S	S
Power door locks:	S	S	S
Power windows:	O	O	S
Tilt steering:	S	S	S
Dual adjustable mirrors:	SEH	SEH	SEH
Alloy wheels:	O	O	S
Anti-theft system:	S	S	S

Colors
Exterior: Black, White, Red, Blue, Yellow, Silver, Green.

Interior: Beige.

AT A GLANCE...

Category:	front-wheel drive sub-compact sedans. **Class : 3**

HISTORIC
Introduced in:	1998
Made in:	Puebla, Mexico.

DEMOGRAPHICS
Model	Men./Wom.	Age	Married	College	Income
New Beetle	NA				

INDEX
Safety:	100 %	**Satisfaction:**	78 %
Depreciation:	20 %	**Insurance:**	$ 995
Cost per mile:	$ 0.37	**Number of dealers:**	650

SALES
Model	1996	1997	Result
New Beetle	Not on the market at that time.		

MAIN COMPETITORS
CHEVROLET Cavalier, DODGE Neon, HONDA Civic SiR, PLYMOUTH Neon, PONTIAC Sunfire, SUBARU Impreza 2.5RS, VOLKSWAGEN Golf.

MAINTENANCE REQUIRED BY WARRANTY
First revision:	Frequency:	Diagnostic plug:
3 000 miles	6 months/6 000miles	Yes

SPECIFICATIONS

Model	Version Trim	Body/ Seats	Interior volume cu ft	Trunk volume cu ft	Cd	Wheel base in	Lght x Wdgth x Hght in x in x in	Curb weight lb	Susp. ft/rr	Brake ft/rr	Steering type	Turning diameter ft	Steer. turns nber.	Fuel tank gal	tire size	Standard tires make	model	Standard powertrain
VOLKSWAGEN	General warranty: 2 years / 25 000 miles; powertrain: 5 years / 50 000 miles; antipollution: 6 years/ 50 000 miles; corrosion perforation: 6 years.																	
New Beetle 2.0	2dr.sdn. 4		84.3	12.0	0.38	98.9	161.1x67.9x59.5	2712	ih/sih	dc/dc	pwr.r&p.	35.4	3.2	14.5	205/55R16	Michelin	Energy	L4/2.0/M5
New Beetle TDI	2dr.sdn. 4		84.3	12.0	0.38	98.9	161.1x67.9x59.5	2778	ih/sih	dc/dc	pwr.r&p.	35.4	3.2	14.5	205/55R16	Michelin	Energy	L4TD/1.9/M5
New Beetle 1.8T	2dr.sdn. 4		84.3	12.0	0.38	98.9	161.1x67.9x59.5	-	ih/sih	dc/dc	pwr.r&p.	35.4	3.2	14.5	205/55R16	Michelin	Energy	L4T/1.8/M5

When Volkswagen developed the new generation Passat, it adopted a whole new approach and strategy. At the dawn of the 21st century, the Wolfsburg firm is exhibiting a fresh, new effervescence and it's busy restructuring as well as expanding on world markets and making some very fine acquisitions. The Passat is the flagship of the VW fleet. Inspired by the Audi A4, it now has a more elegant design and is a bit more upscale, so as to be a serious contender in the fray against the Honda Accord and Toyota Camry models that are in the same league.

MODEL RANGE

The Passat comes in 4-door sedans and station wagons in GLS trim, equipped with a turbocharged 1.8L 4-cylinder conventional engine or a Turbo Diesel TDI 1.9L, and in GLX trim, animated by a 2.8L V6. The five-speed manual transmission is standard and the Tiptronic automatic is optional (standard equipment on the GLX) with gas engines only. Original items on the GLS include power steering, cruise control, manual climate control, dual airbags, radio and tape deck, power locks, windows and mirrors and a theft-deterrent system. The GLX receives all of the above, as well as an antilock braking system, alloy wheels, sunroof and leather trim.

TECHNICAL FEATURES

The Passat's steel unibody benefits from topnotch aerodynamics, yielding a drag coefficient of 0.27. In keeping with current trends, the much more rigid body is more resistant to flexion and torsion. The body is slightly bigger than that of the previous generation model. The new front suspension, derived from that of the A4, includes four pivoting control arms located so as to eliminate torque transmission to the steering system during strong accelerations. The semi-independent rear wheels are affixed to a torsion axle that's mounted on self-leveling components capable of a slight turn angle when there's lateral pull, so it helps cornering into curves and procures stable demeanor during quick lane changes.

PROS

+ LOOKS. This new generation Passat has more flair than the previous one and it has a more energetic character. These stylistic changes have brought the drag coefficient to an amazing 0.27. But one mustn't be fooled, for it's a touched-up Audi A4...

Strategic Offensive...

+ CHOICE. Customers can choose between two body styles, three very different engine models and two trim levels, so everyone can find what they're looking for.

+ PERFORMANCES. The V6 is really the only engine that puts the Passat nicely through its paces, for the 1.8L achieves far less impressive accelerations and pickup and the Turbo Diesel is a compromise when it comes to driving prowess.

+ CABIN SPACE. It's well proportioned to vehicle size and passengers have lots of room all-round, but the trunk is actually a bit smaller than on the previous model.

+ HANDLING. It's taut and neutral at normal speeds on good roads or slightly rough surfaces and understeer is only felt in extreme situations. The new suspension is the master mind behind this improved behavior, along with the precise steering, so you can take wide or tight curves with accuracy.

+ BRAKES. They do their stuff and the below-average emergency stopping distances prove it. Pedal effort is easy to gauge as well.

+ STEERING. It's responsive and accurate, benefitting from a good reduction ratio and power function and the short steer angle diameter allows for slick moves.

+ INSTRUMENT PANEL. It's quite lovely, more so than before, and it's more ergonomic and logical as well.

+ QUALITY. Assembly is robust, fit and finish are carefully executed and posh trim materials are in keeping with the Germanic tradition. Besides, the over-all design is much more attractive and the instrument

panel has a lot of class.

+ RIDE COMFORT. The suspension isn't flexible, in the American sense of the term, but it benefits from more generous travel than was the case and seats are more plush. Noise heard inside the cabin varies with the engine model.

+ FUEL ECONOMY. It's super with the Turbo Diesel engine, the only one of its kind offered in this category, but only penny-pinchers will be crazy about it...

+ CONVENIENCE FEATURES. The nice and square trunk holds lots of luggage, but inside the cabin, there are just the required number of storage compartments, mostly in the front seat area.

CONS

- STEERING. It's vague and springy, so you feel like it's floating. This is partly due to the front suspension that bottoms out as soon as you hit poor roads.

- TIRES. The Continental Contact tires on our test car are to be avoided like the plague. They provide only poor grip and they're noisy as heck.

- TIPTRONIC TRANSMISSION. This system is the ancestor of all current sequential transmissions, but it isn't much fun since the driver only has a partial handle on things.

- PERFORMANCES. The Turbo Diesel doesn't have much oomph, but it's fuel-frugal, which makes up for its wimpy accelerations and pickup.

- VISIBILITY. It's average, since the bulky headrests and thick C pillar get in the way.

- NOISE LEVEL. It's high with all the wind whistling around the windshield (strange with such a good Cx) and road noise is transmitted via the wheel housings and the 4-cylinder engine roars on accelerations.

- TO BE IMPROVED UPON: The cockpit is adequate, but it takes a while to get comfy behind the wheel. The digital screen is absolutely illegible in bright sunlight, the orange-colored instruments are tough to decipher and the radio dials are located below the air conditioning controls.

CONCLUSION

This pared down Audi will no doubt make an excellent Passat, as long as it becomes reliable, once and for all, and if prices stay reasonably competitive. ☺

RATING
VOLKSWAGEN Passat

CONCEPT : 77%
Technology	80
Safety :	80
Interior space :	65
Trunk volume:	80
Quality/fit/finish :	80

DRIVING: 67%
Cockpit :	80
Performance :	45
Handling :	65
Steering :	80
Braking :	65

ORIGINAL EQUIPMENT: 77%
Tires :	75
Headlights :	80
Wipers :	80
Rear defroster :	75
Radio :	75

COMFORT : 73%
Seats :	80
Suspension :	75
Sound level :	50
Conveniences :	80
Air conditioning :	80

BUDGET : 54%
Price :	40
Fuel economy :	60
Insurance :	45
Satisfaction :	75
Depreciation :	50

Overall rating: 69.6%

NEW FOR 1999

- Sedan and wagon in GLS and GLX trim level with 190 hp V6 engine.
- GLX have Syncro 4-wheel-drive with A5 Tiptronic, optional on GLS.

ENGINES | TRANSMISSIONS | PERFORMANCES

Model/ version	Type / timing valve / fuel system	Displacement cu in	Power bhp @ rpm	Torque lb-ft @ rpm	Compres. ratio	Driving wheels / transmission	Final ratio	Acceler. 0-60 mph s	Standing 1/4 & 5/8 mile s	Acceler. 50-75 mph s	Braking 60-0 mph f	Top speed mph	Lateral acceler. G	Noise level dBA	Fuel economy mpg City	Highway	Fuel type Octane
GLS	L4T* 1.8 DOHC-20-EFI	109	150 @ 5700	155 @ 1750	9.5 :1	front - M5*	3.70	9.0	16.8 29.8	6.4	125	137	0.80	67	23	32	R 87
						front - A5	3.70	10.5	17.2 31.2	6.8	131	131	0.80	67	NA		
GLX	V6* 2.8 DOHC-30-SFI	170	190 @ 6000	207 @ 4200	10.6 :1	front - M5	3.39	8.0	15.6 27.0	5.7	128	141	0.83	66	20	29	R 87
						front - A5*	3.70	9.3	16.7 30.2	6.5	131	137	0.83	66	18	29	M 89
TDI	L4*T1.9 SOHC-8-DI	116	90 @ 3750	149 @ 1900	19.5 :1	front - M5*	3.16	14.5	19.0 37.5	6.5	131	109	0.80	70	31	44	D

PRICE & EQUIPMENT

VOLKSWAGEN Passat	GLS 4dr.sdn.	GLX 4dr.sdn.	GLS 4dr.wgn.	GLX 4dr.wgn.
Retail price $:	20,750	26,250	21,300	-
Dealer invoice $:	18,676	23,589	19,167	-
Shipping & handling $:	500	500	500	500
Automatic transmission:	O	S	O	S
Cruise control:	S	S	S	S
Power steering:	S	S	S	S
Anti-lock brakes:	O	S	O	S
Traction control:	O	S	O	S
Air conditioning:	SM	SA	SM	SA
Leather:	O	S	O	S
AM/FM/radio-cassette:	S	S	S	S
Power door locks:	S	S	S	S
Power windows:	S	S	S	S
Tilt steering:	S	S	S	S
Dual adjustable mirrors:	SE	SE	SE	SE
Alloy wheels:	O	S	O	S
Anti-theft system:	S	S	S	S

Colors

Exterior: White, Red, Blue, Green, Gray, Black, Purple, Silver.

Interior: Gray, Black, Blue, Beige.

AT A GLANCE...

Category: front-wheel drive compact sedans & wagons. **Class :** 4

HISTORIC
Introduced in: 1973-1998
Made in: Emden, Germany.

DEMOGRAPHICS
Model	Men./Wom.	Age	Married	College	Income
Passat	72/28 %	44	70 %	60 %	$ 40 000

INDEX
Safety:	80 %	Satisfaction:	75 %
Depreciation:	50 %	Insurance:	$ 1 135
Cost per mile:	$ 0.46	Number of dealers:	650

SALES
Model	1996	1997	Result
Passat	19 850	14 868	- 25.1 %

MAIN COMPETITORS
BUICK Century-Regal, CHRYSLER Cirrus-Stratus, HONDA Accord, MAZDA 626, NISSAN Altima, OLDSMOBILE Alero, PONTIAC Grand Am, SUBARU Legacy, TOYOTA Camry.

MAINTENANCE REQUIRED BY WARRANTY
First revision:	Frequency:	Diagnostic plug:
3 000 miles	6 months/6 000miles	Yes

SPECIFICATIONS

Model	Version Trim	Body/ Seats	Interior volume cu ft	Trunk volume cu ft	Cd	Wheel base in	Lght x Wdgth x Hght in x in x in	Curb weight lb	Susp. ft/rr	Brake ft/rr	Steering type	Turning diameter ft	Steer. turns nber.	Fuel tank gal	tire size	Standard tires make	model	Standard powertrain
VOLKSWAGEN		General warranty: 2 years / 25 000 miles; powertrain: 5 years / 50 000 miles; antipollution: 6 years/ 50 000 miles; corrosion perforation: 6 years.																
Passat	GLS	4dr.sdn.5	95.4	15.0	0.27	106.5	184.1x68.5x57.4	2646	ih/sih	dc/dc	pwr.r&p.	34.1	3.33	18.5	185/60HR14	Continental	Touring	L4T/1.8/M5
Passat	GLX VR6	4dr.sdn.5	95.4	425	0.27	106.5	184.1x68.5x57.4	2756	ih/sih	dc/ABS	pwr.r&p.	34.1	3.08	18.5	215/50HR15	-	-	V6/2.8/A5
Passat	TDI	4dr.sdn.5	95.4	425	0.27	106.5	184.1x68.5x57.4	-	ih/sih	dc/dc	pwr.r&p.	34.1	3.33	18.5	195/60HR14	Continental	Touring	L4TD/1.9/M5

After reworking the 70 series sedans and wagons, Volvo decided to use this as a base for a coupe and a convertible. This unusual step is understandable considering their willingness to diversify and expand into new, untraditional markets. Built on the S70 platform, the C70 coupes and convertibles rise to a level of luxury previously unknown to Volvo.

MODEL RANGE

The C70 is available as a 2-door coupe or convertible in a single trim, powered by a 2.3-liter 20V 2.3-liter engine putting out 236 horses, with a standard 5-speed manual or optional 4-speed automatic transmission. Standard equipment includes cruise control, power steering, antilock brakes, air conditioning, two front and two side airbags, heated front seats, stereo, adjustable steering column, power windows, doors, etc., alloy wheels and an anti-theft system. The convertible top automatically tucks away.

TECHNICAL FEATURES

The C70 series steel unibody splits the weight 60/40. The rounder shape improves the drag coefficient to a remarkable 0.30 on the coupe and 0.34 on the convertible. The front suspension is outfitted with MacPherson struts, and the semi-independent rear axle, called «Delta-Link», a Volvo creation designed to control roll and flexibility, is assisted by an anti-roll bar. The four-wheel disc brakes are controlled by an anti-lock system, and a balancing system between front and rear evenly distributes braking force.
The engine is identical to the 5-cylinder turbo on the sedans and the sporty T-5 wagons.

SIMPLY SUPER

++STYLING is still traditional and very Volvo, but it exudes class. Several small touches bring Jaguar to mind, and the copper color on the coupe adds to the allure.

PROS

+SAFETY. A great deal of research was conducted to guarantee that the structural rigidity of these vehicles would

Winds Of Change...

match that of the sedans and wagons. The convertible required special attention because it is more susceptible to damage in the event of a crash, and has been reinforced in several key spots. The body includes two retractable roll bars that activate as soon as the car begins to turn over. Both vehicles also include two front and two side airbags as well as headrests on rear seats.

+INTERIOR SPACE. Seemingly compact, the body is comparable in size to the sedan, making the interior unusually large for this kind of car. The rear-seat passengers can be relatively comfortable in both the coupe and the convertible.

+PERFORMANCE. Once the Turbo reaches a good cruising speed, acceleration and passing are superb, worthy of Grand Touring cars.

+QUALITY. With these two cars, Volvo has reached a level of luxury never before seen by this manufacturer. The half-wood, half-leather steering wheel, as well as the fine leatherwork, is very «Jaguaresque.»

+DRIVING. In spite of the power under the hoods of these cars, they are most enjoyable driven at normal speeds on Arizona back roads and in chic California area. At most, the 6-cylinder in the S80 would be better than the Turbo for this

kind of American-style touring.

+REMARKABLE. The eight-speaker stereo system is of unusual quality and depth for vehicles of this price.

+WELL DESIGNED. The molded rubber sections around the windshield are refined and well-finished. The wind-breaking cover for unoccupied rear seats is efficient, even though some effort is required to put it on.

CONS

-THE TURBO. The slow response time ruins a bit of the fun, but is less bothersome under normal conditions.

-BRAKING was less impressive than on the sedans and wagons. Note that the vehicle that was made available to us was seriously mistreated by some of our less scrupulous colleagues.

-ACCESS. Getting to the rear seats takes some work since the front seats don't move forward enough, and the powered seats move only very slowly, which becomes exasperating in the rain.

-VISIBILITY. The height of the rear and the top of the convertible create large blind spots, which doesn't help when parking.

-STORAGE. There is a lack of storage space since both the glove box and the center console are quickly filled up and the side-door pockets are tiny.

-WORTH REVIEWING. The speaker in the middle of the dashbord looks a little out of place and a little odd, but this is the price you pay for such outstanding sound.

CONCLUSION

Volvo risked adding two cars to its model range that will help to expand its client base in a market where it has the necessary expertise to succeed.

RATING
VOLVO C70

CONCEPT :   72%
Technology	85
Safety :	90
Interior space :	60
Trunk volume:	45
Quality/fit/finish :	80

DRIVING: 78%
Cockpit :	80
Performance :	80
Handling :	70
Steering :	80
Braking :	80

ORIGINAL EQUIPMENT: 81%
Tires :	80
Headlights :	80
Wipers :	85
Rear defroster :	80
Radio :	80

COMFORT :   67%
Seats :	80
Suspension :	75
Sound level :	30
Conveniences :	70
Air conditioning :	80

BUDGET :   55%
Price :	0
Fuel economy :	70
Insurance :	40
Satisfaction :	95
Depreciation :	70

Overall rating: 70.6%

NEW FOR 1999

- Convertible version of the C70 coupe.

ENGINES

Model/ version	Type / timing valve / fuel system	Displacement cu in	Power bhp @ rpm	Torque lb-ft @ rpm
C70	L5T* 2.3 DOHC-20-MPSFI	141	236 @ 5100	243 @ 2700

TRANSMISSIONS

Compres. ratio	Driving wheels / transmission	Final ratio
8.5 :1	front - A4	2.56
	front - M5*	4.00

PERFORMANCES

Acceler. 0-60 mph s	Standing 1/4 & 5/8 mile s	Acceler. 50-75 mph s	Braking 60-0 mph f	Top speed mph	Lateral acceler. G	Noise level dBA	Fuel economy mpg City	Highway	Fuel type Octane
6.8	14.8 26.5	4.8	131	146	0.85	67-74	19	25	S 91
NA							18	25	S 91

PRICE & EQUIPMENT

VOLVO C70	Coupe	Conv.
Retail price $:	38,995	42,995
Dealer invoice $:	34,795	-
Shipping & handling $:	575	575
Automatic transmission:	O	O
Cruise control:	S	S
Power steering:	S	S
Anti-lock brakes:	S	S
Traction control:	S	S
Air conditioning:	S	S
Leather:	SC	SC
AM/FM/radio-cassette:	S	S
Power door locks:	S	S
Power windows:	S	S
Tilt steering:	S	S
Dual adjustable mirrors:	SEH	SEH
Alloy wheels:	S	S
Anti-theft system:	S	S

Colors

Exterior: Black, White, Red, Blue, Green, Silver, Graphite, Gray, Sand, Teal.

Interior: Blue, Taupe, Gray.

AT A GLANCE...

Category: front-wheel drive luxury coupes & convertibles.   **Class :** 7

HISTORIC
Introduced in:	1992-1997
Made in:	Birmingham, England.

DEMOGRAPHICS
Model	Men./Wom.	Age	Married	College	Income
C70	75/25 %	42	81 %	73 %	$ 70 000

INDEX
Safety:	90 %	Satisfaction:	93 %
Depreciation:	30 %	Insurance:	$1 135-1 475
Cost per mile:	$ 0.65-0.71	Number of dealers:	405

SALES
Model	1996	1997	Result
C70	NA		

MAIN COMPETITORS
MERCEDES-BENZ CLK.

MAINTENANCE REQUIRED BY WARRANTY
First revision:	Frequency:	Diagnostic plug:
Tbo : 5 000 miles	Tbo : 5 000 miles	Yes

SPECIFICATIONS

Model	Version Trim	Body/ Seats	Interior volume cu ft	Trunk volume cu ft	Cd	Wheel base in	Lght x Wdgth x Hght in x in x in	Curb weight lb	Susp. ft/rr	Brake ft/rr	Steering type	Turning diameter ft	Steer. turns nber.	Fuel tank gal	tire size	Standard tires make	model	Standard powertrain
VOLVO		General warranty: 4 years / 50 000 miles; corrosion: 8 years / unlimited; antipollution: 5 years / 50 000 miles.																
C70	Coupe	2dr.cpe. 4	-	14.2	0.29	104.9	185.7x71.5x55.5	3214	ih/sih	dc/ABS	pwr.r&p.	38.4	3.0	18.5	225/45ZR17	Michelin	Pilot SX	L5T/2.3/M5
C70	Convertible	2dr.con. 4	-	8.0	0.34	104.9	185.7x71.5x56.3	3631	ih/sih	dc/ABS	pwr.r&p.	38.4	3.0	18.5	205/55R16	Pirelli	P6000	L5T/2.3/M5

The 70 series is the end result of previous 850 series and the powerful 750. These models were always the key to all sales made by the Swedish manufacturer, who is now trying to expand its model range above and below the 70 series. Besides the exterior, the S sedans and V wagons have undergone a great many changes in order to further improve the handling and comfort, bringing them up to the same level as their closest competitors. And we haven't even mentioned the Cross Country version, Volvo's first foray into the sport-utility world.

MODEL RANGE
The 70 series includes base sedans and wagons, the GLT, the T-5, and the AWD wagon. The base models come equipped with a 2.4-liter, 20V, 168 bhp engine, while on the GLT and AWD wagon, horsepower increases to 190 bhp. The T-5's turbo-charged 2.3-liter puts out 236 horses. Depending on the model, a manual 5-speed or a 4-speed automatic is standard. The base model includes such standard features as cruise control, power steering, ABS brakes, air conditioning, two front and two side airbags, heated front seats, cassette stereo, adjustable steering column and the regular power doors, windows, etc.. Options include automatic transmission (standard on the GLT), traction control (standard on the AWD) and alloy rims. Also, the GLT, T-5, and AWD all come with a sunroof and antitheft system.

TECHNICAL FEATURES
The 70 series has a steel unibody, with the weight split 60/40. The rounder shape improves the drag coefficient to 0.32. The front suspension is outfitted with MacPherson struts, and the semi-independent rear axle has been christened, «Delta-Link», a Volvo creation to control roll and flexibility. An anti-roll bar is also included. The four-wheel disc brakes are controlled by an anti-lock system and a balancing valve between the front/rear circuits that better distributes braking energy.

SIMPLY SUPER
++ THE AWD MODEL. The phi-

Deep inside Volvo...

losophy behind this model opens new horizons, similar to Subaru, but at a higher level of quality and finish. This proves that it is possible to take advantage of all-wheel drive without having to drive a truck.

PROS
+ STYLING. Though rounder, it stills holds true to tradition, and still easily recognizable as a Volvo. The styling continues to exude the same solidity and durability that it has for generations, while at the same time opening up new evolutionary possibilities to the Swedish manufacturer, who seemed enclosed in a world where all lines was straight.

+PERFORMANCE. The Turbo is superb. Because of very quick acceleration and passing, sporty driving is truly enjoyable. Putting this engine under the hood of a wagon took a certain daring. Performance on the base model isn't as exhilarating, but neither is it anemic, because even with the automatic transmission, there is enough power to make driving fun, thanks to the dual selection transmission.

+BRAKING is among the most efficient ever seen on a production car. Emergency stopping distances are very short, in spite of the heavy weight and the anti-lock system.

+HANDLING has been seriously improved by a more rigid body, but the soft suspension on the base model doesn't make it any

sportier, since the roll causes it to understeer (easily controlled). The AWD is remarkable in snow-bound lands, holding the road better than anything else.

+INTERIOR space easily accommodates five with luggage, and the rear seat folds down for larger loads.

+COMFORT. The well-designed seats offer good support, the noise level is normal at cruising speeds and climate controls are a breeze to use.

+INSTRUMENT PANEL. The design is better and more ergonomic, which also breaks from the rugged aspect of previous models.

+QUALITY. The construction, fit and finish of material is comparable to Japanese models, with complete equipment, though not luxurious.

CONS
-THE PRICE, upkeep and fluctuating resale value exacts a lot from the fans of these Swedish beauties.

-THE GEARBOX of the automatic transmission is rougher with the base engine than with the Turbo.

-COMFORT. The hard suspension on the sporty models give you the exact depth of every crack in the road.

-GREMLINS. It's surprising that such high-quality vehicles squeak and rattle.

-CONTROLS. The unconventional controls require a certain getting used to. Several are placed too low and the steering wheel is still too large.

CONCLUSION
The success of the Volvo 70 series supports the unending improvements of these renewed Swedish models. There's one for everybody, but not for every budget. ☺

RATING
VOLVO 70-Series

CONCEPT :		**78%**
Technology	85	
Safety :	75	
Interior space :	70	
Trunk volume:	80	
Quality/fit/finish :	80	
DRIVING:		**71%**
Cockpit :	80	
Performance :	65	
Handling :	60	
Steering :	80	
Braking :	70	
ORIGINAL EQUIPMENT:		**81%**
Tires :	80	
Headlights :	80	
Wipers :	85	
Rear defroster :	80	
Radio :	80	
COMFORT :		**72%**
Seats :	80	
Suspension :	70	
Sound level :	50	
Conveniences :	80	
Air conditioning :	80	
BUDGET :		**56%**
Price :	20	
Fuel economy :	70	
Insurance :	40	
Satisfaction :	90	
Depreciation :	60	
Overall rating:		**71.6%**

NEW FOR 1999

- **No major change.**

ENGINES

Model/ version	Type / timing valve / fuel system	Displacement cu in	Power bhp @ rpm	Torque lb-ft @ rpm
S, V 70	L5* 2.4 DOHC-20-MPFI	148	168 @ 6200	162 @ 4700
GLT	L5T* 2.4 DOHC-20-MPFI	148	190 @ 5100	199 @ 1800
AWD	L5T* 2.4 DOHC-20-MPFI	148	190 @ 5100	199 @ 1800
T-5	L5T* 2.3 DOHC-20-MPFI	141	236 @ 5100	243 @ 2700

TRANSMISSIONS

Compres. ratio	Driving wheels / transmission	Final ratio
10.3 :1	front - M5*	4.00
	front - A4	2.74
9.0 :1	front - A4*	2.74
9.0 :1	front - M5*	4.00
8.5 :1	front - M5*	4.00

PERFORMANCES

Acceler. 0-60 mph s	Standing 1/4 & 5/8 mile s		Acceler. 50-75 mph s	Braking 60-0 mph f	Top speed mph	Lateral acceler. G	Noise level dBA	Fuel economy mpg City	Highway	Fuel type Octane
8.9	16.7	29.9	6.5	121	127	0.78	68	20	29	S 91
9.6	17.0	31.5	7.0	128	124	0.78	68	20	28	S 91
9.0	16.6	30.0	6.4	131	137	0.78	68	19	27	S 91
9.2	16.8	30.3	6.5	134	131	0.80	68	19	25	S 91
6.0	14.2	25.5	4.0	134	143	0.80	68	18	25	S 91

PRICE & EQUIPMENT

VOLVO 70	base	GLT	T-5	AWD
Retail price $:	26,985	32,440	34,010	40,995
Dealer invoice $:	24,785	30,040	31,060	36,795
Shipping & handling $:	575	575	575	575
Automatic transmission:	O	S	O	-
Cruise control:	S	S	S	S
Power steering:	S	S	S	S
Anti-lock brakes:	S	S	S	S
Traction control:	O	O	O	O
Air conditioning:	S	S	S	S
Leather:	O	O	O	S
AM/FM/radio-cassette:	S	S	S	S
Power door locks:	S	S	S	S
Power windows:	S	S	S	S
Tilt steering:	S	S	S	S
Dual adjustable mirrors:	S	S	S	S
Alloy wheels:	O	O	S	S
Anti-theft system:	O	S	S	S

Colors
Exterior: Black, White, Red, Blue, Green, Silver, Graphite, Gray, Sand, Teal.

Interior: Blue, Taupe, Gray.

AT A GLANCE...

Category: FWD & AWD luxury sedans & wagons. **Class :** 7

HISTORIC
Introduced in: 1992-1997
Made in: Gand, Belgium: Torslanda, Sweden: Halifax, Canada.

DEMOGRAPHICS

Model	Men./Wom.	Age	Married	College	Income
70	75/25 %	42	81 %	73 %	$ 70 000

INDEX
Safety:	90 %	**Satisfaction:**	91 %
Depreciation:	40 %	**Insurance:**	$1 175-1 500
Cost per mile:	$ 0.67-0.73	**Number of dealers:**	405

SALES
Model	1996	1997	Result
850-70	-	51 567	-

MAIN COMPETITORS
ACURA 3.2TL, AUDI A4, INFINITI I30, LEXUS ES 300, NISSAN Maxima, SAAB 9[5]-9[3].

MAINTENANCE REQUIRED BY WARRANTY
First revision:	Frequency:	Diagnostic plug:
10 000 miles	10 000 miles	Yes
Tbo : 5 000 miles	Tbo : 5 000 miles	Yes

SPECIFICATIONS

Model	Version Trim	Body/ Seats	Interior volume cu ft	Trunk volume cu ft	Cd	Wheel base in	Lght x Wdgth x Hght in x in x in	Curb weight lb	Susp. ft/rr	Brake ft/rr	Steering type	Turning diameter ft	Steer. turns nber.	Fuel tank gal	tire size	Standard tires make	model	Standard powertrain
VOLVO		General warranty: 4 years / 50 000 miles; corrosion: 8 years / unlimited; antipollution: 5 years / 50 000 miles.																
S70	base	4dr.sdn. 5	100.7	14.7	0.32	104.9	185.9x69.3x55.2	3115	ih/sih	dc/ABS	pwr.r&p.	33.4	3.2	19.3	195/60VR15	Michelin	MXV4	L5/2.4/M5
V70	base	5dr.wgn. 5	93.6	37.1	0.32	104.9	185.4x69.3x56.2	3214	ih/sih	dc/ABS	pwr.r&p.	33.4	3.2	19.3	195/60VR15	Michelin	MXV4	L5/2.4/M5
S70	GLT	4dr.sdn. 5	100.7	14.7	0.32	104.9	185.9x69.3x55.2	3116	ih/sih	dc/ABS	pwr.r&p.	33.4	3.2	19.3	195/60VR15	Michelin	MXV4	L5T/2.4/A4
V70	GLT	5dr.wgn. 5	93.6	37.1	0.32	104.9	185.4x69.3x56.2	3214	ih/sih	dc/ABS	pwr.r&p.	33.4	3.2	19.3	195/60VR15	Michelin	MXV4	L5T/2.4/A4
S70	T-5	4dr.sdn. 5	100.7	14.7	0.32	104.9	185.9x69.3x55.2	3116	ih/sih	dc/ABS	pwr.r&p.	33.4	3.2	19.3	205/55ZR16	Michelin	XGTV4	L5T/2.3/M5
V70	T-5	5dr.wgn. 5	93.6	37.1	0.32	104.9	185.4x69.3x56.2	3214	ih/sih	dc/ABS	pwr.r&p.	33.4	3.2	19.3	205/55ZR16	Michelin	XGTV4	L5T/2.3/M5
V70	AWD	5dr.wgn. 5	93.6	37.1	0.32	104.9	185.4x69.3x56.3	3263	ih/sih	dc/ABS	pwr.r&p.	33.4	3.2	19.3	205/65R15	Continental	Eco Plus	L5T/2.3/M5

VOLVO S80
Non-Conformist...

Since their breakup with French manufacturer Renault, the Swedish Volvo has kicked it into high gear. Their problems with securing anything for the future and the disappointment of the failed collaboration have made Volvo stronger and more definite at setting it's own somewhat risky course on the world scene. On their own and without a partner, the lords of Gothenbürg are masters in their own land, but sooner or later they will have to merge with a larger company in order to reduce costs, share research and production methods to stay competitive on a global scale. In the meantime, it's full steam ahead at Volvo, where, after freshening up the sedans and wagons and introducing the 70 series coupes and convertibles, comes the arrival of the S80.

Within the reorganized and expanded model range, made up of only two principle lines, the S80 doesn't really replace the old 90, which used to be considered the top of the line. A new 100 will overtake the 80 at the high end, while the present 70 will give way to the low end 40, which will soonbe available in North America. The first thing you'll notice on the S80 is the unusual styling for a Volvo. It borrows the sculptured stripe that runs from the rear taillights all the way around from the ECC prototype, giving it a powerful, dynamic look. The only thing that remains of the traditional Volvo look is the front grille and the Volvo faceplate. Things seems more Spartan inside than outside. The smooth lines of the dash don't mini-

mize the harsh-looking instrument panel or the central console that is extremely like the Acura RL. The main controls also reflect this Scandinavian penchant, absolutely in line with the northern European countries. The other unique feature on the new Volvo S80 is the transverse-mounted
6-cylinder engine, the same engine that powered the 90. The Geartronic gear box that comes standard was researched and developed by General Motors. It has the advantage of being very compact, as well as sequential meaning it can be used in manual mode without a clutch or as an automatic, like the famous Tiptronic by Porsche. The S80 is the first Volvo to adopt a Multiplex electric circuit. On a single wire it sends different instructions that can only be understood by the intended system. Lincoln began to use this system on the Continental two years ago. This reduces the complexity of the circuit while increasing the amount of information it is able to transmit. It's not possible to discuss a Volvo without mentioning safety. Besides the front-impact and side-impact airbags, the S80 has introduced an inflatable curtain to protect occupants' heads from windows. In addition, the front seats include a whiplash protection system that activates in the event of an accident. These models are also assisted by anti-lock brakes, and an anti-skid system.

With the new S80, Volvo has made a 180 degree turn. Forget about the sharp lines and the conservative side that only pleased the intellectuals. The S80 has a strong personality and futuristic technology, and aims to conquer a new market. This is the first model to be based on the new large-size Volvo platform, and is the forerunner to the future high-end model, the S100, which, rumor has it, will have a V10 engine! There's quite a bit of anticipation for the future of the Swedish automaker.

MODEL RANGE

The S80 is a luxury sedan available in two trims, the base and the T6. The S80 emphasizes the luxury side with a 2.9-liter, inline, 6-cylinder DOHC engine, while the T6 goes for performance with a 2.8-liter inline-6 bi-turbo. There's room for five, and the front power seats are fully-adjustable. Both models have leather upholstery but not the same quality, and the T6 has real walnut trim, while you'll have to make do with faux wood on the base model. The steering wheel is fully adjustable. Standard equipment includes dual zone climate control and a 60/40 folding rear seat. The T6 adds foglights and an auto-dimming rearview mirror. A sunroof is optional for both.

TECHNICAL FEATURES

The aerodynamics of the steel unibody are outstanding, with a drag coefficient of 0.28. Both the front hood and rear trunk are made of aluminum. The fully independent suspension has MacPherson struts on the front, while the rear has a multi-arm system mounted on the undercarriage, attached to the chassis with rubber bushings. Both front and rear incorporate anti-roll bars. Brakes are all disc with a three-channel anti-lock system and an electronic brake distribution system (EBD). Standard equipment also includes traction control. Finally, the power steering adapts to vehicle speed. The S80 sets itself apart because of the transverse-mounted inline 6 engine

and the compact automatic transmission.

Both versions offer more interior space and a larger crumple zone to better protect passengers in a collision. Both engines include a variable valve timing system. The T6 bi-turbo also maintains maximum torque longer (from 2000 to 5000 rpm) and is mated to a Geartronic sequential automatic transmission, allowing you to change gears like a manual, but without the clutch. This model also includes a differential viscocoupler. In addition to the front-impact and side-impact airbags, passenger safety is heightened with an inflatable curtain in the front, and the bucket seats are equipped with a whiplash protection system.

PROS

+**STYLING** differs greatly from previous models that have been around for generations. With a more sculptured shape, the S80 is very similar to the 1992 ECC prototype.

+**SEATS.** The bucket seats in the S80, as in all Volvos, demonstrate what comfort should be. The high back and well-shaped seat provide excellent support. And they're heated.

+**TRUNK.** Because of the 60/40 rear folding seat, storage space can nearly double. The trunk is very deep and flat.

+**PERFORMANCE.** Accelerating and passing in the bi-turbo is inspiring. Too bad Volvo didn't put switches on the steering wheel like Porsche did with their Tiptronic.

+**HANDLING** is very smooth. The suspension dampens any roll and minimizes bumps.

+**INTERIOR SPACE.** The rear bench is very comfortable. There's enough room for heads, shoulders and legs. Headrests are adjustable, which improves rear window visibility slightly, so long as no one is sitting there.

+**BRAKING** is smooth and easy to gauge, even on difficult mountain passes.

CONS

-**MANEUVERABILITY.** Volvos are well-known to be maneuverable, except for the S80. The transverse-mounted engine increases the width, resulting in a greater turning radius than on the S90.

-**VISIBILITY.** In a car that puts so much emphasis on passive and active protection systems, rear window visibility is seriously limited. The high trunk makes backing up an uneasy undertaking in this large car. There's no way to see where you're going. Maybe they'll have to add a radar detection system to avoid this.

-**STEERING.** On the T6, the power steering is too much and quickly becomes light and uncertain on center. Steering in the base S80 is more enjoyable.

-**TRANSMISSION.** You can feel the Geartronic transmission in the T6 change in certain condition, especially when you disengage the automatic to downshift.

-**PERFORMANCE** of the base S80 is uninspiring since both acceleration and passing are mediocre at best.

-**TIRES.** In spite of the superior performance available on the T6, Volvo has simply installed the same touring tires equipping the S80. Thankfully, Michelin MXX3 «Z»'s are available as an option.

CONCLUSION

The S80 is a radical turn away from the S90 that it replaces. Engine performance is noteworthy and the amount of room is remarkable. It signals that a change is in the wind for the Swedish manufacturer. We'll just have to wait and see if buyers give it the same amount of attention they gave to its rival, the Audi A6. ☺

RATING VOLVO S80

CONCEPT :   **80%**
Technology 80
Safety : 100
Interior space : 70
Trunk volume: 70
Quality/fit/finish : 80

DRIVING: **74%**
Cockpit : 80
Performance : 70
Handling : 60
Steering : 75
Braking : 85

ORIGINAL EQUIPMENT: **81%**
Tires : 80
Headlights : 80
Wipers : 85
Rear defroster : 80
Radio : 80

COMFORT :   **78%**
Seats : 80
Suspension : 80
Sound level: 70
Conveniences : 80
Air conditioning : 80

BUDGET :   **46%**
Price : 0
Fuel economy : 60
Insurance : 30
Satisfaction : 90
Depreciation : 50

Overall rating: **71.8%**

NEW FOR 1999

- Entirely new version to replace the S90.
- Two new inline 6-cylinder transverse-mounted engines, a 2.9-liter and a 2.8-liter bi-turbo.
- New Geartronic sequential 4-speed automatic (S80 T6).
- New inflatable curtains to better protect front occupants.

ENGINES / TRANSMISSIONS / PERFORMANCES

Model/ version	Type / timing valve / fuel system	Displacement cu in	Power bhp @ rpm	Torque lb-ft @ rpm	Compres. ratio	Driving wheels / transmission	Final ratio	Acceler. 0-60 mph s	Standing 1/4 & 5/8 mile s	Acceler. 50-75 mph s	Braking 60-0 mph f	Top speed mph	Lateral acceler. G	Noise level dBA	City	Highway	Fuel type Octane
S80 2.9	L6 2.9 DOHC-24-EFI	178	201 @ 6000	207 @ 4200	10.7 :1	front - A4	3.73	9.0	16.8 30.0	6.4	121	124	0.78	66-70	17	26	S 91
S80 T6	L6T 2.8 DOHC-24-EFI	170	268 @ 5400	280 @ 2000	-	front - A4	-	7.2	15.4 26.6	5.2	125	149	0.78	66-70	16	25	S 91

PRICE & EQUIPMENT

VOLVO S80	2.9	T6
Retail price $:	35,820	40,385
Dealer invoice $:	32,520	36,585
Shipping & handling $:	575	575
Automatic transmission:	S	S
Cruise control:	S	S
Power steering:	S	S
Anti-lock brakes:	S	S
Traction control:	S	S
Air conditioning:	SE	SE
Leather:	SH	SH
AM/FM/radio-cassette:	SCD	SCD
Power door locks:	S	S
Power windows:	S	S
Tilt steering:	S	S
Dual adjustable mirrors:	SEH	SEH
Alloy wheels:	S	S
Anti-theft system:	S	S

Colors
Exterior: Black, White, Blue, Silver, Java, Turquoise, Gray, Emerald.
Interior: Taupe, Graphite, Granite.

AT A GLANCE...
Category: front-wheel drive luxury sedans.   Class : 7

HISTORIC
Introduced in: 1999
Made in: Torslanda, Sweden .

DEMOGRAPHICS

Model	Men./Wom.	Age	Married	College	Income
80	80/20 %	52	88 %	62 %	$ 65 000

INDEX
Safety: 100 %   Satisfaction: (S90) 88 %
Depreciation: 50 %   Insurance: $ 1 400
Cost per mile: $ 0.68   Number of dealers: 405

SALES

Model	1996	1997	Result
S90	Not on the market at that time.		

MAIN COMPETITORS
ACURA RL, AUDI A6, BMW 5-Series, CHRYSLER 300M, LEXUS GS 300, MAZDA Millenia, MERCEDES-BENZ C 280, SAAB 9[5], TOYOTA Avalon.

MAINTENANCE REQUIRED BY WARRANTY
First revision: 3 000 miles   Frequency: 6 000 miles   Diagnostic plug: Yes

SPECIFICATIONS

Model	Version Trim	Body/ Seats	Interior volume cu ft	Trunk volume cu ft	Cd	Wheel base in	Lght x Wdgth x Hght in x in x in	Curb weight lb	Susp. ft/rr	Brake ft/rr	Steering type	Turning diameter ft	Steer. turns nber.	Fuel tank gal	tire size	Standard tires make	model	Standard powertrain
VOLVO		General warranty: 4 years / 50 000 miles; corrosion: 8 years / unlimited; antipollution: 5 years / 50 000 miles.																
S80	2.9	4dr.sdn.5	99.9	15.5	0.28	109.9	189.8x72.1x57.1	3421	ih/ih	dc/ABS	pwr.r&p.	35.7	-	21.1	215/55HR16	-	-	L6/2.9/A4
S80	T6	4dr.sdn.5	99.9	15.5	0.28	109.9	189.8x72.1x57.1	3421	ih/ih	dc/ABS	pwr.r&p.	35.7	-	21.1	225/55HR16	-	-	L6T/2.8/A4

The Best Buys in Each Category

Once again, in keeping with our long-standing yearly tradition, the Road Report team has tested more than fifty models and has carefully assessed each car's performance parameters that, taken as a whole, indicate the vehicle's real worth. Our test pilots wrote up their general impressions and also analyzed performance figures arrived at by using various testing instruments.

The vehicles are classified according to very specific categories, depending on size and mechanical features. Performances are evaluated according to a check list that we've developed over the years. Ninety per cent of these marks are attributed according to objective, scientific mathematical data, so each and every vehicle gets a fair chance. Each set of marks is then calculated to arrive at a comprehensive percentage score, so the various models can be evaluated and compared.

This evaluation system allows for some adjustments. For example, a minivan usually gets top marks for interior space and seat access, but it might get a lower rating as far as road performance or handling are concerned, and the opposite applies for a sports coupe.

No system is fool-proof, but ours is particularly stringent. Of course, as you'll notice, there are sometimes variations between the test pilot's subjective remarks and the score that the vehicle actually gets when all the nitty-gritty mathematical data is calculated. How you feel when you're behind the wheel of a particular vehicle can be influenced by any number of factors, but the analysis data is much more objective, even ruthlessly so.

It's easy as pie to measure a vehicle's exterior dimensions or cabin size, but putting a numerical value on seat-fabric quality or on how finely road-tuned a suspension is, is quite another matter. The same holds true for assembly quality or finish details, since there aren't really any specific existing criteria that define these factors.

See page 8 for the scoring scale and related clarifications.

3s Class: sub-compact for less than $ 13,000

1st   ACURA EL   70.8%

2nd   NISSAN Sentra   68.8%

3rd   HONDA Civic 68.6%

Rank	Models	Concept	OUR CLASSIFICATION Driving	Equipment	Comfort	Budget	Rating
1	**ACURA EL**	70	66	78	70	70	**70.8 %**
2	NISSAN Sentra	63	59	73	69	80	68.8 %
3	HONDA Civic	69	62	74	65	73	68.6 %
4	TOYOTA Tercel	61	56	72	65	79	66.6 %
5	HYUNDAI Accent	61	59	70	59	79	65.6 %
6	CHEVROLET Metro	62	46	69	57	72	61.2 %

Rank	YOUR CLASSIFICATION Models	97 Sales
1	**HONDA Civic**	315 546
2	NISSAN Sentra	122 468
3	CHEVROLET Metro	55 629
4	HYUNDAI Accent	40 355
5	TOYOTA Tercel	31 651

Class-3: Compacts from $13,000 to $16,000

1st TOYOTA Corolla 71.8 %

2nd SATURN SL-SW 69.4 %

3rd MAZDA Protegé 68.8 %

Rank	Models	Concept	OUR CLASSIFICATION Driving	Equipment	Comfort	Budget	Rating
1	**TOYOTA Corolla**	72	64	75	**72**	76	**71.8 %**
2	SATURN SL-SW	**73**	63	68	**72**	71	69.4 %
3	MAZDA Protegé	72	60	75	67	70	68.8 %
4	VW Golf	69	**67**	**76**	71	57	68.0 %
5	CHEVROLET Cavalier	66	63	74	69	67	67.8 %
6	FORD Escort	67	59	75	64	73	67.6 %
7	SUBARU Impreza	70	57	74	67	65	66.6 %
8	CHRYSLER Neon	69	62	68	59	72	66.0 %
9	HYUNDAI Elantra	59	60	69	64	70	64.4 %

Rank	YOUR CLASSIFICATION Models	97 Sales
1	**CHEVROLET Cavalier PONTIAC Sunfire**	**404 321**
2	FORD Escort	283 898
3	SATURN SL-SW-SC	251 099
4	TOYOTA Corolla	218 461
5	CHRYSLER Neon	208 652
6	MAZDA Protegé	53 930
7	HYUNDAI Elantra	41 303
8	VW Golf	30 241
9	SUBARU Impreza	24 242

Class-4 Compacts from $16,000 to $20,000

1st NISSAN Altima 73.0%

2nd BUICK Century 71.6 %

3rd INFINITI G20 71.2 %

Rank	Models	Concept	OUR CLASSIFICATION Driving	Equipment	Comfort	Budget	Rating
1	**NISSAN Altima**	75	**72**	77	**75**	66	**73.0 %**
2	BUICK Century	**80**	65	**79**	74	60	71.6 %
3	INFINITI G20	72	69	**79**	72	64	71.2 %
4	OLDSMOBILE Alero	75	68	76	73	58	70.0 %
5	FORD Contour MERCURY Mystique	69	66	76	66	**72**	69.8 %
6	CHEVROLET Malibu	74	60	**79**	70	65	69.6 %
7	MAZDA 626	75	65	75	71	61	69.4 %
8	VW Jetta	69	67	76	71	57	68.0 %
9	VW New Beetle	71	60	78	61	68	67.6 %
10	CHRYSLER JA	69	62	70	64	69	66.8 %
11	PONTIAC Grand Am	69	62	73	65	63	66.4 %
	SUBARU Legacy	71	55	73	70	63	66.4 %

Rank	YOUR CLASSIFICATION Models	97 Sales
1	**GM N-Series**	**326 605**
2	CHRYSLER JA	203 088
3	FORD Contour-MERCURY Mystique	192 098
4	CHEVROLET Malibu	164 654
5	NISSAN Altima	144 483
6	VW Jetta	90 984
7	MAZDA 626	75 800
8	SUBARU Legacy	40 870

Not classified :
INFINITI G20
VW New Beetle

Class 5-Mid-Size from $ 20,000 to $ 25,000

1st CHRYSLER LH 73.6 %

2nd TOYOTA Camry 73.4 %

3rd HONDA Accord 72.2 %
3rd OLDSMOBILE Intrigue 72.2%

			OUR CLASSIFICATION				
Rank	Models	Concept	Driving	Equipment	Comfort	Budget	Rating
1	CHRYSLER Concorde Intrepid	**83**	66	82	76	61	**73.6 %**
2	TOYOTA Camry	75	68	79	**78**	**67**	73.4 %
3	HONDA Accord	77	66	78	74	66	72.2 %
3	OLDS Intrigue	78	64	**84**	73	62	72.2 %
4	BUICK Regal	80	65	79	74	60	71.6 %
5	PONTIAC Grand Prix	77	67	79	68	59	70.0 %
6	NISSAN Maxima	75	**70**	71	69	63	69.6 %
	VW Passat	77	67	77	73	54	69.6 %
7	FORD Taurus MERCURY Sable	78	58	73	70	60	67.8 %
7	CHEVROLET Lumina Monte Carlo	76	63	71	72	57	67.8 %
8	HYUNDAI Sonata	70	62	72	68	64	67.2 %

	YOUR CLASSIFICATION	
Rank	Models	97 Sales
1	FORD Taurus-Sable	469 562
2	TOYOTA Camry	397 156
3	HONDA Accord	384 609
4	CHEVROLET Lumina Monte Carlo	299 994
5	CHRYSLER LH	162 455
6	PONTIAC Grand Prix	142 018
7	NISSAN Maxima	123 215
8	BUICK Regal	50 691
9	OLDS Intrigue	23 460
10	HYUNDAI Sonata	22 128
11	VW Passat	14 868

Class 6- Full Size from $ 20 000 to $ 25 000

1st OLDSMOBILE 88 69.6 %

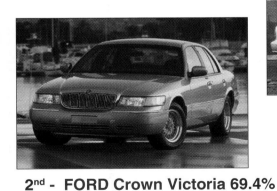

2nd - FORD Crown Victoria 69.4%
2nd MERCURY Gd Marquis 69.4 %

3rd PONTIAC Bonneville 68.8 %

			OUR CLASSIFICATION				
Rank	Models	Concept	Driving	Equipment	Comfort	Budget	Rating
1	OLDSMOBILE 88	80	**66**	75	71	56	**69.6 %**
2	FORD Crown Vic. MERCURY Gd Mar.	83	55	**77**	**75**	**57**	69.4 %
3	PONTIAC Bonneville	78	**66**	76	71	54	68.8 %
4	BUICK LeSabre	79	65	74	69	52	67.8 %

	YOUR CLASSIFICATION	
Rank	Models	97 Sales
1	OLDS 88 PONTIAC Bonneville BUICK LeSabre	296 783
2	FORD C.Vic MERCURY Gd Mar.	217 411

Class 7- Luxury sedans under $ 35,000

1st TOYOTA Avalon 74.4 %

2nd LEXUS ES 300 72.4 %

3rd ACURA TL 72.0 %

		OUR CLASSIFICATION							YOUR CLASSIFICATION	
Rank	Models	Concept	Driving	Equipment	Comfort	Budget	Rating	Rank	Models	97 Sales
1	**TOYOTA Avalon**	**84**	69	77	78	**64**	**74.4 %**			
2	LEXUS ES 300	75	72	80	**82**	53	72.4 %	**1**	**TOYOTA Avalon**	**71 309**
3	ACURA TL	76	67	80	78	59	72.0 %	2	LEXUS ES 300	58 428
4	CHRYSLER 300M							3	VOLVO S/V70	51 567
	LHS	**84**	67	**82**	74	52	71.8 %	4	BMW 3-Series	44 530
5	VOLVO 70 S/V	78	71	81	72	56	71.6 %	5	MERCEDES C-Class	32 543
6	INFINITI I30	78	66	73	77	58	70.4 %	6	INFINITI I30	31 303
7	MERCEDES C-Class	74	70	79	74	53	70.0 %	7	CADILLAC Catera	25 411
8	AUDI A4	76	64	80	73	56	69.8 %	8	OLDS Aurora	25 404
9	BMW 3-Series	69	**79**	79	71	50	69.6 %	9	ACURA TL	23 151
10	CADILLAC Catera	78	68	78	79	44	69.4 %	10	SAAB 9³	22 949
11	MAZDA Millenia	75	66	77	72	52	68.4 %	11	AUDI A4	20 171
11	OLDS Aurora	74	68	76	78	49	68.4 %	12	MAZDA Millenia	18 020
12	SAAB 9³	74	68	78	70	50	68.0 %			

Not classified:
CHRYSLER 300M-LHS

Class 7- Luxury sedans from $ 35,000 to $ 60,000

1st BMW 5-Series 73.8 %

2nd   CADILLAC Seville 72.2 %

3rd   VOLVO S80 71.8 %

		OUR CLASSIFICATION							YOUR CLASSIFICATION	
Rank	Models	Concept	Driving	Equipment	Comfort	Budget	Rating	Rank	Models	97 Sales
1	**BMW 5-Series**	80	**75**	**85**	**82**	47	**73.8 %**	1	**CADILLAC DeVille**	**104 743**
2	CADILLAC Seville	84	68	80	**82**	47	72.2 %	2	LINCOLN Tow Car	92 297
2	CADILLAC DeVille	**89**	67	78	80	47	72.2 %	3	BUICK Park Avenue	68 777
3	VOLVO S80	80	74	81	78	46	71.8 %	4	MERCEDES E-Class	42 883
4	AUDI A6	82	70	80	78	48	71.6 %	5	BMW 5-Series	31 347
4	LEXUS GS	78	73	82	75	50	71.6 %	6	LINCOLN Continental	31 220
4	MERCEDES E-Class	83	71	78	75	**51**	71.6 %	7	Seville	29 837
5	ACURA RL	76	68	82	79	49	70.8 %	8	ACURA RL	16 004
6	LINCOLN Continental	82	72	79	73	43	69.8 %	9	BUICK Riviera	14 097
7	LINCOLN Town Car	86	62	77	73	45	68.6 %	10	AUDI A6	9 949
8	BUICK Park Avenue	78	65	75	72	**51**	68.2 %	11	LEXUS GS	7 713
9	BUICK Riviera	75	66	74	76	49	68.0 %			
10	SAAB 9⁵	86	62	78	69	44	67.8 %			

Not classified:
VOLVO S80
SAAB 9⁵

Luxury sedans over $ 60,000

1st BMW 7-Series 76.4 %

2nd AUDI A8 73.4 %

3rd LEXUS LS 400 73.0 %

Rank	Models	Concept	OUR CLASSIFICATION				Rating
			Driving	Equipment	Comfort	Budget	
1	**BMW 7-Series**	**92**	**78**	**87**	**87**	38	**76.4 %**
2	AUDI A8	88	73	83	83	40	73.4 %
2	MERCEDES S-Class	**92**	72	82	84	37	73.4 %
3	LEXUS LS 400	81	73	80	80	**51**	73.0 %
4	INFINITI Q45	74	72	84	82	48	72.0 %
5	JAGUAR XJ8-XJR	75	74	81	80	40	70.0 %

Rank	YOUR CLASSIFICATION Models	97 Sales
1	**LEXUS LS 400**	**19 318**
2	BMW 7-Series	18 273
3	MERCEDES S-Class	16 119
4	JAGUAR XJ8-XJR	12 588
5	INFINITI Q45	10 443
6	AUDI A8	2 085

Class 3s- Sports coupes under $ 20,000

1st SATURN SC 69.4 %

2nd ACURA Integra 68.4 %

3rd HYUNDAI Tiburon 68.2 %

Rank	Models	Concept	OUR CLASSIFICATION				Rating
			Driving	Equipment	Comfort	Budget	
1	**SATURN SC**	**73**	63	68	72	71	**69.4 %**
2	ACURA Integra	62	70	76	71	63	68.4 %
3	HYUNDAI Tiburon	64	67	76	**73**	61	68.2 %
4	TOYOTA Paseo	61	56	72	65	**79**	66.6 %
5	FORD ZX2	62	60	75	63	71	66.2 %
6	MAZDA Miata	52	**71**	**78**	53	62	63.2 %

Rank	YOUR CLASSIFICATION Models	97 Sales
1	**ACURA Integra**	**38 331**
2	MAZDA Miata	17 218
3	HYUNDAI Tiburon	9 391

Not classified :
TOYOTA Paseo
FORD ZX2
Saturn SC

Class 5- Sports coupes from $ 20,000 to $30,000

1st TOYOTA Solara 70.4 %

2nd ACURA CL 69.8 %

3rd HONDA Prelude 69.0 %

Rank	Models	Concept	Driving	Equipment	Comfort	Budget	Rating
			OUR CLASSIFICATION				
1	**TOYOTA Solara**	**75**	69	79	74	55	**70.4 %**
2	ACURA CL	68	66	**82**	71	62	69.8 %
3	HONDA Prelude	61	72	77	**76**	59	69.0 %
4	CHRYSLER Sebring						
4	DODGE Avenger	71	60	69	68	**68**	67.2 %
5	TOYOTA Celica	62	68	77	67	61	67.0 %
6	FORD Mustang	61	**75**	75	65	57	66.6 %
7	MERCURY Cougar	66	64	78	64	60	66.4 %
8	CHEVROLET Camaro	62	70	78	58	50	63.6 %
9	PONTIAC Firebird	62	69	77	58	48	62.8 %

Rank	Models	97 Sales
		YOUR CLASSIFICATION
1	**FORD Mustang**	**116 610**
2	Chevrolet Camaro	55 973
3	CHRYSLER Sebring	35 365
4	Pontiac Firebird	32 524
5	Chrysler Avenger	31 943
6	ACURA CL	28 939
7	HONDA Prelude	16 678
8	TOYOTA Celica	9 021

Not classified:
MERCURY Cougar
TOYOTA Solara

GT sports coupes over $30,000

2nd MERCEDES-BENZ CLK 69.4 %

1st VOLVO C70 70.6 %

3rd JAGUAR XK8 68.0 %

Rank	Models	Concept	Driving	Equipment	Comfort	Budget	Rating
			OUR CLASSIFICATION				
1	**VOLVO C70**	**72**	78	81	67	**55**	**70.6 %**
2	MERCEDES CLK	69	74	**84**	69	51	69.4 %
3	JAGUAR XK8	68	77	80	**70**	45	68.0 %
4	PORSCHE BOXSTER-911	62	83	81	60	53	67.8 %
5	AUDI TT	64	79	81	67	41	66.4 %
6	CHEVROLET Corvette	65	86	79	55	43	65.6 %
6	MERCEDES SLK	56	74	80	69	49	65.6 %
7	BMW Z3	57	82	64	64	54	64.2 %
8	DODGE Viper	61	**88**	78	46	43	63.2 %
9	PLYMOUTH Prowler	48	70	72	40	50	56.0 %

Rank	Models	97 Sales
		YOUR CLASSIFICATION
1	**CHEVROLET Corvette**	**22 724**
2	BMW Z3	19 760
3	JAGUAR XK8	6 915
4	PORSCHE Boxster	6 996
5	MERCEDES CLK	6 890
6	PORSCHE 911	5 980
7	DODGE Viper	1 458
8	MERCEDES SLK	1 236
9	PLYMOUTH Prowler	120

Not classified :
AUDI TT
VOLVO C70

THE BEST BUYS OF 1999

Minivans

1er HONDA Odyssey 71.2 %

2nd CHRYSLER T&Country-Caravan-Voyager 70.8 %

3rd FORD Windstar 70.6 %

Rank	Models	Concept	OUR CLASSIFICATION				Rating
			Driving	Equipment	Comfort	Budget	
1	**HONDA Odyssey**	79	**63**	78	70	**66**	**71.2 %**
2	CHRYSLER NS	79	59	74	**78**	64	70.8 %
3	FORD Windstar	84	61	74	72	62	70.6 %
4	TOYOTA Sienna	75	59	76	72	64	69.2 %
5	NISSAN Quest	76	61	76	70	58	68.2 %
6	OLDS Silhouette	71	52	**81**	70	**66**	68.0 %
7	VW EuroVan	**87**	53	76	71	51	67.6 %
8	PONTIAC Montana	71	52	79	70	64	67.2 %
9	CHEVROLET Venture	67	52	**81**	70	65	67.0 %
10	MAZDA MPV	73	51	73	70	49	63.2 %
11	GM Astro-Safari	72	52	65	69	54	62.4 %

Rank	YOUR CLASSIFICATION	
	Models	97 Sales
1	**CHRYSLER NS**	**518 445**
2	FORD Windstar	205 356
3	GM U-Series	153 990
4	GM Astro-Safari	146 977
5	MERCURY Villager	55 168
6	NISSAN Quest	46 858
7	HONDA Odyssey	20 333
8	MAZDA MPV	15 599
9	TOYOTA Sienna	15 180
10	VW EuroVan	1 792

Compact Sport-utility

2nd HONDA CR-V 68.8 %

1st TOYOTA RAV4 69.2 %

3rd SUBARU Forester 68.0 %

Rank	Models	Concept	OUR CLASSIFICATION				Rating
			Driving	Equipment	Comfort	Budget	
1	**TOYOTA RAV4**	70	58	**77**	71	**70**	**69.2 %**
2	HONDA CR-V	**74**	58	75	**73**	64	68.8 %
3	SUBARU Forester	69	**62**	**77**	66	66	68.0 %
4	JEEP Cherokee	66	54	**77**	61	57	63.0 %
5	CHEVROLET Tracker	60	53	75	61	63	62.4 %
6	JEEP TJ	54	45	60	43	55	51.4 %

Rank	YOUR CLASSIFICATION	
	Models	97 Sales
1	**JEEP Cherokee**	**130 041**
2	JEEP TJ	81 956
3	TOYOTA RAV4	67 489
4	HONDA CR-V	66 572
5	CHEVROLET Tracker	33 354
6	SUBARU Forester	15 988

Mid-size Sport-Utility

1st MERCEDES-BENZ Classe M 70.0 %

2nd JEEP Grand Cherokee 68.0 %

3rd DODGE Durango 67.0 %

OUR CLASSIFICATION

Rank	Models	Concept	Driving	Equipment	Comfort	Budget	Rating
1	**MERCEDES M-Class**	78	69	**79**	75	49	**70.0 %**
2	JEEP Gd Cherokee	78	**70**	**79**	74	39	68.0 %
3	DODGE Durango	79	56	77	74	49	67.0 %
4	INFINITI QX4	76	62	78	73	45	66.8 %
5	ISUZU Rodeo	76	61	76	64	**55**	66.4 %
5	LEXUS RX 300	**80**	59	77	71	45	66.4 %
6	TOYOTA 4Runner	71	58	78	70	52	65.8 %
7	FORD Explorer	77	55	77	66	53	65.6 %
7	MERCURY Mountaineer						
8	NISSAN Pathfinder	72	57	75	70	52	65.2 %
9	GM Blazer-Jimmy	73	58	74	67	52	64.8 %
10	OLDS Bravada	73	57	74	67	52	64.6 %

YOUR CLASSIFICATION

Rank	Models	97 Sales
1	**FORD Explorer**	383 852
2	GM Blazer-Jimmy	297 217
3	JEEP Gd Cherokee	260 875
4	TOYOTA 4Runner	128 496
5	NISSAN Pathfinder	73 365
6	ISUZU Rodeo	63 627
7	MERCURY Mountaineer	45 363
8	OLDSMOBILE Bravada	28 281
9	DODGE Durango	20 263
10	INFINITI QX4	18 793
11	MERCEDES M-Class	14 569

Not classified :
LEXUS RX 300

Full-size Sport utility

1st LEXUS LX 470 67.0 %

3rd GM C/K 64.6%

2nd LINCOLN Navigator 66.6 %
2nd FORD Expedition 66.6 %

OUR CLASSIFICATION

Rank	Models	Concept	Driving	Equipment	Comfort	Budget	Rating
1	**LEXUS LX 470**	84	56	76	**76**	43	**67.0 %**
2	FORD Expedition	85	53	78	71	**46**	66.6 %
2	LINCOLN Navigator	**86**	48	**80**	75	44	66.6 %
3	GM C/K	77	57	75	68	**46**	64.6 %
4	ISUZU Trooper	77	**59**	76	66	41	63.8 %
5	AMG Hummer	81	38	62	50	43	54.8 %

YOUR CLASSIFICATION

Rank	Models	97 Sales
1	GM- Yukon-Tahoe-Sub	307 412
2	FORD Expedition	214 524
3	LINCOLN Navigator	26 231
4	ISUZU Trooper	10 964
5	LEXUS 450	6 785

Not classified :
AMG Hummer